SAMS
Teach
Yourself

Microsoft®
Windows® Vista™

Greg Perry

SAMS 800 East 96th Street, Indianapolis, Indiana, 46240 USA

Sams Teach Yourself Microsoft® Windows® Vista™ All in One

International Standard Book Number: 0-672-32889-5

Library of Congress Catalog Card Number: 2005937037

Printed in the United States of America

First Printing: December 2006

09   08   07   06   4   3   2   1

Trademarks

All terms mentioned in this book that are known to be trademarks or service marks have been appropriately capitalized. Sams Publishing cannot attest to the accuracy of this information. Use of a term in this book should not be regarded as affecting the validity of any trademark or service mark.

Microsoft is a registered trademark of Microsoft Corporation. Windows Vista is a trademark of Microsoft Corporation.

Warning and Disclaimer

Bulk Sales

Sams Publishing offers excellent discounts on this book when ordered in quantity for bulk purchases or special sales. For more information, please contact

U.S. Corporate and Government Sales
1-800-382-3419
corpsales@pearsontechgroup.com

For sales outside of the U.S., please contact

International Sales
international@pearsoned.com

Safari This Book Is Safari Enabled

The Safari® Enabled icon on the cover of your favorite technology book means the book is available through Safari Bookshelf. When you buy this book, you get free access to the online edition for 45 days. Safari Bookshelf is an electronic reference library that lets you easily search thousands of technical books, find code samples, download chapters, and access technical information whenever and wherever you need it.

To gain 45-day Safari Enabled access to this book:

- Go to http://www.samspublishing.com/safarienabled
- Complete the brief registration form
- Enter the coupon code MFEP-4UIF-5QVJ-X6FR-XK1G

If you have difficulty registering on Safari Bookshelf or accessing the online edition, please e-mail customer-service@safaribooksonline.com.

Associate Publisher
Greg Wiegand

Acquisitions Editor
Loretta Yates

Development Editor
Todd Brakke

Managing Editor
Gina Kanouse

Project Editor
Dan Knott

Copy Editor
Mike Henry

Senior Indexer
Cheryl Lenser

Proofreader
Suzanne Thomas

Technical Editor
Diana Huggins

Publishing Coordinator
Cindy Teeters

Interior Designer
Ann Jones

Cover Designer
Gary Adair

Composition
Bronkella Publishing LLC

Contents at a Glance

Table of Contents

Part II: Getting Started with Windows Vista

Part VII: Running Windows Vista in a Connected World

Dedication

I'm so thankful that Rex and Ginni Jones entered our lives. In a short time they've become friends greater than gold. We count the Jones family as one of the most cherished blessings we have. Rex and Ginni, we love you both.

Acknowledgements

Loretta Yates kept me on track as I wrote (and wrote and wrote...) this book. She was there when I needed something. When I got too busy, she asked if I would take on more work. (Pearson Education needs to give her a raise because there aren't many who would have done that!) I know, however, Loretta asked for more because she trusts me and I am so very appreciative of that trust. I don't ever want to let her down and I hope we have many projects together in the future.

Todd Brakke, this book's Development Editor, did a superb job. Although this is the first time we've worked together, Todd is one of the first DEs I've worked with who seems to know a Beta version of Windows as well or better than I do. His insight during this book's review process was invaluable. Todd, you saved me on several issues when I needed extra help with a buggy beta and I thank you greatly.

Dan Knott, the Project Editor, wore multiple hats during this book's creation. More important, though, was the fact that Dan was always there when I needed him. During the middle of this book, my *Sams Teach Yourself Office 2007 All-in-One* title fell into his lap and he worked extra hard on that while staying on top of this and the other projects he was responsible for. It's obvious to me that Dan is a conscientious worker and he made this book far better than it could have been without him.

Copy Editor Mike Henry had the eagle eyes to correct my flawed writing. Mike, the book reads so much better after leaving your hands than before. Thanks so much. In addition, Diana Huggins spotted errors that I missed. If an error still resides between these covers I'd be surprised, but if so it's my fault alone. The overriding accuracy you'll find throughout this work, however, is due to Diana.

Kimberly Stowe of PortalPlayer Preface™ (at www.PortalPlayer.com) came to my rescue by providing information and a digital photo of Vista's cool, new Sideshow feature you'll learn about in Chapter 4. Sideshow will change the way we all use our laptops and portable devices and it's a feature I wanted you to learn about. The trouble is, no laptop maker had released a Sideshow-ready computer when this book went to press. Kimberly was extremely kind and was willing to help with whatever I needed. For your Sideshow-based laptop you should first check out PortalPlayer to see what features are available.

Finally, I want to express massive thanks to readers who keep coming back to my titles. Teaching you how to do something is nothing but a pleasure for me.

I love hearing from you so feel free to write. Depending on my workload, I always do my best to answer. Travel and deadlines sometimes push email down to a low priority, but when I can respond I do. You can contact me at Vista@BidMentor.com (the BidMentor.com comes from my eBay domain; I teach others how to be successful on eBay). Of course, in today's world some valid emails get filtered out due to high-octane spam filters that filter improperly; nevertheless, in general, my email system is highly reliable and I should get what you send.

—Greg Perry

We Want to Hear from You!

As the reader of this book, *you* are our most important critic and commentator. We value your opinion and want to know what we're doing right, what we could do better, what areas you'd like to see us publish in, and any other words of wisdom you're willing to pass our way.

As an associate publisher for Sams Publishing, I welcome your comments. You can email or write me directly to let me know what you did or didn't like about this book—as well as what we can do to make our books better.

Please note that I cannot help you with technical problems related to the topic of this book. We do have a User Services group, however, where I will forward specific technical questions related to the book.

When you write, please be sure to include this book's title and author as well as your name, email address, and phone number. I will carefully review your comments and share them with the author and editors who worked on the book.

Email: feedback@samspublishing.com

Mail: Greg Wiegand
         Associate Publisher
         Sams Publishing
         800 East 96th Street
         Indianapolis, IN 46240 USA

Reader Services

Visit our website and register this book at www.samspublishing.com/register for convenient access to any updates, downloads, or errata that might be available for this book.

Introduction

You probably are anxious to get started with your Windows Vista training. Windows Vista is an exciting operating system by Microsoft, a completely revamped operating system from the Windows XP operating systems that were used previously. Vista is all new—developed from the ground up—and is not the result of putting together legacy Widows code and adding some extra features.

Windows Vista is cool.

Windows Vista is the first operating system environment that truly puts you in control of all your media, from video to music to pictures, and enables you to synchronize that digital multimedia data with mobile devices, cameras, scanners, projectors, and televisions. Windows Vista, using the famed Aero graphical interface, is a visually stunning operating system honed to a detail before unimagined. Even the window icons you see on the screen are often live depictions of what those icons represent.

Windows Vista is far more than a multimedia-centric operating system, though. Vista is the safest Windows operating system developed. Security measures flow throughout the system to guard you and your computing experience from outside attacks and from bugs inside your programs. Vista offers a robust work environment for the home, small office, or corporate enterprise. Even though Vista integrates an online experience into almost everything it offers, you can rest far easier knowing that Vista contains safety features that protect you while you work.

This book's goal is to get you up to speed as quickly as possible. Take just a few preliminary moments to acquaint yourself with the design of this book described in the next few sections.

What This Book Will Do for You

Although this is not a reference book, you'll learn almost every aspect of Windows Vista from the everyday user's point of view. This book does not take up your time with those many advanced technical details that most of you will never need. I know that you want to get up to speed with Windows Vista, and it's this book's goal to do just that. From the first chapter, you'll learn hands-on, practical ways to make Vista work better for you and to help you get your work done while using Vista.

I present only enough background and theory that a new Windows Vista user needs. In addition to the background discussions, this book is practical and provides a vast array of useful step-by-step tasks that you can work through to gain hands-on experience. You'll glide through that tasks and learn every common Windows Vista action you'll need to make Windows Vista work for you, instead of you working to use Windows Vista.

As with Vista, this book is graphical, using far more figures and callouts than normal to teach you what's going on every step of the way. Enough pages are here, however, to give you the textual background and instructions necessary to learn quickly and thoroughly without wading through a boatload of theory and history.

Who Should Read This Book?

This book is for both beginning and advanced Windows users. Readers rarely believe that lofty claim, for good reason, but the design of this book and the nature of Windows Vista make it possible for this book to address an audience that wide.

Windows Vista is extremely similar to previous versions of Windows in many ways. The Start menu is there. The taskbar is there. Windows Explorer is there. Vista, however, begins where those kinds of features left off. Vista takes each feature to the next-higher notch and offers an added graphical experience to go along with the usual Windows feature.

The bottom-line result is that a beginning user of Vista needs to know far less about Vista to use it than beginning users of previous Windows needed. In addition, there is enough under Vista's hood to make the most tech-hungry computer pro love working inside the operating system.

Conventions Used in This Book

In addition to text, pictures, and step-by-step guides, you'll also find the following special elements are included to set off different types of information to make them easily recognizable:

Special By the Way notes augment the material you are reading in each hour. They clarify concepts and procedures.

You'll find numerous Did You Know tips that offer shortcuts and solutions to common problems.

The Watch Out! sections warn you about pitfalls. Reading them will save you time and trouble.

What to Do Now

With the introduction out of the way, it's time that you began learning what Windows Vista has in store for you. Turn the page to start learning about Microsoft's exciting redesigned operating system that makes your computer come alive.

PART I

Introducing Windows Vista

CHAPTER 1

Welcome to Windows Vista

In This Chapter:

- ▶ Preview Vista's new features
- ▶ Understand the different Windows Vista versions
- ▶ See Vista's amazing Aero Glass in action
- ▶ Gain an understanding of Microsoft's goals for Windows Vista

Move over Windows XP, there's a new kid in town!

Windows Vista dramatically changes the face of Windows, but the extent of those changes is hardly just skin deep. In addition to putting on that new face, Microsoft redesigned Windows Vista internally to provide you more power, more flexibility, and more ways to do the things you want to do while at the same time adding advanced security features that help keep you safe.

It's best to experience Windows Vista from a high level when you first learn about it. There's no need to get into the nitty-gritty details right now. By getting an overview of the operating system early, you'll quickly get a better feel for what Vista can do for you right now.

A Complete Redesign of Windows Awaits You

More than five years passed after Microsoft released XP before Vista arrived on the scene. Microsoft hopes that the underlying code of Vista will be the basis of your operating system for the next decade, twice as long as the expected lifespan of XP. As with any other product, Microsoft will surely release updates throughout Vista's life.

One reason Microsoft hopes that Vista lasts for a decade or longer is the extraordinary effort required to produce this new and improved operating system. As hardware gets more advanced, and the needs of end users matures, the operating system must keep up that pace and take advantage of features the hardware offers, while allowing users to accomplish more tasks in less time. It just takes longer to produce a fresh, rewritten, and revamped operating system today, so its shelf life needs to be longer to give Microsoft (and competing vendors) time to produce the next one.

When you first experience Vista, you'll notice several things. As you look at Figure 1.1, notice the following:

▶ Vista initially sports a clean interface without a lot of icons (you can always add icons).

▶ The Welcome Center is a window set to load automatically when you first install or upgrade to Vista. The Welcome Center is a window that displays common tasks a typical new user to Vista might wish to do. You can turn off the Welcome Center's display by clicking the Run At Startup option at the bottom of the window if you don't wish to see it each time you start Windows Vista. Chapter 2, "Exploring the Welcome Center," describes how to make the Welcome Center work best for you.

▶ Vista shows more detail in its icons.

▶ Although it's clearly different, if you've used a previous version of Windows, Vista's user interface (UI) will still be familiar to you.

FIGURE 1.1
When you first look at the Vista screen, you don't see much there and you don't see a lot of difference from Windows XP and other Windows versions.

At first glance, therefore, Vista is not too impressive, right? Hang on! The nice thing about Windows Vista is that it is familiar to you. You wouldn't want to adapt to a dramatic change when moving from one version of Windows to another. Having said that, from this point forward, you'll start to notice how differently Windows Vista acts when you actually start to use it. Don't worry about having to adapt, though. These differences really just represent evolutionary improvements that allow you to achieve your computing goals better.

Your screen might look different from Figure 1.1's because your desktop's background (called **wallpaper**) might be set to a different picture. In addition, your computer might show far more icons than the figures in this book. It all depends on your PC's vendor (if Vista was preinstalled), what was on your PC previously (if you just upgraded the operating system), and what you've added to Vista since it was installed. This book's Vista computer was set up with nothing installed other than Vista, Microsoft Office, and a few utility programs. This keeps the screens more universal, but it also means you might see a few things on your screen that won't always appear in this book's figures.

Graphical Differences with Aero Glass

Just for grins, look at Figure 1.2. This shows how Windows remains the same but ups the ante by boosting what it does for you. The mouse cursor is pointing to one of the taskbar's open program buttons. Instead of text telling you what the window is, you see a miniature image of the actual screen, called a **thumbnail**. At the same time, Figure 1.2's user is pressing Alt+Tab to move between open programs. You've surely done that many times in Windows XP and earlier versions. This time, you don't see icons representing those programs you're tabbing through; instead, you see thumbnails there as well! No more guessing as to which open program you want to select.

You're seeing an example of Windows Vista's **Aero Glass** mode. Aero Glass is the name Microsoft gave Vista's advanced graphical features, such as the ability to see thumbnails in the taskbar and task switcher. In addition, Aero Glass gives the edges of your open windows a transparent effect so that you can see what one window is covering.

Aero Glass also features complete and true **scalability** of fonts and graphics. This means you can resize just about anything on your screen, from text to graphics to thumbnails without having an image become a pixilated mess. You can even rescale web pages that were not designed with text and graphics that normally could be zoomed in or out. If your monitor's resolution makes text on a web page or a Word document difficult to read, you can increase the size of the font. Although you could *sometimes* increase the viewing font size of web pages and graphics before, Vista's Aero Glass capabilities make this a more universal feature that just plain works better for almost anything and everything you do on your computer.

Alt-Tab shows thumbnail
images of each open program

FIGURE 1.2
Windows Vista
is more graphi-
cal than previ-
ous Windows
and provides
thumbnail
images of
your open win-
dows on the
taskbar and
task switcher.

Mouse pointer produced thumbnail

For another Aero Glass feature sporting a graphical *wow* factor, look at Figure 1.3.
Here you can see several open windows in a 3D presentation called **Flip 3D**. With
Flip 3D you can switch between all your running programs and open windows by
pressing Windows+Tab to see this 3D representation of everything. From here, you
can use your mouse's wheel to scroll through a live view into each program. By
looking down through these 3D windows you can more easily select the program to
which you want to switch. (The Alt+Tab task-switching feature still works as shown
in Figure 1.2, but doesn't display your programs and windows in the 3D format.)

Windows Vista requires a fairly powerful computer. Just about any medium- to
high-end computer made from 2005 forward should handle most or all of Vista's
capabilities. Even if you have a machine powerful enough to run Vista, your graphics card might not be able to support the Aero Glass mode. If not, you will still
enjoy most of Vista's other features. Instead of seeing the Aero Glass interface,
however, you'll see a more traditional windowing effect, as Figure 1.4 shows.

If you've been reading about Vista, you might have already seen some of these Aero
Glass changes. Although the graphics are impressive, Vista is more than just a
graphical remodeling of previous Windows versions. The next few sections touch on
more highlights of Vista.

FIGURE 1.3
Press Windows+Tab instead of Alt+Tab when you want to see this Flip 3D representation of your running programs and open windows.

FIGURE 1.4
Without a graphics card capable of handling DirectX 9 (or higher) and 3D graphics, your Windows Vista screen loses the capability to use transparent windows and displays icons in place of the thumbnails that would otherwise appear as you work.

Not all Vista installations support all features. Later in this chapter, in the section titled "The Vista Editions," you'll learn what Vista flavors are available and how they differ.

By the Way

A Leaner and Cleaner Start Menu

The first thing you click in Vista will probably be the Start button (which is no longer labeled Start, and instead is the Windows logo). The Windows Vista menu pops up as expected but, unexpectedly, as you select options from inside the menu, you'll immediately notice that the menu stays in one column instead of spreading all over your Windows desktop like the plague.

Instead of cascading through layers of menus, Vista's menu lets you drill down into menus and submenus by changing the Start menu to reflect what you've selected. For example, if you select Start, All Programs, Accessories, your Vista menu will look something like the one in Figure 1.5: a single-columned list of all the options in the Accessories menu. Keeping the clutter away from Vista's menus means that you can see more of your screen, which is often useful when you're using the Start menu to look for data or programs related to something you're doing.

FIGURE 1.5
The Start menu stays in one column, letting you see more of your screen and keeping the menu options more concise.

Vista Has Vastly Improved Security

Windows XP was been a major upgrade over Windows 9x or Me, but there's no question it was still a security nightmare. Microsoft worked diligently to make Vista far more bulletproof than XP. In defense of Microsoft's job on XP, many of the security risks that affected users over the past few years were certainly unexpected. They were often the result of new hardware or software technology that wasn't foreseen at the turn of the millennium when Microsoft released XP. Many security pitfalls were often the unexpected outcome of innocent and unsuspecting users clicking the wrong thing, such as an unexpected attachment from an email sent by a suspicious source or masked as being from someone they know.

No matter how much more secure you might have wanted XP to be, when you first begin using Vista, you might think that Microsoft worked *too* diligently on security due to how much you'll have to interact with Vista's warning and permission security messages.

Windows Vista introduces *User Account Control*, or *UAC*, which verifies that system changes and some system-related programs should run before actually running those programs and causing potential problems. The UAC permeates much of Vista and even if you are logged in as an Administrator you'll be prompted to verify certain tasks as you use Vista. When you attempt to run a program such as the Disk Defragmenter, Vista opens a dialog box entitled User Account Control and requests that you confirm you want to run the program. If you're not logged in as an Administrator user then you must enter an Administrator user account's password to run the program.

Vista must adapt to the way you want to work. Because Vista errs on the side of caution, it's extra secure and blocks some things you won't want blocked. Fortunately, Vista usually asks permission to block things at first and you can train Vista, over time, to know what to allow and what to block. (Although there will always be actions that require your confirmation to execute.)

Many home users and users of standalone computers that might or might not be connected to the Internet are considered Administrators, or the masters of their computers. By being an Administrator, you in effect have full control over the computer as opposed to some user accounts that you might set up that are more limited. Non-Administrator accounts are called **standard accounts**. Some standard accounts on your computer, for example, might not be allowed to install new programs (very wise if you share your computer with other members of the family, especially those who love to download and install lots of games).

By setting up the Administrator account for yourself (the first account set up after you install or begin using Vista on a new computer), and the more-limited standard accounts for others in your family or those who work with you on your computer, you help protect your system from programs and downloaded problems later. The standard accounts can allow others to use the computer and run programs but not change any significant system properties or install possibly malicious programs.

By the Way

Vista provides several layers of parental controls so that you can determine exactly what members of your family can and cannot do. You can even go so far as to control what days of the week and times of day they can log in to and use the system. You, as Administrator, can adjust those parental control settings. Users without your Administrator use privileges cannot adjust the settings.

Both Vista and XP offer you the ability to create accounts with various capabilities as just described. In many instances, Vista asks the Administrator whether to allow something before doing it. For example, if you connect a new device to your computer and Vista needs to install a software driver for that device, Vista asks your permission, even if you are using the primary Administrator account (which most of you will probably be using if you're the primary user of your computer or the one who set up the computer).

By the Way

A **driver** is a small program that tells the operating system how to interact with a hardware device. Every piece of hardware on your computer, from your mouse and keyboard, to your printer to your graphics card has drivers that tell Vista how to make use of them.

You'll see many more requests like the driver installation request as you use Vista. If you have permission to grant or deny the request, Vista follows the marching orders you give it. If others who use your computer on a more limited basis try to grant or deny such a request, Vista ignores their response and waits for you to decide when you get back to your Administrator account.

Did you Know?

Even if you are your computer's Administrator, you might want to add a second user account for yourself that is a Standard user giving you more limited access than the Administrator account. Using the more limited account until you gain more familiarity with your computer might be wise so that you don't inadvertently allow or deny something incorrectly that pops up and needs your attention. Besides, Vista allows you to run any program as an administrator by supplying an administrative password.

Of course, Vista's security also extends to online activities. Vista offers a stronger **firewall**, a program that monitors online and network activity and tries to keep other users' computers from snooping through your files and possibly wreaking havoc with your programs and data. Unlike the Windows XP firewall, Vista's firewall can be setup as a **two-way** firewall, meaning that Vista monitors all outgoing online and network activities as well as incoming. (XP only monitored incoming

traffic.) Monitoring outgoing traffic is important because some Trojan horse programs can infect your computer and begin using your Internet and network connection for activities you didn't authorize. The 2-way firewall goes a long way toward
intercepting and preventing such unauthorized attempts.

> Chapter 27, "Managing Your Windows Security," explores the many ways that Vista
> protects you and explains how you can set up and control Vista's security to work
> in your computing environment.

By the Way

Find So Much More So Much More Quickly

Vista offers an integrated search feature that runs circles around XP's cranky, bulky
search operations. Perhaps you've used a desktop search system in the past such as
Google's or MSN's desktop search engine. Such desktop search engines index files
and data all over your computer and quickly locates them when you search for
them.

Vista includes such a search window, accessible by clicking Search from the Start
menu. You can hunt for specific files or hunt for text inside files. The text for which
you're searching can reside in any number of file types, ranging from text documents, to spreadsheets to email (and more), making both much faster and more
dynamic than the old Windows XP Search program.

Vista helps you craft your search in many ways. In Figure 1.6, the user is searching
for the word *stocks*. But as the user types *stoc*, a list of files appear that either include
the letters *stoc* in their filename or include the letters *stoc* inside the files somewhere.
(Even if the files are MP3 digital music files, all the MP3 tag information is
searched.) That's why you see so many files in the list until you finish typing your
search term in the Search box. The Vista Search box looks through websites you've
stored in your Favorites folder, as well as other files, news, and even email you've
collected onto your computer.

By matching your search text as you type it, you don't always have to finish entering the complete search word or phrase before locating what you want to find. If the
file or text you're looking for appears in the search results before you finish typing
the search phrase, just double-click that item to open it without finishing your
search phrase.

> Windows Vista's search results window is really just a specialized Explorer win-
> dow. That's why the window is referred to as a *Search Explorer* window.

By the Way

When you type stoc here...

FIGURE 1.6
Vista provides
high-speed
searching and
begins to return
matches even
before you
finish typing
what you're
looking for.

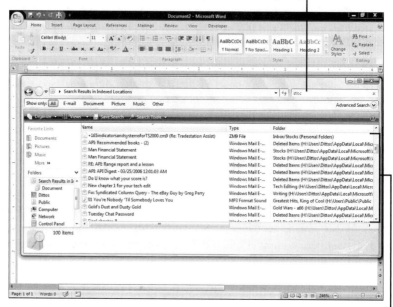

...Vista shows
all results with
stoc here.

You can search for programs and data from many places inside Vista. It's almost as though Microsoft reads your mind because when you need a search box, it's there. You'll even find a search box at the bottom of the Start menu! Just begin typing letters for something you want to find in the Start menu's search box and the results appear right there on the Start menu (see Figure 1.7). One reason Vista is so quick to locate results is because Vista constantly indexes files, emails, MP3s, pictures, visited websites, and everything else you store on your computer in an effort to locate any of these items quickly if you search for text that matches any of the indexed terms found in those files.

You're never limited to searching your own computer. When you search for anything, click the Search the Internet option in the search panel and Vista hands off your search to an online search engine (that you can specify) and displays the online results.

FIGURE 1.7
You can type your search word or phrase at the bottom of your Start menu and Vista searches programs, stored web pages, news, and emails that match your results.

...Vista shows results with ca here.

When you type ca here...

Click to see all results

Manage Meetings and Appointments

You're not used to seeing a Calendar program inside the Windows environment. Vista introduces Windows Calendar with which you can plan events, track appointments, and manage your activities.

When online or working over a network, you can share your calendar with other users also to make collaboration simpler when you schedule meetings. The Windows Calendar is a full-featured calendar that looks and operates a lot like Microsoft Outlook's Calendar feature with one exception: Windows Calendar seems to be leaner and operate more efficiently, so you might find yourself using it more and Outlook's Calendar less if you don't require some of Outlook's more advanced calendar-related features. (You'll learn more about the Windows Calendar in Chapter 20, "Dating with Windows Calendar.")

Vista Introduces a Better Internet Explorer

Although Internet Explorer isn't technically an operating system feature, Internet Explorer got its first major upgrade in almost a decade when Vista brought us Internet Explorer 7.

As you might expect already, Internet Explorer (*IE*) takes advantage of graphics in ways that previous versions didn't. Vista's Aero Glass feature means that you can scale website text larger or smaller even if the site isn't designed to offer scalable text (and many sites are not). In previous versions of IE, you simply could not change the text size of some sites to make them more readable or to show more text on the screen, but Vista makes it possible now to do just that.

In addition, IE finally offers tabbed browsing. As Figure 1.8 shows, you can open multiple websites inside a single IE window. A tab marks the name and location of each open website. Click a tab to make its website appear on top in the window.

FIGURE 1.8

Click a tab to see that page inside a single IE window.

Click to see new Internet page

Each tab is an open Internet page

With older versions of Internet Explorer, you'd have to open a new IE window to see a different website if you wanted to keep several sites open at once. You can still do that, but after you begin using the tabbed browsing feature, you'll find that your Windows taskbar is far less cluttered with multiple open IE windows.

Although the tabs toward the top of the IE window tell you what each website contains, you can click the Quick Tabs button (or press Ctrl+Q) to see a full-screen preview of all the tabbed windows, as Figure 1.9 demonstrates. These thumbnail views show the page that each IE tab represents. Click any thumbnail image to display that web page (in effect, moving that page's tabbed page to the top of the IE stack of tabbed websites).

Before, you might have had to click through several open IE windows to get to the open Web page you wanted to work on next. The tabbed browsing and thumbnail previews make browsing the Internet more intuitive and quicker to manage.

The Quick Tabs button

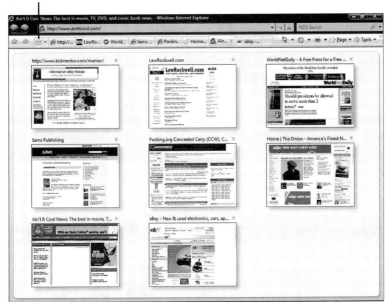

FIGURE 1.9
A preview of your open web pages makes locating the page you want to browse next simple and accurate.

IE adds other new features such as **RSS feeds** (*Really Simple Syndication*; feeds that alert you to new web content instead of you having to browse to it) and security enhancements such as a *phishing detector* that lets you know when you're browsing a site that isn't what it appears to be. **Phishing** is a deceptive tactic spammers and other nefarious Internet types often use to make their emails look like another company's and provide links to a website that looks like an official site, but is a mocked-up version that is trying to trick you into entering your password or other personal information (like bank account numbers). For example, an email might direct you to a phony-but-real-looking eBay site. These phishing sites are far less dangerous with Vista than with earlier operating systems in part because the new IE maintains a reference database of known phishing sites and it can warn you if the site you're browsing is one of them.

> If tabbed Internet browsing, thumbnail previews, and RSS feeds seem familiar to you, it's because other browsers such as Firefox have offered similar features for years. True, IE is behind the times, but Vista's Internet Explorer works great and is a welcome improvement in spite of its tardy feature set.

By the Way

Pictures and Multimedia Improve in Vista

Microsoft revamped XP's anemic My Pictures window to provide organizing tools that makes the Windows Photo Gallery vastly more usable and helpful. In addition to new tagging and organization features, you can perform routine photo editing, too.

With the Photo Gallery, you can organize and track both pictures and videos. When you search for pictures and videos, Vista limits the search to the items in your Photo Gallery. You can select which items the Photo Gallery includes because Vista doesn't force you to use one folder, such as My Pictures, to hold the pictures (and videos) it tracks.

Figure 1.10 shows the Windows Photo Gallery with some of the options available. A thumbnail image appears for each picture and each video you include in the Photo Gallery. The thumbnails used for each video represent the first video frame of each video.

Make edits to the selected photo

FIGURE 1.10
The Windows Photo Gallery not only organizes your photos and videos, but also enables you to make routine edits to your pictures.

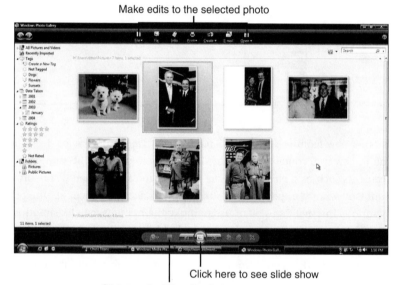

Click here to see slide show

Click to adjust thumbnail sizes

From the Photo Gallery, you can

▶ Adjust picture colors

▶ Change the photo brightness and contrast

▶ Crop pictures

▶ Remove red eye

▶ Add ratings to your photos so that later you can more easily locate the best of the bunch

▶ Assign tags to pictures to add comments and search terms to your photos and videos so you can locate them later

In other words, Vista's Windows Photo Gallery performs many tasks that you had to purchase photo-editing software to do before. Although photo-editing software such as Photoshop Elements has far more features than Windows Photo Gallery, you'll find yourself using Photo Gallery for many routine editing tasks without having to start another program to make simple adjustments, and for adding tags and ratings to your pictures.

If you've been using a different photo album utility, such a the album feature in Adobe Photoshop elements, note that any tags you've applied to those photos do not carry over when viewing them through Photo Gallery.

Watch Out!

Given Vista's superior capability to resize text and graphics on the fly (if your graphics hardware and Vista version support the Aero Glass feature), it's also worth noting that you can also easily resize your Photo Gallery images. Hold the Ctrl key and move your mouse scroll wheel (or your trackball's wheel) to resize the thumbnail images on the fly.

Did you Know?

Although the Windows Photo Gallery organizes and keeps track of both pictures and videos, you'll still use the Windows Media Player to play videos and music. The Media Player has gotten so powerful over the past few years that many users use it exclusively and no longer rely on outside (and costly) programs to play music and video, transfer music to a disk (called **ripping**), and burn music CDs.

Vista's Media Player is more graphical, representing more content with graphics from the original CD cases and album covers. You'll locate music and videos faster using Vista's integrated search tool that you've already read about in the earlier pages of this chapter. Start typing a song you want to listen to and as you type the characters, Media Player displays matching results right away.

Your Computer Is Now a Media Center

In Chapter 14, "Going Multimedia with Vista," you'll see that Microsoft included Media Center software inside Vista that was formerly reserved for the Windows XP superset operating system called *Windows Media Center*. To make your computer a full-featured media center, Microsoft changed the entire multimedia interface. For example, not only is Media Player completely upgraded, but your computer is also now a complete media center capable of interacting with entertainment devices, including your television and home stereo, that is, assuming your PC has the necessary hardware to do so. (Chief among the requirements for TV is a built-in TV tuner that Vista is able to recognize and use.)

Other related changes are somewhat more subtle but are just as important. For example, Microsoft completely redesigned the way the volume control works in Vista. Instead of getting a volume control for each device (such as microphone and speaker), you get a volume control for each application. This means that you can keep the volume on a game high and the volume on your easy listening Media Player library soft.

The Cool Windows Gadgets

Vista introduces *Windows Sidebar* **gadgets**, which displays several *Gadgets* small programs (sometimes known as *applets,* making one think of tiny applications). Vista includes a handful of gadgets but you'll be able to download more, often without any charge, from Microsoft and other sites.

These gadgets, which are similar in nature to the widgets available for the Mac OS, are little programs that do something simple you need. Perhaps it's just a clock showing you the time. Perhaps it's a stock ticker symbol scrolling by. Perhaps you want a calculator always handy. The possibilities are really quite limitless.

The nice thing about Windows gadgets is that you dock them to the side of your screen in the Windows Sidebar, as shown in Figure 1.11. The gadgets remain there for you to use when you need them. You can easily hide the Sidebar and bring it back by right-clicking the gadget icon in the **notification area** (the lower-right part of your screen to the right of your Windows taskbar).

Did you Know?

If you use multiple monitors, you can place the Sidebar on either monitor to keep it out of your way but still make it available for quick access.

Chapter 9, "Working with the Sidebar and Gadgets," explores the many ways you will be able to use gadgets with and without the Sidebar.

Sidebar   Gadgets

FIGURE 1.11
Put gadgets—small applications that help you accomplish tasks you need done routinely—on your Windows desktop's Sidebar for one-click access to them.

Notification area

At first, some users cannot see a gadget's advantage. For example, you can quickly start the Windows Calculator program from the Start menu or simply add an icon for the Calculator to your Taskbar's Quick Launch toolbar (as Chapter 6, "Taking the Taskbar to Task," explains). By being on your desktop and open, the Sidebar's programs make them always visible. A single glance tells you a latest stock price, for example, without you having to click an icon to start a program.

By the Way

Vista's New Features Keep on Coming

Vista offers so much. You're surely anxious to get started trying many of them out, now that you've read about them in this chapter.

Your Vista new feature preview won't end here, though. Vista offers so many new features that you'll be running across new features and easier ways to do your work all throughout this text and beyond. Not only that, of the new features I've discussed here, I've hardly scraped the surface of what many of them can do. As this book leads you through the use of Windows Vista and shows you how to make Vista do the work you want it to do, you'll see many new bells and whistles as well as improved functionality of old favorites.

The Vista Editions

For years, Microsoft has offered various editions of each Windows release. Windows Vista is no exception. These editions are similar because each is a subset of Vista, but the features differ among them.

It's true that the various Vista editions, especially when you first hear about them, seem a little confusing. Microsoft certainly doesn't offer the various editions to confuse anyone. Instead, it's Microsoft's goal to provide an operating system that best serves your needs no matter what computing environment you work in and no matter what hardware you use (as long as your equipment isn't *too* outdated). Not only that, but if you don't have a need for some of Vista's more advanced or niche features, getting a "lighter" version of Vista can save you some money, too.

By the Way

> Any medium- or high-end computer manufactured after 2005, and most higher-end computers made after 2003, should run some Vista edition with little or no problem. To see if your hardware is Vista-capable, the following link takes you to a Microsoft Web page that installs the Windows Vista Upgrade Advisor tool. With that you can learn how well your machine will run with Vista and you'll learn ways you can make your computer more Vista-ready if it's not currently: http://www.microsoft.com/windowsvista/getready/upgradeadvisor/default.mspx.

As time goes by, the release versions of Vista might change, so this information is as current as it can be at the time of this writing. In the past, Microsoft has released additional flavors of Windows long after the initial products debuted; Microsoft has also removed some flavors in the past.

In general, there are three home versions of Vista. Even though these are considered "home" versions, many small businesses will probably adopt and use one or more of these as well. Here is a rundown of the home Vista versions:

- ▶ **Windows Vista Home Basic**—A features-"lite" version, similar to Windows XP, that easily runs on lower-level computers. Even if you happen to have an adequate graphics card, note that no Aero Glass features are present in this version.

- ▶ **Windows Vista Home Premium**—This middle-of-the-road Vista flavor is probably what most home and very small business or home office users will use. Aero Glass, Media Center multimedia functionality, networking, Tablet PC support, and most of the operating system's feature set are included.

- ▶ **Windows Vista Ultimate**—Everything possible in Vista (including the Business and Enterprise versions) is available in this ultimate version, including advanced networking support, extra efficiency routines that make high-powered games run smoothly, and an upgraded support service agreement to get quicker response to your questions and concerns.

In addition to the home versions, Microsoft is offering Windows Vista Business, a version similar to the Vista Home Premium but includes extra utilities and better networking tools that corporate users might find useful.

Microsoft also is offering a deeply trimmed-down version called Windows Vista Starter. Developing nations with generally limited hardware can use many of Vista's simpler features without slowing their older computers to a crawl. As such users upgrade to more modern hardware, they will be able to take advantage of the higher-end Vista flavors.

Business users who need more power than Vista Ultimate or Vista Business will require Windows Vista Enterprise. This operating system is tweaked to work well in enterprise environments, which maintain large networks in multiple locations and require advanced security, more control, and wholly integrated file sharing. A slightly narrower Vista without the vast networking (enterprise) features is called Vista Business.

Microsoft is releasing some Vista flavors without Media Player in an attempt to appease some competing media player firms that offer similar media products. The N releases are primarily sold for European users to help alleviate some antitrust cases related to Windows. If the name of your Windows Vista has an *N* in it (such as Windows Vista Home N), you won't have the Media Player and you won't be able to save files in the Windows Media Audio format with the .wma filename extension unless you have third-party software that will do so. You can download Media Player from Microsoft's Web site at www.Microsoft.com if you want to use Media Player.

Windows Vista comes on a DVD and a DVD can hold a *lot* of information. When you install Vista, you install the edition you purchased a license for (such as Vista Business, Vista Home Premium, or whatever). At any time, you can upgrade to a higher edition such as moving from Vista Home Basic to Vista Home Premium using the *Windows Anytime Upgrade* option on your Windows Start menu's Extras and Upgrade folder. At the time of this writing, you pay only the difference in price between that which you originally purchased and the Vista version to which you want to upgrade.

Chapter Wrap-Up

Vista's Aero Glass graphical interface is only the beginning of the changes Vista offers over XP. If you used XP in the past, it might seem odd that XP's now considered archaic, but it truly is. Microsoft developed XP when hardware was simpler, security wasn't as big an issue, and although the world was getting more wired, only a small percentage of users had always-on, high-speed broadband Internet service.

Now you need to understand more of what Vista represents from a 10,000-foot view; it's time to look a little closer. Chapter 2 discusses the Welcome Center window, a window that provides new Vista users with tools they frequently need to begin using Windows Vista. After you get that background, you'll dive right into using Windows Vista's more routine features starting in Chapter 3, "Clicking Your Start Button."

CHAPTER 2

Exploring the Welcome Center

In This Chapter:

- ▶ See the best place to begin using Windows Vista
- ▶ Improve your computer's performance
- ▶ Locate hardware devices not yet set up
- ▶ View the Control Panel
- ▶ Preview Windows basics
- ▶ Transfer Windows settings from one PC to another
- ▶ Register Windows
- ▶ View your computer's details

This chapter continues your introduction to Windows Vista. In Chapter 1, "Welcome to Windows Vista," you learned how Vista is a completely redesigned Windows operating system that focuses on a graphical interface. With tools such as Vista's integrated search feature that permeates almost every Windows program, and improved security that lets you work with more confidence in a less than safe connected world, Vista is an operating system worthy of respect.

The best place to begin when learning to use Windows Vista is the new Welcome Center window. Microsoft designed the Welcome Center window to give new Vista users the most common tools and features they would need to get Windows up and running.

After you finish this chapter's continued introduction to Vista, you'll be ready to tackle some of the more specific Windows Vista tools.

The Welcome Center: Vista's Welcome Wagon

When you log in to a Vista-based computer, you will see the Welcome Center window, like the one shown in Figure 2.1. The Welcome Center window is a great place to get used to Windows Vista and learn about its features.

FIGURE 2.1
The Welcome Center window introduces the newcomer to the operating system.

> Depending on who used your computer in the past and the settings they changed, you might not see the Welcome Center when you start your Vista-based computer. If the Welcome Center window doesn't appear, you can start the Welcome Center from the Windows Accessories menu or open your Control Panel from your Windows menu and select the System and Maintenance option. Select the Welcome Center option to view the Welcome Center window.

By the Way

Highlights of the Welcome Center

The top of the Welcome Center contains information about your computer. Suppose that you upgrade to Windows Vista and your computer runs sluggishly. The Welcome Center displays information about your computer hardware at the top. If your computer is getting outdated (which in today's terms means it's a couple of years old or more), it might be your hardware and not your Vista installation causing the sluggishness.

To some computer users, knowing the processor model, computer speed, and memory size of their computers is second nature and not something they ever have to look up. To most of us, those facts get fairly hazy after we buy the computer because we're busy just trying to use it, and learn all we need to know to stay on top of the latest programs and updates.

In previous versions of Windows, locating the list of hardware features and speed required opening the Control Panel and then opening the System resources window. The Welcome Center puts much of that information at the top of its window so that it's easy to find. If you cannot get Vista's Aero Glass feature to work, for example, look at the top of your Welcome Center to see what graphics adapter your computer uses. You then can go to your graphics card's website and see if the manufacturer has updated drivers that might allow your graphics card to work with the Aero Glass feature.

Speaking of the Control Panel's System window, clicking the Welcome Center's Show More Details link opens a Control Panel window that shows even more specific information about your computer's hardware, as detailed in the next section.

Did you Know?

Improving Your Performance

Vista is a powerful operating system. But to get that power, your hardware must be robust. You'll see that the computer used for Figure 2.2 has a Windows System Performance Rating of only 2.6, whereas 3 is considered the bottom of the adequate range (if you want to run with all of Vista's features enabled). The higher the performance rating, the smoother your Vista experience will be. The owner of Figure 2.2's computer is either going to have some sluggish computing ahead or he might have to disable some of Vista's glitzier options, such as the Aero Glass user interface. He can either upgrade the computer in an attempt to get the rating higher, switch to a newer and faster computer, or live with substandard performance.

When you click the Windows Experience Index link next to the rating, Vista analyzes your computer and makes suggestions as to things you can do to improve Vista's performance. Figure 2.3 shows a number of suggestions that appear on the computer rated as a 2.6. A few performance issues stand out as low and they relate to the graphics adapter bring used. A sluggish graphics adapter will make your Vista experience sluggish especially if you run Aero Glass mode. The graphics problems rate between 2.6 and 2.9 and are significant given that the CPU, memory, and hard disk all rate a 4.2 or higher. The numerous graphics problems bring the rating down to the 2.6 level, which is considered unacceptable; workable, but unacceptable.

FIGURE 2.2
The Welcome Center can give you more detail by automatically opening the Control Panel's System window.

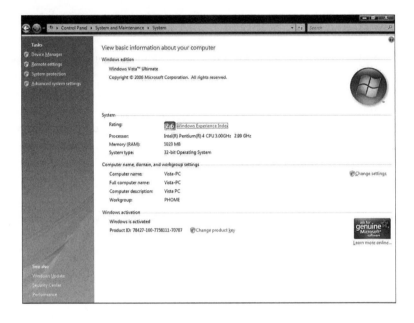

Watch Out!

Because Vista is the foundation of all you do, you need Vista to run smoothly and quickly or your applications will dramatically slow down and otherwise perform erratically.

Substandard scores plague this PC's graphics adapter

FIGURE 2.3
This computer's graphics adapter needs to be replaced before its 2.6 rating will go any higher.

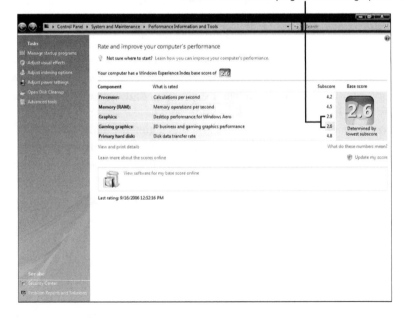

It's not the purpose of this Welcome Center overview to go into detail on how to fix every problem because each subrated computer offers unique challenges. As a rule, however, if your problems lie primarily in your hardware, you need to replace it because there is little you can do to speed up the hardware you have. If your problem lies in drivers, the problems are often easily fixed. Click the Learn How You Can Improve Your Computer's Performance link to get help on ways to improve your machine's performance.

The Get Started Items

In the center of your Welcome Center window are the Get Started items. These options give you links to common Vista options and settings that a new Vista user might want to adjust. Several show by default (refer to Figure 2.1), and you may see more or fewer depending on your Vista version and release. You can click the Show All Items link to see all the options the Welcome Center makes available; the ones that show initially are default options and are the most common that a new Vista user may need.

> Clicking each option causes the top of the Welcome Center window to change to describe that option. For example if you click to highlight the Add New Users option the top green area of your Welcome Screen changes to describe what you can do if you select that option.

Did you Know?

Double-click an option to select it. Double-clicking some of these options might cause Vista to display a User Account Control dialog box that asks for an authorized user to confirm or permit the action (which is to say, those users with Administrative access). This confirmation dialog box appears even if you logged in as an administrator on your computer. If you did not log in as an administrator, you'll have to provide an administrator password to continue.

The following sections explain some of the more critical Get Started options and describe why you might want to review them before learning more about Windows Vista.

View Computer Details

By selecting the View Computer Details, Vista shows you the same Vista Basic Information About Your Computer window that you saw when you clicked the Welcome Screen's Show More Details link (refer to Figure 2.2). Vista has a lot of redundancy as you'll see when you learn more but at the same time this redundancy means that you can locate what you need when you need it.

Transfer Windows Settings from One Computer to Another

Changing computers has long been a chore computer users dread, and for good reason. Getting all your programs and settings onto the new computer is daunting and time-consuming. Programs exist that transfer some programs, but no application transfers everything. You want to transfer not only your programs to the new machine; you want to transfer your Windows settings and folder structure, too.

Although Windows XP included a way to transfer some system settings, Windows Vista has been able to take things a step further. Click the Welcome Center's Transfer File and Settings link to open the Windows Easy Transfer screen shown in Figure 2.4. Windows Easy Transfer cannot transfer your applications, such as Microsoft Office, but Easy Transfer can quickly make your new computer behave a lot like your old one by transferring user accounts, data files and folders, some program settings, your Internet settings (such as your Favorites links), email account settings, contacts, and messages within programs such as Outlook.

FIGURE 2.4
Transfer your previous Windows settings and folder structure to your Vista-based machine.

As you click Next to walk through the process, Vista tells you when to make the connection between the two machines and steps you through the process of making the transfer.

Windows Easy Transfer requires that you close all open programs before you begin the transfer.

Easy Transfer uses one of six methods to transfer depending on your current computer setup:

- ▶ CDs
- ▶ DVDs
- ▶ A USB flash drive
- ▶ A local area network (LAN)
- ▶ An external hard disk, such as a FireWire- or USB-connected disk drive
- ▶ A USB Easy Transfer cable (available at your local computer store)

The method you use depends on your older machine's hardware setup. For example, if the older computer has no way to write to DVDs, that option is out for you. The simplest is to use a network connection but both computers must be attached to the network (and be able to recognize each other). The fastest transfer occurs with the USB Easy Transfer cable, but it requires you to have and connect the cable before you can begin, not to mention have the computers close enough together to make the connection.

The transfer process can take as long as a couple of hours or more to complete depending on the method you choose for the transfer and the number of settings that you must transfer. Still, the automated transfer is much simpler than users had just a few years ago when they had to transfer everything by disk and manually adjust all settings on the new machine.

Learn What's New in Vista

Although you'd be hard-pressed to get better information than you get from the book you're currently holding, the entry in your Welcome Center labeled What's New in Windows Vista opens the Windows help window and displays a list of text and links describing your Vista version's primary features. Figure 2.5 shows one such window that appears if you use Windows Vista Home Premium.

Add New Users to Your Computer

When you want to set up a new user on your computer, you can access the User Accounts and Family Safety window shown in Figure 2.6 by selecting the Welcome Screen's Add New Users link. Not only can you add new users but you can change the settings for current users (as long as you do so from an Administrator's account). For example, you can change the picture associated with your user's account by selecting a user and clicking the Change Your Account Picture link.

FIGURE 2.5
Let Vista tell you about its new features.

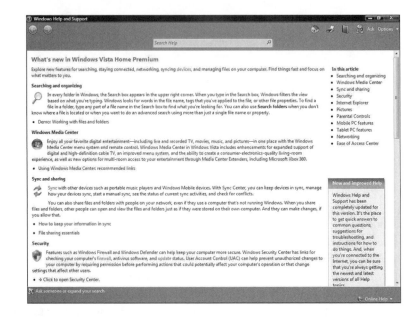

FIGURE 2.6
Add and edit user accounts on your shared Windows Vista computer.

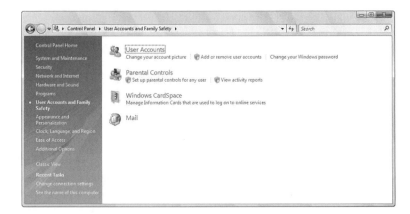

Chapter 26, "Separating Users Gives Each the Access They Need," explains how to set up new users and modify user accounts.

Some items on the Welcome Screen are not necessarily for novice users. For example, you must have an Administrator's account when setting up new users, and you must understand something about a computer's hardware to raise your computer's performance rating as discussed earlier in the chapter in the "Improving Your Performance" section.

The Welcome Screen isn't designed for novice users necessarily but newcomers to Windows and Vista can do a lot with the Welcome Center without having any in-depth knowledge. Microsoft's choice of items for the Welcome Screen lay more with choices that users of a new Vista installation might require regardless of whether they are newcomers or experts.

The bottom line is this: Use the Welcome Screen window as much as you want, but don't feel obligated to go through every option and adjust something. If Vista works well for you, why change anything? However, when you do need to set up something new or modify the way Vista behaves, the Welcome Center might be the best place to start.

Personalize Windows

If you're new to Windows, and even if you are experienced with Windows but new to Vista, you might want to wait before making any personalization changes to your Windows interface. Vista's interface differs quite a bit from Windows XP and Windows 2000. Give yourself some time to become acquainted with Vista before you make any changes.

When you select the Welcome Center's Personalize Windows, you're greeted with the Control Panel's Personalize Appearance and Sounds window shown in Figure 2.7. Here you change the visual appearance, sound effects, and behavior of Windows Vista.

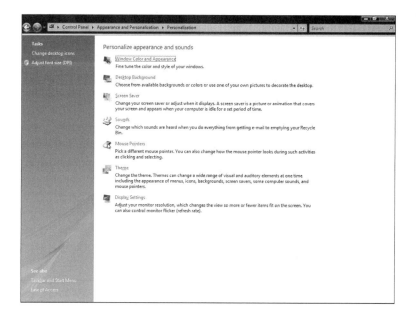

FIGURE 2.7
When you explore Windows Vista, you'll probably have to adjust Vista's appearance and behavior using the Control Panel's Personalize Appearance and Sounds window.

Did you
Know?

If you set up multiple user accounts on your Vista computer, each user can personalize Vista to his or her liking. Upon logging on to their own account, each user works in his or her own personalized environment and that environment doesn't affect the environment of other users on the computer.

Chapters 7, "Changing Windows Vista's Look" discusses ways to use these personalized settings to make Vista behave the way you want.

Connect to the Internet

When the Internet was still an infant, connecting to it often posed challenges. But today, with more standard DSL, cable modem, and dial-up connections, you rarely have to do much to make the connection other than connect cables and plug the power into your modem and possibly your router if you use one.

The Welcome Screen's Connect to the Internet option appears in case you opted not to connect to the Internet when you installed or upgraded to Vista. During the installation or update, Vista asks whether it can attempt to locate your Internet connection. This is important because Vista registers itself and downloads needed updates during the installation. You *can* install Vista if you don't connect to the Internet at that time, but soon after you'll have to connect if you want to do much with your computer.

By the
Way

If you purchased a new computer with Vista preinstalled, an installation routine ran that asked about an Internet connection when you first turned on the system. Assuming that you opted to connect then, you already have Internet access just as you would if you upgraded an older PC to Vista and connected during Vista's upgrade.

If you set up your Internet connection during Vista's installation but still choose the Welcome Center's Connect to the Internet link, Vista displays a dialog box that tells you the connection already exists and gives you the chance to browse the Internet. If you haven't connected to the Internet before, the Connect to the Internet Wizard walks you through the process, asking for the type of connection (such as DSL, cable modem, or dial-up modem), analyzing the connection, and getting you online.

Registering Windows

When you select the Register Windows Online link, the Welcome Center opens Internet Explorer and displays the Windows Vista registration page. You'll need to sign into the Vista registration page with your Windows Live ID name and password. This can be your MSN email address and password, your Hotmail email address and password, your Microsoft Passport name and password, or your Windows Live ID name and password. (Basically, they're all now different names for the same thing.) If you have none of those, you must click the Sign Up Now button to register for a Windows Live ID name and password before you can log in and register your Windows Vista operating system.

Watch Out!

Depending on your Internet browser's settings, you might get a warning before the registration page displays. Microsoft must install an ActiveX control onto your computer for the registration process to complete. It's fine to accept this control when presented with a choice. If you see a yellow bar across the top of your Internet Explorer browser, you have to click that yellow bar and select Install ActiveX Control to complete the process.

After you sign in, the Vista product registration asks for your name and address information. Microsoft usually knows this information and fills it in for you from your Windows Live ID. You also have to enter a product ID, which you can get by pressing Alt+H and selecting About Internet Explorer. Write down the product ID, close the Help dialog box, and type your product ID into the box at the bottom of the screen.

When you click the Register button, the Thank You screen appears and you can close your web browser. You only need to register Windows Vista once unless you have to restore your computer back to its factory-original state using a disc that came with your computer. You'll only do this if you have a problem and your Windows system disk gets damaged, a far less likely occurrence than before Windows Vista's safer computing environment arrived on the scene.

Previewing Windows Basics

The Welcome Center's Windows Basics link opens the Windows Help and Support window that contains link after link of introductory topics. (As with all the Welcome Screen options described in this chapter, if you don't see one, click the Show All Items link to display all your Welcome Center options.) Figure 2.8 shows this window. Ranging from using a keyboard to working with digital pictures, these help-related links walk you through many of Vista's major components. If you don't see the Windows Basics option, click your Welcome Center's Show All Items link to display all Welcome Center items not displayed by default when you first view the Welcome Center screen.

Unless you're brand new to the Windows environment, you won't need to worry about many of these. People who have used Windows in the past almost surely will bypass these as quickly as most of us bypass manuals when we get a new camera and want to start using it right away.

FIGURE 2.8
Scan the list of Windows Vista topics to locate a subject you want to know more about.

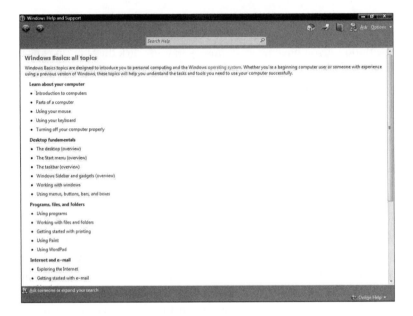

Did you **Know?**

If you're not new to Windows but you also don't consider yourself a Windows guru, you should browse through the topics that appear and click some that interest you. You'll get an introduction to what Windows Vista offers. This text goes into far more detail about how to maximize Vista's features, but this Windows basics overview will whet your appetite to learn more.

Watching a Windows Vista Demo

Selecting Windows Vista Demos from the Welcome Center's options opens the Windows Help and Support Vista Demos window shown in Figure 2.9. Here you can watch various video tutorials and demos that walk you through common Windows tasks such as using your desktop and mouse as well as understanding parts of your computer.

Viewing the Control Panel

Chapter 24, "Controlling Windows Vista," teaches you the most important aspects of your computer's Control Panel window (see Figure 2.10). The Control Panel is available from your Windows Start menu, but you can also get to the Control Panel from the Welcome Screen by selecting the Control Panel link.

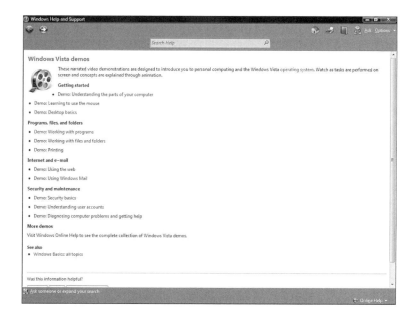

FIGURE 2.9
View any demo that might give you insight into Windows that you didn't know before.

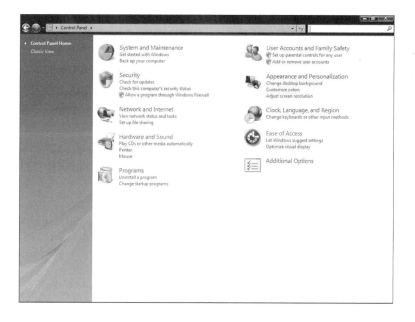

FIGURE 2.10
The Control Panel gives you access to your computer's hardware and system settings.

The Control Panel isn't as difficult to use or understand as it was in the earlier days of Windows. Nevertheless, the very nature of hardware and system settings can still pose a challenge at times. Much of the Control Panel, such as the Personalize

Appearance and Sounds window that appears when you click the Control Panel's Appearance and Personalization link, requires no hardware or system knowledge to use. The link simply offers new ways to personalize the way Windows Vista looks and behaves. (As you may recall from earlier in this chapter, the Welcome Center's Personalize Windows link opens the Control Panel's Personalize Appearance and Sounds window too.)

Even if you're new to some aspects of Windows, such as adding new accounts for family users, Vista's geared to helping you get through the previously ambiguous screens so that you can set up family members and co-workers without knowing a lot about networking or the internals of user accounts. The Control Panel's User Accounts and Family Safety link is where you set up new accounts. In addition, you can access user accounts by selecting the Welcome Screen's Add New Users link.

Did you Know?

If you are the only one who uses your computer, you will be the Administrator and might never need an account other than Administrator to do what you want to do with Windows. Windows Vista allows only Administrator accounts to change a setting. Chapter 27, "Managing Your Windows Security," explains more about user accounts and security.

Although Vista makes using much of the Control Panel easier than ever before, certain parts of the Control Panel can still be tricky. For example, make sure that you understand what's taking place when you access the System and Maintenance window because you can change some memory or system driver settings that freeze your computer. If you're unsure, contact a computer professional when you experience a problem and are unsure how to fix it.

By the Way

Fortunately, Windows Vista is more stable than previous versions of Windows. Reboots due to problems will be infrequent, if they occur at all. Microsoft separated many parts of the operating system from the internal system core, such as sound drivers, so if you have a problem with one aspect of your computer that problem rarely if ever brings down your entire system, as it would in Windows XP and older versions.

The Offers Section

In the Welcome Center's Offers From Microsoft section you'll see options you can order online, some of which are free and others cost money. You can download Microsoft's instant messaging tool named Windows Live Messenger (Messenger does not come with Windows Vista as it did in previous versions of Windows) and you can sign up for a Windows Live OneCare account, Microsoft's online security and protection tool to keep your computing safe and secure.

The Windows Marketplace opens an Internet window where you'll find many of Microsoft's products for sale (see Figure 2.11 for a sample) as well as other vendors' products that you may be in the market for. You'll find freeware that you don't ever have to pay for (such as the Spider-Man Web browser for kids) but most of the site is obviously designed to promote software for sale.

FIGURE 2.11
The Windows Marketplace is Microsoft's software web site where you can purchase and download programs such as games and utility applications.

Chapter Wrap-Up

The Welcome Center is the first window that most new Vista users will see. Spending an early chapter discussing the Welcome Center is critical because the Welcome Center window holds many links to tasks you're most likely to perform when you begin using Vista.

Now that you've read a couple of chapters that discussed Vista's capabilities, you're ready to tackle the specifics. The next chapter, "Clicking Your Start Button," begins your hands-on Windows Vista training.

PART II

Getting Started with Windows Vista

CHAPTER 3

Clicking Your Start Button

In This Chapter:

▶ Master Vista's Start menu

▶ Modify your Start menu's look and behavior

▶ Locate and run programs

▶ Search from your Start menu

▶ Pin programs to your Start menu

It's time to jump into Windows Vista! The quicker you learn the ins and outs of Vista's interface the quicker and easier you'll get your work done and have time to enjoy some Media Player music, movies, or perhaps a game.

Just about everything begins with a single click of your mouse—a click on your Vista's Start button. (You can also display Vista's Start menu by pressing your Windows key.) With that one click, you gain access to all your programs, computer settings, and Vista interface. Even some Windows veterans are somewhat taken aback when they first deal with Vista's Start menu. Here is where you first start to see that as much as the UI looks similar to XP, Vista is actually quite different once you start actually using it. Just remember, these differences only serve to help you get more done with less effort.

About Vista's Start Menu

Clicking your Start button produces Vista's Start menu, shown in Figure 3.1. Your Start menu will surely look somewhat different from the one in Figure 3.1 because the programs installed on your computer will differ. In addition, the Start menu changes, depending on what you've recently done, in an attempt to adapt to your behavior.

FIGURE 3.1
Vista's Start button produces your Start menu from which you can launch your programs and perform just about any nec-essary task.

Recently-run programs

Search box

Start button | Common files, folders, settings, and features

All menus appear in a single column

Did you Know?

If you don't see your Start button, your taskbar is probably set to Auto-Hide mode. By hiding the taskbar except when you need it, you make more room for your other windows. Just move your mouse pointer to the bottom of your screen and the taskbar should appear. In Chapter 6, "Taking the Taskbar to Task," you'll learn how to hide and display your taskbar.

As Chapter 1, "Welcome to Windows Vista," explained, Vista's Start menu doesn't cascade all over your desktop the way Windows XP's did. This leaves you with more desktop space so that you can better see what you were doing and where you're headed. One, two, or three clicks are usually all you need to start programs and adjust settings on your computer from the Start menu.

By the Way

When you install new programs on your computer, those programs add themselves automatically to your Start menu, in most instances. Chapter 28, "Adding and Removing Programs," discusses how to add and remove programs from your computer.

Locating and Running Programs

Once you start using your favorite programs on a regular basis, just like XP, you'll find that they will start to appear on your Start menu in the left column. Windows Vista tracks the programs you use the most and tacks them onto the Start menu. After all, the odds of you running the same program you've run every day for a week are greater than you starting up a program that you haven't run in months. By keeping your most recent programs in the Start menu's recent program list, Vista makes them available to you again with a single click once you've displayed the Start menu.

All your other programs are available on the Start menu even if they don't appear in the recent list of programs to the left. Click the All Programs option above the search box to change the list of programs from your recent programs list to a new menu with your major program categories, as shown in Figure 3.2. After you display the Start menu, you can press your keyboard's up-arrow and down-arrow keys to select All Programs or any other Start menu option.

Your computer's programs
and program folders

FIGURE 3.2
When you select the Start menu's All Programs option, Vista displays a list of programs and program folders from which you can select.

Select to see programs inside

If you don't see the program you want to run, click any program folder to see more programs and menu options. For example, you could click the Accessories folder to see all programs and folders (sometimes called **subfolders** or **submenus**) within the Accessories menu. You could then click the System Tools folder, shown in Figure 3.3, to locate a program you want to run, such as the Disk Cleanup program. If you rest your mouse pointer over a menu option, a pop-up description typically appears that describes that program or option.

Did you
Know?

Vista keeps the Start menu as compact as possible while still showing you what you've selected which is considered what you're most interested in at the time. Click the menu's up or down arrows (or press your keyboard's up-arrow and down-arrow keys) to scroll through the menu if too many options appear on it to show all at once. You can also drag the vertical scrollbar. By allowing this scrolling of Start menu items at each menu and submenu, Vista keeps the Start menu a manageable size and doesn't encroach on the rest of your screen.

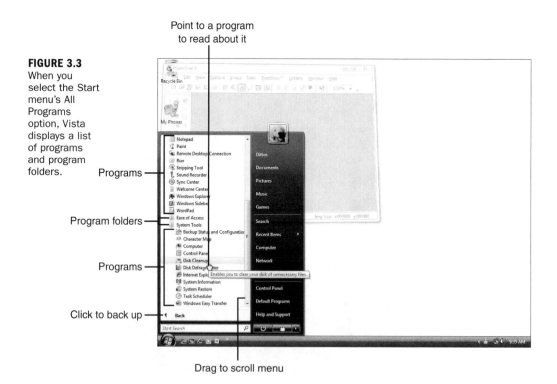

FIGURE 3.3
When you select the Start menu's All Programs option, Vista displays a list of programs and program folders.

Point to a program
to read about it

Programs

Program folders

Programs

Click to back up

Drag to scroll menu

Did you
Know?

If you click to select a Start menu's program folder and then want to back up to where you selected that folder, click the Start menu's Back button to back up one level at a time until you're at the Start menu location.

When you click a program (or press the Enter key after highlighting to select a program with your arrow keys), Vista starts the program and the Start menu disappears.

Searching Is Simple with Start

As I mentioned in Chapter 1, Vista offers many places to search for data. Computer disks are so vast these days and so many programs and data files can appear on them that Vista offers you the opportunity to search for whatever it is that you need at the time from many places throughout Vista.

One of the most useful search boxes to appear in Vista is always ready at the bottom of your Start menu. Just display the Start menu and start typing when you want to search for something because Vista always puts your cursor in the search box until you move it to select a program or select another Start menu option. The reason a search box appears on the Start menu is twofold:

▶ The Start menu is so easy and fast to access that it provides an easy on-ramp to searching for anything on your computer.

▶ If you're unsure of the name of a program you want to run, or if a program is not listed on your Start menu (it's rare, but it does happen), you can begin typing the first few letters of the program and let Vista locate the program for you. When the result appears in the list, you can select the program to run it.

The Start menu changes from its normal list of programs to your search results as you enter a search term. Figure 3.4 shows a search for Microsoft Access, a database program included with some versions of Microsoft Office. Instead of drilling down into the menus for Microsoft Access, you can type the letters in Access and as soon as the program appears, you can select it with your mouse or keyboard.

Did you Know?

With previous versions of Windows, some users opened applications via the Run command, by selecting Run from the Start menu or by pressing Windows+R. Most of the time this was done to run programs that were not on the Start menu. If you didn't know the exact name of the program, however, it was a hit or miss effort as to whether or not it would work. Vista makes the rather archaic Run command almost worthless. By typing the first few letters of the program in the search box and looking at the results, you're far more likely to run the correct program the first time you try.

FIGURE 3.4
You don't have
to locate a pro-
gram within the
Start menu if
you know the
first few letters
of the program's
name.

Click to start Access

Searching for Access

Other Start Menu Features

Up to this point I've focused primarily on the Start menu's left pane, the left half of the Start menu. You've no doubt noticed that the right half, the right pane, is loaded with menu items, too. If you've ever used another version of Windows, you'll be familiar with many of these options in your Start menu's right pane. As with every-thing, Vista tries to keep familiar features that work the way you expect, but attempts to improve on them instead of trying to replace what you already know with foreign situations.

Table 3.1 lists the most common items that appear in the Start menu's right pane. Some, many, or all of them will appear on your Start menu, depending on how your computer is set up and depending on how your Start menu is configured.

TABLE 3.1   Common Menu Programs, Folders, and Options That Appear in the Start Menu's Right Pane

Start Menu Option	Description
YourUserName	Opens the folder where you store most of your files including your documents, videos, pictures, and other data files.
Documents	Opens the folder where you generally will keep your non-multimedia files, such as word processing documents and program data. Previous versions of Windows called this the My Documents folder.
Pictures	Opens the folder where you keep photographs (determined by your Windows Photo Gallery settings, as Chapter 16, "Going Digital with Your Camera or Scanner," explains).
Music	Opens the folder where you keep your digital music.
Games	Opens the folder that contains all your games. Unlike previous versions of Windows, Vista can easily organize all your games in one location: in the Games folder. Your games don't have to reside in the Games folder physically because Vista can put shortcuts to all your games there. Chapter 11, "Taking Time Out with Windows Vista Games," explains how to add your own games to the Games folder to give you quick access to them.
Search	Opens the Search window to perform searches on your computer. The Search window provides more options than the Start menu's simpler search box.
Recent Items	A list of documents and files you've recently accessed and used.
Computer	Displays your hardware and allows access to changing properties of your hardware (formerly called My Computer).
Network	Displays your network hardware and software settings and gives you access to modify them (formerly called My Network).
Connect To	Enables you to connect to the Internet (useful if you have a dial-up connection) or other computers on a network.
Control Panel	Provides access to many common hardware and software settings.
Default Programs	Enables you to specify which programs run under certain conditions (such as which player automatically runs when you select an MP3 file from a list of music files).
Help and Support	Provides access to the Vista help system, where you can get help from Vista's help files as well as go online for more in-depth support.

By the Way

As you point to each entry on the Start menu's right pane, an icon appears at the top of the right pane to indicate the nature of each item. For example, when you point to Games, a deck of cards appears as an icon over the right pane.

In addition to the entries in Table 3.1, two buttons appear at the bottom of your Start menu's right pane. The left button, the Power button, saves your open work and puts your computer into a sleep mode that you can quickly come out of when you're ready to work again. This allows you to shut down almost all the power without having to turn the computer back on from a completely off state, which takes much longer.

The right button, called the Lock button, locks your computer so that nobody can use it without logging in (often with a password). Chapter 4, "Starting and Stopping Windows," explains how to use these buttons and related options to turn on and off your computer as well as place it in sleep mode. (You can change the behavior of this button in your Control Panel's Hard and Sound group's Power Options window.)

Customizing Your Start Menu

You can change the behavior and look of your Start menu so that it works best for your specific needs. To change Vista's Start menu, right-click on the Start button and select Properties. When the Taskbar and Start Menu Properties dialog box appears, click the Start Menu tab (see Figure 3.5).

FIGURE 3.5
Vista enables you to customize your Start menu to perform the way you want.

Selecting the Start Menu Type and Recently Displayed Programs and Documents

The primary options on the Start menu dialog box let you select between the Start menu option and the Classic Start menu option. Unless you or someone else has changed it, the Start menu option will be selected. This allows Vista to display its Start menu to operate in the Vista style of a one-column set of programs, as explained earlier in this chapter. The Classic Start menu changes your Vista menu to perform more like the Windows XP Start menu that cascaded out to the right as you selected from submenus.

> If you're new to Windows Vista, you might be tempted to select the Classic Start menu option so that the menu works the way you're used to. Resist the temptation until after you've used the Vista Start menu style for a while. You'll probably find that it won't take long for Vista's style to grow on you.

Watch Out!

The Privacy section provides two options that determine whether recent documents and programs will appear on your Start menu. The default option displays the programs you've recently run on the Start menu's left pane. The programs you run in the future or the submenus of other programs as you select them from the Start menu will replace the displayed programs.

The Store and Display a List of Recently Opened Files option determines whether the Recent Items entry on the Start menu's right pane (from Table 3.1) appears on your Start menu.

Customize the Start Menu's Right Pane

When you click the Customize button to the right of the Start menu, the Customize Start menu shown in Figure 3.6 appears.

The top half of the Customize Start Menu dialog box determines how menus look and behave on the Start menu. You determine whether most of the items on the Start menu's right pane display (from Table 3.1) by selecting the appropriate option next to each entry. For example, if you click Don't Display This Item under the Control Panel entry, the Control Panel disappears from your Start menu's right pane until you again open this Customize Start Menu dialog box and select either Display as a Link or Display as a Menu.

FIGURE 3.6
You control just about every element that appears on your Start menu.

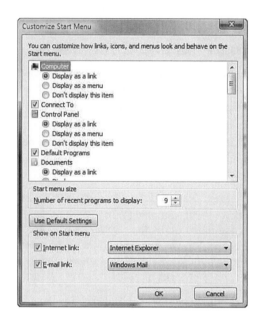

The difference between the two display options—Display as a Link or Display as a Menu—becomes apparent when you display the Start menu. If you selected the Display as a Menu option for any item on your Start menu's right pane, such as the Control Panel, the Control Panel appears with a small arrow to the right of its entry. This indicates that when you point to Control Panel, a cascading menu showing the Control Panel options flies out to the right of the Start menu—not unlike the Start menu in previous versions of Windows.

Figure 3.7 shows a Start menu with several of the right pane's entries set to display as a menu. Notice the arrows next to them that indicate a submenu will cascade out to the right when a user clicks that item (or rests the mouse pointer over the option). When the user selects an item that appears without an arrow, a folder window opens instead of a submenu flying out to the right of the entry.

Even if you set up some of your Start menu's right pane to display submenus instead of opening new windows, you can still open any menu option in its own window by right-clicking that Start menu option and selecting Open from the contextual menu.

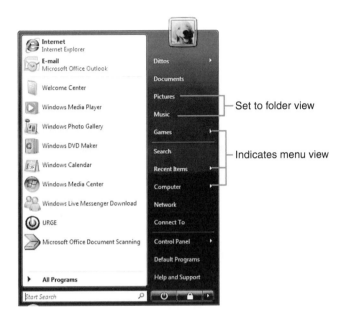

FIGURE 3.7
You can change the Start menu's right pane to display submenus or to open the sub-menu's contents in a folder view when you select the entry.

Modifying Additional Start Menu Settings

The list of options in the Customize Start Menu dialog box doesn't just support changes to the right pane's display. Other options are useful for making your Start menu look and behave according to your preferences. Additional Start menu options in the Customize Start Menu dialog box include the following:

▶ **Enable Context Menus and Dragging and Dropping**—When selected, you can right-click a menu option to display a menu known as a *context menu* (sometimes called a *shortcut menu* or a *pop-up menu*). In addition, you can drag any menu or submenu option to another location on the Start menu. If you don't like the default alphabetical order of your Start menu, drag any entry to another location by clicking and holding that option down with your mouse, and then dragging that item to another Start menu location before releasing your mouse.

▶ **Highlight Newly Installed Programs**—Highlights new entries that represent programs on your Start menu. After you install a new program, that pro-gram's menu will be highlighted for several days until you use the program a few times or turn off the highlighting by clicking to uncheck this option.

▶ **Open Submenus When I Pause on Them with the Mouse Pointer**—Opens submenus when you pause your mouse pointer over them instead of requiring that you click your mouse to open the submenu. Some users prefer that

Windows not open submenus automatically because they want more time to look at the Start menu before it changes to show the submenu. By clicking to uncheck this option, you must click a menu item before a submenu will open. This is also true of the right pane when you have set its entries to display menus instead of displaying in folder views.

▶ **Sort All Programs Menu by Name**—Ensures that all new programs and entries added to your Start menu appear alphabetically (with submenu folders on the bottom, as opposed to the default on Windows XP where the folders appeared at the top). If you uncheck this option, Vista adds new entries to the bottom of your Start menu.

▶ **Use Large Icons**—Determines whether Vista uses large or small icons to represent Start menu entries. Small icons enable you to see more items, but some displays don't easily lend themselves to adequate viewing of the small icons.

By default, the Run command does not appear on your Start menu, but you can add it by selecting the Run Command option from the Customize Start Menu dialog box. As stated earlier in this chapter, the Run command is less necessary in Vista than in previous Windows versions because of the powerful search box that resides at the bottom of the Start menu.

The Number of Recent Programs to Display option determines how many recently run program icons Vista tacks to the Start menu's left pane. Some users feel that the default value of eight is too many. If you routinely run only three or four programs, you might want to decrease this value to a lower number. If you increase the option's value to a higher number, you probably will have to uncheck the Use Large Icons option to see the recent programs without having to scroll to see them all.

By the Way

> The Number of Recent Programs to Display option value has no purpose if you've unchecked the Start menu's Store and Display a List of Recently Opened Programs option (refer to the earlier section titled "Selecting the Start Menu Type and Recently Displayed Programs and Documents").

Returning Your Start Menu to Its Default State

At any time, you can click the Use Default Settings button to return your Start menu settings back to their original, newly installed state. You won't be able to put back your customizations after you click the Use Default Settings button unless you've backed up your computer or set a restore point (see Chapters 31, "Restoring Your Windows System to a Previous State," and Chapter 35, "Protecting Your Data and Programs").

Determining Your Start Menu's Internet Browser and Mail Programs

By default, Windows Vista reserves the two top entries in its left pane for your Internet browser and email programs. For example, the user in Figure 3.8 uses Internet Explorer for Internet browsing and Windows Mail for email. You can elect not to display one or both of these and you can change the program your Start menu uses for each of these items.

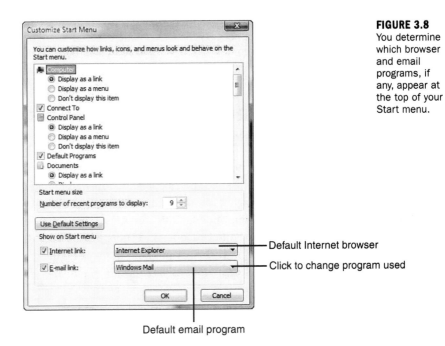

FIGURE 3.8
You determine which browser and email programs, if any, appear at the top of your Start menu.

Default Internet browser

Click to change program used

Default email program

The reason the Start menu reserves the top spots for these two entries is because Internet browsing and email are the two most-used applications today. By putting them in the top spots, Vista ensures that they are never more than two clicks away at any time.

> You might see more than an Internet browser and email program atop your Start menu. You can **pin**, or attach, additional programs to this area and they will remain fixed instead of being fluid as the recent programs lower in the list are. The next section explains how to pin and unpin additional programs and folders here.

By the Way

Keep the checks next to Internet Link and E-mail Link at the bottom of the Customize Start Menu dialog box if you want to keep these entries. To change the programs Vista uses for these entries, click the down arrow and select a different program. For example, if you want to use Windows Mail instead of Microsoft Office Outlook, you can click the down arrow to open the list of available email programs on your computer and select Windows Mail.

After changing any Start menu settings, click the OK button and then click it again to close the Taskbar and Start Menu Properties dialog box to put your new settings into effect.

By the Way

> Your Taskbar and Start Menu Properties dialog box enables you to change the look and behavior of not only the Start menu but also those of the taskbar area at the bottom of the screen. Chapter 6 explores these additional options.

Modify Your Start Menu Without Using the Customization Dialog Box

You can make some changes to your Start menu directly from the Start menu itself without opening the Taskbar and Start Menu Properties dialog box. As you learned earlier in this chapter, you can move menu items from one place to another by dragging them with your mouse. (This works if you've allowed it by checking the Enable Context Menus and Dragging and Dropping option in the Customize Start Menu dialog box.) Right-clicking a program in the left pane (your recently run programs list) produces several options, as shown in Figure 3.9.

By the Way

> Different entries produce a different right-click menu when you right-click your mouse over them. For example, when you right-click over Music in the Start menu's right pane, two options that use the Media Player appear. These options don't appear when you right-click over other entries such as the Control Panel. Vista always tries to give you **contextual help**, meaning that Vista looks at what you're doing and where you are and offers various options specific to that location.

Some common Start menu right-click options you'll see are as follows:

▶ **Open**—Runs the program or opens the folder determined by whatever entry you right-click over.

▶ **Pin to Start Menu**—Affixes the program to the top of your Start menu's left pane to take a fixed place among your Internet browser and email programs. You can right-click over any program pinned to the top of the Start menu and select Unpin from Start Menu to move it out of the top of the Start menu's area. (To unpin your Internet browser and email program from atop the Start menu, you must uncheck those programs from within the Customize Start Menu dialog box, as shown in the previous section.)

FIGURE 3.9
Right-click a Start menu entry to see a list of tasks you can perform related to that item.

Rick-click menu

Your Quick Launch toolbar

▶ **Add to Quick Launch**—Places an icon for that program or folder on your taskbar's Quick Launch toolbar. Chapter 6 explains more about your Quick Launch toolbar.

▶ **Send To**—Opens an additional submenu that enables you to select one of several locations you want to send that item to, such as to a disk, an attachment in an email, or to your desktop as a shortcut icon. This option is most useful for single documents and files such as pictures, music, and video files that you want to put somewhere else or send to someone. Generally, you cannot send programs to another location although you might want to place an icon of a program you frequently use on your desktop. After you place a program icon on your desktop, clicking that icon, which is just a shortcut or pointer to the actual program, executes that program without requiring the assistance of the Start menu.

> ▶ **Remove from This List**—Removes the item's entry from that place in the Start menu's recent programs list.

> ▶ **Rename**—Enables you to change the name of a Start menu entry.

As stated before the previous list, you'll find other right-click options appear when you right-click over other Start menu programs and entries. The most common options are shown in this list. The rest should be self-explanatory as you run across them. For example, right-click on your Start menu's email program and you'll see the Read Mail option. Click Read Mail and your email program opens directly to your inbox.

Chapter Wrap-Up

The Start menu is your ally. With the Start menu, you have access to all your computer's programs and data. You're not even limited to your computer because from the Start menu you can search and browse over your network and the Internet.

Because Microsoft engineered Windows Vista to make your work more efficient, Vista attempts to help you do things more intuitively and naturally. You'll learn in the next chapter how Microsoft changed the way Vista starts and shuts down. More security and less hassle are the welcome results of those changes.

CHAPTER 4

Starting and Stopping Windows

In This Chapter:

▶ Master the shutdown options
▶ Protect your computer from prying eyes
▶ Understand the benefits of Vista's new sleep mode
▶ View mobile sideshow on your laptop

Hit the power button and it instantly turns on. Hit the power button again and it instantly turns off. No, not your computer! It's your radio that turns on and off so nicely. Wouldn't it be nice if your computer responded so quickly and consistently when you wanted to turn it on and off?

One of Microsoft's stated goals for Windows Vista is a carryover from the wishlist of previous Windows versions: that is, to get Windows to load faster and shut down more quickly. When you first install Vista, that seems to be the case. If you've experienced fast computers and new operating systems before, you've probably seen this speed improvement initially only to find out a few months later that things begin to grind to a crawl again as you load your computer with new programs and change system settings. Only time will tell whether Vista remains a quicker on-and-off operating system. In the meantime, you should understand some of the startup and shutdown options Vista provides.

Microsoft designed Windows Vista with a new feature called **Superfetch**. Vista monitors what you do and takes note of the programs you load most frequently. Vista then loads some of those programs into memory automatically (doing so when you're not busy doing another task and without sacrificing any memory you might need for something else you're doing). The goal is to speed the launch of your programs.

By the Way

Starting Vista

Vista loads automatically when you start your computer. The exception to this rule is if you installed Vista alongside another operating system such as Windows XP or Linux. If so, a few seconds after you turn on your computer, you have to choose which operating system you want to start. Select Vista and it begins to load. In many instances, Vista loads faster than XP on the same computer.

Watch
Out!

> Resist the temptation to begin using your computer too soon after your Windows Vista desktop appears. Most of the time Windows continues to load drivers and utility programs, such as the Windows Firewall and any antivirus software you have installed. If you begin to use your computer before everything loads, at best, things will work sluggishly for a while. You might even have to close programs you opened and open them again. Vista's built-in protection is such that you probably won't do any damage to anything in the meantime.

It's difficult to know exactly when your computer has completely started. You can get an idea of whether the computer has settled down by monitoring the notification area's icons. As Figure 4.1 shows, your notification area contains several icons representing many of the programs loaded at startup.

FIGURE 4.1
The icons in your taskbar's notification area indicate the startup status of your computer.

Notification area

Until you get better accustomed to knowing which icons to expect in your notification area and you get a good feel for how long it takes Vista to load, give your computer extra time the first several times you boot up. Let the computer's startup loading sequence have plenty of time to settle down. If you see an arrow icon appear in the notification area, it means there are some icons that Vista is hiding to prevent the area from becoming too cluttered. To see these icons, just click the arrow.

Most computers have a light on the case that indicates when disk activity is taking place. Save a large file to your disk and the light blinks. Vista often works in the background. For example, if Vista notices you're not performing any heavy tasks such as displaying high-resolution graphics, it might take advantage of that downtime to index some files to keep your searches fast. This means that you can't depend on that disk activity status light going out to indicate that Windows Vista has finished loading.

By the Way

Vista's Shutdown Options

Today's computers are left on far longer than they used to be. Many users, especially in office environments, don't power down their systems at all, if for no other reason than to avoid having to sit through a lengthy startup sequence.

For example, with an always-on high-speed Internet connection, you might want to run to your computer to check out movie start times. In the past, when you had to dial a connection and wait for a slow movie site to load, it was far simpler to check a newspaper. Now it's easier, faster, and more informational to look online. With the computer left on, this is possible. If you had to turn on your computer each time you needed to quickly reference some small bit of information, you probably wouldn't bother with the hassle, even if Vista does start up faster than previous versions of Windows did.

Although you'll leave your computer on more often, sometimes 24/7 as so many people do, you won't always want to walk away from the keyboard without changing the state somehow. For example, if several members of your family have their own user accounts, you will probably want to log off your account, especially if your account has Administrator privileges. You wouldn't want a younger member of your family installing a game without your knowledge, possibly overriding some firewall warning intended to safeguard your data from prying eyes.

Not only are accidents possible when you leave your computer without at least logging off, security might be an issue for you. If you work in a Payroll department at a business, for example, and you've been running some reports, you don't want to leave your computer where others without proper authority and access can view files while you're at lunch. You'll certainly want to log off, or possibly shut down your computer to a power-off state or a sleep mode, and you'll want to make sure that your user account is password-protected so that nobody can turn on your computer and easily log in to your account.

Is Powering Off Your Computer Always Best?

Certainly leaving your computer turned on is the easiest way to get back to work when you return to your machine. Are there consequences to leaving your computer on all the time, even at night when you sleep or aren't at work?

This debate has raged for years.

People worried about the environment don't like computers left on because doing so uses resources. That's true, although the power consumption of modern computers isn't bad at all, especially if you enable Vista's power-saving features. Others don't like the machine left on because it uses resources but in a different way: The resources it uses cost money! With energy prices heading upward so steeply these days, cost is a real concern.

Only you can decide which end of the cost-versus-usability spectrum you want to adopt. In general, your computer consumes very little power when operating and still less when you stop working and your PC enters one of its automatic power-saving modes. Unless your monitor is extremely old (pre-1995), Vista can usually turn off your monitor's power as well, or at least put your monitor into a sleep mode that consumes virtually no power until you return and press a key or move your mouse to wake your computer back up. Keep your computers turned on (although you might have to log off your account if others share your computer as mentioned in the previous section) so that when you return to your desk, a quick push of the display's power button puts you right back where you were when you left your machine, ready to work again.

Chapter 34, "Saving Power with Windows Vista," explores Vista's power-setting features that determine when your computer's energy-saving features kick in.

Vista's Sleep Mode

At the bottom of your Start menu's right pane are two shutdown buttons and an arrow you can click to display additional shutdown options (see Figure 4.2).

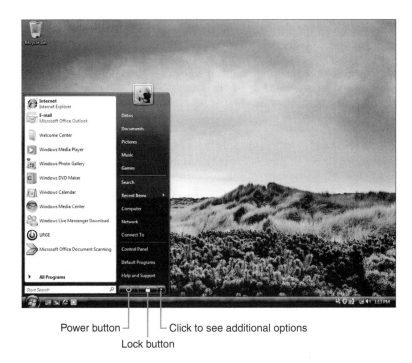

FIGURE 4.2
Your Start menu provides buttons with which you can shut down your computer in various ways.

Power button — ⌐ Click to see additional options

Lock button

The Power button is slightly misleading. By default, it doesn't actually turn your computer completely off. Instead, the Power button puts your computer in a **sleep mode** that greatly reduces the amount of power your computer consumes.

When you click the Power button to select the sleep mode option, Vista saves all your current settings to main memory, including your open programs and open window locations. When it's finished, it goes into sleep mode in which it consumes only enough power to keep the settings active. When you press your computer's actual power button (the physical one, not the Start menu's Power button), Vista quickly starts back up and displays the login screen unless you're the only user and have no password on your account. When you select your user account (and optional password if you set one up for your account), your screen will be right back where it was when you clicked the Power button. If you were in the middle of typing a letter, for example, the letter will be right where you left it.

While going to sleep mode, Vista writes a snapshot of your computer to your disk drive so that if power does go out, everything will be the way you expect it when you turn your computer back on.

Returning from sleep mode is far faster than rebooting your computer from a powered-off state. And you don't have to reopen any of the programs you were working in when you entered sleep mode.

By the Way

Previous versions of Windows supported a standby mode, a hibernate mode, and a sleep mode. The standby and hibernate modes consumed a little more power, but started more quickly than sleep mode. These somewhat similar but different options confused more than they clarified and users often were unsure which to use. Vista's single sleep mode demystifies the situation. You now can put your computer to sleep for a quick wake-up or power it off completely.

Laptop users will see that Vista enters sleep mode automatically when they close their laptop screens. When they reopen their laptop, Vista puts them right back where they were. Sleep mode cannot last forever on a laptop battery, however, because the battery's power will eventually drain away and the laptop will shut down to a power-off state. Because Vista saves an image of your workspace to disk no matter how you enter sleep mode, your work should be fine when you charge your battery.

Your Power Button Sometimes Works Differently

Some circumstances make your Start menu's Power button behave differently. Instead of putting your computer to sleep, your Power button might close your programs and shut down Windows completely. If this occurs, Vista prompts you to save any unsaved work in documents that might still be open. It all depends on how it has been configured to work.

When your Power button displays a circle with a line inside it (as opposed to a partial circle with a line coming out of the top), your PC's administrator disabled sleep mode from the Power Options window (see Chapter 34) or, possibly, your hardware doesn't support sleep mode. If your Power button has a yellow shield on it, Windows Vista is telling you that updates have been downloaded to your computer and you need to restart your computer (instead of going into sleep mode) to install them.

Your Computer's Lockdown

If you click the Start menu's Lock button, Vista instantly logs you off and displays your username in the center of your screen; unless you have a screensaver set up, in which case Vista logs you off and launches your screensaver. Chapter 7, "Changing Windows Vista's Look," explains how to set up a screensaver. When you return to your computer, you only have to click your username and enter a password, if you set one up with your account, and you'll be right back where you were before you locked down your machine.

The Lock button is the quickest way to put your computer into a state in which nobody can use your account, but you can return easily and continue where you left off, with all open programs intact after you log back in.

If someone shares your computer with you and he or she gets to the locked machine before you do, that person can still use the computer. Instead of clicking your username, they only have to click the Switch User button and they will be given a user list from which they select their user account.

Vista's Other Shutdown Options

Figure 4.3 shows the six shutdown options available to you when you click the arrow to the right of the Lock button on your Start menu. The options are as follows:

▶ Switch User

▶ Log Off

▶ Lock

▶ Restart

▶ Sleep

▶ Shut down

Shutdown options

FIGURE 4.3
Click the arrow next to the Start menu's Lock button to see all the shutdown options available.

The option you select depends on what state you want your computer to be in when you leave it. If all you want to do is let someone else use the machine, select the Switch User option. Vista will log you off and display a list of users set up to use your computer. When you eventually return to the account you switched from, all your open programs and windows will be intact.

Did you Know?

> If you are using a standard, non-Administrator account and want to switch to your Administrator account, select the Switch User option to log in as Administrator. You may also run an administrative program from a non-administrative account if you know the password. Just right-click the program's icon and select Run as Administrator.

If you select the Log Off option, Vista assumes that you do *not* want to save your desktop and return right where you left off. The Log Off option tells Vista you want to shut down all running programs in your account; when you return to the computer, you're ready to begin at a startup state.

If you have programs running when you select Log Off, Vista will ask whether you want to save any unsaved data. For example, if you were working on a Word document and selected Log Off before selecting Save, Vista would ask whether you want to save your document before logging you off.

As an extra precaution, if you log off with programs running, Vista displays a list of all running programs and asks you to verify that you really want to log off (see Figure 4.4). If you haven't yet responded to the prompt to save unsaved data in a program when this screen appears, you'll see a new message that says: This program is preventing you from logging off your computer.

You have unsaved data in an Excel worksheet

FIGURE 4.4
Before logging you off, Vista gives you a chance to verify that you want to log off and prompts you to save any unsaved data before continuing.

Protect Your Data

The reason you aren't prompted to save unsaved data when you select Switch User as opposed to Log Off is because Vista assumes that you want to return to the place you were working when you return to the machine. Because Vista isn't logging you off and closing your programs, the Switch User option doesn't tell you about unsaved data. Still, as an extra safety measure, you *should* save your unsaved data before selecting the Switch User option or clicking the Lock button. This keeps your data safe just in case the unexpected happens, like a power failure or if your laptop's battery runs out of juice.

Saving unsaved data is especially critical if you're on a laptop running on battery power that could drain away before your return to your computer and save your work. When entering sleep mode, Vista always attempts to save your data before shutting down, but if your laptop battery is draining too quickly, this isn't always possible.

If you click any entry in the open programs list, such as one that might have unsaved data preventing you from logging off, Vista returns to that program and cancels the log-off process. You then save your unsaved data and close any open programs you want to exit. If, instead, you click the Log Off Now button, Vista honors your request and logs you off, closing your programs—even those with unsaved data.

Selecting the Lock option from the options menu does the same thing as clicking the Start menu's Lock button. Vista logs you off, but it won't close your open programs and current work. You must log back in, entering a password if your account requires one, before you can return to your work. If another user logs in to your computer in the meantime, he or she can work in their account until they log off or select the Lock option.

The Restart option does everything the Shut Down option does except power off your computer. Instead, Vista shuts down and then restarts your computer just as if you had turned off the machine and then turned it back on.

Did you Know?

Many contend that a system Restart is easier on your equipment than turning your PC all the way off and then turning it back on again. (It's also faster.) Think about when a light bulb most often goes dead: when you flip the switch to turn it on. A sudden rush of current shocks any electrical device. Your computer is made to withstand that shock and you have nothing to fear from turning it off and on, but if all you want to do is clear or reset system settings (as is often required when you install or remove a program, especially a utility program such as a disk-imaging program), select Restart. Doing so is probably better for your computer—and quicker and easier for you—than shutting down the system completely and then turning it back on again.

The Sleep option saves your work to memory to the disk and then powers down your computer to very low-power state. Sleep performs the same action as clicking the Power button does. When you resume from Sleep mode, all your previously open windows and programs will be right back in the state you left them when you entered the Sleep mode.

The Shut Down option is the big one. Select it and Vista prompts you to save any unsaved documents or data. When you do that, Windows Vista closes your open programs and turns off your computer. Always shut down your computer before installing any internal hardware such as a new graphics card or hard drive. If you still use a mouse attached to a PS/2 port (instead of a USB-connected mouse or keyboard), you should shut down your computer before plugging it in or unplugging it from your PC.

> PS/2 mouse ports are sensitive and can go bad when you connect a mouse to them with the power on. Because they're designed to be hot-swappable, you don't need to shut down your system when connecting a USB- or FireWire-based device.

As you use Vista for more things, you'll run across other modes you might never have seen. Vista supports an away mode that disables your power button. When in away mode, your computer appears completely turned off, but your PC is actually doing something such as recording a television show or burning a DVD from inside Vista's Media Center. By allowing an interruption such as an accidental press on the power button on the front of your computer, such activity would be severely affected and you would lose your work or have a half-burned CD or DVD that is unusable. When in away mode, the power button will neither put the computer to sleep nor turn it off until the activity finishes.

Help for the Stubborn Computer

The promise of sleep mode (and the old standby mode) is just fine until it stops working. Every version of Windows since Windows 3.1 has had problems shutting down via the keyboard on some systems. Whether going into one of the sleep modes or turning off completely, some hardware just won't obey. If you're like some users, your sleep mode and shutdown modes work fine initially, but after several months of installing new programs and updates your computer freezes instead of turning off or going to sleep.

Vista's design *should* make such problems less frequent, but one would have to be extremely naïve to believe such problems will disappear entirely. Only time will tell, but if you have a stubborn computer that doesn't want to go to sleep or shut down, make sure that you've downloaded and installed all the latest updates and drivers. You might even have to update your motherboard's BIOS (basic input/output system), a process that differs from manufacturer to manufacturer and can be dangerous to the integrity of your system if you're not sure of what you're doing. (BIOS updates can also be notoriously difficult to find.)

If you must resort to shutting down your computer manually by pressing the power button on the front of the machine, you might have to hold the button in for five seconds or so before your computer turns off. Powering down your computer manually is typically required when it locks up instead of entering sleep mode or shutting down properly from the keyboard.

Did you Know?

Resist the urge to turn off your computer by its power button. If your system seems unresponsive to conventional mouse and keyboard input, try pressing Ctrl+Alt+Del in an attempt to get your computer's attention. Pressing Ctrl+Alt+Del usually grants you access to Vista's log off and shutdown options. If it's a specific application causing the lockup, switching to the Task Manager usually allows you to close the offending program.

Always give your computer a few seconds to return control to you before resorting to using the actual power button. Your computer's power-up state may take longer because Windows might have to repair some driver files that get corrupted if you don't shut down properly from the keyboard. Of course if your computer is really frozen there's little more you can do but press the power button. And if even that doesn't work, the worst case scenario is to simply pull the plug. Avoid going this route if you can.

Watch Out!

If you've logged off and no other users are on your computer, you can safely turn off your computer by the power button in most cases. However, the preferred and safest way to turn off your machine is through the keyboard, if you have that option.

Using Vista's Mobile Sideshow

Sideshow is an entirely new feature to Windows. If your laptop supports its features, you won't believe what you can do with Vista's Sideshow! Requiring a laptop with a small display screen on the outside of the laptop (often on the screen's case), Sideshow can display information from your laptop even with your laptop turned off. Figure 4.5 shows such a laptop and Figure 4.6 shows a close-up of the Sideshow display.

FIGURE 4.5
Listen to MP3s and read emails without having to open your laptop's case using the Sideshow feature, such as this version powered by PortalPlayer Preface™ technology.

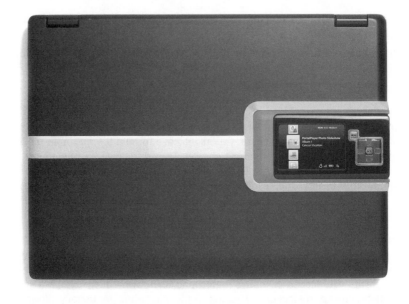

FIGURE 4.6
Without raising the lid and turning on your laptop, you can use Sideshow to get information from your laptop computer.

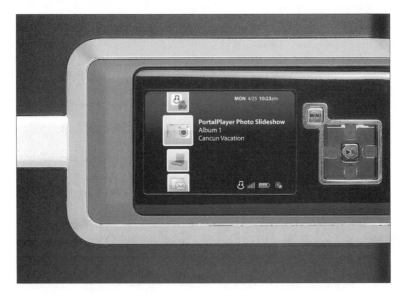

The biggest Sideshow advantage is saving your laptop's battery. As long as your laptop has some battery power remaining, and Sideshow's tiny display doesn't consume much power, you can access Sideshow. Sideshow displays data from various programs, not unlike the Windows Gadgets on Vista's Sidebar (see Chapter 9, "Working with the Sidebar and Gadgets"). Depending on your Sideshow's configuration, you can look at appointments in your calendar, play an MP3 file stored on your laptop, and check an email you received earlier when your laptop was on and connected to the Internet.

The idea behind Sideshow programs is to give you quick and small bits of information without requiring you to turn on your laptop completely. Microsoft will be working with vendors such as PortalPlayer (www.PortalPlayer.com) to release more Sideshow applications over time.

Sideshow applications work more like the small and lean gadget applications in that you shouldn't expect Sideshow to present you with a full-fledged application such as Adobe's Photoshop. Sideshow applications must be small enough and require only enough light disk access to work with very little battery power to ensure that Sideshow doesn't drain your battery as fast as using the full laptop would.

Chapter Wrap-Up

Windows Vista offers different startup and shutdown options but, as you've seen, Vista's startup and shutdown options are more intuitive and safer than those that came with Windows XP and earlier versions of Windows. Data safety and giving you quick access to your computer when you return to do more work seem to be primary goals of Vista's shutdown options.

Starting up and shutting down is even more critical for laptop users than for table-top PC users. Vista respects your laptop's battery life by going to sleep mode when there's enough juice, but writing your workspace to the disk drive for safekeeping when the battery begins to run dry. The Sideshow application is Vista's way to give you quick access to useful bits of information on your laptop without consuming extra power or requiring you to open and turn on your laptop.

In the next chapter, you'll see all the ways that Vista helps you manage your programs. Your programs are the workhorses of your computer productivity and you need quick and reliable access to them.

CHAPTER 5

Managing Your Programs

In This Chapter:

▶ Master program and window control

▶ Utilize see-through window borders

▶ Switch between windows and programs

▶ Use icons to give you live previews in file lists

▶ Change icon sizes when needed

As you know, Windows Vista is an operating system. An operating system serves many purposes, but primarily, it exists so that your hardware can talk to your software. The operating system sets up a uniform data exchange so that your programs recognize all the different devices you've attached to your computer.

The operating system also serves as a conduit between you and your programs. With Vista you interact with your programs by entering information, triggering hardware device activity (such as printing), and adjusting programs and windows so that they behave the way you need them to behave.

Only after mastering Windows Vista's interface and understanding its nuances will you be able to tackle multiple, open programs and windows effectively. In this chapter, you'll learn how to arrange and switch between your windows in an efficient manner. Then you'll leverage this chapter's tools in the next chapter as you learn ways that the Taskbar and help speed up what you want to do. Vista enables you to have full control over your windows and taskbar, modifying the way they all work to suit your preferences.

Manage Multiple Programs and Windows

Unless you're brand new to computers, you know by now that an operating system such as Windows enables you to run several programs at the same time. In your word processor, you could begin to print a long document, then you can start your email program and retrieve your Inbox messages, and while those messages are loading, you can fire up Media Player and listen to some music. Your computer multitasks all these operations in separate windows. Even if you see only one of the open windows, the activities you began in the other windows keeps moving.

Being an efficient and effective computer user means that you have the ability to manage all your open windows. Knowing how to arrange the windows and how to manipulate them enhances your ability to use your PC.

Even if you're a computer pro, you'll be thankful for Vista because it improves on the old XP-style ways of managing your open programs and windows. As with much of Vista, you'll still do much of your window management using the old, familiar ways but Vista usually has a new trick in store.

Working with the See-Through Windows

If your computer supports the Aero Glass feature, just a quick glance at your desktop reveals little ways that Vista improves on past Windows versions. The goal of Vista is to give you tools to help you do your job more quickly, easily, and effectively. One way that Windows Vista does this is by offering you somewhat transparent window borders called **translucent windows.** Some windows display more transparency than others do; the border is always translucent and often more parts of the windows are.

As Figure 5.1 shows, the border of the smaller window allows some of what lies underneath to show. (Note that a window's title bar might not always display a title.) With previous versions of Windows, when one program window covered another, you had no way to know what was under the top window without dragging it to the left or right to see what was underneath.

By the Way

> Sure, you can't typically read clearly what's under a window's border because the border is only semi-transparent. Generally, however, you're somewhat familiar with the programs you run on a regular basis. The semi-transparent effect is often enough to let you know what's beneath a window when you have multiple windows open at the same time. In addition, Windows sometimes pops up a window with a warning or error message and those pop-up windows are often transparent to some extent so as not to cover up more than necessary.

Maximize

Transparent border   Title bar   Minimize | Close

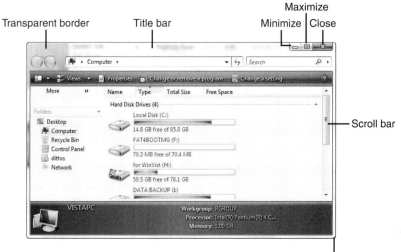

Scroll bar

FIGURE 5.1
In addition to the transparency feature that Aero Glass provides, you can move and resize Vista windows exactly the way you're used to if you've used previous versions of Windows.

Drag here to resize window

If you don't have hardware that supports Aero Glass, you don't have the transparent border effect. However, because routing tasks such as moving and resizing windows still works in the usual way, much of this chapter applies to you, whether or not you get to see Vista's transparency effects in action.

If you want to turn off the Aero Glass effect and return to a Windows XP interface style, right-click over your computer's desktop background and select Personalize. Click to open the Theme group and change the current theme to Windows Classic. Your translucent window borders will go away, and the Aero Glass effect will change back to more of the icon-like views that Windows XP offered. You can switch back to Aero Glass by selecting the Windows Vista theme once again.

Did you Know?

When you maximize a window, its borders are not translucent. A maximized window displays its border in a solid color hue (often black), but the exact color depends on the Windows settings you've set. When you restore the window back to a smaller-than-maximized state (but not minimized), the window's borders and sometimes part of the window's background again turns translucent.

You'll notice from Figure 5.1 that the control buttons are the same for Vista as for other versions of Windows (although the Maximize button has a slightly different look). To move a window, just click and hold anywhere within its title bar and drag the window elsewhere. If you use multiple monitors, you should be able to drag a window from one monitor to another without any problem.

To resize a window, point to an edge or corner of the window. When you do, your mouse pointer changes to a double-pointing arrow and you can drag the edge of the window to change its size.

**Watch
Out!**

> You won't be able to resize all windows. Windows such as dialog boxes and other windows designed by programmers to be a fixed size won't allow you to resize their borders.

Always remember that you can resize most File, Open dialog boxes such as the one in Figure 5.2. When your disk drive contains lots of files, being able to expand the Open dialog box is useful for quickly traversing a long list of files to locate a particular file.

FIGURE 5.2
Being able to resize Open dialog boxes allows you to locate files more easily when you have a large disk and folders with lots of files.

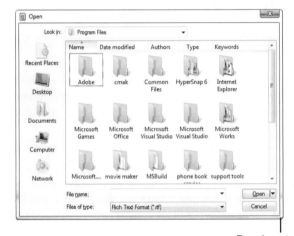

Drag here to resize

Make sure that you know the difference between a closed window and a minimized window. If you start a program such as the Calculator and click the Calculator's Close button, Vista shuts down the Calculator program and you can no longer use it (without restarting the program again).

If, instead of the Close button, you click the Minimize button on the Calculator program's window, Vista removes the program from your screen but keeps the program active and in memory. The taskbar will still show a button for the Calculator program and you can return to the Calculator without reopening it by clicking its taskbar button or by pressing Alt+Tab or Windows+Tab until the Calculator appears again.

Switching Between Windows

If you don't close a program or open folder window, you can still open another. Keeping more than one window open at a time is how you multitask computer programs. You can start your Calculator program, and then start your word processing program without closing and without minimizing the Calculator program first.

After you open several programs, you have to switch between the programs. One way is to click the taskbar button that corresponds to the program to which you want to switch. To help you determine which open program or folder window you want to switch to, Vista's Aero Glass feature displays a thumbnail image of the window as you move your mouse over each open program window button on your taskbar (see Figure 5.3).

Foreground window

Background window

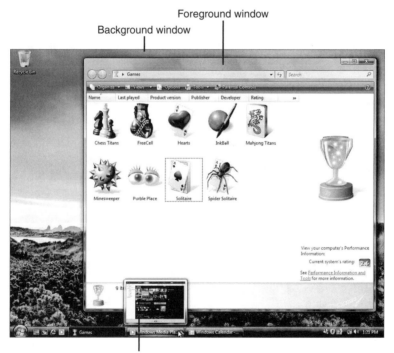

Thumbnail image of program window

FIGURE 5.3
Point to any taskbar button to see a thumbnail image of that program currently running on your computer.

Thumbnails like the one shown here are live, so if you have a video program playing, for example, the taskbar button's thumbnail image shows a live feed of that video. This is especially helpful if you have multiple windows of the same program open at the same time because the thumbnail image helps you quickly locate the specific window you want to work with next.

If your graphics hardware doesn't support Aero Glass, the name of the program or folder appears as you move your mouse pointer over the taskbar buttons.

By the Way

Although you can have multiple programs and windows open, you can work in only one at a time. The window that is currently in view, with its title bar showing, is the **foreground window**, and all other windows are **background windows**. No other program's window covers your foreground window. As you switch to a program, Vista brings the program window to the top of the stack of windows on your desktop. If the window was minimized on your taskbar before you switched to it, the window will now be visible.

Instead of clicking the taskbar buttons to switch between programs, you can press Alt+Tab. Doing so pops up the task switcher window shown in Figure 5.4. Each thumbnail image represents an open program window. As you keep pressing Tab while holding down the Alt key, the next thumbnail in the task switcher highlights. The thumbnail image you stop on is the one whose program will become active in the foreground.

FIGURE 5.4
Press Alt+Tab to switch between programs.

Show Desktop icon   Minimizes all open windows

Vista always includes the Show Desktop thumbnail when you press Alt+Tab. The Show Desktop thumbnail allows you to quickly minimize—but not close—all open windows and display your desktop. Therefore, instead of stopping on a program or folder window, if you stop on the Show Desktop thumbnail image when pressing Alt+Tab, Vista minimizes all your open windows and takes you to your desktop. You can also click your taskbar's Show Desktop icon to minimize all open windows.

> Anytime you want to clear your desktop of all open windows without closing all your windows, the Windows+D shortcut command is often quicker to use than clicking the Show Desktop Taskbar icon and quicker than clicking Alt+Tab until the Show Desktop thumbnail highlights. Press Windows+D again and your open windows reappear where you left them.

Did you Know?

If you don't have Aero Glass–compatible graphics hardware, Vista displays icons and descriptions instead of thumbnails as you Alt+Tab between your open windows.

Pressing Windows+Tab produces the Vista's new Flip 3D effect that enables you to scroll through your program windows. Shown in Figure 5.5, as you press Windows+Tab, the open programs rotate through the scrolling list of screens. If you don't have Aero Glass–compatible hardware, Windows+Tab switches among your taskbar buttons, highlighting each one as you press the keys. In addition to scroll through the windows using Windows+Tab you can also scroll your mouse's wheel to scroll the Flip 3D windows. Left-clicking on any window in the Flip3D view activates that window.

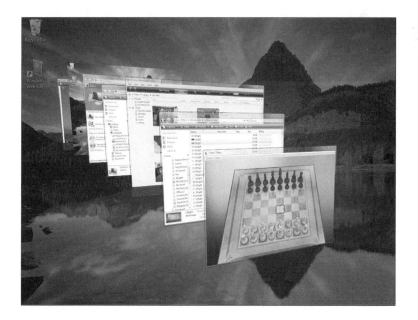

FIGURE 5.5
Press Windows+Tab to switch between programs using Aero Glass's Flip 3D rotational display.

Vista supports numerous keyboard shortcuts such as Windows+Tab and Alt+Tab. For a list of the most useful keyboard shortcuts, see Appendix A, "Common Vista Keyboard Shortcuts."

Even if you have a graphics card that supports DirectX 9.0 or higher (the requirement to use Aero Glass), you still won't see Aero Glass features if you're using the Vista Starter or the Windows Vista Home Basic versions of Vista.

Visual Icons All Over

Windows Vista is more visual than any operating system before. You'll notice signs of Vista's graphics base just about everywhere you look.

For example, when viewing a list of files, such as you would do in Windows Explorer, Vista uses icons that actually represent the contents of each file in folders. These are called **live icons** because they represent the exact picture of the graphic file (which might be a video) they represent. For example, in Figure 5.6, the icon to the left of each graphic image is a tiny thumbnail of the actual picture. Instead of every JPEG image using the same standard icon (unless you don't have the Aero Glass feature), your icons visually show you the contents of files. This holds true for many kinds of files. For example, a Word document's icon is a thumbnail image of that document's first page.

FIGURE 5.6
Small icons reflect the contents of your files.

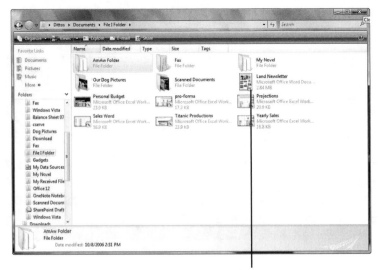

Icons

Although the default size of the icons is small, having them gives you one more shortcut when using Vista. Instead of opening a file to see its contents or clicking to change the view of the Explorer window, the icon itself gives you a clue as to the file's contents.

By the Way

For those times when the icons next to files in a list are too small, select from the pull-down View option, shown in Figure 5.7, to display larger icons for your files. Move the slider control up and down to resize the live icons so that you can see them comfortably.

Select icon size

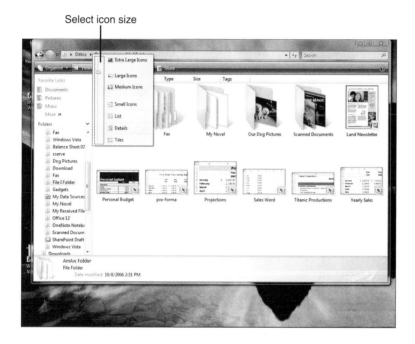

FIGURE 5.7
Each window's View option provides several icon sizes you can select to see your file contents better.

Chapter 8, "Mastering Vista's Explorer Windows," goes into more depth on the various Vista Explorer windows, menus, and options.

Chapter Wrap-Up

This chapter explored some of the ways you can use Vista's functionality to get your work done faster and more effectively. Microsoft modified much in Vista to improve your computing experience. Sometimes only a minor tweak, such a showing you live icons of your documents and pictures in Windows Explorer, is a tiny change that can make you far more efficient as you use your computer.

Another vital Windows Vista element is your taskbar at the bottom of your screen. You've already noticed some of the taskbar's advantages, such as displaying thumbnail images of the open programs and windows the taskbar buttons represent. Many more ways exist to utilize your taskbar effectively.

Many people use the taskbar only for switching between open programs and for seeing the current time, but the taskbar does far more than that. After you master the next chapter, you'll be using the taskbar in ways you might not have known were possible. The taskbar can actually replace some of your Start menu's functionality, making you more efficient at your computer.

CHAPTER 6

Taking the Taskbar to Task

In many ways, Vista's taskbar at the bottom of the screen is like a customized computer dashboard. At the ready are programs, windows, and icons with which you can control your computer and work with programs faster and more efficiently.

The taskbar is generally underutilized. Many people use Windows for years, and understand a lot about Windows, but they don't know how they could use the taskbar more effectively. Vista adds even more power to your taskbar than previous Windows versions.

You will find that if you begin to adjust your taskbar to suit the way you work, you will use your Windows Start menu less and less. The taskbar reduces your keystrokes and saves you time. The taskbar also provides information about your computer, such as the status of devices and programs.

Your Taskbar Awaits You

Unless you're brand new to computers, you know by now that your taskbar is your primary means of controlling the programs and windows you're currently using on your computer. As Figure 6.1 shows, a button appears on your taskbar for each open program. In addition, if you've opened windows such as the Control Panel or a Windows Explorer window, a button appears for each window as well.

Three Windows Explorer windows on one button

FIGURE 6.1
A taskbar button
appears for every
open program
and window.

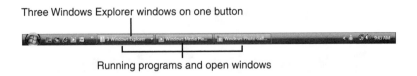

Running programs and open windows

Put Your Taskbar Where You Want It

The taskbar's default location is at the bottom of your screen. It doesn't have to stay there! You can move your taskbar to any edge of your screen, including the top of your screen. If you move the taskbar to the top of your screen, the thumbnail images (assuming that your hardware supports Aero Glass) drop down from the buttons instead of appearing above them as when the taskbar lies at the bottom of your screen. If you move your taskbar to either the left or the right edge of your screen, the thumbnail images appear to the side of their respective buttons.

You lose no functionality when you move your taskbar away from the bottom of your screen. Some users prefer the taskbar somewhere other than the bottom of the screen; perhaps because they use programs with information along the bottom edge that is more visible without the taskbar in the way.

Moving your taskbar to any of the four screen edges is easy; simply drag it to the new location as follows:

1. Locate a blank spot on your taskbar and point to the spot with the mouse cursor. Be sure that you're pointing within the taskbar and not at a button.

2. Drag the taskbar to another edge of your screen. As you drag the mouse, the taskbar moves with the mouse and appears at the edge of the screen.

3. Release the mouse button to anchor the taskbar at its new position.

Figure 6.2 shows the taskbar against the right side of the screen.

If you have multiple monitors, you can move your taskbar to any one of them. For example, if you use three monitors, your Windows Vista workspace becomes three screens wide and you can move windows and programs between your monitors and extend windows over more than one monitor. On a three-screen system, you might want to move your taskbar to the center screen to keep it handy in relation to the other screens.

FIGURE 6.2
You can move your taskbar to either edge of your screen or to the top of the screen.

By the Way

If you find that you cannot drag it to another edge of your screen, your taskbar is locked into place. Right-click on your taskbar (over an unused area) and click Lock the Taskbar to uncheck that option. When locked, a taskbar cannot be moved or resized (see the next section). When you unlock your taskbar, you can move it. After you move your taskbar, right-click and select Lock the Taskbar again to select that option to keep your taskbar in place and safe from inadvertent movement or resizing.

Remember that your Windows Vista Start button appears on your taskbar. That means that when you move your taskbar, you also move your Start button. Your Start menu will fly out from wherever the Start button resides. Therefore, if you move your taskbar to the top of your screen, your Start menu will fall down from the top of your screen instead of coming up from the bottom of your screen.

Some users prefer to put their taskbar on either screen edge because the taskbar buttons don't have room to display the full program or window title when multiple programs are open at one time. This is less of a problem with the Aero Glass feature due to the thumbnail images, but there are still times when you need to read a button's full title. By placing the taskbar against the left or right edge of your screen, you can expand the taskbar's width to read more of the title on each taskbar button. Of course, doing so significantly reduces the amount of screen real estate available to open program windows.

Resize Your Taskbar

You can change the size of your taskbar as follows:

▶ If it is on the bottom or top of your screen, you can change the height of your taskbar.

▶ If it is on the left or right edge of your screen, you can change the width of your taskbar.

To resize your taskbar, first make sure that it isn't locked. As explained in the previous section, right-click on your taskbar and click to uncheck the Lock the Taskbar option if it's checked. To resize your taskbar, point to the edge closest to the center of your screen. In other words, point to the top edge of your taskbar if it's on the bottom of your screen or point to the bottom edge of your taskbar if it's on the top of your screen. Your mouse pointer changes to a double-pointing arrow. Drag the edge closer to the center of the screen. As you drag, your taskbar increases in size one row at a time. If you find it difficult to drag the edge of your taskbar without instead dragging a window edge that might reside close to it, first minimize the window close to your taskbar.

Generally, you'll want to keep your taskbar no taller than two rows or it will consume too much of your screen space. Figure 6.3 shows a two-row taskbar. By giving the taskbar two rows, you have more room for taskbar buttons, the buttons can show more of the open program or title, and your taskbar is less cluttered.

FIGURE 6.3
Adjust your taskbar's height (or width if you've placed it on the left or right edge of your screen) to see more at one time.

Did you Know?

> By resizing your taskbar to at least two rows, Vista is able to display not only the time in the lower-right corner's notification area but also the date. The date is handy to keep displayed.

Using the Taskbar Menu

As you saw in the previous sections, a right mouse button click over your Taskbar produces the same result as a right mouse button click over many Windows programs and elements: a pop-up menu appears. This menu, sometimes called a *context-sensitive menu*, displays several options available to you at the time you right clicked. To determine what task-appropriate options appear in this menu, Vista looks at what you are doing when you right-click.

You can change the appearance and performance of your taskbar and of the windows controlled by your taskbar from this menu. Just locate an empty spot on your taskbar, right-click it to open the contextual menu shown in Figure 6.4.

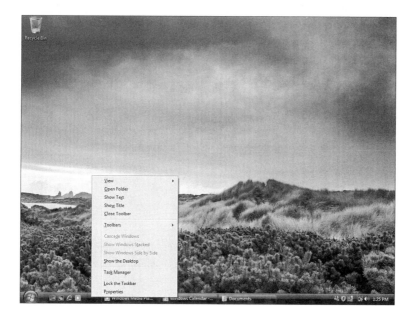

FIGURE 6.4
A right-click on your taskbar's blank area displays this contextual menu.

The taskbar menu is not necessarily one you'll need to display often. Most users play around with various taskbar settings for a while until they find preferences that suit them best. Thereafter, those users might rarely use the taskbar properties menu.

The taskbar actually displays several menus, depending on where you right-click and how you've configured the taskbar. For example, if you right-click over the notification area, several more options appear that don't otherwise show if you right-click over other parts of your taskbar.

The Taskbar Properties Menu

When you select Properties from your Taskbar menu, the Taskbar and Properties dialog box appears as shown in Figure 6.5.

By the Way

If you have too many windows open to locate a blank spot on your taskbar to right-click on, you can display the Taskbar and Start Menu properties dialog box by right-clicking over your Start button and selecting Properties.

In the previous chapter, you learned how to use the Taskbar and Start Menu Properties dialog box to adjust your Start menu's behavior and appearance. You'll use the same dialog box to change your taskbar. Three of the four tabs across the top of the Taskbar and Start Menu Properties dialog box relate to your Taskbar: Taskbar, Notification Area, and Toolbars.

FIGURE 6.5
Adjust your taskbar and Start menu settings from this properties dialog box.

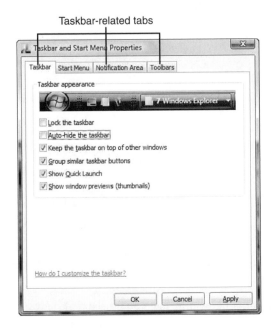

Table 6.1 describes the taskbar page's settings. One of the settings used most frequently is the Auto-Hide setting, which keeps the taskbar hidden until you move your mouse pointer to the bottom of the screen to display the taskbar. This leaves the taskbar out of the way until you're ready to use it, allowing for more screen real estate for your open program and folder windows.

TABLE 6.1   The Taskbar Property Settings

Setting	Description
Lock the Taskbar	Fixes your taskbar so that you cannot move or resize it.

TABLE 6.1 Continued

Setting	Description
Auto-Hide the Taskbar	Hides the taskbar so that you see it only when you move your mouse pointer to the bottom of your screen.
Keep the Taskbar on Top of Other Windows	When the taskbar appears (whether you always display it or when you point to the bottom of your screen and the previously hidden taskbar appears), it appears on top of all other windows if you select this option. Otherwise, your taskbar might be hidden by one of the open windows on your computer.
Group Similar Taskbar Buttons	When selected, Vista watches how you open windows and if the taskbar is already full of buttons, Windows ensures that only one taskbar button appears for all files you open with the same application. In other words, if you've unchecked this option, you can open three Word documents and all three buttons will appear next to each other on your taskbar, even if you opened another program before you opened the three documents. If you've selected this option, Vista will use only one button to represent all three documents, but you'll see a down arrow to the right of the button. When you click the down arrow, a list of titles appears, representing each program or window the button represents. (If you use Aero Glass, a thumbnail of whichever program or folder you move your mouse over in the list will appear.)
Show Quick Launch	Places the Quick Launch toolbar on your Taskbar (see next section).
Show Windows Previews (Thumbnails)	Determines whether thumbnail images appear as you point to each button on your taskbar.

Using the Quick Launch Toolbar

Your Quick Launch toolbar, shown in Figure 6.6, is extremely helpful for speeding up how you start programs that you want to run routinely. Each icon on the Quick Launch toolbar represents a program or folder that you can open with a click of that icon; the only exception is the Show Desktop icon, which minimizes all open windows with one click and returns those windows to their previously open state when you click the Show Desktop icon again.

Show Desktop icon

Quick Launch toolbar

FIGURE 6.6
The Quick Launch toolbar puts your favorite programs on your taskbar.

Your taskbar's Quick Launch toolbar might only show two or three icons to begin with, such as the Internet Explorer, Show Desktop, and Windows Media Player icon. If you upgraded from a previous version of Windows and your previous version contained a Quick Launch toolbar with more icons, Vista should also display those same icons after you install Vista.

To start a program, just click its icon. Unlike the taskbar buttons, when you point to a Quick Launch icon, a thumbnail will not appear but a description of the icon's program will.

Many users add several icons to their Quick Launch toolbar. You can do the same. Add those programs you run often such as your word processor. If you put too many icons on the Quick Launch toolbar, the icons can get unwieldy and consume too much room on the taskbar that would be better used for running program and open window buttons. By putting those programs you often use there, the Quick Launch toolbar button means you don't have to open your Start menu to run a program.

If you increased the height of your taskbar, your Quick Launch icons will not be squeezed for space and you'll more easily see and distinguish them. If your taskbar is only one row high, you might have to click the Quick Launch toolbar's down arrow to see additional icons you've placed there, as Figure 6.7 shows.

FIGURE 6.7
If your Quick Launch toolbar shows a button with an arrow on it, you can click the arrow to see additional Quick Launch icons.

To add a program to your Quick Launch toolbar, locate the program on your Start menu and right-click the program name. Select Add to Quick Launch from the contextual menu and Windows Vista puts an icon on your Quick Launch toolbar that represents the program while keeping that program in your Start menu. After you place the icon on the Quick Launch toolbar, simply click the Quick Launch icon to start the program without having to display your Start menu first. Put icons that represent the programs you frequently start on your Quick Launch toolbar to keep them just one click away at any time.

To remove a program from your Quick Launch toolbar, right-click that program's icon on the toolbar and select Delete. Vista removes the icon from your Quick Launch toolbar.

Vista doesn't erase the program from your disk that you remove from your Quick Launch toolbar using the Delete command. The icons on your Quick Launch toolbars represent shortcuts to your programs, not the programs themselves. A **shortcut** is simply a pointer to the disk location where that program resides. Removing that pointer, or the shortcut, erases only the toolbar's path to the program but not the actual program.

By the Way

Understanding Your Notification Area

Vista's notification area, also called the **system tray** or **systray**, appears in the lower-right corner of your desktop's taskbar. The notification area holds the system clock and icons that represent programs or utilities loaded into your PC's memory, such as a communications icon when you're online and memory-resident programs that start when Vista starts, such as your anti-virus and firewall programs.

Depending on what you do on your computer, other icons and information appear in the system tray. For example, if you've increased the size of your taskbar to two rows, the date appears along with the current time.

If you're running a laptop, an icon usually appears that indicates whether your laptop is running on AC power (plugged into an outlet) or, if running on battery power, how much battery life remains.

Often, the notification area icons are not as useful as the information that appears when you point to them. For example, Figure 6.8 shows the message `Windows Security Alert` when the mouse pointer rests on an icon. When you see a message such as this one, you can double-click the icon to open a program or control panel to adjust the settings for the message. For example, when you double-click the shield shown in Figure 6.8, a message might explain that your antivirus program hasn't started and you'll know that you need to start it (or install one if you haven't installed one yet).

Message appear

Notification area

FIGURE 6.8
Your notification area contains icons and messages that display the status of your computer.

If you double-click a notification area icon and no program starts, try right-clicking the icon and selecting the program from the contextual menu that appears.

As you use your computer throughout the day, messages might automatically pop up from the notification area informing you of the status of certain activities. For example, if Vista or another program on your computer, such as your antivirus program, has recently downloaded updates, a message might pop up to let you know that you need to click to install those updates. Depending on the program, the updates might be applied automatically and the message will let you know that the program was updated after the fact. When you receive an email, an icon might let you know that your inbox has a new entry.

Because of space limitations, Vista doesn't always display all the notification area icons. Instead, Vista hides inactive icons and displays a clickable arrow to the left of the icons. Clicking the icons shows all active and inactive icons.

The notification area tab on your taskbar and Start Menu Properties dialog box, shown in Figure 6.9, gives you various ways to adjust your notification area settings. Most users prefer to keep the inactive icons (or those with little activity) hidden by keeping the Hide Inactive Icons option checked.

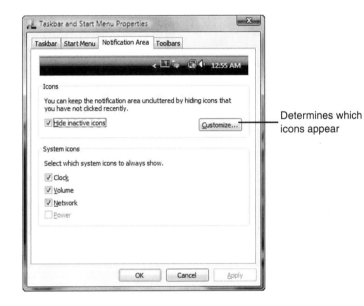

Determines which icons appear

FIGURE 6.9
You can adjust the properties of your notification area.

> Click the Customize button on your Notification Area dialog box page to specify exactly which icons you want to hide. You'll select from a list of available icons that might appear on your notification area depending on which programs are installed on your computer.

Did you Know?

The remaining options enable you to determine whether you want a clock, volume control, network status icon, or power indicator (useful for laptops) on your notification area. You control the appearance of these four icons yourself through this dialog box. You will control the other icons that appear by clicking them or by right-clicking and selecting from their contextual menus.

The volume control is handy for controlling your overall system volume. By keeping the volume control on your taskbar in the notification area, you can always adjust your volume settings no matter which program you're running at the time. Just click the speaker icon in your notification area and the volume control appears, as Figure 6.10 shows. Drag the volume control up or down to adjust your overall system speaker volume.

FIGURE 6.10
Click the speaker icon any time to adjust your system volume.

Click to mute or unmute
your speaker

Managing Multiple Windows with Your Taskbar

Right-click over a blank area of your taskbar and you'll see a menu that enables you to modify the way programs and windows behave. Even advanced Windows users forget these options are available to help make multiple windows more manageable.

When you open two or more windows at once, they can be difficult to manage individually. You could maximize each window and display only one window at a time. There are many reasons to keep more than one window open and displayed at the same time, however. You might need data from one program window to use in another.

The more monitors you use, the easier it is to keep multiple windows open and in your viewing area at the same time. Nevertheless, even with multiple monitors, you sometimes need a quick way to arrange your open windows.

When you want to see more than one open window at a time, your taskbar can help you. You don't have to drag and resize all windows yourself. You can let the taskbar do this for you. Three ways exist to organize several windows that are open at once: You can cascade them, horizontally stack them, or vertically show them side by side. The following steps demonstrate these window placement options:

1. From a clean desktop without any open windows, open your Computer Explorer window by selecting Computer from your Start menu's right pane. If your Computer Explorer window (formerly called *My Computer* in Windows XP) opens maximized, click the Restore button to shrink the window down in size.

2. Open your Control Panel window.

3. Open the Help and Support window. These windows are open just to put some things on your desktop to practice with here.

4. Start your Windows Media Player.

5. Now that you've opened four windows, ask Vista to organize those windows for you. Right-click over a blank spot on your taskbar, and select Cascade Windows. Vista instantly organizes your windows into the cascaded series of windows shown in Figure 6.11.

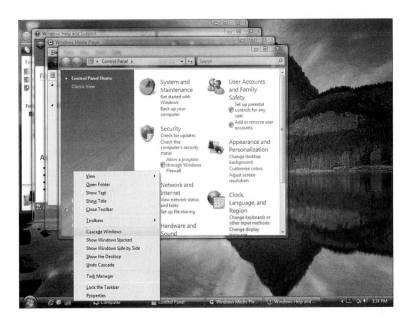

FIGURE 6.11
Your windows are now more manageable with only window borders showing for the windows in the background.

Notice that the title bars of all your open windows are placed where you can read each one. When you want to bring any hidden window into the foreground, click that window's title bar and the window rises to the top of the window stack. The cascading effect always gives you the ability to switch between windows. As long as any part of a hidden window is peeking out from under another, you can click the title bar to bring that hidden window into view.

6. Sometimes you need to see the contents of two or more windows at the same time. Vista enables you to *tile* the open windows so that you can see the actual body of each open window. Vista supports two kinds of tiling methods: vertically stacked or horizontally side-by-side.

Display your taskbar's contextual menu and select Show Windows Side by Side. Vista will properly resize each of your open windows, as shown in Figure 6.12.

FIGURE 6.12
Your windows
are now tiled.

At first glance, side-by-side tiling might seem too limiting. After all, to fit those open windows on the screen at the same time, Windows cannot display much of any one window.

Keep in mind that you can move any window by dragging its title bar with your mouse as long as the window is not maximized to your full-screen size. You can also point to an edge of a window and drag the edge to resize that window.

After you've tiled several open windows, you can still use the moving and resizing feature of the individual windows to arrange your desktop. After tiling the windows, you can move the Help window toward the top of the screen if you want to see more of the Help window. (Scrollbars automatically appear in tiled windows if the contents of the window consume more space than can be displayed at once. Click the arrows at each end of the scrollbar to move window contents into view.)

7. The vertical tiling method, called **stacking**, produces windows that are fairly thin but offer another kind of open window display. Close two of your windows because stacking works best when you have two windows open. Its purpose is to enable you to move data between two windows easily. Select Show Windows Stacked from your Taskbar's pop-up menu and Vista reformats your open windows once again (see Figure 6.13).

FIGURE 6.13
Two windows are now stacked.

8. At any point you can undo one of the stacking options. Undo appears on your Taskbar's pop-up menu only after you've selected a Cascade Windows, Show Windows Stacked, or Show Windows Side by Side option.

No matter how you cascade or tile your open windows, each window's Maximize, Minimize, and Restore buttons work as usual. Therefore, you can maximize any cascading window by clicking that window's Maximize button.

Did you Know?

Chapter Wrap-Up

You now know virtually everything there is to know about using your taskbar to control programs. Your taskbar acts like your dashboard, putting items where you need them and giving you options to arrange open programs and windows as you choose.

Your desktop's background itself is a useful place to manage your programs. The icons that appear there offer a handy place to locate programs you start often and windows you commonly open. In addition, the background holds the graphical wallpaper image that shows when Windows Vista loads. In the next chapter, you'll learn how to manage your desktop, change your wallpaper image, add and remove icons to and from your desktop, and even trigger screensavers to keep prying eyes away from your sensitive data when you leave your computer.

CHAPTER 7

Changing Windows Vista's Look

In This Chapter:

- ▶ Change the look of your desktop
- ▶ Put icons where you want them
- ▶ See more on your monitor
- ▶ Change your desktop's background image
- ▶ Set up a cool screensaver
- ▶ Change the sounds that Windows Vista makes
- ▶ Modify your mouse's behavior to work the way you do

No two people are alike, so why should your Windows desktop look like everyone else's? Whether you're an animal lover and want your PC to reflect that, or you simply cannot stand the thought of staring at the same desktop background day in and day out, you'll be happy to know that you can change all that and more.

In this chapter, you'll learn ways to change your computer desktop's appearance. Along the way, you'll add more functionality to what you can do. Windows Vista is highly customizable and you can arrange Vista to sport an interface that not only reflects your aesthetic preferences but that also minimizes the time it takes you to do tasks.

Managing Your Desktop Icons

Although Vista's initial desktop background is clutter-free with only a few icons, more icons will show up over time. In many cases, as you install new programs, new icons appear. If you bought your computer with Vista preinstalled, almost certainly there are several icons on your desktop that aren't specific to Vista, but represent programs your computer's manufacturer installed for you.

The icons represent programs and windows. When you activate an icon—which usually means double-clicking the icon with your mouse—the program represented by the icon launches or the window opens as would be the case for a folder of your pictures that you might have saved to the desktop as an icon.

By the Way

> Any desktop icons that have small blue arrows pointing to them represent shortcuts to the actual programs and windows. Therefore, you can delete such a desktop icon without worrying that you're deleting the actual program from your computer. All deleted icons go to your Recycle Bin, so they're easy to restore if you change your mind. If you're unfamiliar with the Recycle Bin you'll learn about it in the next chapter, "Mastering Vista's Explorer Windows."

Rearranging Your Desktop Icons

If you want to move a certain icon from one location to another on your desktop, simply click and drag it into position. Perhaps you want to group your icons so that the game-related icons all appear together and your work-related icons appear in another section of your desktop.

Watch Out!

> If you move an icon and Vista snaps the icon to a different location or back to its original place, you have one of the automatic arrangement settings turned on. The next section, "Changing Your Icons' Display," explains what's going on and how to avoid it.

For more global and general changes in your icon layout, right-click on a clean spot on your desktop (any part of your background picture that has no icons or text) and select Sort By from the pop-up menu (see Figure 7.1). This produces a menu of choices for arranging your desktop icons including by name, size, file extension, or date modified. Just click the desired option to arrange your desktop in the specified order.

By the Way

> When you change your desktop icons, as well as all the other elements such as your background wallpaper throughout this chapter, keep in mind that the changes affect only your login account but not the accounts of other users who share your computer. Each user sets up his or her own appearance, icons, background, screensavers, and themes. That way, each user works within a personalized and unique desktop setting.

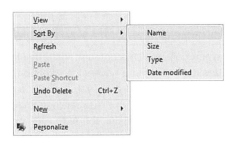

FIGURE 7.1
Rearrange your
desktop icons
using this con-
textual menu.

Changing Your Icons' Display

When you right-click your Vista's desktop wallpaper and select the top option, View, you'll see how you can change the way Vista displays icons. Table 7.1 describes the options you see on the View menu.

TABLE 7.1   Your Desktop Icon View Settings

Setting	Description
Large Icons	Displays oversized desktop icons, which is useful if you have a huge monitor (as you might have if your computer is connected to an entertainment system with a large television) or vision challenges. For the typical computer, the large icon display consumes too much screen to be practical.
Medium Icons	The default icon size that you see when you first install or boot Vista for the first time. This selection is an effective balance of size and space.
Classic Icons	Displays smaller icons than either of the other views. This setting is called *Classic* because the icons are sized identically to Windows XP's default icon size.
Auto Arrange	Arranges your icons as Vista sees fit, generally following an up and down pattern in columns from the upper-left corner to your lower-right corner of the screen. The Auto Arrange option, when you check it, is always on and this means that Vista will constantly monitor the location of icons and adjust them as it deems necessary. This keeps the icons nicely aligned but also means you cannot move icons to just any place you want.
Align to Grid	If you've moved icons to various locations on your screen and then select the Align to Grid option, Vista will arrange your icons in a row and column format. Unlike Auto Arrange, Vista won't insist that every icon be placed on top of each other forming columns across your screen; instead, the Align to Grid option adjusts your icon as close to where you move it as possible so that it stays nicely placed in a grid-like pattern. You'll see how the Align to Grid differs from the Auto Arrange option immediately following this table.

TABLE 7.1 Continued

Setting	Description
Show Desktop Icons	When selected (the default), Vista displays icons on your desktop. When you uncheck this option, Vista hides all your desktop icons and gives you a desktop completely free of any clutter except for your taskbar (assuming that you haven't hidden your taskbar using the Auto Hide option described in Chapter 6, "Taking the Taskbar to Task"). When you hide desktop icons, Vista remembers their location and puts them right back if you show the icons once more. If you install new programs with the icons hidden, those icons won't display until you enable this option to show the icons once more.

Figures 7.2 and 7.3 visually show you the difference between the Auto Arrange option and the Align to Grid option. Before Figure 7.2, the icons were dragged into similar purpose groups all over the desktop. Figure 7.2 shows what happened when the user selected the Align to Grid option. The icons are nicely aligned in rows and columns, but they generally stay in the same area where the user put them.

Figure 7.3 shows the same desktop immediately after selecting the Auto Arrange option. The icons no longer have the freedom to be placed in groups around the desktop. Instead, they all align in columns against the left side of the desktop.

FIGURE 7.2
After Align to Grid, the previously scattered icons are grouped in a more visually appealing, row-and-column manner.

FIGURE 7.3
Auto Arrange moves all the desktop icons over to the left side of the desktop and begins forming columns.

If you prefer to have lots of icons on your desktop, organizing them in groups so they reside together depending on their function is helpful. For example, you might group all icons that represent your graphics programs in one area of your screen and group all your financial icons together in another area. If you then select Align to Grid (not Auto Arrange, which will move them all to the left side of your desktop), Vista straightens their layout by placing them in rows and columns but keeps them in the same general vicinity and in the groups you put them in.

Did you Know?

Adding and Removing Desktop Icons

Deleting an icon is easy. Click to select the icon and press your Delete key. You can also right-click an icon and select Delete. Vista makes sure you really want to delete the icon with the verification shown in Figure 7.4. Click Yes and Vista erases the icon from your desktop and sends it to your Recycle Bin.

Until you delete another icon, Vista adds an Undo Delete option to your desktop's right-click menu so that you can restore the icon to its original position if you change your mind.

FIGURE 7.4
Vista makes
sure you really
want to delete
the icon before
proceeding.

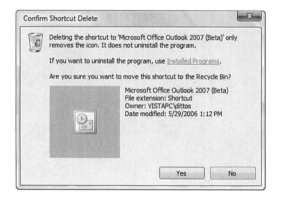

When you want to add new icons to your desktop, there are several approaches you can take. Usually, you'll want to add a desktop icon for a program you frequently run. Instead of wading through the Start menu each time you want to run the program you can double-click the desktop icon. The simplest way to add a desktop icon from a program in your Start menu is to display your Start menu and locate the program there. Right-click the program and select the Send To option from the contextual menu. Choose Desktop and Vista creates a shortcut icon on your desktop for that program.

Did you Know?

You can right-click a Quick Launch toolbar button or any program in an Explorer window to send that item to a desktop as a shortcut icon. If you want to move an icon from your Quick Launch toolbar to your desktop, instead of putting a copy of the icon on your desktop, click and drag the Quick Launch toolbar icon to your desktop.

If you right-click over a blank area of your desktop (not over an icon) and select New, the menu shown in Figure 7.5 appears. From this menu, you can choose from a variety of items that you may represent with a desktop icon. For example, if you routinely use an Excel worksheet for home budgeting, you can create an icon that represents that home budget worksheet: First select Microsoft Office Excel Worksheet to create a shortcut to Excel and then right-click the icon that appears, select Properties, and locate the worksheet file you want to open from the icon. This is a little cumbersome, but works fine. Obviously, if you don't have Excel installed, Vista won't display Excel as one of your options on the New menu.

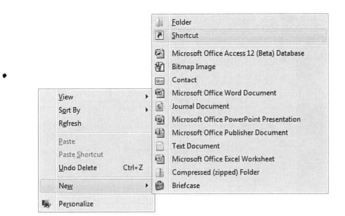

FIGURE 7.5
You can add desktop icons that represent many kinds of programs and files.

Personalizing Your Desktop

You can customize the way your desktop looks. People have different preferences. Some people like to see more information at the cost of small icons and text while others prefer to see less but make what they see larger. Some people don't care what background image appears on their desktop while others like to change their desktop's wallpaper regularly. As with most aspects of Vista, you can change the way your desktop looks.

To customize your desktop, right-click your desktop and select Personalize from the contextual menu. The window shown in Figure 7.6 appears. From here, you can customize your desktop and Windows Vista settings in several ways. The following sections explore some of the personalization settings available to you.

Change Your Display Settings to See More

The first option on the Personalize Appearance and Sounds window is the Display Settings option.

> Depending on your graphics adapter, you might see far more display settings than described here. For example, some adapters support high-resolution 3D graphics that require personalization to match your monitor. These settings will show as extra tabbed pages in your Display Settings window.

By the Way

Most users modify settings in their Display Settings window when they want to adjust the resolution of their screen. **Resolution** refers to how many **pixels** (tiny dots that collectively construct an image) you can fit onto your screen at one time, both vertically and horizontally. In addition, if you use multiple monitors, Vista enables you to control the resolution of each monitor separately.

FIGURE 7.6
Customize the
look and behav-
ior of your
desktop with
these
Personalize
options.

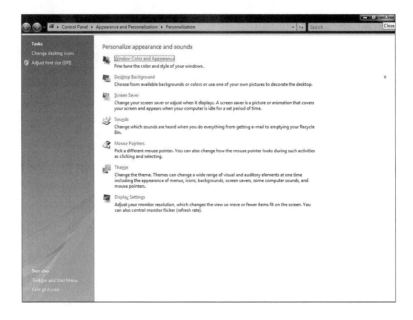

To adjust the resolution of a monitor, click the monitor you want to adjust (you
don't have to do this if you use only one) on the Display Settings window and drag
the slider control labeled Resolution to the left or right. Decreasing the resolution
magnifies objects on your screen, but you won't be able to see as much at one time.
You'll find that you must scroll up and down and left and right when viewing web
pages if your resolution is too low. If your resolution is higher (meaning you slid the
Resolution slider more to the right), you'll see more at one time but everything will
be smaller. You'll have to adjust your resolution to suit your own needs.

On modern systems, especially those capable of running Windows Vista, I recommend you don't set your screen resolution lower than 1024×768, although
1280×1024 is often preferable for screens of 19" (diagonal) and larger. If you have
an LCD panel, note that it was designed for a specific "native" screen resolution and
will display its best image only when operating at that resolution.

**Watch
Out!**

If you use a television for your primary display, your choice in screen resolutions is
likely to be much more limited, particularly if it is not a high-definition TV.

After you adjust your resolution, you generally won't have to do much more with
the Display Settings window again.

Changing Your Vista Theme

Vista enables you to give your Windows a complete facelift, both in appearance and even sound by giving you themes to choose from. A **theme** is a collection of sounds and colors and icons that change the entire look of Windows at once. Your theme permeates all of Windows Vista, including dialog boxes you open in programs such as Microsoft Word.

To apply a new theme, follow these simple steps:

1. Select Themes from your Personalize Appearance and Sounds window to open the Theme Settings dialog box shown in Figure 7.7.

2. Click the down arrow to display the list of themes. For example, if you select Windows Classic, all your desktop, icons, sounds, and dialog boxes will take on the more traditional 2D appearance of Windows XP. As you select from the various themes, Vista displays a window on a desktop under the Sample label to show you what your new theme will look like.

3. Vista doesn't change your current theme to your selected theme until you click Apply or OK. You can still change to another theme, if you prefer, before you click OK to close the dialog box.

FIGURE 7.7
Select a new theme for Vista.

The themes available to you will be either somewhat limited or vast depending on whether you had extra themes when you upgraded to Vista from XP, or perhaps you bought your computer preinstalled with Vista and your computer's manufacturer added new themes to the small set of themes that come standard with Vista. Whether you have a lot or only a few, many more themes are available to you.

You can install a wide variety of themes containing unique and appealing sounds and animations. You can turn your PC into a virtual jungle complete with monkey noises, lion roars, and birds calling among other possibilities. Some desktop themes come with animated mouse pointers that change depending on where and how you move your mouse.

Although you might not have many themes at your disposal now, the Internet is usually just a click away. Microsoft offers a small number of themes at Microsoft.com, but other sites, such as www.themeworld.com, offer far more. There, and on similar theme sites, you'll find themes based on TV shows, cars, music stars, cartoons, animals, and just about anything imaginable.

Watch Out!

> Theme websites that provide themes for free or for small download charges often have their own installation instructions depending on what the theme has to offer. This is one time when you won't want to bypass the instructions because you can mess up your current theme and still not properly install the new theme if you don't follow the directions for specific themes.

Changing Your Desktop's Color Scheme

There are times when you don't want to change your entire set of Windows icons, dialog boxes, and sounds, but you might want to select a different color scheme.

Selecting Window Color and Appearance from your Personalize Appearance and Sounds window produces the Change Your Color Scheme dialog box shown in Figure 7.8.

FIGURE 7.8
You can change your Windows color scheme without changing the entire theme.

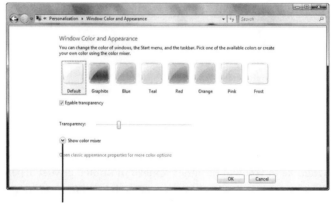

Click to customize border colors

The color scheme you select changes the colors of the following elements from your Windows environment:

▶ Window borders, edges, corners, and interior parts

▶ Start menu

▶ Taskbar

Click to pick one of the sample color schemes at the top of the dialog box to change your Windows color scheme to one of the options.

By clicking to check or uncheck the option labeled Enable Transparent, you determine whether or not the Aero Glass transparency stays on your windows. If you choose to keep the transparency, the slider labeled Transparency determines how much of a see-through effect appears. If you want to create your own colors, click the Show Color Mixer option to get access to color, saturation, and brightness controls.

> Windows XP also allowed you to change your color scheme from the Appearance dialog box. If you're familiar with XP's way of supporting color changes and want to use XP's more familiar dialog box, click the option labeled Open Classic Appearance Properties For More Color Options to adjust your Windows settings with the dialog box you know already.

By the Way

Changing Your Desktop Background

You're never stuck with the default picture Vista uses for your desktop's background. The desktop background image was called *wallpaper* in previous Windows versions. You can change your desktop's background image by following these steps:

1. Select Desktop Background from the Personalize Appearance and Sounds window. The Choose a Desktop Background dialog box appears, as shown in Figure 7.9.

2. With Windows Wallpaper selected for the Picture Location option, several Vista-supplied background images appear. You can select one and click Save to switch to that background desktop image.

3. If you click the Picture Location down arrow and select Pictures or Public Pictures, a preview image of your pictures from your Pictures folder, or one from a system-wide pictures folder (if your computer has one) will appear. You can select one of those images to use as your desktop background.

4. Some images, as will often be the case for your picture files, aren't framed properly to fill the entire desktop. You can select how the image appears (stretched, normal size with a blank border, or tiled) from the options under the question, How Should the Picture Be Positioned?

5. If you elect to place the image unsized in the center of your desktop without stretching or tiling it to the borders, you can choose the border image color you want to use by clicking the Change Background Color button that appears when you click to select this image option.

FIGURE 7.9
Select from several Vista desktop background options or use your own graphic image.

By the Way

If you upgraded to Vista from an earlier Windows version or if you bought a computer with Vista preinstalled, you might have several more wallpaper options available to you than those shown in Figure 7.9.

SOS—Save Our Screens!

Almost everyone has heard of *screensavers*. Computer stores and software distributors on the Internet sell several programs that display pictures of your favorite television characters, cartoons, and geometric and 3D designs. Microsoft designed Windows Vista to include several screensavers, so you don't have to buy one unless you want more than you can find in Vista and online free of charge.

Do Screensavers Protect Your Equipment?

Want to know the worst-kept insider computer industry secret? Here you go: Screensavers really don't save many screens these days.

In the past, computer monitors, especially the monochrome green-letters-on-black-background kind, would burn in characters when left on too long without being used. In other words, if you left the monitor on for a long time and did not type anything, the characters on the screen would begin to leave character ghosting that would still be visible even when something else was being displayed on the screen. Occasionally, you might even have continued to see this with the monitor turned off.

To combat character burn-in, programmers began to write screensavers that blanked the screen or displayed constantly moving letters and pictures if the system went unused for a set period of time. The blank screens had no burn-in problems and the moving text never stayed in one place long enough to burn into the monitor.

For the most part, today's monitors don't have burn-in problems. Yet screensavers are more popular than ever before, mostly because they can be fun! Screensavers greet you with designs, images and animated cartoons when you would otherwise look at a boring screen. It's *cool* to use a screensaver.

That said, screensavers aren't only for fun and games. Windows screensavers offer an additional benefit over entertainment in the form of password protection. If you need to walk away from your screen for a while but you want to leave your computer running, associating your account password with a Windows screensaver requires that password to be input before the screensaver can be deactivated. Although you can always manually lockdown your system, setting a screensaver to pop up after 10 minutes of inactivity adds an extra layer of insurance, just in case you forget.

Computer stores often display their PCs with password-protected screensavers to keep customers from tampering with the systems.

Windows contains several screensavers from which you can choose. Through the Screen Saver dialog box, you can set up a blank screensaver or one that moves text and graphics on the screen. You control the length of time the monitor is idle before the screensaver begins. The following steps explain how to initialize your screensaver:

1. Select Screen Saver from your Personalize Appearance and Sound Effects window. The Screen Saver Settings dialog box shown in Figure 7.10 appears.

2. The drop-down list box—directly below the Screen Saver prompt—that you display when you click the down arrow contains a list of Windows-supplied screensavers. Click the box now to see what's on your computer. When (None) is selected, no screensaver will be active on your system.

Preview

FIGURE 7.10
The Screen
Saver dialog
box controls
your screen-
saver's timing
and selection.

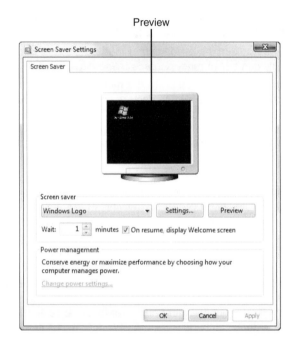

3. If you select Blank, Windows Vista uses a blank screen for your screensaver. When the screensaver activates, your screen goes blank and a keypress returns the screen to its previous state (or prompts you to enter your password, if it's configured to do so).

   The remaining screensavers are generally more fun than a blank screensaver. If you want to see the other screensavers, click them in the list (such as the colorful Ribbons) and Vista displays a preview of each one on the little monitor inside the dialog box.

4. The animated screensavers can move fairly quickly. To adjust their speed, click the Settings button. In some cases, you can also adjust the number of animated items that appear on the screensaver. Sometimes, a screensaver is so basic that there are no options available when you select it. Click OK when you're done changing settings.

5. The Preview button enables you to view the screensaver full-screen if you want a better preview than the small screen inside the dialog box provides. Click Preview to see the actual screensaver in action. Press any key or move your mouse to terminate the screensaver preview and return to the dialog box.

6. The Wait prompt determines how many minutes your computer must remain idle for the screensaver to activate. By pressing Alt+W (the shortcut key combination for the Wait prompt), you can enter a new minute value or click the up-arrow and down-arrow keys to change to a new minute value.

7. When you click the OK button at the bottom of the dialog box, Vista activates the screensaver. The screensaver remains active for all subsequent Windows sessions until you change it by using the Screen Saver Settings dialog box once again. (Other users are unaffected by the screensaver you select.)

The screensaver operates in the background and never shows itself, even on the taskbar, until your computer sits idle for the specified time value. If you keep your hands off the keyboard and mouse for the waiting time period, you'll see the screensaver kick into action. Press any key (or move your mouse) to return to your desktop.

Vista enables you to create your own screensaver. Save the digital images you want to use in your screensaver and select Photos from the screensaver list. Click the Settings button to select the path where your digital pictures are stored. Vista then uses your pictures, rotating them randomly, when your screensaver time limit expires.

Did you Know?

Making Windows Sound Off

When you do something with Vista, such as shut down your system or click an option that causes an error message, Windows often produces a sound to give you audio feedback related to what you're doing. Sometimes the sound is helpful. Sometimes not.

As with most other Windows features, you can control when and how Windows produces sounds. When you select the Sounds option from the Personalize Appearance and Sounds window, Vista opens the Sound dialog box shown in Figure 7.11.

If you want Windows to remain silent, click the down arrow to open the list box under the Sound Scheme label and select No sounds. Program-generated sounds such as music from Windows Media Player will still play, but notification and warning sounds from Windows Vista won't.

Did you Know?

FIGURE 7.11
You control
what produces
a sound and
which sound is
produced as
you work with
Windows Vista.

The Program list contains a list of common Windows operations, such as opening a dialog box, receiving email, and logging off your user account. If a speaker icon appears to the left of one of these events, a sound will be heard when that event occurs. If an icon doesn't exist next to an option, such as the Close Program event, Windows does not produce a sound when that even happens.

To add a sound to an event, select it and then brows to a folder with the sound you want played when you click the Browse button. The sound file that you select should be a wave file. You may need to right-click the file and select Properties to see if the file ends in the 3-letter .wav filename extension. To stop a sound from playing when an event happens, click to select the event and then select (None) from the list that opens under the Sounds label.

When you display a sound in the Sounds list, click Test to preview that sound. After you assign a sound, the sound isn't actually attached to that Windows event until you click the OK button to close the dialog box. If you click Cancel, none of the sound changes will be retained.

As you scroll through the list under Program, you'll see other programs in the list such as Windows Explorer and Windows Photo Gallery. Whatever programs appear in the list are the programs whose events you can assign sounds to. It's surprising how few software vendors add their programs to the Windows Sounds dialog box. If more did so, you would have more control over which sounds were produced and you could better customize the sounds to suit your preferences.

If you assign a lot of sounds to events, you might want to save that set of sounds as a sound scheme. By creating one or more sound schemes, you can save different sets of Windows sounds and load whatever set, or scheme, you want to use when you're ready to do so. After you assign sounds to some Windows events, you can click the Windows Sounds dialog box's Save As button and save that customized set of sounds in a sound scheme that you name. That named sound scheme will thereafter appear in the drop-down list box under the Sound Scheme label when you click the down arrow to see what sound schemes are stored on your system.

Did you Know?

Making Your Mouse Work the Way You Want It To

While working with a mouse may seem pretty straightforward, you can actually control many aspects of its operation. Changing a mouse's behavior is one of the simplest ways to customize your computer to match the way you work and yet even computer gurus often forget what's possible with the mouse. Even if you've seen the Mouse Properties dialog box in the past, you owe it to yourself to review it from time to time. You might find an option that was of no use to you before, but could now be highly beneficial. To learn more about how you can customize your mouse, follow these steps:

1. Select Mouse Pointers from your Personalize Appearance and Sounds window. The Mouse Properties dialog box appears.

2. Although the Pointers tab is active when you arrive, click the Buttons tab to display the Buttons dialog box page shown in Figure 7.12.

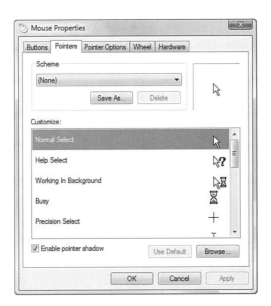

FIGURE 7.12
You can change the behavior of your mouse.

3. If you're left-handed but your mouse is set for a right-handed user, you can select the Switch Primary and Secondary Buttons option to change the mouse button orientation. The buttons will change their functionality as described in the text beneath the option. (The change takes effect immediately—even before you close the Mouse Properties dialog box or click the Apply button.) You can change the button back to its original state by clicking the option again.

4. Dragging the speed slider between Slow and Fast adjusts the speed that produces a double-click. If you find that you aren't clicking quickly enough to trigger the double-click effect when you want one, drag the slider closer to the slower edge. Test the setting by double-clicking the folder to the right of the Speed control. The folder will open or close when you double-click your mouse properly. Keep adjusting the Speed control until you can easily double-click the folder and trigger the folder's movement reliably.

5. The ClickLock option is designed to help some users select text more easily. Instead of clicking and dragging your mouse over text that you want to select, as you might do in a word processing program, you only need to click and keep your left mouse button down for about a second to anchor the selection, and then drag without pressing your mouse button to select text. When you click once more, the text will be selected to that point.

6. Click the Pointers tab to display the Pointers dialog box page. Here you can change the default appearance of your mouse. Scroll through the list to see all the kinds of mouse pointer shapes that appear when certain Windows Vista events take place.

7. To change the default mouse pointer (called Normal Select), double-click the row with the Normal Select text. Vista displays another dialog box, shown in Figure 7.13, with various mouse pointers you can use. The mouse pointers are stored in files on your computer. Some pointers (those whose filenames end with the .ani filename extension shown if you've elected to display filename extensions in any Windows Explorer window) are animated cursors that move when you select them and use the mouse. Click Cancel to close this dialog box for now.

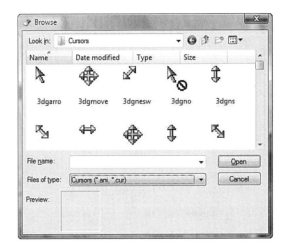

FIGURE 7.13
Select a mouse pointer shape from one of the files.

8. Vista can change the theme or overall look of all your mouse pointers to make them uniform. Click the down arrow next to (None) inside the Scheme area and you'll see several mouse schemes available to you. Instead of changing just a single mouse pointer, you'll change all possible mouse pointers when you select a scheme. Some people especially like to use an extra large mouse scheme when using a laptop so that they can locate their laptop mouse pointer more easily than with the smaller, default size.

   If you select a mouse pointer or scheme that you don't want, click the Use Default button to return to Vista's standard mouse scheme.

9. The Pointer Options tab displays the Pointer Opens dialog box (see Figure 7.14). You can speed up or slow down your mouse pointer on the screen as you move your mouse on your desk. In addition, many users find the Snap To option quite useful because when a dialog box appears with this feature enabled, your mouse instantly jumps to the default button. This often speeds up your computing because the default button is typically the one you'd be moving your mouse to and clicking. That said, a lot of users find the Snap To option's propensity for hijacking the pointer to a new location more than a little annoying.

The Snap To option takes some time to get used to. Don't get rid of it just because you dislike it the first time. The reason some people don't like it is because it's easy to inadvertently click the default button when you might have wanted to select a different button. Some dialog boxes with Yes or No buttons, for example, might default to an answer that you didn't want to select. However, when you set the Snap To option, you'll find yourself automatically clicking as soon as a dialog box appears, and out of habit you'll click a button that you didn't want to click simply because it was the default button.

Watch Out!

FIGURE 7.14
The Pointer
Options can
automate some
of your mouse
clicks and make
locating your
mouse pointer
easier.

The Visibility option is especially useful for laptop users with screens that aren't always highly visible in all light. The Visibility option enables you to set up a trail of mouse pointers, not unlike a comet's trail, as you move your mouse over the screen. The trail helps you locate your mouse pointer more easily.

The option labeled Hide Pointer While Typing causes your mouse pointer to disappear whenever you begin typing text into a text box. Sometimes you'll click a text box to enter text and your mouse pointer overwrites some of the box as you type. You must move your mouse out of the way to get the pointer off the text box so that you can see what you type. With this option, Vista automatically hides your mouse pointer when you begin typing any text and displays the mouse cursor again when you move your mouse.

10. The remaining tabs on the Mouse Properties dialog box differ depending on what kind of mouse you use. If you use a trackball, your remaining Mouse Properties dialog box tabs might relate to your trackball settings, such as allowing you to determine which programs automatically run when you click a predetermined set of buttons.

If you aren't yet comfortable with a mouse, or if you get a new kind of mouse or trackball and aren't used to it yet, the best place to become familiar with your mouse is by playing a few hands of Solitaire. (See Chapter 11, "Taking Time Out with Windows Vista Games," to learn more about Vista's Solitaire game program.)

Chapter Wrap-Up

You now know how to personalize many of Windows Vista's settings to suit your tastes. You spend a lot of time at your computer and you might as well make your computer do some of your work. You can even make your computer more appealing to you by putting a pleasant desktop background on the screen and by creating a screensaver of photos of family and friends.

Vista gives you control over just about anything and everything including mouse pointers, mouse buttons, sounds, colors, display resolution, and so much more. This chapter gave you the whirlwind tour of customizations you can perform.

Although it seems as though there are zillions of customization options all through-out Vista, you now understand the most important ones. In the next chapter, you'll begin to use Vista more to explore some of your disk space by learning how Vista enables you to manage your files and folders.

CHAPTER 8

Mastering Vista's Explorer Windows

In This Chapter:

▶ Quickly navigate files and folders

▶ Clean files of unnecessary data

▶ Restore previous versions of files

▶ Maximize use of your Explorer toolbar

▶ Master Explorer window breadcrumb trails

▶ Rename files effortlessly

▶ Copy and move effectively

▶ Set Explorer options

Here you will work with Vista's Explorer windows. In the Explorer windows, you view and manage your files, folders, and devices. Unlike the Internet Explorer program that browses the Internet, the Windows Explorer windows enable you to browse files on your own computer.

If you're accustomed to Windows XP's Windows Explorer, you should expect some improvements in the way you work with your files. Vista added needed facelifts and functionality improvements to its Explorer windows. As you explore different kinds of files, you'll see that Vista's Explorer windows look and behave differently. Your Pictures Explorer window (often just called the **Pictures window**) always shows enlarged thumbnails of your photos, for example, whereas your Documents folder (called *My Documents* in previous Windows versions) appears in more of a list view with smaller thumbnails. Your Music Explorer window (called *My Music* in previous Windows versions) shows *tag* data such as artist, album title, genre, duration, and more.

By the Way

Not only do the entries in various kinds of Explorer windows look different, but also the toolbar buttons across the top of the windows change to reflect your most likely needs for the kinds of files you're viewing. For example, a Slide Show button appears at the top of your Pictures Explorer window to give you a quick slideshow presentation of all the pictures in that folder.

Navigating Files and Folders with Windows Explorer

Windows Explorer, often shortened to *Explorer*, graphically displays your system of files in a hierarchical tree structure. With Explorer, you have access to everything inside your computer (and you can even view files outside your computer on a network or on the Internet if your network connection allows such viewing). You'll find Windows Explorer listed in your Start Menu under the Accessories option. When you select the Windows Explorer menu option, a list of files and folders appears as shown in Figure 8.1. When you open Windows Explorer, you'll see the contents of your Documents folder.

FIGURE 8.1
Windows Explorer's opening window shows files and folders located in your Documents folder.

Your user name

Back

Address bar

Common file locations

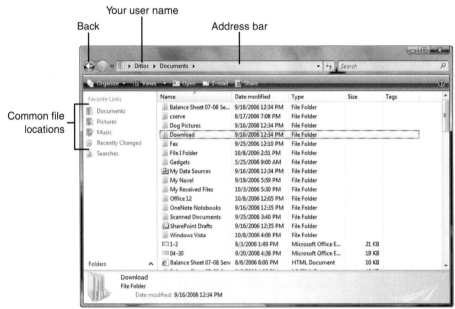

Did you Know?

To display Windows Explorer without using the Start menu, press the Windows+E shortcut key. This opens your Computer's Explorer window, showing your drives. Click the Documents folder in the left pane and you'll see the files located there.

The default location that Windows Explorer first displays is your Documents folder but you can easily traverse to other disk locations by using the techniques taught throughout this chapter. If you're used to previous versions of Windows, it will take just a little time to get used to Vista's folder structure, but Vista didn't change so much that it's entirely foreign to you.

> Vista's Explorer window won't display a menu at the top as did Windows XP Explorer windows. If you want to see the menu, press your Alt key and the window appears.

By the Way

The user ID created when you set up your Vista account determines where your data folders are located. The user's name in Figure 8.1 is *Dittos* and you can see from the Address bar that the documents shown in the figure are listed under a folder named dittos.

> Chapter 26, "Separating Users Gives Each the Access They Need," explains how to set up and manage separate user accounts for each person who uses your computer. When you or your computer's Administrator sets up a new user, that user gets his or her own disk space with a folder name based on the user's ID. Below that folder in Vista's file structure is a Documents folder, a Pictures folder, and other standard folders available to that user. When that user creates a new document, that document is stored in that user's Documents folder and is available only to that user, unless the user gives access permission to others for the file.

By the Way

Depending on what you've done with your computer since you installed Vista, you are likely to see far more files and folders than you see in Figure 8.1. If you upgraded from a previous Windows version, you surely see more files and folders.

Clicking Files and Folders

When you double-click a file inside an Explorer window, Vista analyzes the type of file it is (as determine by its filename extension, the last 3 letters of the filename) and opens the program that works with that file when possible. Therefore, if you double-click a document called MyWork.docx that resided somewhere in the Explorer window, Vista would start Microsoft Word 2007 (if installed) because Vista understands that Word 2007 works with such files. If you don't see the file's extension (that information is hidden, by default), you'll quickly learn which icons go with different file types. The Word document icon has Word's flying *W* on it for instance. You can also click to highlight a file and look in the bottom Explorer pane to see what type of file it is; the file type appears beneath the filename there.

Did you Know?

If you don't see your filename extensions, click to highlight the file and the information bar at the bottom of your Explorer window will describe the file (see Figure
8.2). This information bar is called the **preview pane**. Such a description might
read *Text Document* or *JPEG Image* or *Microsoft Office Word document*. You can
force Vista to display filename extensions with one of the Explorer option settings,
as you'll learn in the "Setting Explorer Options" section, later in this chapter. Most
of the time, you won't need to display filename extensions because the file icons
indicate the kinds of file or folder each file represents.

FIGURE 8.2
Click to high-
light a file to
see more infor-
mation about
the file.

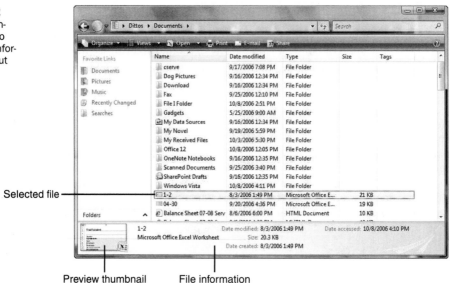

Selected file ——

Preview thumbnail   File information

By the Way

If you double-click a program file, Vista starts that program.

When you right-click on a Windows Explorer file, a pop-up menu of options
appears. If you select the Open With option, Vista gives you a list of currently
installed programs that can work with the file you've selected. Therefore, if you
have multiple MP3 audio players installed and you right-click an MP3 file and
select Open With, you'll be able to select which program you want to use to listen to
that MP3 audio file.

The list of programs that appear when you select the Open With option depends on
what you've done in the past. If, for example, you've used Media Player and
MusicMatch and QuickTime to play MP3 files, those programs will appear on your

Open With menu. Otherwise, Vista displays only the program currently set to play MP3 files which is typically Media Player. (Some programs change your file type association preferences when you install them so the default program can change.) You can also determine which programs open specific file types from the Vista Control Panel's Programs group's Default Programs option as Chapter 25, "Setting Up Windows Program Defaults," explains.

Instead of letting Vista guess which program to use to open a specific file or instead of using the Open With option to select the program, you can right-click the file, select Open With, and then select Set Default Program to override Vista's guess and specify exactly which program you want to use for that type of file in the future. Figure 8.3 shows the dialog box that appears, which allows you to specify the program to use. After you specify a default program to use for that type of file, Vista subsequently uses that program to open that file (unless you change the default again or install a program that sets itself to become the default).

FIGURE 8.3
You can specify which program Vista should use to open a particular type of file.

Instead of double-clicking a specific file, if you double-click a folder, that folder opens and becomes the new focus of your Windows Explorer window. That folder's own files and folders (sometimes called **subfolders**) would then appear. To go back to the previous Explorer you viewed, click the Back button just as you would go back to a previous web page you viewed last in Internet Explorer.

Some keyboards now have Internet browsing buttons such as Back and Forward. Those keyboard buttons work in Windows Explorer, allowing you to go back and forth between Explorer window locations just as you can use them to go back and forth on the Internet.

If you select a file, meaning click once to highlight the file but not twice to open it, depending on the type of file you select, the preview pane that displays information at the bottom of the Explorer window changes. For example, a music file will show song title and album name (although that information isn't always necessarily available for all digital music files on your computer).

By the Way

If you hold the Ctrl key down while clicking on multiple filenames in your Windows Explorer window, the preview pane reflects information about all your selected files as a group, such as their combined file size.

You can update the information about a file, often called the file's **metadata**, by changing the file's properties. Right-click the file's icon and select Properties to open a Properties dialog box such as the one shown in Figure 8.4. More advanced users might want to change the attributes of the file, which can be done by clicking the General tab. For example, if you want to ensure a file cannot be accidentally deleted or altered, without specific user acknowledgement, you could designate it as a read-only file.

FIGURE 8.4
A file's properties specify informative details about that file.

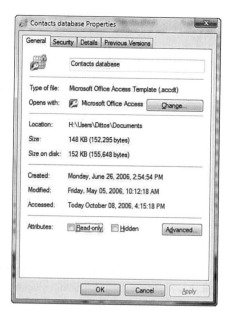

Click any selected Explorer item's field at the bottom of the Explorer window to add or change whatever metadata for the file appears there. For digital music, for example, you can rate such files with stars to designate favorites and also update information such as the Artist and Genre as Figure 8.5 demonstrates.

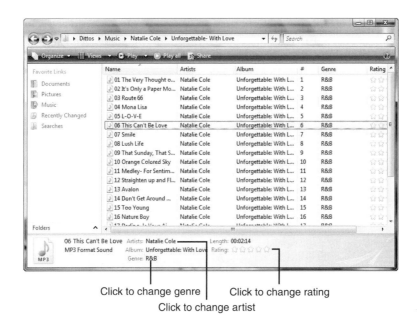

FIGURE 8.5
You can change metadata attached to any file from within Windows Explorer.

Click to change genre | Click to change rating
Click to change artist

To delete a file, just click to select the file and press Delete. You can also select multiple files and folders in your Explorer window and delete all that you select. To select all files and folders press Ctrl+A (you can also choose Select All from the toolbar's Organize option) and press Delete to remove all the contents of a folder. To select a list of continuous files, click at the beginning of the list, hold down the Shift key, and click the last file that you want to include in the list. To pick and choose the files you want to select, hold down the Ctrl key when selecting them.

Going Back to Previous Versions of a File

One of the most powerful features Vista introduces is its Previous Version file feature. At any point, you can return to a previous version of a file (sometimes called a *shadow copy*) that has been updated or altered! This is a huge advantage. Sadly, users of Vista Starter Edition, Vista Home Basic, and Vista Home Premium don't have this feature. Many Home users will be working in a business environment, however, that might support previous versions of files using Vista Business Edition or higher.

Suppose that you're working on a novel and you write Chapter 1, and then make changes, and then add and remove some material, and after a week of hard work you have the chapter just the way you want it. You print the chapter for a final edit only to discover that along the way you deleted an entire section when you meant to delete only a paragraph.

If you saved the document regularly as you wrote and edited it, Vista will often be able to produce an older version of your document. In that older version, hopefully, will be the missing section that you can copy to the Widows Clipboard and then paste into the most recent version of the chapter.

To see a previous version, right-click the file and select Restore Previous Versions. Vista opens the Properties dialog box shown in Figure 8.6. A list of all versions that Vista has saved will appear.

FIGURE 8.6
When you change a file too much, just ask Vista to restore an earlier version.

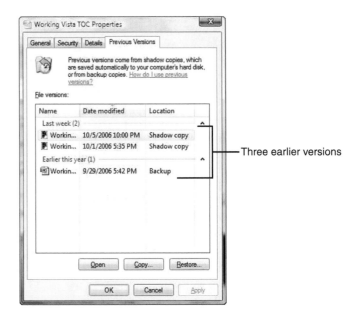

Three earlier versions

Click to select one of the shadow copies of the file that you think might contain the data you need and then click Open. If the file isn't the one you want, close the file and select another. The Copy button sends the file's contents to your Windows Clipboard where you can paste it elsewhere. The Restore button takes that older version and makes it the current version of your file.

Use Your Explorer Toolbar to Your Advantage

Vista's Explorer toolbar seems to be far more useful than previous Windows Explorer was. Table 8.1 lists the options most commonly found on the Explorer toolbar. Depending on the kinds of files you display, the toolbar changes to reflect actions you can perform based on the types of files you're viewing at the time. If a button doesn't have a text label that describes the button, point to the button and Vista will pop up a message that describes the button.

TABLE 8.1 Vista's Windows Explorer Common Toolbar Buttons

Button	Description
Configure Explorer's Layout	Changes the way Explorer displays files and folders. For example, you can set an option that forces all Explorer windows to display all filename extensions. See "Setting Explorer Options" later in this chapter for more information about how and why you might want to customize your Explorer windows.
Views[1]	Changes the view of the files and folders you see in the Explorer window. Enables you to view larger or smaller icons, show file details in a list, and tile the files in a mixture of an icon and descriptive display.
Organize	Enables you to create a new folder, paste a file or folder that you copied to the Windows clipboard from a different location, or select all the contents of a Windows Explorer folder. Depending on the file type, you'll see additional Organize options such as an E-mail option that enables you to send the selected file to another user without first having to open your email program manually.
Explorer	Appears when you click a folder and enables you to change the Windows Explorer window to display the contents of the folder. You can double-click a folder name in any Explorer list to produce the same results.
Open	Starts a program that works with your select file and opens that file as a data file in that program. If you click to select an Adobe Photoshop image file and then click Open, Vista starts Photoshop and loads the image so you can edit the image. (This assumes that you have Adobe Photoshop installed.) Double-clicking a filename has the same effect as selecting the file and clicking this Open option.
Share	Displays the File Sharing window, as Figure 8.7 shows, and enables you to determine who can share the selected file or folder. (Hold Ctrl and click multiple files first to set up the sharing of more than one file at the same time.) You can designate another user as a reader (meaning the user cannot change the file), contributor (meaning the user can add but not delete information from the file), co-owner (meaning the user has the right to add and remove information from the file), and remove to disconnect file sharing from one or more users.

TABLE 8.1   Continued

Button	Description
Print	Sends the file to your printer. Vista will first display the Print dialog box so that you can set print settings and select the appropriate printer to use.
Synch with Other PCs	Enables you to mirror a file, folder, or multiple files and folders on other computers networked to yours. If you modify a synched file, the file on the other computer is modified as well. The other computer must be using Vista, be a part of your network, use the same username and password as you are currently using, and have turned on the Synch feature on that machine. Many users use a secondary PC as a backup for important files and the Synch feature is one way to implement such a backup.
Previous versions	Enables you to return to a previous version of the file as described in this chapter's previous section.

[1]You can drag the View slider up and down to increase or decrease the size of the live icons that represent the file contents in your Windows Explorer window.

FIGURE 8.7
Vista lets you decide who can view and edit your files.

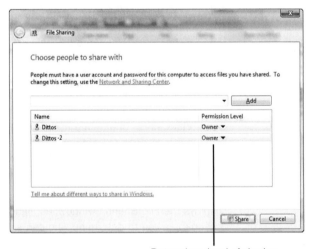

Determines level of sharing

Visually View Your Shared Files

Over time you can forget which files you've allowed to be shared and which cannot be shared. It's a good idea to review your shared file list regularly. You don't want to allow a file to be shared if it now contains sensitive data that you no longer want made available on your network.

To view a list of files you're currently sharing, open your Control Panel's Network and Sharing Center. Click the link labeled Show Me All the Files and Folders I Am Sharing. Click this to open a window with your currently shared files. Figure 8.8 shows such a window. Routinely check this window if you often share files as a security precaution and stop sharing any files that no longer need to be shared.

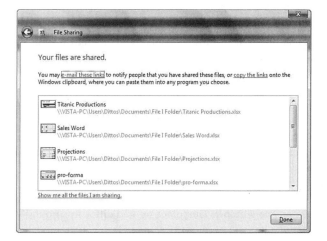

FIGURE 8.8
Vista can produce a list of shared files for your review.

The Always-Present Vista Search Box

As you might expect after reading this book's earlier chapters, all Windows Explorer windows provide you with a handy Search box. Start typing the name of a file or folder you want to locate and Vista starts displaying matching files as you type. When you see the file you want to work with, double-click the filename. If it's a folder, Windows Explorer will open the Explorer window inside that folder.

Explorer searches for files only in the current Explorer folder and lower. If a file matches your search result but the file is located elsewhere on the disk and not somewhere below your current Explorer window's hierarchy, Vista won't find the match. This is done on purpose so that you can more easily restrict a search only to a targeted location.

Watch Out!

Your Trail of Breadcrumbs

Vista introduced a slight twist to the Windows Explorer address bar. At first, you might not notice a difference but as you begin to use your Explorer address bar you'll see the advantage.

Vista calls the links in your Explorer address bar **breadcrumbs**. These breadcrumbs leave a trail of where you've been and provide a simple means for you to go other places as you explore your computer's files and folders.

In previous Windows, the address bar would display a different kind of path to your files. If you navigated to your My Documents folder from the My Computer window, your Windows Explorer address bar would display the My Documents folder even though the full path to get there might be C:\Documents and Settings\JulieD\My Documents\. If you navigated to the My Documents folder from the C:\ drive, the full path would show.

Vista displays the path to your folder in the address bar but it makes the folders clickable. This dramatically adds functionality to your Explorer window! If, for example, the Explorer window's address bar read dittos\Documents (Vista often hides the front part of the file location and doesn't show the full path starting with C:\), you could click on the folder named dittos in the address bar and display that folder's contents instead of the Documents folder contents.

Doing so would change Figure 8.1 to the Explorer window shown in Figure 8.9. Notice the folders in the window. The folder named dittos has no individual files but only folders so Vista changed the view to an icon view, which often makes folders easier to navigate.

However, what if you didn't want to just back your way up the folder list, but wanted to go to a specific folder in that chain? Instead of clicking a breadcrumb to display a new folder, you can click on the arrow next to one of the folders in your address bar. Clicking the arrow produces a drop-down list of that folder's contents, as shown in Figure 8.10. You can click any of those drop-down folders to jump directly to that folder.

By the Way

With previous versions of Windows, when you wanted to traverse to a folder location earlier in your disk tree, you would have to use the toolbar buttons to navigate, folder by folder, to your destination. Sometimes this necessitated clicking through several folders to locate one in the path you wanted to go to. This new system of breadcrumbs allows you to navigate to most locations on your PC in just two or three clicks.

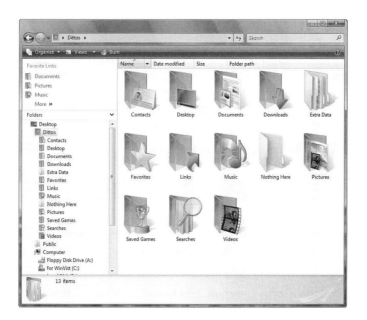

FIGURE 8.9
When a folder contains other folders, Vista changes the view to a more appropriate setting such as this icon view.

FIGURE 8.10
Instead of clicking a folder, when you click the arrow between two folders in your breadcrumb, Vista displays a list of all folders located at that position on your disk.

You aren't limited to clicking to traverse your computer. You can, at any time, directly type an exact path into your Explorer address bar and Windows Explorer takes you to that location and displays the files and folders there. You can also type the name of the folder if it's one of Vista primary data folder names such as Documents, Music, Favorites, Videos, or Pictures.

View Additional Folders

You're not limited to your user account-owned files and folders when you use Windows Explorer. Your user account and permission settings determine what you can do with files and folders but that doesn't completely limit you from seeing the names of files and folders on your computer. If you have administrative privileges you'll often want to view, modify, and arrange files in locations other than your standard user files.

By clicking the arrow next to the Folders option toward the bottom on the left side of a Windows Explorer window, you can display a directory of the primary folders and locations on your computer. Figure 8.11 shows such a list.

On a network, the Folders option gives you the ability to traverse your network to view and manage files on other computers.

To traverse to any location in the Folders list, double-click that item, such as Computer, and Vista takes you there. Keep in mind that your Windows Explorer window can change dramatically as you view different kinds of information in them. For example, your computer's Explorer screen shows graphical representations of your disk and CD and DVD drives instead of files and folders but when you open Explorer from the Start menu the window shows your folders and files. If you click the leftmost breadcrumb arrow, you can traverse straight to one of these folders:

- ▶ Desktop

- ▶ Computer

- ▶ Recycle Bin

- ▶ Control Panel

- ▶ Public

- ▶ Your user name's folders and files

- ▶ Network

Once you land in one of these primary folders you can traverse from there using the icons in the Explorer window.

Click to hide folders

FIGURE 8.11
You can view various folders and other locations on your computer.

Instead of minimizing all open windows to work with your Recycle Bin, you need only display a list of folders from any Explorer window and choose the Recycle Bin entry. You can erase all or some of the files there.

Did you
Know?

A Recycle Bin Review

Although most readers have probably used Windows before, a little review never hurts and a review serves to bring newcomers up to speed quickly with all the rest.

Just in case the idea of the Recycle Bin is cloudy to you, note that the Recycle Bin is a special location inside Windows that holds the documents you delete. The Recycle Bin's icon appears on your Windows desktop. The Recycle Bin's icon shows a bin with trash when your Recycle Bin holds at least one file and changes to an empty bin when you empty your Recycle Bin. Windows always gives you one last chance to recover deleted files and folders. When you delete anything in a Windows Explorer window, Vista sends that file to the Recycle Bin. The item is then out of your way but not deleted permanently. Only after you empty the Recycle Bin is the file gone for good.

You can open your Recycle Bin by double-clicking the Recycle Bin icon on your desktop or selecting the Recycle Bin from a list of folders in any Explorer's left pane. If you right-click on the Recycle Bin icon or Explorer entry you can select Empty Recycle Bin to permanently erase all contents there. If you open the Recycle Bin, you can click to select a single file, or hold Ctrl and click to select multiple files, and then permanently delete those files while leaving the other Recycle Bin contents in the bin for later consideration.

If you select a file or folder in any Windows Explorer window and press Shift+Delete, Vista deletes the file permanently without first sending the file to your Recycle Bin. Obviously, you'll only press Shift+Delete when you're absolutely certain you no longer want to keep the file.

Copying and Moving Files and Folders

From an Explorer window, a file icon's right-click menu offers advanced copying and moving operations. You'll use Vista's Clipboard as the go-between for most copy, cut, paste, and move operations. In a way, the Clipboard is like a short-term Recycle Bin that holds all deleted files until you're ready to remove them permanently. The Clipboard holds deleted (or copied) documents and files but only until you send something else to the Clipboard or exit and log off Windows Vista. The Clipboard holds only one item at a time so when you send something to the Clipboard, the new item replaces the previous Clipboard contents.

When you want to copy a file from one place to another, you send a copy of the file on your Clipboard. When you do, the file is on the Clipboard and out of the way until you go (in Explorer) to where you want the file to be copied. You'll then paste the file to the new location, in effect copying from the Clipboard to the new location. When you copy a file to another location, the file remains in both its original location while the copy is placed elsewhere.

Watch Out!

If you attempt to copy or move a file from one location to another and a file with the same name exists on the destination, Vista displays a dialog box like the one in Figure 8.12. Click whichever icon is the one you want to keep at the destination and then click Resolve. If you click the option labeled Keep Both, Windows Vista places both files on the destination and adds the word *Copy* to the name of the new one.

When you move a file from one location to another, Vista first performs a cut operation. This means that Vista deletes the file from its current location and sends the file to the Clipboard (overwriting any pre-existing data on the Clipboard). When you find the location to which you want to move the file, Vista copies the Clipboard contents to the new location, which might be a different folder or another disk drive.

Whether you copy or move a file, the file's extension never changes between its original location and its destination. The file type doesn't change just because you moved the file. Follow these steps to practice copying a file using the Clipboard technique:

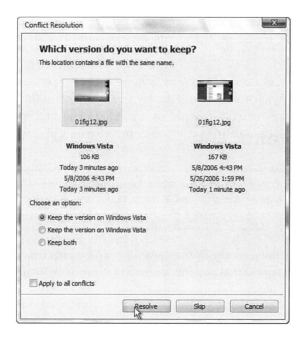

FIGURE 8.12
When you attempt to copy or move a file with the same name to another location, Vista gives you a chance to resolve the discrepancy instead of overwriting the destination file without asking.

1. Open Windows Explorer and view your Documents folder.

2. Right-click a file you want to copy.

3. Select the Copy command from the right-click menu (or press Ctrl+C). Windows Vista sends a complete copy of the file to the Clipboard. The Clipboard holds the file until you replace the Clipboard's contents with something else or until you exit Windows. Therefore, you can send the same Clipboard document to several places once it's on the clipboard.

4. Move to a different location in any Explorer window.

5. Right-click the list of files and select the Paste command from the contextual menu (or press Ctrl+V). Vista sends a copy of the Clipboard file to that location in Explorer.

6. Right-click the file you just pasted. You'll see the Cut command. This time, select Cut instead of Copy (or press Ctrl+X). Windows erases the file from the folder and places it on the Clipboard. Actually, Windows doesn't fully erase the file's entry from that original folder; instead, Vista changes the filename and icon to half-brightness and when you close the folder or paste the file elsewhere, Vista completely removes the reference from that folder. If you cut a file but decide not to paste it elsewhere, Vista does not remove the file from

its original location. Therefore, if you do want to delete a file you cut but didn't paste, you'll have to select the file and delete it by pressing the Delete key.

7. At any time, you can undo a copy or move right after performing either operation. The right-click menu will display an Undo Copy or Undo Move until you copy or move a different file, close that Explorer window, or perform a different task such as deleting a file. You can also press Ctrl+Z to undo an action.

By the Way

You can make a copy of a file in the same folder. When you do, Vista names the copied file the same as the original file but appends the word *Copy* to the end of the filename.

For a faster move using no keystrokes, open a second Explorer window. Adjust the two Explorer windows so that you can see both of them, as in Figure 8.13.

Source folder   Destination folder

FIGURE 8.13
When you open two Explorer windows at once, you can drag files between them to speed the copy process.

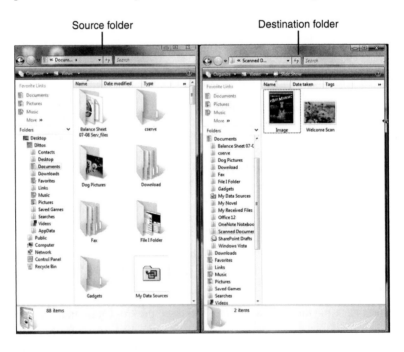

In the second Explorer window, traverse to the destination where you want to move the file. Click and drag the file from its original Explorer window to the second window. When you release your mouse button Windows anchors the file into its new location.

If you first press your Ctrl key before dragging the file, Vista makes a copy of the file in the second Explorer window but keeps the original file in the first window. After you drag to copy or move a file, you can right-click the destination window and select Undo Move or Undo Copy to reverse what you did.

> If you drag a file from one computer to another over a network, or from one disk to another, Windows always performs a copy and not a move. Windows Vista moves the file only when you drag it from one Explorer window to another on the same computer's disk without holding down the Ctrl key.

Renaming Files

Windows Vista makes it simple to rename a file. Right-click to display the pop-up menu and select the Rename command. (You can also click to select the filename and press F2 to rename the file.) Windows highlights the name in the Explorer list and you can edit or completely change the name to something else. Press Enter to keep the new name.

If you start to rename a file and change your mind, press Esc before pressing Enter and Windows keeps the original filename.

> Don't supply an extension when you rename the file unless you've turned on the filename extension display. For example, if you renamed a text file named `Readme` (whose actual filename is `Readme.txt` but you won't see the `.txt` filename extension in the Explorer list) to `NewName.txt`, you just renamed the file to `NewName.txt.txt`! Although this doesn't affect how Vista sees the file, it could certainly make things confusing for you after a while.
>
> Even though you can configure Vista to show file extensions, doing so leaves you open to accidentally removing or modifying a file's extension. Fortunately, Vista warns you if you change a file's extension and gives you a chance to change your mind.
>
> The way Vista keeps track of a file's type is by its extension, so if you do inadvertently change the extension, it will affect how Windows treats the file. For example, changing `readme.txt` to `newname.blog` would cause Vista to no longer recognize it as a text file, meaning that if you were to double-click it, Vista wouldn't know what program to use to open it.

Changing Explorer Settings

Explorer settings are simple to change and you'll want to make Windows Explorer work according to your preferred options.

Clicking the down arrow on the Organize button icon (the far left icon on your Explorer window) to display a drop-down menu. You can add a menu bar to your Explorer window that mimics that of Windows XP's Explorer menus. (Pressing Alt is the shortcut key to add the menu.) Most Vista users don't miss the menu due to the added functionality of Explorer in Vista compared to that of XP.

From the Organize, Layout menu, you can determine whether you want Explorer to display one or more of these panes:

▶ **Search pane**—Adds an advanced Search box at the top of every Explorer menu that enables you to narrow the choices you search for to email, documents, pictures, music, or other files.

▶ **Details pane**—Adds the information bar at the bottom of the Explorer window that describes a selected file's properties.

▶ **Preview pane**–A window pane to the right of your file list that displays a preview of a selected file such as the one in Figure 8.14.

▶ **Navigation pane**—The Folder list at the left of your Explorer's file list (which you display when you click the arrow to the right of the label Folders).

Preview pane

FIGURE 8.14
You control how your Windows Explorer window looks and the window panes it displays.

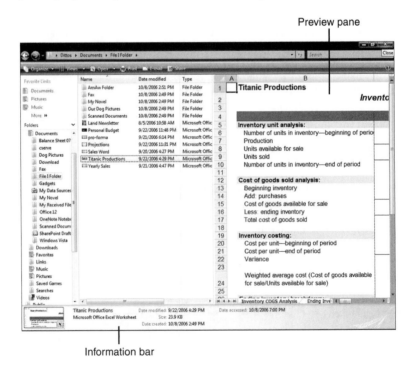

Information bar

Using the General Tab Settings

By clicking the Tools, Folder Options entry from any Explorer's drop-down menu, available when you press your Alt key, you will open the Folder Options dialog box shown in Figure 8.15. The General tab shows a dialog box page that enables you to choose from among three sets of options:

▶ **Tasks**—Changes between Vista's Explorer look and a more traditional (meaning pre-Vista) Windows view without a folder list to the left or any of the three panes

▶ **Browse Folders**—Determines what happens when you double-click a folder inside another Explorer window. You control whether you want a new Explorer window to open with the new folder displayed, or the current Explorer window updated to display the selected folder's contents.

▶ **Click Items as Follows**—Specifies your preference when opening Explorer items. The default is to double-click an item before it opens and letting a single click select an item. If you change to a Single-click selection (the first option in this dialog box section), you open items with one click on them. This takes some getting used to but does slightly speed your work when using Windows. To highlight or select an item you only need to point to it, whereas before you would click once over it. (You also determine how Windows underlines an item you select.)

Click for more options

FIGURE 8.15
The Folder Options dialog box enables you to determine how Explorer displays its contents.

If you change your folder options too dramatically and want to return to their normal state, click the Restore Defaults button.

Using the View Tab Settings

The View tab produces far more folder options than you can manage. Figure 8.16 shows a partial list of these options.

At the top of the dialog box is the Reset All Folders button. If you've changed the type of view (perhaps some Explorer windows display using the Large Icon view, some use the Details view, and so on) for various folders and want to make them all appear uniformly again, click the Reset All Folders button. After you click the OK button to close the Folder Options dialog box, every Explorer window's view will be set to Vista's default view for that type of folder.

At the bottom of the dialog box, you'll see a Restore Defaults button. This is your panic button. By clicking this button, you restore all folders back to their original condition. If you upgraded to Vista from XP, and have made several changes to your folder options over the years, resetting back to Vista's default state might be quite dramatic, so be sure you want to do that. If you're unsure, search through the list of options for whatever you want to change and see whether you can be satisfied with the changes you make manually before resorting to changing back to the default condition of all folder options.

FIGURE 8.16
You can control just about any and every aspect of Window Explorer folders.

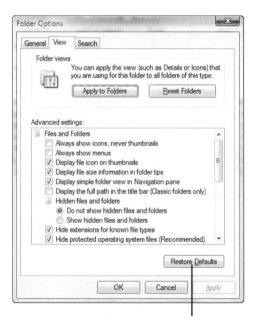

Click to restore Vista's default options

At this point in this book, you don't need a comprehensive description of every folder option available to you in the Folder Options dialog box. Instead, you need to know the highlights, the more common options that users routinely set. Pick and choose from the following that might help you get your work done in a more effective way:

▶ **Always Show Icons, Never Thumbnails**—Even if your hardware supports Aero Glass, you can request that Vista display only icons and not thumbnails to represent your files in the Explorer windows you use.

▶ **Always Show Menus**—If you miss XP's Explorer menus, check this option to place the menu at the top of all Explorer windows you open thereafter.

▶ **Display the Full Path in the Title Bar (Classic Folders Only)**—At first, a Vista user who's used to using Windows XP might be tempted to check this option. Resist the temptation for a while. Given Vista's powerful search box and the breadcrumbs trail in the Explorer address bar, you'll not need to know the exact path of a folder as much as you did in previous versions of Windows. In addition, this option only works when you've set Explorer to display in classic view from the General tab so you lose additional functionality (including the clickable breadcrumb trails!) that Vista's Explorer windows give you there as well.

▶ **Hidden Files and Folders**—Certain files are hidden from view by default. These consist primarily of system files that Windows needs to do its job. You might never need to see these files so the Windows default state is to keep these files hidden so you don't inadvertently delete them some time when working with other files in your folders. If you want to see these normally hidden files, select Show Hidden Files and Folders. This is typically recommended only for advanced users who need to work with a system file and even then the recommendation is to again hide the files by restoring this option back to its default state.

▶ **Hide Extensions for Known File Types**—A filename extension is usually a three or more letter suffix that goes on the end of a filename. Starting with Windows 95, the extensions were hidden by default. With recognizable icons representing file types, extensions were not needed as much as before. Yet, many computer users still prefer to see the entire filename in Explorer listings and Windows will do just that if you uncheck this option.

▶ **Remember Each Folder's View Settings**—Requests that Vista remember specific folder views when you set them. For example, you might want to change the view of your Documents folder to Small Icons. If you do, Vista will always use the Small Icons view when you display the contents of your Documents folder as long as you've checked this option. Vista won't show other folders in the Small Icons view however, unless you've specifically changed the view in them as well.

From time to time, display your Folder Options and review them. You might run across an option later that you see a need for whereas today you might not have a use for that setting.

Chapter 42, "Vista's Ten Best Tips that Save You Time and Grief," revisits these Explorer options and explains how to use more of them to maximize your use of your Explorer windows.

Exploring Vista's Various Explorer Windows

So far in this chapter, you've learned about the Windows Explorer window, which enables you to manage your files and folders. Windows Vista uses the Explorer concept all throughout the Windows environment. Whether you want to view pictures, disk drive information, or music files, the Explorer window gives you a uniform set of familiar commands and options to manage that information.

There is a Pictures Explorer window, a Computer Explorer window, and more. Even though all the various kinds of Explorer windows are similar, each one does offer unique options and capabilities because the data they represent requires different ways of handling the data.

Throughout the rest of this text, you'll be using the various Explorer windows to view and work with information inside Windows Vista. To give you a preview of what to expect, the following sections briefly walk you through several of the more common Explorer windows you'll work with in Vista.

The Pictures Explorer Window

When you view your Pictures folder (or any other folder that contains digital images), you'll see an Explorer window that looks similar to Windows Explorer but offers additional options.

One of the most interesting changes in the Pictures Explorer is the Slideshow button on the toolbar. Click the button and Vista generates an impressive slideshow that displays your photso in a full-screen mode. Right-click on any photo to display the Slideshow controls to change the behavior of your Slideshow (see Figure 8.17).

FIGURE 8.17
Instantly generate an impressive slideshow from any pictures folder.

The Slideshow controls

Click to select any picture in the folder and the toolbar adds more options including:

▶ **Print**—Prints the picture using an enhanced print dialog box that enables you to print multiple prints on standard photograph-sized paper (such as two prints each 5" by 7") and a contact sheet with 35 small images on the page.

▶ **Preview**—Enables you to select a program installed on your computer that supports digital images to edit that image.

▶ **E-mail**—Opens a new email message window and attaches the selected picture (or multiple selected pictures) to the email.

You can right-click any picture to rotate the image clockwise or counterclockwise. Selecting Set As Desktop Background from the right-click menu changes your desktop background image to the selected picture. If your windows cover up your desktop, you'll see the image there the next time you close or minimize your open windows.

By the Way

> Windows includes a standalone program called Windows Photo Gallery, which has similar features to Pictures Explorer, but adds more advanced editing commands. You'll learn about Photo Gallery in Chapter 16, "Going Digital with Your Camera or Scanner."

The Music Explorer Window

When you open your Music Explorer window, Vista displays the Music folder associated with your user account. Typically, this folder lists your song titles using the Details view so you can see information about the music such as album title, genre, year recorded, and other aspects of the files. Vista gets this information from a music file's **tag**, which is data encoded into the file about its contents. If your music files don't have any tag data, you can enter it manually using the Music Explorer's Edit Properties option, or use Windows Media Player to look it up.

A Play button appears on the Music Explorer window so that you can play the song using one of your installed music players such as Windows Media Player. You'll learn more about music and how Vista integrates with music files in Chapters 14 and 15.

The Computer Explorer Window

Depending on your hardware, when you open the Computer Explorer window (by pressing the Windows+E shortcut key or selecting Computer from your Start menu's right pane), you'll see an Explorer window open that graphically shows your computer's disk, CD, and DVD drive storage devices like the ones shown in Figure 8.18.

FIGURE 8.18
Vista can quickly show you the free and used disk space on all your disk drives from the Computer Explorer window.

Notice that you graphically see how much storage space is consumed on your drives. The toolbar updates to give you hardware-specific options such as the Change setting button that takes you directly to your Control Panel so you can make system changes as needed.

> Vista even considers the Control Panel as an Explorer window.

By the Way

Sort Explorer Windows Contents

When multiple files and folders fill your Windows Explorer window, as is often the case with your Documents folder, you can change the way the entries appear. If you click any column heading, such as Name or Date Modified, Vista instantly sorts the entries in the Explorer window in alphabetical order with the folder names appearing at the top of the list and entries that begin with numbers appearing before those with letters. Click the same column heading again and Vista sorts the list in the opposite direction from high to low.

If you don't like the order of the columns in the window, click and drag one to another location. For example, you might want to drag the Type column over so that it appears to the left of Authors on Explorer windows that show those columns.

> Right-click over any column heading to see a list of additional column headings available. Click to select or deselect any column heading you wish to see for the open folder. Figure 8.19 shows several column headings available for the open Explorer window. By clicking the More option you can see even more headings.

Did you Know?

A powerful way to view your files is to point to any column heading, such as the Type column, and click the down arrow that appears. A list of file types in that window appears. Click to select a file type and Vista changes the Explorer window so that the only files of that file type are displayed. If you click to select multiple file types, Vista displays each file that matches that file type within your window but not any other files. The selection works as a filter to enable you to locate only those files you have interest in at the time.

If you select multiple file types (or select any other column's filter by clicking its arrow) and then click the Group command, Vista sorts files into groups as shown in Figure 8.20. Instead of all the files appearing together of different types, you see files grouped by type or by whatever column you filtered and grouped.

FIGURE 8.19
Select only the columns you want to see in any Explorer window.

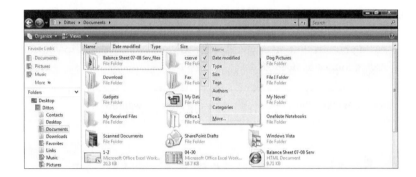

FIGURE 8.20
Filter out the files you don't want to see and then select Group to organize them.

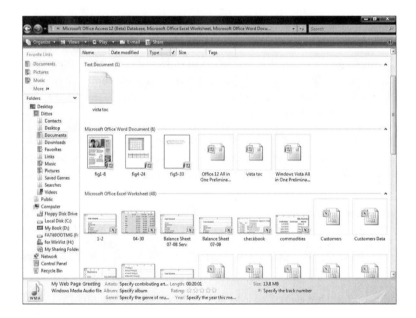

By the Way

If you select the Stack option instead of Group, Vista stacks all your filtered files into stacks. If you clicked to filter only application files and folders in an Explorer window, and then clicked Stack instead of Group (as was done in Figure 8.20), Vista would create two piles, or stacks, of file icons with each stack containing the files from each group you selected. When you double-click a stack, Vista opens that stack to show each item individually in your Explorer window.

Chapter Wrap-Up

You're no doubt tired from all the exploring you did in this chapter!

In this chapter, you learned about all there is to know about the Windows Explorer window, the window in which you manage and view your files and folders. Vista adds several new twists to previous Windows versions' Explorer windows. One of the most useful features is the breadcrumb trail that enables you to click to traverse your disk folders more easily than before. In addition, if you mess up a document you're working on, just ask Vista to restore an older version and you'll get things back to an earlier date where you can make different edits.

After you've mastered the Windows Explorer window, you already know a lot about the other Explorer windows that appear as you use Windows Vista. They differ only in their specific support for the data inside that window. For example, you'll find hardware-related options and toolbar buttons when you open your Computer Explorer window.

The next chapter begins a new part of the book titled "Working with Windows Vista." Much of what you've covered so far has been an introductory feature review and some theory about Vista's structure and important abilities. Starting in the next chapter, you'll get less review and background material and master more practical, hands-on activities that you'll follow as you learn how Vista works.

PART III

Working with Windows Vista

CHAPTER 9

Working with the Sidebar and Gadgets

In This Chapter:

- ▶ Understand the Sidebar's purpose
- ▶ Work with gadgets on your Sidebar
- ▶ Add new gadgets to your computer
- ▶ Change Sidebar and gadget options
- ▶ Look for more information about writing your own gadgets

The Windows Sidebar is a feature new to Vista. When enabled, it resides on an area of your screen that you can make visible at all times, typically as a vertical column with icons on it along the right side of your screen. On the Sidebar, you can place **gadgets**— small programs that give you routine information that you like to have available such as a calendar, calculator, or stock quotes.

The Sidebar always puts information at hand and is just one of the many ways you can customize Windows Vista to give you the data you need in the manner you want it. Throughout this chapter, you'll learn ways to customize your Sidebar and add gadgets to it.

A Sidebar Overview

Figure 9.1 shows the Sidebar on a Vista desktop. As you can see, the Sidebar itself is see-through, so if there were no gadgets on it, you wouldn't know it was there. Also, sometimes a window might position itself under the Sidebar area, and being able to see between the Sidebar gadgets enables you to see what's under the Sidebar.

Sidebar control icon

FIGURE 9.1
Your Sidebar
sits against an
edge of your
screen and
makes small
programs called
gadgets avail-
able.

Gadgets

One of the nicest features of the Sidebar is its ability to load and stream live data.
The Sidebar can display information that you'd otherwise have to open Internet
Explorer to find, such as stock quotes and a weather summary.

When you first start the Sidebar, you'll probably see at least two gadgets there.
Depending on what's happened on your computer before or how your computer's
manufacturer set up Vista on your computer, you could see additional gadgets or
perhaps none at all. The clock is almost always one of the gadgets set to reside on a
Sidebar. Other gadgets, such as the Stock quote gadget, might also appear there.

Your Sidebar might already be showing but if not, open your Start menu's
Accessories option and select Windows Sidebar. To see which gadgets are currently
running, right-click the Sidebar icon on your Taskbar's notification area and select
Properties from the pop-up menu. Click the View List of Running Gadgets button,
and the View Gadgets dialog box shown in Figure 9.2 opens. Each item in the list is
a separate gadget.

By the Way

Gadgets can run on your desktop's Sidebar, your Vista desktop itself, or often on
a Windows Sideshow screen on the outside of some laptops and other peripheral
computer equipment. Chapter 4, "Starting and Stopping Windows," describes
Sideshow.

FIGURE 9.2
You can always check to see the names of the gadgets currently running.

Adding Gadgets to Your Sidebar

Before you can add a gadget to your Sidebar, you have to know which gadgets are currently available on your system. Over time, you will obtain gadgets from www.Microsoft.com and other websites. To see what gadgets you currently have installed, right-click the Sidebar's icon on your Notification area and select Add Gadgets.

The Add Gadgets dialog box shown in Figure 9.3 will appear. The gadgets shown in Figure 9.3 are a sample of gadgets that Microsoft shipped with Windows Vista. The next section explains how to download additional gadgets from Microsoft. Other sites will supply gadgets for your Sidebar as well as Microsoft.

By clicking the Show Details option, you can learn more about a selected gadget as shown in Figure 9.4. The Show Details button produces an Information bar that lists the selected gadget's version number and distributor. To hide the Information bar click the Hide Details link.

To add a gadget to your Sidebar, double-click the gadget's icon. To remove a gadget, just point to the gadget on your Sidebar to display its Close and Options buttons and click the Close button.

FIGURE 9.3
Each gadget has its own options dialog box with which you can control the gadget's properties.

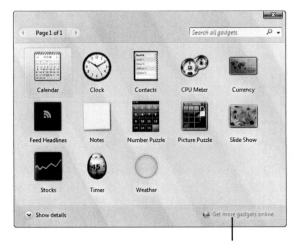

Click to locate more gadgets online

FIGURE 9.4
You can view additional information about a selected gadget such as its version number and distributor.

By the Way

A gadget begins running the moment it appears in your Sidebar. You need to do nothing more to trigger the gadget's operation.

If you ever want to remove a gadget from your system, right-click the gadget's icon in the Add Gadgets dialog box and select Uninstall.

Instead of removing a gadget from your Sidebar, you can drag the gadget from the Sidebar to another location on your screen. The gadget floats over your programs and is not anchored on your desktop.

Did you Know?

Download Additional Gadgets from Microsoft

You should search the Internet for companies that sell or give away new gadgets you might find beneficial. Microsoft offers additional gadgets and you can see what Microsoft has by clicking the Get More Gadgets Online link in your Add Gadgets dialog box.

A web page like the one in Figure 9.5 appears. You can scroll down the list of gadgets to locate one or more you're interested in. You'll find games, utilities, and more.

FIGURE 9.5
Microsoft and other companies offer websites from which you can download additional gadgets to your computer.

Click the Download button next to a gadget you want to install on your computer. When the File Download dialog box appears, you can select Save to save the gadget to a folder on your computer or select Open to install the gadget directly from the website without saving the gadget's installation file on your computer.

Did you
Know?

> The default location for the gadgets you download is your Documents folder. Instead of saving the new gadgets there, you can create a new subfolder named Gadgets and save the gadgets to that folder to keep your downloaded gadgets together.

When the download completes, click the Open button. (Assuming that you saved the gadget to your computer. If you didn't, the gadget begins installing automatically.) The gadget will install itself on your computer and become available in the list of gadgets when you display the Add Gadgets dialog box.

Modifying Gadget Properties

Most gadgets running in your Sidebar have three buttons that appear in their upper-right corner when you point to them with your mouse. These are a Close button designated with an *X*, an option button designated with a wrench icon, and a grab button which you can click to drag the gadget to another location on your screen or elsewhere in your Sidebar.

Clicking the Close button closes the gadget and removes it from your Sidebar. Clicking the Options button opens a dialog box with which you can control the various options that gadget supports.

Clicking the Options button on the World Clock gadget produces the World Clock options dialog box shown in Figure 9.6. There you can select a time zone that you want to display from a list of worldwide time zones. In addition, you control whether the clock displays a second hand moving around the clock in real-time and you can select a time zone.

FIGURE 9.6
Enter a clock name and a time zone for your Sidebar's world clock.

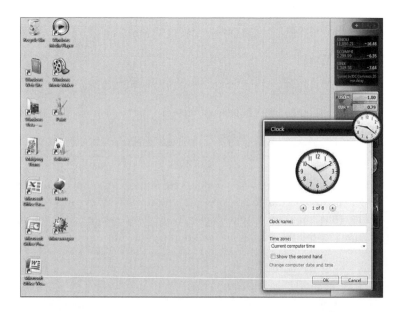

If your Sidebar fills up with gadgets, Vista creates additional pages for it. To see the gadgets that aren't currently in view, click the left or right arrow at the bottom of your Sidebar's control button panel.

Organize Your Gadgets

Vista supports several ways you can organize and use your gadgets. You don't have to keep them on your Sidebar to use them, but the Sidebar keeps them together and always available. You can add a gadget to your desktop, too.

To move a gadget from your Sidebar to your desktop, drag the gadget's grab button and drag the gadget away from the Sidebar. If you want all gadgets placed on your desktop, you should hide your empty Sidebar from view so that it won't get in your way. To hide your Sidebar, right-click over an empty spot toward the bottom of your Sidebar and select Close Sidebar from the contextual menu. Your Sidebar icon still remains on your Taskbar's notification area where you can display the Sidebar again if you wish.

Modifying Your Sidebar Properties

Your Sidebar might become hidden without you intending for that to happen. If you maximize a program or folder window after you display your Sidebar, that window will appear on top of your Sidebar. If you want your Sidebar to remain in view no matter what else you do (which is often the reason why you want the Sidebar to begin with), right-click over an empty spot at the bottom of your Sidebar and select Properties. The Windows Sidebar Properties dialog box opens as shown in Figure 9.7.

FIGURE 9.7
You can control the Sidebar's appearance and behavior.

From the Windows Sidebar Properties dialog box, you can control several aspects of your Sidebar. To keep your Sidebar on top of all windows, even those you maximize, select the option labeled Keep the Sidebar on Top of Other Windows. After you select that option, any windows you maximize afterward will maximize only to the extent of your screen's width that doesn't include your Sidebar.

Did you Know?

If you don't want your Sidebar to stay on top of all other windows at all times but you want to see your Sidebar temporarily, right-click the Sidebar gadgets icon in your taskbar's notification area and select Bring Gadgets to Front. Vista instantly places your sidebar on top of all open windows but does not set up your Sidebar to stay on top of all windows you subsequently open.

The option labeled Start Sidebar When Windows Starts will, when checked, ensure that your Sidebar remains open the next time you start Windows. You won't have to start Sidebar manually because it will appear when your computer starts.

By the Way

Your Sidebar placement and gadgets affect only your user account and not the accounts of others who use your computer. Their Sidebar settings are unique to their accounts.

The default location for your Sidebar is the right side of the screen, but if you click the option labeled Left, Vista places your Sidebar to the left of your screen.

If you have multiple monitors, you can determine which monitor Vista places your Sidebar on. Click the arrow next to the number for the Display Sidebar on Monitor option to use the selected monitor for the Sidebar. If you use three monitors, for example, you might want your Sidebar placed against the right edge of the far right monitor's screen or perhaps the left edge of the far left screen. Using the Windows Sidebar Properties dialog box, you control the exact placement on the monitor that works best for your needs.

Did you Know?

If you're a programmer, you can write gadgets and share them with others. Microsoft provides support for writing new gadgets at http://microsoftgadgets. com/Build. Figure 9.8 shows the website, and as you can see from the menu across the top, the site contains a lot of resources for anyone who wishes to write their own gadgets or gadgets for others to use. A gadget consists of HTML and script code. To see the exact steps required to write, test, and run new gadgets, this page will walk you through the entire process: http://microsoftgadgets.com/ Sidebar/DevelopmentOverview.aspx.

FIGURE 9.8
The Gadget Builder Depot website contains the answers you need to build your own gadgets.

Looking at Vista's Gadgets

One of the best ways to learn how the Sidebar works is to use it. The following sections review a few of the gadgets that Microsoft supplies with Windows Vista.

The Feeds Headlines Gadget

The Feeds Headlines gadget, shown in Figure 9.9, supports **RSS** (an acronym for *Really Simple Syndication*, which allows you to receive live updates from your favorite blogs and websites. Chapter 38, "Staying in Touch with RSS and Instant Messaging," explains more about RSS feeds and how you can subscribe to them on your favorite websites.

The Feeds Headlines gadget defaults to showing you Internet Explorer–related information. If you subscribe to RSS feeds in Internet Explorer, the Feeds Headlines will display those feeds as well.

When you click the wrench icon to display the options window, all RSS feeds that you subscribe to will be presented in a scrolling list. Select an RSS feed and the Feeds Headlines gadget displays information from that feed.

The Notes Gadget

The Notes gadget, shown in Figure 9.10 with its option window open, is an always-ready notepad that you can jot notes on while you work. The Notes gadget is nice because you don't have to open Word or WordPad to type quick notes that you want to refer to later.

Click to see options

FIGURE 9.9
Get live RSS
streaming infor-
mation from the
Internet.

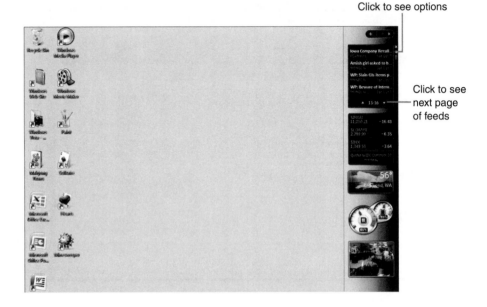

Click to see
next page
of feeds

FIGURE 9.10
Notes is a gadg-
et that's always
ready to record
your notes like
a sticky pad
next to your key-
board.

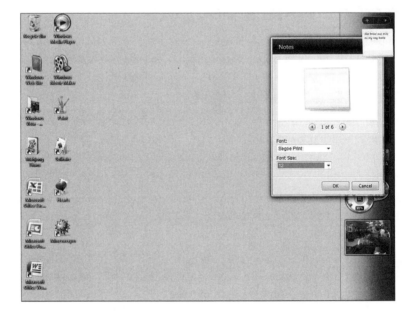

To use the Notes gadget, click on the Notes gadget and begin typing. You cannot
adjust the side of the Notes except if you drag the Notes gadget off your Sidebar,
Vista will increase the size a little for better viewing. If a note takes more than the
current note size, the note scrolls down as you type past the bottom line.

Notes can keep track of multiple notes, not just one. When you're ready to add another note to your Notes pad of notes, click the plus sign and a blank note appears on top of the pad. Click the Note gadget's left and right arrows to move back and forth among the notes that you've created.

The World Clock Gadget

Earlier in the chapter you saw the World Clock gadget. The clock shows the time for any time zone you select. A second hand display is also available in the options window.

> If you have friends or family who are traveling, you could display their time zone in the World Clock. You'll be able to keep track of their time and better know the hours when you could call them. Changing your Sidebar's World Clock's time zone doesn't change your computer's time zone shown in the notification area of your taskbar.

By the Way

The Slide Show Gadget

The Slide Show gadget is another Vista-supplied Sidebar gadget. When you first install Vista and display the Sidebar, it might not hold the Slide Show. But you can easily add Slide Show by following the steps in the previous section, "Adding Gadgets to Your Sidebar." Figure 9.11 shows the Slide Show gadget atop the Sidebar with its Options window open.

When you point to the Slide Show gadget, a set of control buttons appear at the bottom of the display. With these controls, you can do the following:

▶ Look at the picture displayed before the current one.

▶ Pause the display on the current picture.

▶ Move to the next picture. (This is useful for stepping through the pictures at a faster speed than the current rate.)

▶ **Reveal** the current image (meaning, in Slide Show talk, that you display the current picture in its own program window in your Photo Gallery Viewer).

If you want to display images from a folder other than your Pictures folder (which is the folder Vista defaults to), click the check mark to display the Slide Show's options window and change the Directory entry to the folder you want to use for the Slide Show. You can change the speed of both the fade from image to image and the amount of time Slide Show uses to display each picture before moving to the next one.

FIGURE 9.11
The Slide Show gadget steps through your pictures.

Chapter Wrap-Up

The Sidebar is just another tool Windows Vista gives you to get work done. The Sidebar in and of itself does little more than stay against one side of your screen and run little programs, called **gadgets**, that you can refer to as you use your computer. While the Sideshow gadgets are running, you can open other programs and use Windows just as you'd normally use Windows.

Windows Vista provides lots of programs like gadgets that help make you more productive. Your Start menu's Accessories menu option is filled with other programs. In the next chapter, you'll learn about the accessory programs that come with Vista.

CHAPTER 10

Exploring the Windows Vista Accessories

In This Chapter:

- ▶ Familiarize yourself with Vista's accessory programs
- ▶ Use Vista's Calculator accessory program
- ▶ Write with Vista's free word processor
- ▶ Create pretty pictures with Paint

Windows Vista comes with several application programs you can use right away without having to install anything else. The names of these programs indicate their purpose in most cases; for example, Calculator and Paint are self-explanatory.

This chapter introduces these programs to you. They reside on your Start menu's Accessories folder. If you've used previous versions of Windows, some will surely be familiar but others are new to Vista, such as the Mobility Center.

Looking at the Accessories

Open your Start menu, select All Programs, and then select Accessories. Depending on your Vista's installation, you might see a different list of programs from this book's but many will overlap. Windows users often find themselves using these programs more than they first thought they would. The programs load quickly because they're fairly small, unlike larger applications such as Adobe's Photoshop, which is why many Vista users put some of the accessory programs on their Sidebar. The following list describes programs that Vista users commonly find on their Accessories menu.

▶ Calculator—Performs quick calculations; handy for arithmetic that doesn't require a worksheet program. Calculator includes an option to change its display to a scientific calculator for more complex calculations such as statistical and trigonometric operations.

▶ Command Prompt—Sometimes known as the **DOS prompt** due to the pre-Windows, DOS-like window that the Command Prompt emulates. Figure 10.1 shows the Command Prompt window that appears when you select Command Prompt from the Accessories menu. To close the Command Prompt window type **exit**.

Right-click here for options

FIGURE 10.1
Use the
Command
Prompt window
when you want
to work in a
DOS-like environment.

Did you
Know?
You can adjust the way the Command Prompt window behaves by right-clicking on its title bar and selecting Properties. (This isn't obvious because there is no button or label or link to tell you about the right-click option.) On the Command Prompt Properties dialog box that appears, you can adjust the Command Prompt window's size, colors, font used, and more.

▶ Connect to a Network Projector—Connects your computer to a networked projection system (as opposed to one directly connected to your computer). Such a network projector, whether wired or wireless, is becoming more common.

When you give a presentation at a hotel or board meeting, instead of connecting to a projector, you now can simply access the company's network and your screen output will appear on the network's projection system.

▶ Notepad—A text editor somewhat useful for writing web pages in HTML and scripting code and for writing programs. Vista's Notepad is slightly primitive even compared to most of today's low-level editors. The advantage of Notepad is that Notepad is always available and ready to use.

Notepad isn't intended to be used as a word processor. You won't find the typical word wrap in Notepad (you can turn on word wrap, but it's not on by default) and Notepad can edit only files stored in a textual format. If you want to do simple word processing, even if you just want to type some quick notes into a file, use WordPad or another word processing program.

▶ Paint—A simple but effective drawing program that you can use to create colorful pictures. If you're a good artist, you can use one of your Paint creations (or one of your children's, which will please them greatly, if you do) for your desktop's background.

▶ Remote Desktop Connection—Allows you to connect to a remote computer, such as one at a different location from your physical address. You might wish to access your home computer's files from work, for example, and a remote desktop connection will enable you to do that.

▶ Run—Enables you to run programs from an operating system level if you know the exact name of the program and where it's located if its not a system program that Windows expects to be ran from the Run dialog box. When you select Run, the Run window shown in Figure 10.2 appears. Windows+R is the shortcut for the Run command.

If you type the command cmd in the Run window, Windows Vista opens a Command Prompt window on your desktop just as if you'd selected Command Prompt from the Accessories menu. Some Run commands execute quickly and then close their window before you've had a chance to see what the program did. When this happens, type cmd to open a Command Prompt window, which remains open after a command executes, allowing you to see (or scroll up, if necessary) the results it generated.

FIGURE 10.2
You can execute
commands by
typing their
name from
inside Vista's
Run window.

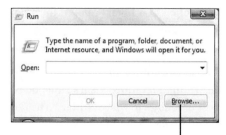

Click to locate a program to run

▶ Snipping Tool—Starts a program that enables you to capture some or all of your screen as a graphic image.

▶ Sound Recorder—Enables you to record sound from your computer's microphone jack and save it to a file. Unlike previous versions of Windows, the Sound Recorder provides no rudimentary editing on the sounds you record and save. Chapter 18, "Recording Simple Audio," shows you how to use the Sound Recorder.

For most versions of Windows Vista, Sound Recorder saves its recordings using the Windows Media Audio (WMA) file format. However, if you have a Business or Home version of Vista with an N designation (Windows Vista Business N, for example), your sound files are saved as Wave (WAV) files. The N versions of Windows are primarily intended for distribution outside the United States.

▶ Sync Center—Enables you to synchronize the files on other computers and devices connected to your computer such as **PDAs** (Personal Digital Assistants such as Palm Pilots and PocketPCs). In Chapter 39, "Synchronizing Your Computers with Other Devices," you'll learn how to use the Sync Center.

▶ Welcome Center—Displays Vista's Welcome Center described in Chapter 2, "Exploring the Welcome Center." If you click to uncheck the option labeled, Click to Run at Startup, the Welcome Center window will cease opening when you start Vista. This Accessories option turns it back on once again.

▶ Windows Explorer—Opens the Windows Explorer window in which you can manage files and folders. Chapter 8, "Mastering Vista's Explorer Windows," explains how to use Windows Explorer.

▶ Windows Sidebar—Produces the Sidebar that contains gadgets as the previous chapter explains.

► WordPad—A simple word processor with which you can create formatted, word-processed documents.

The rest of this chapter gives you an overview of most of these programs. Some, such as Windows Explorer, you'll learn about in subsequent chapters.

Calculate Results

The Calculator program performs both simple mathematics and advanced scientific calculations. Throughout your working day, you use your computer constantly, perhaps writing letters, printing bills, and building presentations. As you work, you'll often need to make a quick calculation and, if you're anything like computer book authors, your handheld calculator ends up buried underneath a mountain of papers stacked a foot high on your desk. With the Windows Calculator program, however, a handy calculator is never farther away than a simple mouse click or three.

Calculator actually contains two calculators: a standard calculator and a scientific calculator. Most people need only the standard calculator that provides all the common mathematical operations typically required for day-to-day affairs. The scientific calculator contains additional operations, such as statistical and trigonometric operations.

Did you Know?

So, sell your desk calculator on eBay and start using Vista's. The Calculator program even enables you to copy and paste the calculator results directly into your applications.

Follow these steps to practice using the standard calculator:

1. Click Start, All Programs, Accessories, Calculator (see Figure 10.3). If you see a calculator window with many more buttons than is shown here, select View, Standard from the Calculator's menu to work with the nonscientific calculator.

You cannot resize the Calculator window. You can only minimize the Calculator program to a Taskbar button and move the window.

Watch Out!

FIGURE 10.3
The Vista Calculator program goes beyond a pocket calculator.

2. It doesn't take a rocket scientist to use Calculator! Calculator performs standard addition, subtraction, multiplication, and division. The Calculator also includes memory clear, recall, store, and memory add capabilities.

By the Way

All the Calculator operations produce running totals, meaning that you can continuously apply operations such as addition to the running total in the calculator's display.

Watch Out!

The Calculator program has keyboard-equivalent keys. Instead of clicking with your mouse to enter 2 + 2 for example, you can type **2 + 2** = (the equal sign requests the answer). Not all keys have obvious keyboard equivalents, however. For example, the C key does not clear the total (Esc does). Therefore, you might need to combine your mouse and keyboard to use the calculator effectively.

3. Click the number 1, and then 2, and then 3 (or type the numbers with your keyboard, but make sure that your Num Lock key is turned on first). As you click, the numbers appear inside the display.

4. Click the multiplication sign (the asterisk).

5. Click 2.

6. Click the equal sign, and Calculator displays the result of 246.

7. Click C or press Esc to clear the display.

Did you Know?

Click the Backspace key to erase any numbers that you type incorrectly.

8. The percent key produces a percentage only as a result of multiplication. Therefore, you can compute a percentage of a number by multiplying it by the percent figure. Suppose that you want to know how much 35% of 4000 is.

Type **4000** and then press the asterisk for multiplication. Type **35** followed by the percent key (Shift+5 on your keyboard). The value **1400** appears. The result: 1400 is 35% of 4000. The word *of* in a math problem almost always indicates that you must multiple by a percentage. Calculating 35% of 4000 implies that you need to multiply 4000 by 35% (or .35).

9. When you want to negate a number in the display, click the +/- key. Suppose that you want to subtract the display's current value, 1400, from 5000. Although you can first clear the display and perform the subtraction, it's faster to turn the 1400 into a negative number by clicking the +/– key, press the plus sign, type **5000**, and press the equal sign to produce 3600.

10. To store a value in memory, click MS (memory store). Whenever you want the memory value to appear in the display, click MR (memory recall). MC (memory clear) clears the memory and M+ adds the display to the total in memory. If you want to store a running total, click the M+ button every time you want to add the display's value to the memory. The M disappears from the memory indicator box when you clear the memory.

> The Calculator program displays a letter M above the four memory keys when you store a value in the memory.

By the Way

> When you want to switch your application to Calculator to perform a calculation and then enter the result of that calculation elsewhere (such as in your word processor's document), select Edit, Copy (Ctrl+C) to copy the value to the Clipboard. When you switch back to the other Windows program, you will be able to paste the value into that program.

Did you Know?

The program's standard calculator performs all the operations most Windows users need most of the time. The interface is simple. The scientific calculator supports many more advanced mathematical operations. Despite its added power, the scientific calculator operates almost identically to the standard one. The standard keys and memory keys are identical in both versions.

To see the scientific calculator, select View, Scientific. Vista displays the scientific calculator shown in Figure 10.4. You'll see that the scientific calculator offers more keys, operators, and indicators than the standard calculator, including trigonometric and statistical operations.

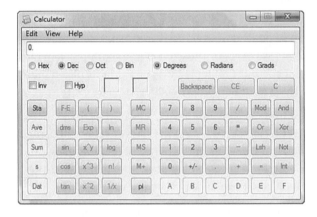

 Did you Know?

The scientific calculator even supports binary, octal, and hexadecimal calculations.

Write with Flair

Vista contains a word processor called WordPad, which appears on your Accessories menu. Although WordPad does not contain all the features of a major word processor, such as Microsoft Word, WordPad does contain many formatting features and can accept documents created in some other word processing programs.

By the Way

Notepad also appears in your Accessories menu group, but despite the similarity of its name to WordPad, Notepad is a scaled-down version of WordPad and offers very few of the capabilities that WordPad offers. The most important WordPad feature omitted from Notepad is its lack of rich text-formatting abilities as well as a word wrap feature that's turned on by default. A text editor used for writing programs, which is one of Notepad's reasons for being, doesn't require a rich assortment of formatting tools and word wrapping could cause program problems if it automatically wrapped text from the end of one line to the start of the other.

WordPad edits, loads, and saves documents in all the following formats: text documents (TXT) and Rich Text Format (RTF) documents. As a result, when you open an RTF document that contains formatting such as underlining and boldfaced characters, WordPad retains those special formatting features in the document.

Figure 10.5 shows the WordPad program window. WordPad contains a toolbar that you can use to help you access common commands more easily. In addition, WordPad supports the use of a ruler and format bar that help you work with WordPad's advanced editing features. When you type text into WordPad, you won't have to worry about pressing Enter at the end of every line. WordPad wraps your text to the next line when you run out of room on the current line. Press Enter only when you get to the end of a paragraph or a short line such as a title that you don't want combined with the subsequent line. (Pressing Enter two times in a row adds a blank line to your text.)

Toolbar   Format bar   Ruler

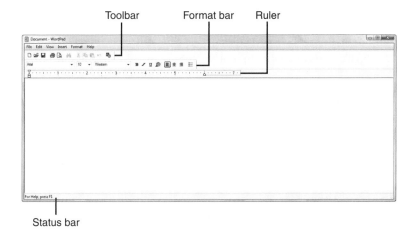

Status bar

FIGURE 10.5
WordPad offers many word processing features.

To practice using WordPad, follow these steps:

1. Start WordPad from the Accessories menu. You'll see the WordPad screen shown in Figure 10.5.

If your WordPad screen does not look exactly like the one in Figure 10.5, you can use the View menu to add a check mark to each line of the first four commands—Toolbar, Format Bar, Ruler, Status Bar—so that you can display each of these four optional tools.

By the Way

---

2. For this task, you'll practice entering and formatting text. Type the following text: **A large line**.

3. Select all three words by highlighting them with your mouse or keyboard. With your mouse, select by pointing to the first character and dragging the mouse to the last character. With your keyboard, you can select by moving the

text cursor to the first letter and pressing Shift+Right Arrow until you select the entire line.

4. Click the format bar button with the letter B. The text stays selected but something changes—the text becomes boldfaced. Press any arrow key to get rid of the highlighted text and see the boldfaced text.

5. Select the three words once again. Click the second format bar button with the letter I. WordPad italicizes the text. Now click the third format bar button with the letter U. WordPad instantly underlines the selected text. Keep the text highlighted for the next step.

By default, WordPad selects a **font** (a typestyle) named Arial. You can see the font name directly below the format bar. The font's size, in *points* (a point is 1/72 inch), appears to the right of the font name (the default font size is 10 points).

You can change both the font and the font size by clicking the drop-down lists in which each appears. When you select text, choose a font name and Word Pad changes the font to the new name's style. After selecting the text, display the font name list by clicking the drop-down list box's arrow and select a font name. If you have the Comic Sans MS, use that font; if not, select another that sounds interesting.

Open the point size drop-down list box and select 36 (you can type this number directly into the list box if you want to). As soon as you do, you can see the results of your boldfaced, underlined, italicized, large-sized text displayed using the font name you selected. Press the left or right arrow key to remove the selection. Figure 10.6 shows what your WordPad window should look like.

FIGURE 10.6
The text is formatted to your exact specifications.

WordPad applied all the previous formatting on the three words because you selected those words before you changed the formatting. If you select only a single word or character, WordPad formats only that selected text and leaves all the other text alone.

Although this example uses a lot of different formatting options, when you write you should avoid overformatting your titles and documents. If you make your text too fancy, it becomes cluttered, looks cheap, and your words lose their meaning amid the italics, underlines, and font styles. Use italics, boldfacing, and underlining only for emphasis when needed for select words and titles.

6. Press Enter. Click the B, I, and U format bar buttons once again. This resets the boldface, italics, and underline buttons so subsequent text you type doesn't have those formatted properties. Return the font name to Times New Roman. Lower the font size to 20. Press Enter three times to add some blank lines after the title and then type the following: **Windows Vista is fun** and press the Spacebar. If you don't like the font size, click the down arrow to the right of the font name list and select a different size.

7. Click the italics format bar button again. Subsequent text you type will be italicized. Continue typing this on the same line: **and I like to use WordPad**. As you can see, you don't have to select text to apply special formatting to text. Before you type text that you want to format, select the proper format command and then type the text. WordPad then formats the text, using the format styles you've selected, as you type that text. When you want to revert to the previous unformatted style (such as when you no longer want italics) change the style and keep typing.

Controlling Fonts

Ctrl+B, Ctrl+I, and Ctrl+U are the shortcut keys for clicking the B, I, and U format bar buttons. You can also change the formatting of text characters by selecting Format, Font. WordPad displays a Font dialog box, as shown in Figure 10.7, on which you can apply several formatting styles.

As you change the style, the Font dialog box's Sample area shows you a sample of text formatted to the specifications you provide. When you close the Font dialog box, WordPad formats subsequent text according to the Font dialog box settings.

FIGURE 10.7
The Font dialog box provides all formatting specifications in a single place.

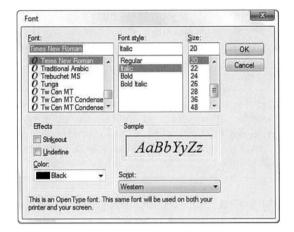

8. Select File, Print Preview to see a thumbnail image of how your document will look if you were to print it. By looking at a preview before you print your document, you can tell whether the overall appearance is acceptable and if the margins and text styles look good. You can quit the preview and return to your editing session by pressing Esc.

9. Close WordPad. You don't need to save your work when WordPad prompts you to do so.

You now have a taste of the text-formatting capabilities available. In addition to the standard editing commands you saw in the previous walk-through, here are additional features that give WordPad enough power to handle almost all simple word processing chores:

▶ The ruler indicates where your text appears on the printed page when you print the document. Each number on the ruler represents an inch (or a centimeter if your WordPad is set up for a metric setting in the View, Options dialog box). As you type, you can watch your ruler to see where the text will appear when you print your document. If you select the Format, Paragraph command, WordPad displays the Paragraph dialog box in which you can set left and right indentions for individual paragraphs as well as tab stops.

You can place tab stops quickly by clicking the ruler at the exact location of the tab stop you want.

▶ The toolbar's Align Left, Center, and Align Right buttons left justifies, centers, and right justifies text so that you can align your text in columns as a newspaper does. The Center alignment format bar button is useful for centering titles at the top of documents.

▶ If you have a color printer, consider adding color to your text by clicking the toolbar's color-selection tool after highlighting the text you want to apply a color to.

▶ The far-right format bar button adds bullets to lists you type. Before you start the list, click this Bullets button to format the list as a bulleted list.

Paint a Pretty Picture

Paint provides colorful drawing tools. Before you can use Paint effectively, you must learn to interact with Paint and you must understand Paint's tools. The Paint screen contains five major areas, as Figure 10.8 shows. Table 10.2 describes each area.

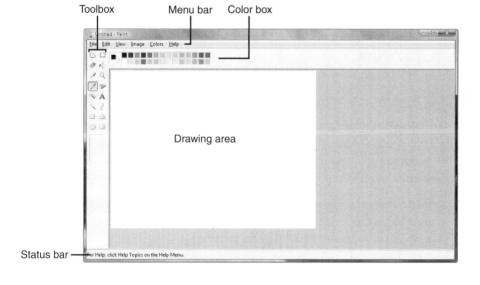

FIGURE 10.8
The five major areas of the Paint screen enable you to create and edit your graphic images.

Paint does not contain a toolbar with buttons, as do WordPad and many other Windows programs. Paint contains a toolbox that is the most important area of Paint. It is from this toolbox that you select and use drawing tools.

By the Way

TABLE 10.2   Paint's Five Areas Help You Draw

Area	Description
Drawing area	Holds your drawing as you create it. When you want to create or modify a drawing, you work within this area.
Color box	Produces a list of possible colors you can choose to add color to your artwork.
Menu bar	Displays the commands that control Paint's operation.
Status bar	Shows important messages and measurements as you use Paint.
Toolbox	Holds the vital drawing, painting, and coloring tools with which you create and modify artwork.

The two scrollbars on Paint's drawing area enable you to scroll to other parts of your drawing. The drawing area is actually as large as a maximized window. If, however, Paint initially displayed the drawing area maximized, you wouldn't be able to access the menu bar or the toolbox or read the status bar. (Paint was originally designed before the concept of floating toolbars was invented, and Microsoft didn't add them in this version for Vista.) Therefore, Paint adds the scrollbars to its drawing area so that you can create drawings that will, when displayed, fill the entire screen.

The easiest way to learn Paint is not to see a list of commands but actually to draw something. The following steps walk you through Paint's major features:

1. Start Paint from your Accessories Start menu option.

2. Maximize Paint's program window to your full screen size. Paint is one of the few programs in which you'll always want to work in a maximized window. By maximizing the program window, you gain the largest drawing area possible.

3. If you don't see the toolbox, the status bar, or the color box, open the View menu and click to view each of these important screen areas to ensure that you see all five shown as you follow along here.

4. Figure 10.9 labels each of the toolbox tools. Each tool contains an icon that illustrates the tool's purpose. The tools on the toolbox compose your collection of drawing, painting, and coloring tools. When you want to add or modify a picture, you have to pick the appropriate tool.

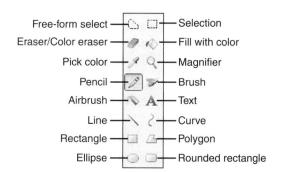

Free-form select — Selection
Eraser/Color eraser — Fill with color
Pick color — Magnifier
Pencil — Brush
Airbrush — Text
Line — Curve
Rectangle — Polygon
Ellipse — Rounded rectangle

5. Click the Pencil tool.

6. Move your mouse pointer over the drawing area and the pointer changes to a pencil (the same icon that's on the Pencil tool itself).

7. Hold down your mouse button and move your mouse pointer, the pencil, all around your drawing area. Make all sorts of curves with your mouse. Notice that Paint keeps the pencil within the borders of your drawing area. Figure 10.10 shows what you can do if you really go crazy with the Pencil tool.

8. The default color for pencil drawings is black. Click a different color on the color bar, such as red or green, and draw some more. The new lines will appear in your selected color. Select additional colors and draw more lines to beautify the picture further.

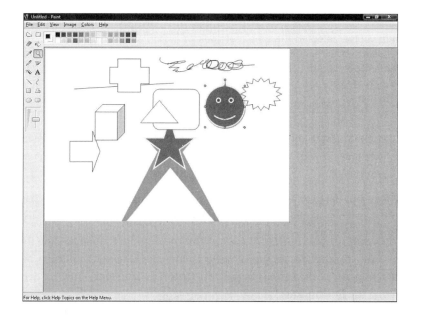

FIGURE 10.10
The Pencil tool enables you to doodle; no criticism of the artist will be tolerated!

> Every time you change a tool or color or draw a separate line, Paint saves the next group of changes to your drawing area. As with most Windows Vista programs, Paint supports an Edit, Undo feature (Ctrl+Z or Alt+Backspace are both shortcuts for the Undo command). You can undo up to three previous edit groups. Therefore, if you've just drawn three separate lines, you can remove each of those lines by performing the Undo command three times.

9. Erase your drawing by selecting File, New. Don't save your current drawing (unless you really want it, for some reason). Paint clears the drawing area so that you can begin again.

10. Click the Line tool. Use the Line tool to draw straight lines.

   A straight line is defined by two coordinates: the starting coordinate position and the end coordinate position. To draw a line, you must anchor the line's starting position and extend the line to its ending position. Paint automatically draws a straight line from the starting position to the end position. You can draw lines using the Line tool in any direction.

   Get used to reading the coordinate pair numbers in the status bar. The numbers tell you the number of drawing points from the left and top of your window. Move your mouse around the drawing area without clicking a button and watch the pair of numbers at the right of the status bar change.

11. Select a different color and draw another line. Paint draws that line in the new color.

> Now that you've selected the Line tool, look at the area below the toolbox. You'll see five lines with each line growing thicker than the one before. By clicking a thick line, the next line you draw with the Line tool appears on the drawing area in that new thickness. You can change the thickness using the line size list for any geometric shape.

12. Click the thickest line in the line size list. Draw a couple of lines to see the thicker lines. If you change colors before drawing, the thicker lines appear in the new color.

13. The rest of the geometric shapes are as easy to draw as the lines are. Select File, New to clear the drawing area. Don't save any changes.

14. Click the Line tool to change the line thickness size to the middle line thickness (the third thickness size). Always change the Line tool's thickness before selecting one of the geometric drawing tools. The Line tool's line size determines the line thickness for all geometric tools.

15. Select the Rectangle tool. Rectangles, like lines, are determined by their start-ing anchor position and the rectangle's opposite corner's position. Begin draw-ing a rectangle at coordinates 190, 75. After anchoring the rectangle with the mouse button, drag your mouse until it rests at position 385, 270. The status line indicator will show 200,200 meaning that the rectangle is 200 by 200 drawing points. When you release your mouse button, you will have drawn a perfect square.

Drawing a perfect square is not always easy because you have to pay close atten-tion to the coordinates. Paint offers a better way to draw perfect squares than try-ing to draw them manually. Hold down the Shift key while dragging the mouse and the rectangle always appears as a square. Shift also draws perfect circles when you use the Ellipse tool.

Did you Know?

The three rectangles below the toolbox don't represent the line thickness of the rectangles. They determine how Paint draws rectangles. When you click the top rectangle (the default), all of the drawing area that appears beneath the next rectangle that you draw shows through. Therefore, if you draw a rectan-gle over other pictures, you see the other pictures coming through the inside of the new rectangle. If you click the second rectangle below the toolbox, the rec-tangle's center overwrites any existing art. As a result, all rectangles you draw have a blank center no matter what art the rectangle overwrites. If you select the third rectangle, Paint does not draw a rectangular outline, but draws the interior of the rectangle in the same color you've set for the interior (the default interior color is white).

16. Now that you understand the rectangle, you also understand other geometric tools. Click the Ellipse tool to draw ovals (remember that Shift enables you to draw perfect circles). Click the Rounded Rectangle tool to draw the rounded rectangles (or rounded squares if you press and hold Shift while dragging).

17. Click the top rectangle selection (to draw see-through shapes) and click the Ellipse to draw circles. Click the rounded Rectangle tool and draw rounded rec-tangles. Fill your drawing area with all kinds of shapes to get the feel of the tools.

18. A blank drawing area will help you learn how to use the Polygon and Curve tools so select File, New (don't save) to clear your drawing area.

19. Select the Polygon tool. The Polygon is a tool that draws an enclosed figure with as many sides as you want to give the figure. After you anchor the poly-gon with the mouse, drag the mouse left or right and click the mouse button.

Drag the mouse once again to continue the polygon. Every time you want to change directions, click the mouse once again. When you finish, double-click the mouse and Paint completes the polygon for you by connecting your final line with the first point you drew.

20. Clear your drawing area again. The Curve tool is one of the neatest but strangest tools in Paint's toolbox. Click the Curve tool (after adjusting the line thickness and color if you wish to do so).

21. Draw a straight line by dragging the mouse. After you release the line, click your mouse button somewhere just outside the line and drag the mouse around in circles. As you drag your mouse, Paint adjusts the curve to follow the mouse's movements. When you see the curve that you want to keep, release your mouse button so that Paint can stabilize the curve.

22. The Eraser/Color Erase tool erases whatever appears on your drawing area. The Erase/Color Eraser tool comes in four sizes—A small eraser that erases small areas up to a large eraser that erases larger areas at one time. When you select the Eraser/Color Eraser tool, you can also select an eraser thickness. (The color you choose has no bearing on the eraser's use.) Select the Eraser/Color Eraser tool now and drag it over parts of your drawing to erase lines you've drawn.

23. Exit Paint.

By the Way

Paint can read and save files in several popular graphic file formats including bitmap files with the .bmp filename extension, JPEG files that end in .jpg and .jpeg, Graphic Interchange Files (with the .gif extension), and TIFF files with .tif and .tiff file extensions. Certain image files are better for some things than others. For example, bitmap images work best for your desktop background images and JPEG images often work well for nonphotographic web images that you want to keep small so that they load quickly.

Because formats like JPEG compress data to achieve a smaller file size, they're also prone to degrading overall image quality. It's generally not a huge issue, but if you absolutely do not want to lose image quality due to file compression, save your image in an uncompressed format, such as TIFF.

Paint doesn't just put lines and colors on your drawings, it can also add text. The Text tool enables you to add text such as photo captions and titles, using any font available within your Windows Vista's font collection. You can control how the text covers or exposes any art beneath the text. After clicking the Text tool, drag the text's outline box (Paint text always resides inside this text box that appears when you first place text onto a drawing). When you release your mouse button, select the font and style, and type your text. When you click another tool, your text becomes part of the drawing area.

Did you Know?

Chapter Wrap-Up

This chapter reviewed many of the programs that Vista provides in the Start menu's Accessories folder. You learned how to use three of these programs—Calculator, WordPad, and Paint—in some depth. The accessory programs are designed to give you simple but quick access to common features that you'll need as you use Windows. Although more powerful programs exist, the accessory programs come free with Windows Vista and even if you use additional programs such as Photoshop or Microsoft Word, you'll still find times when the smaller accessory programs come in handy. Therefore, you should know something about how to maneuver in them and this chapter gave you enough background to do just that.

In the next chapter, you'll learn about the games that Windows Vista supplies. Many of these you've no doubt seen before. That's fine. Unlike recent versions of Windows, though, Vista updated some of these games to make them more graphically appealing and added a few new ones. In addition, if you play more advanced games available that aren't included with Windows Vista, you should understand Vista's new Games Explorer window, which allows you to organize all your games into one location in your Start menu, along with basic information about them, like a game's publisher and ESRB rating.

CHAPTER 11

Taking Time Out with Windows Vista Games

In This Chapter:

- ▶ Learn about Windows Free Games
- ▶ Master Solitaire
- ▶ Tread carefully with Minesweeper
- ▶ While away free time with FreeCell
- ▶ Enjoy a fast-paced game of Spider Solitaire
- ▶ Play Hearts against three imaginary players
- ▶ Battle your computer at Chess Titans
- ▶ Discover the Orient with Mahjong
- ▶ Teach your kids with Purble Place
- ▶ Set parental controls for games
- ▶ Understand the Games Explorer window

Many people use Windows Vista to help them get their work done. Many use Windows Vista to help them run the latest games. Many do both!

This chapter gives you somewhat of a time out from learning the aspects of Windows Vista because it focuses on gaming. Some games come with Vista and although you might have played them before, Vista has given them an attractive makeover. In addition, Vista makes it possible to more easily organize all the games you install on your computer, providing you with access to all your computer's games from one location, even if they reside in separate locations around your computer (as they often do).

All work and no play makes Jane and John dull people...take a breather and learn how you can turn an idle ten minutes of downtime into some enjoyable brain calisthenics.

The Games Vista Supplies

Open your Start menu, click the Games entry in your Start menu's right pane and you'll see the games that Vista supplies in a window (see Figure 11.1). For users of previous Windows operating systems, Vista's list of games will generally be familiar, but you'll see a few newcomers that you haven't seen before. When you select a game, its computer performance recommended rating appears along with the current computer's rating, so you'll know if the game will run sluggishly or efficiently.

Click to determine who can run what

FIGURE 11.1
Vista offers a few games to while away your idle time.

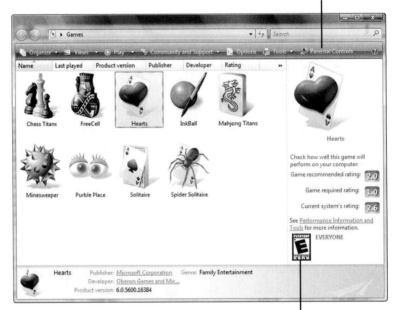

Each game's Parental Control rating appears here

The following sections quickly run through some of Vista's games and explain how to run and play them. They are intended to provide you with a basic overview, as opposed to detailed instruction guides.

As you click to select each game in the Games window, you'll see a rating in the lower-left corner of the window. You can set parental controls to keep certain users from accessing games of a particular rating if you want to do so. The "Setting Game Parental Controls" section later in this chapter explains how to control user access to games.

The Old Standby: Windows Solitaire

Solitaire has been around since some of the earliest versions of Windows and Vista didn't buck the trend. Solitaire is fun, doesn't require intensive mental alertness, which makes for a nice time-out during the day. Solitaire also offers a benefit in that people getting used to a new mouse or trackball find that playing a few rounds of Solitaire gets them familiar with the mouse quicker than most other means.

To start Solitaire, double-click the Solitaire icon in your Games window. Vista runs the Solitaire game and you'll see the Solitaire window that looks something like the one in Figure 11.2. Vista changed the look to make the game more visually and audibly appealing than it has been for more than a decade.

Remaining cards in deck   Suit stacks

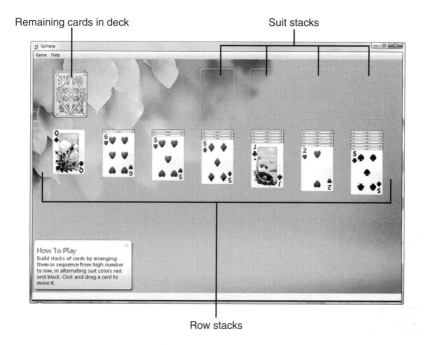

FIGURE 11.2
The Solitaire game mimics that with real cards.

Row stacks

This chapter spends a little more time explaining Solitaire than the rest of the games because Solitaire is by far the most-played of all the Windows games.

By the Way

The purpose of Solitaire is to place all the cards in the four blank areas in the upper-right area of the window. These four stacks are called **suit stacks** because each area will eventually hold a stack of cards from the same suit.

You must build the suit stacks from Ace (the low card) to the King (the high card). After you've sent all 52 cards from the rest of the screen to the suit stacks, you win the game and see an animated card dance. Winning is a challenge and requires both skill and luck.

You can change the pictures shown on the cards as well as Solitaire's background image. Select Game, Change Appearance to display the Change Appearance window shown in Figure 11.3. Select a different picture and click OK to change to that deck and background. You can change either the deck or the background in the middle of a game without affecting the game's status.

FIGURE 11.3
You can change the cards or background at any time during play.

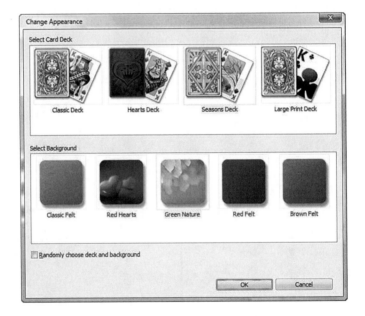

If an Ace fully appears anywhere on the screen without being partially covered by one or more other cards, at any time, you can double-click that Ace to send the Ace to start a new suit stack. After you send an Ace, you can send a two, three, and so on until you build the entire suit in each stack. Whenever you see the next card from any of the suit stacks, you can double-click that card to put the card on the stack. If there is no Ace showing, you cannot place a card on a suit stack yet. You'll have to begin rearranging and displaying cards in the lower portion of the screen to find cards to send to the suit stack.

You can also drag the card from the lower area of the screen to the suit stack. After playing Solitaire for a while, you'll be a pro at dragging with your mouse.

Before building a suit stack, you have to find cards on the screen that go there. The seven stacks of cards, called the **row stacks**, that you see in the center of the screen build downward. Row stacks are made from high cards to low cards and alternate from red to black. In other words, you always can place a red 8 on a black 9 and you can always place a black Queen on a red King.

If you can drag-and-drop a card from any of the row stacks onto another stack, you should do so. For example, the 10 of hearts (a red card) from the bottom of one row stack can be dragged onto a jack of spades (a black card) on the bottom of another stack. Dragging such a card frees up the card beneath the stack that originally held the 10 of hearts for use elsewhere.

On the back of the row stacks are cards that are hidden and you see only the card backs. When you move all the shown cards from a row stack, Solitaire turns over the card that's on top of the row stack and makes that card available for play.

You can move more than one card from one row stack to another. For example, if several cards on a row stack appear with descending ranks and alternating colors, you can move all those cards to another stack if the destination stack is a card that works with that group.

Did you Know?

After you've moved all the cards possible among the row stacks, you'll have to deal from the deck in the upper-left corner that holds all the cards left in the deck that don't appear elsewhere in the window. Click the deck to deal the cards from that stack.

Solitaire always deals three cards at a time from the deck, as is the standard Solitaire rule. You can change the number of cards dealt through the Game, Options menu if you want to make the game more or less difficult.

Watch Out!

If you can place the card showing on the top of the three dealt cards onto a suit stack or a row stack, you can drag the card to that location. If you can do nothing with the dealt card, you'll have to deal again. After you deal all the cards, you can deal again by clicking the deal stack twice. Solitaire monitors all your moves to ensure that you don't place the wrong card somewhere. If you attempt to move a card where it does not belong, Solitaire will move the card back.

If you run out of moves and can do nothing further with the cards you have left, Solitaire tells you that in a dialog box and offers to undo the last move you made or let you quit the game.

The game continues until you run through all the dealt cards without being able to drag one to another stack. You win if you successfully build all four suit stacks.

Search and Destroy with Minesweeper

The goal of Minesweeper is simple. You set out through a minefield trying to locate all the mines without getting blown up.

> Minesweeper is a fast game to play. Therefore, if you want something to do while waiting on hold, you can play a quick round to pass the time.

Start Minesweeper by double-clicking its icon in the Games window. Your Minesweeper window will look something like the one in Figure 11.4.

FIGURE 11.4
Muster your courage to traverse the minefield.

For such a simple game, Minesweeper contains several options that you can change. Choose your level of play by displaying the Game menu and selecting Beginner, Intermediate, or Expert. Each level of play determines the starting mine field size and the number of mines hidden in the field. The beginning player (the default) gets an 8-by-8 grid with 10 hidden mines. The intermediate player gets a larger minefield in 16-by-16 grid with 40 hidden mines. The expert player gets a 16-by-30 grid with 99 hidden mines. (You can customize the height, width, and number of hidden mines in each level by typing new numbers in the Options window.)

When you first load Minesweeper, Vista starts a new game. Unless you want to change an option, you can begin playing immediately. Your job is to click squares on the minefield grid to try to locate mines hidden under some of the squares. If you click on any square with a mine, you blow up and the game ends there. Your first click (and possibly some thereafter) is just a guess as to whether a mine is hidden there or not. After you click one square (without landing on a mine), you can begin to use logic to determine which remaining squares you can successfully click on. You win if you click to reveal all squares without mines.

The thing that appears when you click a square determines what happens next:

- If a number appears when you click a square, that number represents the number of mines that appear in the eight connecting boxes that surround the square. For example, if you click on a square and the number 2 shows on that square (instead of a mine blowing you up), two of the eight squares around that one contains mines and 6 do not.
- If a blank appears under a square, the blank indicates there are *no* surrounding mines. In addition, Minesweeper clears all the squares showing either more blank squares or numbers for clues to the rest of the minefield. A mine never appears in the squares cleared by Minesweeper when you land on a blank square.

Every game is different, so you cannot follow along with this example exactly. Nevertheless, consider what happens if, after clicking the upper-left corner square, the minefield in Figure 11.5 appears.

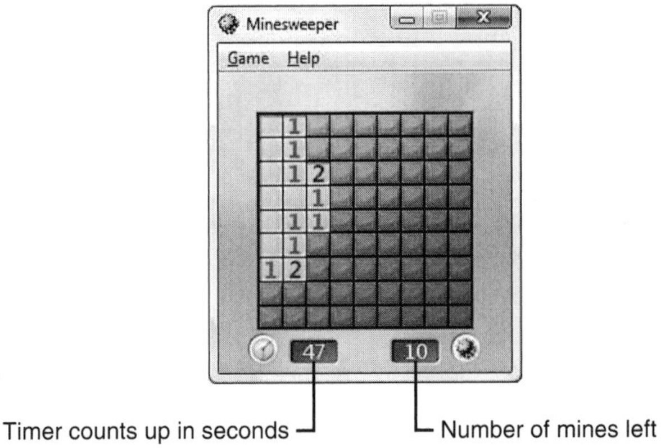
Minesweeper
Game Help
47
10
Timer counts up in seconds
Number of mines left

FIGURE 11.5
One click, especially in a corner, tells you a lot about the surrounding squares in the minefield.

The click over the upper-left square produced lots of helpful information. In addition, none of the upper-left corner's surrounding squares had mines on them. Therefore, Minesweeper automatically blanked those surrounding squares as well as additional squares that had either numbers or blanks.

For those squares where a number 1 appears, only one mine touches that square. Where a 2 appears, two mines touch that square somewhere on one of the eight sides. You continue playing, using deductive logic to uncover squares, with the numbers on top of the squares to guide you. When you suspect that a mine exists under a square, right-click that square to flag it as a mine and don't click that square again. As you progress, the numbers and blank squares give you information to help pinpoint where some or possibly all the mines are hidden.

When you successfully right-click over all hidden mines to flag them without getting blown up, the game displays a Game Won window and shows your time.

FreeCell

FreeCell has a loyal following as it offers a different twist on the more traditional Solitaire game. At the end of 2005, NBC's comedy *The Office* discussed FreeCell to the delight of the many players who love the game. When you first start FreeCell, you see eight stacks of cards, as shown in Figure 11.6.

Holding area   Suit stacks

FIGURE 11.6
FreeCell is
based on
Solitaire's con-
cept.

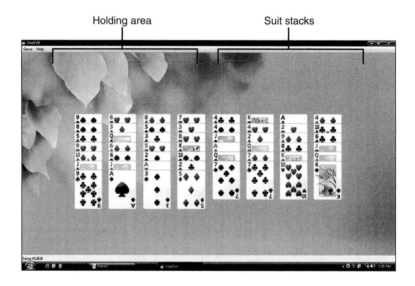

FreeCell contains a suit stack area in the upper-right corner just as Solitaire did and the goal is to send all cards to that suit stack. Whenever an Ace appears at the bottom of any of the eight stacks, you can drag that Ace to the suit stack to begin building that suit's stack and eliminating cards from the area below. Depending on your skill, you might run out of legal moves and not be able to finish with a successful win.

By the Way

It's said that every game in FreeCell is beatable. Your author certainly hasn't been able to prove that as true!

Although the cards in the eight stacks first appear randomly, it's your job to drag them into descending stacks of alternating colors not unlike Solitaire. You can drag from one to four cards to the holding area in the upper-left corner to move them out of the way while you arrange the bottom stacks. When you first begin, if no Ace appears at the bottom of any of the eight stacks, you'll need to send one or more cards to the holding area in the upper-left corner and rearrange some cards onto other stacks to uncover an Ace to send it to the holding area. Once an Ace is there, you then work on uncovering that suit's deuce (the 2 card) and sending it to the suit stack, and so on.

Figure 11.7 shows a game in progress. Both Aces remaining on the cards below are difficult to get to because they are so deep in the rows, so begin uncovering those rows as best you can to reveal the Aces.

Ace is deep in row

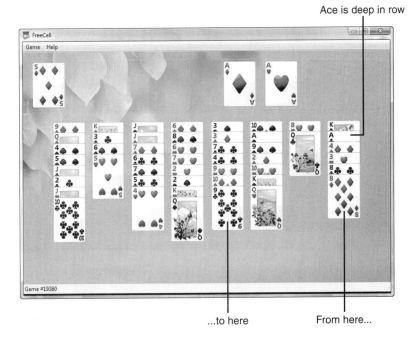

FIGURE 11.7
Keep trying to get to the low cards first to form your suit stacks.

...to here   From here...

If this seems confusing, it's because FreeCell is relatively easy to play, but trying to keep track of your potential moves adds an engaging layer of complexity. For anyone who enjoys Solitaire, however, you'll see that FreeCell produces a little more action and is beatable more often than regular Solitaire is.

A Quick Glance at Spider Solitaire

Spider Solitaire seems to be an even more convoluted Solitaire game than FreeCell. The goal, as usual, is to eliminate the cards from the playing field as quickly as possible. At its default level, beginning, you only have to worry about rank because alternating suits aren't part of the level. You get only two decks of spades to move. As you increase the playing difficulty in the game's Options window, you can require that you work with two suits or all four.

When you start Spider Solitaire, you see 10 columns of 5 or 6 cards with the top card showing face up. As shown in Figure 11.8, Spider Solitaire uses two sets of cards so you'll see two 6 of spades in the game, two King of spades, and two of every other spade (at the beginning level).

Ace from here...   ...to here removes 13 cards from this row

FIGURE 11.8
When you create a full run of cards from King down to Ace, the game removes all those cards from play for you.

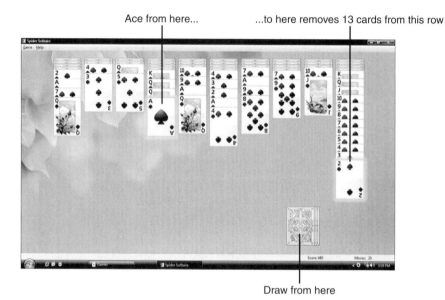

Draw from here

The goal is to move cards until you can complete a full run from King down to Ace using the same suit. Keep moving cards from high to low until you can form a complete run. In Figure 11.8, the tenth column is almost ready to lose 13 cards, which is good. After you drag column 4's Ace to the 2 at the bottom of column 10, the game removes all 13 cards from the King down to the Ace, so you have fewer cards to manage.

If you can do nothing further with the cards in the columns—meaning you've moved as many cards as possible and have no more legal moves—click the rest of the deck in the lower-right corner. Spider Solitaire deals ten cards from the deck and places one on the bottom of each stack and you can again try to form a complete ranked column to eliminate.

Eliminate all the cards and you win the game. Of the three Vista Solitaire games, Spider Solitaire is both the easiest to win (at its beginning level) and the most difficult to win (when having to match all four suits in both decks).

Play Three Imaginary Players in a Game of Hearts

The Hearts game is intended for four players, unlike the other card games in Vista. When you start the game, you're dealt your cards and the other three players' cards are hidden from you (but each of them sees his or her own cards and not yours), as shown in Figure 11.9. The computer simulates the other three players.

You will no longer find Internet versions of Hearts, Backgammon, Checkers, Reversi, and Spades in Windows Vista. Unlike Windows XP, Microsoft removed the online, multiplayer versions of these games and you can no longer play Hearts over a network. The games are still available over an Internet connection, however, from the MSN Games website at http://games.msn.com.

Click to close

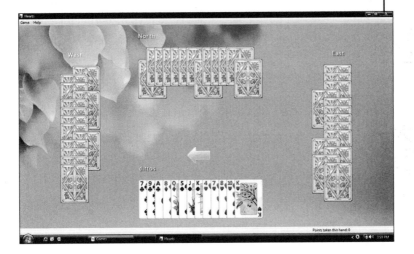

FIGURE 11.9
Hearts is a multiplayer card game.

Hearts is identical to the real-life card game that's always played in quartets. Your goal is to get rid of all your cards with the fewest points. You get rid of cards by setting down three cards in the center of the game. These cards are called the **trick**.

You don't want the trick because then you must take all 12 cards and the goal is to get rid of all your cards as soon as possible. The person who puts down the highest card of a suit takes the trick.

In addition, you get points when you take tricks that contain hearts and the Queen of spades. The more points you have, the less likely you will win. As in golf, in Hearts, you don't want the high score! As soon as someone gets 100 points, the game ends and the low score wins.

Hearts has lots of rules that can seem foreboding at first but you'll get used to them quickly. For example, the person with the 2 of clubs is the first person to add to the first trick. In every fourth hand, no cards are put down in the trick. You will **shoot the moon** when you collect all the hearts and the Queen of spades, but that's a good thing because you get zero points for that round and all other players get 26 points each.

Given that the rules are somewhat tricky at first means that playing Hearts on a computer makes things go more smoothly than playing the game with actual cards. The computer monitors the score and makes sure that the rounds go according to rules. You can focus on strategy.

Chess Titans—You Against the Machine

Chess Titans is a traditional chess game where you play against the computer. You can rotate the three-dimensional board to see various views during the play. Figure 11.10 shows a game in progress and white has already lost a queen and a bishop.

FIGURE 11.10
Play chess against your computer and may the best strategist win.

You can also play against another person by selecting New Game Against Human from the Game menu. After you make a play, the board turns around so that your opponent can use your keyboard to make a move.

This certainly isn't the place to list the rules of chess but, as with Hearts, your computer monitors the game whether or not you play against another person or the machine, and ensures that all moves are legal. In addition, the computer keeps track of your win record so that you can see how you're improving over time.

Chess games can take a while to play. During a game, you can save the board to continue at a later time.

Mahjong Titans—Tosses Tiles to Trick You

Mahjong Titans is an extremely simple and enjoyable game based on an Asian tile game. When you start Mahjong Titans, you're presented with a series of tile patterns to choose from. After you click to select one, an actual game begins. Figure 11.11 shows the beginning of a game.

A matched pair

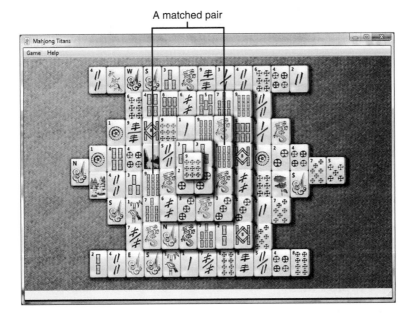

FIGURE 11.11
Point to two matching tiles whose left or right sides aren't both bound by another tile to remove the tiles.

The goal is to get rid of all the tiles. At first, the three-dimensional aspect of the board adds slightly more challenge to the game than will be there after you grow accustomed to the way the board works. As you play, you must always view the tiles like stacks of tiles on a table. The game adds shadowing along one edge of the tiles so you can more easily see which tiles are on top of other tiles.

The goal is to locate two matching tiles and remove them. You select one, and then find its match, and click it to remove both tiles. The only rule is that there must be a left or right edge on each of the matching tiles before you can remove them. If you try to remove a pair and one of them has tiles on both its left and right edges you won't be allowed to remove the pair of tiles and you must select another matching pair if one is available. You win when you remove all tiles from the stack. You lose if you run out of pairs available to remove.

In Figure 11.11, there are two tiles you can remove. They are the tiles with 9 blocks on them (other moves are possible, too). As you can see, the left one isn't quite as obvious, at least in the figure where the shadowing effect is somewhat lost, because the left one is stacked on top of the tiles beneath and doesn't have any tile on its left edge. The tiles that appear to be on its left in the figure actually are on the stack of tiles beneath that level. To remove them, you would point to one then the other and your computer would remove both from the stack. When you remove tiles, you free up additional tiles that were not available for movement before. If a tile has an actual color picture on it (called a **season tile** in the default game appearance) as opposed to a design or number of some kind, as a few have each game, you can find another color picture and remove both even if they don't match.

If you see no tiles you can remove, press H and the game gives you a hint.

Experience Purble Place

Purble Place is a collection of three games. The style of the games is certainly geared more toward younger audiences than the other games in your Games Explorer window. When you first start Purble Place, a colorful little town scene opens like the one in Figure 11.12.

The goal of Purble Place is to help children learn memory skills, colors, and shapes.

Playing Purble Pairs

Clicking the schoolhouse opens a concentration-like game that tests the player's memory (see Figure 11.13).

Schoolhouse   Comfy Cake Factory   Purble Shop

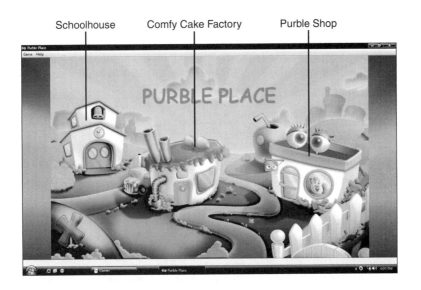

FIGURE 11.12
Purble Place opens with a town that acts as the main menu.

Players click a square to reveal what's underneath and that square remains shown until the player displays the contents of a second square. If they both match, they are erased from the board. If they don't match, the computer covers them up again. You keep clicking pairs of squares trying to recall where a match might be. Keep matching up pairs until you get rid of all the pairs and the game ends.

FIGURE 11.13
Purble Pairs tests your memory and concentration.

Sneak peeks

You can get a sneak peek at all the tiles by clicking on one of the gold tokens in the lower-left section of the game window. Each time you get a sneak peek, a sneak peek token goes away. Occasionally you'll see a bonus tile with a token in its corner. If you can match a bonus tile with the token showing, you gain another sneak peek gold token to use.

Playing Comfy Cakes

Comfy Cakes is a Purble-based color and shape-training game. You're presented as a worker in the cake factory. An order comes in for a cake. Look at the picture and try to build the cake that the customer wants.

Figure 11.14 shows the Comfy Cake factory in progress. At each station along the assembly line you must choose the correct shape and color to build the cake shown.

FIGURE 11.14
As the cake moves down the assembly line, you must put together the correct shapes and colors to build the cake that the customer ordered.

Target cake

Select to add correct decoration

Playing Purble Place

In Purble Place, you actually build Purbles themselves! In a game that's somewhat like the Comfy Cake game, your charge is to build a Purble. Figure 11.15 shows a game in progress. The game is an extremely loose translation of the traditional board game of Clue.

Behind the curtain is a Purble and you must build a Purble to match the one behind the curtain. You'll select eyes, a nose, and mouth. When you finish adding all three facial features, you click the check mark to see how many you got right. The first time is just a guess, but then you're told how many of the three parts are correct. You must then deduce which should be changed and how.

Goal hides behind the curtain

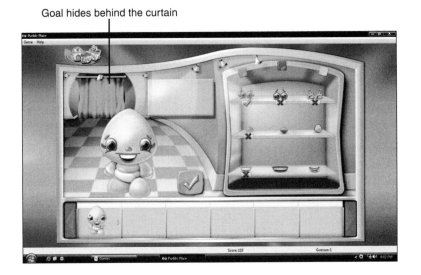

FIGURE 11.15
Build Purbles to match the one behind the curtain.

Setting Game Parental Controls

The Parental Controls button on your Games window toolbar enables an administrator level user to set controls on who can run games. When you click the button, Vista displays a list of users authorized to use your computer. You click to select a user and Vista displays a window that determines what that user can do on the computer. (Chapter 26, "Separating Users Gives Each the Access They Need," explains how to set up and manage user accounts.)

Initially parental controls are set to off, but when you click the On option, Vista provides options that you can designate for that user. The user you're setting control access to cannot have an administrative account because an Administrator can modify all settings on the computer, including parental controls.

You must have administrative privileges to set and change parental controls for other users.

When you select the Games option, Vista displays the Games Control window shown in Figure 11.16. You can block all games from the account (meaning that you block all games listed in the Games Explorer window, as the next section explains) and you can elect to allow the user to play games that meet a certain rating. This rating, set by the Entertainment Software Rating Board (ESRB), is one generally followed by all major game makers to restrict usage to an appropriate player, just like movie ratings. It ranges from Early Childhood to Adults Only. However, it's a broad system and you can also restrict games with specific types of content, such as animated blood or intense violence (assuming that Vista recognizes the game or if the game itself is designed to tell Vista what it contains). The highest rating you assign to a user's account determines the highest rating that user can play on your computer.

FIGURE 11.16
You can set up user accounts so that they can play games of a specific rating.

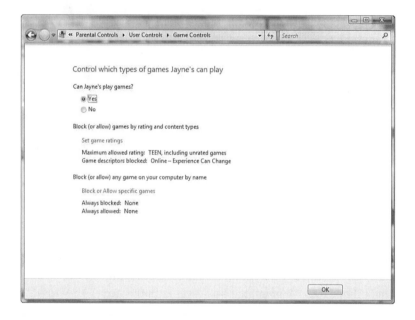

If you click the Block or Allow Specific Games option, Vista will look not just at ratings but also specific games you have installed and monitor the user's account anytime the allowable and blocked games run. If a game is blocked, Vista refuses to start the game for that user.

By the Way

Chapter 27, "Managing Your Windows Security," explains more about the parental controls and how to apply them to other areas of computing such as online activity.

Your Games Explorer Window

When you open the Games Explorer window in the Start menu's right pane, you aren't actually looking at a specific disk location. Instead, you're looking at the location of games installed on your computer. Those games will appear in various locations around your hard disk folders.

As you install new games on your computer, most recently released games should automatically appear in Vista's Games Explorer window. That is, the games are supposed to if the game vendors wrote the games properly for Vista. Some older games or those not written specifically for Vista will still appear in your Games Explorer window because Vista monitors common games and can recognize many of them.

Still, there are sure to be plenty of game titles that, when installed, won't show up in the Games Explorer window. That doesn't mean, however, that you can't get them there. To put a game's shortcut in the Game Explorer window manually, you need to open both Windows Explorer and Games Explorer. Adjust the size of each window so that you can see both on your screen at the same time without overlapping. In Windows Explorer, locate the folder where you installed the game. Drag the game's executable file entry to your Games Explorer window. A shortcut moves to the Games Explorer window so that all your games are accessible from one place. To remove a game from the Games window, right-click the game and select Remove from List.

A game must appear in your Games Explorer window before you can set parental controls for the game.

By the Way

Chapter Wrap-Up

This chapter gave you a break from the mundane by showing you the games that come with Microsoft Vista. By utilizing a single repository for all your games, Microsoft ensures that you can control access to every game installed on your computer. The Games Explorer window should contain an entry for each game on your computer. Not only will the Vista-installed games appear, but also the games you install from outside sources.

In the next chapter, you get help on help! You'll learn all the ways that Vista offers to help you through problems and the locations where you can find information on just about any topic related to Vista. Vista's help system goes far beyond that of a traditional program's online help system, as you'll see.

CHAPTER 12

Calling for Help

In This Chapter:

▶ Understand Vista's Help and Support window

▶ Differentiate between local and online help

▶ Maximize your use of the Help and Support window's toolbar

▶ Ask Microsoft a question

▶ Search the massive Knowledge Base

▶ Request or offer remote assistance

▶ Use Windows Communities

▶ Understand application-based help

This chapter shows you how to help yourself. That is—how to help yourself find help that you need as you use Windows Vista.

This book is *really* all you'll ever need to use your computer effectively (humility was never a problem with your author). But when you get confused, as might happen at times when something doesn't go the way you expect it should, Vista offers an extraordinary set of tools that you can access to find out how to accomplish a specific task. If you've recently upgraded to Vista from a previous version, you will notice that Microsoft added a lot to the Windows help system.

Introducing Vista's Help and Support

Even Windows experts need help with Windows every now and then. Windows is simply too vast, despite its simple appearance and clean desktop, for users to know everything about the system. Windows Vista includes a powerful built-in help system, which can connect to the Internet when needed so that in addition to the built-in help on your disk, there's also up-to-the-minute help available from Microsoft's website.

Help is available whenever you need it. For example, if you're working within a Windows Explorer window and have a question, just search the online help system for the words *Windows Explorer* and Windows gives advice about how to use Windows Explorer.

Microsoft calls the Windows Vista help screens the *Help and Support window* (or sometimes the *Help and Support Center*). The Help and Support window goes far beyond the standard online help you might be used to in other applications.

You can request help in a number of ways while working in Windows Vista. And there are numerous places from which you can get help. This chapter focuses on the most common ways that you can use online help and offers tips along the way.

By the Way

> To use every help feature available to you in Windows Vista, you need Internet access. Microsoft keeps up-to-date advice on the Web, such as bug reports and add-on programs to Windows Vista that you can download to improve your effectiveness as a Windows user.

The taskbar is always available to you at the bottom of your screen no matter what else you're doing in Windows. Even if you've hidden the taskbar behind a running program, the taskbar is available as soon as you press your Windows key to display the taskbar and Start menu.

You'll find Vista's Help and Support command on your Start menu's right pane. Selecting Help and Support displays Figure 12.1's Help and Support window.

FIGURE 12.1
The Help and Support window offers all kinds of help.

Don't worry if your Help and Support window looks slightly different from the one pictured in Figure 12.1. Depending on which Vista upgrades and service packs have been installed on your system, along with other factors such as your computer vendor (who might have customized the Help and Support window with its logo), there is often variation in how the Help and Support window appears.

By the Way

The Help and Support window offers two kinds of help:

▶ Local help that searches your PC's help files for answers to your questions

▶ Web-based help that provides a vast resource of help from Microsoft's online site

As with most of Vista's Explorer-like windows, the Help and Support window contains a toolbar that works like a web-browsing toolbar. As you move through the help screens, you can click the Back button to back up to something you read earlier. Click the Forward button to return.

Did you Know?

The great thing about Vista's help being both local and online is that you aren't limited to your own system help files. Although you can get many answers from your PC's local help files, Microsoft's online help window makes it easy to get the latest answers you need.

Obviously, you need to have an Internet connection to use the online help. Most readers of this book have that; however, if your connection is dial-up and not an always-on, high-speed connection, the effectiveness of the online help will be diminished slightly. If you're not logged on to the Internet when you need to get online help, your computer must first dial in to your service provider to connect to the Internet. When that process is complete, Vista can locate the help files you need and download them. If the files are graphical, as many are, they will be slow to load on a dial-up connection. You certainly will benefit from the online help but the connection to it won't be as seamless as if you had an always-on Internet connection.

If you use dial-up and don't want Vista to search online automatically every time you request help, you can request that Vista search only your local disk space when providing routine help. The section, "The Help and Support Window Options" later in this chapter, explains how to set Vista's help system to search only your local machine when you request help.

Did you Know?

If you've used Windows Help in the past, you're likely to notice at least one omission. Unfortunately, Windows Vista's Help and Support window does not support a

History button on the toolbar atop the screen as previous versions of Windows did. The next time you have Bill Gates over for dinner, you should ask him why he removed that helpful feature.

Using the Help and Support Window's Toolbar

Figure 12.2 shows the toolbar that resides atop your Help and Support window. You will use the Help and Support window toolbar quite a bit as you traverse Vista's help system.

FIGURE 12.2
You'll use the Help and Support window's toolbar quite a bit.

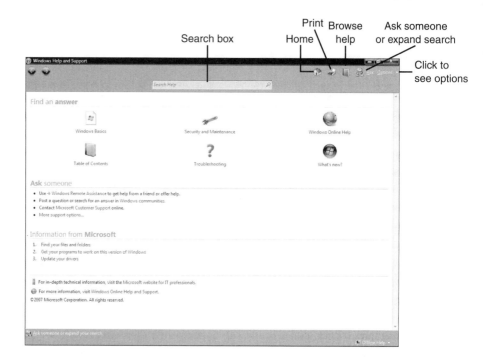

In the upper-left corner are the Back and Forward buttons described in the previous section. In the upper-right corner reside the rest of the help buttons. The following sections explain the use of each button.

Help's Home Button

When you click the Home button from any help page, Vista displays the original Help and Support window again. This is a quick way to return to the top-level help page on your system without having to click Back over and over to get back to the original Help and Support window or opening the Start menu to display the first Help and Support window again.

Help's Print Button

Anytime you want to print a help page you've displayed, click the Print button. Vista opens the Print dialog box from where you can print that page.

Help's Browse Button

When you click the Browse toolbar button, the Help and Support window changes to show you all the top-level topics on your computer's local help system (see Figure 12.3).

FIGURE 12.3
The Browse button produces a window of high-level help topics.

When you have a general question, the browsed topic list is often a good place to begin. For example, assume that you just got a music CD and you want to send the CD's music to your computer's hard disk—called **ripping**—to play while you work. Although you could search the help system for *CD* and *music* and *ripping*, you'll get a better introduction to using your computer's CD player to rip music by browsing the topic called *Music and sounds*. That high-level, music-related topic gives you a much better introduction to ripping CD music than a search for the specific word *ripping* would.

Help's Ask Button

Perhaps the most powerful of all the Help and Support window features is the Ask button. When you click Ask, the Help and Support window changes to display the Get Customer Support or Other Types of Help window as shown in Figure 12.4.

Click for remote assistance

FIGURE 12.4
A massive amount of personalized help is available to you here.

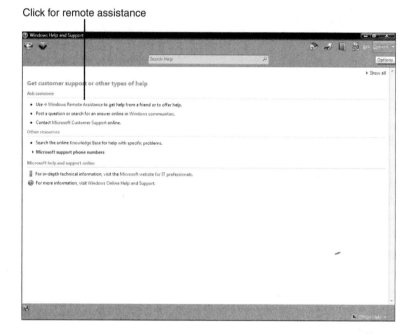

The Ask Someone window's list of help contacts also appears in the lower-half of the Help and Support window's home page.

The Ask button puts you in touch with personalized, third-party assistance and Internet-based information that can help you get past problems.

Contacting Remote Assistance

When you have a problem with your computer, wouldn't it be nice to ask an expert to look over your shoulder and explain what's going on? In a way, Windows Vista does just that.

When you click the Windows Remote Assistance link, you gain access to a system that allows others connected to your computer via the Internet or local network to temporarily take over your computer from their own Windows desktop. This allows them to see your display and work with any running applications with the goal of finding a solution to whatever problem you have.

Remote Assistance is one of the most innovative features of Vista's help system. When you click the Windows Remote Assistance link, you'll see the screen shown in Figure 12.5, which explains what will occur when you make a connection with a remote user.

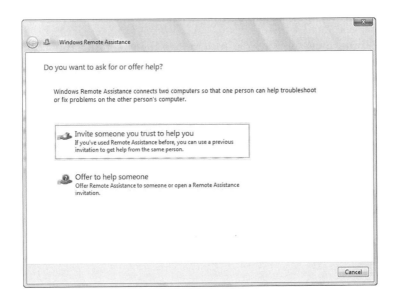

FIGURE 12.5
Anther user can connect directly to your computer and run your programs remotely to locate problems.

During the remote session, you and the remote user are able to chat in a pop-up chat window. You'll use the chat window to explain what is happening and to answer questions the remote user has.

Your remote user must be using Windows Vista or Windows XP, and must also have Internet access or access to your computer through a local area network. Some computers that you might connect to might have firewalls attached that add security from unauthorized break-in attempts. Such firewalls sometimes wreak havoc with the Remote Assistance feature. You and the remote user must be able to modify or temporarily disable firewall settings if this occurs to allow the remote access. Because this is done differently for all of the kinds of hardware and software firewalls available, you'll have to check the firewall's documentation to learn how to do this. (Although it can be easier to simply disable your firewall rather than reconfigure it to allow Remote Assistance to run, you should avoid doing so if at all possible.)

Watch Out!

So many variations of equipment and connections exist that it would be virtually impossible to walk you through the steps that would work in all readers' cases. Nevertheless, the general steps that you must take to connect to a remote user are fairly common. Here are those general steps you'll go through when using Remote Assistance:

1. Display the Help and Support window.

2. Click the Ask button on the Help and Support window's toolbar.

3. Click the Windows Remote Assistance link.

4. Click the Invite Someone You Trust to Help You link. Before connecting to a remote user, you have to send that user an invitation to connect to your system. As Figure 12.6 shows, you can send an invitation as an email link or save the invitation in a file that you then must attach to an email and send to your remote user. (The latter approach is required if you use a web-based email service such as Hotmail.) You can also save or copy the file to a remote user over a network folder, or save it to a disk that the remote user can then read to make the remote connection. The file contains instructions that the remote user's computer can understand to connect to your computer.

FIGURE 12.6
The Windows Remote Assistance window offers two ways to send an invitation to a remote user.

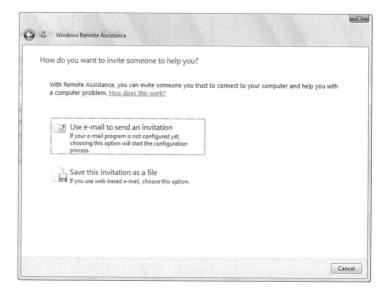

By the Way

You must type a password twice and your remote user must know that password before any computer can connect to your computer. This ensures that if the file falls into the wrong hands, the owner of those hands won't be able to use the file to access your computer.

5. After the remote user responds to your invitation and agrees to help you out by clicking the appropriate link on the remote computer, Windows Vista connects your machine to the remote user. At that time, the remote user can watch everything you do on the remote computer's screen. You can chat back and forth and if you've been getting an error that you don't understand, the

remote can see everything you do to generate that error and might be able to help you around the problem.

During the remote session, you'll notice only two differences from normal Windows operation. Your desktop background will be blank. To help keep the connection as fast as possible, Vista temporarily hides any desktop background image you may have selected. In addition, a remote session window will be available to you. Using this window, you can send a file to the remote user, start and stop a chat session, and terminate the remote connection when you finish.

Don't send an invitation to a remote user you don't trust. Obviously the ability to access your computer's resources is not a gift you'd offer to someone you don't know or isn't a representative of a trustworthy support operation. More and more software and hardware firms will surely offer remote assistance through Vista's Remote Assistance service. Generally, if you initiate the session, your files should be fine as long as you know, or trust, the remote user. You can terminate the remote session any time you want.

Using Windows Communities

Instead of getting help from someone in particular, as you do with Remote Assistance, you can request help from Microsoft-based websites and other online areas of chat and email related to Vista.

When you click the Windows Communities link, your web browser opens to the screen shown in Figure 12.7. Here you can access Microsoft Windows Vista newsgroups, a gathering of people from both Microsoft and its customer base who chat, post files, and troubleshoot problems.

A newsgroup is like a community bulletin board. Chapter 41, "Accessing a World of Information in Newsgroups," explains more about newsgroups and how to use them.

Type a word or phrase that describes your problem in the Search For text box and click the Go button to see the newsgroup information related to that search topic. To the left of the newsgroup web page, you'll see a list of Vista-related newsgroups that you can explore.

FIGURE 12.7
Search
Microsoft's
newsgroups for
answers you
need.

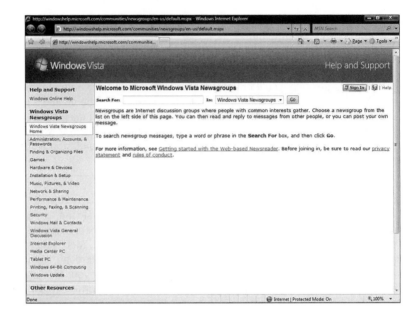

Contact Microsoft Support

Click the Contact Microsoft Support to open link and the web page shown in Figure 12.8. On this website are the various ways you can contact Microsoft for additional help, from email support to phone support.

FIGURE 12.8
Sometimes you
need to contact
Microsoft to get
an answer.

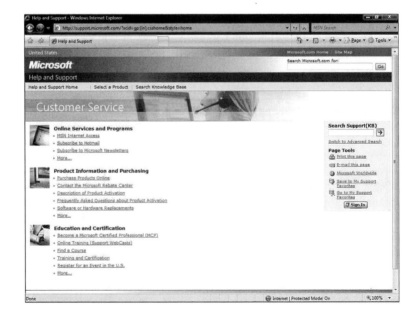

Not all the contacts on the Microsoft Support page are free. Some cost money, such as some of Microsoft's phone-related support contacts.

Watch Out!

If you know you want to call Microsoft Support for something, you don't have to search the Support web page to locate phone numbers. Instead, click the Microsoft Support Phone Numbers link on the Ask page of the Help and Support window and a list of numbers will appear.

Did you Know?

Search Microsoft's Knowledge Base

Knowledge Base is a specific location on Microsoft's website that holds the largest repository of helpful information about Windows Vista you can find. In addition, Microsoft's Knowledge Base contains a massive amount of information on all of Microsoft's products.

When you click the Search Knowledge Base link, Vista takes you to Microsoft's online Knowledge Base website shown in Figure 12.9. Here you select the product for which you want help, and type a phrase for which you want to search, in hope of getting help on a problem.

For example, if you cannot get Vista to recognize an old CentStar LP5 dot-matrix printer that you've connected to your computer, you might want to search Knowledge Base for the search phrase *CentStar LP5* or *dot-matrix* and see whether anybody in the past has run across or solved your problem. (By the way, there is no printer company named CentStar, so you won't find anything on that if you're following along on your keyboard. You can search the Knowledge Base for something else.)

Additional Online Help

You'll find two additional online help resources on your Ask page.

If you're an IT professional, such as a programmer or Network Engineer, you might want a more technical and specialized help and support location. Click the link labeled Microsoft Website for IT Professionals to go to a page geared toward and run by a more technical crowd than the average PC user.

In addition, if you click the Windows Online Help link, Vista sends you to the more general Vista help page shown in Figure 12.10. Here you'll find a well-structured website that you can dig down into for extremely specific and technical advice, but also a website that is better organized than the IT Professional website.

FIGURE 12.9
Microsoft's
Knowledge
Base is a mas-
sive database
of help topics
with tens of
thousands of
articles.

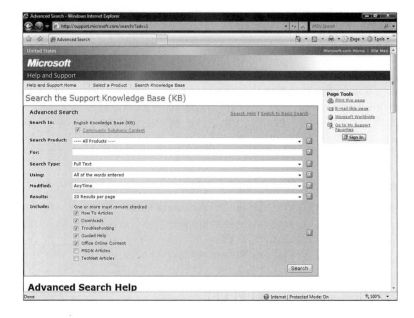

FIGURE 12.10
The Windows
Vista Help and
Support web
page contains
the most gener-
al interface of
all the Vista
help sites.

The Help and Support Window Options

A few options are available when you click the down arrow next to the Options button on your Help and Support window toolbar. Most are self-explanatory but a couple of them are extra useful.

On some monitors, your help screens might display text that is too small to read. Depending on your graphics card's resolution, you might have to enlarge the text on your help screens to make it more readable. To increase the text size (or decrease it if too little of the help screen shows), click to open the Options menu and select Text Size. You can change the text size from Largest to Smallest; the default is Medium.

Another option you might want to select is the Settings option, which displays the Help Settings dialog box shown in Figure 12.11.

FIGURE 12.11
The Help Settings dialog box enables you to set two specific Vista help settings.

By clicking to uncheck the top option, Vista no longer searches online when you request help from within the Help and Support window. This option is most useful for dial-up users without high-speed broadband connections who don't want to connect to the Internet every time they request help.

The second option turns on Microsoft's Experience Improvement program. When you get help on a topic, Microsoft might send certain information about your request and your machine to the Microsoft servers. By collecting the most common problems, Microsoft is better able to provide updates that can help users avoid those problems in the future. The information that goes to Microsoft is anonymous.

There's an even faster way to request that Vista offer local-only help or both local and online. Click the Online Help button in the Help and Support window's lower-right corner and click either the Get Online Help option or the Get Offline Help option depending on whether you want Vista to use the Internet to provide help.

Did you Know?

Other Forms of Help

The help you obtain in Windows Vista does not always come from the help system itself but from auxiliary help systems that adds support to the programs with which you work.

Using Application Help

When you use a Windows Vista program, you often need help with the program rather than Windows. Almost every application's menu bar includes a Help option that you can click for help with the program.

For example, if you select Help, Help Topics from the Vista Calculator program, a help dialog box appears for Calculator. The help is fairly standard and looks and works a lot like Vista's help system in that the help is link-based and you can traverse the help topics back and forth just as you might a web page.

In addition, a search box appears at the top of each application's help window. When you type a topic or term in the search box for which you want help, the help system will search only the Calculator-based help. Therefore, application-specific help searches search only that application's help files.

Some applications you run will have been written before Vista appeared on the market or perhaps the software authors decided not to follow Vista's exact requirements for software development. In those cases, you are likely to run across help windows that look more like the help windows in previous versions of Windows, such as the one shown in Figure 12.12.

FIGURE 12.12
Some programs produce more traditional help windows that were more common in pre-Vista Windows versions.

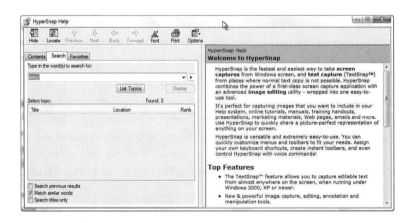

On these older Help dialog boxes, you'll find three tabs at the top of the screen with help divisions called Contents, Search, and Favorites (and possibly others). The Contents pages offer a general overview of the program. The Search tab enables you to search for specific help topics on that program.

Vista's Guided Help

A powerful help feature you'll also find embedded within many of Vista's help screens is the *guided help* feature. Guided help will actually perform an action for you, such as open a window or start a program that you need help with.

For example, if you click your Start menu's Help and Support button and type **defrag** in the Search box, you'll see a list of help topics related to Vista's disk defragmentation program. Selecting the Start Disk Defragmenter option opens Figure 12.13's help screen. Not only does the help screen explain how to start the Disk Defragmenter program, the help screen provides a link that opens the Disk Defragmenter program for you. By clicking the link, therefore, you don't have to follow the start instructions under the Note section to start the program.

The Disk Defragmenter can only be run by a user with Administrative user account privileges, so you'll have to confirm your Administrator user account before you can run the program even if the guided help system is the reason the program is starting.

By the Way

Click to open Disk Defragmenter

FIGURE 12.13
Vista's guided help actually starts programs and opens windows for you when needed.

Chapter Wrap-Up

This chapter showed you how to access Vista's powerful Help features. When you have a question about Windows Vista, you can ask Vista for help. There are several ways to access the helpful dialog boxes that cover a variety of topics. The most common way is to open the Help and Support window from your Start menu. You can access your PC's local files, search the Internet for answers you need, or ask a remote user to look at your problem. Most Windows programs contain a Help command that displays a tabbed dialog box containing different kinds of help search screens.

In the next chapter, you'll become a master at searching for information on your computer. Windows Vista's power search boxes appear in several places so that you can locate what you want when you want it. With disk drives so much larger than ever before, being able to locate information quickly is more critical than ever.

CHAPTER 13

Finding Information All Over Windows

In This Chapter:

- ▶ Find files and folders fast
- ▶ Search when you don't know a file's location
- ▶ When to use the Search folder
- ▶ Narrowing your search results
- ▶ Modifying search locations
- ▶ Perform Boolean searches
- ▶ Save searches to reuse later

Hard disks are getting big...*very* big. As a terabyte of space—that's 1,000 gigabytes—comes closer to becoming a standard storage capacity, you have more room to store more data in more places than ever before. When you want some of that data, you want to be able to locate the data quickly. (If you can't find it quickly, the data isn't very helpful.)

Windows Vista comes to the rescue with an entirely redesigned search system that permeates your entire operating system environment. Unlike the sluggish search features that previous versions of Windows offered, Vista's search is quick and helpful. Vista's Search boxes—called Instant Search boxes—are all over Vista; you'll find them on your Start menu and throughout your Explorer windows. Vista's Instant Search is a desktop searching tool that scans your files and folders at lightening speed locating data you want to find. Many times you don't even have to know exactly what to search for or exactly how to spell what you want to find, and still Vista can usually find what you're looking for.

Introducing Search

Open the Start menu and you'll see an Instant Search box, located at the bottom of the menu, just above the Start button. As Chapter 3, "Clicking Your Start Button," explained, Microsoft put a Search box on the Start menu to make Search easy to get to.

You don't even have to click your mouse button to search for something on your Start menu. The moment you open the Start menu, your text cursor is already in the Search box. The moment you start typing, Vista goes to work. Figure 13.1 shows a search in progress. The user typed the letters *co* and Vista instantly began looking for programs and folders whose names begin with the letters *co*.

FIGURE 13.1
Vista provides intelligent and quick help that starts showing you search matches before you finish typing what you want to find.

...Vista provides search results here

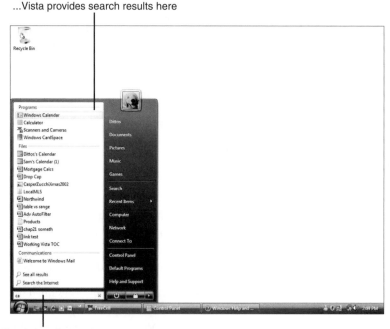

As you type here...

Notice that when you search from the Start menu, the search is intelligent enough to look for programs and folders (but not documents and music files) that begin with the letters *co*. Throughout your use of Vista, Vista's Search boxes look for context-related data. If you display your Music Explorer window and search for something with the Search box, Vista knows to look through your music files first and only then look through unrelated program and folder names.

> Surprisingly, one of the few places where the Search box does not begin display-
> ing results the moment you start typing is in the Help system's Search box. You
> must type your search term in the help system's Search box and press Enter to
> start a search for help related to that topic.

By the Way

Searching for Files and Folders

When searching in a large folder such as your Documents folder (formerly called *My Documents*), manually locating a particular file might be daunting. Your Documents folder will grow with files and subfolders as you use your computer. In such a Windows Explorer window, your Search box helps you locate the files and folders you want to locate. The Search box locates files whose filenames contain the characters you're searching for as well as the file contents themselves. For example, search for *Colt 1911* and Vista returns a list of files with *Colt 1911* in their filenames as well as a list of files (including emails, spreadsheets, and anything else that might include the search test) from locations outside the current folder that contain the text, *Colt 1911*. Such an intensive search would have taken a long time in previous Windows versions but since Vista constantly updates its search indexes the search is rapid.

It's important to note that when you search from within a Windows Explorer window, such as your Documents window, Vista searches Documents and all the subfolders within Documents, but no location outside the Documents hierarchy. If the search fails, the file or folder you're looking for might not reside in Documents at all. (Another possibility is that you typed a wrong or misspelled name in the Search box.) Figure 13.2 shows the contents of a folder named My Novel that appears inside the Documents folder.

You'll notice that two files whose names both start with the letters *Opening* appear in this folder. The files are Opening-A and Opening-B. It's good to see what takes place when you start typing Open in the Search box at the top of the window.

The moment you type *O*, Vista instantly begins filtering out all the files from the current folder that don't match that criteria. Figure 13.3 shows that five files now display because only those files contain *Open* in their filename or inside the documents themselves. The nice thing about the incremental way that Search box searches and locates files as you type the name is that you don't have to spell out the entire search term. Usually, just three or four letters will enable you to zero in on the file you want to locate.

FIGURE 13.2
Before you start
searching, all
files appear in
the folder's
window.

Name of current folder

Search box

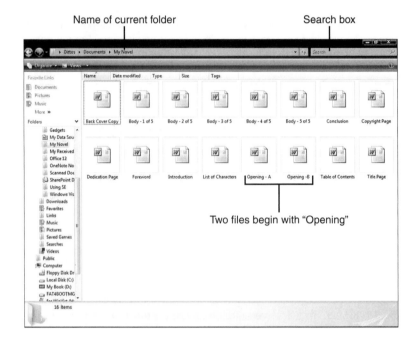

Two files begin with "Opening"

FIGURE 13.3
Vista filters out
all files that
don't match
your search
term as you
type the search
term's letters.

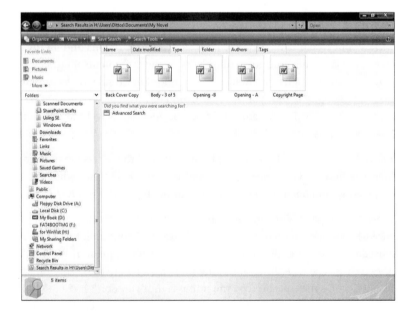

After the Search box filters enough of the file and folder entries down in the Explorer window, you'll see the file you're looking for.

How to Search When You Don't Know a File's Location

Using the Search box from your Documents or other Explorer window is nice when you know the general location of a file. Because you'll store most of the data files that you create with your word processor and other application programs in your Documents window, you're likely to begin your search there, as the previous section explained.

Other times you'll need to locate a file or folder that might not be in your Documents folder. Perhaps it's a program file or a downloaded utility folder that you want to copy to another computer. Before you can copy the item, you must find where it's located.

When you want to locate something but you don't know its general location, use the Search folder. The Search folder is a general-purpose search window that acts a lot like the other Explorer windows when you use their Search box, but the Search folder is more generic in where it looks. To open your Search folder, click your Start button and then select Search from your Start menu's right pane. A Search folder like the one in Figure 13.4 opens.

Filter buttons   Search box

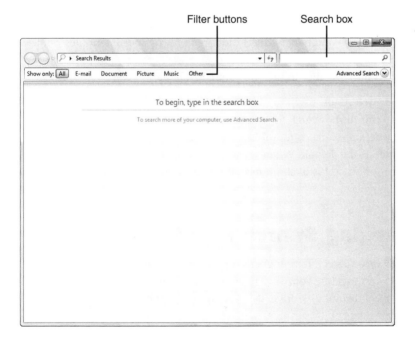

FIGURE 13.4
Use the Search folder when you have no idea where a file or folder is located.

Should You Always Use the Search Folder?

Why not just use the Search folder to locate every file and folder you need regardless of whether you know the location? After all, the Search folder looks over your entire disk, including your Documents folder.

The reason you need to understand how the Explorer Search box searches work, as explained in the previous section, is because you'll often already be looking inside a Windows Explorer window when you realize you need to search for something you can't find. You'll spend a lot of time browsing your Documents Explorer window, for example, because that's where your data files usually reside. The Search box is there at the top of the window and is a lot easier and quicker to use than first opening the Search folder to look for a file that's probably located somewhere in your Documents folder hierarchy.

As you type a search phrase into the Search folder's Search box, Vista begins displaying matching files in the search result area. The files don't necessarily begin with your search phrase, but they will contain it.

Narrowing the Search Folder to Specific File Types

If you're looking for a document file, and you use the Search folder to find it, you'll get matching file and folder names that aren't always document files. Some results might be an audio file; for example, if a CD whose music you ripped to your hard disk has a name similar to the one you're looking for.

If your search results begin to fill with too many unrelated matches, click one of the filter buttons in the Search folder's toolbar to narrow your search to a specific type of file. The default search is for all files and folders, so the Search folder uses the All filter button as the default. When you click another filter button, such as the Document button, Vista eliminates all files from the search results that are not document file types.

Changing Search Locations

The Advanced Search button opens a panel at the top of your Search window with several ways to refine your search. For example, you can search in locations outside your typical default disk drive. By clicking the Location button you can search your computer (which by default includes your internal hard disk drives, but not external drives, USB flash memory, or CD and DVD drives), all drives and devices, a specific user's files, or a specific location on any drive on your computer.

If, for example, you wanted to search an external drive set up as drive I: on your system, you would click the Advanced Search, then click Location. From the locations that appear, you could scroll down and select the H: drive (see Figure 13.5).

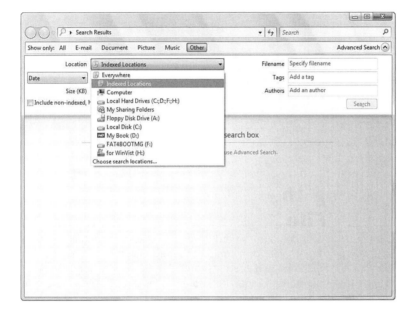

FIGURE 13.5
You can select a specific location anywhere on your computer or network to search for.

Clicking the Choose Search Locations button on the Location drop-down list produces the Choose Search Locations dialog box shown in Figure 13.6. Here you can build a specific list of locations where you want to search. Suppose, for example, you had two folders where you routinely stored your work and you wanted to search only those folders. Inside the Choose Search Locations dialog box, you would click to select the first folder and Vista would begin to build a search list with that location showing. You then can scroll to a different folder, click there to add a second search location, and so on. You've now specified exactly where Vista is to look for a particular file or folder.

FIGURE 13.6
You can select a specific location anywhere on your computer or network to search for.

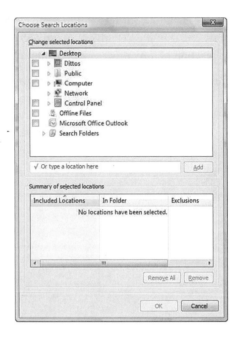

Watch
Out!

Searches outside your computer's hard drives can take substantially longer than searches you perform on your own computer's hard disk drives. Vista continually indexes your hard disk and updates its search list as you use your computer so that it finds files quickly. Vista does not, however, index CDs, DVDs, and external and networked drives that your computer doesn't recognize as being always-connected drives. Therefore, Vista must perform a file-by-file, folder-by-folder search on those places when you look for something there. You must press Enter every time you search a nonindexed location such as a DVD drive so that Vista knows you've finished typing the search phrase and that the search is to begin.

Narrowing Your Search

The Advanced Search button provides several additional tools that can help you refine your searches. In addition to multiple locations as you learned about in the previous section, you can search for a specific date range or file size. You can also limit your search to specific filenames, tags, and authors who create those files.

Click the Date drop-down listbox to select from one of these two options:

▶ Date

▶ Date Modified

▶ Date Created

When you select the kind of date you want to limit your search to, you then select from the second drop-down box one of these three options:

▶ Is

▶ Is Before

▶ Is After

You then select a date. Therefore, these kinds of searches are possible that you've limited by date:

▶ Date Modified Is Before July 7, 2007

▶ Date Accessed Is After September 1, 2008

To limit your search to files of a certain size, select from the drop-down listbox to the right of the Size entry one of these options:

▶ Any

▶ Equals

▶ Is Less Than

▶ Is Greater Than

These options allow you to narrow a search down to all files whose file size is less than a specific value that you enter.

In the Filename box you can enter letters to limit the search to specific filenames. For example if you typed **opening** then only files with the word *opening* in their title would be searched.

> The Tags and Authors option boxes change depending on the type of file you're searching for. If you click the E-mail button to limit searches to emails, Vista changes the Filename box to a Subject box and the Tag and Authors boxes to From Names and To Names option boxes. Clicking Picture to limit the search to picture files changes the Author box to a Title box so you can easily search through your picture titles (the digital image files you've added titles to). If you limit a search to music files, then the Tags and Authors boxes change to Artists and Album.

By the Way

You can combine these Advanced Search options. Figure 13.7 shows a search in progress looking for all files modified before *October 16, 2006* with the word *dog* in the filename and the names *Casper* or *Zucchi* (or both) in the tag.

Advanced Search Option pane

FIGURE 13.7
You can build advanced searches to locate files with the exact pattern you require.

Saving Your Search Results

If you find yourself routinely performing the same searches, you can save your searches. Vista calls this *saving your search results* and you'll see that phrase in Vista's help screens, but it is somewhat misleading. You don't actually save the search results from a specific search. If that were the case then no matter what changes you made to your files, the originally saved search would repeatedly show the same search results from the first time you saved the search.

Instead, when you save search results, what you're really doing is saving a set of search commands and options. Vista creates an Explorer window for each search you save. Every time you open that window to view it, you'll see the current results of that saved search. If you add or remove files that would produce a new set of search results, you see the updates when you reopen that saved search's window.

After completing a search that you might want to perform again, click the Search window's Save Search button on the toolbar. Vista requests a name for the search and then saves your search in the Searches folder, which is located within your User folder (see Figure 13.8). Instead of rebuilding a complicated set of options each time you wish to search for something again, you need only open your Searches folder and select one of the searches you've saved; Vista performs the search again and opens the results window.

Before you save a search, Vista already has a list of common searches that you might perform. When you click Searches from any Windows Explorer window, you'll see a list of searches as shown in Figure 13.8. As you create saved searches, your search results folders will appear in the Saved Searches folder.

Did you Know?

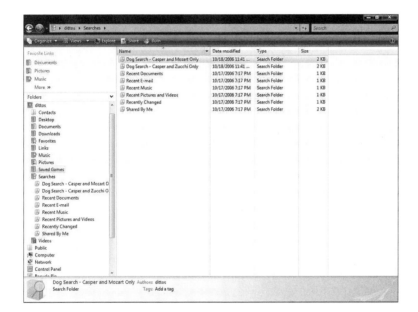

FIGURE 13.8
Vista comes pre-supplied with common searches and you can add your own.

Chapter Wrap-Up

This chapter helped you find information you need on both your own PC and any networked computers. Get in the habit of using the Search box and the Search folders to locate the things you need. You can search for any file and folder using a myriad of methods that Vista offers. When you locate the file or folder you are looking for, double-click that item to run the program, open the data file, or display the contents of the folder you found.

The next chapter begins a new part in the book called "Making Things Happen with Windows Vista." The next few chapters explore Vista's multimedia capabilities. Vista's multimedia support goes far beyond any previous version of Windows. The role of the computer has morphed into a computing and entertainment system, and Windows Vista is up to the task of helping you manage your multimedia files such as songs, videos, pictures, and slideshows.

PART IV

Making Things Happen with Windows Vista

CHAPTER 14

Going Multimedia with Vista

In This Chapter:

- ▶ Look, play, and listen to Vista's multimedia offerings
- ▶ Learn how Vista combines several multimedia tools into its programs
- ▶ Access all your media from one program
- ▶ Organize pictures, music, and videos
- ▶ Make your own recordings
- ▶ Edit movies and videos
- ▶ Put a media center in your living room

Computers form the heart of most multimedia experiences and those experiences are no longer limited to amusement parks and movie theaters. In your own home you now can perform the following tasks that are considered ordinary whereas just a handful of years ago they would have been amazing:

- ▶ Watch and record TV shows
- ▶ Play DVD movies
- ▶ Play CD music and save that music to your disk (called **ripping** the CDs) for later playback
- ▶ Enjoy pictures
- ▶ Create slideshows with sound
- ▶ Edit your movies
- ▶ Edit and touch-up digital photos

If you've used Windows in the past, you're probably familiar with the Windows Media Player. Vista not only improves on the Windows Media Player with lots of new features but it also includes an updated application called the *Media Center*, which boosts your computer's multimedia experience to levels only seen on stand-alone media center PCs in the past.

This chapter gives you an overview of all Vista's multimedia features and ends with a more detailed focus on Vista's Media Center application. Subsequent chapters discuss Vista's multimedia capabilities in more detail.

Windows Vista Advances Multimedia

A computer without multimedia is like...like a computer from the Stone Age!

Since the early 1990s, almost every computer sold has supported sound, video, and CD audio. DVD-based video followed suit by the turn of the century, and now DVD-recording (and using recorded DVDs for high-volume data backups) is the norm. Although each version of Windows from Windows 3.1 forward supported some form of multimedia, Windows 95 launched true integrated multimedia support throughout its applications. More than a decade later, Windows Vista provides a multimedia experience not even dreamed of at the time of Windows 95 (such as the ability to pause live TV shows).

Multimedia Is No Longer for Geeks

Getting video to work on a computer, especially if you wanted to watch television shows or make DVDs by editing your own digital video clips used to be a time-consuming, nerve-racking process. Windows Vista is so multimedia savvy that it no longer seems like such a chore to put together a bunch of video clips and record your movie to a DVD.

Such tasks are available to all who use Windows Vista, and Vista integrates audio and video tasks into virtually every one of its nooks and crannies. Play a DVD you bought from the store in Windows Media Player without having to add a special DVD driver. Listen to sound clips from the Internet or touch-up photos from your digital camera before using them in an eBay auction. It's all a snap in Windows Vista.

When it comes to usability, little things can mean a lot. One problem that Windows users had in the past—and this was a problem that many of us didn't even realize *was* a problem until we see how Windows Vista works so much better—was the lack of an application-specific volume control.

At any one time, you might be running several Windows programs. Perhaps you're playing some music in the background using the Windows Media Player, you're waiting for a Microsoft Outlook alarm to sound telling you about a phone call you need to make, and you want to play a game while you wait. Before Windows Vista, you had only one volume control. Each individual application might or might not give you a volume control for that application; the only thing you could count on was that Windows had a universal volume control named Main (with a secondary one that sometimes came in handy, the Wave volume control). When you wanted to hear your game's sounds, you turned up the volume on all programs.

Doesn't it make more sense to have a separate volume control for each application that produces a sound? That's a reasonable request with Windows Vista. Figure 14.1 shows the Windows Vista Volume control panel. The Main volume control still exists because there are times when you want to lower or mute the volume on all running programs. Other times during the normal course of computer use, however, you might want to adjust only one or two applications' volume levels. With Vista, you select the running application to adjust and move its volume level. You don't disturb the other programs' volume levels.

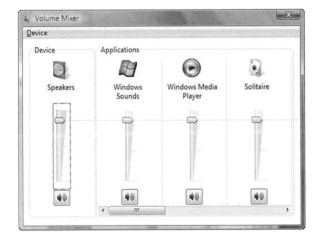

FIGURE 14.1
When you run multiple applications with sound, Vista gives you multiple volume controls: one for each application plus a Main volume control for your computer's overall volume level.

The title of this section is "Multimedia Is No Longer for Geeks." Multiple volume controls might actually seem a little geeky. And they are really. Perhaps a better title would be "All Vista Users Can Now Be Geeks!" We've arrived.

By the Way

Before Windows Vista, programs that produced sound added a strain on the computer's processor. If you played music, for example, the playing music would stress your processor, and if you also wanted to perform some calculations with a spreadsheet program, your spreadsheet program would hesitate during some of the music's playback. Windows Vista's sound architecture uses twice the internal memory size (32 **bits**, or **binary digits**, as opposed to 16), so sound no longer affects the performance of your running programs as much as before.

Access All Your Media

Networks used to be reserved for large corporations. Now even small homes have networks. When replacing a PC with the latest and greatest, one of the best things to do with your old one is to connect the two (with wires or wirelessly) into a network and use the old one to serve up files or perhaps give the hand-me-down PC to a young family member. By networking them, you can access all the files on both computers.

With Windows Vista, not only is setting up such a home or business network simple, sharing multimedia files is effortless as well. You can access all your photos, music, movies, and recorded TV shows from the other computers on your network.

By the Way

If you have an Xbox 360, Microsoft's game machine, you can connect it to your home network and access its files, as well as use it to play music and videos from the other computers on your network.

Introducing Windows Vista's Multimedia Tools

As described throughout the previous pages of this chapter, Vista's multimedia experience goes far beyond that of other Windows operating systems and is almost ubiquitous given its embedding in the Windows environment. Therefore, one of the best ways to begin to get a handle on Vista's multimedia elements is to review the following list of the major players in Vista's multimedia offerings:

▶ **Windows Photo Gallery**—Organize, edit, and print your digital pictures.

▶ **Windows Media Player**—Play, watch, and manage your music, DVDs, and pictures.

▶ **Windows Sound Recorder**—Record your own digital audio from within Windows Vista.

▶ **Windows Movie Maker**—Edit, splice, and put together your own digital video with sound and special effects.

▶ **Windows Media Center**—Use your computer as the center of your entertainment universe by accessing all your multimedia files from across your network and viewing them on your family's living room television for maximum enjoyment. The Windows Media Center also enables you to record televised broadcasts, pause live television, and other set timers for recording when you're away.

Each of the following sections gives you an overview of these products. Some readers won't need more detail to enjoy most of these Windows Vista multimedia offerings. If you need more detail, however, such as how to edit your photos to ensure sharp images for putting up on the Web, the next few chapters go into more detail.

Organize Your Pictures with Windows Photo Gallery

Windows users are accustomed to the Windows photo-viewing Explorer window, shown in Figure 14.2, which appears when you click My Pictures from the Windows XP menu. You couldn't do much other than organize photos, rename files, print pictures, and send them to a CD or to an email recipient. Third-party software makers, such as Adobe, did well creating replacement photo-editing and management programs such as Photoshop Elements.

FIGURE 14.2
Vista's Photo Gallery runs circles graphically around the old My Pictures Windows XP menu offering.

Windows Vista provides the Photo Gallery application. Photo Gallery doesn't replace the extensive functionality and features of a dedicated program such as Photoshop Elements, but Photo Gallery offers enough bells and whistles that you won't be forced to use a third-party program nearly as often as before.

Chapters 16, "Going Digital with Your Camera or Scanner," and 17, "Modifying and Sharing Photos," explore how to use Photo Gallery to augment your camera and scanner to create and organize your digital image collections. A quick overview here not only whets your appetite but also prepares you for the more in-depth coverage in Chapters 16 and 17. In addition, throughout this chapter you must remember that even though photos don't move, digital images do make up an important piece of the multimedia framework. For example, you can drop a digital picture into a movie with Windows Movie Maker and use that picture as an opening shot, scene change dissolve, or put text on the picture for a fancy final credits screen with music playing in the background as the slideshow runs.

When you first start Photo Gallery from your Windows Start menu, you might see only a blank window where you'd normally expect pictures to appear. You have to click the File toolbar button to display a menu and select Add Folder to Gallery to select your primary (or top-level) pictures folder, and from there you can begin to manage and edit your current pictures.

Photo Gallery initially looks in your Public folder's Pictures subfolder for pictures to display. If you have pictures there, they will appear even if you don't specifically tell Photo Gallery about them. As you add more pictures to that location, Photo Gallery constantly updates its screen to include the new pictures.

When pictures begin to appear, whether Photo Gallery finds them in your Public folder or you tell Photo Gallery where they are, Photo Gallery begins to fill its screen with thumbnail images sorted by picture date (see Figure 14.3). You will soon learn many ways to organize and group your photos.

A Photo Gallery control panel appears at the bottom of the Photo Gallery program window. Using its controls quickly enables you to perform the following actions:

▶ Increase or decrease the zoom level of the thumbnail images that appear in Photo Gallery.

▶ Set the thumbnail's default size.

FIGURE 14.3
Photo Gallery
initially displays
thumbnail
images of your
photos.

Display controls

▶ Move back through your photos one at a time, which is especially useful when viewing your images one at a time in the editing mode. How you view your photos determines the meaning of *back*; for example, if viewing by date, the Back button selects the next photo earlier in time.

▶ Play a slideshow of your photos in the current folder.

▶ Move forward through your photos one at a time, which is especially useful when viewing your images one at a time in the editing mode. How you view your photos determines the meaning of *forward*; for example, if viewing by date, the Forward button selects the next photo later in time.

▶ Rotate a photo 90 degrees counterclockwise (a quarter of a complete rotation).

▶ Rotate a photo 90 degrees clockwise.

▶ Delete a photo. You must confirm the deletion before Photo Gallery sends the deleted image to your Recycle Bin.

After you begin to populate Photo Gallery with photos, you will start to organize them by date, subject, or even rating, using a five-star rating system. You can also edit photo images to adjust exposure and color, crop a photo to decrease its size, and fix the red eye effect that can appear when photographing people or animals with flash photography.

By the Way

> You now have enough information to get started using Photo Gallery. If you need more help, Chapters 16 and 17 explore Photo Gallery's feature set in more detail.

Stop, Look, and Listen with Windows Media Player

Windows Media Player has been around since Windows 95. Microsoft had updated Media Player more times than Internet Explorer, showing a strong commitment to the player and a desire to improve the entertainment experience available to Windows users. Vista's Media Player is an extraordinary player that enables you to view pictures (a feature that's been available in Media Player for years and even some power users don't know about it), listen to music, and watch videos.

If you've used Windows Media Player in the past, you'll be pleasantly surprised at how simple to use the new features are and yet how they dramatically amplify the functionality of Media Player. Start Windows Media Player from your Start menu or by clicking the Media Player icon on your Taskbar's Quick Launch area. From a brand new interface (see Figure 14.4) to lots of new features that take advantage of today's entertainment needs, there's a little for everyone.

FIGURE 14.4
Vista's Media Player ups the digital player ante with a new interface and new features that take advantage of today's entertainment environment.

At the risk of letting this turn into something that sounds like a Microsoft-paid commercial, let me say that I've used Media Player for years and although I've bought most of the major digital media players, including MusicMatch, QuickTime, and RealPlayer, I find myself returning time and time again to Media Player. It's always there, it loads quickly, and its feature set leaves little to be desired. In Vista's Media Player, you can

- ▶ Easily organize your pictures, videos, and music

- ▶ Show pictures, play music, and watch videos

- ▶ Rip music from audio CDs

- ▶ Burn music to CDs and DVDs by dragging and dropping files onto the interface

- ▶ View album cover art that comes from the Internet when you rip music from CDs, and search through your music by browsing the album covers just as you might do in your CD rack

- ▶ Synchronize portable devices with your music library

- ▶ Buy music that you download from MTV's new Urge service

<table>
<tr><td>You will notice as you work in Media Player, Photo Gallery, and other types of Windows Vista Explorer–like windows that many new features overlap each other. For example, you can sort your music by date or by rating preference (based on a five-star rating) just as you can organize your photos in Photo Gallery. Keep in mind that Windows Vista is about as integrated as possible. By offering similar features and interfaces, you'll create synergy as you use Windows. For example, you can display pictures in Media Player just as you can in Photo Gallery. It makes sense to retain the same five-star ratings system and organization abilities in both programs so that you can locate what you want quickly. Even the playback control at the bottom of Windows Media Player looks quite a bit like the Photo Gallery control at the bottom of the Photo Gallery window that you saw in the previous section.</td><td>*Did you* **Know?**</td></tr>
</table>

Certainly, Windows Media Player is one of the programs you'll want to start using right away if you enjoy music in the background as you work on your computer. If you start Windows Media Player and don't see any music, video, or photo files, you'll have to add those files to Media Player's library. (This also holds true if you store your files on a network drive or on an external USB drive.) To add your files so that you can enjoy them in Windows Vista, click the toolbar's Library button and select the Add to Library option to display the Add to Library dialog box shown in Figure 14.5.

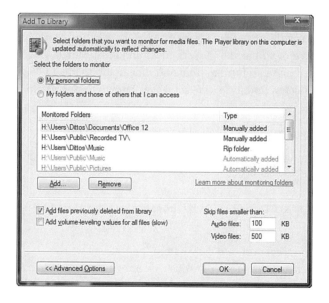

By default, Windows Media Player asks whether you want it to monitor your personal folders for the presence of music files or both your personal folders and those of other users (if you have permission to view them). If you store all your digital audio files in the default Music folder, clicking either option and selecting OK is all you need to do. However, if you store your music files elsewhere, you can click the Advanced Options button to locate your multimedia files and tell Media Player to index them.

Opening the Advanced Options portion of this dialog presents you with a list of folders that Media Player monitors for the presence of audio files. To add a folder location to that list, click the Add button and navigate to the folder you want to add (when you select a folder, any subfolder that resides within it is also monitored). After you add one or more locations, Media Player will always look to those locations in the future to update and refresh its library of multimedia files.

The Windows Media menu is hidden by default. You can press Alt to select an option from the menu (such as Alt+F to open the File menu). In addition, you can display the menu by pressing Ctrl+M or select Classic Menus from the View menu if you wish to see the menu.

Now that you've added your multimedia files to Media Player's library, click the Library button to browse through your music. You'll see album covers for some, but not for others, depending on whether Media Player has downloaded information for each track's albums. Figure 14.6 shows such a browsing session, although you can browse and search through your music in many different ways in addition to browsing through titles and album covers. To play a song, just double-click the file's icon.

FIGURE 14.6
Browse through your online music collection by album cover, title, rating, or by song.

As long as you have an active Internet connection, Media Player searches through your music library and fills in the album cover pictures when it finds a match in the online music databases. Depending on the number of music files you have, this could take a while, but you can work in Media Player and other Windows applications while Media Player collects the pictures.

Did you Know?

If an album cover (of course, that means CD cover today, although *album cover* is still the preferred term even when referring to CDs) fails to appear, you will learn how to correct that in Chapter 15, "Managing Your Entertainment Experience with Media Player."

By the Way

Media Player can also display any photo in your Picture library if you happen to use Media Player to open a Picture folder. Just click the arrow at the bottom of the Library button at the top of the screen and select Pictures to view your pictures. In the same manner, you can locate video files and recorded TV shows if any exist on your computer or your networked files. Media Player uses the first frame from your video as a thumbnail picture so that you can quickly locate the video you want to watch. To play a CD or DVD, simply insert the disc into your CD or DVD drive (often the same drive); Media Player starts automatically, if you haven't already started it, and you can begin enjoying the disc's contents.

Did you Know?

The Library button is the primary button you will use to move between types of entertainment data in Media Player.

You might wonder why Media Player displays photos and enables you to search for them using a similar interface to Photo Gallery. Why have Photo Gallery if Media Player does the same thing? Actually, Media Player does not have Photo Gallery's full feature set. Photo Gallery supports the editing of photos as well as gives you the ability to create a slideshow with the click of a button. Just as Media Player doesn't support the editing of movies (Movie Maker does that) but plays movies, Media Player doesn't support the editing of photos, but does display photos when you want to view them. Each application in Windows does what it was designed to do well, but several Windows Vista applications overlap in their features in the name of offering you more flexibility. The idea is to give you what you need when you need it.

Record Audio with Vista's Sound Recorder

Surprisingly, Windows Media Player doesn't provide a way for you to record from a microphone or an external sound source. One underutilized Windows program that's been around for many years is the Sound Recorder application, shown in Figure 14.7. Chapter 18, "Recording Simple Audio," explains how to use Sound Recorder and how to get the best sound.

FIGURE 14.7
Sound Recorder's recording meter, shown here at low volume, visually shows your recording's peaks and valleys as you record.

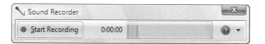

If you've seen previous versions of Sound Recorder, Vista's Sound Recorder might seem rather lean. Microsoft stripped Sound Recorder of many of its features but its primary purpose, recording audio, is still functional and quite usable. Vista does not restrict the length of recordings you can make as previous versions of Windows did and Vista automatically compresses your recorded audio using files in the Windows Media Audio (WMA) format.

Why might you want to use Sound Recorder? One place it's used quite extensively, for those who know to do so, is on a laptop, recording meetings and lectures. Instead of taking copious notes during a meeting, start Sound Recorder and plug an external microphone into your laptop to begin recording. Many laptops have built-in microphones, so if the sound's volume is strong enough and you don't need high-quality, high-fidelity recording, you'll find that your laptop's built-in microphone should capture what you need.

> Always test your recording volume before relying on your laptop's built-in microphone.

By the Way

Windows Movie Maker Puts Hollywood's Tools at Your Disposal

Windows Movie Maker, shown in Figure 14.8, is often overlooked as a video-editing tool. That's a shame because since Microsoft released Movie Maker 2 for Windows XP, Movie Maker has had a feature set that includes all the standard video-editing tools you might want for simple movie creation, with enough extras, such as special effects, to satisfy those who want to add some pizzazz to their movies.

With the introduction of Windows Vista, Microsoft again updated Movie Maker with new special effects and scene transitions. Before Vista, Movie Maker previewed movies in a small 320 × 240 pixel window. Now you can preview your movies as you edit them in a much larger preview screen, enabling you to see the details you want to see. You can also add menus and chapters to your movies so that when you burn them to a DVD, your DVD's audience members can search and scan to their heart's content.

> In spite of its improvements, Movie Maker is no competitor to more complete video-editing applications such as Adobe Premiere Elements, but Microsoft didn't design Movie Maker to compete with such programs. Movie Maker is a workhorse that's always there, giving you a way to edit your videos and put them together into full-length movies using a simple interface with enough bells and whistles to satisfy many of introductory video-editing requirements. For some people, Movie Maker *is* the only video-editing program they need to do what they want to do.

By the Way

FIGURE 14.8
Movie Maker includes a feature set that enables you to put together video clips and edit movies.

If you're new to editing videos but you want to put some home movies onto DVD, Movie Maker is probably the best place to begin. Chapter 19, "Making Movies with Windows Movie Maker," teaches you how to use Movie Maker's basics. Given that this chapter's intent is to give you the bird's-eye view of Windows Vista's multimedia tools, here is a list of features Movie Maker offers:

▶ Import video from files or a video camera

▶ Combine multiple video clips from any source in a single movie

▶ Delete and rearrange portions of a movie

▶ Place movie clips on a storyboard and timeline to synchronize and arrange your movie until it's just the way you like it

▶ Add sound and narration over your entire movie or parts of it with a microphone or with audio files

▶ Use CD or MP3 music as a background to your movie or opening and closing credits

▶ Add opening titles and closing credits

▶ Publish your movie to a DVD, recordable CD, email, or videotape

Introducing Your New Entertainment Center for the Twenty-First Century: Vista's Media Center

Now that you've seen what multimedia applications await you in Windows Vista, it's time to spend a few pages covering what might be new to some Windows users, even those who have used Windows quite extensively in the past: the Windows Vista Media Center.

Media Center, which was first released a few years ago as its own version of Windows, provides a customized user interface that's basically glued on to of the existing Windows user interface with the intent of making your computer the center of your home's entertainment center. At its heart, Media Center is an application, just another program as Photo Gallery and Media Player are. In addition, Media Center includes several hardware-related drivers and accessory programs that enable you to use your PC with the Media Center software in your living room to access and control all your video, music, and pictures. For some, the idea of moving the computer out of the office or bedroom and into the living room seems strange, but your computer is a great tool to organize all your entertainment from a central location.

Before Windows Vista, Microsoft licensed Media Center for use in **Media Center PCs,** computers that ran a special version of Windows XP with Media Center embedded throughout the operating system. Instead of the usual Windows opening screen, users saw a Media Center menu when they turned on the computer. From that menu, they could select what they wanted to do: see pictures, watch a movie, listen to music, or watch (or record) from television.

Media Center Isn't for Everybody...Yet

Now that Media Center is included with Windows Vista instead of being a stand-alone product, any computer that meets its hardware requirements can become an entertainment center. Not every reader has a need for Media Center and not every reader has all the media connections, such as a television tuner, available at their computer. Media Center assumes that your computer has television access, your computer is situated close to your family television, and everybody's ready for the computer-controlled entertainment experience.

Such an experience is nice. But we're not all ready to put a computer in our living rooms.

Therefore, given that Media Center is not a Vista program quite ready for universal use, the rest of this chapter explores some of Media Center's setup and operation. Instead of devoting a complete chapter to Media Center, this chapter introduces you to Media Center and shows some ways you can benefit from it. If you decide to take the Media Center plunge and use it to control your home's primary entertainment activities, that's great, and you'll be ready for a more detailed step-by-step tutorial.

Setting Up Media Center

Vista requires you to set up Media Center before you can use it. The setup makes sense because each home (or business) that uses Media Center will have its own combination of entertainment devices and sources. Media Center can make no assumptions about what kind of media connections await it.

When you first start Media Center (by selecting Media Center from the Windows menu), an opening screen welcomes you, as shown in Figure 14.9. This screen begins the Setup Wizard that walks you, step-by-step, through Media Center's setup.

FIGURE 14.9
Follow the Setup Wizard to inform Media Center about the entertainment sources you have connected to your PC to control.

Click Next at the Welcome screen to continue the setup. The second screen informs you that the setup works in two stages: the required setup and the optional setup. The first setup is required because Media Center must know what networking and Internet connections your computer uses. To take advantage of Media Center's features, you'll need an always-on, high-speed Internet connection. To be able to access media content on other computers on your network, you'll need to have a wired or wireless network that Media Center can access.

The optional setup isn't truly optional because to use Media Center to its fullest, you have to tell it about your needs, entertainment desires, and so on. This setup is optional only in the sense that you don't have to complete the optional setup at once. As you want to do more with Media Center, you'll have to run the optional setup again to change and update the settings to suit your current needs.

Running Media Center's Required Setup

The required setup is straightforward. In a way, it's redundant. Windows Vista knows about your Internet connection, and yet Media Center asks whether you have an always-on Internet connection. (If you don't, Media Center's feature set is reduced dramatically—almost to the point that you should wait to set up Media Center until you do.) After you tell Media Center that you have an always-on Internet connection, Media Center runs a quick test to verify that the connection is working properly.

After verifying the Internet connection, the Media Center setup asks whether you want to read a privacy statement that describes how Microsoft and related online partners will use information you supply. Click the down arrow to read the rest of the privacy information. In today's world many people are concerned about how and where information about them is used.

As with software warranties, the privacy statement can be a little vague and legal-sounding. Still, by reading it, you'll have a better idea of how Microsoft handles information about you and your activities that it learns through your Media Center use. If learning "about you and your activities" seems somewhat ominous, it's not really that way. Microsoft has a vested interest in keeping your information anonymous and confidential, and the privacy statement is Microsoft's attempt to reassure you that it will do so as much as it can.

By the Way

Click the Done button when you finish reading the privacy statement to continue your Media Center setup. You'll be greeted with a screen titled Help Improve Media Center and an offer to join the Customer Experience Improvement Program. If you elect to join by selecting Yes, your computer will periodically send anonymous reports about your Media Center performance so that Microsoft can analyze the data and determine whether updates are required to Media Center to improve certain performance measures.

Did you Know?

There are times when, through your use of Media Center (the Windows Media Player also has this capability), you'll send personal information over your Internet connection. When you subscribe to a music service, for example, and purchase songs for playback, you'll have to give information for the transaction to go through. The privacy statement explains the steps that Microsoft takes to help guard your personal data whenever and if ever you have to send it through the Media Center.

The Customer Experience Improvement Program, which comes up next, does not monitor the same information covered in the Privacy Statement. The Customer Experience Improvement Program is a way for Microsoft to send **actions** (that is, the ways that people use Media Center) without receiving personal data of any kind. As Microsoft learns the ways that people use Media Center, it can issue updates to make Media Center more enjoyable, more workable, and more efficient for you and other users. Figure 14.10 shows Media Center's request to join.

FIGURE 14.10
If you allow Media Center to send anonymous information about your use habits periodically, Microsoft can better analyze how you and others use Media Center and provide updates that make the software better over time.

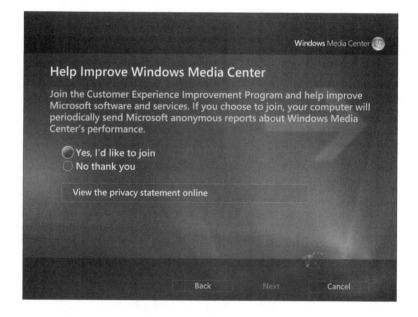

Should you join? It's not like a club you join and, by using the term *join,* Microsoft somewhat masks what you're agreeing to. With that in mind, there are benefits to joining, although they are indirect to you. As more people join and send more usability information to Microsoft's servers, Microsoft will improve on Media Center, and you and other users will be the beneficiaries of those improvements. If nobody agreed to send this periodic information, Microsoft would have no feedback as to how people use Media Center, or what problems they encounter, and improvements would come more slowly and be less helpful.

Joining is up to you. The data sent to Microsoft's servers is small, so it won't bog down your Internet connection. Therefore, don't let that be a reason to stop you from agreeing to the program. If extreme privacy is a concern for you, you might be averse to sending such information and that's fine, too. It's nice that Microsoft gave us a choice.

The Enhanced Playback screen now appears, as shown in Figure 14.11. Just as Media Player goes to the Internet to download album covers, so can Media Center if you allow it by selecting Yes on the Enhanced Playback screen. Most people like the album cover photos to appear when browsing or playing music and videos, and if you're one of them, select Yes and then click Next.

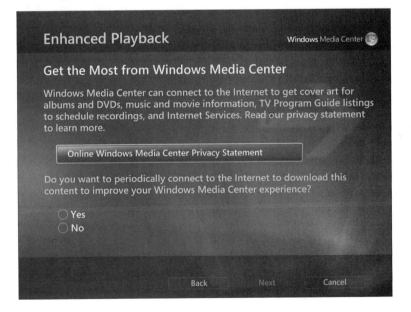

FIGURE 14.11
If you give Media Center permission, Media Center can download album covers to accent your music's playback and browsing.

After you inform Media Center of your decision to download album cover art, a final screen appears telling you that the required setup is finished. Click Next to move to the optional setup.

Running Media Center's Optional Setup

Media Center's optional setup provides the two following options:

▶ Optimize your Media Center's screen output

▶ Set up your Media Center's speakers for the best sound possible

Many people will elect to skip these steps and return to them if problems or adjustments must be made later. Doing so is fine, but running through the setup isn't time-consuming.

To set up video playback, Media Center runs a short video so that you can determine whether playback on your display is adequate. A computer running Media Center often connects to a large television through some kind of digital input. Because Media Center isn't talking to a normal computer video screen, the playback of video and photos can be somewhat off-center or perhaps off-balance in color or brightness. By watching the video, you have a chance to learn about potential video problems early and correct them now. As you play the video, the video's narration describes ways to correct problems you might see and make your Media Center experience more enjoyable.

When the video finishes, the Setup Wizard walks you through the video setup. You'll provide information about the type of display you use so that Media Center can send the best output for that device. For example, if you use Media Center on a traditional computer monitor or TV display, the shape of the screen differs greatly from the shape of a widescreen monitor or HDTV. In addition, but the cabling you use to connect your PC to a display can vary as well. During the video setup, you'll supply information about the connection, including whether to use your PC's TV tuner card (if it has one), and Media Center adjusts its display and functionality accordingly.

After setting up your video playback so that you get the most from your display, you can optionally run through a similar (and shorter) setup for your audio playback. The Audio Setup Wizard enables you to inform Media Center about speaker placement and the type of sound system you have connected to move the sound from your computer to the speakers that people ultimately hear.

Using Media Center

After you set up your Media Center program, using it is simple. Keep in mind that Microsoft designed Media Center as an entertainment-controlling program for the entire family. For that to be successful, Microsoft had to make the software simple to use. A menu such as the one in Figure 14.12 appears when you start Media Center.

You'll find that you can most easily scroll through the Media Center menu using your Up Arrow and Down Arrow keys. The menu includes the following options:

▶ **Pictures + Videos**—Gives you access to your digital picture and online video collection.

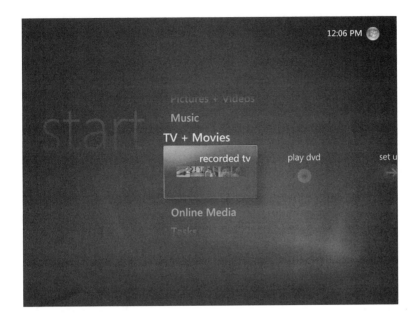

FIGURE 14.12
Media Center's menu gives you quick access to your entertainment options.

▶ **TV + Movies**—Enables you to play DVDs and movies you've saved to your disk or network. When you select a movie, Media Center displays a synopsis of that film. In addition, you can record television shows, pause live broadcasts, and watch television.

▶ **Music**—Enables you to play music from your digital music collection, from a CD, or play broadcasts from an Internet radio broadcasts.

▶ **Online Media**—Provides an online showcase of music, TV shows, movies, music, Internet radio, news, sports, games, and lifestyle-related media that you can enjoy from the Media Center.

▶ **Tasks**—Gives you the option to burn CDs or DVDs with digital content, synchronize your portable media players with your Media Center library, shut down Media Center, and adjust some options related to the optional Media Center Extender program (available by subscription). Several tools are also available so that you may adjust your Media Center settings, such as specifying startup and window behavior, electing to use visual and sound effects, adjusting parental controls to protect family members from certain rated content, adjusting your tuner and music settings, and other options that control the way Media Center operates for you.

By the Way

Some movies are available for download through Media Player's Urge service or another download site. Some allow you to play the movies only from the computer you download them to, due to copyright restrictions.

Did you Know?

When you arrive at a Media Center menu option, such as Music, press your Left Arrow and Right Arrow keys to see additional options, such as selecting music from your saved music library or playing a radio broadcast from an Internet radio station.

As you move through the menu and select options, move your mouse to the top-left corner of your screen to click the Back button. The Back button works somewhat like a web browser's Back button by taking you back one menu option at a time. (There is no Forward button to return to where you were before clicking Back.) If you have a keyboard with Internet-related buttons, your keyboard's Back button will return you through Media Center's menus.

Did you Know?

You'll find that your Media Center's experience is richer if you use a wireless mouse and keyboard so you're not tethered to your computer while you enjoy your entertainment selections.

One of the best ways to learn your way around Media Center is to use it. You'll find that many elements overlap each other. For example, from the Music menu, you can locate Internet-fed TV shows and movies that you can watch or download to your computer, many of which are free.

Media Center will usually recognize your Media Player's library contents and add your media to its library. When you first enter the Music Library section, Media Center asks if you have additional folders you want to add to the library (see Figure 14.13). If you do, you'll have to go through the same add-to-library process that you do with Media Player by telling Media Center where additional music files are stored.

After you add music to your Media Center library, Media Center gives you all sorts of ways to access your music. You can search by album cover, artist, genre, song title, and so on. As expected of a Windows Vista application, Media Center makes locating your music and other entertainment files easy.

FIGURE 14.13
You'll need to tell Media Center where your music folders are so that it adds those titles to its library.

You must have some television connection attached to your computer to use the television features. For example, you can connect an antenna or cable television cable (this won't include any pay or digital cable channels to which you subscribe) to a PC tuner card to access the television-related features. When you watch a show, Media Center offers VCR-like controls that enable you to pause the show or to start recording it. In addition, you'll find a VCR-like timer that enables you to record shows that will play some time in the future.

The Online Media provides an interesting catch-all Media Center menu option. When you select the Online Media option and scroll through it, you'll see that you can access games located in your Vista Games folder (refer to Chapter 11, "Taking Time Out with Windows Vista Games") and select to run those games on your Media Center display, as Figure 14.14 shows. Even Solitaire takes on a new life when you play it on a 42-inch plasma television!

When playing movies located on your computer or network (as opposed to playing DVD movies, which is also possible from the Movie menu option), Media Center can display information about the movie, such as the title, the date and time you recorded it, a summary, the cast and crew, and more. You can even access this information while playing a video. (Useful when your friend asks, "Who's that actor? I forget his name!") Move your mouse to the top-left corner of the movie and the Back arrow will appear. Click the arrow to see the movie summary. If you don't pause the movie first, the movie still plays in a small screen at the bottom of the summary to ensure that you don't miss anything as Figure 14.15 shows.

FIGURE 14.14
Play games located in your Games folder from within Media Center.

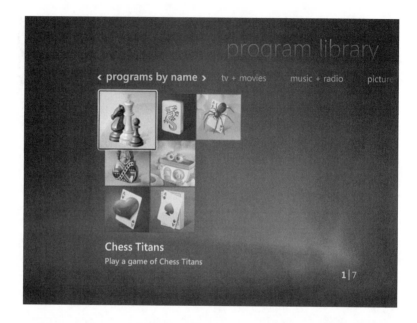

FIGURE 14.15
Media Center can display summary information about movies you're watching.

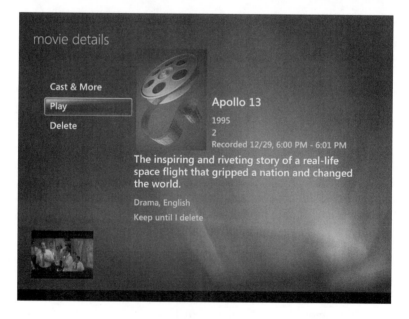

Some people might wonder, when do I use Media Player and when do I use Media Center? Both have their place. Media Player is better suited for a PC user who wants to listen to music or watch a movie while using the computer to do other tasks. The Media Center application consumes quite a few computer resources, even on the fast computers of today. As a result, you'll find that running Windows programs outside of Media Center while it plays content isn't always optimum. Your Windows program will be slow to respond. Media Center truly is designed to be a center of your family's entertainment control, and not necessarily your home's primary computer. Most users who begin to utilize Media Center find that dedicating a computer solely for Media Center operations and using another computer for regular computing is the best option.

By the Way

Chapter Wrap-Up

You just got a whirlwind tour of Vista's multimedia offerings. It was a quick run-through, but it was enough to give you an overall impression of Vista. If you don't want to dedicate your computer to Media Center, you'll find that Media Player and Photo Gallery will serve your entertainment needs just fine in most cases. To utilize Media Center fully requires a constant television signal connection to ensure that you get the shows you want to record. That implies that your Media Center–dedicated computer stays with your family TV, while you use another computer to perform routine computer tasks, and watch an occasional movie or listen to music while doing so.

This chapter only introduced Media Player, Photo Gallery, Sound Recorder, and Movie Maker; the next several chapters more fully cover those Windows Vista programs.

CHAPTER 15

Managing Your Entertainment Experience with Media Player

In This Chapter:

▶ Master Media Player's interface

▶ Browse your music in different ways

▶ Edit music file properties

▶ Add album cover art to your music collection

▶ Create and use playlists

▶ Rip music from a CD

▶ Burn music to a CD

Microsoft calls Vista's Windows Media Player the *next-generation digital music software.* Media Player is more than music software, however. It's a way to experience your music, movies, and photos from one program that puts you in control of your entertainment-related digital files.

Media Player plays CDs and DVDs. Just insert a disc and Vista can take you where you want to go. You can send CD music to your disk drive by ripping the tunes to your PC; afterward, you can store the CD with the rest of your music collection and play the files digitally from your PC or from any PC on your Vista network. The original disc stays in mint condition and acts as a backup when you need it.

Users of previous Media Player versions will be pleased with the more intuitive and considerably more attractive Media Player interface. When you want to listen to music, watch movies, or look at some family photos, you don't want to wrangle with the program—you want to see your media. Vista's Media Player minimizes the time you spend getting to your media and maximizes the experience.

Getting to Your Music, Videos, and Pictures

Media Player's interface is simpler than previous versions. You will find yourself using Media Player's menu less than before because the buttons across the top provide most routine features you'll use. That's why the menu is hidden by default although you can display it once more by pressing Ctrl+M. With the toolbar, the menu isn't as important as it was in previous versions. For example, when you start Media Player and want to play music from your digital music library, click the down arrow beneath the Library button and select Music. Media Player displays the music library files from which you can select (see Figure 15.1).

Refer to Chapter 14, "Going Multimedia with Vista," to learn how to add digital music files you already have on your computer and network to your Media Player library. You'll learn how to rip CD music to digital files and burn CDs from digital music files later in this chapter.

Did you Know?

Store music, photos, and videos you want to share with others across your network—perhaps on a PC you dedicate as your media center—in your Public folder. The files in your user account's folder are private and viewable only from your account. The Public folder and its subfolders are shareable across a network. The Public folder includes Public Documents, Public Downloads, Public Music, Public Pictures, Public Videos, and Recorded TV subfolders where you can conveniently make your media files available to other users and computers.

Double-click a song (or click the song and then click the Play button at the bottom of the screen) to listen; Media Player begins playing your selected song and continues down the list on your screen after that song ends. Double-click an album to play that album without moving to the next album or song in the list when the album finishes.

Although you'll use Media Player for music, video, and digital pictures, the vast majority of most users' Media Player libraries are comprised of music. You can browse, search, and play videos and show pictures using similar onscreen tools to the ones you use to browse, search, and play music.

Because music is often the library used most in Media Player, it makes sense to cover music first, and the next section begins doing just that. Keep in mind that when you learn how to browse through music files, you are learning much of what is required to browse through your digital photographs as well. Media Player works in a similar manner no matter what kind of data you want to access.

Select how to view music

FIGURE 15.1
Select Music from the Library drop-down button to browse your music files.

Stop, Look, and Listen the Way You Want

You might not like the way Media Player browses through your files. For example, in Figure 15.1, Media Player organizes the music by song title. You'll notice that Songs is selected in the left column. Although it appears that Media Player organizes the music by album, that's misleading. When you browse through a bunch of CDs or record albums, you generally look at the album covers and if one piques your interest, you look at the song list. In the default music display, shown in Figure 15.1, the songs get in the way. It's difficult to browse through the albums because you must scroll through so many songs.

If you rip only one song from a CD to your digital music collection, and later view that song, Media Player displays the album cover for that song if it's available. This means that you also get album information such as the title and release year next to the album when you view the song in the default music list shown in Figure 15.1. When you browse by song title, it appears you have a lot of albums, but only one or a few songs will appear on some of the albums in your list.

Viewing Music in Various Ways

To browse by album covers alone, which gives you far more screen space for the album covers and eliminates the song lists on each album, click the Album entry in the left selection column. Figure 15.2 shows the result.

Playlists appear here

FIGURE 15.2
When you browse by albums, you see only the covers to give you more albums on the screen at one time.

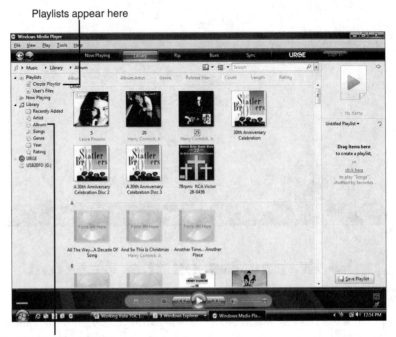

Displayed by album cover

From the selection column to the left, you see that you can browse your music library in these ways:

▶ **Recently Added**—Shows your songs in reverse date order based on when you added them to your collection.

▶ **Artist**—Shows album covers arranged alphabetically by artist name. If you have a Harry Connick, Jr. album and a Herman's Hermits album in your collection, both album covers appear in the H's.

▶ **Album**—As Figure 15.2 illustrates, the Album view arranges your albums alphabetically by album title.

▶ **Songs**—As shown in Figure 15.1, this view displays your music collection arranged by artist, showing album covers and each song from each album.

▶ **Genre**—Shows album covers arranged by genre, such as Ballad, Blues, Country, Gospel, Instrumental, Rock, and so on. As shown in Figure 15.3, if more than one album appears in a genre category, those albums are depicted as stacked one on top of another. When multiple albums appear for a genre, double-click the album icon shown to see all albums in that genre arranged alphabetically. (This also applies to the Artist, Year, and Rating views.)

Breadcrumb trail   Multiple albums in Country genre

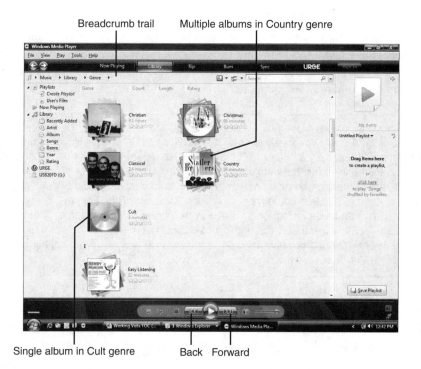

FIGURE 15.3
When viewing by genre, an album cover shows one or multiple albums in your collection from that genre; double-click a multiple-album cover to see all albums in that genre.

Single album in Cult genre   Back Forward

▶ **Year**—Displays your music in reverse year order, beginning with the latest. If a stack of album covers appear for a year, your library includes multiple albums from that year. Double-click a stack to see all albums from that year.

▶ **Rating**—Shows music by rating based on a five-star rating scale. As you add music and albums to your library, you can rate the music according to your preference. That way you can rank your favorites as well as the duds and quickly get to your favorites. The next section, "Editing Music Properties," shows you how to rate a song or album.

If you click to select Library in the left selection column, as opposed to clicking a specific library selection such as Rating or Artist, Media Player displays the following additional ways to sort and view your music library: by contributing artist, composer, parental rating, online store item, and folder. Not all of these values are available for every song in your library. Over time you will be able to fill in these values as appropriate, as the next section explains.

When viewing your music, video, and photo libraries in Media Player, you change views quite often, as you might imagine. Just as you can back up to a previous web page by clicking your web browser's Back button, you can move back and forth among the various views you've used to browse your collections with Media Player's Back and Forward buttons.

A breadcrumb option is available in Media Player, just as in other Vista Explorer windows. Using it, you can locate music based on location, genre, artist, or another factor. Click the arrows in the breadcrumb trail toward the top of the Media Player screen to access these viewing options.

Did you Know?

If you want to see an alphabetical list of every song you own, click the Songs selection, and then click the Title column. Every song in your music collection appears alphabetically as Figure 15.4 shows. If an album cover picture is present, a small icon shows for that album in the Album column but the album cover's picture doesn't consume so much screen space that you cannot see many song titles at once. Clicking a column heading such as Album, Title, Length, Rating, and Artist sorts your music selection's display in that order. Click the same column again and get a reverse sort (arranged in descending order). Your actual music library doesn't change or reorganize on your disk drive; you're only changing the way Media Player offers your digital music to you.

FIGURE 15.4
Display a complete, alphabetical song list on your screen at one time by clicking the Title column.

Click column to sort

There are times when you want to play a certain song. Just one song. Perhaps you want to play it for a friend and you would like to go straight to the song and not browse in any way to get to it. As with most of Vista's programs, Media Player includes an Instant Search box. Type the first few letters of the song title, and Media Player immediately goes to work locating those letters and displays matches by artist, album, and song title. Getting to what you want has never been easier.

Editing Music Properties

After you start building your digital music library, you soon realize that regular maintenance is required. When you rip music from a CD, Media Player goes to the Internet and attempts to transfer as much information as it can find about that CD and its contents to your Media Player library. In a best-case scenario, Media Player should locate your exact CD online, download the album cover, artist, song titles, track numbers, length, contributing artist, and so on.

The data stored in the music fields, such as the genre and rating, is **metadata**.

By the Way

The reality is that *most* of the time, Media Player finds *most* of that information and *most* of it is accurate. For missing data, you can either ignore those fields or fill them in yourself. Obviously, no music data service can rate music for your tastes. Therefore, all music enters your collection with a generic three-star rating. Media Player colors these three stars gray to indicate that the rating was the default rating and not a rating that you or someone else with access to your computer gave the song. When you rate a song, the stars turn yellow. Therefore, a song with three yellow stars is a song that you or someone else on your computer rated as a three-star song. When you change a song's rating, every user on your computer that accesses that song also sees the new rating.

If you never fill in this missing data, that's fine. Some people prefer not to mess with the rating system. Others rely on it to quickly scan their music for their all-time favorites. Others create extensive **playlists**, lists of songs arranged in a preferred order, that match their moods, needs, and favorite preferences and rely on them to decide what to play next. (We cover playlists in the "Create and Use Playlists" section later in this chapter.) Media Player often sorts missing data into the Other category. For example, if a song or album doesn't have a specified genre, that item appears in the Other category when you display your music library by genre.

By the Way

When you notice that music is missing data, Media Player makes it simple to fill in the missing information. For example, if you were to rip songs into your Music Library without having an active Internet connection to help identify the CD, Media Player wouldn't be able to fill in any information about the CD's artist or the songs on it, other than the track number. In this case, it's up to you to fill in all the details. Most of the time, your Internet connection will be active and it might be that Media Player just isn't able to fill in a few types of fields.

One of the easiest ways to complete details for an album is to display the album and all its songs on the same screen. As the previous section explained, when you browse by song, Media Player also shows the album cover. You can browse by album cover or artist also. No matter how you locate the album, when you double-click the album cover, it displays a list of songs (see Figure 15.5). To get to Figure 15.5's screen, for example, you would click Artist from the Navigation pane on the left.

Right-click to change any field   Click a star to rate song

FIGURE 15.5
Editing album information is simple when you display the album and song details on the same Media Player window.

Did you Know?

Want to make your song-editing session more enjoyable? Start playing any song on the screen while you edit. Media Player plays the album while you edit its details.

The following fields are to the right of the album cover: Album Title, Artist, Genre, and Year. It will be obvious if any information is missing. If the Year field shows Unknown Year instead of an actual year, that information was unavailable when Media Player saved the album to your library.

In the song list to the right of the album appears the track number, the song title, the length in minutes of each song, your rating, and any contributing artists. (If no contributing artists appear in the data, Media Player places the artist in the contributing artist field.)

Before manually changing any data other than the song rating (which is a personal field left up to you), you might see whether Media Player can locate information about a song or album with your help. Right-click the album picture or a song, and select Find Album Info. Media Player goes to the Internet and attempts to locate a matching album. Sometimes more than one album appears, so you have to locate the album, if it appears, that matches the one in your library. Click to select that album and Media Player updates the album's information. The information will be as complete as possible, but you still might have to fill in a field or two—especially the rating field if you want to rate the album.

Figure 15.6 shows several albums found by Media Player's Internet search for the album titled *Comin' Right Up*. Clicking the first entry in the list, the matching album in this case, causes Media Player to update the album cover picture and the rest of the data, such as the track numbers that are currently missing. (You didn't know that Bruce Willis recorded some vocal albums a few years ago, did you? He's very good.)

Click to update Media Player

FIGURE 15.6
Media Player often finds several possible matches. Click the one that matches your library's album and Media Player updates the information.

For albums and songs that Media Player cannot locate online, changing or adding new data is simple. To edit any album field, right-click the field and select Edit from the pop-up menu. For example, you would right-click Unknown Year to change the year to the album's year. To change song information, right-click a song and select Edit. Changing a song's rating is even easier; just click a star. If you click a song's fourth star from the left, you'll give that song a four-star rating.

The cover picture, when missing, requires a little more effort on your part to update. If the online update doesn't fill in the picture, you'll have to locate a digital picture of the album cover and paste it over the missing picture in your music library. You can scan the album or CD or take a digital picture of it. Chapter 16, "Going Digital with Your Camera or Scanner," explains how to do just that. In addition, you might be able to locate the album cover online in an online music store such as www.CDNow.com. If you can locate an album's picture online, right-click the album cover and select the pop-up menu's Save Picture As option. Save the image to your disk. The default folder will be your Pictures folder.

After you save the image to your disk, copy the picture to your Windows clipboard. Media Player and Photo Gallery both handle pictures extremely well. But the fastest way to copy the picture to your clipboard, surprisingly, is to open Windows Explorer (using the Windows+E shortcut key), display your Pictures folder, right-click the album's image, and select Copy from the pop-up menu. Return to Media Player, right-click the blank album image, and select Paste. The album cover will now appear with your music.

By the Way

That's quite a bit of work to place the album cover but, fortunately, Media Player is often successful at locating albums and their pictures when you request the online update.

Create and Use Playlists

You now can browse your music collection, locate and play songs, and rearrange the library to see things in the way that works best for you. As you use Media Player, you'll quickly come to realize why playlists are important to create.

Did you Know?

If you updated your computer to Windows Vista from XP, Media Player will automatically recognize any playlists you had already created.

You can create as many playlists as you want. It's important to understand that a playlist doesn't reorganize your actual music files, nor does a playlist change any of the data attached to music files, such as the genre or rating. A playlist is nothing more than a list of songs that you create from your music library. After you create a playlist, instead of playing music by song title, album, or date, you can play the playlist. Media Player then plays only those songs located in the playlist. You create and manage playlists from within Media Player.

When first learning of playlists, some people confuse them with genre. For example, you *could* create a playlist of all Classic Rock music in your music library. Depending on what you own, that might be a huge playlist. The size of a playlist isn't a factor in whether a playlist is good or bad, but as a general rule of thumb, if a playlist grows to include 100 or more songs, it means one of two things:

▶ You need to break up the playlist into multiple playlists.

▶ You're confusing a playlist with a genre, artist, or rating.

Most often, it's the second problem that has occurred if your playlist becomes too long, but let's take the first possibility first: You need to break up the playlist into multiple playlists.

Suppose that you want to create a playlist for party music. As you add to the playlist, you begin to see that the playlist has grown to a rather large number. As you'll see in a moment, Media Player makes it easy to add songs to a playlist, so creating a playlist of 100 or more songs isn't difficult at all. When you surpass 100 songs, you should begin to ask yourself how helpful the playlist truly is. How long will it take to play 100 songs? The party is going to have to last a long time!

When that occurs, you should consider creating multiple party playlists. For example, you might have a tropical party playlist for parties with an island theme. You might create a New Year's Eve party playlist with *Auld Lang Syne*, *Anthem to the New Year*, and other songs appropriate for a New Year's Eve party. You'll end up with better playlists because each targets a particular type of party.

A playlist can contain other playlists. If you know several of your party's guests like easy listening (and your other guests won't scream too loudly when they hear it!), you can create a new playlist for a specific New Year's Eve party and include your New Year's Eve playlist to bring in all those songs and add a few easy listening tunes to mix it up a bit. Media Player makes it simple to organize and even quickly delete playlists you no longer need, so creating such a one-time playlist makes sense.

Did you Know?

More often, a person will confuse a playlist's purpose with one of the song's fields such as genre. For example, it would be ill-advised to create a playlist of all your jazz music and call that playlist Jazz. The genre field is better suited to label your jazz tunes. Perhaps you take your jazz seriously and you want to break your jazz collection into Jazz Vocals, Ragtime, Pre-1960s Jazz, and so on. Depending on the size of your collection, even those playlists can become huge and the genre field might be a better location to label the songs with those categories. Then, when you browse by category you can easily locate all your Pre-1960s Jazz genre music.

If every person in your 4-member family enjoys a different type of jazz, with some overlap, you might begin to see how playlists can help that situation. For example, you might create Mom's Jazz Favorites and add all of her favorite hits to that playlist. Mom then can quickly play her playlist that will include only her favorite music. It doesn't make sense to label the genre of those songs Mom's Jazz Favorites because genre is a more generic field used to describe a type of music, not who likes it best. The right pane of Media Player is where you manage and create your playlists. If you don't see the playlist area, click your Library button and select Create Playlist to add a playlist to your window. Scroll through your music library, in whatever order you want to view it, and drag songs that you want to add to your playlist to the right pane where it says Drag Items Here. You can drag complete albums to your playlist, too.

By the Way

The first song you drag will begin playing and its album cover will appear atop your playlist. Media Player isn't naming your playlist with the album name or assigning that cover to the playlist; the playback occurs only so that you have something to listen to while you create the rest of the list. You can immediately click the control panel's Stop button at the bottom of Media Player to stop the playback.

You can select multiple songs by holding your Ctrl key while clicking song titles and you can select an entire range of songs by clicking the first song to select it, scrolling down to the last song in the range, holding Shift, and clicking that song. Media Player selects the entire range of songs and you can drag them to your playlist in the right pane.

Feel free to drag and drop songs from your playlists to a different location. If the second song works better for you later in the list, click and drag it toward the bottom of the playlist. When you finish adding all the songs you want to add, click the Save Playlist button. Type a name for your playlist and press Enter to save it.

As Figure 15.7 shows, the playlist title appears at the top of your playlist and the new playlist is added to your selection of Playlists in Media Player's navigation pane. Click the down arrow next to your playlist's title button to see options in a pop-up menu that enable you to clear the list, shuffle the list randomly, rename the playlist, and save the playlist under a second name (useful for two similar playlists when you want to start with a copy of another and then modify the copy).

New playlist appears

FIGURE 15.7
Your playlists specify sets of titles you want to listen to.

When you click a playlist in the left-hand pane's selection area, that playlist fills Media Player's large, central window pane so that you can adjust the order, rate songs, and click Play to enjoy that playlist.

Play a Music CD

Playing a CD is perhaps the easiest way to use Media Player. The only thing you have to do is insert the CD. Media Player begins playing the CD. If the CD is a common title, Media Player retrieves the album art and song titles and displays that information for you as the CD plays. You can work in other Media Player areas and create playlists from your digital music library, while listening to the CD play. You can go to the CD's song list anytime by clicking the Now Playing button atop your Media Player window.

If Media Player does not retrieve the album information, click the Now Playing entry in Media Player's left pane to show the missing album cover and song contents. You can right-click the album cover and select Find Album Info as described earlier in this chapter to locate and store the album information in Media Player. If the information is not found, as sometimes happens for privately produced or custom mix CDs, you can manually enter the information.

If you hold down one of your Shift keys while inserting the CD into your computer, Media Player will not start playing the CD automatically.

Rip Music from a CD

If you want to rip the music from a music CD to your disk, insert the CD and retrieve or edit the album information. Although you can add the album and song details after ripping the music, you save a step or two by doing it now versus filling in the details after you rip the album.

Click the Rip button at the top of your Media Player to display the album's information. By default, Media Player selects all the songs to rip to your disk, but you can click to uncheck certain songs if you don't want the rip the entire album.

Click the down arrow at the bottom of the Rip button to check some options before beginning the rip process. The following options determine how your music will rip:

▶ **Format**—Determines the digital music format of your ripped music. The default is Media Player's Windows Media Audio, a standard format used by Media Player and several other portable music players that use the .wma filename extension. Three other Windows Media options are available: Pro, Variable Bit Rate, and Lossless. Pro uses slightly less storage space, but is not as widely supported in handheld devices as the other choices. Variable Bit Rate offers superior quality, but marginally increased file sizes. Lossless offers the best quality you can get from your rip, but has monumentally larger file sizes. Only use the Lossless format if you're an audiophile to the *n*th degree, with hundreds of gigabytes of free hard drive space to devote to your music collection. MP3, being the most widely accepted music format in the world, is also an option. Finally, Media Player offers the WAV Lossless format, a higher-quality format than the standard .wav file and one that most web browsers can play with little trouble, but not a format that most will want to save their music collection. Music players often cannot play .wav files, so if you want to use a lossless format, go with WMA Lossless.

Lossless versus lossy audio formats refer to the use of compression to achieve small music files sizes. **Lossy** formats crop out sounds that are generally outside the bounds of human hearing in order to reduce the size of music files. **Lossless** formats achieve minimal compression without losing any data from the recording.

▶ **Bit Rate**—Determines the quality of the music playback. The higher the bit rate, the better quality the audio playback will be, but the larger the digital music file will be too. A bit rate of 192Kbps is considered the minimum for near-CD playback quality, although 256Kbps and higher come nearer to achieving true, near-CD quality that the human ear can hardly distinguish from the original source. The format you choose determines which bit rate options appear. For example, if you select MP3, you can select a bit rate that goes as high as 320Kbps, but if you choose to save your music in the Windows Media Audio, 192Kbps is the highest bit rate available. In fairness to the .wma format, 192 Kbps for .wma files is considered to sound about as good as MP3 files recorded at 256Kbps. Note that because a variable bit rate (VBR) WMA file automatically bases its bit rate on each individual song, you cannot specify a custom bit rate when ripping to this format; the default bit rate for WMA files is 128 Kbps.

▶ **Rip CD Automatically When Inserted**—Allows you to specify when to rip CDs. Generally, you will want to rip CDs only when you click the Rip button and start the process. If, however, you have multiple CDs to rip, you might want to change this option to Always to speed up the process temporarily until you rip all the CDs you are working with.

▶ **Eject CD After Ripping**—Click to request that Media Player eject the CD after the ripping process finishes and all your music is digitally recorded to your disk drive.

▶ **More Options**—Displays the Options dialog box, shown in Figure 15.8, with multiple rip options available to you. The Options dialog box opens when you select Options from the Tools menu. Press your Alt+T to see the Tools menu if you don't see your menu. Many of these are similar to what the Rip drop-down button gives you already, such as music format and bit rate. You can change the default location of your ripped music by clicking the Change button and entering a new disk location, and you can click the Options dialog box's tabs to modify other Media Player options.

To ensure compatibility with as many music players and computer software programs as possible, save your audio in the MP3 format. Many audiophiles cringe at this advice, but they have to admit that no other format is supported worldwide as much as MP3. Although the other formats, especially the lossless formats, can produce better sound quality, as long as you use a decent bit rate of 192Kbps or better, most people won't be able to tell a difference in quality when playing back an MP3 file or any other digital music format.

Did you Know?

Changes music file format

FIGURE 15.8
The Options dia-
log box enables
you to set
music-ripping
options as well
as other Media
Player options.

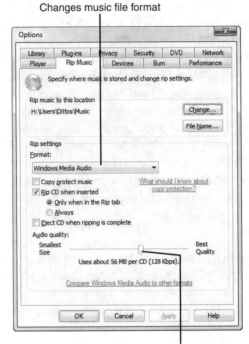

Drag to change bit rate

If you use an Apple iPod portable music player, do not record your audio in any WMA format. Because the iPod is incompatible with WMA, if you use Media Player to rip your audio CDs, you have to stick with MP3.

After you set the music-ripping options, you're ready to rip the CD contents onto your disk. Click the Start Rip button and Media Player begins saving your music. Depending on the speed of your computer and the bit rate you set, a standard CD should take only a few minutes to rip and often completes in less than five minutes.

When ripped, your music becomes part of your Media Player library and you can put your CD safely away.

Burn Music to a CD

The opposite of music ripping is music **burning**. When you burn music to a CD, you transfer a copy of your digital music files to a CD. Other CD players can play that CD.

Throughout this Media Player discussion, this chapter has been discussing playing, ripping, and burning music files. Many CDs don't contain music files. For
example, audio books distributed on CDs contain recorded speech and not music.
Audio is audio, and all the same concepts apply whether you're working with a
music CD or a CD with other content, such as a narrator.

**By the
Way**

You have two ways to burn music to a CD:

▶ Burn a standard audio CD, playable in any drive that plays CD music

▶ Burn a data CD

A **standard CD** is one that contains up to a maximum of approximately 80 minutes of content and follows the same format as any CD you'd purchase at a retail
store. Such a CD is playable in any CD player, whether that CD player is a stand-
alone music CD player in a home or car stereo or a computer's CD drive. In addition, most DVD players can play back standard audio CDs.

A **data CD** is one that contains any kind of computer files. When you burn a CD
with audio files and use the data CD format instead of the standard CD format, you
can store about 10 hours of music (depending on the music quality). In addition,
you can use the data CD to make backups of any files on your computer. If you save
MP3 or other Windows Media Player files to a data CD, some CD players can recognize that the CD contains music and play back all 10 hours. This eliminates a lot of
disc-swapping that takes place with regular music CDs that hold only a little more
than an hour's worth of music.

All computer CD and DVD players can play digital music files from data CDs and
many car and home stereos and DVD players now can play them as well. Before
creating a lot of data CDs for playback off your computer you'll want to burn one
and test it where you want to listen to the CD to ensure that your player can play
music from these CDs. For example, if you're taking a long car trip, a couple of ten-
hour CDs burned with a set of MP3 or WMA files is a lot easier to manage than 20
one-hour conventional music CDs. Also, burning a couple of data CDs is less time-
consuming.

When you insert a blank, recordable CD into your computer's CD drive, the
AutoPlay dialog box shown in Figure 15.9 appears.

FIGURE 15.9
Windows Vista asks what kind of CD you want to burn when you insert a blank CD into your computer's CD burning drive.

After you select the kind of CD you want to burn, Media Player opens and the Burn button is selected. From here you can select the music you want to burn to the blank CD. Click the down arrow at the bottom of the Burn button to ensure that all the burn options are set to your liking. The burn options are usually less critical than the ripping options you learned about in the previous section.

Did you Know?

Media Player automatically selects the Apply Volume Leveling Across Tracks on Audio CDs option. This option helps to normalize your CD volume levels so that some tracks aren't extremely loud whereas others are too soft to hear. Music purists might want to uncheck this option, but for most people, who simply want to enjoy music on their trip or elsewhere, volume leveling means you don't have to adjust your CD player's volume control throughout the music.

The Burn button's More Options choice opens Media Player's Options dialog box for a few additional options shown in Figure 15.10. If you find that some CDs you burn don't play well in your CD player, you might need to slow down the burn speed by clicking the Burn Speed button and choosing Fast, Medium, or Slow as opposed to the default Fastest option. Some CD players are more sensitive than others and the slower you burn your CD, the less likely (in many cases) you'll have trouble playing back the CD. The only drawback to slowing down the burn speed is that it will take longer to burn the CD.

You must now select music to burn. Media Player's right pane will hold your burn list as you drag files to it. Just as you dragged music files from your library to this pane to create playlists, you drag songs to this pane to create a burn list for the blank CD in your drive.

Changes burn speed

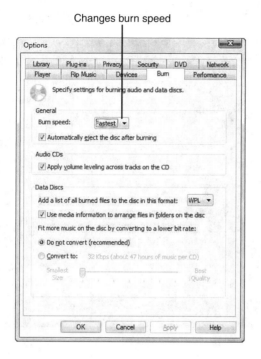

FIGURE 15.10
Additional burn
options are
available, such
as the burn
speed.

If you send more music files to your burn list than will fit on one CD (this limit differs depending on whether you elected to burn a music CD or a data CD), Media Player inserts a dividing line in the burn list and starts a new list below the first one for the next CD. Figure 15.11 shows a burn list with multiple CDs ready to burn. As you keep adding music to send to your CDs, the burn list keeps adding as many CDs as needed to hold all the files in the list. When you start the burn, Media Player burns the CDs in the order of the burn list and prompts you to insert a new CD when it's time to burn the next one.

By the Way

You can drag to rearrange the burn list order if you want to burn songs or CDs in a different order from the burn list you originally generate. You can also select and press Delete to delete selected songs that you decide against recording to the CD.

Did you Know?

Second CD to burn

FIGURE 15.11
Your burn list
holds one or
more CD's
worth of music
you want to
burn.

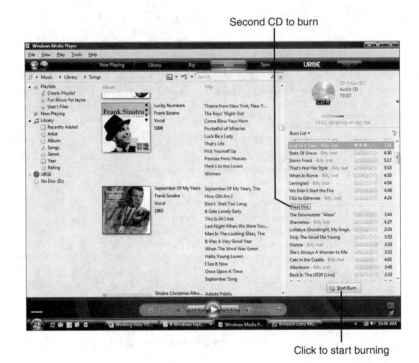

Click to start burning

When your burn list contains all the music you want to save to the current CD (or
to multiple CDs, if you've created a burn list that will go to several CDs), click the
Start Burn. Media Player begins the burn. Depending on the burn speed you selected
and your CD burning drive's speed, the burn process can take several minutes.
Usually, burning a CD takes longer than ripping music from a CD.

The Urge Music Service

Microsoft brokered a deal with MTV to create a new Media Player environment
called Urge. Urge, available when you click Media Player's Urge button, provides up-
to-date news about the music industry, artist interviews and blogs, CD-quality and
commercial-free online radio stations, and free music downloads, and has more
than two million paid music track downloads available. Figure 15.12 shows an Urge
screen within Media Player.

FIGURE 15.12
MTV's Urge service gives you online access to music and artists.

Click a genre at the bottom of the Urge window to view Urge content on your favorite type of music.

The heart (and real reason) of Urge's existence, however, is to make music available to you, giving you an online store of millions of downloadable tracks without requiring that you leave your Media Player environment. You must subscribe to Urge to download music. At the time of this writing, after you subscribe, you can purchase individual tracks to download or buy an All Access pass by paying a monthly fee and downloading as much as you want. Once you download music, Media Player automatically adds the tracks to your library and you can play the music on your portable music devices (using Media Player's Sync button to transfer the music) or on your computer.

Depending on the music you download, you will face *Digital Rights Management* (*DRM*) restrictions. DRM is used by vendors of online content such as music and video to control how the files can be used. For example, DRM could determine that a music file can be played only on the one computer it's downloaded to or perhaps not copied in any form. DRM can limit the number of times the content is played, such as a digital movie you download that you can copy anywhere but it can only be played three times before it refuses to play again. The license related to the content you purchase on sites such as Urge determines what you can do with music. Windows Media Player and Media Center both honor any DRM rules they come across.

By the Way

What About Video and Photos?

The chapter began by discussing how well Media Player handles music, video, and photos. The bulk of the chapter then concentrated on music and little else! This is intentional for a couple of reasons. First, music is what most people use Media Player for most of the time. Given the size of music files compared to digital video files, people who have digital content often have far more music files than the massive files required for digital videos of any size. Therefore, learning how to organize, manage, and play music as was explored throughout the earlier sections makes the most sense.

Concerning digital photographs, many computer users today have many digital pictures. Photo Gallery is the best place to manage your pictures. Media Player is a good place to view photos and you can organize and rate them from within Media Player also. But the added features of Photo Gallery mean that you'll probably work within Photo Gallery primarily (or within another digital photo program, such as Adobe's Photoshop Elements) when you manage your photos. You'll use Media Player when you're already inside Media Player doing other things, such as downloading or listening to music, but you want to look at some pictures and perhaps print or email them to others without leaving the Media Player environment.

Possibly the best reason not to include a lot of separate coverage for accessing and managing videos and digital pictures is that Media Player's interface doesn't really change when you view and manage videos and pictures. Figure 15.13 shows a Media Player screen displaying a video file library. You view digital files just as you view music files. Instead of album art, Media Player shows a captured image from early in the video. To watch a video, double-click it and Media Player starts playing the video. Accessing and managing digital photographs works the same way, too.

To play a DVD, insert it in your drive and Media Player starts playing the movie. All the normal DVD-related menu options work, so you can play the DVD extras or jump to a specific scene if the DVD supports those features.

You can add parental controls to limit the DVD ratings that play back in Media Player. Select Tools, Options and click the DVD tab. Click the Change button in the DVD Playback Restrictions section of the Options dialog box to determine the highest rating (such as G, PG-13, and R) that can be played on Media Player.

FIGURE 15.13
You'll access, watch, and manage digital videos using the same tools you access, listen, and manage digital music files.

If you have a DVD drive capable of writing to blank DVDs, you can save music and your digital video and photo library to DVDs. The capability to play that DVD in a standalone DVD player depends on many factors, such as the type of blank DVD media you use and the number of DVD formats your DVD player can read. Your DVD player's manual should be your first step in determining whether you can play DVDs that you create in Media Player.

> One thing Media Player does *not* allow you to do is to rip DVDs to your digital library. Programs exist to do that, but you face copyright laws and copy protection schemes that change constantly. Is it as legal to make a backup of a DVD as it is to rip a CD to your hard disk? At first glance, there seems to be very little difference, but Microsoft chose the path of least (legal) resistance and opted not to allow DVD ripping. At the end of the day, you can do it so long as you're not circumventing a built-in copy-protection mechanism in order to do so. Because most commercial DVDs do have built-in copy-protection, this does in fact make backing up those DVDs illegal.

By the Way

DVDs hold a tremendous amount of storage, from about 6 to 20 or more times the amount of data that a data CD can hold. Therefore, using DVDs for data backup makes a lot of sense. Routinely sending your digital music, pictures, and videos to a data DVD, even if you don't ever plan to watch that DVD on a stand-alone DVD player, serves as a good back-up for your digital media collection (and your regular data too!). You can burn your digital files to DVD using the same procedure you used to burn CD digital files in the "Burn Music to a CD" section.

Chapter Wrap-Up

You're now a Windows Media Player pro! You learned in this chapter how Media Player acts as a repository and management system for your digital music, videos, and photographs. You can view and play music and videos easily. Browse through your photograph collection. Create playlists and go online to download new content.

Media Player's true power comes in its ability to handle digital music. Media Player easily rips music from music CDs, burns music to CDs, and provides an electronic jukebox of music that can encompass your entire music library no matter how vast it might be.

Although Media Player enables you to view and manage your photographs, Photo Gallery does a better job because you can edit your pictures in Photo Gallery and Media Player's music and video options don't get in your way. The next two chapters move you away from this chapter's music-themed discussion to cover Windows Vista's work with digital pictures. You'll see how to get pictures onto your computer easily, and edit and manage those pictures after they're there.

CHAPTER 16

Going Digital with Your Camera or Scanner

In This Chapter:

▶ Get pictures onto your Vista computer

▶ Use a network to transfer pictures

▶ Transfer pictures from a camera to your PC

▶ Import pictures to Windows Photo Gallery

▶ Grab pictures from your scanner

Vista's Photo Gallery program is a welcome addition. Windows XP's My Pictures folder didn't allow for digital photo editing or extensive picture management. Photo Gallery enables you to organize your pictures, perform routine edits, and perform common picture tasks with your digital photos such as sending them to friends and family via email.

Before Photo Gallery can work with pictures, you must get those pictures on your computer. You might already have some pictures on your computer, but if you have a brand new PC, you'll want to get the pictures off your other PC so that Vista can work with them. In addition, you might use a digital camera or scanner to take digital pictures and want a quick way to get pictures from those devices to your computer.

This chapter shows you how simple it is for Vista to download pictures from your camera or scanner and how to transfer pictures from your older PC, if you have any there. When the pictures arrive on your primary Windows Vista machine, you can use Photo Gallery to rate and tag them; that kind of organization allows you to find any picture you want when you need it.

Getting Pictures onto Your Computer

If you purchased a new computer with Windows Vista and want to get your older computer's pictures to your new Vista-based machine you can transfer files by copying them from the older computer to your new one if you network them. Without a network, you'll have to back them up to an external hard disk or a removable storage medium, such as a CD, DVD, or USB flash memory drive.

By the Way

> If you installed Windows Vista as an upgrade to a previous version of Windows, any digital pictures you already had stored on that computer are still there and available to you.

The following sections explain some of the best ways to get pictures onto your Windows Vista computer.

Moving Digital Photos to Your Vista-Based Computer Over a Network

When you buy a new computer, a common question is, *What do I do with the old one?* You might choose to donate it to a private school or perhaps give it to charity. If your family has several members, younger members often get the computer hand-me-downs and are usually grateful when that occurs.

By the Way

> Society's come a long way hasn't it? Hand-me-down clothing was the way families traditionally get extra life out of their needed items. Now, it's hand-me-down computers. Computers go out of date so rapidly these days, technically, that second-hand computers aren't worth much more money than second-hand clothing!

If you end up with multiple computers in your home, there's no reason not to network them. You don't even have to run cables, with wireless network hardware available at such low prices.

By the Way

> This section's procedures work not only for digital pictures but also for any files you want to transfer from one computer to another.

Before transferring your pictures from the older computer over your network to the new computer, you must make sure that the pictures are stored in a shared folder. Most Windows XP computers have a folder called Shared Documents that you can see in any Windows Explorer window.

Data is relatively simple to transfer from one computer to another. Computer programs, such as Adobe Illustrator, are virtually impossible to transfer over a network from one computer to another. Programs do exist to help you transfer programs from one computer to another, but they are rarely 100% successful. The only way to ensure that you successfully transfer programs is to reinstall the program from the original program CD or downloaded installation file on your second computer. (Most copyright restrictions don't permit you to run the program on two computers at once.)

After you connect the computers in a network, open two Windows Explorer windows in Vista. The shortcut key to open an Explorer window is to press Windows+E (or open the Start menu and click the Computer or Documents links). Adjust the windows so that each takes up half your screen. That way you can see the contents of each Explorer window. One window acts as your source window and shows the older computer's disk contents. The other window acts as your target window and shows your new computer's contents.

On the target computer, your new Vista machine, locate the folder where you want to store photographs. Assuming that you don't have any security issues, the simplest location is to place them in your Public folder's Public Pictures folder (beneath your Public folder) because your Vista machine will readily accept files there and then users on your Vista computer can grab the pictures they need from the Public Pictures folder and store them in their individual accounts' Pictures folders. Use your Vista Explorer window's Folder navigation pane (the Explorer window's left window pane) to locate the folder to which you want to copy the pictures from the older computer.

Even though Vista offers a custom Pictures folder for each user account on the system, you can create a new folder for the transferred pictures if you like. Locate the place where you want to store the pictures, right-click in the Explorer window, and select New, Folder. Give your folder a name, such as OldPCPics. When the new folder's icon appears in your Explorer window, double-click it to open that folder and you can transfer your pictures there.

In your computer's other Explorer window, the one that shows the older PC's files that you moved into your Shared Documents folder, select Network in your Vista's left navigation pane (in the Folders section that appears when you click the arrows to the right of the word Folders in your Navigation pane) and scroll down until you see the other computer's name. Double-click the computer's name to display all that computer's shared folders. Locate the shared folder where you stored the pictures to move and double-click that folder to display the photo files it contains.

To move the pictures, simply select the pictures to move on the source computer's Explorer window and use your mouse to drag those pictures to the target computer's Explorer window. Figure 16.1 shows the result of such an operation. The pictures from the older, source computer in the bottom Explorer window are now on the Vista-based computer as the top Explorer window shows.

FIGURE 16.1
Copying between two Explorer windows is perhaps the simplest way to transfer files between computers.

...to here

The target Vista-based PC

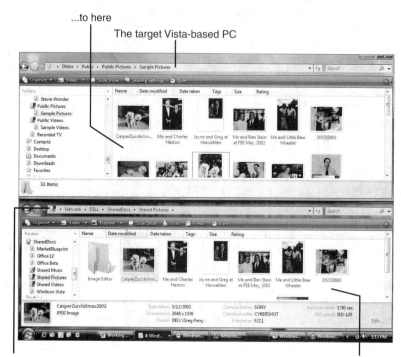

Older source computer

From here...

When dragging files between two network computers, Windows performs a copy and not a move. Therefore, the files still reside on your older, source computer after the operation finishes. If you want to move the files instead of copying them, use your right mouse button to drag the files to your target computer's Explorer window. When you release your right mouse button, a pop-up menu appears. Select Move and Vista knows to remove your pictures from the older computer after they transfer to your new computer.

If you don't have your computers networked, you will have to copy the photos and other data that you want to transfer to data CDs or DVDs. Chapter 15, "Managing Your Entertainment Experience with Media Player," explained how to create data CDs and DVDs from within Media Player.

Getting Pictures from Your Digital Camera

If you've used your digital camera often, you will find that Vista quickly recognizes it and can access the pictures there with ease. When getting pictures from your camera to your computer, you generally have the following options:

▶ Remove your digital camera's memory card and insert it into your computer's card reader.

▶ Use a USB cable to connect your camera to your PC.

> Some digital cameras now include a wireless networking option. If yours does, your camera's instructions explain how to get your computer's network to recognize your camera. From there you can easily drag files from the camera's memory to your computer's disk using the method described in the previous section.

By the Way

Transferring Pictures with a Memory Card and Card Reader

If your Vista computer has a memory card reader that can read the same memory sticks (sometimes called **memory sticks** or **compact flash**) that your camera uses, you may find that it's faster and easier than cabling your camera to your computer. Instead, just pull out the memory card from your digital camera and insert it into your computer's card reader. When you insert the card, Vista displays the AutoPlay dialog box shown in Figure 16.2.

FIGURE 16.2
The AutoPlay dialog box appears when you insert your digital camera's card into your computer's card reader.

If you select View Images, Photo Gallery appears and displays the first image in its viewing area. Actually, you are seeing the Photo Gallery Viewer, a version of Photo Gallery that enables you to manage single pictures at a time. You can edit, crop, resize, and do various other tasks with your pictures, as well as click the control buttons at the bottom of the Photo Gallery Viewer to see additional pictures on your camera's memory card, but you are not working within the full-featured Photo Gallery.

You can also select the Media Center option to view your pictures. This option is nice if you're on a computer dedicated for use as a Media Center machine and you want to show your pictures on a larger TV screen connected to the computer. You also might not want to store the pictures on the computer. For example, you might just want to show off pictures you have on your camera to friends and family using their Windows Vista PC.

Most of the time, you will want to transfer pictures from the memory card to your computer. The Import Using Windows option is by far the easiest way to do this. Select the AutoPlay dialog box's Import Using Windows option. If you accept all the defaults and click OK, Vista begins transferring a copy of the memory card pictures to your Pictures folder, as shown in Figure 16.3. Vista creates a new folder and names it with the current date, such as 2007-10-29. After the pictures are on your disk, you can use Photo Gallery to edit and manage them.

You can add tags to your imported photos now, or later in Photo Gallery. A **tag** is a descriptive word or set of words attached to your pictures. It acts as a property for the pictures just as the filename and file size properties do. In Photo Gallery (and in Media Player) you can view your pictures' tags, search on tags, and organize pictures by their tags.

If you just returned from vacation in Italy, you might want to tag the pictures Italy Vacation 2007, for example. You can change and add tags later but by adding an initial tag now, you'll be better able to tag this group of digital photos more accurately, making them easier to sort out from all your other photos. You can add multiple tags when prompted by separating the multiple tags with semicolons.

Transferring Pictures Directly from Your Camera to Your Computer

When you connect your digital camera to your computer with the camera's USB cable, your computer should recognize your camera and treat it as a disk drive with the pictures on the camera's memory card acting like files on a disk.

FIGURE 16.3
Vista shows the progress as the pictures transfer from your camera's memory card to your computer.

You must turn on your camera before your computer will sense your camera's presence. When the connection is established, the AutoPlay dialog box shown in Figure 16.2 appears and you can make your selection. As when using a memory card in your computer, when connecting your camera to your computer, the Import Using Windows option is the fastest and easiest way to get the pictures onto your computer's disk where you can work with the pictures in Photo Gallery.

Email is not an effective way to transfer lots of images from one computer to another. Email often has size restrictions and if your images are large, you cannot send many of them in a single email.

Watch Out!

Importing from Your Camera or Scanner Directly into Photo Gallery

Photo Gallery enables you to import digital pictures directly from your digital camera or scanner. If you often work within Photo Gallery, this makes more sense than using the methods in the previous sections. The methods described earlier in this chapter, however, work for everybody who wants to get digital pictures onto a Vista-based computer, whether or not they use Photo Gallery extensively. Some might feel that Media Player provides all the power they need to manage their pictures and so they open Photo Gallery only to edit photos.

If you work in Photo Gallery, though, you might as well take advantage of Photo Gallery's import procedure. By using Photo Gallery, you can directly import pictures from your digital camera or from your scanner.

Your digital camera can hold any number of pictures, depending on how much storage space it has. Your scanner scans one picture at a time. When importing pictures from your digital camera, you start Photo Gallery, start the import, select your camera, and then import the pictures. When you import a picture from your scanner, however, Photo Gallery doesn't actually import a picture that's already there. Instead, Photo Gallery starts your scanner and captures a picture of whatever you scan. Therefore, you can grab only one picture at a time, as you scan it.

Click the File button's down arrow and select Import from Camera or Scanner. The Import Pictures and Videos dialog box opens, and from there you can select your camera or scanner. Assuming that you want to scan pictures into Photo Gallery, select your scanner and click the Import button. Photo Gallery displays the New Scan dialog box shown in Figure 16.4.

FIGURE 16.4
You can scan photos directly into Photo Gallery.

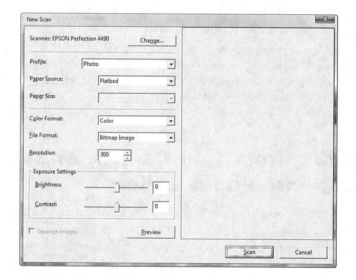

Set your scanning preferences. It's usually best to scan at one of your scanner's highest resolutions. This ensures that the scan is as accurate as possible and you don't lose color and crispness. Having said that, some scanners produce tremendous digital picture sizes, so you might want to work with the resolution to determine the best resolution for you.

If you're scanning items for a web page, such as you might do for an eBay auction, the default resolution is often too large because the load times for the web page with your pictures will be too long. A good resolution to scan such items is 300 **dpi** (**dots per inch**) although you'll still have to reduce the picture size and resolution further. A 300 dpi resolution ensures that the scan is crisp and true, but not overly large (although in most cases you still should reduce the size of a 300 dpi picture if you send it as an email attachment). The higher the resolution, the longer it takes to scan an item, so you must weigh your time against your image requirements.

If you're unsure of which settings will work well for you, the default scanning settings are not too bad and you should try them to see whether they suffice.

After setting your scanning preferences, you can get a sample of your scan by clicking the Preview button. Photo Gallery quickly scans your item and shows the scanned image in the preview area as seen in Figure 16.5. If the item is off-center or somehow not properly placed on your scanner, you can adjust the item and keep clicking Preview until you like the image.

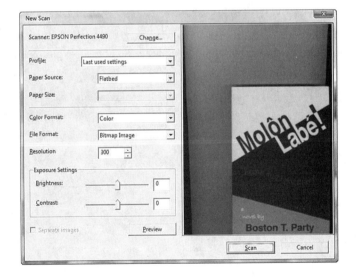

FIGURE 16.5
Photo Gallery allows you to preview your scanned item.

When the preview is to your liking, click Scan and the true scan begins at the resolution and format settings you set. After the scan finishes, Photo Gallery prompts you for a tag for the scanned item in a small Importing Pictures and Video dialog box and saves the image in its gallery.

A scanned image is rarely final. You'll want to crop the image in almost every case. As mentioned earlier in this section, you'll probably need to reduce the picture size before sending the picture as an email attachment. As you'll see in the next chapter, you can crop the scanned photo within Photo Gallery. Photo Gallery includes a few extras that come in handy as well, such as giving you a way to reduce the image size before sending it as an email attachment.

Chapter Wrap-Up

You can now get pictures to your Vista computer. The way you transfer pictures depends on the hardware you have. If you network your Vista computer to another computer with images, you can transfer those images (and videos) over the network. You might elect to save the images to a CD or DVD.

Getting pictures from a digital camera or scanner is simple too. You can transfer using your camera's memory card or a USB cable connection hooked between your computer and your camera. With Photo Gallery, you don't need standalone scanning software because Photo Gallery can grab an image from your scanner directly and store that image in your picture gallery.

Now that you've got pictures on your Vista computer, you're ready to edit and organize them. The next chapter, "Modify and Share Photos," explains how to do just that.

CHAPTER 17

Modifying and Sharing Photos

In This Chapter:

▶ Organize, manage, and edit digital pictures

▶ Import pictures into Photo Gallery

▶ Display both images and videos

▶ Master Photo Gallery's control panel

▶ Fix common picture problems

▶ Print pictures from Photo Gallery

▶ Put pictures on CDs and DVDs

In the previous chapter, you learned how to get pictures onto your Windows Vista computer. Whether you transfer from another computer, download from the Internet, import from a digital camera, or scan a picture directly into Photo Gallery, you should have little trouble getting a picture to your computer's folders.

Photo Gallery is the best place in Windows Vista to organize, manage, and edit your photos. This chapter explains how to maximize your use of Photo Gallery to get the most from the program. Almost every digital image library can use some organization and photo retouching—with Photo Gallery you now have the tool to do that.

Working in Photo Gallery

Start Photo Gallery by selecting Windows Photo Gallery from the Windows Start menu. Photo Gallery appears with one or more pictures in the central Photo Gallery window pane, as Figure 17.1 shows.

FIGURE 17.1
Photo Gallery is
the best place
to organize,
manage, and
edit pictures in
Windows Vista.

Navigation pane

If you see far fewer pictures, or none at all, but you know digital pictures reside on
your computer, Photo Gallery doesn't yet know that you have digital pictures on
your computer. You will learn how to add images to Photo Gallery, just as you add
media files to Media Player's library, in the next section.

Telling Photo Gallery You Have Pictures

Photo Gallery displays only pictures contained in your Pictures folder and the subfolders within it. If you have pictures located elsewhere on your computer and you
don't want to move them to your Pictures folder, you can tell Photo Gallery to display those pictures by adding their location to Photo Gallery's digital image gallery.

When you tell Photo Gallery to display pictures and videos from a folder other than
your Pictures folder, Photo Gallery adds that folder to the Folders entry in the left
navigation pane. This enables you to browse and manage that folder's picture contents and subfolders as easily as you can the Pictures folder and its subfolders.

To add folders to Photo Gallery's picture gallery, click the File button at the top of
Photo Gallery and select the Add Folder to Gallery option. A dialog box appears
from which you select the folder you want to add to Photo Gallery's picture gallery.

Click to select the folder and click OK. Photo Gallery adds the folder to its picture gallery and displays the Add Folder to Gallery dialog box shown in Figure 17.2. Click OK to close the dialog box and review your navigation pane.

FIGURE 17.2
Photo Gallery confirms the addition of the new folder to your picture gallery.

Photo Gallery now displays the newly added folder in its Folders list along with the Pictures folder and any other added folders. All folders listed are now available for your work within Photo Gallery. As you organize your photos, it's important for you to realize that Photo Gallery treats all the folders as one big collection—your picture gallery. Using this picture gallery, you can tag the pictures, and group and browse them in various ways without worrying that some are stored in different folders on your disk drive. After you add a folder, the pictures in that folder are on equal footing with the pictures that Photo Gallery displays; the only difference is that the pictures don't share the same top-level folder.

Displaying Photo Gallery's Images and Videos

Depending on how you want to view your photos in the current session, you might want to change the way Photo Gallery displays pictures. Instead of small thumbnail images, you might prefer to see one photo at a time, enlarged so that you can see the details. Just double-click the thumbnail image to see the picture in a large area (such as the one in Figure 17.3), where you can edit the image, email it to someone, or print it. Click the Back to Gallery button to return to the gallery of images.

If you hold the Ctrl key on your keyboard and move your mouse or trackball's scroll wheel, your picture thumbnails increase or decrease in size (depending on the direction you scroll).

Did you Know?

Click to rate picture

FIGURE 17.3
When working
with a single
image, Photo
Gallery shows
you only that
image and not
the thumbnail
list of other pic-
tures that would
get in your way.

Did you
Know?

In both the thumbnail and single picture views, you can easily change the rating of
any photo by clicking the appropriate star in Photo Gallery's right window pane.
(Click Info if you don't see the rating pane.) In addition to giving a picture a star
rating, you can click the Add Tags button below the rating area to add one or more
tags, separated by semicolons, to the picture. If a tag hasn't been used before, a
new tag appears in your navigation pane when you expand the Tags entry. If you
apply a tag that's been used, the picture appears along with the other matching
tagged pictures when you click that tag in the navigation pane.

Because doing anything with your digital picture collection requires that you view
the pictures in a manner that suits the job you must do, learning how to view pictures in various ways is important. There are times when you need a bird's eye view
of your pictures and the thumbnail images are more helpful than a close-up view of
individual pictures.

Did you
Know?

When viewing thumbnails, if you point to a thumbnail image, Photo Gallery temporarily pops up a window that is larger than the thumbnail view, but smaller than
the full-screen, single image view, so you can see more of the picture's detail without having to change from the thumbnail view in many cases.

Fortunately, Photo Gallery uses methods similar to Media Player, so how you view your picture files will be familiar to you. The navigation pane on the left side of your Photo Gallery window is the place you should go first. Click on any of the items: Recently Imported, Tags, Pictures, Videos (Photo Gallery enables you to manage your videos if you want to, just as it does your photographs, although Media Gallery is a better place to view videos), Date Taken, Ratings, and Folders.

If you don't see all the pictures that you expect to see in your Photo Gallery window, you might have to click the navigation pane's Folders entry and locate your Pictures folder. From there, you can open subfolders to view any pictures in those folders.

Always keep in mind Photo Gallery's navigation pane at the left of your screen. Some people get confused about where pictures reside (and video locations because Photo Gallery enables you to tag and track videos, too) and how to display them.

The Folders entry, shown in Figure 17.4, contains every folder that Photo Gallery currently uses. If you see only the Pictures folder in the Folders entry, click the arrow to the left of Pictures to see subfolders from which Photo Gallery is also getting pictures to work with.

Click to expand   Click to see all videos

Click to see all pictures

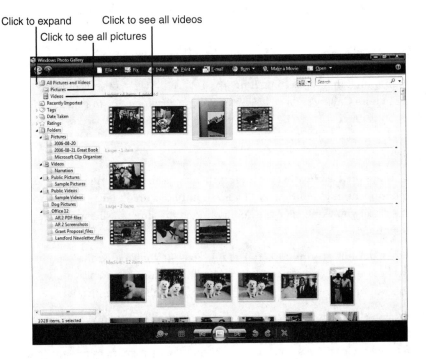

FIGURE 17.4
You can see individual folders of pictures or all your pictures at once.

When you click a folder, Photo Gallery shows you all pictures from that folder and any subfolders beneath that folder. If any of those folders also have videos, Photo Gallery displays the videos, too. Instead of clicking a folder, if you click the Pictures entry toward the top of your navigation pane, all pictures from all of Photo Gallery's collection appear. If you cannot see images that you know reside on your disk somewhere, follow the directions in the previous section to add that location to your Photo Gallery's image gallery. After you do so, the images' folder appears under the Folders entry and the images will appear when you click the Pictures link under All Pictures and Videos.

You can click any entry in the navigation pane to expand or collapse that entry. For example, to see every tag you've given to pictures, click the Tags entry, and Tags expands to list all tags available for every image in Photo Gallery. Click Tags again and the list collapses back to the single Tags entry. Click Recently Imported, Date Taken, or Ratings to see images ordered by those criteria.

You can view your images in all these ways, but when you want to see all your pictures, or perhaps all your videos, don't mess with the Folders, Tags, or Ratings entries. Just click Pictures or Videos under All Pictures and Videos, and Photo Gallery lists every single item with a thumbnail view in its center window pane.

Using Photo Gallery's Control Panel

The control panel that looks something like a video player's controls appears at the bottom of Photo Gallery's screens. Whether you're viewing a list of thumbnails or working on a single image, the control panel is there to give you access to some common Photo Gallery tasks. Figure 17.5 labels each of the control panel's controls as follows:

▶ **Change the Display Size**—Changes the image size of the image or images that appear in Photo Gallery; if your thumbnails aren't large enough to see the detail you want, click the Zoom button and drag the slider up to enlarge the images.

▶ **Reset Default Thumbnails to Default Size**—If you've used the Zoom control to change the level of zoom used in the Photo Gallery window, you can click this button to reset the display to the default level of magnification.

▶ **Previous**—Moves the selection one image to the left. When viewing thumbnails, the Previous button only moves the highlighted image back one image. But when viewing a single picture, clicking Previous changes the image to the image that falls before it in the current view. For example, if you clicked a navigation pane Tag entry named Summer Vacation 2008, the thumbnails would show only the images with that tag. If you double-clicked to show only one of that summer vacation's images, and then began clicking Previous, Photo Gallery would move backward through the summer-vacation-tagged images. When it got to the first tagged image, the next time you clicked Previous the images would wrap around so that the last summer vacation picture would appear.

▶ **Play Slide Show**—Displays your images (all or only some, depending on what you're viewing at the time) in a full-screen slideshow presentation. In doing so, Photo Gallery transitions between the images smoothly and slowly changes depending on which theme you've selected. By moving your mouse during the slideshow, a slideshow control panel appears. Using it, you can change the theme and speed, manually move forward or backward through the slideshow, pause the slideshow, change the volume of the background music (this assumes that you selected at least one video to display, along with optional pictures, before starting the slideshow), and end the slideshow.

Press Esc to end the slideshow.

Did you Know?

▶ **Next**—Moves the selection one image to the right. This button operates in the same way as the Previous button. So, when viewing thumbnails, the Next button moves the highlighted image forward only one image, but when viewing a single picture, clicking Next changes the image to the one that appears after it in the current view.

▶ **Rotate Counterclockwise**—Rotates the selected image 90 degrees (a quarter of a complete rotation) to the left.

▶ **Rotate Clockwise**—Rotates the selected image 90 degrees (a quarter of a complete rotation) to the right.

▶ **Delete**—Erases the selected picture (or video). Photo Gallery erases the picture from your disk drive, so be sure that you want to delete the picture or video before clicking Yes at the verification prompt.

FIGURE 17.5
Use Photo Gallery's control panel to move through your images and perform routine maintenance.

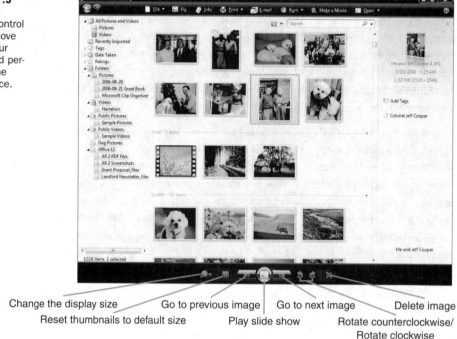

Change the display size   Go to previous image │ Go to next image   Delete image
Reset thumbnails to default size   Play slide show   Rotate counterclockwise/
                                                                    Rotate clockwise

Fix a Photo with Photo Gallery's Editing Tools

If you need to make routine edits to an image, Photo Gallery will help. When editing a photo, Photo Gallery displays the image in full-screen mode to prevent thumbnail images of other pictures from getting in the way.

To edit a picture, double-click it. Alternatively, you can click to select the image and click the Fix button from the toolbar. Photo Gallery displays the full-screen view of the picture and puts editing tools in the right window pane, as shown in Figure 17.6.

By the Way

> The Fix button isn't available when viewing your video thumbnails because Photo Gallery cannot edit videos. Chapter 19, "Making Movies with Windows Movie Maker," explains how you can use Movie Maker to edit videos.

Too dark

Editing tools

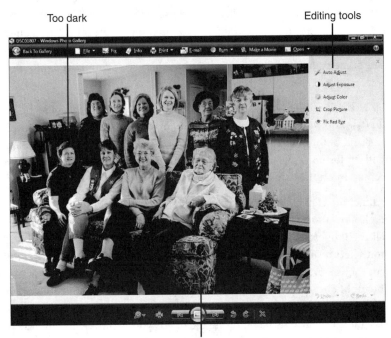

Picture needs to be cropped

FIGURE 17.6
Photo Gallery's editing tools enable you to crop and fix routine picture problems.

In Figure 17.6's picture, the image needs cropped. It was scanned and the scanner's bed was much larger than the image itself. In addition, the image is dark and doesn't contrast well.

One of the first edits you'll want to make to any photo that needs fixing is to click the Auto Adjust link. Auto Adjust corrects and sometimes sharpens your images. Auto Adjust doesn't modify brightness or cropping, but can sometimes fix a picture all by itself.

> Ctrl+Z, the Undo command, reverses any fix you make to your photo. If Auto Adjust or any other fix changes a picture too dramatically, press Ctrl+Z to reverse the fix. An Undo button also appears at the bottom of your tools pane to enable you to undo the most recent edit or revert the image back to its original, unedited state.

By the Way

You don't have to rely on Photo Gallery's skill at auto-adjusting your photos. You can take the reins yourself. If you want to adjust the picture's brightness or contrast, click the Adjust Exposure link. Two slider controls open that enable you to adjust the picture's brightness and contrast. Click the Adjust Color link to display slider controls for Color Temperature, Tint, and Saturation. Bad or artificial lighting often affects these three properties when taking a picture. By using these controls on a picture where some colors seem to overwhelm the others, you can fix the color problems.

The Crop Picture tool allows you to cut off an unwanted portion of the picture. One reason to crop a picture is that you scanned an image into Photo Gallery and you want to get rid of the blank area that surrounds the scanned image. Cropping is also useful for losing the surrounding area in a photo where you would prefer to have zoomed in on the subject.

To crop a picture, click the Crop Picture tool link. A rectangular highlight appears over the photo with resizing handles at its four corners. Click to open the drop-down list under the Proportion title to see a list of common picture sizes such as 8 × 10. When you select a size, the cropping highlight changes to that size and proportion. With your mouse, drag any resizing handle to move, expand, or shrink the highlight. The highlight will change but retain the proportions of the picture size you first selected. Click within the highlight to move the highlight without changing its size. The goal is to retain as much of the picture as you require, filling up the proportion that you need. If you're going to print this picture on wallet-sized 3 × 5 photo paper, you would select the 3 × 5 proportion to ensure that the final cropped image is in that proportion.

Did you Know?

If you click the down arrow to display the Proportion drop-down list in the tool area and select Custom, two more resizing handles appear on the crop's highlighting area. You can now drag any of the six resizing handles in or out to cover those areas. The Custom proportion is useful if you want to use an image on the Web, or perhaps view the picture only in a slideshow or from Media Center when you don't have to worry about a common printed picture proportion size such as 3 × 5 or 8 × 10.

By the Way

The Rotate Frame button rotates the cropping frame so that instead of using a 3 × 5 frame, for example, the cropping highlight frame rotates to a 5 × 3 proportion (longer than taller). You might want to rotate the frame when you work on landscape pictures.

After you move and size the highlight to the part of the picture you want to save, click the Apply button and Photo Gallery crops the picture. Figure 17.7 shows Figure 17.6's picture after editing. The cropping worked to make the entire picture fill the frame area by eliminating all the blank space around the image. In addition, the Auto Adjust and Adjust Exposure tools sharpened the picture and brought it into a better light and exposure.

FIGURE 17.7
A badly cropped and underexposed picture now looks better.

Red eye occasionally occurs when taking pictures of animals or people with flash photography. Sometimes, the eye's response to the flash causes a reddish tint to occur on the eye. To fix red eye problems, select a picture with red eye and click the Fix button to display the image repair tools. Click the Fix Red Eye link and then drag your mouse to form a rectangle around one of the eyes in the picture with the red eye problem, as shown in Figure 17.8. When you release your mouse, Photo Gallery analyzes the problem and adjusts the picture to reduce or eliminate the red eye.

When you click the Back to Gallery button to return to the thumbnail image gallery after fixing a picture, the thumbnail will reflect your repairs on that picture.

FIGURE 17.8
Photo Gallery can reduce or eliminate red eye problems in your pictures of pets and family.

Printing Pictures from Photo Gallery

To print one or more pictures, select the picture or pictures you want to print. Press Ctrl+A to select every picture whose thumbnail is in view. After you select the pictures to print, click the Print button's down arrow and select Print. Photo Gallery's Print Pictures dialog box appears.

Watch Out!

You cannot print videos or their thumbnails from within Photo Gallery.

As you can see in Figure 17.9, Photo Gallery's Print dialog box doesn't look like most Windows applications' Print dialog boxes. Printing pictures offers some unique challenges in comparison to printing documents and charts to paper. Pictures often print based on standard sizes to match frames, wallets, and other traditional picture holders. If you have a photo printer, you probably purchased photo paper based on one of the standard sizes and Photo Gallery will ensure that the picture conforms to the size you need.

If you selected multiple pictures to print, the Print Pictures dialog box shows only the first picture so that you can tell Photo Gallery how you want that picture printed. You then can click the right arrow below the picture preview area to display and adjust the print settings for each subsequent picture.

Scroll to see more sizes

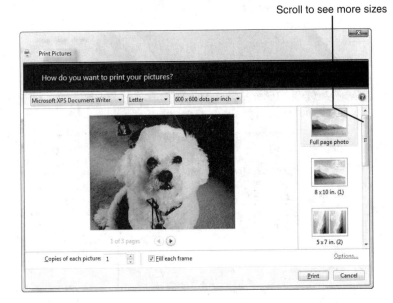

FIGURE 17.9
Photo Gallery's
Print Pictures
dialog box
ensures that
you can print
your pictures
based on tradi-
tional picture
sizes when the
need arises.

Click to tell Photo Gallery how many copies you want to print of each picture by changing the value next to the Copies of Each Picture prompt.

Scroll down to see additional picture sizes. Some of the sizes provide for more than one picture per page. For example, suppose that you select three pictures to print and you want to print wallet photos of those pictures. When you scroll to the Wallet size, you'll see that you can print up to nine pictures on each page of wallet-sized photos.

How do you want to print those nine pictures? If you tell Photo Gallery that you want nine copies of each picture, Photo Gallery will print three pages with nine wallet-size pictures on each page, one page for each of your pictures. If, instead, you tell Photo Gallery you want to print only three of each of the pictures, Photo Gallery will print all three pictures on one page for nine wallet-size photos as shown in Figure 17.10.

Select the printer you want to print to, the paper size, and the resolution you want to use by clicking and selecting from the three buttons across the preview area. You might want to print a sample page at a low resolution to save on printer ink. If the sample comes out the way you want, you can reprint multiple copies at a higher print resolution. After setting the appropriate options, click the Print button to start printing.

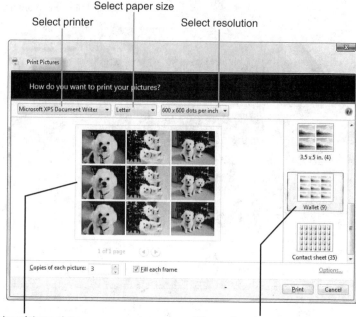

FIGURE 17.10
Photo Gallery adjusts the number of prints you want to the number of prints per page to maximize your page use.

The figure shows labels: Select printer, Select paper size, Select resolution, Three copies of three pictures, Nine wallet pictures selected.

The Options link in the Print Picture dialog box's lower-right corner provides picture-sharpening, color-management, and printer properties options you can select, depending on what your printer allows.

Send Your Photos to a Professional Photo Service

Through Photo Gallery you can order prints online and the professional service you choose will mail your prints to you. If you want to explore this option, select the pictures you want to send away for printing and click the Print button's arrow to display the Order Prints option. Select a service from those listed, such as Shutterfly, and click Send Pictures.

It's always possible that Microsoft *could* add or change services used for your photo processing over time. If you sign up for a service and Photo Gallery stops accepting that service, you can almost surely stay with that service and access it through your web browser. If Microsoft no longer has a Photo Gallery relationship set up, that only means that you cannot access the service through Photo Gallery.

Photo Gallery opens a new window for the service, such as the one shown in Figure 17.11. If it's the first time you've made use of the service, you'll be required to go through a preliminary sign-up process. Signing up often includes a free trial membership, such as 15 free prints the first time you order, but in any case you're usually required to tell the service who you are, create an account, and provide credit card payment information. (Even if your initial print order is free, odds are good that you'll still have to pay shipping fees.) After you have an account with a service, however, you'll only need to sign in by clicking the Sign In button, and entering your username and password. At that point, you can order as many prints as you like.

FIGURE 17.11
Photo Gallery offers at least one online professional photo service that you can send your digital images to for processing.

When you sign in, you specify the number and size of prints you want. Prices are given next to each size. Scroll down to make sure that you complete the specifications for each image you select to print. After you place your order, the prints usually arrive within a few days.

Look through the options available in the photo printing service, or services, available before you decide on one. You might want to try the free trial membership of all services before selecting one to do business with on a more permanent basis. Some of them will offer to put your images on coffee cups, T-shirts, mouse pads, and other fun things.

Did you Know?

If you have no photo printer and don't want to use one of the online services, most picture processing drugstores and department stores (such as Wal-Mart) accept a CD or DVD burned with your images. They'll produce prints for you, often for less than an online service can do. It means you must travel to the store to leave your CD or DVD and pick up the prints instead of getting them in the mail, but the service is typically cheaper and faster. (Although Wal-Mart and other retailers allow you to upload to their websites, so the only thing left to do on your part is to pick up the prints.)

The next section explains how to store Photo Gallery images on a data DVD.

Put Pictures and Videos on DVDs

Photo Gallery can put your pictures and videos onto DVDs for others to watch in the PC's DVD drive or in a standalone DVD player. Photo Gallery does this in one of three ways:

- ▶ A data DVD
- ▶ A video DVD
- ▶ A movie that you edit and place on a DVD

The following sections explain each of these methods.

Creating a Backup Data DVD

With Photo Gallery, you can easily back up your pictures to a DVD. To create a DVD backup, place a blank DVD into your writeable DVD drive. Click the down arrow on Photo Gallery's Burn button and select Data Disc. Photo Gallery opens the Burn a Disc dialog box that you can add a title to. When you click Next, Photo Gallery begins preparing the DVD.

First, Photo Gallery must format your DVD. This can take a while, sometimes 15 to 20 minutes if you have a slow DVD burner. When formatting finishes, Photo Gallery sends your selected pictures and videos to the DVD. Put the disc in a safe place, preferably at a location different from your computer so that a disaster such as a fire won't ruin both sets of your pictures.

To back up your entire Photo Gallery image and video gallery, click All Pictures and Video in the navigation pane (the top option) before making the data disc. Photo Gallery sends all your pictures and videos to the DVD as a backup disc (assuming that they'll all fit). If you have a large collection of high-quality image files, you might need more than one disc.

Creating a Video DVD Using Windows DVD Maker

Photo Gallery can create DVDs that do more than work as simple data backups for your pictures and videos. You can create DVDs with Photo Gallery that become video DVDs. Many DVD players can play video DVDs that present your pictures in a slideshow fashion. In addition to the pictures, you can add video and audio to the DVD slideshow. You can even set up DVD menus to give quick access to various parts of your video DVD.

Photo Gallery accesses a Windows Vista program called Windows DVD Maker to create your video DVDs.

By the Way

To begin creating a video DVD, click the arrow below Burn and select Video DVD. Photo Gallery opens the Windows DVD Maker window shown in Figure 17.12 and displays your pictures in a scrolling list. Rearrange the pictures and videos by dragging them to a different order one at a time, or by selecting one and clicking the Move Up and Move Down buttons. Add items you failed to select by clicking the Add Items button and remove items you decide against putting in your video DVD by clicking the Remove Items button. As you add more and remove items, the running time of your video DVD updates in the window's lower-left corner.

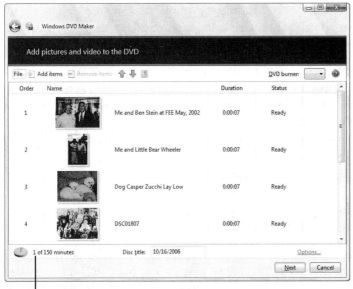

FIGURE 17.12
Photo Gallery produces video DVDs from your videos and pictures.

Time consumed by your video DVD

The Options link in the lower-right corner opens an Options dialog box where you can specify your DVD's

▶ Aspect ratio (4:3 or 16:9, depending on the type of display you use; the default is the standard computer monitor's ratio of 4:3)

▶ Playback style (you can choose to loop the video automatically or use a DVD menu)

▶ Video format (either NTSC [the North American video standard] or PAL, which most other countries use)

After you select the pictures, videos, and their order, click Next to work on the DVD's menu, assuming that you chose to use a menu in the Options dialog box. On the menu window, select the menu style you want to use from the options at the right by scrolling through the list. As you click to select sample menu styles, the preview window changes to show you how the DVD's menu will look. Some get rather fancy; however, you should consider not only the style but also the options. Most menu themes enable anyone viewing the DVD to select Play or Scenes so that they can play the video DVD straight through or select from one of several scenes that Windows DVD Maker will insert in your video at fixed time intervals.

After you select the menu style, click Menu Text and type a disc title (so that the date you create the DVD, which is the default title, isn't used in place of something more appropriate). In the Notes field, you can enter notes that the user will see when her or she clicks the Notes option before or after playing the video DVD.

Click Save to save the DVD menu, title, and notes. To customize your video DVD further, click Customize. On the Customize window, you can select foreground and background videos that play during the menu sequences and an audio file that plays anytime the user displays the video DVD's menu. If you want a still image to appear behind your menu select a digital picture instead of a video. After you finish setting these customization options, the final step is to click Slide Show if your video DVD is comprised of pictures and not videos or a combination of videos.

Your video DVD does imitate Photo Gallery's slideshow when the video DVD contains only pictures to display. The music and transition effects can make such a movement from picture to picture much more enjoyable for your viewers. You can turn the slide show into a training video if you record narration over the slides, but getting the timing correct is not an easy thing to do. If you want to create slideshow training video DVDs, you should probably transfer the training images to Movie Maker and create the training video there, where you have much more freedom in the synchronization between audio clips and the video scenes.

Did you Know?

If you begin to change something on your video DVD, such as the menu style, and decide you want to go back a step in the process, click the Back button in the Windows DVD Maker's upper-left corner.

At the Slide Show Settings window, you can add music that the DVD plays while the user views the pictures. You can set a default time, in seconds, for each picture to appear, and select a transition effect that occurs every time the video DVD changes from one picture to another.

Click Save to save your Slide Show Settings and return to the primary Windows DVD Maker window. You're almost done now. Figure 17.13 shows a sample DVD Maker window that has all its options completed. You can click the Preview button to generate an onscreen preview before burning the DVD. If the preview has problems, you can change the video DVD settings. After you finalize your video DVD, place a blank, writeable DVD in your writeable DVD drive and click Start Burn to burn your video DVD.

FIGURE 17.13
Photo Gallery reduces the size of pictures you send to others in email attachments.

When Windows DVD Maker finishes writing your video DVD to the DVD, Windows Vista ejects the disc from your DVD drive and displays a small dialog box asking whether you want to create another DVD of the video. You can keep clicking the Duplicate This Disc option and burn as many DVDs as you need. When you finish burning the final DVD, click Close and you return to Photo Gallery.

Creating a Movie from Photo Gallery Images and Videos

If you click the Make a Movie button, Photo Gallery, automatically starts Windows Movie Maker and transfers any selected pictures and videos to Movie Maker. From there, you can edit together the movie you want to make and save the movie to a DVD. Chapter 19, "Making Movies with Windows Movie Maker," explains how to use Movie Maker.

Send Pictures and Videos in Email Messages

Surely there will be times when you want to send pictures and videos to someone else. Email is a quick choice as long as you are careful not to overload your recipient's inbox with huge files. It's not considered appropriate to send tens of megabytes of pictures to someone as email attachments unless you've written or spoken to them first. If your recipient has a dial-up Internet connection, several megabytes or more of email attachments will bog down both email and web browsing activities, so make sure that the recipient expects a large attachment and knows to give it some time.

Even if your recipient has high-speed Internet, such as a cable modem, DSL, or T1 line, you should get permission to send large attachments. Some email services limit the size of an email attachment to around 5MB and your email might never get through.

Always send a follow-up email telling the recipient how many emails you sent with attached pictures and videos. That way, if their email service blocked your emails, your recipient can let you know that your items didn't get through. You might decide to send a CD or DVD with the pictures instead of using email.

The nice thing about Photo Gallery is that if you do want to send some pictures to someone else using email, Photo Gallery will give you the option of reducing those pictures to a smaller size before sending them.

Photo Gallery will not reduce the size of videos you send. Surprisingly, short videos can be massive, easily reaching 10 or more megabytes of space even though the video might only be seconds long. It's typically unwise to send all but the smallest of videos to someone as an email attachment. CDs and DVDs sent by regular mail are much better options.

When you select pictures or videos to send to someone as an email attachment, Photo Gallery displays the dialog box shown in Figure 17.14. Click to open the drop-down list next to Picture Size and select the size you want Photo Gallery to use for your pictures in the email. The total estimated file size is the size of *all* your selected pictures. If you find that the smallest size still results in an email attachment that's too large, you might have to cancel the email request and select fewer pictures. Sending eight emails that are 1.5MB each is wiser than trying to send one email with a 12MB attachment.

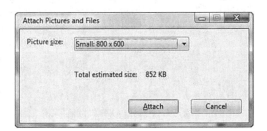

FIGURE 17.14
Photo Gallery will reduce the size of pictures you send to others in email attachments.

You will want to select the highest size possible that won't bog down the email. When you approach 3–4MB or higher, you're beginning to reach the limit and you might want to reduce the size or the number of emails you select to send at once.

When you get the best-fit size and number, click the Attach button. Photo Gallery compresses the images according to the size you selected, opens an email message, and fills in the attachment field as shown in Figure 17.15. The email system used is your system's default mail program. Generally, this will be Windows Mail (formerly Outlook Express), Microsoft Outlook, or Eudora. If you use an online email service, such as Hotmail or Gmail, that service's message window will open if you've set that service as your default email provider. You now must fill in the recipient's email address and subject, and click Send to send your message with the attachments.

Photo Gallery shrinks the image sizes that you send as attachments but does *not* actually change the stored images themselves. They retain their original resolution. Only the attachments are smaller.

By the Way

FIGURE 17.15
Photo Gallery opens a new email message and automatically attaches your compressed picture files.

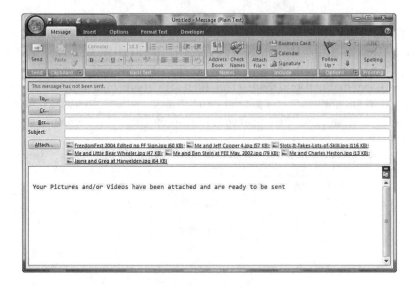

Chapter Wrap-Up

As you've seen in this chapter, Photo Gallery not only enables you to organize and view your pictures and videos, it also gives you a way to edit your pictures and correct problems such as poor lighting and red eye.

After you get your images in shape, you can print them to your photographic printer using photo paper for picture-quality prints. If you don't have a photo printer, you can use one of Photo Gallery's available online services to send your images over the Internet and go to your mailbox in two or three days to retrieve your prints.

Although Photo Gallery doesn't give you all the features of a more complex program, such as Google's free Picasa and Adobe's full-featured Photoshop Elements, it is a major functional leap past Windows XP's picture tools.

Now that you've learned how to work with digital images and videos, it's time to switch over to sound. The next chapter shows you how to use the Windows Sound Recorder to make recordings.

CHAPTER 18

Recording Simple Audio

In This Chapter:

▶ Understand how recorded digital audio can be helpful

▶ Learn about Sound Recorder's format and file quality

▶ Get sound to your computer

▶ See which microphone works best

▶ Make a test recording

▶ Review helpful recording tips

Windows Vista includes a small application called Sound Recorder that enables you to make recordings and save them as digital audio files on your disk. The program doesn't have lots of bells and whistles, but it's stable and provides a reliable way to record sound that you can use for narration, note taking, and recording other sounds and events that you want to save digitally.

To record audio with Sound Recorder, all you need is a source for the sound. That might be a direct cable you run from a stereo or a microphone plugged into your computer to record your voice. Sound Recorder has been around since the early days of Windows. Surprisingly, in Windows Vista, Microsoft *removed* rather then added features to the Sound Recorder application. What appears in Windows Vista is lean and mean, and this short chapter explains how you can use Sound Recorder to get the most out of your digital audio.

Why Audio

In addition to the obvious need to add sound over videos and slideshows, you might want to record sound and save the recording to your computer for a variety of reasons. Consider these possibilities:

▶ **Record meetings and lectures**—With your laptop you can record meetings and lectures instead of taking copious handwritten notes. By recording the meeting or lecture, you can listen better and concentrate on what's going on. Later, your recorded audio file serves as a backup if you want to refer to something that was said.

▶ **Record quick notes**—With your laptop, you'll never need a miniature tape or voice recorder. Laptops eliminated the need for portable CD players, DVD players, and pocket organizers years ago and now you can toss your portable recorder, too. Your laptop might be larger than all those devices but you need to carry only the laptop now, instead of carrying your laptop *and* all those other devices when you travel.

▶ **Record speech for emails**—Say hello to friends and family when you travel. Record audio files and send those files as email attachments.

▶ **Record vinyl records**—Get an appropriate cable from your local electronics store and you're ready to use Sound Recorder to record those old vinyl records you no longer listen to because of the hassle of playing them on a turntable. Put the files on your PC and then record them to a CD so that you can listen to them in your car on your next cross-country trip.

▶ **Record audio for web pages**—How can you put your voice into digital audio files that you want to send to the web or a blog? Sound Recorder works well for doing just that and if you create Podcasts you can drop your Sound Recorder files right onto your site's Podcast launcher.

Sound Recorder is adequate for these kinds of jobs. Anything more would be overkill and would create high-quality sound files that would quickly consume disk space and would not load fast with a web page. Worse, sending a huge audio file in a high-quality format would clog some email systems, causing them to reject the emails you send with those kinds of attachments.

If you want a full-blown, PC-based recording studio, you'll certainly need something other than Sound Recorder. Programs such as Cakewalk and Composer do a good job and you can connect your computer to good recording equipment that will turn sound into high-quality digital files before sending those files to your computer for processing. Sound Recorder doesn't compete with those high-end programs and your computer doesn't compete with the high-end hardware. Instead, Sound Recorder is meant to give you quick access to simple digital audio recordings.

By the Way

Some complain about Sound Recorder's lack of features that would turn it into a full-fledged recording studio application. Although such a full-featured application might be nice, it wasn't Microsoft's intent to offer so sophisticated a program. When you need a quick and reliable way to get sound into a file for later playback, Sound Recorder does the job nicely.

Perhaps in a future operating system Microsoft will include a sound recorder in Media Player. As it stands now, Media Player cannot record audio; it can only play audio and it plays audio very well indeed.

About Sound Recorder's Format and Quality

Sound Recorder records in the Windows Media Audio format. When you save a recording, the digital audio file has these properties:

- **Filename Extension**—.wma

- **Sound Quality Bit Rate**—96Kbps

- **Size of Audio File**—11KB per second of recording; a five-minute recording consumes about 3.5MB of disk space

- **Sample Rate**—44.1kHz; comparable to a good quality, portable tape recorder using high quality tape

By the Way

You learned in Chapter 15, "Managing Your Entertainment Experience with Media Player," that 192Kbps is the minimum recording rate when you need high-quality audio. Sound Recorder's 96Kbps is half that rate, so the quality is nowhere near that approaching CD quality. Again, this is fine as long as you know the proper role that Sound Recorder plays in your system's multimedia toolset.

If you run a Windows Vista operating system with the letter N in the title, such as the Windows Home Basic N, Media Player is not included in your system; you can download Windows Media Player from Microsoft.com if you want to use Windows Media Player on such systems. Without Media Player, the player for which .wma files were designed, you might not be able to play back .wma files easily. Therefore, for N-based operating systems, Microsoft saves Sound Recorder files in the WAVE form audio format with these properties:

▶ **Filename Extension**—.wav

▶ **Sound Quality Bit Rate**—96Kbps

▶ **Size of Audio File**—1,378K per second of recording; a five-minute recording consumes about 51MB of disk space

▶ **Sample Rate**—44.1kHz; comparable to a good quality, portable tape recorder using high quality tape

As you can see, Media Player's .wma files are compressed and consume far less disk space than file formats of similar quality, such as WAVE files. That is perhaps why so many MP3 players (the iPod excepted) now support the .wma format along with MP3.

Physically Getting Sound to Your Computer

Sound Recorder requires a sound card and speakers (or a headset plugged into your computer sound card's output jack). Some PCs have jacks for a microphone and headset or speakers in the front of the computer as well as in the back. You'll have to locate yours.

If you want to record your voice or meeting and lecture notes, your laptop might have a built-in microphone already. The recording quality of a built-in microphone will not be as good as using a separate microphone, so you should consider using a standalone microphone for all your sound recording. Some PC microphones use a plug that connects to your sound card or front panel microphone-in jack and some PC microphones are USB-based.

Some microphones work as handhelds or can be placed on your desktop, whereas others, such as the one in Figure 18.1, are headset based. Also, webcams often have microphones built into them if you happen to have a webcam attached to your computer. A headset microphone includes one or two earphones as well as a micro-phone that wraps around to your mouth area. A headset microphone creates a much better recording of your voice than a separate microphone that you hold near your mouth.

Obviously, your recording needs dictate the type of microphone you use. A headset cannot record ambient sounds around the room that you would need for recording lectures and meetings.

FIGURE 18.1
A headset-based micro-phone provides far better sound recording quali-ty than a stand-alone micro-phone that you hold or place on a table.

If you connect a stereo cable from a stereo, television, or other electronic device into your computer's line-in or microphone-in jack, you can use Sound Recorder to record the sound. Don't rely on Sound Recorder for high-quality music recording even if you are sending a high-quality signal from a good stereo to your computer. The recorded sound file properties shown in the previous section for Sound Recorder's .wma or .wav files determine the highest quality possible; the sound source doesn't determine Sound Recorder's quality.

Introducing Sound Recorder

Sound Recorder serves as one of the best ways to test your computer's microphone and sound quality even if you're using your microphone for something else. Suppose that you are anxious to try out Windows Vista's speech recognition technology or want to make phone calls from your computer to others with computer-based phone technologies such as eBay's Skype calling (see www.Skype.com). Plug in your micro-phone and start Sound Recorder to create a sample and listen to ensure that your microphone and sound levels are accurate.

> Chapter 23, "Speaking to Your Computer," explains how to access Vista's speech recognition tools.

By the Way

Sound Recorder provides instant feedback that it's hearing sound. It does this through a visual display that shows you a moving, green light that varies with vol-ume and pitch. If you've ever seen a graphic equalizer on a stereo system, Sound Recorder's visual sound gauge works something like that (although not as finely tuned). Look at Figure 18.2 to see a recording in session.

FIGURE 18.2
The louder the sound and the higher the pitch of what you record, the wider Sound Recorder's sound display gets.

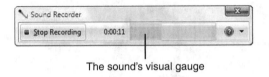

The sound's visual gauge

As you can see, Sound Recorder isn't fancy. It doesn't need to be fancy.

Making a Test Recording

If you have a microphone or line-in jack set up and you want to try Sound Recorder, you can do so by following these steps:

1. Start Sound Recorder from the Windows menu's Accessories option. The only control on Sound Recorder's small window is the Start Recording button.

2. Click Start Recording and speak into your microphone. As you speak, Sound Recorder's green recording bar moves to the right to indicate volume level. If the volume is too great, you can back up from your microphone or speak softer. If your microphone seems to work but is not loud enough, your microphone's recording level might be set too low; you can adjust the volume in your Control Panel.

By the Way

> If your recording source is a stereo jack, you might have to turn down the output from your stereo considerably before Sound Recorder can record at a reasonable volume.

If your microphone is plugged in but no sound appears to be coming from it, you should check the Sound dialog box, available through the Control Panel's Hardware and Sound group, to ensure that Windows Vista is set to recognize your microphone.

Select your microphone from the list of devices and then click the Properties button and click the Levels tab to display the Levels dialog box shown in Figure 18.3. Drag the microphone slider to the right to increase the microphone's volume. You might have to adjust the volume several times before arriving at a good level. When you get to a good microphone level, you'll rarely have to adjust the level in the future. If your recording level is still too low, the Other tab usually displays a MIC Boost option you can check to add volume to your microphone input level.

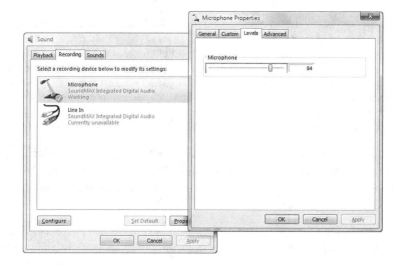

FIGURE 18.3
If your micro-
phone recording
level isn't high
enough, you
might have to
adjust the level
from your Control
Panel's Sound
dialog box.

3. To temporarily stop recording, click the Stop Recording button and click Cancel when the Save As dialog box appears. You can resume the recording by clicking the Resume Recording button.

4. When finished recording, click Stop Recording. Sound Recorder displays the Save As dialog box shown in Figure 18.4.

FIGURE 18.4
When you finish
recording your
message, save
your audio
recording and
specify a name
for the .wma (or
.wav) file.

5. The Save As dialog box does more than specify your digital audio file's name. You can add an artist and album tag. This might be useful when you are recording old LP records from a turntable so that you can listen to your records electronically. The artist and album details will appear in Media Player when you play the recording there, and you can specify further details (such as your star rating preference) about the song when it arrives in Media Player.

If you're not recording record albums or other type of stereo but are recording meeting notes or dictating audio you want to record, you should consider filling in the Artist information field. For the Album Title field, only add a note that describes the recording. This way you'll have more than just a filename to locate the recording in the future. To enter these details, click the Artist and the Album Title fields and replace the placeholder text that appears with more specific and descriptive information about your recording.

Before clicking the Save button, you can click the breadcrumbs at the top of the dialog box's address area to find a disk location where you want to store your recording if you don't want to store the recording in the default Documents location.

If you click the Browse Folders button, your Save As dialog box expands to include far more fields, including a star rating that you can give your recording like the one shown in Figure 18.5. The more information you save with your recording at the time you make it, the more accurate your sound file information will be. It's often difficult to go back a week or more later and remember, based solely on the filename you gave them, what several digital recordings were about.

FIGURE 18.5
Expand the Save As dialog box to enter more labeling information about your recording.

As soon as you save the file, all the descriptive data you attached to the recording in the Save As dialog box is available to Media Player and other Explorer programs that display files.

6. Click Save to save your recording. The Sound Recorder resets and displays a Start Recording button again in case you want to start a new recording.

Simple Recording Tips You Can Use

Audio professionals will tell you that most people, when speaking in a microphone, do it badly. People practically kiss the device by holding it too closely or behave as though they're afraid of it by keeping the microphone too far away. No doubt you've seen this happen on TV when someone in an audience is handed a microphone.

In addition, amateur recorders tend to underestimate how much the sound around them, the **ambient sound**, can contribute to background buzzing and distractions that can impair the overall quality of the recording. For example, if you place your microphone too close to your PC itself, you might pick up the hum of the computer's power supply and internal fans. With that in mind, try these tips for best results:

▶ Position your microphone a few inches from your mouse. This is true for both handheld microphones and headset microphones. It's often best when your mouth and the microphone are not in direct alignment or you will record the pops in your breathing.

▶ Don't place your microphone too close to your PC speakers, telephone, or monitor. You might get a low, humming interference or feedback whine if you do.

▶ Rheostats and fluorescent lights can produce some noisy interference when recording.

▶ If the microphone has its own volume control, start with its volume turned to a medium level.

▶ Turn off or close any programs that beep or otherwise play sounds (such as the tone that plays when new email arrives or when you receive an instant message).

▶ Take a moment to check the background sound level in the room where you record. Try to eliminate any extra sounds.

▶ Plan to make a few test recordings before you try for the real thing. Try different microphone levels and positions to see which work best.

Sound Recorder might not record the highest quality sound, but you don't need to hamper it further by violating some of these recording tips. By keeping these tips in mind, you help to ensure that whatever you record is playable when you want to listen to your recording later.

Chapter Wrap-Up

A microphone adds an important dimension to a computer. With Sound Recorder, you can record web or email audio files. Take your laptop with you to lectures or meetings and record the event to reduce the amount of note-taking you would otherwise have to do.

Although Sound Recorder is simple, that's also its beauty. For reliable and quick recordings, nothing is easier to use. You'll be creating your own sound files quickly. If you don't have costly recording software, you can even use Sound Recorder to record your vinyl record collection that's been gathering dust for the past decade or longer.

Moving from audio to video, the next chapter explores Movie Maker, one of the most fun applications in Windows Vista. When you see what you can do with Movie Maker you will feel like a Hollywood producer.

CHAPTER 19

Making Movies with Windows Movie Maker

In This Chapter:

▶ Understand Movie Maker's past and present

▶ Plan your videos to produce great movies

▶ Understand Movie Maker's busy screen

▶ Get video into your computer

▶ Work with video clips

▶ Produce your movie

▶ Add special effects, movie titles, and credits

Get your director's chair ready because you're about to enter the world of video editing. Unlike the cut-and-splice film days, editing movies digitally requires no special chemicals—only a good program that can take movie clips, piece them together, add special effects when needed, append titles and credits, and enable you to synchronize the sound with the action.

Windows Vista includes Movie Maker, a program that does all that and more. Technically, Vista's Movie Maker is version 3 and is a nice upgrade from Movie Maker 2. But Movie Maker users drop the 3 when referring to Vista's program. Movie Maker has quietly worked in the background for video-editing buffs without a lot of fanfare, as you'll see in this chapter's first section.

Movie Maker often gets lost in the shuffle of all-in-one movie-production programs. That's a shame. Movie Maker is a fair contender in the video-editing arena of programs and unless you need extremely advanced editing features, Movie Maker will fill just about any editing need.

Movie Maker's Past and Present

When Microsoft first introduced Movie Maker to Windows XP, movie-editing users were unimpressed. They had good reason to be. Movie Maker was originally far too simplistic and far too limited in what it could do. You could edit simple videos, but you were limited in how you could save those videos. Movie Maker's first version didn't support the writing of movies to DVD, its special effects and scene transitions were weak, and the program wasn't intuitive.

Microsoft quickly updated Movie Maker. Windows XP updates gave the new version to existing XP users. Movie Maker 2 was stellar given its free-with-Windows price tag, but Microsoft never really touted Movie Maker 2. Consequently, potential users overlooked a nice video-editing program. Many Windows XP owners ignored Movie Maker 2 and purchased video-editing programs. Most of those video-editing programs were vastly superior to Movie Maker 2, but in many cases, users needed only the tools that Movie Maker 2 already provided.

By the Way

In spite of its vast improvements over the first version, Movie Maker 2 still didn't support saving movies directly to DVD. This missing feature was enough for many to try something else and never learn Movie Maker 2. By 2001 or so, when Microsoft released Movie Maker 2, writing videos to DVD was a reasonable feature to expect. That missing feature alone was enough to convince video-editing buffs to go with other programs and understandably so.

Finally, with Vista, Microsoft has brought Movie Maker's third version into the present by supplying DVD-creation tools and a greater assortment of video-editing capabilities. If you need to edit video files or to produce videos from your own PC, you'll find that Movie Maker might be all you need; if not, you can do a lot of work in Movie Maker without a lot of in-depth training and then move to a more advanced video-editing program, such as Adobe Premiere Elements.

Did you Know?

Please note that it would take a complete book to cover all of Movie Maker's features in depth. This chapter can only skim the surface and give you an overview of what Movie Maker does, and offer some insight in how you'll be able to use Movie Maker. If this chapter whets your movie-making appetite enough, you'll want to get a complete book on Movie Maker. One of the best books on Movie Maker ever written (if I do say so myself) is *Digital Video with Windows In a Snap*, by Greg Perry, Sams Publishing, ISBN 0672325691. This text is a step-by-step, task-oriented training course for Movie Maker and is unique in how it approaches the tasks you'll want to perform when making movies with your PC.

Planning for a Great Video

The right hardware goes a long way in making a great video, but a little planning never hurts either. You can do a lot to boost the quality of your movie before you even pick up your video camera. Obviously, you can't plan those spontaneous videos that you find you need to take, but before you go out to make a video, you might find some of these tips helpful.

Keep the Background in the Background

One thing that makes a video sluggish is a low frame rate. As you know, lots of pictures "pasted" together make up a video. When the pictures are very similar from one frame to another, the computer has to do very little work to refresh the screen and move to the next frame, thus speeding up the frame rate. If, on the other hand, you do a lot of panning (moving from one side to the other) across a wide area or shoot with a "busy" or moving background, video performance is bound to suffer.

When possible, choose solid or static backgrounds. If that isn't possible, try focusing the camera on your primary subject by bringing him or her closer to the lens or using a telephoto lens to zoom in on your subject. This reduces the depth of field, making the background fuzzy and less distracting.

Light Up Your Life

It goes without saying that your video subject should reside among adequate lighting conditions. What kind of lighting is best? Soft, diffuse, and—most importantly—consistent lighting gives the best results. Harsh lighting such as direct sunlight might cause shadows or silhouettes to appear instead of your subject.

It might be worth taking some sample shots before you actually begin filming. Take a few videos, return to your computer, and run them through Movie Maker. This isn't easy or possible when you're on vacation or shooting your kids or pets doing something unexpectedly, but when you have time to plan your video, a preproduction test works wonders to ensure that the final filming goes smoother.

After you do some preproduction testing a few times, you'll have a better idea of how your camera works and how lighting and ambient conditions affect the videos you shoot. You will gain practice and be able to adjust your camera and change lighting settings more accurately when you do run across those spontaneous filming sessions.

The Clothes Make the Video

Believe it or not, the clothes that your video subject wears can dramatically affect the quality of your video. Bright colors can bleed onto the subject's face and other surroundings, and stripes can cause distracting **moiré** patterns (video artifacts that make the lines look like they are crawling or moving onscreen).

Presenting Windows Movie Maker

Before you begin working with Movie Maker, it's a good idea to know your way around its workspace. Figure 19.1 illustrates the parts of the Movie Maker screen.

FIGURE 19.1
Learning your way around Movie Maker is the first step toward understanding how Movie Maker works.

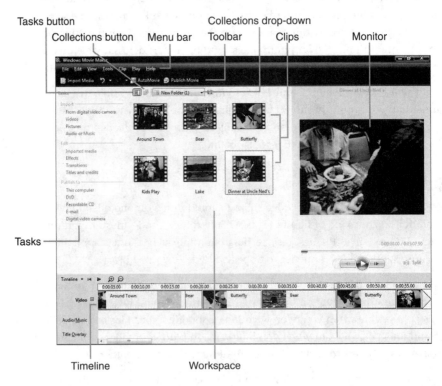

Here is a bit more detail about each element on your screen:

▶ **Menu bar/toolbars**—These elements perform similar functions to their counterparts in other Windows applications. With them you can open and save files, change views, and gain single-click access to unique Movie Maker tasks. You can also move, show, and hide Movie Maker toolbars as with other toolbars you have worked with previously.

▶ **Tasks/Collections area**—In the left pane, you will see a list of available video collections and files or you will see a list of tasks. What you see depends on which button you click: Tasks or Collections. (You can show the Tasks pane and then use the Collections drop-down button to display your video collections, transition effects, and special effects when you want to see a list but not keep it on the screen all the time.) In the right pane, you will see shortcuts to clips contained within the selected file or movie in your collection. After you load a video into Movie Maker's editing area, you can divide that video into separate clips whenever the entire makeup of the frame changes suddenly.

▶ **Monitor**—Drag a clip into the monitor to view it, or play a whole project by selecting Play, Play Storyboard. Use the buttons underneath to control video play much like you did in Media Player. The seek bar above the buttons lets you know how much of the clip or movie has been viewed or has yet to be viewed.

| Select View, Preview Monitor Size to change the size of your Monitor window. | **Did you Know?** |

▶ **Workspace**—This is the strip of workspace near the bottom of the window. It is where you drag all your clips to make a movie. You can view your project in two ways: by storyboard or by timeline. Figure 19.1 shows the Timeline view.

| If you've never used a video-editing program before, Movie Maker's screen might seem a little busy at first. Take your time to look at all the elements and you'll begin to get an idea of what is going on. | **By the Way** |

The clips in the center workspace are videos and still images that you drag, copy, or insert into the current project. You can put them together or use only part of them in your final video. Your final video will appear at the bottom of your screen in a timeline or storyboard display. Figure 19.2 shows a storyboard display, a simpler video project window than with the timeline but also not as detailed when you want to know the timing of certain parts of your video.

You can select a single video clip to play in the Monitor. In addition, you can play the video you're piecing and editing together in the Monitor. You'll rearrange most things by dragging them. For example, if the fourth video clip on your storyboard should actually appear at the end of your movie, just drag the clip from that second position to the end and drop it there.

FIGURE 19.2
The storyboard
view gives you a
higher-level look
at the video
you're putting
together in
Movie Maker.

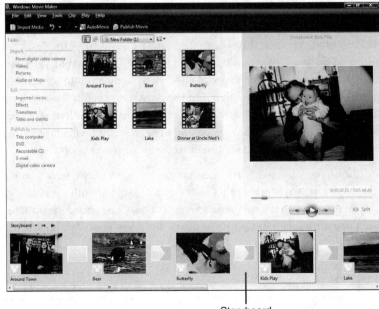

Storyboard

By the Way

The order of clips in the large, center workspace has no bearing on the movie's final order. You'll put clips in the center workspace so that you have them there to edit and use in your final movie that always appears on the storyboard or timeline.

Obtaining Video for Your Movie

Before Movie Maker can work with your video clips, you must be able to get your video clips to your computer. The video could be on a videocassette, in your camcorder, or on your digital camera with video clip capabilities. Regardless, you will have to do the following to make the movie (or movies) and their associated clips available for use in Movie Maker:

1. With your video device attached to your PC, using a Firewire or USB 2.0 cable, copy the files to your hard drive. Often, your computer sees your video camera as a disk drive, so you can use Windows Explorer to move the files.

   If your computer has trouble seeing the video, you'll have to resort to the software that came with your camera. Your mission here is simply to get the content onto your PC's hard drive. Older cameras use various means to transfer video to a hard disk.

2. Next, you will have to import the files into Movie Maker. With Movie Maker up and running (click your Windows Start button; then click Windows Movie Maker), click the Import Media button on Movie Maker's toolbar. Movie Maker displays the Import Media Items dialog box shown in Figure 19.3.

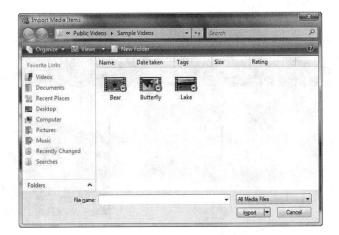

FIGURE 19.3
Movie Maker will import your video clips and still pictures for your movie.

By the Way

Movie Maker can import both video and still images (such as those you manage in Photo Gallery). Pictures work well in videos for backgrounds for titles and credits. Movie Maker imports from your Sample Videos folder located within your Public\Public Videos folder by default, but you can import from any disk location to which you have access.

Did you Know?

Select Tools, Options to display the Options dialog box, and then click the Advanced tab. You can adjust how long Movie Maker uses for each picture's duration. The default value is 5 seconds using a 1.25-second transition to the next picture or video clip. If all you did was import pictures into Movie Maker, Movie Maker could create a slideshow-like movie to which you could easily add narration or an audio clip such as background music. You have more control over a Movie Maker's slideshow movie than Photo Gallery's slideshow, but Movie Maker is slightly more difficult to use than Photo Gallery if all you want is a slideshow of still images.

3. Click your way to the file you want to import and then double-click its name when you find it. Movie Maker takes a few moments to scan the file and create a clip for the video in the center workspace.

4. You can view any imported clips by clicking the clip's picture in Movie Maker's center workspace. Images representing the resulting clips appear in the right Collections Area pane. Film edges on either side of the clip's picture designate the video clip, whereas still images that you import don't have the film edges as you can see in Figure 19.4.

FIGURE 19.4
You can distinguish between video clips and picture clips in the workspace area by the clip image's side borders.

Picture clip

Video clip

Repeat these steps until all the video images you want to use are viewable in the Collections area.

Pasting Clips into a Movie

You can view the movie files as they exist on your hard drive, but you could have a whole lot of fun pasting clips together to make a real movie.

To get started, click View, Storyboard on the menu bar. Remember that the storyboard is where you piece together the actual movie. The storyboard resembles frozen points in your movie where each clip you place eventually becomes an image in the film. This is the best way to see which clips are where in the movie you are piecing together.

To move a clip into the project, click the clip's picture and drag it to the desired position on the storyboard. Don't forget: You may use a clip more than once in the same movie if you want to.

Trimming Clips

You can shorten a clip by using Movie Maker's Timeline view. This is a great way to cut unwanted parts out of your clips, and does not modify the source files in any way. To trim your clips, follow these steps:

1. First, click View, Timeline to change the workspace view from a Storyboard to a Timeline view. Ctrl+T is the shortcut key. As Figure 19.5's timeline shows, each clip varies in length relative to those clips around it, and the width shows you visually how long each clip is to one another. The timeline shows you the exact length of each clip.

Click the Zoom In and Zoom Out buttons across the top of your timeline to zoom into your timeline for more detail and to see a more exact timeline in minutes and seconds when you need more accuracy than Movie Maker first provides.

Did you Know?

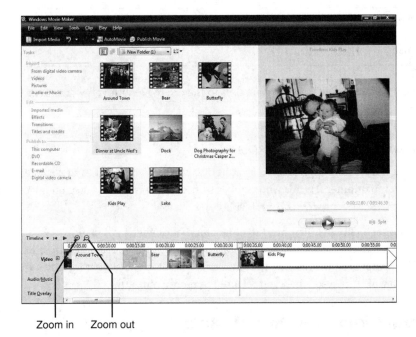

FIGURE 19.5
Each clip's width shows its relative length in your movie.

Zoom in   Zoom out

Keep in mind that this is only a bird's-eye-view chapter, walking you quickly through a simple movie-editing process. You are seeing how simple Movie Maker makes video editing, but you're seeing it at the expense of delving very deeply into all that Movie Maker can do for you.

2. Next, click the clip you want to shorten. You will see the clip's image outlined in blue, its duration on the project timeline shaded, and two gray trim handles (black arrows pointing in toward the clip picture's center) at either end of the clip's timeline.

3. To begin trimming, run your mouse over one of the trim handles until it becomes an east/west double-headed arrow. (Obviously, you will click the left handle to trim from the front of the clip and the right handle to trim from the end of the clip.) This ensures that you are in the right position to grab the trim handle. To make the trim, click and drag the handle in the desired direction and then release it in place. You can use the elapsed time as a guide or keep an eye on the Monitor that displays the frames you are dealing with as you drag the trim handle.

When you click the Monitor's Play button, your selected clip plays. As you trim a clip, you might want to play back the clip to see the results of your trimming process.

Repeat as necessary to get all your clips to the desired length you want them to play.

Rearranging the Clips

As you work with the project, you might discover that you want to move a clip from one spot to another. That is what makes working with a computer so great: You can move pieces of your video around with ease.

To relocate a clip, you first need to enter Storyboard view by clicking View, Storyboard. Next, click the image of the clip you want to move and drag it across the filmstrip. See the dark line that moves as you drag the clip? It indicates where the clip will be placed when you release the mouse button.

Transitioning Between Clips

Real movies can change scenes in various ways other than a straight cut from one scene to the other. You can too! The video and picture clips on your storyboard (or timeline) often represent scene changes. A transition sometimes makes the passing of one scene to another less instant and conveys a sense of change to prepare your audience for the new scene.

When you add one or more transitions to your movie, they appear between your clips on the storyboard. Click the Tasks Transitions entry to display all of Movie Maker's scene transition formats. There are a lot of them. Figure 19.6 shows only a few and you can scroll down the list to see far more.

Scroll to see more

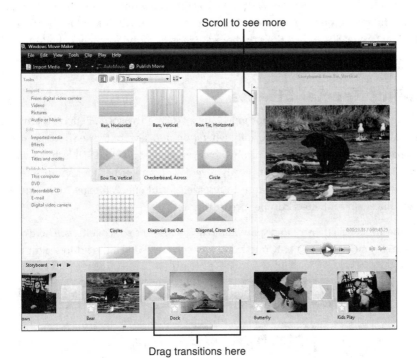

Drag transitions here

FIGURE 19.6
Movie Maker provides numerous transitions from which you can select.

> The more numerous, varied, and fancy your transitions are, the more they distract viewers from your movie. Your movie's message is far more important than the transitions you add. Even if it's a home movie of various family birthday parties through the years, transitions should accent your scene changes and not detract from them. Save dramatic transitions, such as the checkerboard transitions, for rare use, such as cutting away from a funny clip and don't overuse them. Your audience will like your video more, and when you use a transition or special effect, it will mean more and be a surprise to your audience instead of a distraction.

Watch Out!

You can preview a transition just as you can see a preview of a video clip in your Monitor window. Double-click any transition and Movie Maker shows two pictures transitioning from one another in the Monitor window.

Transitions aren't just for video clips. You can transition from one picture to another, or to or from a video and picture. To add a transition to your movie, drag the chosen transition to the area between whatever two clips you want to transition in your storyboard. The transition's icon lets you know the transition will take place between those clips. You can click to select the storyboard's transition and then click the Monitor's Play button to see the transition from one scene to another.

Adding Special Effects

You can add special effects to your video clips. Most of the special effects seem silly when applied to video clips, especially when you add several to the same short movie. The special effects seem to work nicely, however, when you create slideshows with Movie Maker. A special effect can slowly reveal a picture or perhaps spiral into a picture. As with transitions, you'll want to reserve special effects for special moments, but a well-placed special effect can be nice at times.

Click the Tasks Effects entry to display all of Movie Maker's special effects. There are many of them. Figure 19.7 shows only a few and you can scroll down the list to see far more.

FIGURE 19.7
Add special effects to your clips to modify the way they begin.

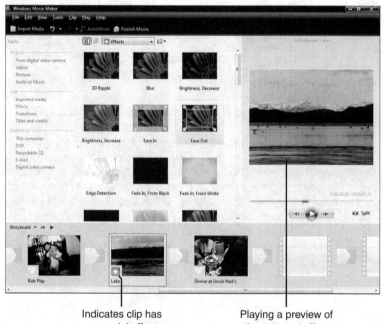

Indicates clip has
a special effect

Playing a preview of
the selected effect

As with transitions, you can click an effect to select it and then click the Monitor's Play button to see what effect that special effect produces. When you locate a special effect you want to use at the beginning of a scene, drag that special effect to the lower-left corner of a storyboard clip where a star appears. The star, when not grayed out, indicates that the clip will begin with a special effect. Figure 19.7 shows a preview of the clip playing in the Monitor. The clip has the Pixelate effect added, so the picture begins displaying in large, chunky blocks that gain greater and greater resolution until the full picture appears.

A video or picture clip can have more than one special effect associated with it.

By the Way

Adding Titles and Credits

Although this book can't go into a lot of detail about adding titles and credits (because the primary goal is to cover Windows Vista and not teach every detail of Movie Maker), you should understand that adding titles and credits to your movie is very simple indeed.

Never be afraid to experiment with Movie Maker. If you're unsure whether you want to add credits to a video, go ahead and add a panel of credits and watch the results in your Monitor. The Undo command reverses any changes you make that you don't like, including removing a complete screen of opening credits. The Undo command, available from the Edit menu (or using the Ctrl+Z shortcut key), undoes special effects, transitions, clip changes, and just about anything else you change your mind about.

By the Way

All you need to do is click your Tasks list's Titles and Credits link. To Movie Maker, a **title** appears at the beginning of a movie, or perhaps before certain clips. A **credit** appears at the end of the movie. Of course, the content is what actually distinguishes the two. You can put your movie titles at the beginning of your movie and use the title sequence for a few credits as well.

After selecting the Titles and Credits link, Movie Maker displays the following list of options:

- ▶ **Title at the Beginning**—Puts your titles at the beginning of your movie before the first clip.

- ▶ **Title Before the Selected Clip**—Inserts your titles before a clip you've selected.

▶ **Title Overlap on the Selected Clip**—Inserts your titles on top of a clip you've selected. You can use a clip as the background to your titles this way.

▶ **Credits at the End**—Inserts credits at the end of your movie.

As you type the text for your title or credit, Movie Maker displays a preview of the title or credit in the Monitor window, as Figure 19.8 shows. The titles normally fade into view but if you click the Change the Title Animation Link, you can select a different way the titles appear. In addition, you can change the font and text color used by selecting the Change the Text Font and Color link.

FIGURE 19.8
Movie Maker previews your titles or credits in the Monitor Windows.

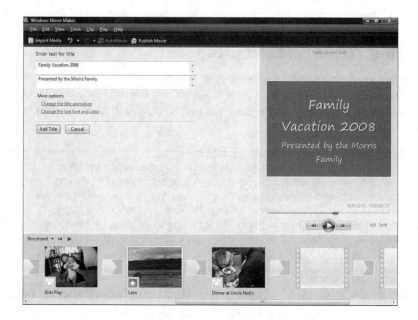

When you finish adding a title, click the Add Title link and your title will appear at the bottom of your Storyboard or Timeline view. As with any item in your storyboard, you can add a transition between the title and the next clip or add a special effect to the title itself.

When you add titles over an existing clip, Movie Maker requires that your movie appear in the Timeline view and not the Storyboard view. This is because overlaid titles are an element of your movie that you can move to a different point in your movie and the timeline enables you to move them accurately.

Figure 19.9 shows such an overlay title. The figure also gives you an indication of the true power of Movie Maker's Timeline view.

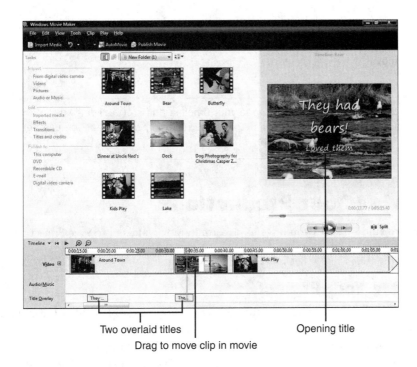

FIGURE 19.9
Use the Timeline view for overlaid titles and for adjusting the start points and end points of various movie elements.

Two overlaid titles

Opening title

Drag to move clip in movie

About the Timeline

The Timeline view shows you the precise point in time the following five elements appear in your movie:

▶ **Video**—The video and picture clips you've added to your movie. The width of each clip shows the relative time that clip consumes in your movie, and the timeline across the top of the clips shows the exact start and end times of each clip.

▶ **Transition**—Shows where one clip transitions to another. By dragging the left edge of the transition on the timeline, you can extend the length of that transition.

▶ **Audio**—Indicates where audio begins and ends throughout your movie. If no audio entry shows for a part of your movie, the movie is silent at that point. The audio has the same name as the recorded audio file, or if the video includes audio, the audio has the same name or date as the video.

▶ **Audio/Music**—You can overlay a second audio track onto your movie. The video's soundtrack, such as voice, might be in one audio track and you can add background music to the second audio track labeled Audio/Music. You can drag audio tracks left or right to change their starting times.

▶ Title Overlay—Shows where each overlaid title or credit begins and ends. You can drag an overlaid title or drag its right edge to change its duration in your movie.

Did you Know? | Select Edit, Clear Timeline to erase your timeline and start building your movie again. Any clips open in your workspace will remain there so that you can again drag them to the timeline or storyboard.

Saving Your Production

The two kinds of saves you have to perform in Movie Maker are Save Project and Publish Movie.

Saving Your Project

Saving a project means that the files you have chosen to work with for the current project will stay intact, as will the edits you have made to them (trims, fades, and so on). When you click File, Save Project, you will have the opportunity to save these elements so that you can go back and work with them at any point. Figure 19.10 shows the Save Project dialog box.

FIGURE 19.10
Saving a project saves your Movie Maker workspace, but does not generate a stand-alone movie file.

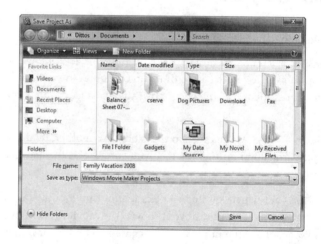

Publishing Your Movie

When you publish a movie, Movie Maker splices all your work together to create a final video file. Click Movie Maker's Publish Movie toolbar button to display the

Publish Movie dialog box shown in Figure 19.11. As you can see, the Publish Movie dialog box gives you several options because different Movie Maker users produce videos for different purposes. The way you plan to use your movie determines how Movie Maker should generate the movie.

FIGURE 19.11
You must give Movie Maker an indication of how you will use your movie so that Movie Maker generates the proper video file.

If your Tasks pane is open, you don't have to click the Publish Movie button to display the Publish Movie dialog box and select a publish option. You can go directly to any of the publishing options, such as Publish to DVD, by clicking the appropriate link in your Tasks pane.

Did you Know?

Movie Maker publishes your movie in the Windows Media file format (with the .wma extension) or the Audio-Video Interleaved format (with the .avi extension). The choice you make depends on how you will play the movie. Computers without Windows Media Player won't be able to play .wma files, so if you plan to share your video with others who don't use Windows but use a Mac, you might have to publish your video as an .avi file.

The Publish Movie dialog box offers the following choices:

▶ **This Computer**—When publishing your movie to play back on your own computer, Movie Maker asks for a filename and a location to which it should publish the file. You then must select a quality setting and optional file format. Generally, if you accept the default option labeled Best Quality for Playback on My Computer, Movie Maker will publish your movie in the highest playback quality possible. Depending on the size of your file, you might have to select a different format if you don't have enough disk space for the movie. As Figure 19.12 shows, the Publish Movie dialog box shows your movie's estimated file size along with your free disk space. These measurements change if you select different quality settings.

Click to change movie quality

FIGURE 19.12
Movie Maker publishes your movie in a high quality format as long as you have enough disk space to hold the movie.

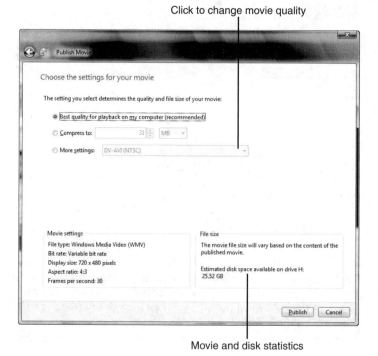

Movie and disk statistics

▶ **DVD**—When you want to publish your movie to a DVD, Movie Maker transfers your movie to Windows DVD Maker to create the DVD. You must have a blank DVD in your writeable DVD drive. Chapter 17, "Modifying and Sharing Photos," includes the "Creating a Video DVD" section that explains how to use Windows DVD Maker. After Movie Maker starts Windows DVD Maker, you can follow the instructions from the section in Chapter 17 to generate your movie.

▶ **Recordable CD**—If you send your movie to a recordable CD, most PCs will be able to play your movie but not all DVD players will be able to. You must make sure that the intended player can play .wmv or .avi files as you'll select one of those formats. Your video should fit on a recordable CD unless it's extremely long and you don't choose a lower-quality format when saving it to the CD. If you want to maintain quality but still place your movie on a CD, perhaps to send to family members who have only CD drives and no DVD drives in their PCs or laptops, you might have to return to Movie Maker's editing screen and divide your movie into two or more separate movies. By the way, Movie Maker does not write in the somewhat standard VideoCD or SuperVCD format.

▶ **E-mail**—Movie Maker can prepare your video and attach it to an email message that you send to others. Obviously, size is an issue here but Movie Maker compresses your video some before attaching it to a new email message. When you attach the movie to the email, look at the size of the movie in the Attach field. Figure 19.13 shows that the attachment includes both the filename and the movie's size. If the movie file is too large for the recipient's email system (and you should *always* ask first), you'll have to break up the movie into multiple parts and send the resulting videos separately. A better option would probably be to save the movie to a CD or DVD and mail the disc to the recipient.

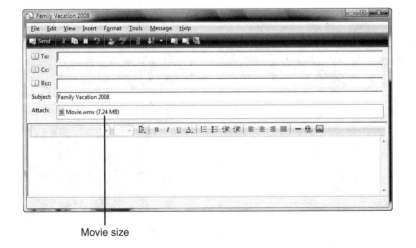

Movie size

FIGURE 19.13
Check the Attach field's file size before sending your movie as an email attachment to ensure that the movie doesn't clog your recipient's inbox.

▶ **Digital Video Camera**—If you want to send your movie to tape (or to a digital video camera's memory), select the Digital Video Camera option. Turn on your camera and connect it to your computer; often this is done using a FireWire connection. Click Next on the Publish Movie dialog box. Movie Maker displays multiple camera options if you have more than one camera connected. Most digital picture cameras have a video-recording mode, so if you have both your digital camera and your video camera attached, you'll have to choose the one you want to write to. When Movie Maker displays the Cue Your Tape dialog box, move to the position on the tape where you want to record the movie and click Next. Set your camera to record and click Yes on the Windows Movie Maker dialog box to begin the recording.

Did you Know?

You can preview the movie as it goes to your video camera's tape or memory by watching the video camera's viewfinder.

Making Movies Automatically

Movie Maker contains an AutoMovie feature that almost does all your work! AutoMovie takes your video and picture clips, analyzes any sound you've selected, and combines them into a movie based on some high-level preferences you select.

When you click the AutoMovie button, the AutoMovie editing style window appears as shown in Figure 19.14. As you can see, several movie styles are available, from an old-time movie that plays as though it's showing on old, used, video tape to an emphasis on action sequences using the Sports Highlights style and a Flip and Slide style that works well for slideshows.

FIGURE 19.14
Movie Maker can analyze your video and sound and create a movie for you.

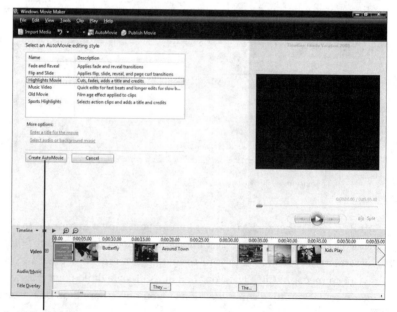

AutoMovie button

When you want to create a movie fast, the AutoMovie button is your answer. Here are the general steps in creating an automatic movie:

1. Locate all the clips and pictures you want to appear in your movie and copy them to Movie Maker's center workspace area.

2. Edit the clips, as needed, to shorten them if some contain extraneous material that you don't want to appear in the movie.

3. Press and hold Ctrl and click every clip you want Movie Maker to include in the final movie. Don't drag any to the storyboard or timeline because doing so defeats the purpose of automatic movie generation.

4. Click the AutoMovie button.

5. Select an AutoMovie style.

6. Click the Enter a Title for the Movie link. Add the title.

7. Click the Select Audio or Background Music link. Click the Browse button and locate one or more audio files you want to put in the movie. Adjust the audio volume level by dragging the volume slider left or right. This adjusts the relative level of audio included with your video clips and audio that you add as background music.

8. Click the Create AutoMovie button and Movie Maker generates your movie. The storyboard and timeline will hold the resulting movie and you're free to adjust whatever elements there you want to change. You can add or remove special effects, titles, and transitions just as you can when you build your own movie in the Storyboard or Timeline window pane.

9. After you preview and finish editing your movie, click the Publish button to save the movie to a disk, DVD, CD, or to send it as an email attachment.

The Undo command cannot undo an automatic movie. If you select an automatic movie style and you don't like the results, you'll have to generate a new movie and select a different style.

Specifying Movie Properties

You can set any of your movie's properties from within Movie Maker. Therefore, you can assign a title, author, copyright message, rating, and comments for your movie. These movie properties travel with the movie and you can view or change them from Media Player.

The rating you assign is an audience rating, such as G or PG, and not a rating based on the five-star rating system you've seen in previous chapters. From Media Gallery, you can assign a star rating to your video file.

Before publishing your movie, select File, Project Properties to display Figure 19.15's Project Properties dialog box. There you can enter the properties for your movie.

FIGURE 19.15
Specify the properties to save with your movie when you publish it.

Add Narration to Your Movie

If you create training videos, or want to talk over a movie you produce, Movie Maker supports a narration feature. Using it, you can plug a microphone into your computer's microphone-in jack and start narrating. Just select Tools, Narrate Timeline, and the Narrate Timeline screen in Figure 19.16 appears. If the Storyboard view was showing previously, Movie Maker changes to the Timeline view.

When you click the Start Narration button, Movie Maker turns on your microphone, starts recording what you say, and plays the movie in your Monitor window. If the movie already has a soundtrack, as is often the case with video clips shot with audio, you will talk over the sound. Movie Maker takes care of timing the narration so that your voice always covers the same timeframe in the video. When you mention something in the video, your narration will accurately stay on track during your movie's playback.

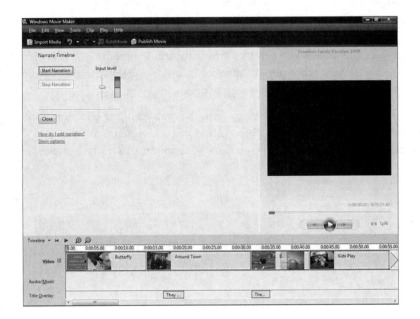

FIGURE 19.16
Talk over your movie, or parts of your movie, if you want to add narration.

When you finish adding the narration, Movie Maker saves the narration in its own file using the Windows Media Audio format and prompts you for a filename in the Save Windows Media File dialog box. As with most audio, you can rate the recording with the five-star rating, specify an artist, album title, and year. Of course those items aren't critical for a movie narration, but you should probably change the Album Title property to describe what you're narrating. Subsequently, when viewing a list of audio files you'll know the purpose of the recording.

> Your narration track appears in your timeline's Audio/Music track, where you can adjust the narration or move it to a different part of the video. Keep in mind that if you move narration, you change the narration's original synchronization with the movie.

By the Way

Chapter Wrap-Up

You now have a video-editing tool that's surprisingly powerful for a program Microsoft tosses in free with Windows Vista!

Although you can purchase more powerful programs, Windows Movie Maker is a great place to begin your video-editing hobby or career. More powerful programs might include additional audio and video tracks on the timeline, provide more control over titles and credits, and perhaps support more output formats, but the general way you edit videos doesn't change from program to program. That is why Movie Maker is a good place to begin; its interface is simple and you can quickly grasp the concepts required for editing movies in its simple interface.

In the next chapter, you'll move away from the multimedia applications that recent chapters have covered. Windows Vista introduces a new program, Windows Calendar, which you can use to keep track of appointments and reminders.

CHAPTER 20

Dating with Windows Calendar

In This Chapter:

▶ Learn to manage your schedule with Calendar

▶ Distinguish between appointments and tasks

▶ Use multiple calendars to your benefit

▶ Change calendar views

▶ Create appointments and tasks

▶ Set alarms for important meetings

▶ Invite others to your appointments

▶ Subscribe to online calendars

Windows Vista Calendar breaks new Windows operating system ground by offering you a calendar not tied to a specific program, such as Microsoft Outlook or Act! Contact Management software. When you use Vista, your Windows Calendar program is there waiting to record a meeting or appointment or task, willing to remind you when something is due, and displaying one of multiple calendars you can set up.

In addition to scheduling and tracking your days, Windows Calendar is also shareable; when you work with others who need access to your calendars or have family members who need to keep up-to-date, Windows Calendar can be where you need it to be. Share your calendars with others and download calendars from the Internet of scheduled items of interest to you.

Introducing Windows Calendar

Windows Calendar, shown in Figure 20.1, tracks your schedule. Although Windows Calendar is comprehensive and supports multiple, overlaid, shareable calendars, don't let its power sway you from using the program when your scheduling needs are simple. One of Windows Calendar's strengths is its ease of use and its simplistic and intuitive interface. Unlike Microsoft Outlook's somewhat bloated calendaring features, Vista's Windows Calendar is lean enough to remain simple to use without overrunning new users with little-used, excess features.

FIGURE 20.1
Windows Calendar's screen can look busy if you have a busy schedule and maintain multiple calendars, but its interface is simple and intuitive.

Three calendars showing   Appointments

Tasks

Navigation pane   Details pane

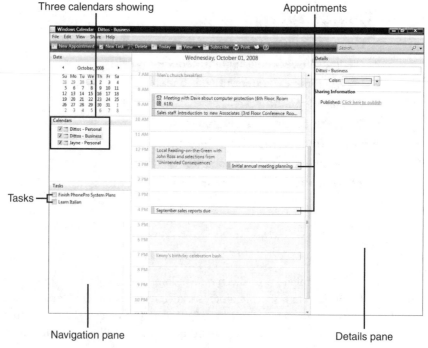

By the Way

Figure 20.1 shows three calendars. When Windows Calendar displays multiple calendars at once, the calendars overlay each other. Each calendar's appointments display in a unique color so that you can easily distinguish between the calendar appointments.

Vista's Windows Calendar works primarily with two kinds of items:

▶ **Appointments**—Items you record in a future time period that have a start and stop date and time, or perhaps lasts all day, such as meetings and parties. Appointments appear in your calendar's screen and are attached to dates and times.

▶ **Tasks**—Items you describe that you want to accomplish at a later date. Tasks can have start and due dates, but aren't generally linked to specific hours on a clock, as are appointments such as meetings. Tasks appear on your Navigation pane under the Tasks section header.

Tasks often have start dates because Windows Calendar uses the date you create a task as its default starting date, but you can change this. Tasks don't have to have end dates unless you want to use Windows Calendar tasks for goal-setting to achieve goals that you enter as tasks within a specific timeframe. Projects, such as business plans that have to be complete by an agreed-to time, also might be tasks for which you specify end dates.

Did you Know?

Windows Calendar keeps its appointments and tasks in the popular iCalendar format so that you can easily share your calendars with others.

Using Multiple Calendars

If you're the only one who uses your computer and if you want to maintain only one calendar, Windows Calendar does the job. You will work with a single calendar. All the dates that display belong to that single calendar. Even if you're the only one who uses Windows Calendar, you can still take advantage of Windows Calendar's multiple calendar feature when you break your own appointments into helpful categories where each category is contained in a separate calendar. For example, you might create a personal calendar and a business calendar.

If you display multiple calendars but want to show dates from only one of them, as you might do if you want to check your personal schedule without your business calendar appointments getting in the way, just click to uncheck the calendar (or calendars) you don't want to see. Figure 20.2 shows the same calendar shown in Figure 20.1 except only the business calendar appointment displays because the other two calendars are unchecked.

Did you Know?

One calendar showing

FIGURE 20.2
Uncheck the calendar you want to hide so that you see only the appointments you need to see.

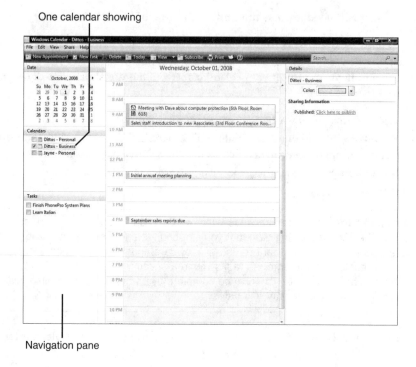

Navigation pane

To create a new calendar, select File, New Calendar. Windows Calendar doesn't clear your screen of any calendars or appointments currently showing. Instead, Windows Calendar simply adds a new entry in the left window pane (called the *Navigation pane*) in the Calendars section and highlights the new name text, New Calendar, so that you can change it to a meaningful name such as Paula's Personal or Mike's Business.

By the Way

Calendar names can be long (256 characters seems to be the limit), but at most only about 27 characters will appear in the Navigation pane's Calendars section depending on your screen's display setting.

You can create as many calendars as you need. You'll learn new ways to use Windows Calendar's multiple, overlaid calendar features. Everyone in a family can create his or her own calendar on the same computer. With all the calendar's checked and displaying, the Calendar screen shows the family's appointments. When someone from the family wants to see only his own appointments, he has only to uncheck the other calendars.

By the Way

Deleting a calendar removes all its appointments, so do so with care. Click the calendar name in the left pane's Calendars section and press the Delete key. After confirming the deletion, Windows Calendar deletes that calendar from your screen and removes all its appointments.

Changing Calendar Views

Now that you've become somewhat familiar with Calendar you're ready to learn how to change the views of your Calendar screen. You can adjust your view to see more or less detail at any one time. For example, you can view a single day's appointments as shown in Figure 20.2, a week's appointments as shown in Figure 20.3, or an entire month's appointments.

Click to change view

FIGURE 20.3
You can see as much detail as you want, including an entire week's worth of appointments.

To view a week's calendar, click the arrow to the right of the View button and select either Work Week (Monday through Friday) or Week (includes weekend days). Select Month to view an entire month calendar. In the Date Navigation pane, you can click any day to change the dates shown in the view. Click the arrows to the left or right of the Navigation pane's month to change months.

After traversing to a day, week, or month that differs from the current date, click the Today button to return to the current day's calendar. You'll still be viewing the current day or week or month, but today's date will be the selected date within that view.

As when viewing a single day's appointments, when viewing a week or month calendar, you can click to check or uncheck calendars in the Navigation pane to see only the appointments for your selected calendars.

Obviously, there is not enough screen space to view all your appointments' text when viewing a week or month at a time. You can close the Navigation pane and the Details pane by clicking the close button in the upper-right corner of either pane. Ctrl+I and Ctrl+D are the shortcut keys to close or open the Navigation pane and the Details pane, respectively. Closing one or both of these panes gives your calendar more room to display appointment text, as you can see when you compare Figure 20.4 to Figure 20.3.

FIGURE 20.4
When you close the Navigation and the Details panes Windows Calendar is able to show more text for each appointment.

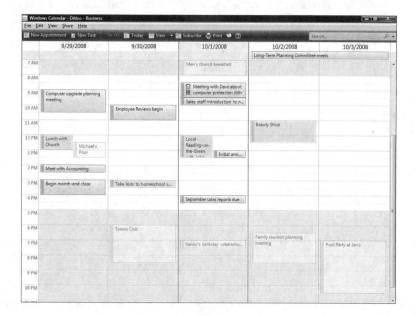

The Details pane includes details about any selected appointment. Therefore, when viewing a week or a month view, the Details pane becomes even more important than when you view a single day where you can read more at each appointment in the calendar. Just click an appointment in any view to see the detail for that appointment. The Details pane includes the following information:

▶ **Details**—Text that describes the appointment.

▶ **Location**—The appointment's location, such as an address or room and floor. The location appears next to the appointment's details in parentheses.

▶ **Calendar**—The calendar this appointment belongs to.

▶ **URL**—A web address (also known as a *Uniform Resource Locator*) related to your meeting or appointment.

▶ **All-Day Appointment**—An option that determines whether the appointment lasts the entire work day or, when unchecked, shows that the appointment time is limited.

▶ **Start and End**—The date and time the appointment begins and ends.

▶ **Recurrence** —An option that designates whether the appointment repeats daily, weekly, monthly, yearly, or at a less common time frame. When you select Advanced, the Recurrence dialog box shown in Figure 20.5 opens so that you can determine how often the appointment repeats, and you can limit the recurrence to a specific number of times or specify that the recurrence ends on a given date.

FIGURE 20.5
You can set up a recurring appointment to repeat as often as needed.

▶ **Reminder**—Determines how far in advance you want to be reminded for the given appointment. Calendar sounds an alarm and displays a reminder dialog box, such as the one shown in Figure 20.6, when it's time to let you know about your appointment.

FIGURE 20.6
Calendar reminds you of your appointments.

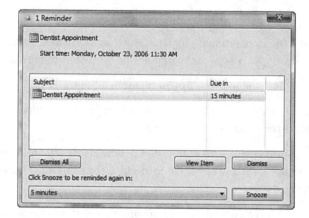

You can click a reminder's Snooze button to get rid of the pop-up dialog box alarm temporarily and reset it to appear at the time you select for the snooze. The default is five minutes, so when a reminder dialog box sounds an alarm and pops up to remind you of an appointment, the dialog box closes when you click Snooze and reappears five minutes later. You can click Snooze as often as you want and select a snooze time to remind you of the appointment again as far away as two weeks. Obviously, for a two-week snooze time to work, the reminder must be set to remind you of an appointment farther in advance than two weeks before your appointment. You might set an important date, such as your anniversary, with a one-month reminder and then select a two-week snooze to be reminded two weeks before the date.

An alarm clock icon appears next to the details of any appointment that contains a reminder to let you know you'll receive a reminder before the appointment is due.

> ▶ **Participants**—Displays the list of optional participants in your appointment and includes an Invite button to invite others from your address book (such as those found in your Microsoft Office Contacts folder or your Windows Contacts entries) to attend, with emails that include the meeting details requesting their presence.

> ▶ **Notes**—Detailed notes about the meeting that are too lengthy to put in the Details box. The Details box contains appointment details that appear in your calendar and reminder and the Notes text supplies more detailed information that you want to attach to the appointment for later reference but that don't clutter your calendar or reminders.

These fields inside your appointment's Details pane are mostly optional. Obviously, if you create an appointment that is not an all-day appointment, you have to specify a beginning and ending time for the appointment. In addition, all appointments require that you type something in the Details box so that you know what an appointment is for when you see it in your calendar or displayed in a reminder dialog box. You fill in these appointment details when you create an appointment.

> Tasks have many of the same details as appointments, but also support task-specific details such as a priority level and a completed option.

By the
Way

Creating an Appointment

One of the quickest ways to create an appointment is to click to select the calendar the appointment goes with. Click the daily calendar view and click the time when the appointment is to begin. When you click the New Appointment button, Windows Calendar creates a colored entry in your current calendar, displays the Details pane, uses the selected day and time for the appointment's start time, and fills in the Details box with the text, New Appointment.

You can then type over the New Appointment text to give the appointment a meaningful description and fill in any remaining details that apply to your appointment. For example, if the appointment lasts two hours, you'll want to override the default 30 minute appointment length and change the end time accordingly.

> You can change the default 30-minute appointment length on Windows Calendar's options page. See "Adjusting Windows Calendar's Options" later in this chapter to learn more about Windows Calendar's options.

Did you
Know?

Click to check the All-Day appointment option if your appointment is to last the entire day. All-day appointments always appear at the top of the day's calendar no matter which view you're displaying at the time. For example, Figure 20.7 shows a day with two appointments (each for different selected calendars) and one all-day appointment, a long-term strategy session. The all-day appointment doesn't have a specific start and stop time because its duration is the entire day. Perhaps Calendar should show such all-day appointments as long, highlighted appointments that show throughout the entire day's calendar, but such an appointment has no start and end times and the appointment would appear to last from one minute past midnight to midnight 24 hours later and that doesn't truly reflect the nature of an all-day appointment.

FIGURE 20.7
All-day appointments appear at the top of your calendar day.

All-day appointment

By the Way

The appointment's colored entry in your calendar expands or shrinks depending on the length of the appointment. If another calendar's appointment overlaps your new one, you can distinguish between the appointments at a glance because each appointment is in that calendar's default color. Windows Calendar puts multiple appointments that overlap on different calendars next to each other and will not put one appointment from one calendar on top of another.

Did you Know?

Instead of entering a stop time, you can drag an appointment's bottom, colored edge down or up to change the appointment's ending time.

To delete an appointment, simply click to select the appointment in any calendar view and press Delete.

Watch Out!

Windows Calendar does not support an Undo command for deleted items! If you delete an appointment or task, you must re-enter that appointment or task all over again.

To change the details of any appointment, click the appointment. Press Ctrl+D if the Details pane isn't currently showing, and change any details related to that appointment.

To designate who is to attend, type the attendees' names or email addresses in the Attendees text box or click the Attendees button to display a list of contacts. From the list, select one or more contacts and click the To button to add them to your meeting attendees.

If you want to invite others to your appointment, click the Invite button and select contacts that have email addresses to invite. Windows Calendar will send those persons an invitation to your appointment and include all the appointment details.

Fill in as many details as possible for the appointment before you invite others. That way, Windows Calendar can include all the appointment's details in the emailed invitations.

Did you Know?

Creating a Task

Creating a task is similar to creating an appointment, but is even easier because tasks don't typically start and stop at preset time intervals and you don't invite others to attend a task as you do for appointments.

Select the calendar the task goes with. Then click any time on the day the task is to begin and click the New Task button. Windows Calendar adds a new task to your Navigation pane under the Tasks section, displays the Details pane, uses the selected day for the task, and fills in the Details box with the text, New Task.

You can then type over the New Task text to give the task a meaningful description and fill in any remaining details that apply. For example, you can assign a priority to your task: Low, Medium, High, or None. The reminder you use for tasks is far less specific than for an appointment reminder that is detailed from five minutes to two weeks. A task reminder must begin on a date you specify and the default is the task's start date.

Unlike upcoming appointments, your tasks always appear on your screen in the Navigation pane's Tasks section, so task reminders might not be as critical as appointment reminders.

By the Way

When you finish a task, click to select the task and its Details pane. Click to check the Completed option to show that the task is finished. You can also click to check the box to the left of the task in your Navigation pane's Tasks section to show the task's completion. All completed tasks remain in your Tasks list, with the completed option checked, for as long as you've set them to do so in Windows Calendar's Options dialog box.

Adjusting Windows Calendar's Options

Select File, Options to display Figure 20.8's Options dialog box. Windows Calendar's options relate to certain behaviors of the program, such as the default appointment length and reminder times.

FIGURE 20.8
You can adjust Windows Calendar's options to modify the default values Windows Calendar uses when you create appointments and tasks.

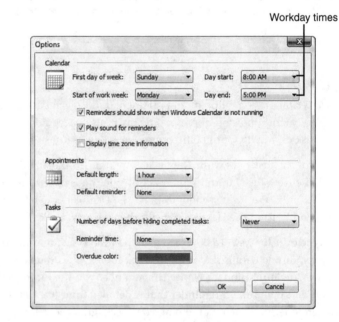

Workday times

You can change the following options in the Windows Calendar program:

▶ **Starting Day of Week**—Determines the day of the week that shows first as well as the start and end times of the workday hours.

▶ **Reminders Display Option**—Determines whether reminders sound their alarm and display reminder dialog boxes whether Windows Calendar is running or not running. Just because you don't start Windows Calendar doesn't mean you don't want reminders of appointments that come due. If you don't want an audible reminder to sound when a reminder box pops up on your screen, click to uncheck the option labeled, Play Sound for Reminders.

If you drag Windows Calendar to your Windows menu's Startup folder entry, Windows Calendar will start every time you start Windows.

▶ **Time Zone Information**—An option that displays time zone information, useful especially if you travel in multiple time zones.

▶ **Default Length and Reminders**—Determines the default length of time Windows Calendar uses for new appointments and reminders for those appointments you request reminders for.

▶ **Completed Task Duration**—Determines how long checked, completed tasks appear in your Tasks list.

▶ **Reminder Time**—Determines the time of day that Windows Calendar reminds you that a task is overdue.

▶ **Overdue Color**—Determines the color used to mark overdue, uncompleted tasks.

After you change an option, click OK to close your Options dialog box and put your option settings into effect.

Searching for Appointments

After you add many appointments and tasks, finding certain ones can be difficult. As with much of Windows Vista, Windows Calendar includes a powerful Search box that quickly locates tasks and appointments you want to find.

Start typing letters in Windows Calendar's Search box that correspond to the appointment or task you want to locate and Windows Calendar immediately begins narrowing the search to appointments or tasks that contain your search term. As Figure 20.9 shows, typing the letters lo in the Search box immediately locates several appointments and tasks with those letters. You can finish typing your search term to keep narrowing down the search, but if you see the appointment or task you want to view in the search results list, double-click that entry and Windows Calendar opens that item's day so that you can read or edit the details for that item.

Search results　　　　　　　　　　　　　　Search term

FIGURE 20.9
As you type letters to include in your search, Windows Calendar begins matching appointments and tasks to your search term.

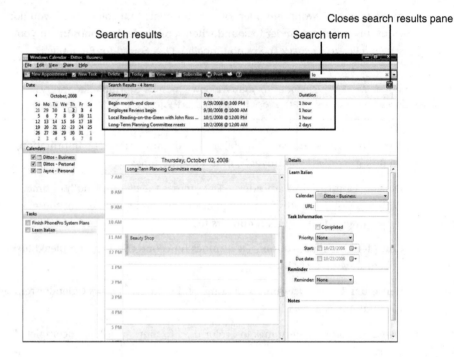

Sharing Calendars

To let others know about your calendars, you can share them with others on your network or in a web folder if your company's network administrators have set up web folders for office sharing. In addition, others can share their calendars with you and you can subscribe to shared calendars of others. (The next section, "Subscribing to Calendars," explains how to subscribe to calendars that others offer to share with you.)

> You must have set up at least one mail profile setup to announce your shared calendar to others on your network. In Windows Mail or Microsoft Outlook (or any similar mail program you might use with Vista) create a new email account if you have not done so already. Without the account, Windows Calendar has no way to get your calendars published or sent by email for others to use.

Follow these steps to share a calendar:

1. Click to select the calendar you want to share (if you use multiple calendars).

2. Click the Share menu option and select Publish. Windows Calendar displays the Publish dialog box shown in Figure 20.10.

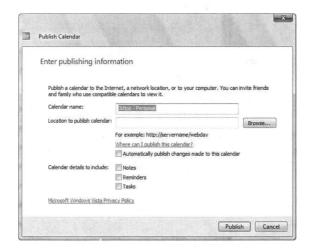

FIGURE 20.10
You'll publish your calendar when you want to share it with others.

3. Type a new name that others will see for your shared calendar if you want to use a different shared name from the one you use in Windows Calendar.

4. Enter a location to publish your calendar. You can enter a network location for which you have access, such as a shared folder, or a web folder that people on the Internet can see. Click the Browse button to select a location to publish to. If you work in a networked, group environment in a business, you might have to contact your network administrator to determine the best location for your shared folder. It must be a location you have write access to and a location that others can read from. For home users, publishing to one of your Public folders ensures that everyone who uses your PC or who networks to your computer in a home or small office environment can subscribe to your calendar and get regular updates automatically.

5. Click to check or uncheck the Automatically Publish Changes Made to This Calendar option. Any time you subsequently change the calendar that you've published, this option ensures that Calendar will apply that change to your published calendar as well.

6. Click one or more options to select notes, reminders, or tasks you want to share with the published calendar. The notes are contained in each appointment's Details pane.

7. Click Publish to send the calendar to the shared location where others can now subscribe to it and see your calendar along with any they have created or subscribed to within their own Windows Calendar program. When it finishes sending the calendar to your shared location, Windows Calendar displays a Publish Calendar dialog box like the one shown in Figure 20.11.

FIGURE 20.11
Calendar lets
you know when
it's time to
announce
your shared
calendar.

8. After publishing your calendar, it's time to let others know that they can subscribe to, or share, your calendar. Click the Announce button to send your calendar to everyone you've created a Calendar profile for in your Control Panel.

9. Users can subscribe to your calendar directly from the email they receive or
   through the website you published your calendar to.

If sharing calendars with family members on your same computer or on other computers in the same household you'll find that using the Share, Send Via E-Mail
option is slightly easier to understand than using the Share, Publish option. While
there is a drawback in that updates are not performed automatically, each user can
still import an emailed calendar when you send one in order to get the latest
updates.

Assume that you maintain a calendar of family events and you want others in your
household to get a fresh copy of your calendar to overlay their own, individual
calendars. To do that, follow these steps:

1. Click the calendar you wish to share and select Share, Send Via E-Mail.
   Windows Calendar opens a new Message window and attaches the selected
   calendar's .ics file.

2. Fill in the recipient's email address. If you want to send the calendar to multiple recipients in your family, separate each email address with semicolons.

3. Click the Send button to send the email to all the recipients in your family.

4. Upon logging into their account, each recipient will then get an email with the current family calendar. They can save the calendar to their Documents folder (or to any folder they wish to create). Even if they use the same computer you used to send the calendars they can receive and save this emailed calendar once they log onto the computer.

5. Each user then selects File, Import, browses to the location of the saved calendar from your email, and clicks the Import button. The updated family calendar now appears along with their other appointments.

If you or someone else imports a calendar with the same name as another calendar, as might be the case if you send a new version of a calendar that you've previously sent to your family members, a new copy of the calendar will appear in their calendar list. Each user can delete the old calendar when the new one arrives to replace it.

Subscribing to Calendars

As Vista matures and more people use Windows Calendar, more websites such as entertainment and sports sites will provide calendars you can subscribe to. A Marvel Entertainment site might, for example, publish calendars that show its upcoming movie release in theaters and on DVD and you need only subscribe to that calendar to know when something that you want to see is about to arrive. The calendars that you subscribe to become just another named, overlaid calendar in your Windows Calendar program window that you can monitor and work with, getting reminders when things are about to take place.

Subscribing to a published calendar on the same computer or on a network, as might be the case in a family or small business environment, subscribing is simple as long as the calendar is located where the other users can access it such as a Public folder. By publishing to a Public folder, any user on your network or who shares your computer only has to click the Subscribe button, type the location and name of your calendar, and click Subscribe to get regular and automatic updates. If you've sent an announcement then a link to do this appears in the announcement email they receive so they don't have to know the exact shared location to subscribe to your calendar. They just need user access to that location.

To subscribe to a calendar online, you can download a calendar from a website and then click the Subscribe button to display Figure 20.12's Subscribe to a Calendar dialog box where you type the location of the saved calendar. Windows Calendar then imports the calendar's appointments and tasks into your collection of calendars.

FIGURE 20.12
Tell Windows Calendar where the calendar you want to subscribe to is located.

Did you Know?

If you don't know of any calendars on the Web that you can subscribe to, click the Subscribe to a Calendar dialog box's Windows Calendar Web Site link to locate useful calendars available for you.

By the Way

If you receive an email of an available calendar you can subscribe to, the email generally has a link to download the calendar so that you don't first have to visit a website to get the calendar.

Printing Calendars

Printing a calendar is simple, but does support slightly more options than printing other items such as a word processed document. You'll need to tell Windows Calendar how you want the printed calendar to look and what date range you want to print. When you click the Print button at the top of your Windows Calendar's screen, the Print dialog box shown in Figure 20.13 appears. Select what you want to print, such as a day, work week, full week, or month, and then select a date range to print using that date view. When you click the OK button, Windows Calendar begins printing your calendar.

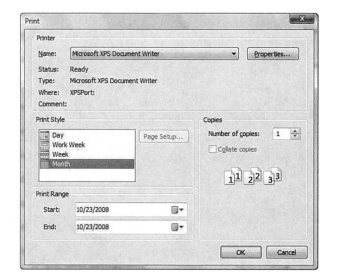

FIGURE 20.13
Tell Windows
Calendar how
you want your
printed calendar
to look and
what date range
to print.

Chapter Wrap-Up

Vista's Windows Calendar is a full-featured calendar tool that enables you to track appointments and tasks, get reminders, invite people to meetings, and share your calendars with others. It's the calendar sharing that turns Windows Calendar into a true, enterprisewide application; you can subscribe to calendars from websites and overlay those calendars onto your own to track multiple kinds of appointments and tasks you're interested in.

The next chapter begins Part V, "Automating Vista," in this book. There you will learn several ways that Vista can automate tasks such as running programs at set times without your intervention. You will also learn new ways to command and control your computer as you see the various ways that Vista's interface stays flexible and accessible to relate to your needs and requirements.

PART V

Automating Vista

CHAPTER 21

Scheduling Tasks to Run Later

In This Chapter:

▶ Learn how to schedule programs to run later
▶ Understand the Task Scheduler's busy screen
▶ Change the way a scheduled task runs
▶ Determine a scheduled program's filename and location
▶ Use program arguments for hands-off program execution
▶ Set up Disk Cleanup as a scheduled task
▶ Run scheduled tasks even when you're not logged on to the computer

When you want to run a program, such as Microsoft Access, you know to click the Windows Start button, locate the program on Windows Vista's Start menu, and click the program's menu entry. If the program's icon resides on your desktop or on your Windows taskbar, you just click the icon to start the program.

Although you're the catalyst that triggers most program executions, you might prefer that Vista run certain programs at certain times. For example, you might want to schedule a backup program to run in the middle of the night when you're away from your computer. Or perhaps you want to run a disk-optimizing program like Disk Cleanup every week or two to keep your system running smoothly.

> Chapter 32, "Improving Disk Performance and Storage," describes Disk Cleanup and explains its options.

> **By the Way**

Windows Vista includes Task Scheduler, which will run the programs you designate at the time and day you designate. You can set up recurring program executions such as scheduling a daily backup of your data files and a monthly backup of your entire system. In this chapter, you learn how to start Task Scheduler and schedule programs to start when you want them to run. Using Task Scheduler to schedule a program isn't difficult, but some programs that you schedule require extra options that aren't always obvious. This chapter uses the Disk Cleanup program as an example of how to schedule programs to run at specific times, and you can apply what you learn here with Disk Cleanup to any program you want to run regularly, such as a backup program.

Opening Task Scheduler

You access Task Scheduler from the Start menu's Accessories, System Tools folder or from your Control Panel's System and Maintenance group. The opening Task Scheduler program window is shown in Figure 21.1.

FIGURE 21.1
The Task Scheduler program window can get busy.

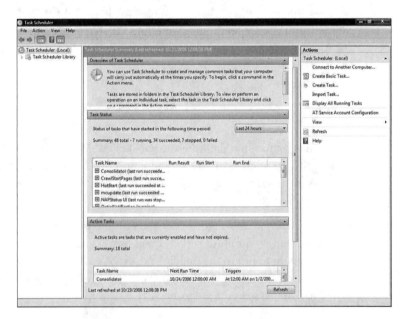

You might have to click Continue to verify that you give Windows permission to start Task Scheduler. Only users with Administrator privileges can start Task Scheduler, although if you're the sole user of your computer, your account is probably designated as an Administrator account.

When you start Task Scheduler for the very first time, you might be surprised by the number of programs listed in the center window pane, titled Task Status. The list of programs might not even look familiar; you'll find entries such as CrawlStartPages. These are system tasks that Vista has scheduled to run automatically, at various times, depending on your system settings. You don't need to concern yourself with them unless you want to adjust the way one of the system programs behaves or cancel a system program's automatic execution altogether.

> It probably goes without saying, but you should never remove a Task Scheduler program that you're unfamiliar with and that you did not add yourself. The system programs listed in Task Scheduler by default can be crucial for the proper execution of Windows Vista.

Watch Out!

Generally, you'll want to add a few programs of your own to Task Scheduler's task list. As you learn more about Vista's offerings and as you add new programs to your computer over time, you will revisit Task Scheduler to add and change the programs that run automatically.

Creating a Task Scheduler Task

When you want to add a program to Task Scheduler, you add a new task to the Task Scheduler program. It might seem as though a better name for Task Scheduler would be *Program Scheduler*, but Task Scheduler can do more than just start programs at specific times.

For instance, Task Scheduler supports specialized features that enable it to send emails to an email address you specify if a certain system problem occurs. Although this feature is rather specialized for typical users, it indicates the nature of Task Scheduler and shows that it's more than a system routine that only runs programs at specific times. Task Scheduler can even run programs after you run other programs, such as Media Player or Internet Explorer. Such events are not linked to a specific time interval, but are triggered by an event such as starting one of those programs.

> Vista cannot run a task if your computer is not turned on. Your computer must be turned on before Task Scheduler can properly execute the tasks you set up. Task Scheduler will still run tasks at scheduled times when your computer is in Sleep mode.

Watch Out!

Most of the time you will create a *basic task* in Task Scheduler. A **basic task**, as you might guess, is most often a program you want to run at a certain time. To the right of the Task Scheduler program window is a window pane labeled Actions. Select the Create Basic Task entry in the Actions pane and Task Scheduler begins collecting information about the program you want to run in the Task Scheduler Wizard dialog box, shown in Figure 21.2.

FIGURE 21.2
The Task Scheduler Wizard screens walk you through the setup of a task.

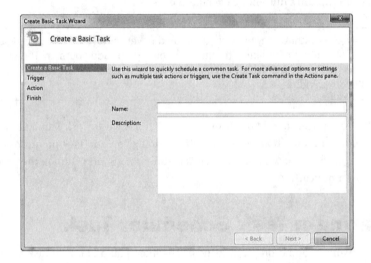

Enter a name and optional description for the task you want to set up. It's best to spend some time creating a descriptive name and an ample description so that you know exactly what the purpose of this task is when you later look through a listing of multiple tasks you've created over time. Click Next to continue with the wizard.

The Task Trigger window, shown in Figure 21.3, now opens. This window is where you designate the frequency of the task you are scheduling.

The Task Trigger window covers almost every possibility. For example, you can request that Vista run your task every day, week, or month. You can also request that Vista execute the task once at a specific date and time, or perhaps when a certain event takes place, such as when you log in to your Windows user account.

By the Way

> The task trigger you select determines what you'll see next. For example, if you designate that you want a task to execute monthly, the Task Scheduler Wizard asks for the day you want the task executed on each month. If you specify that you want to create a task that executes when a specific event occurs, such as when you start Internet Explorer, the Task Scheduler Wizard prompts you for that event trigger.

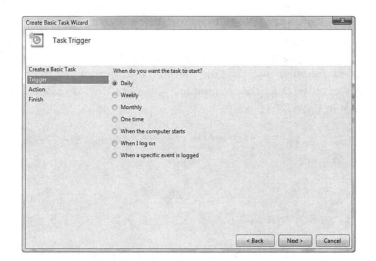

FIGURE 21.3
You will desig-
nate how often
you want the
program to run.

Because most Windows users create tasks to execute programs at specific times, the
rest of this description assumes that is what you want to learn to do. Any deviation
from scheduling tasks to run at specific time intervals changes the task setup procedure only slightly.

To run the Disk Cleanup program every week, you click to select Weekly and then
click Next to designate the day and time in the Weekly window that appears next.
Figure 21.4 shows the Weekly window.

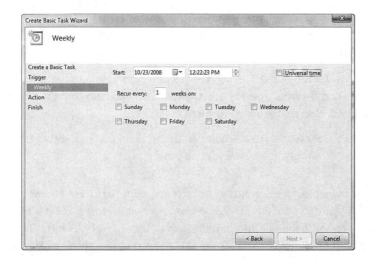

FIGURE 21.4
You must tell
Task Scheduler
the day and
time each week
you want to
schedule the
program to run.

For timed scheduling, such as daily, weekly, and monthly, you must tell Task Scheduler when to begin. The default start date will be the current date, but perhaps you don't want the program to begin running on its schedule until a certain date in the future. You must also enter the time you want the program to start and designate the day of the week for the program to begin. Click Next to see the Task Action screen shown in Figure 21.5.

FIGURE 21.5
Let Task Scheduler know if you want a program to run, an email to be sent, or a message to be displayed.

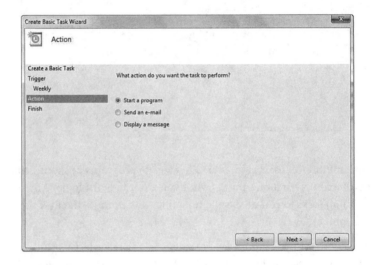

The Task Action screen includes the following three actions from which you can select:

▶ **Start a Program**—Task Scheduler runs a program when the time or event takes place.

▶ **Send an E-mail**—Task Scheduler sends an email to any recipient you designate when the time or event takes place. The email can contain an attached file if you elect to use an attachment.

▶ **Display a Message**—Task Scheduler displays a dialog box with a message you request when the time or event takes place.

The window you next see depends on the action you selected. For example, if you elected that Vista send an email when a certain event or time takes place, Task Scheduler asks for the email information such as the From, To, Subject, Text, and Attachment (if any) fields as well as the SMTP server to use (this is available from your email provider).

You can specify multiple recipients for the email if you separate the To field's email addresses with semicolons.

If you elected to show a message when a certain event takes place, Task Scheduler prompts you for the title and message text that will ultimately appear in a dialog box that pops up when it's time for the action to occur.

If you've requested that a program run, Task Scheduler requests the program information in a Start a Program window such as the one shown in Figure 21.6.

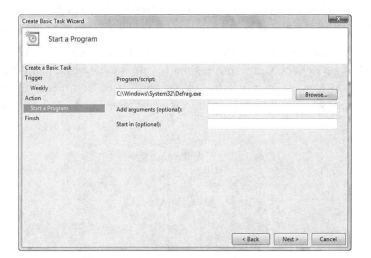

FIGURE 21.6
Task Scheduler needs to know which program to run.

Determining a Program's Filename and Location

One of the tricky parts of task scheduling now awaits you. You must know the filename of the program you want to execute as well as the location on your disk where the program resides. For typical Vista utility programs, such as the Disk Cleanup program, the program will reside in a Windows folder's subfolder named system32.

The reason you must have Administrator privileges to use Task Scheduler is because some programs access parts of the system that should not be available to all users. Many programs in the system32 Windows folder, for example, access security settings or disk management aspects that could cause problems if they are executed without a full understanding of their operation.

Knowing the actual program name can be a challenge. For example, if you click the Start a Program window's Browse button, Task Scheduler opens a file-browsing window for your system32 folder. Scrolling down through the files shows some programs you might recognize (such as SoundRecorder), whereas others are likely unfamiliar system programs (such as shrpubw and mblctr). Many of the items in your system32 folder aren't even programs!

How can you tell the name of the program you want to run and where it's located? It takes some detective work. One would think the Disk Cleanup program's filename would begin with the letter *D* and perhaps have a name something like DiskClean or DiskCleanup. Nevertheless, you can look through every file in the system32 folder that begins with the letter *D* and never locate the Disk Cleanup program.

One way to locate the name and location of a program is to open your Windows Start menu and right-click over the program you want to schedule. Right-clicking over the Disk Cleanup program in the Accessories, System Tools menu produces a pop-up menu. Selecting Properties from the context menu produces the Properties dialog box shown in Figure 21.7.

FIGURE 21.7
Use some detective work to locate the scheduled program's filename and location.

Folder Location

Filename

The dialog box's Target field displays the program's location and filename. The filename is to the right. In the case of the Disk Cleanup program, the filename is cleanmgr.exe, although the .exe typically won't show in a file list. The folder location is the system32 folder on your system's disk drive in the Windows folder. Instead of showing a nice drive letter and Windows folder location, such as C:\Windows, you'll see %SystemRoot%\. That's a shortcut that means wherever your Windows folder is located, that's where %SystemRoot% appears. Some shortcut, huh?

Generally, analyzing the program's properties in this way gives you insight into where the program is located and what its filename is. Therefore, when you click the Task Scheduler's Start a Program window's Browse button, you'll either keep the default system32 folder or select another depending on where the program you want to schedule resides. Then you'll select the program from that folder.

In the case of the Disk Cleanup program, select the cleanmgr filename in the system32 folder and click Open to let Task Scheduler know you want to schedule the Disk Cleanup program. You now must decide whether the program requires user intervention of any kind, and if so, you must locate arguments that bypass such intervention as the following section explains.

Locating and Using Program Arguments

Arguments often pose another problem for most that use Task Scheduler. Some programs require user intervention. Disk Cleanup, although a great program to schedule in the wee morning hours you're away from your computer, is a program that typically requires user intervention before it runs. Disk Cleanup needs to know which disk drive you want to clean up and which kinds of files you want it to wash from your computer. Figure 21.8 shows what happens if you, or Task Scheduler, run Disk Cleanup without using any arguments, as you do when you run Disk Cleanup from the Windows Start menu. The dialog box prompts the user to learn how much of the disk—the current user's folders or all disk locations—the cleanup is to cover.

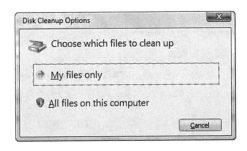

FIGURE 21.8
Some programs require extra information before they execute on their own.

System and other programs often accept arguments, or program control options, that tell the program how to behave if no user is present. For example, one argument is the disk drive letter. If you run Disk Cleanup from within Task Scheduler using the /d c: argument, for example, you're telling Disk Cleanup that it's drive letter C: you want it to clean. When run with that argument, Disk Cleanup won't require you to sit there and select your C: drive, but will instead know that you want it to clean your C: drive.

Almost every program you assign to Task Scheduler needs this added information. For example, if you want Task Scheduler to run a backup of disk files every so often, you have to tell the backup program which disk drive or drives you want to back up and where the backup program is to back up to. When you run such programs manually from the Windows Start menu, specifying this kind of information requires only a few mouse clicks. Telling Task Scheduler how to handle such options, however, requires more work using the program's arguments.

Disk Cleanup requires more arguments than just the drive letter to clean. The program needs to know whether you want to clean up one or more of the following file sets:

▶ Temporary setup files

▶ Old Chkdsk files

▶ Recycle Bin files

▶ Setup log files

▶ Temporary files

Depending on your user privileges and Windows Vista version, you might see additional file options that Disk Cleanup can clean. (Again, you can read more about Disk Cleanup in Chapter 32.) Most of these files are unneeded; for example, after you install a program successfully, its log files just consume disk space. The Setup log files provide a record of an installation so if the install doesn't work properly, the program's technical support team can trace the problem.

Disk Cleanup allows you to create sets of arguments—each uniquely identified with a number—that determine how you want Disk Cleanup to perform. You create a Disk Cleanup set using the sageset argument. The following describes how to do so.

To set up arguments for Disk Cleanup, you temporarily leave Task Scheduler and work with your Windows Vista Start menu. Don't close Task Scheduler's window; leave it open. After you get the proper Disk Cleanup arguments, you'll finish the Task Scheduler entry.

Setting Up Disk Cleanup Argument Sets

Here is how you create a Disk Cleanup argument set. After you create and assign a number to a Disk Cleanup set, you'll specify that argument set in Task Scheduler so that Task Scheduler won't require any user intervention from you when it runs Disk Cleanup.

To create a Disk Cleanup argument set, press Windows+R. This opens the Run dialog box. Type the following: cleanmgr /sageset:1. Your Run window will look like the one in Figure 21.9.

FIGURE 21.9
Use the Windows Run dialog box to create a Disk Cleanup argument set.

The Run dialog box tells Windows Vista to run the Disk Cleanup program. The default folder is the system32 folder for the Run dialog box. The /sageset:1 entry is an argument that tells Disk Cleanup the following:

Run Disk Cleanup and watch which options I select. Save all those options to an argument set that I'll call #1. In the future, when I run Disk Cleanup using that argument set, or when Task Scheduler runs Disk Cleanup using that argument set, don't ask me for any option but go ahead and select the save option I am about to choose and run the program without my intervention.

Click OK to start Disk Cleanup. Run the program and select all the options you want Task Scheduler to select when you're not present. Select the files you want Disk Cleanup to clean from the Files to Delete list, as shown in Figure 21.10. When you specify the files you want to clean, click OK.

FIGURE 21.10
Select the files
you want Disk
Cleanup to
clean.

Did you
Know?

> If you want to specify different Disk Cleanup options to execute at different times, just run through this process again and create an argument set numbered 2, and then one numbered 3, and so on. Each set is a unique set of arguments. After you create an argument set, you can run that argument set from the Windows+R run box or from Task Scheduler as shown next.

After you click OK, Disk Cleanup *will not run*. Instead, Disk Cleanup saves that argument set which, in this case, is called 1. The sageset:# argument is a special argument that tells Disk Cleanup to create a new argument set with the number you specify.

Finishing Task Scheduler's Disk Cleanup Entry

Now you're ready to finish the Task Scheduler's Disk Cleanup entry. Before taking this Disk Cleanup argument detour, you were well on your way to making Disk Cleanup run automatically. You now have all the work done to complete Disk Cleanup's Task Scheduler entry. You created a Disk Cleanup argument set and it's named 1.

By the
Way

> In the future, you'll want to work out which arguments your Task Scheduled program will use before starting Task Scheduler and adding the program. It made sense in this chapter to begin Task Scheduler first so that you'd know where you were heading, and then taking this Disk Cleanup detour when it was required to finish the Task Scheduler entry.

To request that Disk Cleanup use that argument set when Task Scheduler runs Disk Cleanup, return to the Task Scheduler session that you began earlier. In the Add Arguments (Optional) text box, type /sagerun:1 so that Task Scheduler sends that argument to Disk Cleanup when the program runs. This argument tells Disk Cleanup to use the argument set number 1 when it runs. (From the Windows+R run dialog box, you would achieve the same effect manually if you typed cleanmgr /sagerun:1 and clicked OK.)

<table>
<tr><td>If you create multiple Disk Cleanup argument sets, perhaps with one cleaning only your Recycle Bin and another cleaning more, the number you use after the /sagerun: argument determines which one runs when Task Scheduler schedules it.</td><td>**Did you Know?**</td></tr>
</table>

That's all you have left to do to make Task Scheduler run Disk Cleanup without your intervention. Click Next and then Finish to save the Task Scheduler entry for Disk Cleanup. Task Scheduler will run Disk Cleanup at the time you specified as long as your computer is turned on and you're logged on.

<table>
<tr><td>If you want Task Scheduler to run a task whether or not you're logged on, you can schedule it as long as your computer is powered on at the time Task Scheduler needs to run the program. From the center of the Task Scheduler window where your tasks appear, double-click to open any task you want to run during those times you won't be logged on. Click the Properties button in the right pane inside the Selected Item section to display Figure 21.11's Properties dialog box. Click to select the option labeled Run Whether User Is Logged On or Not. If you click to check the Do Not Store Password option, any task you run affects only your user account's files and folders. If you click to uncheck the Do Not Store Password option, the task uses your user account's password to run programs that affect all files and folders you have access to. Therefore, if you have an Administrator account and you don't click the Do Not Store Password option, Task Scheduler can use your Administrator privilege to run your task as needed.</td><td>**Did you Know?**</td></tr>
</table>

Remember, Disk Cleanup is being used here only as an example of how to set up any program you want to run at a specified time. Hardly any space is used to describe Disk Cleanup because it's Task Scheduler that is our focus here. Task Scheduler is one of the first Vista applications you've seen described in this book that requires more extensive setup and knowledge just to use, but don't let that deter you from learning about the program. The technical aspects of Task Scheduler's scheduled programs almost always center on the program's user interface. You can't schedule programs to run automatically unless they provide some kind of argument-based program execution, so you don't have to be there when Task Scheduler starts the program.

FIGURE 21.11
You can specify
that a task
should run even
if you're not
logged on at
the time.

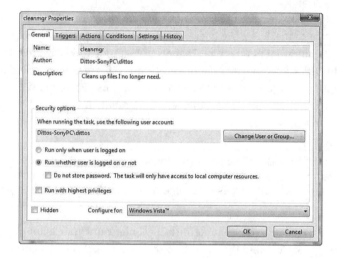

Most programs do require some kind of user intervention, such as Disk Cleanup, that must know which drive and options you want it to use. You'll have to search the program's documentation for *command line arguments* to learn how to specify arguments for each program you add to Disk Scheduler.

Are Scheduled Programs Worth This Effort?

Believe it or not, getting Disk Cleanup to run automatically is one of the *simplest* programs available from your Windows Vista system tools. When you first learn how to automate programs with Disk Scheduler, however, locating the program file-name, location, and setting arguments can seem like a lot of trouble. After you set up a program to run automatically, you rarely have to adjust any option other than the day or time you want Disk Scheduler to run the program, so this initial setup trouble is worth it.

For many users, remembering to run Disk Cleanup and other disk utilities such as Disk Defragmenter regularly doesn't always happen. A disk drive can become cluttered and these kinds of programs, when run regularly, help speed your system and keep your disks optimized. Go through the process of setting up Disk Scheduler and any other programs that you know should be run routinely, such as your backup program. After you go to the trouble of letting Disk Scheduler do the work, your system will operate at its peak performance without you having to intervene to run these mundane system programs.

Running Disk Defragmenter with Task Scheduler

Fortunately, you can schedule some programs to run regularly without going through the motions of locating the program and finding its arguments. Disk

Defragmenter, a program that keeps your disk drive running at its peak efficiency (as Chapter 32 explains), will add itself to Task Scheduler and you can modify the Task Scheduler time without even opening Task Scheduler itself.

Windows Vista normally runs Disk Defragmenter automatically, as it was set up when you installed or upgraded to Windows Vista. When you start Disk Defragmenter from your Start menu, the opening window (shown in Figure 21.12) shows that Disk Defragmenter is already set up to run automatically. This means that your Task Scheduler will have an entry for the program. If you want to modify when Disk Defragmenter runs, you can do so from that program by clicking the Modify Schedule button and changing the scheduled program execution. Chapter 32 goes into more detail about how to schedule Disk Defragmenter.

For this purposes of this chapter, it's important to note that by including this scheduling option in the Disk Defragmenter program itself, you don't need to locate its hands-off, command-line options and set them up through the Task Scheduler. (It's too bad that Disk Cleanup doesn't have this option, considering the effort Task Scheduler can require in setting up Disk Cleanup command-line options as explained in the previous section.)

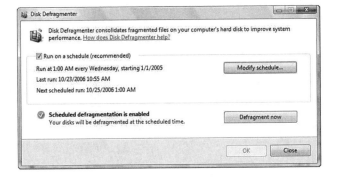

FIGURE 21.12
Select how you want Disk Defragmenter to organize your disk.

Obviously if you or someone else has edited Disk Defragmenter's settings from within that program or within Task Scheduler, Disk Defragmenter won't be set up to run automatically as in Figure 21.12.

Chapter Wrap-Up

This chapter explained how you can make Windows Vista run programs for you at specified times you choose. Much more is possible with Task Scheduler, but most of the time, the majority of users want to run a program such as a backup or disk-related program at a particular time. Even with the simplest of Task Scheduler routines, setting up your programs to run unattended requires more technical work than you might expect at first. You must be able to locate the program and set it up to run using special arguments that eliminate all user intervention that would otherwise be required.

Even though this was a far more technical chapter than the ones that came before it—and more technical than most chapters that come later—the advantages of Task Scheduler outweigh the slight effort needed to set it up.

In the next chapter, you'll learn about the accessibility options that enable you to control Windows Vista's environment in ways you might not have considered. Although the accessibility options were designed for users with special needs, almost anyone can benefit from some of the options that make Windows easier to use.

CHAPTER 22

Making Windows More Accessible

In This Chapter:

▶ Display the accessibility tools

▶ Magnify your screen

▶ Learn which accessibility options might benefit you the most

▶ Change the keyboard's response for combining keystrokes such as Shift+E

▶ Replace visual screen messages with audible signals and alarms

▶ Set the screen's display so that you can read enlarged letters, icons, title bars, and high-contrast screen colors

▶ Use your keyboard to imitate mouse moves and clicks

This chapter describes all the Windows Vista tools that provide help for users with special needs. Everyone who uses Windows Vista is a potential candidate right now for one or more of these tools because they often make a part of Windows easier to use. A good number of Windows users who wouldn't normally consider themselves candidates for the accessibility tools will often find ways to use one or more of the accessibility tools as a shortcut to a way of working or to make something they do easier. Previous versions of Windows supported many of Vista's accessibility features, but Vista offers more tools and makes Windows easier to use than ever before.

The Windows Vista accessibility options change the behavior of the keyboard, screen, and speakers so that they operate differently from their default behaviors. Microsoft designed Windows Vista so that everybody can take advantage of the new operating environment.

Getting to the Accessibility Tools

Open your Windows menu, select All Programs, and then select the Accessories sub-menu. Open the Ease of Access folder to display Vista's accessibility tools. Vista's menu's Ease of Access folder lists a few individual accessibility tools, such as the Narrator, but unless you specifically know you want to use one of those tools, your first foray into Vista's accessibility tools should begin with the Ease of Access Center. There you get an overview of what is available and you can easily select the tools you want to use.

When you select Ease of Access Center from the menu, Vista displays the Ease of Access window shown in Figure 22.1. The moment the window opens, a voice starts talking to let you know how to get additional accessibility tools and describes how to turn the window's links into audible prompts.

Determines what is read when you open this windov

FIGURE 22.1
You'll locate and set Vista's accessibility tools and options in the Ease of Access Center window.

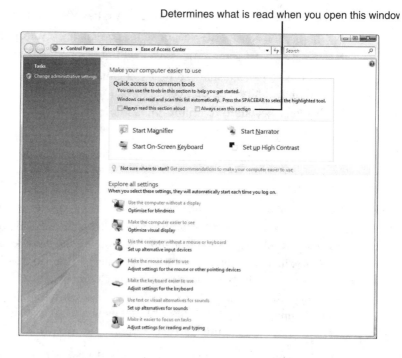

Click the Always Read This Section Aloud link if you want to hear the voice preview every time you display the Ease of Access window. The Always Scan This Section Option link, when checked, causes Vista to highlight each Ease of Access option and describe, in the narrator's voice, each option when you display the Ease of Access window. By slowly highlighting each access option one at a time, and having each option spoken aloud when highlighted, you can turn on one or more options by pressing your spacebar when the reader describes an option you want to set.

The top half of the Ease of Access window enables you to get to common access tools quickly. There you will be able to turn on and off specific accessibility tools described in the following sections.

The bottom part of the Ease of Access window enables you to select from more general requirements you might need. For example, if you want to use your computer without a mouse or keyboard, click the Use the Computer Without a Mouse or Keyboard link. The Ease of Access window then guides you through the accessibility options related to using your computer without a keyboard or mouse, but instead using another means, such as voice control.

> As this chapter's opening stated, just about everybody can benefit from one or more of Vista's accessibility tools. Too many people think they don't need the accessibility tools, so they ignore them—by doing so, those people sometimes overlook features that would help them do their work better and faster. Your author had a forced tour of duty with Windows' accessibility tools when I temporarily lost part of my vision. I was grateful that Microsoft chose to make the accessibility tools available to Windows users. Before that experience I never expected to use them, but I ended up requiring both the speech-to-text capabilities and the text reader. I won't go into more detail here, but my experience is completely documented in the book, *Disabling America*, ISBN 0-785-26225-3, Thomas Nelson Current Publishers.

By the Way

Zoom with the Magnifier

The Microsoft Magnifier is a program that magnifies part of your screen. As you move your mouse around the screen, the magnified viewer updates to show you a magnified view of your mouse cursor's area. If you have trouble reading text on your screen, you might want to try the Magnifier. Although the Magnifier program consumes some of your screen space to show a magnified area, text is much more readable than on the standard Windows Vista screen.

When you click the Start Magnifier option, Vista displays the Microsoft Screen Magnifier dialog box shown in Figure 22.2. (Optionally, Vista reads aloud the option you just clicked to verify audibly that you wanted to select that option.)

> Click and drag the dividing line between the magnified and unmagnified portions of your screen to give more or less room to the magnified area.

Did you Know?

Magnified area moves with your mouse

FIGURE 22.2
As you move
your mouse
pointer around
the lower part
of your screen,
the magnified
upper window
gives you a bet-
ter view of the
details.

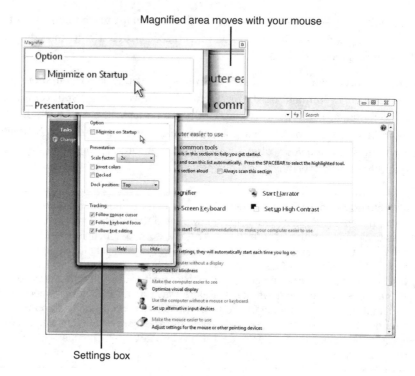

Settings box

In the dialog box, you can change settings such as the scale factor used to magnify parts of your screen. You can invert the screen colors that might make what you're viewing easier to see in the magnified window pane, and determine where the magnified window pane appears: docked at the top of your screen as shown in Figure 22.2 or on one of the other screen edges. In addition, you determine how the Magnifier follows your mouse and keyboard focus so that you can zoom into text that you enter, or stay with your mouse if that works better for you.

By the Way

After you turn on the Magnifier, the magnified window pane appears as you use Windows Vista. Start Microsoft Word, for example, and you'll see the magnified window pane. Surf the Internet and the magnified pane will be there also to help you see what you're doing.

Use the Onscreen Keyboard

If you find it easier to use your mouse than your keyboard, or perhaps you have an alternative input device that imitates a mouse and typing on your keyboard can be problematic, you should check out the onscreen keyboard. When you click the Start

On-Screen Keyboard option at the top of the Ease of Access window, Vista displays a full keyboard at the bottom of your screen as Figure 22.3 shows. The on-screen keyboard stays on your screen no matter which application you later start. To type a key, you can still use your regular keyboard, but you can also click with your mouse or other input device to imitate the typing of a keyboard key.

Num Lock

Scroll Lock

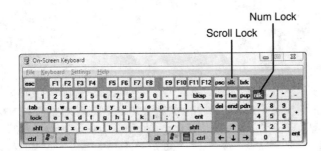

FIGURE 22.3
When you turn on the onscreen keyboard, you can imitate typing on your keyboard by clicking the on-screen keyboard's keys. The on-screen keyboard stays on top of whatever program you run for easy access to the onscreen keys.

To use the onscreen keyboard's Shift, Ctrl, Alt, and Windows logo key combination, click the Shift or Ctrl or Alt or Windows key first and the key stays selected. Then click the next key that makes up the combination you want to trigger. Therefore, to click Ctrl+C, you would first click the onscreen keyboard's Ctrl key and then click the onscreen keyboard's letter C. The Lock key turns on Caps Lock so that what you subsequently type appears on the screen in uppercase letters until you click the Lock key once more.

Did you Know?

Turn On a High Contrast Screen

If you have trouble separating text from a screen's background, or if some colors bleed together for you, you can click the option labeled Set Up High Contrast to change your screen so it takes on a dramatic dark-and-light contrast as shown in Figure 22.4. (You can turn off the high contrast screen by pressing Left Shift+Alt+PrtScrn.)

You can set multiple accessibility options at the same time. Each is explained individually throughout this chapter, but you can combine them. For example, you might want to view your screen in high contrast mode and use the onscreen keyboard also.

By the Way

FIGURE 22.4
The high con-
trast screen
option changes
all the text and
colors on your
screen to a
higher-contrast
set of colors
that makes
viewing the
screen easier
for some users
such as those
with color blind-
ness.

By changing your Windows Vista color scheme to a higher-contrast set, you make
your screen's color contrast more obvious and discernible. When viewing in a high
contrast mode, Vista changes your applications to display them in a high contrast
that makes it easier to distinguish between background and foreground screen elements.

If you find that the high contrast settings don't suit you, change some of the related
settings when you first select the high contrast option and see the options window
shown in Figure 22.5. Here you can select a different high contrast color scheme and
adjust text and icon sizes and other elements such as window border thickness. Click
the dialog box's Apply button to put that contrast scheme into effect and see
whether it works for you.

Did you Know?

> If you find a high contrast display that works fairly well for you, you can right-click
> over your desktop, select Personalize, choose Theme, and click the Save As but-
> ton to enter a new name for your current display settings that you can return to
> again if you ever change away from them.

Surprisingly, when you turn off the high contrast mode, Vista doesn't always return
your screen to the state it was in before you entered that mode. This is a bug that's
been around since Windows XP and doesn't seem to be fixed in Vista at the time of
this writing. If, for example, you were using the Windows Vista Aero appearance settings before entering a high contrast mode, your computer probably won't use the
Windows Vista Aero appearance setting when you leave the high contrast mode.

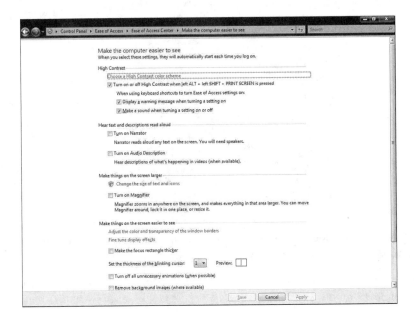

FIGURE 22.5
You can modify
the high con-
trast options to
get better
results.

To fix this, click the Set Up High Contrast option beneath the Ease of Access window's Turn On High Contrast option and select the Windows Vista Aero color
scheme to put your computer back the way it was originally.

Your Computer Can Read to You

When you click to select the Start Narrator option, Vista displays the Microsoft
Narrator dialog box shown in Figure 22.6 and begins reading aloud the dialog box's
contents. When reading dialog boxes, the narrator always reads the title, the main
menu options, the dialog box text, the names of special elements such as check
boxes and option buttons, and their selected state, when they appear.

If you hear no narration within a few seconds of turning on the option, your speaker volume is too low, or a speaker is not plugged into your sound card's output
jack.

The narrator can read to you the following screen elements depending on your
selection:

▶ **Your keystrokes**—As you type, Narrator can speak the keys to you. Typing
   ABC DEF results in you hearing, as you type, "ABC Spacebar DEF." You'll also
   hear an audible confirmation when you click a check box and perform other
   screen selection actions.

FIGURE 22.6
You control the
narrator's
options from
the Microsoft
Narrator
dialog box.

▶ **System messages**—System messages that appear in pop-up dialog boxes, such as shutdown messages, can be read to you.

▶ **Scroll notifications**—Reads new text that appears when your screen scrolls up or down.

▶ **Quick Help**—Clicking this button reads to you help about the narrator feature. You can stop the help's narration by pressing the Ctrl key.

By selecting the Voice Settings button, you can modify the way your computer reads onscreen text to you. You can change the speed, volume, and pitch of the voice that reads to you. If you've installed additional voices (available through Microsoft's website and elsewhere), you can select a different voice to read to you.

Vista Can Suggest Accessibility Tools for You

Although the four individual accessibility tools described in the previous sections are useful and solve specific problems, you might have requirements that demand a combination of the tools. Or perhaps if you're new to the accessibility features, you'd rather let Vista make some suggestions for you.

Previous versions of Windows offered an Accessibility Wizard that stepped users through the setup of one or more accessibility options. Vista's Ease of Access Center

provides a similar but more helpful feature. When you click the Get
Recommendations to Make Your Computer Easier to Use link in the center of the
Ease of Access window, Vista begins a question-and-answer session that steps you
through the setup of accessibility tools customized for your specific needs.

When you click the link, Vista displays the Get Recommendations to Your Computer
Easier to Use window shown in Figure 22.7.

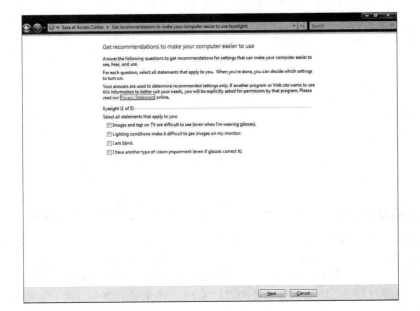

FIGURE 22.7
Windows Vista
can help guide
you through the
accessibility
tools through
this step-by-step
question-and-
answer
process.

The screens help identify your needs. For example, the first window asks for visual
statements that might apply to you. You can select one or more items that describe
your situation. For multiple items, Vista might recommend multiple accessibility
tools to work in tandem that can help make your computing experience far more
useful. If none of them apply to you, don't click any of the options before clicking
the Next button to move to the next step.

The screens collect information about you, and when you finish the five-screen
process, Windows displays a customized screen (such as the one shown in Figure
22.8) to make the best use of Windows for your situation. You have the choice of
selecting any of or all the options available.

FIGURE 22.8
Windows Vista
suggests a cus-
tomized set of
accessibility
tools just for
your needs.

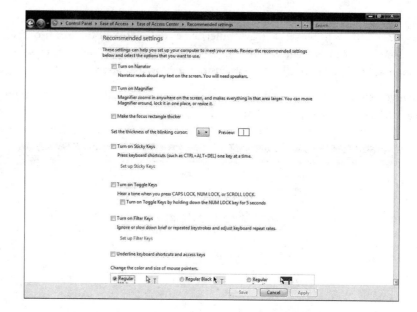

Accessing All the Accessibility Tools

The lower half of the Ease of Access screen provides access to all the tools Windows Vista offers that can help make your computing experience more enjoyable and productive. Keep in mind that the top set of tools shows only the most common six accessibility tools Vista provides. Several more are available and you can select from all that are available from the lower part of the Ease of Access screen.

The following list describes the collection of accessibility tools you can set up based on the settings you'll find at the bottom of the Ease of Access screen:

▶ **Use the Computer Without a Display**—Provides tools that enable the visually impaired to work more effectively on the computer. Places emphasis on sound settings, such as narration, and reduces visually distracting animations.

Did you Know?

These audio tools include a text-to-speech setting that enables your computer to read file contents, such as Word documents, over your computer's speakers.

▶ **Make the Computer Easier to See**—Provides tools that help improve the visual effectiveness of the Windows screens, making objects easier to see, text easier to read, removing background images when possible, and adjusting for a high contrast viewing area.

▶ **Use the Computer without a Mouse or Keyboard**—Enables you to use your computer without a mouse or without a keyboard (or either). You can use voice control to manage your computer and dictate text. Information about additional assistive technologies is available as well.

Chapter 23, "Speaking to Your Computer," explores Vista's speech recognition technology.

By the Way

▶ **Make the Mouse Easier to Use**—Enables you to set up special mouse-related accessibility tools, such as enlarging your mouse pointer, changing the contrast of your mouse pointer, and turning on **Mouse Keys**, which are specific keys on your keyboard you can press to simulate mouse movements and clicks.

▶ **Make the Keyboard Easier to Use**—Provides all of Vista's keyboard-related tool settings—such as Mouse Keys, Sticky Keys, Toggle Keys, and Filter Keys—in one place.

▶ **Use Text or Visual Alternatives for Sounds**—Provides text and onscreen alternatives to actions where sound would normally be heard. For example, you can elect to see flashing visual warning messages and title bars when Windows system sounds would otherwise play over the speaker. A caption display also replaces spoken dialogue when programs take advantage of Vista's caption option.

▶ **Make it Easier to Focus on Tasks**—Enables you to make overall reading and typing actions simpler by bringing together a set of tools that focus better on visual and input tasks. The Reasoning Tasks window, shown in Figure 22.9, is actually a special combination of accessibility tools, such as Filter Keys, narration, and high contrast screen options.

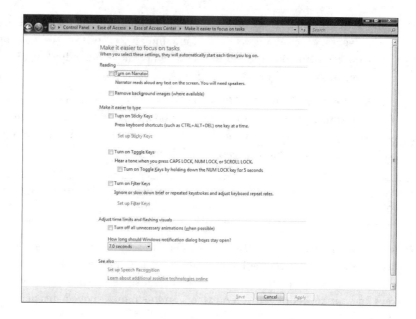

Reviewing Two Common Keyboard Accessibility Tools

Two keyboard tools, Stick Keys and Filter Keys, have been included in the Accessibility Tools since Windows 95 and for good reason. They enable people who might otherwise have problems tackling the keyboard by making the keyboard work for them. The following sections review these tools.

Make Your Keys Sticky

Although you could pour honey on your keyboard to make your keys sticky, the Ease of Access window gives you a much more useful way to produce sticky keys. When you turn on the Ease of Access window's Sticky Keys feature, you can press any modifier key (Shift, Ctrl, Alt, or your Windows logo key) individually instead of having to press them using combined keystrokes. Therefore, you can press Alt, let up on Alt, and then press C instead of combining the two for Alt+C.

The Sticky Keys feature enables you to type more easily using one hand or even one finger if the situation calls for it. If you find that you need the Sticky Keys feature, you don't even have to display the Ease of Access window first. Simply press either Shift key five times and the StickyKeys dialog box shown in Figure 22.10 appears. You can also access the Sticky Keys feature by clicking the Make the Keyboard Easier to Use link on the Ease of Access Center window.

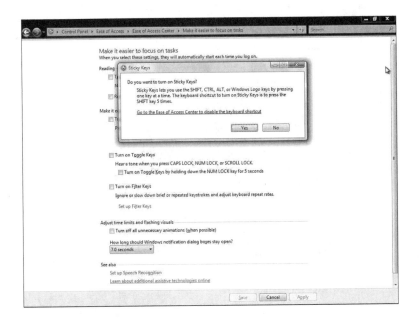

FIGURE 22.10
The Sticky Keys
feature enables
you to trigger
the Ctrl+C key-
stroke by press-
ing Ctrl, letting
up on Ctrl, and
then pressing C.

Turn On Filter Keys

The Filter Keys Ease of Access option includes support for accessibility tools called Repeat Keys, Slow Keys, and Bounce Keys. Inadvertent errors can occur when users hold keys down too long or press keys by using a bouncing motion that can double or triple keystrokes. The Repeat Keys settings control the appearance of such extra keystrokes that can result from holding keys down too long, resulting in typing that would otherwise produce text *lliiikkkkkkkee tthhhiisss*. The Slow Keys option guards against keys being pressed accidentally and accepts a keystroke only if it's held down for a specified period of time. The Bounce Keys setting helps to eliminate extra characters that might appear due to a bouncing keystroke motion.

When you select the Turn On Filter Keys option, you'll almost always want to click the Set Up Filter Keys link to specify how the Filter Keys option is to work. The Configure Filter Keys window, shown in Figure 22.11, appears when you configure Filter Keys from the Make the Keyboard Easier to Use link and click Set Up Filter Keys.

The Set Up Filter Keys window provides several options that control Vista's Filter Keys actions. Most of the settings you might need to adjust are timing-related settings. For example, if you require the Bounce Keys feature, you should specify how long, in seconds or partial seconds, Vista should wait before accepting a keystroke. If you select one second but later bump a key that stays down for less than a second, Vista will ignore that keystroke.

FIGURE 22.11
You can control the Filter Keys settings for Bounce Keys, Slow Keys, and Repeat Keys.

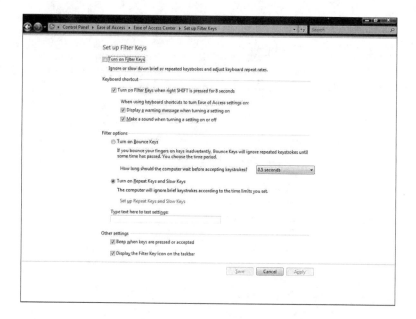

Did you Know?

Users of Filter Keys often find the beep option useful. When you click to select the Beep When Keys Are Pressed or Accepted option, your computer gives you an audible short beep when it accepts a keystroke. You quickly learn to use this beeping feedback as verification that a keystroke was properly accepted.

To set up Repeat Keys and Slow Keys, you must click the link in the center of the Set Up Filter Keys window to access the options related to those features. Again, the timers are the most critical elements to adjust. You might have to try several timer settings as you use your computer before you find the timing that best meets your needs. For example, to help eliminate inadvertent key presses, you can set the Slow Keys setting to one full second. If you press a key for a second or more Vista considers that a valid keystroke.

Watch Out!

People who need the Bounce Keys settings don't require Repeat Keys and Slow Keys and vice versa. These two sets of options are mutually exclusive because any Bounce Keys setting would negate the Repeat Keys and Slow Keys settings. Therefore, you can activate either the Bounce Keys feature, or you can activate the Repeat Keys and Slow Keys features.

Chapter Wrap-Up

This chapter explained how you can control the accessibility options inside Windows Vista. Microsoft designed Windows Vista to be accessible to virtually anyone who needs to use a computer, even if that person requires extra help with the keyboard, video display, or mouse. The accessibility options contain audible and visual clues and a step-by-step guide helps you set the options you need most. These accessibility tools are available for anyone who uses Windows, and just about every user can find something that will make his or her computer use more productive.

In the next chapter, you'll learn about another tool that is part of the accessibility options but almost anyone can benefit from it: Vista's speech recognition tool. You'll learn how to control your computer and dictate into Word and other programs by speaking into your computer's microphone. It took a few years for speech recognition to become mainstream technology, but now that it's included with Windows Vista, it's time to begin using this technology that science fiction writers could only imagine for most of the twentieth century.

CHAPTER 23

Speaking to Your Computer

In This Chapter:

▶ Understand the problems inherent in speech recognition
▶ Set up your computer's microphone properly
▶ Train your computer to understand what you say
▶ Take Vista's speech recognition tutorial
▶ Master speech recognition commands so that you can control your computer
▶ Dictate text into your documents

Why mess with a keyboard and mouse when Vista understands what you say?

The day is finally here, long-promised in science-fiction stories from long ago. Computers understand people. Speak into your computer's microphone, and you can control your computer and dictate words into your word processor. Speech recognition used to be error-prone at best. Although some improvement is still called for, a Vista-based computer is extremely capable of understanding what you say with a high degree of accuracy.

Vista integrates speech recognition technology into its full line of features. You'll need a microphone. You'll need to spend a few moments training Vista which, in effect, enables Vista to pick up on your specific voice characteristics. You'll then be able to command your computer with your microphone.

Preparing for Speech Recognition

Think of all the languages that people speak. Each language brings a different set of grammar and pronunciation rules. Within one language, people sound much different; women sound different from men. People from the east coast sound different from those on the west coast. People in the same family sound different from each other. Vista has quite a chore ahead of it if it's going to understand and respond to what you say.

Until recently, computers really were not powerful enough to interpret spoken words with a high degree of accuracy. You'll find that today's speech recognition systems are extremely capable and highly accurate, but 100% accuracy is still a few years— and perhaps a lot of years—in the future. Having said that, today's technology is certainly accurate enough to be useful. One way that you can gain more speech recognition accuracy with Windows Vista is to train Vista to recognize your voice characteristics.

Without a microphone, Vista cannot hear you. You can find many computer microphones at your local computer store and online. If you plan to do much with speech recognition, a headset is the best way to go. With a headset, you don't need a microphone stand and can adjust the microphone to where it works best, and keep it at that location relative to your mouth while you speak. Another advantage to headset microphones is that they don't pick up other noises from the room as readily as desktop microphones.

By the Way

You'll find microphones that plug into your computer sound card's input jack as well as USB and Bluetooth microphones. Currently, it seems as though USB-based microphones are the most universal and easiest to install. So, if you have a choice, use a USB-based microphone for your Vista speech recognition.

Did you Know?

The accuracy of Vista's speech recognition is tied to the quality of microphone that you get for your computer. Generally, if a microphone came bundled with your computer, it's not a high quality microphone and you might encounter more problems than you would if you upgraded to a higher-quality microphone. As with many things, you generally get what you pay for. When looking for a computer-based microphone, don't get one of the cheaper models. Buying a computer microphone that falls in the middle or higher end of the price scale is worth the added cost if you plan to do much with speech recognition.

Setting Up Your Microphone

If you get a USB-based microphone, the microphone often comes with installation instructions and a CD-ROM. Vista will probably recognize the microphone the moment you plug it into an empty USB slot, but follow the instructions that come with your microphone just to be sure that you get the microphone installed correctly. If your microphone has a silver, 1/8" plug that plugs into your sound card's input jack, the microphone might not include an installation CD-ROM because your computer should be able to monitor the microphone the moment you plug it in.

After you install the physical microphone, you must set up the microphone in Vista. Open your Control Panel and select the Ease of Access group. Open the Speech Recognition Options to display your Control Panel's Speech Recognition window, as shown in Figure 23.1.

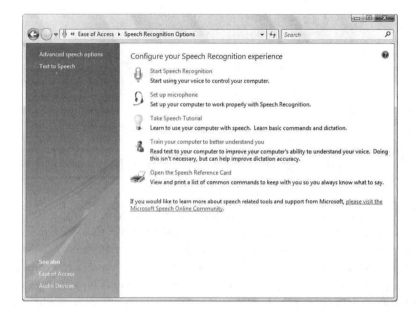

FIGURE 23.1
The Control Panel's Speech Recognition window supports Vista's speech recognition capabilities.

It is from the Speech Recognition window where you will work most with speech recognition, especially when you first begin to train your computer to understand your voice better.

The first thing you should do is set up your microphone by selecting the Set-Up Microphone option. Although you've already installed your microphone hardware, Vista needs you to tell it some specific details about your microphone because Vista adjusts its sound settings differently for different types of microphones.

When you select the Set Up Microphone option, Vista starts the Microphone Setup Wizard. You'll first be asked to select the type of microphone that you connected to your computer from these options: Headset Microphone, Desktop Microphone, or Other (such as handheld microphones and array microphones). Select your microphone type and click Next.

If you selected the Headset Microphone option, the Microphone Setup Wizard displays the information window shown in Figure 23.2. The window includes instructions for proper headset microphone placement and usage. (The best position for a headset microphone is about one inch away from your mouth.)

Click Next to move to the next microphone setup screen. There you'll see a sentence that you are to read. If your microphone is set up properly, most of your speech will remain inside the green zone and sometimes move into the red zone as you talk. If the bar does not move while you speak, you should check to ensure that your microphone is plugged in fully and installed using the software that came with your microphone, if any did. If the bar is pegged at the right of the red zone while you speak, your microphone volume is set too high. This can occur if you use an amplified microphone that is not designed for computers, or an array-based microphone, or a microphone plugged into amplified equipment whose volume levels should be set much lower.

**Watch
Out!**

> If your microphone has a mute button, make sure that the button is *not* set to mute. Also, make sure the microphone's Mute option isn't selected on the Control Panel's Sound options' Volume Control. No matter how properly installed your microphone is, the mute button will keep it silent when you speak.

After you say the sentence and click Next, Vista lets you know whether the recording level was fine, or if you need to adjust the microphone further and try again. When you get the volume in the range that Vista prefers, click the Finish button to complete your microphone's setup. Unless you change microphones or adjust any amplification equipment that your microphone is plugged in to, you won't need to set up your microphone again.

Train Your Computer to Understand Your Voice

You must now go through a short training session with Vista. Open the Control Panel's Speech Recognition window and select the Train Your Computer to Better Understand You option. There you will be led through a series of screens with text that you read into your computer's microphone. After you finish reading a sentence, Vista prompts you with another sentence.

Before clicking Next to start the training, get ready to read a series of sentences that Vista gives you one at a time. Try not to speak in any way differently from the way you'd speak to a friend next to you. Try not to drawl or use sloppy pronunciation, but don't be overly exact either or else you will come across differently from the times later when you dictate into your computer. Vista recommends that you mimic the voice pattern of a newscaster, meaning that you speak clearly but naturally.

> Depending on the sentence and how you speak it, your computer might not understand every sentence you read. Don't worry about it; a few errors are common.

Watch Out!

When you finish training, Vista displays the concluding Speech Recognition Voice Training window as the one shown in Figure 23.3. You can click More Training to train further or Finish to accept the training you've performed.

Click for more training

FIGURE 23.3
The more training you do, the better Vista will be at recognizing what you say.

> The more you train Vista to recognize your voice, the more accurate the speech recognition will be. If you have time now, this is a great time to train some more by clicking the More Training option.

Train Yourself for Speech Recognition

Now that you've trained your computer, it's time to train yourself to give voice commands and dictation. You need to take Vista's speech tutorial. The tutorial is a series of lessons that explain how to use Vista's speech recognition services. The lesson is invaluable at this time and you might find it useful to return to the lessons later for a refresher course.

The primary information you'll gain from the speech recognition tutorials includes correcting mistakes that you or Vista make during your dictation and voice command work. For example, if while dictating into your word processor you said *recording*, but Vista thought you said *recoding*, Vista would place *recoding* in the document at the cursor's position. To correct the mistake, you could use your mouse to select the word and type it, but correcting with your voice is much faster and easier. Just say, *Correct recoding*. Vista highlights the word *recoding* and offers a series of possible corrections from which you can select.

> Every time you correct a mistake using speech recognition, Vista analyzes your correction and modifies its speech recognition pattern to avoid making the same mistake again. Therefore, every time you correct Vista's speech recognition using your voice, you make the speech recognition more accurate in the future.

Although this chapter could list all the ways to correct and handle voice input, the tutorial is the preferred way to learn because it uses Vista's speech recognition technology to train you and allows you to interact using your microphone. In addition, you further train Vista to recognize your voice patterns properly.

> The speech tutorial uses your speakers for some sound during the lessons. Make sure that your speakers are turned on before you start the speech tutorial.

To start the tutorial, set aside about a half hour. The speech tutorial is meant to be run through in a single sitting. Open your Control Panel's Speech Recognition window and select the Take Speech Tutorial option. The speech tutorial lessons begins with the opening window shown in Figure 23.4. Click Next—or say *Next*—to start the tutorial.

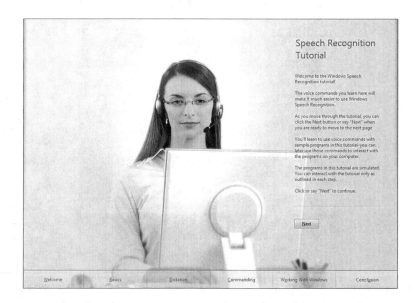

FIGURE 23.4
A 30-minute set of speech recognition tutorials is all you need to become a master at Vista's voice input system.

Here is a summary of some of the speech tutorial's primary lessons:

▶ When you use speech recognition, a small window appears with a microphone button and meter that shows your speech status. Saying *Start listening* tells Vista to begin recognizing your voice, and saying *Stop listening* tells Vista to ignore whatever sounds come from your microphone until you say *Start listening* again. The microphone button also includes a meter that moves as you speak and color-coded feedback, such as orange, which means the computer didn't understand you and you need to repeat the previous command you gave.

▶ Say *Show speech options* when you want to see the speech recognition's context menu, a menu of speech-related commands.

▶ Asking Vista *What can I say?* (as long as you've first said *Start listening* so that Vista monitors your microphone and is awaiting your voice command), displays the basic speech-related commands that summarizes high-level speech recognition actions, as shown in Figure 23.5.

▶ Vista's speech recognition's dictation system will *not* punctuate for you. If your text requires a comma, you'll have to say *comma* to put a comma in the text as you dictate. Vista's speech recognition system is good at capitalizing words at the beginning of a sentence.

FIGURE 23.5
Ask Vista for help by saying *What can I say?* into your microphone during dictation or when giving voice commands.

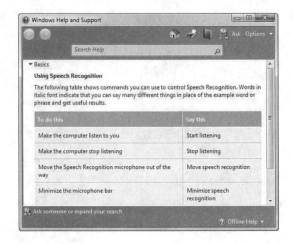

> **By the Way**
>
> Vista automatically separates words with a space between them as necessary.

▶ Saying *Delete that* deletes the last sentence or phrase you spoke. Saying *Undo* undoes the previous deletion, but saying *Undo* also might delete a phrase or sentence you last spoke if you dictated the text right before saying *Undo*. In other words, *Undo* either reverses your most recent command or your most recent text, depending on what you did just before saying *Undo*.

▶ To select text that you've dictated, you can say *Select apple through pear* if you want to select all text between and including those two words. You can then say *Delete that* to delete all the selected text.

▶ To remove a selection from text, say *Clear selection*.

▶ When a list of corrections doesn't show the correct word in a list of possibilities, as might be the case for proper nouns, you can spell the correct word by saying *I'll spell it myself* followed by *Capital B o b b y OK* to use the name *Bobby* for the correction.

▶ Saying *New line* and *New paragraph* simulates pressing Enter once or twice.

▶ Say *Press* and then say the name of any key on your keyboard (such as *Backspace*) to simulate that keypress.

▶ Say *Start* to open Vista's Start menu.

▶ Usually you can say whatever is on your screen when controlling programs. For example, if you're viewing a web page that has an About link, just say *About* to simulate the mouse click over that About link and the web page changes to the About page. If multiple items appear on your screen with the same word, such as multiple Edit buttons, when you say *Edit*, Vista places a different number over each Edit button and then you say the number that matches the button you want to select. Say *double-click* before saying a screen name that you want to open that would normally require a double-click of your mouse. Therefore, saying *Double-click Recycle Bin* opens your Recycle Bin when viewing your Vista desktop.

▶ For dialog boxes and forms that have text boxes, say *Go to name* to place the text cursor in the name field where you can say or spell a name.

▶ Speech Recognition will typically guess correctly at the context of your meaning so if you're text cursor is at the end of a Word document and you begin speaking, Speech Recognition assumes you are dictating. If you say File by itself, Speech Recognition assumes you want to select from the File menu and opens the menu. If, instead, you say *File it away* then Speech Recognition assumes you wanted to dictate the word File and not open the File menu. If Speech Recognition ever gets confused and keeps selecting a menu or command instead of dictating what you want to say, you can say *press capital F press i press l press e* to get the word File in your document.

▶ Say *Switch to Word* (for example) if you have multiple program windows open and want to switch to one of them, such as Word.

After you finish the tutorial, you're ready to use Vista's speech recognition system. Open your Control Panel and select the Start Speech Recognition option. Vista's speech recognition begins and Vista requests that you set up your microphone if you haven't done so already. In addition, speech recognition offers a speech recognition reference sheet in Figure 23.6's window, which produces a Help window of common speech commands that you can print and keep handy as you begin getting comfortable with speech recognition. Within the Speech Recognition window, click Open the Speech Reference Card and then click Common Speech Recognition commands.

FIGURE 23.6
View and print
Vista's handy
speech recogni-
tion reference
sheet.

Chapter Wrap-Up

If you followed along with this chapter, you might have been amazed to see how simple speech recognition can be. Although not 100% accurate, Vista's speech recognition engine is simple to use after you set it up and is relatively accurate. To gain more accuracy, you'll want to get a good computer microphone and you'll want to train Vista to understand your voice through the Control Panel's speech-training program.

You used the Control Panel early in this chapter and you accessed programs from the Control Panel in previous chapters as well. There is so much to Windows Vista that it's difficult to learn everything sequentially. In other words, if an earlier chapter had focused exclusively on the Control Panel—as the next one does—you might not have had enough background to understand the importance of some of the Control Panel's entries.

Now that you're becoming a Windows Vista Master, you're ready to focus more on your Control Panel and learn about what it can do for you. Depending on how you use your computer, you might have a lot or only a little need for the Control Panel. Through the years, Microsoft has made the Control Panel easier to understand and use with each release of Windows. By getting an overview of how the Control Panel operates, you'll be better informed of its benefits and you'll better understand when you can use the Control Panel to get something done.

CHAPTER 24

Controlling Windows Vista

In This Chapter:

▶ Familiarize yourself with Vista's Control Panel's contents

▶ Locate Control Panel options with the Search box

▶ Learn where the Control Panel entries reside throughout Windows

▶ Practice safety when working with the Control Panel's system-related options

▶ Try out several Control Panel features

▶ Walk through the many Control Panel groups

The Control Panel provides access to most of Windows Vista's hardware and software settings. The Control Panel is usually where you go when you need to adjust something about Windows, such as your screen's appearance, or to set up a microphone for speech recognition.

Many of the Control Panel's features are available from outside the Control Panel itself. Over the years, Microsoft has made the Windows Control Panel easier to understand so that users can locate what they need faster and get back to work. You typically won't spend much time working with the Control Panel. Some Control Panel options you might never use. The most important thing you should know about the Control Panel is what it contains so later you'll know that when, for example, you need to adjust something about your mouse, such as the double-click speed, you'll find the doorway to your mouse settings in the Control Panel.

This chapter gives you an overview of the Control Panel and familiarizes you with its features.

Get Familiar with Your Control Panel

Throughout the earlier chapters of this book you've already worked with the Control Panel. That's because the Control Panel covers such a wide range of hardware and software settings that it's difficult to cover most subjects related to Vista without visiting the Control Panel occasionally. For example, in Chapter 3, "Clicking Your Start Button," you worked with the Control Panel when learning ways to modify your Windows Start menu behavior.

Figure 24.1 shows the Control Panel. You access the Control Panel from your Windows Start menu. Click the Start button and the Control Panel appears on the right side. Selecting the Control Panel entry opens the Control Panel window.

FIGURE 24.1
Access your computer's hardware and Windows software settings in the Control Panel.

As you can see, the Control Panel's entries are grouped by function. If you need to make security changes to your computer, the first place to look would be the Control Panel's Security group. Click Security to display further Control Panel settings related to security, such as your Windows firewall and parental controls.

The Control Panel is a window that brings together, in logical and related groups, settings for your computer's hardware and software. You won't find options for specific programs such as Adobe Illustrator in the Control Panel, but you will find options for Windows-related software such as the clock in your taskbar's notification area and hardware-related settings such as your printer options.

> As you traverse the Control Panel, the address bar at the top of the window shows you a breadcrumb trail of where you are so that you can click to return to various areas of the Control Panel. In addition, the Back and Forward buttons in the upper-left corner enable you to move back and forth through the Control Panel's windows.

Did you Know?

As I said earlier in this chapter, Microsoft changes the Control Panel with each version of Windows in an attempt to make the Control Panel easier to access and find what you need. If you're familiar with and prefer the older, Windows 98–style of Control Panel, the style that shows the Control Panel items listed one after another without major grouping, click the Classic View link to display your Control Panel options, listed alphabetically, in an icon view as shown in Figure 24.2.

Returns to grouped view

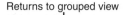
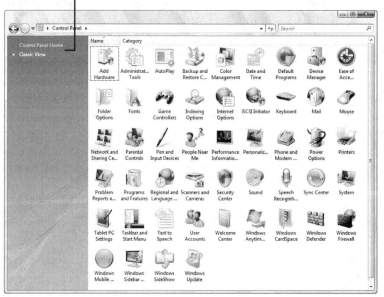

FIGURE 24.2
The Classic view shows your Control Panel items in an ungrouped, more detailed order.

> To return to the Windows Vista view of Control Panel, click the Control Panel Home link.

Did you Know?

Use the Search Box to Locate Control Panel Options

Some users aren't always sure whether the Control Panel holds the options they want to see. For example, when working with speech recognition, it's not intuitive that the speech recognition training wizard is located inside the Control Panel's Ease of Access group. If you just read Chapter 23, "Speaking to Your Computer," that knowledge might be well-known to you now, but if it takes you six months or so to use speech recognition again and you need a refresher course, will you remember that the speech–recognition-related routines are to be found inside the Control Panel's Ease of Access group?

The Search box that permeates most of Vista's windows, described in Chapter 13, "Finding Information All Over Windows," also enables you to locate items in the Control Panel. When you first open the Control Panel to either the Vista view or the Classic view, there don't appear to be enough items to warrant a search. Nevertheless, some options and settings are buried beneath some of the Control Panel's groups and their locations aren't always obvious until you learn the Control Panel's contents more fully.

Therefore, you can type what you want to find in the Control Panel's Search box and Vista displays all the Control Panel items related to your search text. For example, typing speech in the Search box narrows down the Control Panel's options to only two groups—Speech Recognition Options and Ease of Access Center—as shown in Figure 24.3. Both Control Panel groups include speech recognition settings.

FIGURE 24.3
Use your Control Panel's Search box to locate out-of-the way Control Panel options.

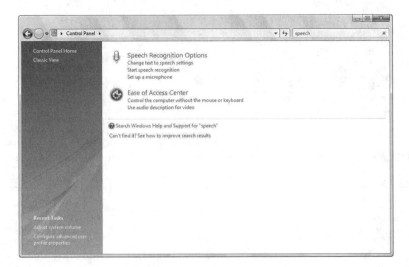

Vista's Search box attempts to remain in context with what you're doing. Therefore, when using the Control Panel's Search box, the search returns Control Panel items. When using the Start menu's Search box, Vista returns Start–menu-related results before showing results that match filenames.

By the Way

Backspace to erase the Search box contents and to return to the full Control Panel screen.

Did you Know?

Many Control Panel Options Appear Elsewhere

You now know that the Control Panel groups hardware and Vista settings so that you can adjust the behavior of things that happen as you use your computer. Many of the Control Panel features are available from other places, too. Microsoft's goal for Vista is to give you access to what you need when you need it. If you often need a Control Panel option when working elsewhere in Windows, Vista puts a link to that Control Panel option elsewhere.

For example, the Welcome Center includes a Personalize Windows option that, when you click it, opens the Control Panel's Appearance and Personalization group's Personalization window shown in Figure 24.4. This same window is available from within the Control Panel when you open the Appearance and Personalization group and then click the Personalization option.

Vista's guided help system often takes you to a Control Panel option. For example, if you search Vista's help using the search term *change screen resolution*, a help window (like the one shown in Figure 24.5) appears that explains what screen resolution means and includes a link you can click to open the Display Settings window. The Display Settings window is located under your Control Panel's Appearance and Personalization group and appears when you click that group's Adjust Screen Resolution link.

FIGURE 24.4
Many Control Panel options are available in several locations.

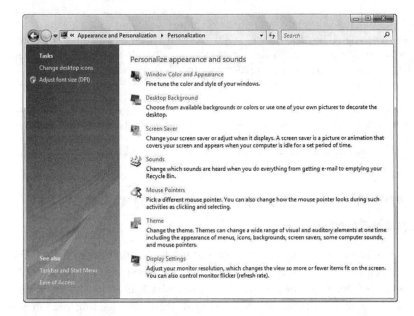

FIGURE 24.5
The Help system often takes you to the Control Panel setting you need.

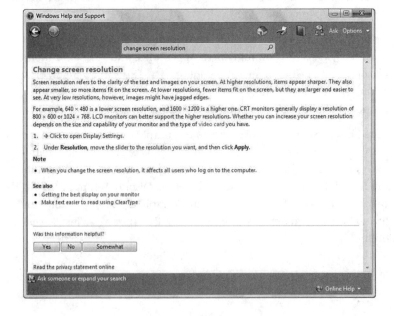

Stay Alert When Using Your Control Panel

Some of the Control Panel's options are advanced computer settings that can cause problems if you or someone else sets certain options incorrectly. But that danger doesn't mean you need to shy away from the Control Panel out of fear that you'll harm your computer.

Many of the Control Panel's options are extremely simple to understand and change depending on your needs. For example, the colors used in Windows and your Windows desktop background picture (called **wallpaper**) should be set to *your* liking. Changing your desktop's picture won't harm any operating system setting and if you don't like the picture you choose, it's simple to change it back to what you had before.

Most of the more critical and potentially dangerous Control Panel settings appear in these two groups: System and Maintenance and the Hardware and Sound groups. In each of these groups you can change settings that may render certain components unusable as might occur if you change a device's driver setting. Despite that, you'll still want to access these groups from time to time even if you don't want to change any critical settings. For example, the Hardware and Sound group includes AutoPlay settings that control the way a CD or DVD plays when you insert the disc into the drive. Settings such as AutoPlay are easily reversible and don't set any system options that could cause something to malfunction if set incorrectly.

Chapter 25, "Setting Up Windows Program Defaults," explains how to set various AutoPlay options so that your audio and video media responds the way you want it to.

By the Way

Use good judgment when making changes to the functions available within Control Panel and you should be just fine. If you know what you want to do and you see the Control Panel option to do it, make the change without fear of harming something in your system. If something more elaborate needs looking at, such as a device driver for an attached peripheral like a modem, you might opt to use more caution and make changes only when you have instructions on how to do so. For example, many modem instruction manuals tell you how to download and install the latest drivers for the modem, and often times you'll update the driver from within the Control Panel's Hardware and Sound group's Device Manager option. As you can see from Figure 24.6, the Device Manager includes several strange-sounding devices whose purpose isn't always obvious.

FIGURE 24.6
Some items
inside the
Control Panel
require exten-
sive knowledge
or detailed
instructions
before you can
safely make a
change.

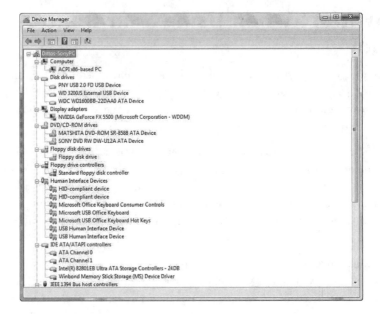

Protect Yourself Before Setting the Wrong Option

If you have to make a system setting inside your Control Panel that might adversely affect your computer's operation, especially when changing device and driver
settings, you can protect yourself by setting a system restore point before changing the Control Panel setting.

Chapter 31, "Restoring Your Windows System to a Previous State," explains how
to create system restore points. If you change a setting incorrectly, or if you ever
want to revert back to a previous system state, you can easily do so as long as
you created a system restore point before making the change.

Therefore, if you're unsure about a Control Panel setting, create a restore point
before you change the setting and you'll be just fine if something goes astray.
You'll be able to return your operating system back to the state it was in before
the change and all will be back to normal.

A Control Panel Walkthrough

As a Vista user, you need to know what the Control Panel offers, but you don't necessarily have to be an expert in all the Control Panel's contents. If you've read
through the earlier chapters of this book, you already know what some of the
Control Panel options are for and you're already comfortable with making changes
to those options when needed.

The most important thing to understand about the Control Panel is that it generally contains settings that you'll access when you want to adjust the way a device behaves or when you want to adjust the way Windows looks or behaves. For example, Windows makes sounds as you work within it and if you want to adjust or turn off certain sounds, the Control Panel should be the first place you look.

Take a moment to open the Control Panel and study its contents. You won't work within your Control Panel daily, and sometimes you might go months without ever opening the Control Panel, but you need to have a general idea of what is there. To give you an idea of the Control Panel's contents, the following sections describe each major Control Panel group and discuss the chapters in this book that focus on specific Control Panel entries when appropriate.

Watch Out!

Depending on your Windows Vista version and the options you have installed, you might see other Control Panel groups not listed here. The sections that follow describe the most common groups that all users of Vista might need to work with at some point.

Did you Know?

The more you use the Control Panel, the smaller it seems! Many options appear in multiple places throughout the Control Panel. You can adjust your screen colors and resolution from several Control Panel groups, for example. At first it might appear that the Control Panel has far too many options to ever remember (not that you *have* to remember every option), but as you visit each of the Control Panel window's groups throughout the rest of this chapter, you'll see that many of the same entries appear in several different Control Panel groups. Vista puts what you need where you need it. If you're working in the Hardware and Sound group, for example, you might be looking there because you want to adjust your Windows desktop's background picture that appears on your monitor. Instead, someone else might look in the Appearance and Personalization group in an effort to change their monitor's background wallpaper image. The option appears in both places.

System and Maintenance

Before clicking the System and Maintenance Control Panel option, notice that beneath the System and Maintenance group are two links: Get Started with Windows and Back Up Your Computer. In an attempt to put often-used items and options where you can locate them quickly, Vista provides these two links that you can click without first opening the System and Maintenance group. If you opened the System and Maintenance group you would see items related to getting started with Windows and backing up, but the upfront links mean you don't first have to open the entire group if you want to perform either of those two tasks.

Clicking the System and Maintenance Control Panel option opens the System and Maintenance window shown in Figure 24.7. The links in the upper-left pane are links to the other Control Panel groups. You don't have to return to the Control Panel's main window to go from System and Maintenance to the Ease of Access group, for example. Just click the Ease of Access link to save a step. The Recent Tasks list in the lower-right pane includes any Control Panel options you've recently visited, and you can return to any of those by clicking one of the links there.

Return to previous window

Quickly select any Control Panel group

FIGURE 24.7
The Control Panel's System and Maintenance group includes options related to updating and backing up your computer.

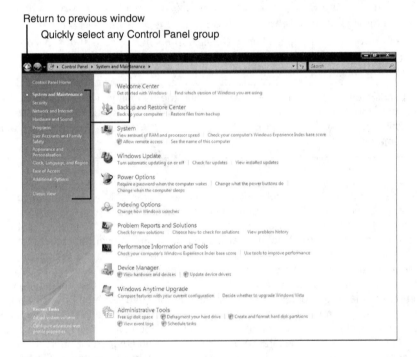

The following describes each of the System and Maintenance entries:

▶ **Welcome Center**—Provides quick access to common programs and settings that you'll often use when you begin using Vista. Chapter 2, "Exploring the Welcome Center," discusses the Welcome Center's features.

▶ **Backup and Restore Center**—Provides links to Vista's backup and restore wizards so that you can save your disk data and protect it from disasters that could cause data loss. Chapter 35, "Protecting Your Data and Programs," shows you how to back up and restore your computer's disk drives.

▶ **System**—Displays an overview of your computer settings and provides links to advanced system-related features such as hardware settings. Most of the settings in the System group are advanced and require that its users understand driver and hardware settings.

▶ **Windows Update**—Displays the status of your Vista system, telling you whether any system updates are needed by going online and comparing the latest updates to your system, as shown in Figure 24.8. Chapter 27, "Managing Your Windows Security," discusses more about how you can apply updates to keep your system running smoothly and as safely as possible.

Change update settings

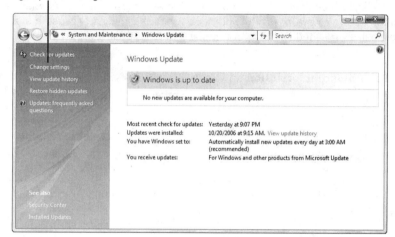

FIGURE 24.8
Keep your operating system up-to-date by checking for the latest updates or automating Vista so that updates apply automatically.

▶ **Power Options**—Determines what happens when you press your computer's power button, shows how your system uses energy-saving features, and offers ways that can extend your laptop battery usage to get the most out of each laptop's charge. Chapter 34, "Saving Power with Windows Vista," explains how you can use the Power Options settings to get optimum performance with the energy levels you want to use.

▶ **Indexing Options**—Provides settings that specify how Vista's searching features work in the background to locate files and provide quick searches.

In general, Vista's indexing options are set for maximum efficiency so that Vista updates its internal search indexes in the background while you work without consuming a great amount of resources. If you use an older computer that causes Vista to perform slowly, you might have to remove some file types that Vista's search feature scans for by deselecting certain file types from the search index.

Watch Out!

▶ **Problem Reports and Solutions**—As you use Vista, problems could occur. Vista does its best to point you in the right direction with helpful advice for more information online. In addition, Vista keeps track of system problems you experience and can sometimes locate a fix that becomes available later. You can track your system problems and read solutions that Vista offers in the Problem Reports and Solutions window.

The internal structure of Vista is designed to keep system problems from bringing down your entire system. Therefore, when a system problem occurs, it's more likely that Vista will be able to analyze the problem and suggest solutions. Such an analysis wasn't always possible in previous Windows versions because a system problem likely resulted in Windows freezing or a reboot being required.

▶ **Performance Information and Tools**—Provides descriptions of your computer's performance, factoring in disk speed, memory size, and graphics card, and suggesting ways you might be able to improve performance while using Vista.

▶ **Device Manager**—Displays the Device Manager dialog box from which you can adjust advanced hardware device settings and install new device drivers.

The Device Manager is also available from the System option inside the Control Panel's System and Maintenance group.

▶ **Windows Anytime Upgrade**—Allows you to upgrade to a more advanced Vista level by paying an upgrade fee; for example, you could upgrade from Vista Home Basic to Vista Home Premium. The capability to upgrade directly from inside Vista makes upgrading easier and faster than ordering an upgrade through the mail or going to a store to purchase a more powerful version of Windows.

▶ **Administrative Tools**—Contains several Vista utility programs that enable you to get better performance out of your disk drive. Chapter 32, "Improving Disk Performance and Storage," describes several programs located in the Administrative Tools group. You can access the Task Scheduler from this group also (refer to Chapter 21, "Scheduling Tasks to Run Later").

Security

Clicking the Security option opens the security-related Control Panel group of options, as shown in Figure 24.9. Here you'll find options that help protect your computer's integrity. Chapter 27 discusses each of the Security group's options in more detail and explains how you can maximize the safety of your computing experience.

FIGURE 24.9
Security must remain in the forefront of the Windows Vista user's priorities to keep computers running properly.

The following describes each of the Security entries:

▶ **Security Center**—Provides a one-stop overview of your computer's current security settings, allowing you to see what's lacking. For example, Figure 24.10's Security Center shows that the computer's malware protection is lacking. **Malware** is bad software that can invade your computer from your Internet connection through such things as email attachments that contain viruses.

> The Security Center provides an overview of the rest of the Security group's options. For example, if Windows Firewall, the second option, isn't turned on, the Security Center will warn you of this.

By the Way

▶ **Windows Firewall**—Controls the state of your Vista firewall and enables you to adjust the firewall's settings.

▶ **Windows Update**—Enables you to modify the way Vista is updated (manually or automatically) and shows you the status of your current updates. This option is available from the System and Maintenance Control Panel group and also resides on your Windows Start menu.

FIGURE 24.10
The Security
Center warns
you of any
potential
computer
weaknesses.

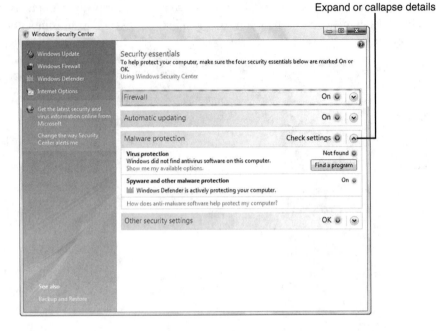

▶ **Windows Defender**—Gives you access and control over Windows Defender, a Vista utility program that monitors spyware.

▶ **Internet Options**—Provides access to Internet Explorer's security settings and offers you the ability to delete pieces of your web-surfing history.

▶ **Parental Controls**—Gives parents a means to control what children and other users of the computer can access. Chapter 27 explains how to institute settings that limit what your computer's users can access based on these settings.

Network and Internet

Clicking the Network and Internet option opens the network-related Control Panel group of options, as shown in Figure 24.11. Here you'll find options that enable you to set up and control the way your computer interacts with any attached network. The network might be external, such as the Internet, or internal, as you'd find in a home or business environment where a network has been established for the various computers on site to share files and printers.

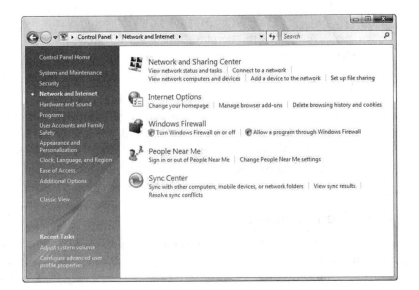

FIGURE 24.11
Maintain and control your computer's access to other computers with the Network and Internet options.

Chapter 36, "Combining Vista, Networks, and the Internet," as well as subsequent chapters devoted to using your computer in the connected world of the Internet, explore many of the options you find in the Control Panel's Network and Internet window.

The following describes each of the Network and Internet entries:

▶ **Network and Sharing Center**—Provides a graphical picture of the network that your computer is connected to as well as shows the Internet connection if you've set one up. The Network Center also provides troubleshooting tools you can use to monitor your network activity and to repair problems that you might be having.

▶ **Internet Options**—Gives you access to Internet Explorer's security and control dialog boxes.

> The Internet Options entries are also available when you select Tools, Options from within Internet Explorer.

By the Way

▶ **Windows Firewall**—Offers another way to access your firewall settings in addition to the Security Center described in the previous section.

▶ **People Near Me**—Adds support for **Windows Collaboration,** technology that enables you to work with others on the same data (such as documents) that a team is preparing for a presentation. The People Near Me option searches for those on your network and displays their name, their computer's name, and their IP address.

▶ **Sync Center**—Makes available tools that you can use to synchronize files on a PDA such as a smart cell phone, to maintain up-to-date files and contacts on the device. Chapter 39, "Synchronizing Your Computer with Other Devices," explains how to use the Sync Center.

Hardware and Sound

Clicking the Hardware and Sound option opens the hardware-related Control Panel group of options as shown in Figure 24.12. If you need to adjust something on any device attached to your computer, such as a game controller or your mouse, you'll find a way to access that device's settings here. In addition to devices stored on your computer, you can adjust your computer's sound settings. These sound settings relate not only to your sound-producing hardware, such as your internal sound card, but also to Vista's sound settings that control the various sounds Vista makes when certain events occur.

FIGURE 24.12
Adjust the settings on all your hardware devices from within the Hardware and Sound Control Panel group.

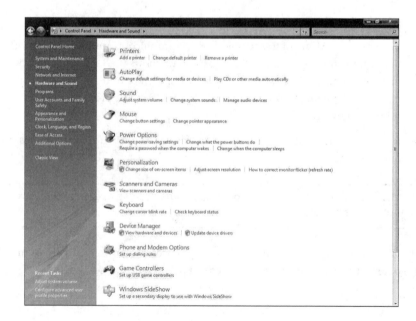

You don't need a walkthrough of each of the Hardware and Sound group because you know what a printer, mouse, and keyboard (as well as the other devices listed in the group) are.

By the Way

Sometimes you'll have to use some sleuthing skills to locate what you need. For example, if you want to adjust the resolution of your monitor, no Monitor or Graphics Adapter option appears inside the Hardware and Sound group. Instead, you use the Personalization option to modify your monitor's resolution settings.

Watch Out!

You might not always have every device listed in your Control Panel's Hardware and Sound group. For example, if you're not using a tablet-based portable computer, you probably have no tablet pen to use as an input device. Nevertheless, you'll see the Pen and Input Device option in the window. It's there for those who need it.

Many of the entries inside your Control Panel's Hardware and Sound group are familiar to you because you've seen them in the other Control Panel groups you've read about in previous sections. For example, the Power Options and Device Manager options appear in the window. Vista constantly tries to make available what you need, so many items overlap throughout the Control Panel groups. The Device Manager, for example, is directly related to both your hardware and also to your Windows system because it's device driver software that allows a hardware component to interact with Windows. That's why Microsoft chose to include the Device Manager both here in the Hardware and Sound group as well as in the System and Maintenance group as you saw earlier in this chapter.

Programs

Clicking the Programs option opens the Programs group window shown in Figure 24.13. Here you'll find options that enable you to view, manage, install, and remove programs as well as purchase additional programs online that you can download to your computer.

User Accounts and Family Safety

Clicking the User Accounts and Family Safety option opens the User Accounts and Family Safety group window shown in Figure 24.14. Here you'll find options related to setting up and maintaining user accounts as well as the parental control options that you read about when you learned about the Security group earlier in this chapter.

FIGURE 24.13
You can manage all your programs from the Control Panel's Programs group.

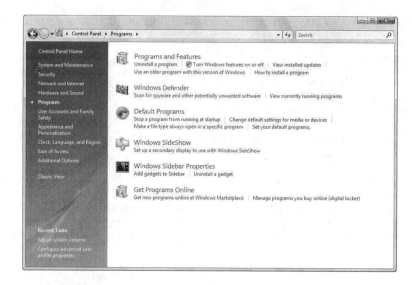

FIGURE 24.14
Manage user accounts and adjust parental controls from your Control Panel's User Accounts and Family Safety group.

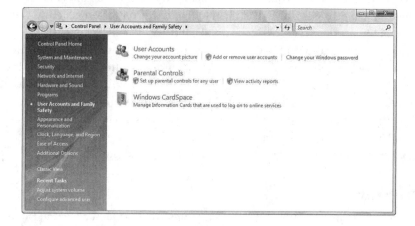

The following describes each of the User Accounts and Family Safety entries:

▶ **User Accounts**—Provides an interface for you to add, change, view, and delete user accounts on your computer. You can set up users with limited or full Administrative privileges here. Chapter 26, "Separating Users Gives Each the Access They Need," describes how to manage the user accounts on your computer.

▶ **Parental Controls**—Gives parents a means to control what children and other users of the computer can access. You also saw this entry in your Control Panel's Security group.

▶ **Windows CardSpace**—Allows you to manage digital security cards that send encrypted data about yourself to sites that you approve. Such digital ID cards will make logging into secure web sites safer and faster but web site designers must begin adopting the Windows CardSpace feature in larger numbers for the feature to be helpful to most users.

Appearance and Personalization

Clicking the Appearance and Personalization option opens the group window shown in Figure 24.15. There you'll find options related to your screen, taskbar behavior, Sidebar, and other Vista elements that determine how your computer projects information and modify the way you interact with your computer.

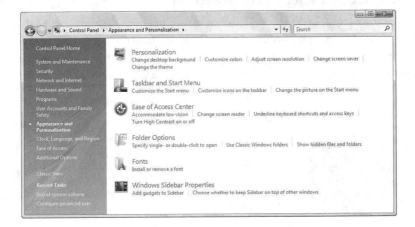

FIGURE 24.15
You can change the way you and Vista interact with one another from the Appearance and Personalization window.

The following describes each of the Appearance and Personalization entries:

▶ **Personalization**—Gives you access to screen settings such as the Vista color scheme, screen resolution, and desktop background wallpaper image.

▶ **Taskbar and Start Menu**—Enables you to customize your taskbar and Start menu's behavior. Chapter 6, "Taking the Taskbar to Task," explains the associated features of this entry.

▶ **Ease of Access Center**—Opens the Ease of Access Center window where you modify your computer's accessibility options. Chapter 22, "Making Windows Vista More Accessible," describes the accessibility options.

▶ **Folder Options**—Provides settings and options that determine how your Explorer windows behave.

▶ **Fonts**—Gives you control over the fonts installed on your computer. You can add and remove fonts from this entry and Windows programs such as Microsoft Word will have access to the set of fonts you manage.

New fonts are available online that you can purchase and download from sites such as www.Fonts.com.

▶ **Windows Sidebar Properties**—Offers Sidebar settings and controls so you can manage your Sidebar. Chapter 9, "Working with the Sidebar and Gadgets," explains how to maximize your use of the Sidebar.

Clock, Language, and Region

Clicking the Clock, Language, and Region option opens the group window shown in Figure 24.16. Here you'll be able to adjust your computer's clock and date (found at the right of your taskbar), add additional clocks in case you travel and want to keep up with multiple time zones, and change regional information such as the default language and keyboard your computer assumes.

FIGURE 24.16
Update your Windows clock and time zone region from the Clock, Language, and Region window.

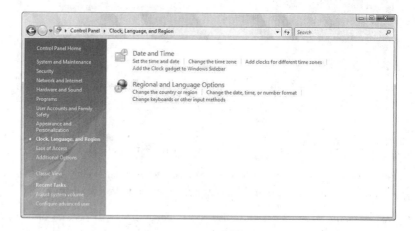

Rest your mouse pointer over your taskbar's time to view the date.

Chapter 33, "Configuring Windows Vista," describes more of these settings.

Ease of Access

Clicking the Ease of Access option opens the Ease of Access group window in which you can manage your accessibility options as well as your Speech Recognition settings.

The Ease of Access Center provides you with options that enable users with special needs to utilize a more appropriate Windows interface. Chapter 22, "Making Windows Vista More Accessible," explains how you can take advantage of these features. Chapter 23 explains how to talk to your computer to control it and dictate without using your keyboard.

Additional Options

The final Control Panel group is Additional Options. The Additional Options group differs from computer to computer, depending on the programs installed. For example, if your computer has Apple's QuickTime media player installed, you can access the QuickTime options and behavior settings from the Control Panel's Additional Options group. Of course, those same settings are available from the QuickTime program itself, but the Control Panel's group gives you the ability to modify QuickTime options without actually starting the QuickTime program.

Chapter Wrap-Up

You have now seen a major overview of your Control Panel's contents. The Control Panel provides an interface for modifying and managing your computer's hardware and Windows Vista settings. Organized in related groups, the options you find change Vista's behavior. Some of the settings, such as the Device Manager, are advanced and should be changed only by knowledgeable users. Other options, such as the Speech Recognition options located in the Ease of Access group, control the way you interact with Vista.

Knowing every option located in your Control Panel is unnecessary. They are there and await you when and if you ever need them, but many users will never select many of their Control Panel's options. Some advanced users (and some who are simply adventurous!) might play around with the Control Panel more than other users in an effort to see the extent to which they can customize Vista to perform in a unique way.

Now that you've seen an overview of the Control Panel, you know in general what awaits you there and you can adjust your Control Panel's settings when and if you need to. The next chapter, "Setting Up Windows Program Defaults," explains how to use some of these Control Panel settings to customize Vista to your needs.

CHAPTER 25

Setting Up Windows Program Defaults

In This Chapter:

▶ Determine what AutoPlay action occurs when you insert a CD or DVD

▶ Learn how Windows Vista recognizes different file types

▶ Limit programs to use only selected file types

▶ Change your folder options to display filename extensions

▶ Associate file types to specific programs

▶ Set your default web browser, instant messenger, email, and media player program

As you use Windows Vista, you'll notice that Microsoft applied several default settings that you might or might not want to keep. Actually, every one of the scores of options in the Control Panel that you read about in the previous chapter are set to values that Microsoft perceived as being the settings most users would prefer most of the time. You might not be one of those typical users, however, and you want to change some of the more common default behaviors to suit the way you work.

This chapter explores the common default settings that users most often change. One of the most common is the action your computer takes when you insert an audio CD or DVD. Do you want Vista to begin playing the contents immediately or do you want to trigger the play by running a program such as Media Player yourself?

This is a *potpourri* chapter in that you'll see how to change default settings across several aspects of Vista. It's not meant to be a tell-all chapter that shows every default value you could ever set; that would waste your time. Instead, you'll learn how to make common system changes often requested by Windows users.

Change Media Actions

Open your Control Panel's Hardware and Sound group and select AutoPlay to change the behavior of your media such as audio CDs and DVDs. The AutoPlay window, shown in Figure 25.1, opens to provide you with the options you can change to reflect your media preferences. All the options on this window describe what happens when you insert or select each type of media content.

FIGURE 25.1
Tell Windows how you want your media and player defaults set.

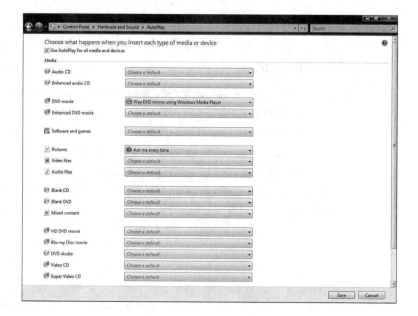

Many of the options will show `Choose a Default` for their selected value. This doesn't mean that Vista doesn't already have an option selected because Vista assumes a value for all its options. In other words, if you haven't selected an action for the Audio CD option, Vista defaults to playing audio CDs with Windows Media Player or, in the case of Vista installations without Media Player, it defaults to a different media player. After you set your own default, that option setting will display.

By the
~~Way~~

It would be helpful if Vista showed the actual setting instead of displaying `Choose a Default`, but it does not.

If, as in Figure 25.1, your DVD movie option is set to Play DVD Video Using Windows Media Player, as soon as you insert a DVD movie in your computer's DVD drive, Windows Media Player begins playing the DVD. If the DVD uses a menu, that menu appears after any initial title and copyright screens appear.

If you'd rather Vista do nothing when you insert a DVD movie into your DVD drive, click the arrow next to this option and select Take No Action, as shown in Figure 25.2. If you regularly burn your own DVD movies and are using Windows Movie Maker, for example, to bring together multiple clips from multiple movies for a collage movie you're creating, if Media Player began playing the movie as soon as you inserted each disc, stopping the movie's playback to return to your Movie Maker editing session would get tiring. After you finish making your movie collage, you can reset the AutoPlay option so that your computer automatically begins playing DVD movies when you insert them if that's your usual preference.

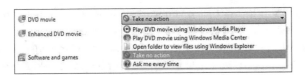

FIGURE 25.2
You can tell Vista not to play DVDs and CDs automatically when you insert them into your computer's drives.

The AutoPlay options change as you install and remove media-related programs. For example, if you've installed Apple's iTunes, you can play video and music with iTunes. If iTunes is your preferred media player, change the Audio CD (and any other AutoPlay options you want to play through iTunes) to the Play Audio CD Using iTunes option. As you can see from Figure 25.3, iTunes entries will appear on the drop-down list. Other media players, such as MusicMatch, might also appear on the drop-down settings, making it simple to select your preferred players. You'll also find Vista's own Media Center appearing throughout the options if you primarily use your computer as a Media Center PC.

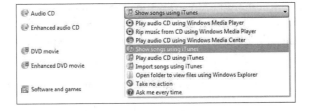

FIGURE 25.3
Other media players, such as iTunes, will appear in your AutoPlay options if you've installed players other than Windows Media Player.

The AutoPlay options include not only audio and video options, but also game and picture options. For example, you can control what Vista does when you insert a game CD into your disc drive.

Did you Know?

If you've set several options and decide that Vista's default AutoPlay options were better, you don't have to change back every option. Instead, scroll to the bottom of the AutoPlay window and click Reset All Defaults. Sadly, this causes the AutoPlay options to list, once again, Choose a Default instead of showing the current setting, but you'll know that the options are back to their original, installed state.

Setting Program-Related Defaults

You don't just work in Vista all day, you work with *programs* that run in Vista. Windows Vista is a means to get to your programs. Of course, Vista is an important tool and with Vista you can manage your programs and data effectively, so understanding Vista is critical as you're learning throughout this book. Nevertheless, your programs are really what matter. No matter what operating system you run, if you use your computer to keep track of your expenses, your accounting program is far more important than the operating system the accounting program runs on.

Therefore, one of the most important aspects of Vista is how it manages and runs your programs. Today's computers are faster than ever before and if your PC is capable of running Vista, particularly if it can run the Aero user interface, the odds are you have an advanced computer. Having said that, speed isn't always the only critical factor when running programs. You'll want to set your Vista-related program defaults so that you get your work done with less effort.

As you saw in the previous chapter, your Control Panel's Programs group includes an entry called *Default Programs*. Selecting Default Programs produces the window shown in Figure 25.4 from which you can control program-related actions, such as which programs start automatically every time you turn on your computer as well as associate file types with certain programs that ensure the associated program automatically runs if you select a file of that type from an Explorer window or elsewhere.

Each of the next few sections explores many of these program-related options.

Specifying Default Program File Types

Programs and data work together. In reality, your data is the more important of the two. You can always reinstall a program, but if you lose your data, you've lost work you've done.

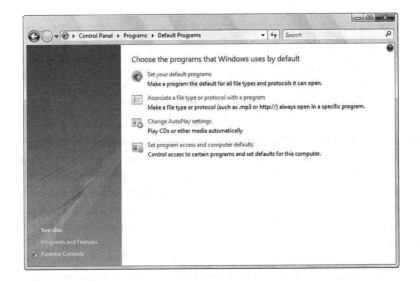

FIGURE 25.4
Set default programs and program-related file types in the Default Programs window.

In earlier days of computing, users started a program and then loaded the program's data. This is still done quite often today. You might, for example, start Media Player and then load an MP3 file to listen to using Media Player's File, Open command. You no longer have to run a program first, however, to work with one of your files. If you double-click an MP3 file from inside a Windows Explorer window, Vista checks to see what program you've associated with MP3 files and automatically loads the program and begins playing the music.

You can change programs and their associations. Before learning to do so, a short detour that explains file types is in order.

About File Types

In the Windows environment, your files have an associated file type. This file type is usually determined by the file's extension which is comprised of three letters at the end of the filename. The file named Word.exe is a program with the extension exe and JanSales.dat is a file with the extension dat. As you can see, a period separates the extension from the rest of the file's name.

Over the years, programmers have used common extensions to indicate the type of files they create. For example, a file with the .exe extension is a program. A file with the .txt extension is a text file.

Nothing requires a file to conform to industry standards. You can create a document in Excel, for example, and save that document with the .exe extension by overriding the default extension Excel normally uses for its worksheets. Using common filename extensions incorrectly can cause problems later, however, so it's best not to rock the boat. In almost all cases, when a program wants to add a certain extension to a file you are saving, accept the program's default extension.

When you view a file in a Windows Explorer window, Windows looks at the file's extension and guesses at the type of file it is. Vista then uses its database of file extensions to select an icon for the file. Figure 25.5 shows several files (and folders). The icons on each folder gives you a visual clue as to the type of file you're looking at. For example, Adobe Acrobat files end in the .pdf filename extension. A file called Success appears in the window and the PDF icon indicates that the file uses the .pdf extension.

FIGURE 25.5
A file's extension determines how Vista displays the file in an Explorer window.

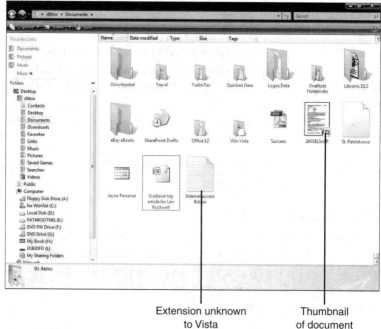

Extension unknown to Vista

Thumbnail of document

Vista normally hides file extensions, but there are two ways to see them. If you right-click a file and select Properties, you can locate the full filename with its extension in the dialog box. In addition, you can open your Control Panel's Appearance and Personalization group and select Folder Options, click the View tab, and click to uncheck the Hide Extensions for Known File Types option. When you close the dialog box, Vista displays all extensions in all filenames shown in all Explorer windows.

Sometimes you'll see more than just an icon that represents an Explorer window's file. You'll actually see a small image of the document, as Figure 25.5's Word file displays. When you save documents in Microsoft Office 2007 and other Vista-aware products, you can select to save a thumbnail image of the first page of the document so you get a mini-preview of the document's contents. Word includes the Word icon along with that thumbnail preview to confirm that you're looking at a Word document.

If Vista does not recognize a file's extension, Vista will not be able to display an icon that represents a file type. Vista goes ahead and lists the file's extension, even if you've hidden file extensions, so you can possibly determine for yourself what file type the extension represents.

Set Program Defaults for File Types

Opening the Set Your Default Programs from your Control Panel's Default Programs group opens the Set Your Default Programs window shown in Figure 25.6. The window includes only Microsoft programs installed with Vista.

Here you determine what file types each of the listed programs can open. Click to select a program and then click the Choose Defaults button. A list of every possible file type (shown with each type's extension) appears. Figure 25.7 shows all the file types that Windows Media Player can play. If you want to use Windows Media Player to play every one of those types, you can click the Select All button and Vista selects every type. If you only want Media Player to play certain file types, click to select only those types.

If you use multiple media players, you might prefer one over the other depending on what you want to experience. For example, you might prefer to use Media Player to listen to your music but prefer QuickTime to watch your videos. To accomplish this, you can set Media Player's file types to music files only and leave the video-related file types unchecked. Then you'll set your QuickTime file types to the video file types you want QuickTime to play.

FIGURE 25.6
You can specify
which file types
certain pro-
grams can
open.

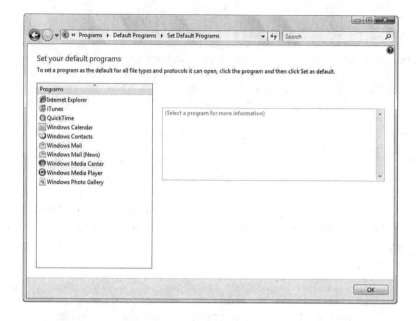

FIGURE 25.7
Select any or all
file types for
the programs to
be associated
with.

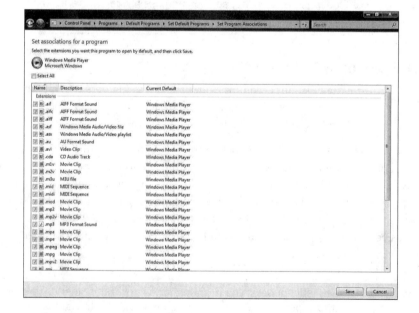

By the Way

Before Vista offered the program default windows you're learning about in this chapter, you would have to open each program and determine which file types that program was allowed to work with. Sometimes it got confusing as to which program was associated with which file type. Using Vista's Set Default Programs window simplifies the process dramatically by giving you a way to see all possible file types and selecting from the master list which types go with each program.

Media-related programs aren't the only programs that you can associate file types to. For example, web-browsing software can display more than just HTML files. You can determine which kinds of web-related pages Internet Explorer and the other web browsers on your computer can access. You might, for example, prefer to use Internet Explorer for HTML files that you view but use an FTP client program such as WS-FTP Pro to view and access FTP-related files. (*FTP* stands for *File Transfer Protocol*; FTP programs enable you to transfer multiple files back and forth across Internet and network connections.)

By the Way

Internet web pages are little more than files that have extensions and are stored on web servers. Vista looks at a web page's extension to determine that page's file type and then picks your preferred program to view that page.

Associating File Types to Programs Revisited

When you select the Associate a File Type or Protocol with a Program option from your Control Panel's Default Programs group, you'll see a list of every known file type on your Vista system and the program that's associated with that type. You might have associated the program yourself using the previous section's window, or perhaps Vista was always set to associate that file type and program and you never needed to change the association.

Figure 25.8 shows this window. You see each filename's extension in the first column followed by a description of that file type and the currently set program associated with the file. Some prefer this file type list when associating programs to file types over the program-centric window described in the previous section. In addition, the Set Your Default Programs window described in the previous section works primarily with Windows-based programs such as Media Player and doesn't always show non-Windows programs in its list.

FIGURE 25.8
Select any or all
file types for
the programs to
be associated
with.

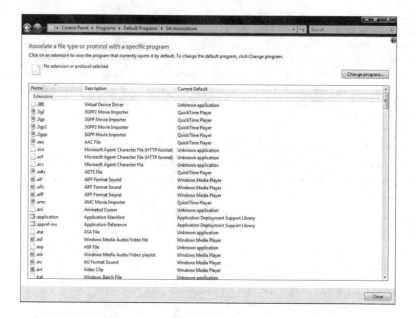

FIGURE 25.8
Select any or all
file types for
the programs to
be associated
with.

Did you Know?

The window you start with, the one that shows a list of all known file types or the Set Your Default Programs window described in the previous section that shows a list of Microsoft programs installed on your computer, depends on your approach. If you want to adjust the file types that a certain Microsoft Vista program works with, you might be better off opening the Set Your Default Programs window and selecting from all the file types that program can work with. If, instead, you have a file type that you want to associate to a certain program, whether or not it's a Microsoft-supplied program, you'll want to use Figure 25.8's window to associate a program to a file type.

Suppose that you want a different program to start when you select a digital image file with the .gif extension. You click to select the GIF Image file type and then click the Change Program button. Vista displays a list of programs in the Open With window shown in Figure 25.9. The programs toward the top of the window are programs that Vista suggests you use from the list of all programs installed on your computer. Below those suggested programs are other programs you might want to select to associate that file type to. After you click to select a program and click OK, Vista associates that program to that file type and if you ever double-click a file of that type in an Explorer window, Windows Vista automatically opens the program you associated with that type and loads the file. If this is a graphics file, you'll see the image on the screen. If it's a music file, the music begins playing when your associated program opens. If it's a video file type, the associated program automatically opens and begins playing that video when you select the file.

There are many reasons why you might want to change an association of a program and its file type. Perhaps the most important reason is your own personal preferences and needs. Photoshop Elements provides far more image-editing capabilities than Windows Photo Gallery. Therefore, you might want to choose all the .gif, .jpeg, .tif, and other digital image file types and associate them all to the Photoshop Elements program you've installed.

Many times, when you install a program such as Photoshop Elements, the installation routine asks your permission to associate certain file types to the program and updates Vista's file association tables automatically.

By the Way

Specifying Default Programs to Run

What Internet browser do you prefer? Internet Explorer? Firefox? Even though Microsoft developed Windows Vista and Internet Explorer, and even though Internet Explorer comes with Vista, you're free to change your default web-browsing software to a different program.

Selecting the Set Program Access and Computer Defaults option in your Control Panel's Programs group opens Figure 25.10's window. When you first open the window you'll see three entries: Microsoft Windows, Non-Microsoft, and Custom. These expand and collapse as you click the arrows to the right of each option.

Click to expand or collapse

FIGURE 25.10
Determine Vista's program of choice when performing common computer tasks, such as browsing the Internet.

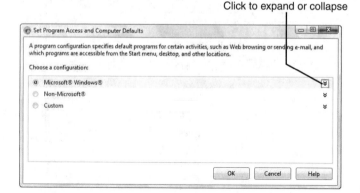

Each of the three groups represents possible program configurations you can set up. If you only have Microsoft-based web-browsing, email, instant messaging, and media-playing programs installed on your computer, click to open the Microsoft Windows program configuration. There you can choose among the programs you want to use for web browsing, email, sending and receiving instant messages, and playing media files. Actually, you won't have many choices, depending on what software you've installed.

For example, if you've installed Microsoft Outlook and set up an email account in Outlook, you will see at least two choices for your email: Outlook and Windows Mail. If you've also installed a non-Microsoft email program, you won't see it as an option in this Microsoft configuration. To set that program as your current email client, you'll need to select it from the Non-Microsoft or Custom configurations.

Just because you set program defaults doesn't mean that you cannot use the other programs when you want to. You can always start Internet Explorer from Vista's Start menu even if Firefox is your default web browser. Some websites are written for specific browsers and most often the browser is Internet Explorer because of its widespread use. If you normally use Firefox to surf the Internet but need Internet Explorer for specific web pages, use Firefox as your default browser and manually start Internet Explorer from the Start menu when you need to look at web pages that work better with internet Explorer.

The program defaults you specify apply to all user accounts on your computer. You cannot set up program defaults for your user account and a different set of program defaults for another user who uses your computer.

Expand the Custom configuration and select the default programs you want to use from a combination of both Microsoft and non-Microsoft applications.

Some people get confused when working with this Computer Defaults window and the Program Associations windows. When is it best to select a default media-playing program in one and not the other? Actually, the Computer Defaults window shown in Figure 25.10 has nothing to do with file associations. Instead, it's a Windows default setting that determines what happens when you click a web link inside a document. Word documents, for example, can contain embedded web links that, when you click them, open your default web browser and send you to the web pages discussed in the document. Other places such as web pages on the Internet include **mailto** links, which are special links that open your default email program and send email to the address in the mailto link. It's these kinds of default program settings you set up in the Computer Defaults window. When you want a specific program to begin when you select a certain file type, tell Vista about that in the Associate a File Type or Protocol with a Program window described in the previous section.

Chapter Wrap-Up

Windows Vista gives you the freedom to customize your operating environment in such a way that Windows behaves the way you want it to. You learned here how you can even tell Vista what to do the next time you insert a CD or DVD into your computer's disc drive.

In an attempt to help you specify your preferred default programs, sometimes Windows Vista helps *too* much by providing many options and windows that perform similar activities. In this chapter, you saw several ways to specify which file types a certain program can access, which programs should execute when you select certain file types, and default programs that run when you trigger them by clicking links, buttons, and other triggers that start email, web-browsing, instant-messaging, and media-playing programs.

The next chapter explains how you can set up your computer for multiple users. Each user has his or her Vista environment, and can often share files with the other users on the computer depending on the security currently set up.

CHAPTER 26

Separating Users Gives Each the Access They Need

In This Chapter:

- ▶ Learn about Administrator and user accounts
- ▶ Assign user account passwords
- ▶ Change user account settings
- ▶ Change your user account's picture
- ▶ Increase or decrease a user account's security level
- ▶ Manage multiple users
- ▶ Protect your user account's files

Microsoft designed Windows Vista to be a multiuser operating system. On one computer, several people can access Vista and manage their own set of files, their own Vista look and behavior, and abide by the security settings given to them by a user on the computer who uses an Administrator user account. When someone first installs Vista on a computer, that user—the first user—has Administrator privileges and can create accounts for other users that might or might not have full privileges. A user account without full system privileges is called a *Standard user account.*

It's not the goal of this chapter to dig too deeply into security because that is a subject that deserves the attention that only a full chapter can give. The next chapter, "Managing Your Windows Security," explains how you can manage your computer's security. This chapter teaches you the first step: how to create and manage user accounts to give other members of your family or business access to your Vista computer.

About User Accounts

When you open your Control Panel's User Accounts and Family Safety group, one of the items you see is the User Accounts option. Selecting User Accounts opens a User Accounts window similar to the one shown in Figure 26.1. Your User Accounts window will certainly look somewhat different from the figures, depending on whether other users are set up.

FIGURE 26.1
You add, view, change, and delete user accounts from the User Accounts window.

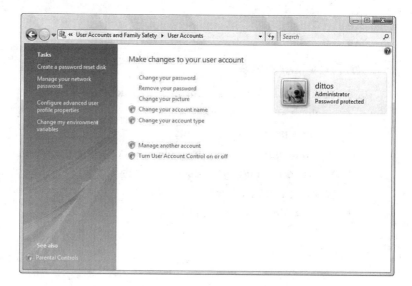

One of the ways you most quickly learn about setting up and modifying user accounts is to begin adjusting the settings of your own user account. The next section shows you how to do just that. After you become familiar with modifying your own account, you'll be ready to set up accounts for others.

By the Way

To modify user account settings, you must have Administrator privileges. If you see your username and the title Administrator, you have that privilege. If you have only a Standard account, you have to gain administrative privileges to change some aspects of your own account and to add or modify other user accounts.

Make the Most of User Accounts

When you have a user account on a computer, you have your own set of files and Vista settings. The desktop background wallpaper image you see might be unique to you and you can change it to suit your preferences. You can adjust your screen's resolution to see more items on the screen or to see fewer items at a larger size. The data files you create are yours, and stored in a Documents folder assigned to your user account.

Your user account name and optional password give you access to your computer defaults. When you finish working on your computer and you want to make it available for someone else, open your Vista Start menu, click the arrow next to the padlock at the right of your All Programs group, and select Log Off (see Figure 26.2). Doing so closes your current session, prompts you to save any data files you have not saved yet, and logs you off the computer. Anyone else who uses your computer will then log on to their user account to access their files, their settings, and the computing environment they have set up. When they finish, they should log off to make it easy for you and others to log on again when you're ready to use the computer. To use the machine once again, you will have to click your username and enter your user password (if you use a password).

FIGURE 26.2
Log off when you finish your computer session to make it easy for others to log on to their user account and to make it difficult for them to use your user account.

Always log off when you finish your computing session if others might possibly need to use your computer. It's incumbent upon you or a user with Administrator account privileges to assign to each user his or her own unique user account. Obviously, if you password-protect your user account, you help protect your account from unauthorized access. Whoever uses your user account will have full access to your files and settings. Even if they intend no malice, another user who uses your account because you forgot to log off can inadvertently change your computer's settings or accidentally delete files that you didn't want removed.

Watch Out!

If you're the only one who uses your computer, you don't have to set up additional user accounts. There is an advantage, however, to setting up a second account for yourself that does not have administrative privileges. You might want to use that account for your routine computer work and save your administrative account for system changes that you must sometimes make. This keeps you and the programs you run from inadvertently changing a system setting that could cause problems. The chance of this is unlikely because even an administrative account user must confirm just about any risky behavior by confirming the action in a dialog box, but it's good peace of mind.

If you share your computer with someone you trust, both of you routinely work with the same sets of files, and both of you prefer the same basic system settings, you don't have to set up an account for each user. You can both use the same account. If you elect to do this, be sure that you and the other users have similar computer knowledge and that both of you know enough to accept system requests such as Vista and security updates. (Only administrative accounts can accept system and security updates when prompted.)

Even if you and one or more others share the same computer, have full trust in the other, and each understands security issues and knows when to accept system updates and such, having multiple accounts still makes the most sense. You can easily set up files and folders that are shareable between users on the computer from different accounts. If you decide not to set up multiple user accounts for now, it's simple to add user accounts later if you decide to.

Working with Your User Account

Select User Accounts from your Control Panel's User Accounts and Family Safety group to display the User Accounts window shown in Figure 26.3. If you've not yet set up a password for your account, you won't see the Password protected notice beneath your user ID, and your password options to the left of your account's picture will differ slightly from those in the figure.

Assigning a User Account Password

If you haven't assigned a password to your account, go ahead and do so now to see how simple adding a password can be. If you don't want to keep a password on your account, you can remove it later. Click to select the Create a Password for Your Account option to display the password entry window shown in Figure 26.4. Type your password twice, once in each of the two text boxes. When you begin typing the first password, the placeholder text New password disappears.

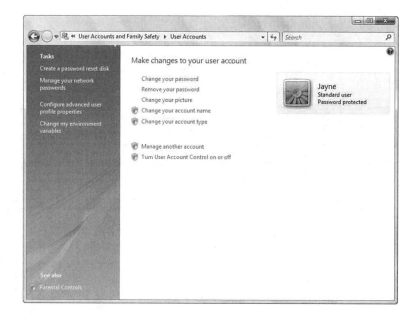

FIGURE 26.3
Making changes
to your own
user account.

As you type, notice Vista doesn't display your password but instead displays dark circles for each character you type. This protects your password from prying eyes that might be looking on. Because your password doesn't show, you could accidentally type a mistake in the password and be unable to log on to your account because you won't know exactly what you typed for the password. By requesting the password twice, Vista helps verify that the password is accurate by assuming that if you type the same password twice, you typed the correct characters. If you make a mistake and the two passwords don't match when you click the Create Password button later, Vista tells you about the problem and displays this screen once more so that you can enter your password more carefully.

Although it's optional, you should type a password hint in the bottom text box. If you forget your password, Vista displays this hint to remind you of what you used for the password.

Suppose you use Chevy97 for your password. Your password hint might be Car and year. Obviously if you have a 1997 Chevy sitting in your driveway that password hint provides a little too much information. Design your hint so that you can figure out by looking at it what you used as a password, but others won't be able to.

When you click the Create Password button, Vista assigns that password to your user account. The next time you log on to Windows, you'll be prompted for that password when you select your user account. Without the password, nobody can use your account.

Placeholder text

FIGURE 26.4
You must enter
your password
twice to verify
its accuracy.

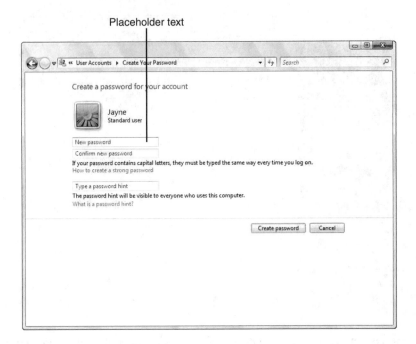

FIGURE 26.4

Deleting a Password

If you ever want to delete an account's password, you must know that account's password before you can delete it. To delete a password, click the Remove Your Password link. Vista prompts you for the password assigned to the account.

This helps protect you in case you walk away from your computer and forget to log off. Someone could quickly go in and delete your account's password without you knowing they did so. By asking for the password before deleting it from the account, Vista helps to ensure that the user deleting the password is the owner of that account.

Changing Your Account's Picture

The user account picture that appears doesn't have any function other than aesthetic purposes, but it's nice to use something you associate with. Perhaps you'll even use your own photo, as might be done in a multiuser business setting. Windows Vista lets you select from a list of pictures or supply one of your own.

To change your picture, click the Change Your Picture link. Vista displays a selection of pictures from which you can choose as shown in Figure 26.5. Your currently selected user account photo (which Vista assigned if you never selected one yourself) is the top photo and a list of choices appears below it.

FIGURE 26.5
Use this window
to select a new
picture to asso-
ciate with your
user account.

If you like one of the pictures in the window, click to select it and then click Change
Picture to change your current account's picture to the new one. If you want to use
your own picture, you first need to store the picture in your account's Pictures folder.
When you click the Browse for More Pictures link, Vista opens your Pictures folder
from which you can select a picture. Select a picture and click Open, and Vista uses
that picture for your user account's photo. Since your user account picture always
appears in a square frame, you should select an image that is already in a square
shape. If your selected image is too wide, Vista will have to squeeze the sides to fit
the image into your user account picture frame and the image will not look as good
if you begin with an image that is already fairly square in shape.

Changing Your Account's Name

To change the your user account's logon name, click the Change Your Account Name
link to display the Type a New Account Name window. Type a new name and click
Change Name to change your account's name. This name will appear on your
Welcome screen as well as the Start menu, and so will your photo, as Figure 26.6 shows.

Vista displays your name and picture above the Start menu in an attempt to keep
your computer as secure and accurate as possible. Suppose that you sat down at
your computer and someone was already logged on. If you were rushed, you might
assume that it's your account, but as soon as you open the Start menu you would
see that someone else is logged on. You then can log off and log on to your user
account to get access to your files.

By the Way

FIGURE 26.6
Windows displays your user account's name and picture atop your Start menu.

Changing Your Account's Type

You can change an Administrator account to a Standard account and you can change a Standard account to an Administrator account. If you own the only Administrator account, however, you cannot change your account to a Standard account. You can add a second user account for yourself and make it a Standard account. Every computer requires at least one Administrator account because no system changes are possible with it.

Working with Multiple User Accounts

The previous sections will come in handy whether you use a single account computer or a computer that you share with others. You can modify your own user account settings as well as other user accounts as long as you have an Administrator account. If you have a Standard account, you can change only your account password and picture. You are not allowed to change your account's name or account type if you own a Standard account.

If you own multiple accounts and one of them is an Administrator account, you can change all aspects of your Standard account even when logged in to your Standard account because when you attempt to change one of the secure Standard account's settings, such as the password, Vista stops and asks you for the Administrator's password. If you type the Administrator password correctly, Vista lets you change one of the secure user account settings, such as the account type.

Did you Know?

When logged in as an Administrator, you can change anyone else's user account settings. Click the Manage Another Account link to display the Manage Accounts window shown in Figure 26.7.

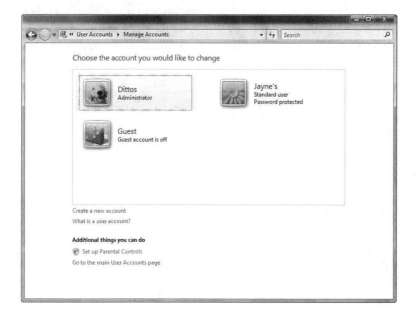

FIGURE 26.7
An Administrator can modify settings of any user account on the computer.

Select the account you want to modify. For example, you might select a Standard account so that you can upgrade that user account to have full administrative privileges. You can also create a new user account here and downgrade another user from an Administrator account to a Standard account. Finally, you can completely delete another user's account by selecting the account after clicking the Delete the Account link.

About the User Account Control

You cannot modify system-level settings when using a Standard account, as you've already learned. In reality, you *can,* but you must know an Administrator account's password if you want to remain inside a Standard account and make system settings.

Suppose, for example, you're logged in to a Standard user's account and you attempt to upgrade your Standard user account to an administrative level. Windows Vista will first display a User Account Control (UAC) dialog box and ask you to type an Administrator user's password. If you type the password correctly, Vista assumes that you have administrative privileges in another account even though you're logged in to a Standard account. At that point, you can make the change you want to make. All the User Accounts window's entries marked with a security shield (see Figure 26.8) require Administrator-user level confirmation before they can be changed.

FIGURE 26.8
The security shield icons mark the items for which you need Administrator privileges before you can change them.

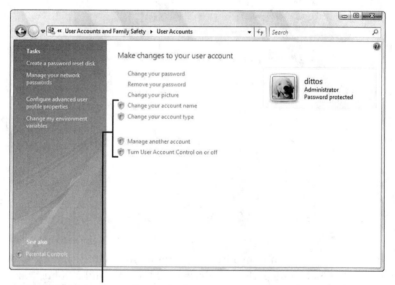

Administrator level security required

By the Way — All Control Panel routines that use UAC to require Administrative privileges to run display the UAC shield next to their names.

Windows Vista utilizes a new security concept named *User Account Control* to protect your system from inadvertent system changes that could affect the system and other users. In a nutshell, the UAC sets up two security levels for every Administrator account and one for each Standard user account. When you log on as a Standard user, you are allowed to access only your own files and have a limited set of tasks you can perform. In general, this will not limit your typical use of your computer, but it does limit any system-level changes you can make, such as being able to upgrade your account from a Standard account to an Administrator account. If you attempt such a task when logged on as a Standard user, Windows prompts you for an Administrator user account's password as described at the beginning of this session.

If you're logged in as an Administrator user, Vista creates two security levels for you. The default security level is a Standard user account. If you, as an Administrator, attempt to run a system program such as the Disk Defragmenter, Vista temporarily blocks you from doing that and asks that you confirm that you truly want to run that system program. All you need to do is click Continue and Vista elevates your security level and allows the program to run. You don't need to type your Administrator user password because by logging in to that user account to begin with, you entered the password.

Think of the confirmation as a reminder to you, an Administrator, that you're about to do something that could cause potential harm or affect files belonging to other users. It's fine if you click Continue and go ahead with the task, but Vista is just temporarily stopping you from doing so to remind you of the critical nature of what you might do next.

By the Way

Previous Windows versions didn't do this. If you had administrative privileges, you always ran as an Administrator. It made Windows easier to use when you were updating other user accounts and running system programs because you weren't stopped all the time to confirm that you really wanted to do what you'd requested. Then again, you didn't have the second-chance warning that the confirmation provides.

Software developers determine the level of the user account needed to run programs. An application is either a Standard user application or an Administrator user application, and Vista determines which it is before running the program so that Vista can let the UAC handle the confirmations when required.

By the Way

If you do not want to see the UAC-based confirmation dialog boxes when logged in as an Administrator, you can turn them off. Select your Administrator user account to modify in the User Accounts window and select the option labeled Turn User Account Control On or Off. As you might now expect, Vista prompts you with a confirmation dialog box before you can even get to the window to turn off the UAC controls on your account. After you confirm, the Turn User Account Control On or Off window, shown in Figure 26.9, appears. Inside the dialog box, Vista recommends leaving the UAC turned on, but if you click to uncheck the option and then close the dialog box, Windows no longer bothers you as an Administrator when you attempt to do anything that requires administrative privilege to run. You will need to reboot your system to implement this change and once you do, you won't see the UAC messages.

FIGURE 26.9
You can turn off your Administrator user account's UAC confirmations, but Windows Vista doesn't recommend that you do so.

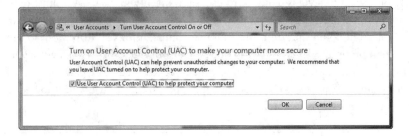

Switching Between User Accounts

When logged in to a user account, whether it's an Administrator user account or a Standard user account, you can switch to a different user account at any time. When you switch user accounts (as opposed to logging off your account first), all the programs and windows you currently have open remain open in your account.

The ability to switch users is helpful when you're working on your computer and someone else with access to your computer needs to do something quickly. The other user can switch to her or his user account without logging you off first, do whatever it is that needs to be done, and then log off. You'll select your user from the list that appears (the message Logged on appears in the user list you select from, indicating that your account wasn't logged off and might still have programs and windows open) and Vista puts you right back where you were before the interruption.

Obviously, before letting someone else switch users from your account, or use their account in any way while yours is still logged on, you should stay there to make sure that nothing takes place inside your account that might cause problems with your files or settings. If your account is password-protected, as *all* Administrator user accounts should be, after another user's account is logged in, your account can no longer be switched back to without your password. Even so, completely logging out of your account before letting someone else take over the computer for a while greatly increases the likelihood that your files will be safe. If the user turns off the power switch, for example, while your account still has open files, you could lose data.

Watch Out!

To switch to another user account without first logging off your account, display the Start menu, click the arrow to the right of the padlock at the bottom of the Start menu's left pane, and select Switch User. Vista displays a user list so that the next user can log on while keeping your programs and windows open in your user account so that you can return to them.

Chapter Wrap-Up

You now understand the importance of user accounts and account settings. The Administrator user level is far more privileged when it comes to making system changes than a Standard user account is. For typical computing, however, the Standard user account provides access to routine programs and that user's data files, so running from a Standard user account isn't a severe penalty unless you need higher access to do something.

Security permeates Windows Vista and, as you've seen in this chapter, security is of prime importance when working with user accounts. In the next chapter, you will learn more about Windows Vista's security features. In today's world, running in a safe computer environment helps ensure that your system runs as smoothly as possible.

CHAPTER 27

Managing Your Windows Security

In This Chapter:

- ▶ Learn to recognize computer security threats
- ▶ Find programs that help you secure your computer as well as possible
- ▶ Enjoy safer online web surfing
- ▶ Correctly respond to Internet Explorer's security warnings
- ▶ Master your Control Panel's security settings
- ▶ Modify your firewall settings
- ▶ Keep your computer up-to-date automatically
- ▶ Use Windows Defender to monitor all files on your machine
- ▶ Set parental controls to safeguard your younger family members

Microsoft is well aware of the security risks Windows operating systems face. When they developed Windows XP, the Microsoft programming team made security a high priority. Nevertheless, the moment Microsoft released Windows XP, the attacks began. In Microsoft's defense, the security flaws that have since been exposed could not have been 100% foreseen because new hardware and software developments since XP's release have allowed Trojan programs, worms, spyware, and virus emails to flood users' systems. Neither Microsoft nor any other developer could have predicted how severe these attacks would become.

Attacks on non-Microsoft operating systems are less frequent than Windows-based systems. This is true, but it's also true that with the much larger installed base of products, malicious hackers are going to go after the largest number of installations and not spend as much time attacking the other environments. However, Microsoft designers certainly could have made XP a little more secure than they did. Having learned from past mistakes, Microsoft has made a valiant effort to keep Vista secure.

In this chapter, you'll learn ways Microsoft designed Vista to protect you. If you've read articles about computer security in the past, you know that security is a subject that quickly gets highly technical. This chapter addresses security from a hands-on approach that enables you to take charge of common security issues without having to become a security technician to understand what you need to know to protect your safety when using Vista.

Vista Security—A Brief Overview

To make proper decisions regarding security settings, it helps to have an overview of some security approaches Microsoft chose when developing Vista. You probably already understand that before you can make any major security decisions you must be running from an Administrator account, as explained in the Chapter 26, "Separating Users Gives Each the Access They Need." Without an Administrator user account, you can run common programs but can do very little with system programs.

Security and the stability of your computer go hand-in-hand. You want your computer to remain secure and you want it to operate as expected. If a security threat gets through your protection, your machine will stop working properly. Vista does its best to protect your system-related folders. If a malicious program attempts to write to your Program Files folder, for example, and doesn't have the appropriate certification to do so, Vista will block the attempt.

Partitioning Danger

Old programs, called **legacy programs**, might write directly to your Program Files folder without going through the normal security clearance routines that Vista-written programs go through. Vista can't simply block these programs altogether because some people still want to run programs they purchased long before Vista arrived.

Vista fools such programs into thinking they are writing to your Program Files folder, but they are actually writing to a folder that looks to legacy programs as if it were the Program Files folder. Therefore, if a malicious coder writes such a program that acts like a legacy program, and the code infects a computer's files, Vista will help ensure that, at worst, the danger will be limited to the user account that was active when the program was installed.

If such a problem occurs, you can log on to another user account and use your computer normally, accessing all the programs you were able to access from your previous account. This is a good reason to create a second, password-protected Administrator account for yourself now and leave it alone until you absolutely must use it because of damage to your original account. All your personal settings in that other account will be lost, so regularly back up your user account's files in case you have to restore them to your new account. (Chapter 35, "Protecting Your Data and Programs," explains how to back up files and folders.) Your user account's files are always stored in a folder named after your user account name. When you open an Explorer window, you see your account's folder in your Users folders list as Figure 27.1 shows.

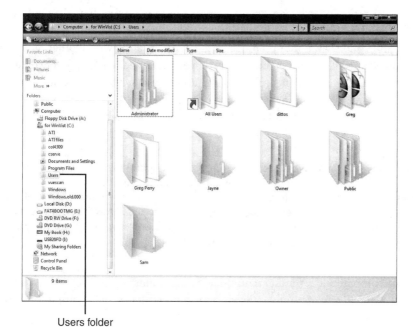

Users folder

FIGURE 27.1
All user folders are located inside the higher-level Users folder.

How Safe Is Vista?

Are Vista's security protection tools adequate to protect you? Vista's security is wonderful compared to what has come before. But Microsoft would be the first to admit that Vista by itself does not provide a completely secure computing environment. Although nothing can fully ensure that you'll be safe when you use your computer, you should augment Vista's built-in versions of the following programs with more complete offerings you can get from known and reputable vendors:

▶ Firewall—A program that guards your Internet data entry and exit points (called **ports**) and keeps your always-on, Internet broadband connection secure from intruders. ZoneAlarm and Symantec's Norton Firewall are two well-known firewall programs. See www.ZoneLabs.com and www.Symantec.com.

▶ Antivirus—A program that helps keep email-delivered viruses from affecting your system, as can happen if you open some emails or click links in others. Norton AntiVirus and McAfee VirusScan are two capable antivirus programs that you can get to help safeguard your email. See www.Symantec.com and www.McAfee.com.

▶ AntiSpyware—Try as you might, some programs can find their way onto your computer. You might download and install a free program that you find online and even if that program is safe, it might bring with it other programs called **spyware** that pop up ads or use your computer's idle time for sometimes innocent and often troublesome uses. www.WebRoot.com and www.Lavasoft.com provide extremely effective spyware removal tools that you may want to try if Vista's own Defender doesn't catch everything for you.

Did you *Know?*

Most security program vendors provide free trial periods during which you can try the program at no cost. In addition, watch the Sunday color ad inserts in your newspaper for computer stores in your area. After-rebate deals are often available that allow you to get these security-related programs absolutely free after rebate. It's the hope of the vendors that if they give you the program for a year, you will pay to subscribe for another year of protection.

Software companies offer most security-related programs on a subscription basis, and you have to pay annually to renew your subscription if you want protection against the latest threats. These vendors attempt to stay on top of the latest problems and send you updates regularly (sometimes daily, depending on what's happening in the world of computer infections). As long as you're paid up, you will get the latest updates.

You Cannot Have Too Much Money, Too Much Good Health, or Too Much Computer Security

Throughout the rest of this chapter, you'll learn how Vista offers protection for each of the problem areas just mentioned. Use Vista as your starting point, base-level security and then build on its security with appropriate programs you get elsewhere.

You cannot be *too* secure, so having a dedicated, standalone program that guards you against each of these problems is wise.

Did you Know?

You don't always need one program for each job. Most of the security software vendors listed in the previous list offer complete packages that do a better than adequate job of protecting you from all the dangers described in the earlier list. Using a single vendor and program means that you have to update the programs less often and there are fewer potential conflicts between the programs. Microsoft even offers Windows Live One Care, a security service that guards against the threats described earlier (www.microsoft.com).

Vista Requires Fewer Reboots

Another advantage to Vista's internal, more secure architecture is that you should rarely have to reboot your computer. A system program you install that modifies the system, such as an antivirus program, should now be able to update all the necessary files without requiring you to reboot your system to complete the installation. It's Microsoft's goal to design Vista so that if a program requires a reboot of your computer to finish installing, you return to the same place you were when the reboot occurred. All your open programs and windows should be intact.

By the Way

Windows XP reduced the number of reboots required during program installation, but did not eliminate them. When updating some antivirus definitions, you might have found yourself rebooting more than once just to download and install all the day's updates.

Perhaps not surprisingly, Microsoft sometimes updates your computer and requires a reboot. This often occurs when one or more Windows Vista system files currently in use have to be changed. In general, don't expect program and folder windows that were open before the reboot and update to be open when Vista restarts. Sometimes inconsistencies are consistent with Microsoft.

Enjoy Safer Online Surfing

Although Chapter 36, "Combining Vista, Networks, and the Internet," discusses Internet surfing while using Vista, you should know that Microsoft has tried to protect you not only from outside attacks that might infect your computer but also from yourself.

Don't Be Phishing Bait

Some people create websites that look like other websites. They might, for example, create a web page that looks just like the sign-in page for eBay or a bank. The design of these sites is to fool you into entering your username and password. The sites store that information so that their owners have access to your account. These are **phishing websites** and Vista includes some antiphishing tools to protect you.

Every time you attempt to access a web page, if warranted, Internet Explorer displays the web address in a color indicating suspicion: yellow if Vista suspects the site of being a phishing location or red when the site you're opening is a known phishing location. You'll see the color in your web page's address bar. Figure 27.2 shows a website that Vista suspects of being a phishing site and sure enough it is. Vista highlighted this faux-eBay web page with a yellow address at the top and displayed the pop-up warning box to let the user know that the site is extremely suspicious. Even though this looks like a valid eBay login screen, it's not, as the lack of ebay.com URL in the web address verifies.

Yellow address bar

FIGURE 27.2
This looks like eBay, but it's a phishing web page set up for the sole purpose of stealing eBay IDs and passwords.

Not really eBay

When the address is red, Internet Explorer is warning you that you're looking at a known, invalid web page that is most likely a phishing site, so don't enter any information there. When address is yellow, double-check the source of the address to ensure that it's reliable.

In general, banking, auction, and other sensitive financial and reliable websites will address you by your name or user ID to indicate they are legitimate when sending you emails with links to websites. They also rarely if ever ask you to provide confidential information.

Did you Know?

Just keep an eye open for the colored address bar; if you see yellow or red, forewarned is forearmed.

Internet Explorer Blocks

Vista runs Internet Explorer in Protected Mode, which disallows much of the malware that can give you problems when you surf the Internet such as **ActiveX controls** (small programs that download and run) and download files that begin downloading when you click a button or a link that triggers them.

The problem today is that you'll many times run across a valid website that needs to place an ActiveX control on your computer or perhaps you'll want to download a program such as Adobe Acrobat Reader to read PDF files. When Internet Explorer blocks an activity, Vista displays a yellow ribbon called the *information bar* toward the top of your screen. You can right-click the information bar and select what you want Internet Explorer to do.

Figure 27.3 shows such a session. The user is attempting to download Adobe Acrobat Reader from the Adobe.com website. This program is a perfectly good program that you can download and install safely, and yet Internet Explorer stopped short of letting the program arrive without alerting you with an information bar.

Vista beeps to help indicate that the information bar appeared, so it's a good idea to keep your speakers turned up loud enough to hear system sounds. Without the beep, it's easy to miss the information bar and not know what to do when you want to install an ActiveX control or download a file.

Did you Know?

Right-clicking the information bar gives you options. You can agree to download the file, in which case Adobe continues sending the program to the computer and the Acrobat Reader installs. Clicking the What's the Risk? option opens the Windows help screen, shown in Figure 27.4, which explains the purpose for the warning and why Vista requires that you confirm the download. Clicking More Information takes you to more-detailed Vista help screens that describe how you can achieve a safer Internet surfing experience.

Information Bar

FIGURE 27.3
Internet
Explorer wants
to make sure
that you want to
download a file.

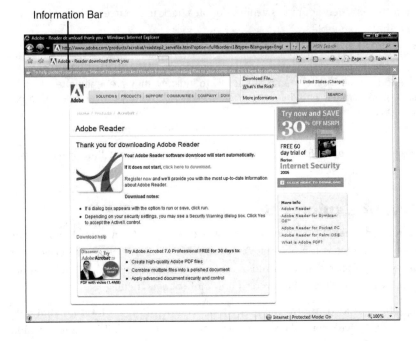

> **By the Way**
>
> Internet Explorer prompts you to confirm such a download whether you're working from within an Administrator or a Standard user account. Your account level does not affect Internet Explorer's operation.

FIGURE 27.4
Vista provides
help that
explains why it
temporarily
blocked you
from download-
ing a file.

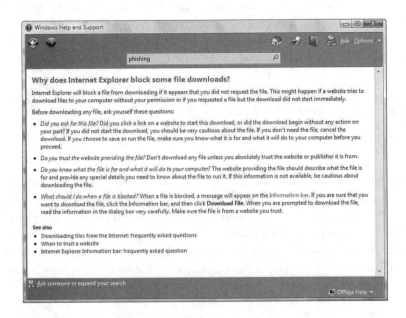

Re-Consider Turning Off Warnings

You can turn off the information bar warning, but doing so invites potential danger to your online surfing. After you click a button that was labeled Free Information or some other innocent-sounding title, a website could install or send a file to your computer without you knowing about it. When the file is on your computer you could be in trouble if your anti-spyware program is off or doesn't yet know to look for that particular kind of infection. (Vista's Windows Defender is such a program, as you'll find out about in the next section.)

If you truly want to turn off the information bar, select Tools, Options from within Internet Explorer. (Pressing the Alt key displays IE's menu.) Click the Security tab and then click Custom Level. Scroll to the Downloads section and select the Enable option on the Automatic Prompting for File Downloads prompt. You can also turn off the information bar's warning for ActiveX controls by scrolling to the ActiveX Controls and Plug-Ins section and select the Enable prompt for the option labeled Automatic Prompting for ActiveX Controls. You might want to turn off these prompts temporarily if you're downloading several files from a known website, or perhaps if you want to allow a known website to install multiple ActiveX controls before you turn on prompting again to protect your subsequent Internet surfing activities.

Internet Explorer, although made by Microsoft, doesn't discriminate. If you attempt to download and install an ActiveX control from Microsoft.com, the information bar pops up and does its job even though the source is valid. IE's goal is to let you do whatever you want to do, but to make sure that you triggered the action intentionally.

Become Familiar with Control Panel's Security Features

You don't have to be a security expert to understand your Control Panel's security-related groups shown in Figure 27.5. Chapter 24, "Controlling Windows Vista," gives you an overview of Control Panel's security groups if you want only a quick impression. But this is a good time to spend a few moments learning more about Vista's security-related offerings; lots of people want to get into your files *right now* and you do not want to let them do so.

Your computer connects to every other online computer in the world every time you check email and surf the Internet—and connects all the time if you subscribe to an always-on broadband connection such as DSL or a cable modem.

FIGURE 27.5
You can go a long way toward making your entire computing experience safer by visiting your Control Panel's Security group.

The Security Center, shown in Figure 27.5, works like a dashboard to give you a bird's-eye view of your computer security status. Depending on what you find, you can explore other options in your Control Panel's Security group. Each section, Firewall, Automatic Updating, Malware Protection, and Other Security Settings shows green if Windows sees at least some protection there, yellow if possible danger exists, and red if probable danger exists. Click the arrow to the right of each section name to expand that section and read more details.

In Figure 27.6, the user is running without virus protection. Although you cannot see color in this book's figures, the group is yellow and not red because the user has no email account set up, so the lack of virus protection isn't as critical as it would be with Outlook installed and running. If you connect to the Internet and you turn off your firewall, Vista will color the Firewall group red because you're running naked without any protection from intruders.

By the Way

As with most of Windows Vista, you can access many of the same security settings from different areas of Vista. For example, you can change Windows Update, Windows Firewall, Windows Defender, and your Internet option settings from the Security Center by clicking the links at the left of the screen.

Quick links to specific
security settings   More help   Expands section

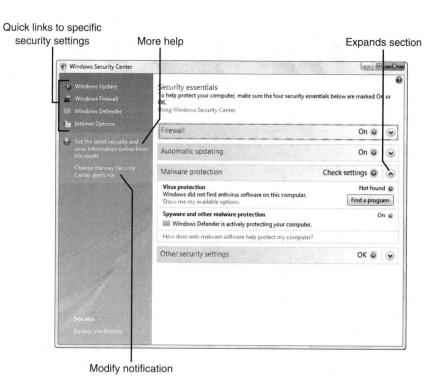

Modify notification

FIGURE 27.6
The Security
Center gives
you an overview
of your security
status.

Click the Windows Security Center's Change the Way Security Center Alerts Me
option to display Figure 27.7's Windows Security Center dialog box. In this box,
you determine how you want Vista to warn you when you have a security problem:
by displaying a pop-up icon and message, displaying just the icon, or keeping quiet
until you elect to view your Security Center status. These days you cannot afford
to be lax in your security, and choosing to see a pop-up icon and message the
moment one of the four critical Windows Security Center's elements is in danger
is the best way to stay notified and safe.

Did you
Know?

FIGURE 27.7
Let Windows make you aware of security holes the moment they appear on your computer.

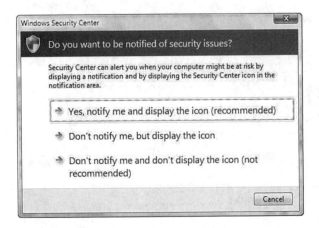

Stay Behind the Firewall

Windows Vista improved on Windows XP's firewall because now the firewall monitors both inbound and outbound Internet traffic. (The XP firewall monitored only inbound traffic.) This means that if you do happen to get an infected program, perhaps from a friend's CD-ROM that had a free game on it, that program cannot use your computer and Internet connection to do its bidding without first getting permission from you.

To access the firewall and its settings, open your Control Panel's Security group and select the Windows Firewall option. A Windows Firewall status screen appears that contains much of the same information you saw at the Security Center in Figure 27.5. Clicking the Change Settings option opens the Windows Firewall Settings dialog box shown in Figure 27.8 (after you confirm that you want to open the dialog). There you can turn off your firewall if you suspect a program conflict with the firewall and want to check to see whether the firewall might be causing the problem.

Watch Out!

Obviously, if you have an always-on Internet connection, never leave your firewall turned off for more than a few moments.

You can click to check the Block All Incoming Connections option to stop all inbound Internet connections. If you want to connect to a network that isn't secure (or that you're unsure of), you can keep all Internet intrusion out of your computer while you work on that less-secure connection. For example, you want to connect your laptop to a network inside a conference room to share files with others, but you're unsure whether the network you're about to connect to has adequate protection on its inbound Internet traffic. You can keep all traffic (other than from the network itself) from getting through to your computer until you disconnect from the network and restore your laptop to its previous state that allowed inbound Internet traffic.

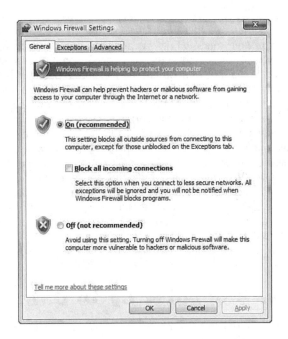

FIGURE 27.8
You can control your firewall settings and even turn off your firewall temporarily.

The Exceptions tab enables you to specify exceptions to the firewall. Generally, you should make changes to this dialog box page only if you're familiar with computer communications. Vista usually makes the Exceptions settings when you perform other tasks. For example, when you elect to share files and a printer with others on a network, you'll usually access this option from your Network window. Vista checks the firewall's exceptions list File and Printer Sharing option when you request that sharing mode. Therefore, in general you won't select or deselect options from the Exceptions tab.

> It helps to think of the Exceptions tab as you inform the Windows Firewall which programs and computer processes are to be let through the firewall without hesitation.

Did you Know?

On the Advanced page, you'll generally see at least one (and possibly more) network connection that you want Windows Firewall to monitor or not monitor. The assumed default is that you want Windows Firewall to monitor your network connections because they generally include Internet traffic coming to your machine from the network.

The Windows Firewall is basic, but often that's all the firewall protection you need. When a malicious hacker wants to enter a computer through its Internet connection, the hacker typically moves on to the next connection if there's any kind of firewall. (In fact, most of the time, a good firewall prevents a potential hacker from even seeing your computer's presence on the Internet.) So few connections are actually protected that finding one without a firewall isn't too difficult, at least until more computer users understand the importance of protecting their systems. (The fact that Windows Vista and Windows XP SP2 turning on their firewalls by default will help to solve this problem as more and more people upgrade their computers.) Despite the fact that Windows Firewall is usually all the firewall protection you need, especially given Vista's outgoing traffic monitoring feature, upgrading to a more robust firewall such as the one offered by Zone Labs (www.ZoneLabs.com) almost guarantees that you'll never have an intrusion problem. So, keep your Vista firewall turned on until you're able to upgrade to a more complete firewall solution to make extra sure that your Internet connection is safe.

Keep Your Computer Up to Date

One of the easiest ways to guard against the latest security threats that develop is to keep Windows Vista updated. When you click your Control Panel's Security group, you'll see the Windows Update option. Clicking that option produces the Windows Update window shown in Figure 27.9. Although Windows Update updates such programs as Internet Explorer and Media Player–related settings and add-ins, it also updates your system with any patches that might help prevent a security threat from entering your machine, whether that threat comes from a program you install or from the Internet.

Figure 27.9 shows that no critical updates are available, but one optional update is. Clicking the View Available Updates link describes what that update contains and enables you to select, download, and apply it. If the update relates to security, Windows does not call the update *optional*—it's an update (or perhaps multiple updates) that you should install without hesitation.

Did you Know? Many Microsoft products now update through the Windows Update system. If you have Microsoft Office installed, the Office programs will update when needed through your Windows Vista update system.

Clicking to select the Change Settings link opens the Change Settings window, shown in Figure 27.10, where you can select the frequency of Windows updates. A daily update setting, as shown in Figure 27.10, isn't unreasonable as quickly as threats can attack these days. Setting updates to occur automatically at 3:00 a.m. or another time when you won't be using your computer will keep your machine as up-to-date as possible.

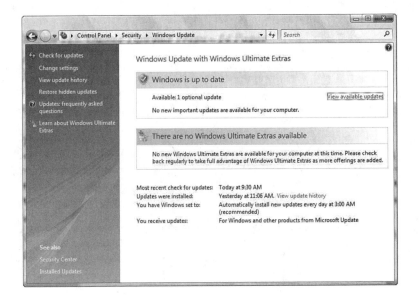

FIGURE 27.9
Keep your computer's system software up-to-date to guard against some of the latest threats.

> **Did you Know?**
>
> Some users prefer to see all updates before they allow the updates to install. Clicking the Download Updates But Let Me Choose Whether to Install Them option ensures that all updates download according to the schedule you select (such as every day at 3:00 a.m.), but doesn't apply them. An icon in your taskbar's notification area indicates that the updates are ready to install. After you review the updates and want to proceed with one or more of them, check the updates you want to install and Windows applies them.

> **Watch Out!**
>
> It's rare, but sometimes Microsoft releases an update that can cause unforeseen system problems. If you're uncertain about an update or perhaps you've read that the update can cause problems (word gets around quickly on the Internet news and blog sites when an update goes badly), before installing that update you can save your system settings by using restore points as described in Chapter 31, "Restoring Your Windows System to a Previous State." Most updates are supposed to create a restore point for you, but they don't all seem to do so.

If the updates relate to your Vista system files, Vista might have to violate its own stated goals and require you to reboot your computer before the changes will take effect. In that case, a dialog box like the one shown in Figure 27.11 pops up from your taskbar. You can click Restart Now to reboot immediately, or select a time for a reminder and click the Postpone button.

FIGURE 27.10
You can deter-
mine when your
computer has
updates
applied.

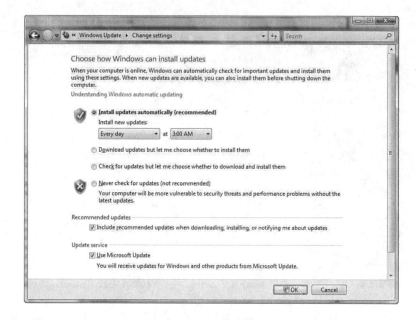

FIGURE 27.11
Vista some-
times needs to
reboot before it
can apply a sys-
tem update.

Let Windows Defender Help Protect Your Files

Vista includes a new security program named *Windows Defender*. Windows
Defender's job is to scan files that you retrieve through Internet Explorer and elsewhere and try to ensure that the files are spyware-free. This means that Windows
Defender scans files on your computer and looks at them to see whether they fit the
pattern of a malicious file that might destroy something or fill your screen with ads
that are difficult to get rid of as some programs can do. (Others send Internet
Explorer off to advertising websites.) Windows Defender, whose window is available
from your Control Panel's Security group, offers the following kinds of protection:

▶ **Real-time protection**—Continually monitors your computer and watches all program installations and system settings, and alerts you if an unexpected and possibly malicious action could result from the program.

▶ **SpyNet community ratings**—You can elect to join SpyNet, a group of other Vista users who have agreed to participate. Each time a SpyNet user accepts or rejects a program due to possible malware involvement, SpyNet records that activity. If the same program threatens you, you can see what others have done in the SpyNet community to determine whether it's safe to install the program.

Just because lots of other users have agreed to install the program doesn't necessarily mean that you can safely install it, although the SpyNet community's decisions are guides for you to consider. You might also be working when a certain problem just became known and very few if any in the SpyNet community have faced the potential threat, so your decision to accept or reject the program can affect what others do. *Generally*, if the program is from a known source, especially from a major software vendor, you can safely install any program Windows Defender warns you about.

Watch Out!

▶ **Scheduled and manual system scans**—You can schedule, or manually request at any time, a complete Windows Defender scan of all your files. Windows Defender then sets off to the task of analyzing every file on your computer looking to see whether spyware has infected anything.

Windows Defender looks at each program installation—whether that program is installed by you, through the Internet (perhaps as an ActiveX control), or perhaps through a link or button you clicked in an email—and looks for a known pattern of actions cause it enough concern to warn you about.

Spyware changes frequently and new kinds of attacks crop up. When you perform a Windows Update, Windows Defender's database of known problems often updates as well to ensure that you have the latest monitoring system.

By the Way

When you open the Windows Defender window, you'll likely see that you system is fine because Windows Defender is always working in the background to let you know about potential threats. You can click the History button to see when Windows Defender warned you about a potential security threat such as the warning shown in Figure 27.12. The history shows the potential offending program and location, as well as the description and advice Windows Defender gave you when you or something you did triggered this program's installation.

FIGURE 27.12
Windows
Defender shows
you a history of
problems it
spotted as
potentially
threatening to
your system.

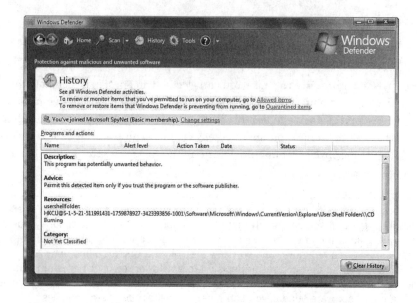

Clicking the Tools button produces a screen where you can change Windows
Defender's settings. Settings include scheduling Windows Defender to perform a full
system check weekly, updating your membership in the SpyNet community, and
viewing **quarantined items** (which are programs Windows Defender prevented from
running on your computer). Others involve the allowed items that Windows
Defender permits to run, or provide quick access to the Windows Defender website,
where you can learn more about Windows Defender's operation.

Did you Know?

If you allow Windows Defender to run a program but then realize you should not,
you can stop the program from running in the future (assuming that the program
hasn't done any damage) by opening the Windows Defender Tools window and
clicking Allowed Items to display the window in Figure 27.13. Click to select the
offending program and click Disable to quarantine that program to keep it from
running until you allow it or click Remove to remove the program from your
machine altogether.

By the Way

You might wonder what happens if you allow spyware to run when you shouldn't.
The worst thing that can happen is that the program can destroy your data. Often,
however, spyware performs less destructive tasks such as monitoring your computer activities and sending reports to an advertising website that sends you targeted, pop-up ads. Disabling or removing such spyware makes your system run
smoother and causes fewer interruptions for you.

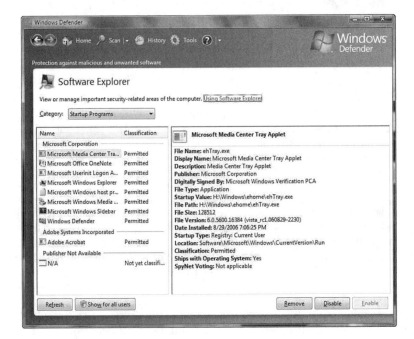

FIGURE 27.13
You can change your mind and quarantine or remove programs you allowed to run in the past.

Parental Controls

Microsoft designed Vista's parental controls so that parents can monitor and limit what their children see through the computer. With the parental controls, you can do the following:

▶ Restrict the running of certain programs to certain users.

▶ Monitor a user's computer usage and view activity reports that list websites visited, blocked websites that were attempted to be viewed, files downloaded, programs run, games played, email sent, instant messages sent and received, and media-related event logs that show what music and DVDs were played (assuming that the title data was available).

▶ Restrict web surfing and downloads to limit the amount of mature content, drugs, and so forth. Not all websites make it clear to the parental control features what they're all about, so accurate web restriction is not usually possible 100% of the time. Parents concerned about web content should allow their children to surf the Web only when adults are present.

▶ Limit computer usage on a user account basis, as you might do to allow a user to use the computer for two hours on a Saturday morning.

▶ Control games by rating, content, or title (when possible).

▶ Allow or block certain programs on the computer from running from the user's account.

By the Way

Modern computer games have ratings that use a system similar to motion picture ratings. Vista can detect those ratings and allow or disallow the program based on the parental controls that you set.

Watch Out!

Some games, including almost all games published before 2002, don't have such ratings, so you have to specify your parental controls by title or content. Even then you might not be able to control older games because they might not display enough information for Vista to recognize them. In addition, the parental controls options cannot control games installed on a **FAT** partition (file access table; that is, a disk drive formatted under an older Windows file system).

To access the parental controls, open your Control Panel's Security group and select Parental Controls to display a list of users. Select a user to display Figure 27.14's Parental Controls window. The Parental Controls window is also available from within the User Accounts and Family Safety Control Panel group.

FIGURE 27.14
Set parental controls on game ratings, monitor computer activities, and restrict computer usage with Vista's parental controls.

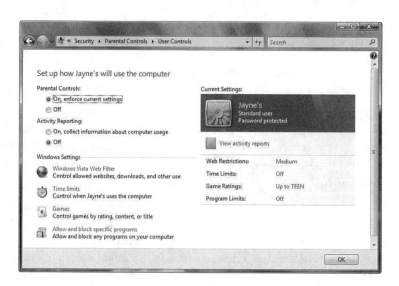

If an Administrator user account exists but has no password assigned to it, any Standard user account can perform any Administrator-level task. For the Parental Controls window options to have any teeth, all your Administrator user accounts must have passwords.

To restrict or allow certain access, click the appropriate link on the Parental Controls window. For example, clicking the Game Ratings screen controls which games the user can run. Clicking the Set Game Ratings link opens a ratings window. Ratings range from EC—Early Childhood to AO—Adults Only, so you can set the highest rating allowed for a particular account.

By its very nature, an Administrator user account must have full access to the entire computer and all its settings. Therefore, you can restrict access only to Standard user accounts.

BitLocker Secures Hard Disks

Windows Vista's BitLocker feature encrypts your disk drive and all its contents with a 48-digit encryption code. When you encrypt a disk drive with a BitLocker encryption key, you will be able to use the disk drive as long as you enter the proper key but nobody else will be able to use the computer.

BitLocker does not encrypt the individual files you specify; instead, it encrypts the entire disk drive. The Encryption File System is useful for encrypting individual files for those who use the Windows Vista Enterprise, Vista Business, Vista Ultimate versions. However, they can encrypt only files located on their Windows drive (this is usually drive C), not on another drive attached to the computer.

When you use BitLocker on your desktop or laptop's disk drive, the disk drive becomes incapable of being read by anyone who removes the drive from your computer and attempts to access your files from another computer. BitLocker also keeps encrypted any files that you send to others over a network, although the recipients can decrypt the files if you tell them the key you used to encrypt the data. By blocking such data, you ensure that snoopers who gain access to your computer over the Internet cannot read anything from any file on your computer, including system files that security threats could corrupt.

To use your computer, you either type your encryption key when you first boot the machine or store the key on a USB drive that you insert to boot your computer and then remove when you're finished. If someone steals your laptop, they cannot access any data on it without the key. You turn on BitLocker from your Control Panel's BitLocker Drive Encryption group.

> BitLocker technology can be problematic for the average user, which is why Microsoft chose not to include the feature in lower-end Vista installations, including Vista Home Premium. Several factors in BitLocker can cause the computer to be unbootable. In addition, managing BitLocker settings and keeping a BitLocker computer running properly requires extra work to protect the encryption and to keep the hardware running smoothly.

Not all hardware that works with Vista is BitLocker-compatible. If yours is not, you will see a window, like the one shown in Figure 27.15, indicating that your computer does not contain a TPM (**trusted platform module**). A TPM is what enables the machine to interact with USB drives and connect key encryptions to the machine's disk drives.

FIGURE 27.15
You must have appropriate hardware before you can apply a BitLocker encryption key to a disk drive on your computer.

Although the primary focus of this book is on home and small business users who will probably be using Vista Home Premium, you need to know about BitLocker to round out your knowledge of Vista's security offerings in case you have a need for such data protection and security. Know that the risks and management of a BitLocker system can become a nuisance but, of course, such nuisances are minor when data is critical.

If you run one of the Vista Home operating systems and feel you need BitLocker protection, display your Windows Start menu, select Extras and Upgrades, and upgrade your Vista installation to a higher version to allow for the BitLocker technology. You should first check your hardware settings to ensure that you have a system that permits BitLocker. The following website contains detailed information to help you decide whether BitLocker technology is right for your needs: http://www.microsoft.com/technet/windowsvista/security/bitexec.mspx.

Chapter Wrap-Up

You now have no reason to be infected with malicious computer threats ever again! Oh, if only that were true! The reality is that no matter how diligent you are and no matter how much forethought Microsoft put into Vista's security, new threats are dreamed up every day that were never before thought of. You must stay updated, you must keep your security-related software installed and active, and you probably should augment your Vista security software with a purchased security suite to increase the likelihood that you'll survive whatever comes your way.

Despite the huge number of security threats that can take down your computer, the world is full of countless programs that help you get your work done and enjoy your computer. The next chapter tells you what you need to know to install and remove programs properly.

CHAPTER 28

Adding and Removing Programs

In This Chapter:

- ▶ Learn about the types of programs available
- ▶ Find new sources of programs you can install
- ▶ Be aware of the dangers that can arrive with new software
- ▶ Master Vista's installation process
- ▶ Uninstall the programs you no longer want

Windows Vista is a means to an end. You use Windows Vista to manage your computer and its files. Vista also enables your programs to talk to your hardware. For example, when you want to print your word-processed document, your word processor sends the document to Vista and Vista handles the printing.

You didn't buy a computer to mess around in Vista. You bought a computer to get work done, or for enjoyment, or both. You need to be able to get your programs onto your computer in the fastest and safest way possible. This chapter addresses some of the issues related to installing—and uninstalling—programs so that they work in tandem with Vista.

All Sorts of Programs

Programs come in many flavors. Windows Vista itself comprises many programs. Programs fall in several different categories. Vista is a system program and, more specifically, an operating system. Other kinds of programs exist, many of which come with windows such as a system restore program (see Chapter 31, "Restoring Your Windows System to a Previous State") and a backup program (see Chapter 35, "Protecting Your Data and Programs"). Windows also provides you with nonsystem programs such as Calculator, which you learned about in Chapter 10, "Exploring the Windows Vista Accessories."

In general, nonsystem programs fall into these categories:

▶ **Entertainment**—Programs that often include games and media-related programs such as Media Player and Nero.

▶ **Education**—Programs that teach their users various subjects; those subjects could be related to school or to post-school interests, such as foreign language tutorials.

▶ **Financial**—Programs that manage and track finances, such as Intuit's Quicken.

▶ **Lifestyle**—Programs that address lifestyle- and often non–computer-related subjects, such as weight-loss and exercising programs that monitor your progress.

▶ **Productivity**—Traditional programs such as word processors and spreadsheet programs (Microsoft Word 2007 and Excel 2007, for instance).

▶ **Utility programs**—Programs that enable you to improve on something you already do on your computer, such as keep track of your list of passwords or check your disk for errors. Some utility programs are also referred to as *system programs* because the line between system and utility is blurred as might be the case for the Task Scheduler (see Chapter 21, "Scheduling Tasks to Run Later").

The reality is that many programs fall into multiple categories. Excel 2007 becomes a *financial program* when used to track and manage expenses, but is referred to as a *productivity program* generically, given its eclectic abilities to track and manage just about any kind of data, financial or otherwise.

Although the distinctions can be blurry, these general program categories are useful for classifying software. No matter what the category, however, if you want to run a program on your computer and that program doesn't come pre-installed when you buy your computer or upgrade to Vista, you must do something to get that program onto your computer.

Most of the rest of this chapter discusses how to do that. The last part of the chapter shows you how to uninstall programs you no longer want.

Sources of Programs

In general, you'll obtain programs in one of three ways:

▶ Buy the program at a store or by mail order and install the program from the CD-ROM or DVD disc the program comes on.

▶ Get the program from a friend who loans you a CD-ROM or DVD or sends the program to you as an email attachment.

▶ Download the program from a website to try for a free trial period offered to you or where you purchased the program online.

The method you use to obtain a program depends on the program's source. Many programs are available both as an online download as well as on a disc you buy at a store.

Warnings Are in Order

The second option, getting your program from a friend, merits a couple of warnings. First, depending on the source, you certainly might be violating copyright issues if you install a program that your friend also installed and is using. You are not allowed to install Adobe Photoshop Elements on your computer if your friend bought Adobe Photoshop Elements and has installed it on his or her machine. Not only are legal issues involved, but technical ones are possible, too; with online product activation, you often cannot install and run a program on a second computer.

Some programs are classified as **shareware**, which means your friend is perfectly justified, legal, and even encouraged to give you the program. The program authors offer anyone who wants to try the program a trial period or perhaps limited use of the program. If you like the program, you send the program author or publisher a fee to unlock it and make everything legal. If you don't like the program, you stop using it, uninstall it, and all is well.

If you get **freeware**, the authors fully intend to give away the program. The program should indicate this somehow. The Phantom Desktop Screen Saver, for example, is available from www.GregoryBraun.com and you can download and install it free. If you put the downloaded file on a CD-ROM or attach it to an email message, you can give it to as many friends as you like.

Why would someone write a program and give it away free? Some developers write freeware and, during installation and perhaps on the Help About screen, ask for an optional donation, usually by PayPal. Given that it's optional, you are under no obligation to pay and you can keep using the program. Developers such as Gregory Braun who designed the free Phantom Desktop Screen Saver program hope that you will like the freeware program enough to check out his other products to see whether they are worth paying for (they are).

Did you
Know?

Given that this chapter follows a chapter titled, "Managing Your Windows Security," you should now be well aware of the dangers inherent in software that you install intentionally, as well as software that installs without your knowledge, such as spyware. When you get a homemade CD-ROM or DVD that contains a program you install, you are risking your computer's integrity when you install that program.

Even if you trust your friend and your friend would never intentionally give you a program with a virus or spyware on it, you don't know whether your friend got the program from an unreliable source. Carefully think twice about the wisdom of installing such a program.

The Ease of Installing Programs Changed

Programs use to be easy to install. Then they got hard. Now they're fairly easy again.

Before Windows came on the scene, you'd buy a diskette, put it in your computer's disk drive, and copy the files to a single place on your hard disk, usually in a new directory folder you created just for the program, using a simple copy command. That got even easier when programmers stored a batch file on the disk, which typed the copy command for you. (A **batch file** is one that contains one or more sets of commands. Such files were most popular back in the pre-Windows days of DOS.)

Then Windows 1.0 was released and things got messy. A simple copy command was severely underpowered to install the program and a batch program wasn't much better, so program developers had to write complex installation scripts and use third-party program installation routines to install programs into all the nooks and crannies that Windows required. To make matters worse, in the first few years of Windows, program standards were available but hardly followed. The programs you installed might or might not work, and often they would conflict with other programs. When you wanted to get rid of them and tried to do so, artifacts of their installation could plague you for a long time even when you followed all the uninstallation procedures the software maker gave you—*if* the software maker gave you any.

> Games have earned their reputation as being notoriously difficult to install at times. Even in the modern world of Windows Vista, which has done a lot to improve the gaming experience on a PC, nobody is fully convinced that we won't continue to experience installation problems with some games.

Now, the tide is turning back in the computer user's favor again. Several factors have converged to make program installations simpler. Not only is Microsoft stricter with its requirements for programs to run under Vista, the entire software industry has slowly settled on some de facto standards that mean most people will install most software the same way and achieve the same results.

Programs written for Vista (as well as those for Windows XP) are supposed to create a Windows restore point so that you can return to your computer's previous state if the installation goes awry or causes your system to malfunction. (You can read about restore points in Chapter 31.) Sadly, not all programs *do* create a system restore point and Vista doesn't warn you if they don't. Therefore, you should get in the habit of manually creating a restore point before you install any program. If something bad happens, you can return Windows to where it was before the trouble began.

Watch Out!

Older programs written long before Vista arrived on the scene are called **legacy programs**. If you want to run a legacy program that doesn't run properly in Vista, you can try running Vista's Program Compatibility Wizard and adjusting settings that might allow Vista to run the legacy software. Vista's help screens guide you through the Program Compatibility Wizard and its options.

Did you Know?

Installing From Discs

If you get a program on a CD-ROM or DVD, this is almost always how you begin that program's installation: insert the disc into your computer's disc drive and follow the onscreen dialog box prompts. In most cases, if you accept all installation defaults, the programs run just as you expect they should.

Have you noticed the terms *disks* and *discs* mean two different kinds of media? Generally, *disk* is used for a hard disk or an older diskette (floppy or the firm, plastic ones that came in a 3.5-inch version) and a *disk drive* is the unit you insert a disk into, or perhaps already has a disk there, such as a hard disk drive. *Disc* is used for a CD or DVD and *disc drive* is the unit you insert a disc into. It's unclear why they changed but, in general, if a device uses magnetic particles for data, it's a disk; if a device uses optically written data, it's a disc.

By the Way

Vista helps you along the way. Just because you insert a disc with a program on it doesn't mean you want to install that disc's contents. Therefore, if you insert a program disc into your disc drive, such as the Adobe Photoshop Elements 4.0 disc, Vista displays the AutoPlay dialog box shown in Figure 28.1.

FIGURE 28.1
Vista gives you a choice when you insert a program disc into your computer.

If you don't see such an AutoPlay dialog box when you insert a program, you have AutoPlay turned off. Open your Control Panel's Hardware and Sound group and select AutoPlay to display the AutoPlay options. Click the arrow to open the Software and Games option and select one of the options there. These options include Install or Run Program, Open Folder to View Files Using Windows Explorer, Take No Action, and Ask Me Every Time. If you want Vista to install or run a program whenever you insert its disc, select the Install or Run Program option. If you want to be asked what to do, as Figure 28.1's dialog box does, select the Ask Me Every Time option.

Photoshop Elements 4.0 is an outdated program version released more than a year before Vista was released. (Adobe released version 5.0 right before Vista came out.) As you can see, Vista doesn't seem to mind the older version. Vista can work with just about any program written in the past decade that you will want to install and run. As usual, it's possible to find a game that causes problems, though.

To install the program, press Enter to accept the dialog box's default or click the selected Run Setup.exe option. After Vista confirms that you want to run the installation program, the program begins and walks you through the installation process, usually in a step-by-step dialog box wizard screen set such as the one in Figure 28.2. Almost always, the installation program will request your name and a serial number or product ID to confirm that you are the rightful owner of the program.

Setup.exe is the name most often applied to a program's initial installation program. No matter how many files are on the disc, if Setup.exe is there, Vista sees it and offers to run it to install the program. The case never matters, so SETUP.EXE works the same as Setup.exe. Although Setup.exe is the industry-standard name for such an installation file, not all software developers call their required install program file Setup.exe. Some use Install.exe and other names. If Vista cannot locate a Setup.exe file, you should select AutoPlay's Open Folder to View Files option to view a list of files on the disc and consult the program's manual to learn which file you need to select to start the process.

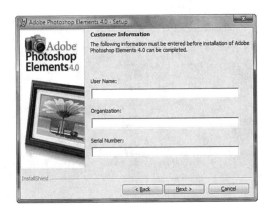

FIGURE 28.2
The program will ask you for some details during the installation.

After you enter all the details required during the installation, the program might offer to display a notes page describing some initial material you should be aware of that might not have gotten into the program manual (if the program even came with a manual). Typically you can click to select or unselect an option that offers to run the program immediately after finishing the installation.

> Due to Vista's more secure architecture, you shouldn't have to reboot your computer after a program's installation as often as before Vista. This might not hold true for system programs you install, such as antivirus programs, because they rewrite some system-level routines and your computer won't be secure until you reboot to switch to that newly replaced system code. Programs not designed for Vista might request a reboot even if Vista does not require one. You should reboot when prompted, even if you suspect that Vista made such a reboot unnecessary.

By the Way

Installing an Online Program to Your Vista Computer

When you visit a website and purchase a program or request a freeware, shareware, or a free trial, you won't have a disc with the program. You will have to download the program's installation file. Whereas on an installation disc many files can appear, to install a program that you get from the Internet, you download a single file. After it is downloaded, that single file will either take over and download any remaining files it needs or you'll have to expand the file into several smaller files that are required for your installation to take place.

Almost always, after you pay for a program or request it online using whatever method is required, you're asked to run or save the program from a prompt such as the one shown in Figure 28.3.

FIGURE 28.3
You'll need to save or run an installation file when you request to install a program from the Internet.

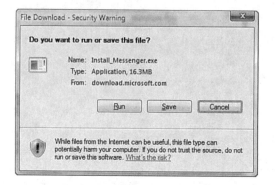

If you select Run, the program begins downloading to a temporary location on your computer and installs itself after it completely downloads. The Run option is the easiest and fastest. The drawback to running the program directly from the install prompt, as opposed to saving the program first, is that if you ever need to install the program again, as might be the case if your disk drive gets damaged, you'll have to download it all over again. If you select the Save option and save the installation file to your computer, you'll only have to select that file from an Explorer window to install the program in the future.

Did you Know?

Vista placed a folder named Downloads in your username's main folder. When you save an installation file to your disk, create a folder just for that installation. For Norton Ghost, for example, you might call the new folder Norton Ghost Install File and direct the Save command to that folder. If you ever need to reinstall the program, just open that folder and select the Setup.exe file to install Ghost again so that you don't have to wait on another download. Keeping all your downloads in their own separate folders in this manner makes it simple to locate them in the future. Just make sure that you back up regularly, or you'll have to download the file again if you ever need to install it in the future.

When the downloaded install file in full gets to your computer, whether you selected Run or Save, you can install the program and follow the prompts that then come to set up the program on your computer.

After the Installation

After many programs finish installing, they offer to go to the Web and update themselves with the latest available updates and patches. If offered, you should accept this option and let the program grab and install the updates. This assures you that you have installed the latest bug fixes and security measures that the program's makers have produced.

Some programs offer optional updates, such as TurboTax. You will have to download your state's tax tables for TurboTax (if your state is unfortunate enough to have state taxes). The program's nature, therefore, dictates whether the initial installation is all you need to use the program.

Did you Know?

Uninstalling Programs

In the ancient days of old, back when DOS ran on computers, to erase a program you just typed a delete command and the program went away. If you delete a program file in Windows, you almost surely will mess something up. Vista will still run, but you'll have program artifacts of that deleted file all over the place because a Windows program actually comprises many different files scattered all over your disk drive.

To delete a program properly, open your Control Panel and select the Programs group. Click the Programs and Features option to display a list of installed programs on your computer that might look something like the one in Figure 28.4. If you don't see the Details pane at the bottom of the window, click the arrow next to Organize, choose Layout, and then click Details Pane to show the pane that displays information about the selected program.

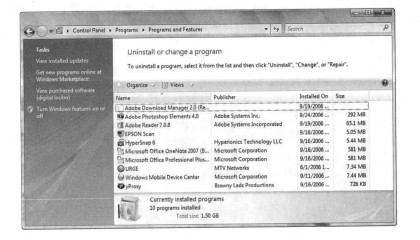

FIGURE 28.4
The Programs and Features option displays a list of programs you can delete.

All programs you installed, as well as a few you might not have known you installed, appear there. The reason that some might seem unfamiliar to you is that one program's installation often lets another program piggyback and install with it. For example, if you download Adobe Acrobat Reader to your computer and install it, the Adobe Download Manager is also installed.

To remove a listed program, click to select the program and click the toolbar's Uninstall/Change button. (Depending on the program and its options, you may see Uninstall and Change on their own buttons across the Uninstall or Change a Program window's toolbar.) After Vista confirms your intent to uninstall the program, the uninstall process begins.

The program's developers typically supply Windows with the uninstall routine that runs, at least for well-behaved programs that follow Microsoft's Windows guidelines. Therefore, when you begin the uninstall, you'll usually see a program screen that guides you through the process.

By the Way

> If you want to change a program's installation options, you will also follow this same procedure. That is why the button you clicked is labeled Uninstall/Change. Microsoft Office is one such program that you might change using this procedure. If, for example, you didn't install Excel when you installed the other Office programs, but later decide you want to install Excel, you will follow this procedure to change your Office installation and select the Excel option when given the chance to do so.

Depending on the program, you might not see a Change option, but you will always see a Remove option and often a Repair option, as Figure 28.5 shows. If you experience new problems with a program you can try the Repair option to see whether it fixes the problem. This option checks the primary program files for consistency and, when possible, replaces any that are damaged.

FIGURE 28.5
You can repair or remove certain program's installations.

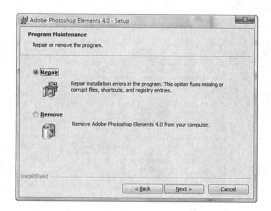

The Remove option will completely remove a program after you confirm that you want to do so.

An uninstall *can* cause a problem, but it's rare. Typically, programs uninstall safely but programs that interact with internal system features, such as anti-virus programs have been known to be problematic to uninstall. To be on the safe side, create a system restore point before you uninstall a program. If Windows Vista behaves funny after the program is gone, you can put your system files back in shape by restoring to that restore point.

Chapter Wrap-Up

In older Windows books, a chapter on installing and uninstalling programs was much longer. Fortunately, the process is getting easier because programmers are following better standards. Your programs are important and you need a reliable way to install them when you need them and remove them when you no longer want them on your system. Vista provides a great interface for handling your program installations.

It's time to move away from your software and concentrate on the hardware attached to your Windows machine. The next chapter begins Part VI, "Interfacing Windows and Hardware." Vista is far easier to deal with when you have to resolve a hardware issue than previous Windows environments were. Installing a new printer, for example, is typically effortless at best and hardly painful in the most trying of times; that's not the way it used to be.

PART VI

Interfacing Windows and Hardware

CHAPTER 29

Printing with Windows Vista

In This Chapter:

- ▶ Understand the various ways printers can be attached to your computer
- ▶ See how simple it can be to install a printer in Vista
- ▶ Designate a printer as your primary default printer
- ▶ Select from multiple printers attached to your computer
- ▶ Preview printing to save paper and time and frustration
- ▶ Manage Vista's print jobs

It used to be said that computers would revolutionize and reduce paper usage in the world. Fortunately for paper manufacturers, computers did the opposite. Thanks to computers, more paper is consumed than ever before. Those who love trees but also understand that only the free market can effectively work to maintain resources should also be grateful that paper manufacturers now plant more trees in a single year than occurred in a whole decade before the 1990s.

It's also been said that the chance a paperless office will ever exist is as slight as the odds that a paperless bathroom will become the norm.

In other words, stock up on plenty of paper because you'll use it. And you'll use a *lot* of it. This chapter discusses how Vista helps you use those paper products by discussing your printer and its relationship to Vista.

**Watch
Out!**

> The last part of this chapter includes more background and theory than most of the other chapters have. That's because a history of how printers used to work with computers helps you understand why they work the way they do today and why all those pesky Windows drivers that we're always told to install are so important. This is a good chapter with which to begin this part of the book because it focuses on hardware. The background you master here will help you better understand the need for some chapters that follow. So sit back and put your history thinking cap on because in a little while you're going to revisit some pre-Windows computing history.

Vista and Printers

No matter what kind of printer you connect to your computer, Vista can probably handle it. For the vast majority of printers, old and new, Vista can handle them effortlessly. Vista "knows" about more printers than any other operating system ever released. Vista's printer database is huge. Vista can recognize older printers that even XP could not recognize, and it recognizes many of them without driver disks and all the rest of the hassles that used to go hand-in-hand with connecting printers to computers. Printers can generally connect to computers in one of four ways, which are as follows:

- **Wired with a printer cable, also called a parallel cable**—This cable is much thicker than a USB cable, sometimes as much as one-half inch thick, and connects to your computer's parallel port using a wide connector on both ends of the cable. The connector is about 2.5 inches wide. Hardly any printer has required a parallel cable, or even supplied a parallel port for such a cable, since USB ascended to popularity in 2000–2001.

- **Wired with a serial cable, also called an RS-232 cable**—This cable is slightly thinner than a parallel cable and has a connector that is slightly more than an inch wide. Fewer printers were made that connected to computers using serial cables than parallel connections and many printers that included serial connections also offered parallel connections. A statistically infinitesimally small number of serially connected printers are in use today.

- **Wired with a USB cable**—Most printers sold today are USB based. One advantage of USB printers is that they typically install themselves the moment you plug them in. In reality, Vista installs them the moment you plug them in, as you'll see in the next section.

- **Networked**—Some printers connect directly to a network hub using a standard networking cable. After installing, all computers connected to that network share and can print to the network printer.

▶ **Wireless printers**—Using the same technology as wireless networks, as well as Bluetooth technology that many wireless headsets use, more and more wireless printers are sold every day due to their ease of installation; put them close to your computer and turn them on. Vista senses their presence and connects to them.

> Even we computer fanatics probably wouldn't have believed you if you told us a few years ago that to install a printer today you'd just need to take it out of the box and turn it on somewhere near the computer. Oh, the nightmares some people used to have getting their computers to communicate with their printers properly!

By the Way

Installing a Printer

Although this chapter will discuss a little about what happens when a printer's installation doesn't go smoothly, you should understand that in most cases, the following are the steps you follow to install and use a printer on a Vista-based computer:

1. Plug your printer's USB printer cable into your computer.

2. Begin printing.

You can eliminate step 1 if you have a wireless network and your computer can connect to the network wirelessly! (Of course, if the Wi-Fi network is secure, you may need to set up the printer to access the wireless network using a password or key.)

Here's an example. The Hewlett Packard LaserJet 4500 printer was manufactured years before Vista. When you plug the HP 4500's USB cable into Vista, the Vista Taskbar pops up the message shown in Figure 29.1.

FIGURE 29.1
Vista senses a new device is present.

After a brief pause that lasts about five seconds, the Vista taskbar pops up the message shown in Figure 29.2.

FIGURE 29.2
Your printer is
now installed.

The pop-up screen isn't printer specific. After you install a printer, verify that Vista really did its job properly by opening your Control Panel's Hardware and Sound group. Select the Printers option to open the Printers window. There you should see your printer listed among any other printer-related devices that were there before. Figure 29.3 shows the Printers window immediately after Figure 29.2's pop-up window appeared. The HP LaserJet 4500 installed properly, and Vista knows exactly what kind of printer it is and named it correctly in its list of printers.

FIGURE 29.3
Vista installed the printer properly and recognized the exact model number and manufacturer.

Default printer   New printer

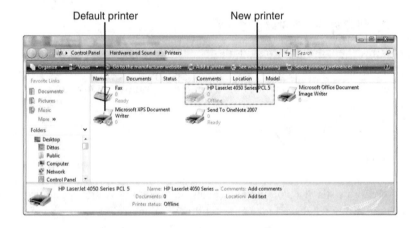

Installing a Non-USB Printer

All this is well and good when it works. Sometimes the printer won't install this easily. If you use a USB-connected or a wireless printer, the printer should install this easily. Some wireless or Bluetooth printers will not install automatically, although others will. If yours will not, check your printer's manual and installation instructions. Some printers require you to insert and install driver software for the printer to be able to communicate with your computer.

Almost always, the way you install a non-USB printer is to open your Control Panel's hardware and Sound group and select the Printers option. Click the Add a Printer button on the toolbar across the top of the window to open the Add Printer dialog box. Select Add a Local Printer (or Add a Network, Wireless, or Bluetooth Printer if you're having trouble installing such a printer), select the type of connection (LPT1: is typically the port you'll use for a parallel printer and COM1: is the port you'll select for a serial printer). You'll then have to select a manufacturer and a model number from the Add Printer dialog box shown in Figure 29.4 and complete the installation.

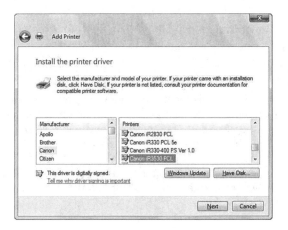

FIGURE 29.4
You will need to tell Windows your printer's manufacturer and model if you install a non-USB printer or install a USB-based printer that does not install automatically.

If Vista doesn't show your exact model, select one that sounds close. Other drivers will often work fine for your printer, although some features might not work properly.

Did you Know?

If you cannot locate your printer in the Add Printer dialog box and nothing else you select seems to make Vista communicate with your printer, you will have to go to the printer manufacturer's website and download the latest drivers for that printer before you can be sure that Vista will communicate properly. Even then, it's possible that a printer might be so old and cranky (due to design, not because of a physical problem) that Vista will never be able to communicate with it properly. This is especially true of serial-cabled printers and some earlier parallel printers.

If all else fails, write to your printer manufacturer's customer support help staff and ask them how to get the printer to work with Vista. Understand, however, that if your printer is old, there's a slight chance that it cannot be made to work with Vista. Sometimes if you install a printer driver from the same manufacturer for a newer printer, you can get the computer to see the older printer well enough to print text to it.

Did you Know?

To make sure that all went smoothly, right-click the Printer window's icon for your newly installed printer and select Properties. The dialog box that appears will differ from printer to printer because different printers offer unique features, but you can click the Print Test Page button to send a test page to your printer. Assuming that your printer is turned on and has paper, the page should print.

If the test page does not print properly, instead of clicking the Close button on the Test Page dialog box that pops up, click the Troubleshoot Printer Problems link. Vista walks you through several potential trouble spots that can occur when the computer and the printer don't communicate properly.

It's easy for me to spend your money but... printers are cheap! Don't waste a lot of time trying to get a cranky old printer to work with Vista. On eBay and other online sites that sell printers, as well as any computer store and just about any discount store you shop at, you'll find printers that run in the low double-digit price range. They might not be the most robust printers that will last for 10 or more years, but they do the job for a time and get you connected and up and running for now. You can upgrade to a better printer later if you don't want to spend the extra money now. Even moderately powerful printers that are somewhat photo-capable are relatively low-priced.

If your computer connects to a network and a network printer is somewhere else on the network or perhaps connected to a different computer on your network, you will have to tell Vista about it because Vista cannot magically know that you want to have access to that printer. The final section in this chapter, "A Note About Network Printing," explains what you do to inform Windows that you want to print to a network printer.

Specify a Default Printer

If you want the new printer to be your default printer—that is, the printer that Vista always selects to print to when you open an application's Print dialog box— right-click over your new printer and select the Set As Default Printer option. The green check mark moves to the new printer and that printer will be used in all subsequent programs that you run as the default printer.

By the Way

If the printer you just installed is the first printing device on your machine, Vista will have already designated it as your default printer, indicated by the green checkmark on the printer's icon.

Overriding the Default

If you have multiple printers or, as many Vista installations will have, one or more printers and possibly a fax modem for sending faxes, you'll see multiple printer icons in your Control Panel's Printers window as the previous sections described. All of your valid printing devices are available for your use—even for those that aren't designated as default printers.

For example, suppose that you use the Microsoft XPS Document Writer for outputting text to XPS files. The Printers window will show the Microsoft XPS Document Writer as one of the printer options. To print a PowerPoint presentation to this print device, as opposed as to the default printer, select File, Print to display the program's Print dialog box and click the Name list to select a different printer.

As Figure 29.5 shows, the HP Laser Jet 4050 is the default printer on the system and that's the printer selected by default in the Name field, but you can click to change that to the Microsoft XPS Document Writer. After the PowerPoint presentation prints to the XPS Document Writer device, the HP 4050 is still the default printer, so no other applications are affected.

Some applications allow you to designate specific printers for specific operations. For example, some financial programs allow you to designate a specific printer for printing checks and another printer for printing invoices and receipts. After you designate these printers, when you print a check, the program automatically sends the check information to the printer with the checks. When you print an invoice or other document that requires plain paper, the program sends that information to the printer with the plain paper.

Did you Know?

Default printer

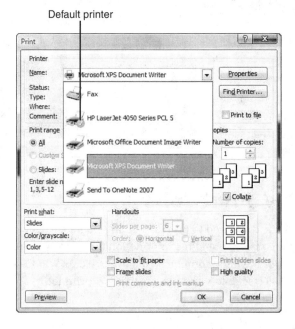

FIGURE 29.5
You can always select a printer that is not your default printer when you want to print something.

Previewing Your Printing

In most Vista applications, you can preview a document before you print it. Getting into the habit of doing just this will save you a bunch of time, paper, ink, and frustration. To select a preview in most applications, select Print, Preview. Sometimes the Preview option is labeled Page Preview. Such a preview screen appears in Figure 29.6, showing a newsletter being edited within Microsoft Word 2007.

Did you Know?

> A button normally resides on the preview's toolbar that enables you to preview more than one or two pages at once. Previewing eight or more thumbnail images of your previews gives you a good idea of how balanced your pages are with titles, headings, subheadings, text, and pictures.

FIGURE 29.6
Always look at a preview of your printed document before spending the time and expense of actually printing it only to find something wrong with the document's format.

Closes the preview

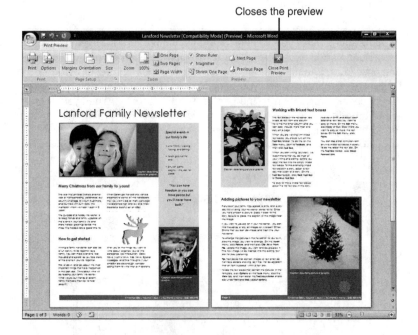

Managing Print Jobs

When you select the command to print something from a Windows Vista application, your program does *not* send the information directly to your printer. Instead, your program sends the information to Windows and asks Windows to print the document. The collected data sent to the printer is a **print job**.

A Little History Helps Explain a Lot

Before Windows, every program had to include printer options for every single printer in existence. In other words, if eight printer manufacturers made a combined total of 114 printers, a program would need to know how to communicate with 114 different printers. When you used the program, you selected your printer from the list.

The problem was this: As soon as the program was written and sold, those pesky printer manufacturers would make new printers that weren't listed in your software! You'd have to wait for the next version or make do with not being able to take advantage of all the printer's new features if you purchased a new printer that was designed and sold after your program.

Such a world is difficult for software developers. They had to monitor all printers made and include as many printers as they could in their software so as not to be outdone by the competition. There was lots of duplicated effort by the software developers. Microsoft would have to write a bunch of printer drivers for each of its programs, Lotus would have to write a bunch of similar printer drivers for each of its programs, and so on. This duplication meant that developers were spending time reinventing the wheel instead of working on new ways to make the software do more for you.

Did you Know?

> By the way, this background might be interesting to you or it might not. If you didn't begin using computers until well after Windows, this old history might seem like a waste of your time. It's valuable background, however. For one thing, only when you know where we've been can you more easily understand why things are the way they are and why things will differ in the future. In addition, knowing that Windows handles all your printer drivers now, as opposed to each software maker having to do so, makes it clearer why the print queue, described in a moment, is so nice.

Microsoft Windows changed all that. Microsoft freed software writers from the drudgery of writing for every printer in existence. Windows also freed software writers from the drudgery of writing for every monitor and graphics card in existence for the same reason. In addition, Windows freed software writers from the drudgery of writing for every keyboard, modem, and every other device that could possibly be attached to your machine. In other words, Windows now talks to the hardware no matter what hardware you have. The only job of your program is to talk to Windows.

If you have both an HP LaserJet printer and an Epson color inkjet printer attached to your computer, the program you buy and install doesn't have to know how to send data to an HP LaserJet or an Epson inkjet. Your program just sends the data to Windows. You tell Windows which printer you want the data printed on. Windows then formats the data to work on your printer.

Now, only one program, Microsoft Windows, has to understand and be aware of all the countless printers, monitors, graphics adapters, modems, keyboards, and so forth. No program has to know any of those details. Software developers are free to add neat, whiz-bang features to programs instead of writing code for printer after printer. Even Microsoft has it easier than before. Microsoft Vista programmers don't even have to write drivers for all the printers and other hardware that exist now and in the future. Instead, Microsoft tells the manufacturers of those devices: If you want to work with Vista, that's great; all you have to do is follow this pattern. Microsoft then gives the printer makers the pattern. As long as printer maker follows the Windows Vista pattern, that printer is guaranteed to work with Windows Vista even if the printer never existed when Vista was released. All the printer maker has to do is supply one driver, a driver that follows Vista's pattern and tells Vista how to speak to that printer.

Using the Print Queue

Now that you see where things have been, you have a good understanding of how Vista printing works today. When you print from an application, your application sends data to Windows. Windows then sends the data to a driver that formats the data for your printer.

Another variable slips into the mix now. Windows is a multitasking machine. You can open several programs at once and they can all run at the same time. Although only one window is active and in focus at any one time, all open programs are running. If Windows couldn't multitask when you opened Media Player and began playing Dean Martin hits, as soon as you opened Quicken to work on your finances, Deano's music would stop playing.

But Dean Martin music never dies.

The Media Player window's songs keep right on playing for your entertainment while you work on your finances.

Consider this, however: What happens if you open Word, load a long document, and begin printing? Before the printing has even gone past the first page, you start printing a report from Quicken. Then before that printing even has a chance to begin, you surf to a web page and you select File, Print to print it. Three programs and one printer could cause problems if Vista didn't perform some fancy footwork. And Vista does just that.

When you print, you print to something known as a *print queue*. You'll never see that term on a window's title bar, but that's its technical name. A **print queue** is an area of memory that holds your printing until Windows has a chance to spool the data from the print queue to your printer. Even the fastest printer is slower than the slowest computer running Vista. When you print, Vista quickly spools output to the print queue. If you don't have enough memory to hold everything that you're printing, Vista uses disk space to hold the data that's lined up to print.

When you send anything to a printer, Windows creates a new print job that contains the batch of data you're printing for that printer. If you print three Word documents to a printer, Windows creates three print jobs for that printer. A printer icon appears on your taskbar. If you double-click the taskbar icon, a window that looks like the one shown in Figure 29.7 opens for that printer. The window informs you of all your print jobs' status for that printer.

Currently printing

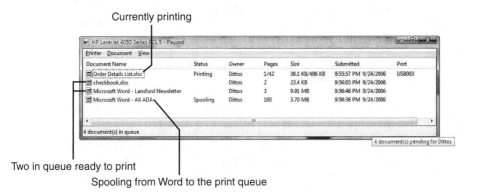

Two in queue ready to print

Spooling from Word to the print queue

FIGURE 29.7
Your printer window informs you of each print job's status for that printer.

In Figure 29.7, the files represent print jobs. The first print job, Order Details List.xlsx, is an Excel worksheet and that worksheet was the first item the user requested be printed. Even if that worksheet has not yet finished printing, if the user prints a second item, as was done here with the checkbook.xlsx worksheet, Vista keeps printing the first file but then queues up the second so that it will begin printing as soon as the first one finishes.

Two more documents have also been requested to be printed. The fourth one, a Word document called All ADA, is still being spooled to the print queue. Until that document spools, Word won't let the user close Word. After the print queue has the entire print job stored and queued up for the printer, though, the Spooling status message changes to blank, which means "ready to print" and the user is free to close Word.

Sending information to the print spool is typically very quick and rarely keeps you from closing a program whose data hasn't yet been completely spooled.

As print jobs finish printing, Vista removes them from the list. The first job is always the first job to finish printing and the first job to disappear from the list. If an error occurs, as might happen if the printer runs out of paper or gets a paper jam, the status for that print job changes.

You cannot rearrange print jobs in the print queue. Such a feature could be useful at times, but Vista doesn't allow it.

If you send one or more items to the printer and nothing prints, open your printer's job window and see whether an error message appears for the top entry. If so, something is wrong and that typically means you're out of paper, you have a paper jam, your printer is not turned on, or your printer cable isn't plugged in all the way. Usually, the moment you fix the physical problem Vista removes the error message and begins printing.

Vista segments printing, organizing it by printer, if you have multiple printers installed. Therefore, if you print a large amount of data to one printer from two different programs, and then start printing a third set of data to a different printer connected to your computer (or to your computer network), clicking your taskbar's printer icon offers two printer windows. In each will be the status of the print jobs sent to each of the two printers.

Vista will typically spool the output very quickly and then begin printing. But if you send something to print and then change your mind, you can open your printer window, right-click on the print job you want to stop, and select Cancel. Some of the document might print, but Vista will delete all that has yet to print from the print queue. You can also right-click to pause printing if, for example, you need to change the paper in your printer and you don't want the rest of the print job to print on the incorrect paper that the first few pages printed on. After you change the paper, you can right-click and select Restart to resume printing. (You'll need to reprint the first few pages that printed on the wrong paper.)

The best way to stop printing is to cancel the job in the printer's window. You might also want to press the printer's Cancel button if there is one. If your printer has a large memory buffer, Windows might think the entire document has finished printing when it actually hasn't. The Cancel button on the printer will take care of deleting all the print data that hasn't yet printed but that the printer has stored and is waiting to print.

A Note About Network Printing

If your computer connects to a network that includes a printer, whether the printer is a network printer connected to a network port or a printer connected to another computer on your network that you want to share, you have to tell Vista that you want to be able to print to that printer. Assuming that the printer is set up for sharing, you can print to it from your computer.

Open your Control Panel's Hardware and Sound group and select the Printers option. Click the Add a Printer button on the toolbar across the top of the window to open the Add Printer dialog box. Select Add a Network, Wireless, or Bluetooth Printer. Windows will scan your network looking for shared printers. When the network printer appears, click to select it and click Next, following the prompting of the printer installation routine. When you finish, that networked printer will be one that your computer can print to. You can make that network printer your computer's default printer or you can make a different printer attached to your computer (called a *local printer*) the default one and select the network printer from the printer selection list when you print something.

Chapter Wrap-Up

There's probably more behind the history of printers than you knew about and almost certainly more detailed in this chapter than you want to know about. Nevertheless, with the background you got here, you are better equipped to understand the nature of Windows driver files, print queues, and print jobs.

Hopefully you're more comfortable with the installation and use of your printer. Some advanced Windows users don't know that they can cancel print jobs in their print queue windows. By understanding the nature of print queues, you are better informed and know how to cancel large print jobs that you start without having to rush to the printer, turn off the printer, and deal with data that shouldn't be printed but keeps getting sent to a printer. Some users who don't know about the print queue window just turn off the computer to cancel the printing. Sadly, depending on the status of the print queue when they turned off their computer, the printing can start right back up again the next time they turn on the computer!

The next chapter discusses additional hardware and software subjects that deal with connections on your computer: faxing and scanning.

CHAPTER 30

Faxing and Scanning

In This Chapter:

- ▶ Get a bird's-eye view of Vista's fax capabilities
- ▶ Fax from within any application you run
- ▶ Install your fax properly
- ▶ Use the new Windows Fax and Scan program
- ▶ Scan any document into digital form
- ▶ Send a quick text fax

Fax machines are a thing of the past. They went the way of eight-track tapes and vinyl records. Some people still need them if they fax physical documents such as legal documents that exist in only one copy with original signatures, but in many ways even that is outdated. If you have a computer and a scanner, you don't need a fax machine in most cases.

With a computer, if you want to fax a document, you scan it into your computer and fax the scanned image to the receiving fax machine or to a computer that's set up to receive faxes. Sure, scanning the document seems like an extra step, but when you fax, the fax machine is scanning the documents so scanning and sending with your computer isn't much more time-consuming than using a standalone fax machine. Plus you have the added advantage of having a stored, digital file that you can reference later without digging through file cabinets to find it.

Even better, with your computer, you can fax documents and files that don't exist in paper form. Instead of printing and then faxing, as you used to have to do when the world only had fax machines and not computers that faxed, you can fax straight from Word, Quicken, Photoshop, or any program that you print from. Instead of sending your data to your printer, select your computer's fax service when printing and off the fax goes.

A Faxing Overview

To fax from your computer, you need one of two things:

▶ **A fax modem**—All phone modems manufactured after the mid-1990s connect to the Internet and they include fax capabilities.

▶ **A fax service**—Online services exist that will accept your digital documents and fax them to recipients. www.eFax.com is one of many that offer this service for a small, monthly fee (see Figure 30.1). The service faxes your files to the recipients you specify, and it provides your own phone number that you give to others who want to fax documents to you. Such services often have local numbers and 800 numbers available. When someone sends you a fax from a fax machine to that number, the online service digitizes the fax and sends it to you as an email attachment. Such services are invaluable for anyone who sends and receives numerous faxes as people in the real estate and legal professions often do. For most users in today's email-intensive world where most items are sent back and forth as email attachments, a fax service is overkill and a fax modem suits them just fine for those once-a-year faxes they send or receive.

FIGURE 30.1
Online fax services, such as eFax.com, make sending and receiving faxes almost effortless for a monthly fee.

The rest of this chapter discusses the first option, faxing from your own Vista-based computer. Almost everybody has a modem installed, so almost everybody has a fax machine inside their PC.

"Would You Like a Modem With That?"

When ordering a new computer from a manufacturer such as Dell or Gateway, many users have DSL or cable modem service for their Internet, so they don't order a phone modem for their new computer. Later they realize they need to fax a file that's on their computer, so they scramble to get a modem. Usually this means printing the document and paying a service to fax it for them until they buy and install a modem in their computer.

Don't let this happen to you.

Modems are cheap and it's easiest to get one installed when you buy a new computer. Even if you don't think you'll ever have to dial up the Internet over the phone lines again, get the modem so that you can send and receive faxes if the need ever arrives. Even a single fax that's a dozen pages or fewer can cost more to pay someone else to send than the cost of an internal modem.

Don't forget the phone line! You need not only a fax modem, but also a phone line that you can connect to your modem. Many homes and small businesses now use wireless phone sets that all communicate with a base unit located elsewhere. Such a phone system eliminates the need for putting phone lines in every room that needs a phone. With a fax modem, the need for the phone line returns, however, so you have to run a phone line to your computer's location to send and receive faxes from your computer.

Watch Out!

If you don't want to run a phone line to your computer's location or you cannot because of physical considerations in the structure of your home or office, it doesn't necessarily mean you'll be without fax capabilities. You can now get a transmitter that sends a phone signal from a device plugged into your phone line's wall jack that transmits the phone's signal to a distant receiver that you put next to your computer. You run a phone line from your modem's phone jack to the receiver. Your modem will think it's plugged in directly to a phone jack when in reality it's plugged into a transmitter that sends and receives the modem's signals to the actual phone jack in another room. You can find these phone line transmitters in the phone accessories location of just about any large discount store or electronics retailer.

If You Can Print, You Can Fax

Vista is set up to install a virtual fax device automatically. As long as you have a modem plugged into a phone line (or into a wireless phone line transmitter) you can fax from Vista. To send a fax, follow these steps:

1. Start the application you want to fax from, such as Photoshop, Quicken, or Word.

2. Load the document you want to fax.

3. Open your program's Print dialog box. This is usually done from the File, Print menu selection or from Office 2007's Office button click followed by clicking Print. You can fax anything you can print. Therefore, if you want to send only certain pages or a selected area of text in the fax, you first select that area or designate the pages you want to send in the Print dialog box.

4. Click to open the Name list and select Fax as shown in Figure 30.2. (If you selected Fax as your default printer, you won't need to select it.)

FIGURE 30.2
To send a fax when you print from any application, select your computer fax.

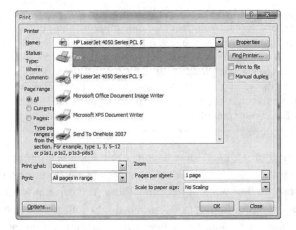

5. Click OK. Instead of printing or sending the fax, the fax program needs extra information such as the phone number to the recipient's fax machine. The first time you fax, Vista will ask whether you want to use a fax modem or connect to a fax server on your network, as might be the case if you work in a networked, business environment. Select the option you want to use.

If you select a fax modem, you'll give it a name on the Choose a Modem Name dialog box that appears next. Subsequently, you'll select this name when you want to print to the fax. Vista then displays the Choose How to

Receive Faxes dialog that enables you to receive faxes or just send one for now, as shown in Figure 30.3. (If you select Notify Me, Vista pops up a dialog box if your phone rings to ask whether you want the fax modem to answer and receive a fax. For most users, this gets annoying quickly.)

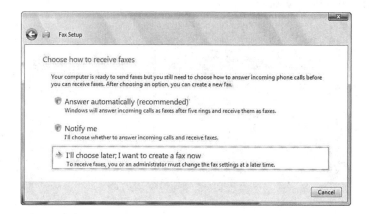

FIGURE 30.3
You can set your fax modem to answer calls after the fifth ring or set your modem to send a fax and not set other options.

6. Because you probably just want to send a fax and not ask your modem to answer calls that subsequently arrive at your location, click to select the I'll Choose Later; I Want to Create a Fax Now option.

7. The New Fax dialog box shown in Figure 30.4 appears and you're finally ready to enter the recipient's fax information. Click to open the Cover Page drop-down list to select a cover page from the list if you want a cover page to arrive at the beginning of your fax. Type a name next to the To text box. (If you have Outlook installed, you can click the To button and select a recipient from your contacts.) The contact you select must have a fax number listed, so in Outlook one of the fax numbers must be entered. If both the Business Fax and the Home Fax entries for that user are filled, Vista will ask which one you want to use. If you don't use Outlook, you can select File, New Entry from the Select Fax Recipient dialog box and create a new name and fax number entry that you can reuse later if you ever need to.

Make sure that Dialing Rule is set to My Location if you're calling from your typical location, such as your home or office. This uses your area code to determine whether the call is local or long distance.

Complete the Subject text box and Cover Page Notes text box if you elect to use a cover page. Don't worry about the strange filename in the Attach field. Vista renames the document you're printing when it converts the document to the required faxing format.

Next, complete the area at the bottom of the dialog box. There resides a mini-word processor with formatting tools to format a message for the recipient. This message gets sent on an initial page whether or not there is a cover page, so the cover page is often redundant when you fill in this sheet. Whether you fill it in is up to you.

FIGURE 30.4
Windows Fax and Scan is a Vista application that forms your complete fax management center.

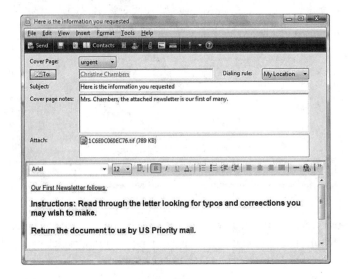

8. Click Send to start the fax. Your computer dials the fax number and transmits the fax while showing a status screen as the fax progresses.

If you need to fax a printed document, instead of sending a fax from a digital document already on your computer, you need only scan the document first. After you scan any document into your computer, that document exists as a digital image on your disk drive. Whether it has graphics or only text doesn't matter. You can fax the document once it's there. The rest of this chapter discusses scanning.

By the Way

You can usually fax right from your scanning software just as you can fax from any other program.

Using Windows Fax and Scan

Vista includes the Windows Fax and Scan program, a program not offered in earlier Windows versions. With Fax and Scan, you can send and receive faxes. Of course, you can do that from any Windows program, as the previous section explained, but the Fax and Scan program is a complete fax management center that keeps track of your sent and received faxes, allows you to manage your contacts, and more.

Before you can fax, you must install your scanner. For USB-based scanners, installing the scanner usually requires only that you plug your scanner into your Vista computer. Vista often recognizes the scanner and installs it automatically so that when you start to scan, the scanner is there and ready to scan. Before faxing a printed document, you have to scan the document. Follow these steps to scan the document before faxing it:

1. Open your Windows Start menu and select Windows Fax and Scan from the All Programs option. The Fax and Scan screen opens. If you've scanned and faxed in the past, the window will display those activities. If this is the first time you've used the program, Fax and Scan displays an introductory window as shown in Figure 30.5.

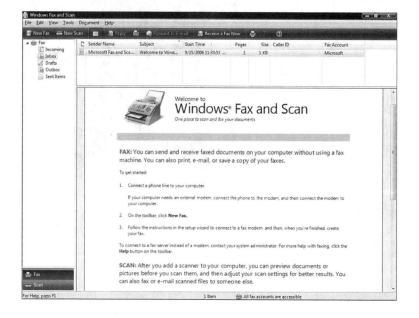

FIGURE 30.5
Windows Fax and Scan welcomes you with initial fax connection instructions the first time you start the program.

2. Click the New Scan button to display the New Scan dialog box. Adjust the controls on the New Scan dialog box to suit your needs. For example, if you're scanning a color photograph and want to obtain the highest quality possible, you might change the resolution to a higher one than the default (which is usually 300 *dpi*, or *dots per inch*).

3. Click the Preview button to see what the scanned image will look like. After the preview appears, drag the sizing handles around the picture to crop the picture so that only the part of the scan you want to keep remains with the scan. (To **crop** means to remove all but that you want to keep; cropping is common when working with digital images.)

After you crop down your image, your New Scan dialog box will look something like the one in Figure 30.6. Depending on your scanner's capabilities, you will see a dialog box with more or fewer options than the one shown in Figure 30.6 for the Epson Perfection 4490 scanner.

FIGURE 30.6
After you crop the image, click Scan to finalize the scan at the selected full resolution.

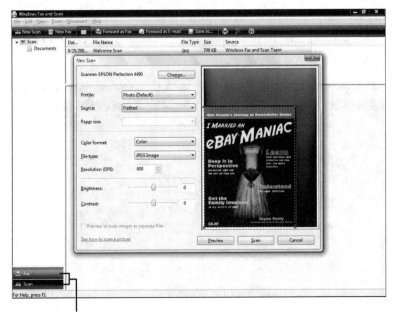

Click to change views

4. Click the Scan button to finalize your scan. The Fax and Scan program will re-scan the image at the resolution you selected, but will not scan the area you cropped off. When the scan completes, the image appears on your screen and a new entry appears in the scanned images list above the image.

By the Way

The Fax and Scan program has two primary views: fax and scan. Click the Fax button or the Scan button in the lower-left corner of the Fax and Scan program window to change views. The Fax view lists all your faxes and the Scan view lists all your scanned images.

When you have scanned the image, you can fax it to someone. The image remains cataloged in the Windows Fax and Scan program in case you ever need to work with the image again or fax it to someone else. If this was a one-time scan and fax, you can right-click the scanned image's Scan View entry and delete the scanned image after you fax it to someone else.

If you right-click any scanned image and select View, Vista opens the scanned image in the Windows Photo Gallery. You can use the editing tools you learned about in Chapter 17, "Modifying and Sharing Photos," to change the image before faxing it.

Faxing the image you just scanned will be extremely simple for you now that you've read the earlier sections of this chapter. Windows uses the Fax and Scan's fax routine for all faxing that you do from within Vista. Therefore, when you select Fax and the printer to fax a document on your computer, Windows starts Fax and Scan's faxing routine.

If you right-click your scanned image—or any image you've scanned that is listed in the Fax view's fax list—then select Send To Fax, the Fax and Scan program opens the same New Fax dialog box you learned about in the previous section (refer to Figure 30.4). Complete the New Fax dialog box's To, Subject, and Comments fields, and click Send to send the fax.

Instead of selecting Fax, if you select Mail Recipient from the Send To menu, Vista opens an email message, attaches the scanned image to the email, and lets you fill in the recipient's email address, the Subject line, and the email body so that you can send the scanned image as an email attachment. Figure 30.7 shows the email message window that opens if you have Outlook 2007 installed on your system. Fax and Scan uses Outlook if it's installed, or Windows Mail, or your own email program to send the email, depending on the default program setting in the Control Panel's Programs group's Default Programs option. (Chapter 25, "Setting Up Windows Program Defaults," explains how to designate a default email program.)

FIGURE 30.7
Once you scan
an image or
document, you
can easily send
that scanned
item as an
email attach-
ment.

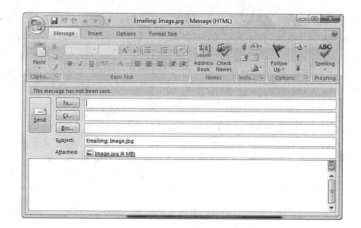

Send a Quick Text Fax

If you need to send a quick fax that doesn't require images or well-formatted text,
you can use the Fax and Scan program to send a fax quickly from scratch. To send
a quick fax to one of your fax recipients, click the Fax view, click the toolbar's New
Fax button to open the New Fax dialog box, complete the To and Subject fields,
optionally select a cover page, and type your message in the body of the New Fax
dialog box.

You won't send any attached files. The message you type will be the fax. The
Windows Fax and Scan program sends your fax the moment you click the Send
button.

If you rarely receive faxes but are expecting a fax to be sent to you, when your
phone rings open the Windows Fax and Scan program and click the Receive a Fax
Now button. The Receive Fax Status window shown in Figure 30.8 opens and the
Fax and Scan program receives the fax. After receiving the fax, the window closes
and the new fax appears in your Fax view's Inbox list. Double-click the fax entry in
your Inbox to view and, optionally, print the fax.

FIGURE 30.8
You can receive a fax even if you rarely get them and you don't normally want Vista to answer the phone.

Chapter Wrap-Up

You're coming along well with your Windows Vista education! You saw in this chapter that Vista's fax and scanning capabilities work to give you just about all the fax and scanning capabilities you'll ever need. From faxing a document within any program to using the Windows Fax and Scan program to manage your faxes and scanned images, there are plenty of tools to give you the power you need without getting in your way when you don't need them.

The next chapter explains how you can create system restore points. Such restore points enable you to return your Windows Vista system to a better state if something happens to make Vista work improperly. The restore points will not help in times of major disasters where you cannot boot your computer as can be the case with disk failures—that's the job of your backup and restore programs—but system restore can put your Vista system back in shape, often within seconds, if damage occurs.

CHAPTER 31

Restoring Your Windows System to a Previous State

Computers are complex machines. The software you run on computers, however, is far more complex than the hardware. Windows Vista is the most comprehensive operating system ever written, with more code under its hood than any operating system to date. Given what's there, it's amazing that it works at all! How *well* Vista does work is a tribute to those who developed it.

Due to Vista's complexity, it doesn't take much to mess up the operating system. One lone bit (a **bit** is just one-eighth the size of a character in memory) in the wrong place and Vista will behave erratically at best, and crash and refuse to run in the worst of cases.

When you install a program that isn't fully debugged, and some major software programs are released with bugs, that program can harm Vista if even one out of its billions of bits goes awry. Vista is designed to keep this from happening as much as possible, but ways still exist for system problems to occur. Saying that Vista will improve when it's randomly changed by one bit is as absurd as saying that the human body gets better and gains new features through random mutation. Vista doesn't gain a new feature when a bug changes one of your system files—quite the opposite. Vista gets very cranky indeed when that takes place.

Fortunately, there is a way that you can turn back the clock and put Vista right back where it was before the problem appeared on your computer. This chapter shows you how to create system restore points to protect against such problems.

Why You Need System Restore

Sometimes Vista just stops working well. Perhaps your computer begins to run very slowly. Perhaps Vista stops responding completely. If your computer was recently working well and now it does not, you can put it right back to the way it was with the System Restore program that comes with Vista.

One of the times that your system is at risk occurs when you install a new program or a new hardware device. If you immediately see a system problem right after you install a program, obviously one of the wisest things you can do is uninstall that program or device. If you do that and Vista works well, you're okay, and you can and should contact the program's support department to learn what the problem might be.

A hardware device, such as a graphics card that you insert into your computer, can cause system conflicts. It's not the hardware that actually causes the problem; it is the software, the drivers responsible for letting Vista know how to communicate with that device. When you install new hardware, you should check out your system thoroughly. Make sure that the new hardware works as expected. After you do that, before installing any additional hardware or programs, use your computer for a few hours and run the programs you routinely run to make sure that the system is okay with the new hardware.

If a problem arises, look at the hardware's website for possible clues into the problem. Make sure that you download the latest drivers for the program. If everything seems to be correctly installed but Vista still acts up, you probably should remove the hardware and uninstall the drivers that came with it until you can contact the hardware vendor's customer support and get further instructions.

Sometimes you can remove the hardware and the driver and Vista will still act up. As long as you used the System Restore program to create a restore point just before installing the hardware, you can be right back where you were before the problems began. That's nice to know!

By the Way

> You must have administrative privileges before you can create a restore point or restore one. Restoring your computer back to a restore point can affect programs installed after the restore point. A restore point saves the system, but not any programs installed. You might have to reinstall a program after restoring a restore point, so administrative privileges are required.

System Restore does not save or restore any of your data. This is good. Your data remains intact on the disk so that whatever data you saved after the restore point will still be there when you send your system back to a previous restore point. The system, therefore, goes back to an older, better-working state, but your data does not go back. This eliminates the need for you to reconstruct all your data after you restore your system. Make sure that you back up regularly, however, because doing so is the only way to ensure that your data is safe. Chapter 35, "Protecting Your Data and Programs," explains how to use Windows Backup to make copies of your data so that you can restore your data if the need arises...and the need *will* arrive some day.

Did you Know?

What System Restore Actually Does

Think of System Restore as a recording of your computer's system files. When you use System Restore to create a restore point, System Restore takes a snapshot of your system files at that point in time. When you run System Restore, you can name each restore point that you create. Later you will be able to locate the system restore point you need from the name you give it.

For best results, get in the habit of creating a lot of system restore points, especially when you get a new computer and begin loading it up with programs and changing its hardware. Before you install a program or a new device such as a graphics adapter, create a restore point. Creating restore points takes only about a minute in most cases and it's time well invested.

The restore point captures your system files so that if one or more of the files gets damaged you can restore a restore point that you created before the problem surfaced. Although it's not a computer backup, it is a computer system file backup. System restore will back up critical system files and your registry.

Your **registry** is a large database of system settings that Windows Vista monitors, updates, and reads to keep track of hardware and software settings throughout your computer. The registry tells Windows exactly how you want your desktop to look. The registry tells Windows what hardware and device drivers are installed on your computer. The registry contains many of your installed program settings so that when you return to a program, you don't have to reset all your preferences each time.

By the Way

System Restore Protects You from Itself

When you restore your system to a previous restore point, Vista first creates a new restore point for you automatically. Therefore, if you restore your system back to a point in time when you think things will work better—and the opposite happens—just select System Restore's Undo System Restore link to restore back to the restore point that Vista created just before you performed the restore and you'll be back to where you started.

Of course, your original problem will still be with you, but you won't have the problem that the restore added. This can occur if you accidentally restore a newer restore point than one you meant to restore. By allowing you to undo a restore, in effect, the System Restore program makes a valiant effort to keep you running as smoothly as possible at all times.

Vista Creates Restore Points Automatically

When you install a new program, install a new hardware device, or update your hardware drivers, Vista creates a restore point for you. Given this information, you might wonder why it's incumbent on you to create restore points yourself. Problems can occur because some programs are not well behaved and they don't always go through the proper Vista channels to install themselves on your computer.

If Vista doesn't recognize the fact that a new program or driver is being installed, Vista cannot be expected to create a restore point. Knowing this means that you'll spend a minute or so creating a restore point before you make any change to your hardware or software. This extra safety measure pays ample dividends the one time you might need the restore point you created that wouldn't have been created otherwise.

> In addition to monitoring system events such as hardware installs, and creating restore points then, Vista creates a restore point for you every day whether or not you change your system. This gives you a worst-case system restore scenario of going back at most a day to get your system running properly again.

Although multiple restore points exist on your computer and more are placed there as you and Vista create them, it's best to select a restore point that is as recent as possible without going back too far. The best restore point to restore is the one that either you or Vista created immediately before the problem began.

Restore points don't remain on your computer forever. In general, the System Restore program uses about 15% of your hard disk space and once that space gets close to capacity, System Restore removes older restore points when new ones are created. You can erase all restore points on your computer by turning off System Protection in your Control Panel's System and Maintenance group's System option. The System Protection link is at the right of the window as Figure 31.1 shows.

Click to turn on or off your System Protection services

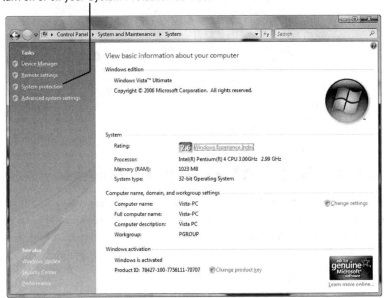

FIGURE 31.1
The System Protection link opens the System Properties dialog box that enables you to turn on or off System Protection.

When you click the System Protection link, Figure 31.2's System Properties dialog box appears. Click to check or uncheck the disk drives you want to create restore points for. In general, you keep your system disk's restore point creation turned on by leaving that drive's check box checked. If you uncheck the drive and close the dialog box by clicking OK, all your restore points will be erased. You then can turn System Protection back on by returning to the System Properties dialog box and checking your Vista's system disk drive again.

FIGURE 31.2
Vista creates
restore points
for those drives
you check;
you'll generally
just check your
Vista disk drive.

Creating Manual Restore Points

As you now know from this chapter's earlier sections, Vista creates restore points but you need to know how to create them, too. To create a restore point, open your Windows Start menu, select All Programs, Accessories, System Tools, and select the program named System Restore. After confirming your Administrator user privileges, the System Restore screen shown in Figure 31.3 appears.

FIGURE 31.3
You'll create
and restore sys-
tem restore
points from the
System Restore
program.

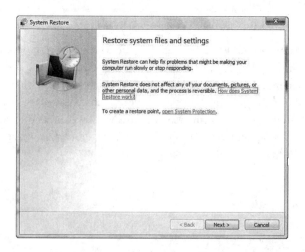

The System Restore program is designed to do just that: restore your system to a previous restore point that you or Vista created. To create a restore point, click the Open System Protection link on your System Restore program window. The same System Protection window opens that you saw in Figure 31.2 where you could turn on or off the restoration feature.

Make sure that your system disk is checked, and click the Create button to begin the creation process. Vista displays the Create a Restore Point window where you type a description for the restore point. It helps to link the description to the event you're about to perform. For example, you might create a restore point just before updating your graphics card drivers, so you might name that restore point *Pre-Graphics Driver Update* as done in Figure 31.4.

Name of restore point

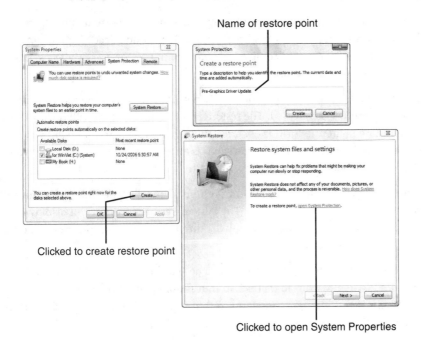

FIGURE 31.4
Give your restore point a good name so that you'll be able to link it to an event later.

Clicked to create restore point

Clicked to open System Properties

Click the Create button to create your newly named restore point. Vista saves your files and the process usually takes a minute or less. As Vista saves the restore point, a status bar lets you know that the restore point is in progress. Vista displays a message box stating that the restore point was created when the process finishes.

Another reason you should create your own restore points before installing a program, changing hardware in any way, or updating a driver, is that you can name the
restore points that you create, as you saw in this section. The names that Vista
gives its own restore points aren't always clear, and you might or might not know
which one was created just before you installed a new graphics driver yesterday
that you noticed is giving you problems today. When you create a restore point
and give it a name that you'll remember, such as *Before installing new graphics
driver*, the next day you can look at a list of all the restore points and know exactly which one was created before you updated that specific driver.

Restoring a Saved Restore Point

To restore a saved restore point, run the System Restore program again. Open your
Windows Start menu, select Accessories, System Tools, and select the program
named System Restore. After confirming your Administrator user privileges, the
System Restore screen appears.

Vista will suggest a restore point for you. Generally, this will be the most recent
restore point that Vista created. The restore point's date and time will always appear
on the restore point and Vista is good at telling you why the restore point was made.
The restore point might have a name such as *Install: Device Driver Package*. If you
want to restore back to this point, click Next to begin the restoration.

If, instead, you've created a more recent restore point, click the Choose a Different
Restore Point option and click Next. The System Restore program will display a list
of restore points from the most recent back through several previous restore points.
Figure 31.5 shows such a list.

Click to select the restore point you want to go back to and click Next. Vista confirms that you really want to go back to that restore point. Click Back if you accidentally chose the wrong restore point so that you can choose another. Click Finish
if you're ready for Vista to restore back to that point.

It's worth noting that system restoration is an important process that you should
never quit while it's still running. You cannot undo a system restore until it's fully
finished restoring, and trying to stop a system restore in the middle of a restore
might cause system problems. The System Restore program will warn you about
all this—heed the warning. Click yes to the warning message box when you're
truly ready for the restore to begin.

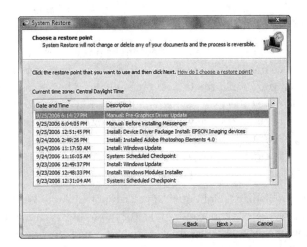

FIGURE 31.5
Several restore points should be available for you to choose from.

When the restoration begins, a status bar will appear in a small message box window to tell you the initial progress being made. Once started, Windows forsakes its Vista-never-needs-reboots promise and shuts your system down to a system window for the restore to take place. Fortunately, Vista will ask you to save any unsaved work in any applications you might still have open before rebooting.

> System restoration takes far longer than the creation of a restore point. Sometimes a system restore can take 10 or more minutes. Often the process takes about 3 minutes. The speed of your computer and the number of system files on it determines the time required.

By the Way

When Vista starts back up, your system files will be in the same place they were at the time of the restore point's creation. Vista will display a message in the center of your screen telling you that the restore point is in effect. You should be restored to that point and if your computer was acting up before the restore, things should work as expected now.

> To undo a restore point, you can immediately return to the System Restore program and click the Undo System Restore option that will already be selected when you see the System Restore screen. Keeping this selection and clicking Next reverses the latest restore.

Did you Know?

Chapter Wrap-Up

You now know to save restore points routinely to help you maintain a fully functioning computer as much of the time as possible. Before changing anything drastic on your computer, you should create a restore point. Even before installing a program that should never affect your system files, such as a game, you should consider creating a restore point. (Actually, you should *always* create a restore point before installing any game.) You'll never regret having too many restore points. They take hardly any time to create and they can put you back in good working order quickly when you need them.

A major system problem, as might occur if you cannot reboot to Windows, is certainly more than System Restore can handle. For those cases, you might need to restore a backup image of your disk drive if you've created one or perhaps reinstall Windows and all your programs before restoring your data from a backup. Either way, a major problem that requires such a massive restoration will be time-consuming and isn't any fun. System Restore cannot cope with such a problem, but it was not designed to do so. System Restore is there to revert your system back to a point in time when things were working great that are cropping up with problems today.

Now that you've learned how to keep Windows Vista streamlined and running smoothly, it's time to give your disk drive a checkup. The next chapter explains how to use Vista's disk optimizing tools to clean up your disk drive, maintain its speed, and maximize your storage space.

CHAPTER 32

Improving Disk Performance and Storage

In This Chapter:

- ▶ Understand how disk fragmentation can adversely affect performance
- ▶ Detect fragmentation problems
- ▶ Let your disk run efficiently by letting Disk Defragmenter clean up potential disk problems
- ▶ Use Disk Cleanup to keep your disk drives free of clutter

Everybody seems to need more disk space eventually no matter how much they already have. Some get external drives that hold as much as a *terabyte* or more of information (that's one thousand gigabytes, or approximately 1,000,000,000,000 characters of data!). They get this storage for their music files only to begin storing video files as well that quickly eat up the massive excess space they thought they would have for years.

This chapter shows you how to get more disk space and use your disk more efficiently with two of the more useful Windows Vista disk-related system utilities: Disk Defragmenter and Disk Cleanup.

As you use your computer over time, your disk becomes cluttered, not only with extra programs and Windows Vista components that you don't need, but also with file **fragments**, small pieces of files that slow down the overall operation of your computer. You'll be able to eliminate those fragments and combine them into a more efficient disk that Vista can access quicker.

Fill in the Holes

Disk Defragmenter is a Vista program that reorganizes data on your disks to make retrieving it more efficient. As you add and delete files, the deleted space leaves free holes around the disk. Vista eventually fills those holes with other data as you add files and programs to your system. However, the more erasing and rewriting that occurs, the more the data for programs and even individual files can end up scattered in multiple locations on a disk. Over time, your disk response time will slow down as you add or delete files to and from your disk.

To put it another way, in a perfect world, large files are always stored as one continuous file. That occurs only if there is enough space to do so and only if you never change that file and other files physically located close by on the disk. Windows tries its best to reuse fragment space left over from a deleted file, but chances are great that a file you create won't exactly fit in a fragment left behind by a previous file's deletion. Windows stores as much of the file as it can in a free fragment and puts the rest in other fragments. Over time, the number of these file fragments can grow considerably and slow down your PC when you access a fragmented file.

By the Way

It's important to remember that if a file is badly fragmented, it's stored in several chunks, the file fragments, over different parts of your disk drive. For you, Vista acts as though the file is still one continuous single file, but every time you do anything with that file Vista must collect all the fragments, which slows things down. You don't know Vista is doing this except that your disk drive's access gets slower, especially for large, badly fragmented files such as big databases.

Disk access slows down on a fragmented disk drive because Windows must jump to each file fragment when retrieving a file. If you run Disk Defragmenter often enough (once or twice a month for the average user ought to be enough), Windows keeps the fragments to a minimum and, thus, increases your disk access speed. Disk Defragmenter not only closes empty disk gaps but also rearranges your disk drive so that often-used programs run faster.

Did you Know?

Although the Windows Task Scheduler has its own schedule for running Disk Defragmenter, you can also manually start Disk Defragmenter and then do other things with your computer. You might notice a slowdown as Disk Defragmenter runs in its program window, defragmenting your disk drive, but you can still do other work in other programs. Generally, it's best not to work on your computer while Disk Defragmenter runs, but you can.

Correcting Disk Fragmentation

To use Disk Defragmenter to consolidate your disk drive's fragmented file portions, follow these steps:

1. Open the Start menu and select All Programs, Accessories, System Tools, Disk Defragmenter. Windows confirms that you want to run the program and that you have Administrator user account privileges to do so before opening the Disk Defragmenter's start window as shown in Figure 32.1.

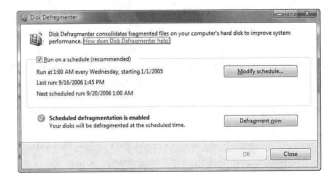

FIGURE 32.1
You can schedule Disk Defragmenter to run on a schedule or you can defragment your disks now.

As Chapter 21, "Scheduling Tasks to Run Later," explained, Disk Defragmenter can run at a preset time, such as when you normally are away from your computer. This is good because Disk Defragmenter can take a few hours if your disk drive is large or badly fragmented.

> The more often you run Disk Defragmenter, the quicker the defragmentation completes.

Click to uncheck the Run On a Schedule option if you don't want Disk Defragmenter to run on a schedule. If you do this, make sure that you run Disk Defragmenter manually every so often to keep your disk drive running smoothly in a defragged state.

2. If you want to change the schedule on which Disk Defragmenter runs, click the Modify Schedule button to display Figure 32.2's Disk Defragmenter Modify Schedule dialog box and select the recurring schedule you want to use for the scheduled defragmentation. A weekly scheduled defragmentation will really pay off in disk performance for you over the years as you add, change, and delete files from your disk drive as you use your computer. Click OK to accept the schedule and close the scheduling dialog box.

FIGURE 32.2
Modify the
recurring sched-
ule you want to
use to defrag-
ment your
disks.

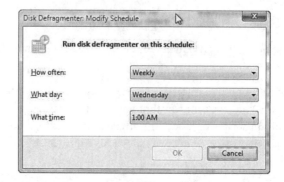

3. Even if you keep your Disk Defragmenter program on a schedule, you can run
   Disk Defragmenter manually whenever you want. To do so, click the
   Defragment Now button to begin your disk defragmentation.

   Vista begins defragmenting your disk drive. The process can take from a few
   minutes if you've defragged recently to a few hours, depending on the condition of your drive. If you want to cancel the disk defragmentation, click the
   Cancel Defragmentation button and, after a brief pause, the program will
   stop. Depending on how long it ran before you stopped the program, a portion of your drives will be defragmented although not fully because you can-
   celled the operation early.

By the Way

Users of previous Windows operating systems might be surprised that Vista's Disk
Defragmenter doesn't display the usual map of the defragged disk drive the way
that Windows XP and earlier Windows did. A map such as the one shown in Figure
32.3 was helpful in learning how badly fragmented a disk was. In previous versions, you could request such a visual report without actually starting the defragmentation process. If you saw that you disk wasn't badly defragmented, you could
skip the disk defragmentation to save time. Vista doesn't do that; the Disk
Defragmenter interface is rather bare of options. When you or Task Scheduler runs
Disk Defragmenter, the program begins and defragments all your hard disks active
on your Windows Vista system.

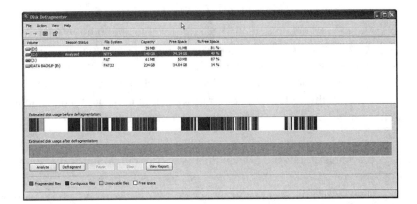

FIGURE 32.3
Older Windows versions enabled you to see how badly fragmented your disk was before starting the defragmentation process.

Disk Defragmenter's Biggest Danger: A Power Failure

Never turn off your computer when you're running Disk Defragmenter. Actually, you should never turn off your computer no matter what you're doing except in two instances: your computer has frozen and you cannot get it to do anything, including a reboot using the Ctrl+Alt+Del key combination. Or you logged off or shut the system down using the Start menu's Shut Down button and your computer didn't power off on its own after enough time has passed for it to do so (due to a device conflict that can sometimes occur and keeps computers from fully responding to a shut down command).

Turning off your system at other times could cause you to lose data, but turning off your system when running Disk Defragmenter can completely damage the system files on your computer and keep your computer from starting properly the next time you turn on your machine. You probably don't have any intention of turning off your computer during Disk Defragmenter's execution. Nevertheless, you should understand what can happen and know that a power-down is possible even if you never intended to power off you computer.

If you run Disk Defragmenter, or if Task Scheduler runs it, and the power goes off at your home or office where the computer is running, the power failure can very easily cause Disk Defragmenter to leave your files left in a critical half-written state. Your computer could have severe issues and might not even boot the next time you turn on the computer.

This does not imply that you shouldn't run Disk Defragmenter due to the possibility of a power failure. Instead, this should encourage you to obtain an uninterruptible power supply, also called a *UPS*. You plug your computer and monitor into the UPS and then plug the UPS into a power outlet. A UPS contains a powerful battery that continuously charges from the power outlet while it also powers your computer. If the power goes out, the battery keeps your system running without a glitch long enough for you to cancel the Disk Defragmenter and shut down your computer properly.

Of course, you might not be there when the power goes out. Many of the mid-range and better UPS models sold in the last few years usually include a USB connection that, when the power fails, begins shutting down your Windows system properly so as to not cause the disaster of a disk problem that would otherwise occur if the power went out and Disk Defragmenter were still running.

By the Way

> Unlike previous Windows versions' defragmenter program, you cannot specify which disk drives Disk Defragmenter defragments. Instead, Disk Defragmenter defragments all your disk drives.

Cleaning Up Your Disk

Disk Cleanup is a utility program that comes with Windows Vista that enables you to free your disk drives of clutter and make more space available. Over time, your disk drives fill with temporary files and other information that you don't have to retain. Disk Cleanup can keep your free space at a maximum.

Did you Know?

> When combined with a regular use of Disk Defragmenter, Disk Cleanup ensures that your disk drives will perform at their optimal level and that you'll always have as much disk space as possible for your data.

If you read the chapters prior to this one, you're already familiar with Disk Cleanup because Chapter 21 used Disk Cleanup as its sample program to show you how to schedule automatic program execution.

The following steps walk you through the process of using Disk Cleanup to remove clutter from your drive. Although you will probably use Task Scheduler to set up Disk Cleanup to run automatically, it helps to run through the Disk Cleanup process at least once to learn what kinds of files Disk Cleanup handles.

1. Display the Start menu and select All Programs, Accessories, System Tools, Disk Cleanup. Windows displays the Disk Cleanup Options window, shown in Figure 32.4, from which you can specify whether Disk Cleanup is to clean up only your user account's files or the files from all users on the computer.

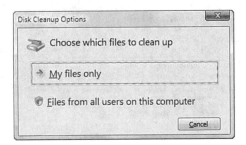

FIGURE 32.4
Disk Cleanup keeps the clutter from your files or from all users' files.

If you elect to clean up files for all users, Disk Cleanup requires that you run the program from an Administrator user account, or be able to enter the password from your Administrator user account.

2. Select the option you want to use. If you choose Files from All Users on This Computer, Disk Cleanup asks for a confirmation before continuing, showing that you're aware that only Administrator user privileges can clean up the files across user accounts.

3. Open the Drive Selection window's drop-down list and click the disk drive you want to clean. All hard disks, internal and external, are available from the list.

You cannot clean up disk drives on computers networked to yours. Disk Cleanup must be run from those computers.

4. After selecting the disk drive you want to clean up, Disk Cleanup shows how much space will be freed in various areas such as Temporary Internet Files and your Recycle Bin. Click to check or uncheck any option you don't want to erase and click OK in this window shown in Figure 32.5.

5. Often, your Recycle Bin holds files that you no longer want. Disk Cleanup offers to delete all the files from your Recycle Bin. First, you can click the View Files button to open your Recycle Bin window and review everything there.

FIGURE 32.5
Determine the
kinds of files
you want to
clean.

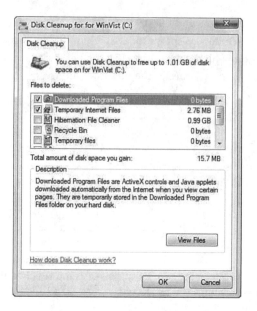

6. If you want to delete the files from your Recycle Bin, click the check mark next to the Disk Cleanup's Recycle Bin option.

7. Windows Vista includes an indexing feature that operates when you search for data. In addition, other files (such as installation log files, cached Internet files, and power-related hibernation files) build up over time and you do not need to keep them. Click to check each of the file categories you want Disk Cleanup to remove.

Did you Know?

Click to select each type of file set on the Disk Cleanup dialog box to read a description about those files. For example, if you click the Hibernation File Cleaner entry, Vista displays several sentences that describe how the hibernation-related files get onto your computer.

8. Click the OK button and Vista issues a final confirmation that you want to permanently delete the selected files with Figure 32.6's message box.

9. Click the Delete Files button to begin the cleanup. Disk Cleanup permanently removes the files you selected. Disk Cleanup displays a status box that shows you the progress. Depending on how cluttered your disk is, Disk Cleanup can take from a few seconds to several minutes to complete.

FIGURE 32.6
Disk Cleanup is
about to clean
up several
areas of your
disk drive.

Did you Know?

If you're extremely low on disk space, Windows Vista and your applications will begin operating at a sluggish rate. Programs require ample disk space to store temporary files and Windows Vista requires ample disk space to function. Although you should run Disk Cleanup regularly, if you are low on space, your sluggish computer will let you know. Given the relatively low cost of an additional disk drive today, if you find yourself needing to run Disk Cleanup more and more often, consider purchasing a second disk drive. You'll gain a tremendous amount of storage and your computing experience will be much better.

Users of previous Windows versions might be surprised that Vista's Disk Cleanup program eliminated some of the options that Windows XP and earlier operating systems provided. Most of these options related to operating system components and programs, as Figure 32.7 shows.

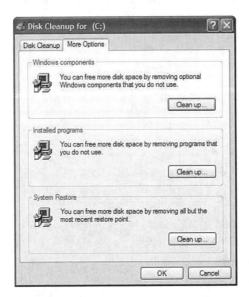

FIGURE 32.7
Disk Cleanup
used to provide
system- and
program-level
cleanup
options.

As with Disk Defragmenter, Microsoft decided to slim down Disk Cleanup and make it more of a temporary file-related cleaning program and removed the system-level and program-level modification options. It's probably best because system changes are best left to more focused tools that you find in your Control Panel, and program-related removals are best done from the Programs group, which is also located in the Control Panel.

Chapter Wrap-Up

This chapter described the two primary Windows Vista disk utilities: Disk Defragmenter and Disk Cleanup. Both utilities work to make your disk drives operate faster and with more disk space. If your disk begins to slow down, run Windows Vista's Disk Defragmenter to eliminate the empty holes in your drive so that your disk access runs at top performance. If you find yourself needing more free disk space than you currently have, run Disk Cleanup to see whether you can remove some unwanted clutter.

In the next chapter, you'll learn how to configure Vista and fine-tune the operating environment further to be more efficient and to work the way you want Vista to work. Now that you know how to keep your disk drives tuned up, in the next chapter you'll learn how to keep Vista running like a well-oiled machine.

CHAPTER 33

Configuring Windows Vista

In This Chapter:

- ► Change your computer's startup options
- ► Modify the programs that load when Vista loads
- ► Set your computer's clock and calendar
- ► Change regional settings when you travel
- ► Add a second or third clock to your taskbar
- ► Synchronize your computer's clock to accurate Internet time
- ► Change event sounds
- ► Work with Windows themes
- ► View all your system settings

Throughout a lot of this book you've been configuring Windows Vista. You customized your screen's theme and colors as well as its background image in Chapter 7, "Changing Windows Vista's Look." You set up speech recognition and trained your computer to understand your voice in Chapter 23, "Speaking to Your Computer." You learned how to upgrade your entire Windows Vista system to a higher version in Chapter 24, "Controlling Windows Vista." You changed default programs that Vista automatically runs in Chapter 25, "Setting Up Windows Program Defaults." You learned how to change your user account picture in Chapter 26, "Separating Users Gives Each the Access They Need." Just about every time you learn something new about Vista, you learn a way to make Vista behave in a way that suits *your* computing needs better.

Microsoft had to make a lot of guesses when determining which features and options would be included and turned on for each new Windows Vista installation. Although the default Vista installation truly is a remarkable tribute to a programming effort that produced an amazing operating system, Microsoft knows that everybody works a little differently and that everybody likes various combinations of features. That's why Windows Vista is so customizable.

This chapter works as a catch-up chapter, filling in some of the configuration gaps that didn't really fit elsewhere. So much of Vista is changeable. You can change which Windows programs load at startup. You can change the behavior of your taskbar's clock. You can even change the sounds that Vista makes. In this chapter, you'll learn these and other ways to keep your computer running accurately and behaving the way you like it.

Configuring Startup Options

Although it's highly technical and can cause severe problems if you inadvertently change the wrong settings, there might come a time when you need to run the System Configuration program to make a change to your Windows startup settings. You start System Configuration in one of two ways and neither is all that elegant:

▶ Click your Start button to display your Start menu and begin typing **System Configuration** in the Search box. Windows locates the program and lists it in your Start menu as shown in Figure 33.1.

▶ Press Windows+R to open Vista's Run dialog box, type **msconfig**, and press Enter.

FIGURE 33.1
Use the Search box to locate your System Configuration program.

Program found

Search term

Whichever method you use to start the System Configuration program, you'll soon see the program window open as shown in Figure 33.2. As usual, Vista confirms your administrative privileges before opening the System Configuration program.

Msconfig.exe is the filename of the System Configuration program. Because it's located in the Windows/system32 folder—a folder that's always searched in when you type a filename in the Run box—Vista locates the program and executes it.

System Configuration is a system program that can change the way Windows behaves and can dramatically affect your operating system's performance and behavior for all users on the computer. Only an Administrator user account has the power to make such universal changes, so Vista verifies your administrative privileges before allowing you to work in the program.

FIGURE 33.2
The System Configuration program enables you to make changes to your Windows Vista's behavior.

Although the System Configuration program enables you to adjust several internal system services, the most common reason that people run System Configuration is to change the way Windows starts up. Click the program's Startup tab to display your current Vista startup settings. You will see a window that looks something like Figure 33.3 although, depending on your computer settings and the programs you've installed, the details of your Startup page might be very different from what's shown here.

If you're following along, from this point forward be very careful about what you click inside the System Configuration window. Any change you inadvertently make will change the way Vista starts up.

Drag the column dividers left or right to see more room in whatever column you're interested in. For example, the default column width for the Startup Item is so narrow that you probably can't read most of the items there. This first column is important, so drag the Command or Location column divider to the left to make more room for the Startup Item column. It would be nice if Microsoft would allow users to maximize this window to full-screen size. Users have been requesting this since Windows 95 arrived on the scene. For more than a decade (and with Vista it appears that another decade might go by before it changes), the small, fixed System Configuration window size has been woefully inadequate to work in safely; it's too easy to change something incorrectly because it's so difficult to see all the words in each column.

Drag here to widen or narrow columns

FIGURE 33.3
The Startup tab displays the System Configuration program's Startup page where you control which programs load and which don't the next time you start Windows.

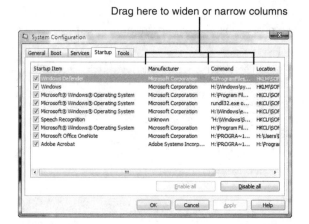

You'll notice that each item listed in your System Configuration program has a check mark next to it. (If a check box in your program window is not checked, someone or some process has already turned off one of your startup routines.) Each entry on the Startup page is a program that runs automatically every time Vista starts up. In Figure 33.3, for example, Windows Defender always starts first. This helps ensure that the files on that computer have protection from spyware, as explained in Chapter 27, "Managing Your Windows Security." The rest of Windows loads afterward.

It's true that many programs, especially those supplied by Microsoft, are difficult to discern. Because of the Windows entry that follows Windows Defender and the four subsequent entries labeled *Microsoft Windows Operating System*, it appears from the Startup page shown in Figure 33.3 that Windows loads five times.

A little sleuthing will tell you what most of these Windows programs really are. It's not true that Windows is loading five times.

Locate the web site http://sysinfo.org/ and add it to your Favorites Center. There you can type names of programs you find in your System Configuration window and find out what those programs are used for.

Did you Know?

Expanding the Command column enough to see the rightmost portion of its data reveals many of the programs that start, as Figure 33.4 shows. It's not easy to know what all the processes do, but the Sidebar is the third item that loads on the system. The Welcome Center runs next, opening the Welcome Center window that you learned about in Chapter 2, "Exploring the Welcome Center." Following that is a program named ehTray.exe, which is the taskbar and notification area that you see at the bottom of your screen as you use Windows. As you can see, looking at the command gives you insight into what is taking place for those system processes with inadequate names.

The SideBar

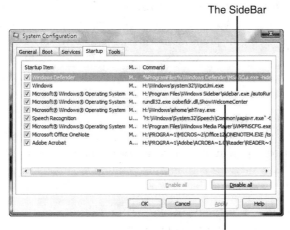

The Welcome Center

FIGURE 33.4
After adjusting the column widths and scrolling to the right (if necessary), you can see the actual files that run during startup.

Here's how you can use this knowledge: Suppose that you notice Windows isn't starting properly because of a system error that appears on your screen. Or perhaps your display won't stay in a high-resolution state. You should first attempt to load a restore point from back at a time when Windows started better. This gets tedious, but the best way to do it is to restore the latest restore point that you think will solve the problem, reboot, and see whether the problem goes away. If it does not, redo the restore as you learned how to do in Chapter 31, "Restoring Your Windows System to a Previous State," and restore the next restore point back in time. Continue restoring and undoing until the problem goes away.

The problem will persist or you'll solve it. If it persists, you should suspect that one of your startup programs is causing your problem and start working on that theory. Open System Configuration, click to display the Startup page, uncheck one item, and then reboot. It's best to work your way back, so uncheck the bottom item first, and reboot to see whether the problem goes away. If so, in the case shown in Figure 33.3, you would then uninstall Adobe Acrobat Reader. If Windows still reboots nicely, either leave Adobe Acrobat Reader off your computer or reinstall the latest version from the Adobe.com website.

It would be highly unusual if Adobe Acrobat Reader causes you any startup problems. It just happens to be the final item loaded in Figure 33.3 and because you always work your way back, Adobe Acrobat Reader is the example used here.

Why not just uninstall Adobe Acrobat Reader and omit the Startup page process where you click to uncheck Adobe and then reboot? The reason is your problem might not *be* Adobe's Acrobat Reader and probably is *not* Adobe Acrobat Reader, so completely uninstalling the program just in case is a lot of work and a potential waste of time. It's far easier to leave Adobe Acrobat Reader installed but turned off so that it doesn't load automatically. You can then rule it out or determine it's the reason for your startup problem.

If Adobe is not the problem, click to check Adobe Acrobat Reader (using Figure 33.3's example) so that the program starts the next time you reboot and click to uncheck the OneNote program, the next-to-last program in Figure 33.3. Then reboot to see whether OneNote is the culprit. After you find the troublesome program, you should uninstall the program and reinstall it or stop using it altogether.

Another use for the System Configuration Startup page is to turn off certain startup programs just because you don't want them to run for some reason unrelated to system problems. For example, you might want to install Dragon Naturally Speaking, a powerful speech recognition program. You could turn off Vista's speech recognition program temporarily by clicking to uncheck it from your set of startup programs. Vista will not load its own speech recognition program as long as you have the program unchecked on your Startup page. If it turns out that you don't want to use Dragon Naturally Speaking, you can uninstall Dragon and click to check Vista's speech recognition option.

System Configuration has a Disable All button that disables every program that Vista loads at startup so that you start with a vanilla Windows Vista environment the next time you reboot. If you are experiencing major problems but you can boot to Windows, you might have to resort to turning all your startup programs off. Doing so allows Windows to settle down long enough to install a driver that you need to install or perhaps to copy some data files that weren't saved on your most recent backup off the computer so that you can reinstall Windows and start with a clean slate. Such a restore is dramatic but sometimes required if Windows is damaged badly enough.

Did you Know?

Configuring Your Clock, Language, and Region

Far less technical than your System Configuration options, the clock in your taskbar's notification area sits there quietly updating the time as you work. Point to your taskbar's time and Vista pops open a small window above your taskbar to show you the date as well. If you followed the tip about increasing the size of your taskbar in Chapter 6, "Taking Your Taskbar to Task," you won't have to point to the time to see the date because you'll always see both the time and the date on your taskbar, as in Figure 33.5. (If you moved your taskbar to the left or right edge of your screen, drag its inner edge toward the center of your screen to see the date.)

Date and time

Two-row Taskbar

FIGURE 33.5
After you increase your taskbar's height, you can see both the time and the date.

If you cannot resize your taskbar, right-click a blank area in your taskbar and click the Lock the Taskbar option to uncheck it. After you resize the taskbar, you can right-click and check the Lock the Taskbar option again. By locking your taskbar in place, you keep your taskbar from being moved, resized, or changed inadvertently.

Did you Know?

When you increase the size of your taskbar, you reduce the amount of room on the rest of your screen. That's why Vista's Auto-Hide feature is so nice. When turned on, Auto-Hide hides your taskbar until you move your mouse cursor to the bottom of the screen, which causes the taskbar to appear. That way you see the Taskbar only when you need to, but it's always there for you when you do. Many Windows users use Auto-Hide even for their one-line taskbars to maximize their screen real estate. Refer to "The Taskbar Properties Menu" section in Chapter 6 to learn how to turn on and off the Auto-Hide feature.

Quickly Display a Clock and Calendar

Click your taskbar's time and Vista opens a window containing an analog clock and a complete calendar for the month, as Figure 33.6 shows. Click the arrows to the left or right of the month and the calendar shows you future or previous months as you click to scroll through them. Click today's date at the top of the window to return the month view to the current month.

FIGURE 33.6
The pop-up time and date window does more than display today's date and time.

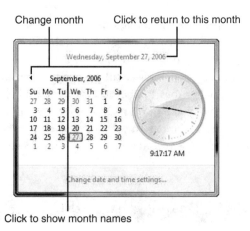

Change month   Click to return to this month

Click to show month names

Click the month name above the monthly calendar and the names of the 12 months of the year appear. Now when you click the arrows to the left or right of the year, you move forward or backward one year. This is handy if you want to see what day a certain meeting or vacation falls on.

Go back to the year of your birth to learn what day you were born on!

If you really want to move forward or backward in time, click the year at the top of the window in the year view and the window changes to show 12 years at a time through which you can quickly move forward and backward. Click once more to see an entire century! This helps you zero in on a far-off year that you want to look at for a specific day. You'll be able to confirm such trivia as the fact that the Wright Brothers flew the very first airplane on a Thursday (December 17, 1903).

To close the clock's window press Esc, select a desktop icon to start a program, or display your Start menu.

> Unfortunately, the Windows clock does not interact at all with Windows Calendar, Microsoft Outlook, or any other appointment-making program, so the Taskbar clock shows no indication of reminders when appointments are scheduled.

By the Way

Change Your Date and Time Settings

To change your clock or date settings, click your taskbar's time to open the clock window described in the previous section. Click the Change Date and Time Settings link to open the Date and Time window shown in Figure 33.7.

FIGURE 33.7
The Date and Time window does much more than it first appears.

If the time or date is incorrect, first check the time zone displayed in the center of the window to make sure that your time zone is set. You can change the time zone by clicking the Change Time Zone button and selecting the correct time zone from the drop-down list box. If your state adjusts for daylight saving time, make sure that option is checked. (Some states such as Arizona and Hawaii don't.)

Did you Know?

> Notice that Windows offers to display a reminder a week before the daylight saving time change. The reminder enables you to get a lot of sleep the week before you lose an hour due to the spring time change. You can use this reminder to check batteries and electrical connections if you follow the extremely wise advice of checking your smoke detectors every six months when the time changes.

Assuming that the time zone is set correctly, you can adjust the computer clock's date or time by clicking the Change Time Zone button. After Vista confirms your administrative privileges, the Date and Time window opens. You can click to select the correct date; click an hour, minute, second or AM/PM indicator to change any part of the time. When you click OK, your computer's internal date and time will update.

Watch Out!

> An internal backup battery maintains your computer's time. If you notice that your date and time are always wrong and you've been using the same computer for a couple of years or more, it's possible that you need to replace the battery inside the unit. This usually requires a trip to a computer repair center or a trip to the manufacturer's website to determine which battery to replace. Usually, more than your time and date will be affected—your internal default settings might also be reset. The typical internal computer battery lasts at least five years, which in the world of computers is a very long time indeed, longer than many people keep a computer before upgrading to a more powerful machine. If you pass down your computer to other members of your family and network the old ones to the new ones, there's a good chance that you'll own the computer more than five years, so keep the replacement possibility in the back of your mind when it becomes obvious that the computer's battery has gone bad.

Adding a Second Clock

If one clock is nice, why not add a second one to your taskbar? You can add a second and even a third clock. Click the Additional Clocks tab to display the Additional Clocks page shown in Figure 33.8.

The reason you might want to monitor one or two extra clocks is because when you travel, your laptop can monitor the time in up to two places you're traveling while you keeping track of the time at home for those daily phone-home calls. You can keep up to two clocks selected. In Figure 33.8, the two clocks are for Rome and New Zealand. (If you travel to those two places often, you are extremely fortunate indeed.) In addition, you can click to check the country you're going to on your laptop's time, and uncheck the country you aren't going to on the current trip. Both clocks stay set up, but only one secondary clock is active. Clicking the taskbar's time displays both your home and your travel clocks, as Figure 33.9 demonstrates.

FIGURE 33.8
Add a second clock to Windows Vista to keep track of the time in two locations.

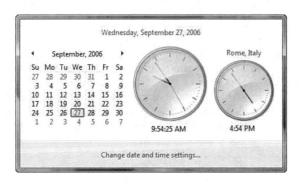

FIGURE 33.9
You can now easily monitor the time both where you travel and back at home.

Set Your Clock to Synchronize with the Internet

Your computer's clock can access the http://time.windows.com online clock and access the correct time. The website is not a page you can browse with your browser, but contains a special interface that Windows understands and can access if you want to keep your clock up-to-date and accurate.

To set up your computer to synchronize with Internet time, click the Date and Time window's Internet Time tab to display Figure 33.10's Internet Time Settings dialog box. (Vista first confirms you have administrative privileges.) Several clock-setting sites are available and you can choose one from the Server drop-down list box. The default site, http://time.windows.com, works well and there's really no reason to change it unless the site goes down for some reason, or you notice your clock's time or day settings are out of sync and you suspect the site is faulty.

FIGURE 33.10
Let the Internet set your computer's clock so that you don't have to.

The website sets your time based on Greenwich Mean Time. Vista takes that time and adjusts your computer clock to the time zone you selected.

The Internet clock-synchronizing feature is on by default when you install or upgrade to Windows Vista. Vista synchronizes your computer's clock to the website's once a week. This, of course, requires an active Internet connection.

You can click the Internet Time Settings window's Update Now button to correct the time immediately instead of waiting for the weekly Vista check. You might do this if you just replaced your computer's battery and want to set the clock accurately based on the Internet clock's time. You can also do this any time you need an exact time setting; a radio station, for example, schedules commercials, songs, and talk to the exact second each needs to happen. If you work at a station, you might find it best to update your computer's clock daily to keep the seconds accurate on your machine.

Each week, Windows Vista synchronizes your computer's clock in the background (as long as there's an Internet connection) and doesn't bother you with the process or open any web pages to do so.

Customizing Your Region and Language Options

Your Control Panel's Clock, Language, and Region group contains a Regional and Language option you can select to open Figure 33.11's Regional and Language Options window. In general, after these settings are correct you won't need to change them. If you bought a computer from someone who lives in another country, though, you're almost sure to need to change the settings. In addition, if you move to another region, you'll need to change your computer's settings. Last, if you interact often with others who live in other regions and countries you might want to change your computer's region settings temporarily so that the work you do reflects that region's usage.

The programs you work with often use your Windows Vista region settings to determine how to display numeric formats, currencies, and your own keyboard's layout. For example, in the United States, the decimal point is a period and commas separate numeric amounts after every three digits. In Europe, decimal placement uses a comma and periods separate numeric amounts every three digits.

When working with Excel, therefore, if you format a cell as currency, Excel looks at your regional settings and uses that settings structure to display the money format. If you select a European region, all Excel currency amounts will use the comma for the decimal. If you are working on a worksheet that you plan to fax or print to mail overseas, by adopting that country's region settings while you work on the worksheet, it will appear normal to those you send it to. You then can change back your regional settings for your own country's use.

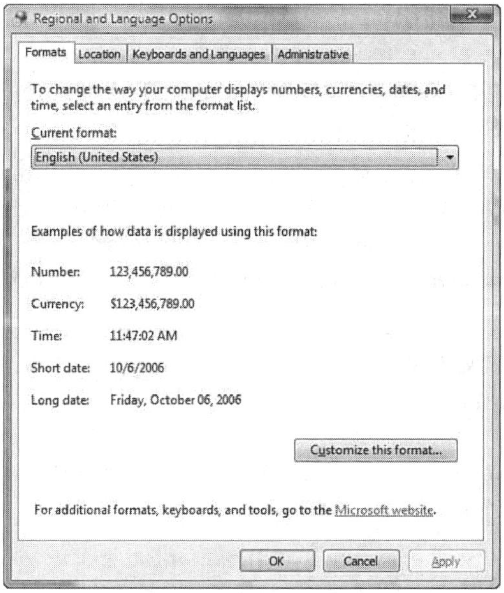

By the Way

FIGURE 33.11
Change the region settings that your computer should assume when you want to work with that region's settings for your program options and keyboard layout.

The Location tab of the Regional and Language Options dialog box controls the country you want your computer to assume. This option might at first seem redundant to the Formats tab, where you select a current format such as English (United States), German (Austria), German (Germany), and Hebrew (Israel), but your computer uses the Location tab for a different purpose from the Formats tab. The

Formats tab controls the currency format and other data-related program settings that produce data for that region or language; the Location tab tells software what country the computer's user actually resides in (no matter what language or country is set in the Formats tab) so that country-specific information such as the weather or local news will be accurate.

> To help clarify the distinction between the Formats tab and the Location tab, suppose that you're an American vacationing overseas in Florence, Italy. You would keep your Formats tab set to English (United States) because the writing and financial work you brought with you has to remain American-based so that the formats will be correct when you get home. While in Florence, however, you might change the Location tab to Italy so that the programs you work with that access weather, news, and sports access the local Italian information—that way you know what's happening in that part of the world. (It might also help if you speak Italian, so *parla l'italiano bene!*)

Not all countries adopt the same alphabet and not all countries use the same keyboard. Therefore, if you are working on a dramatically different keyboard layout, as you would if you are in Greece, you have to tell Windows about the keyboard layout so that Windows properly interprets your keys and does not assume a standard American layout, for example.

Click the Keyboards and Languages tab to change the keyboard layout and language Windows Vista assumes. Suppose that you travel to Greece for business quite a bit, you're well versed in Greek, and you take along a Greek keyboard to use with your laptop when you want to manage your Greece-related work.

You would click the Change Keyboards button to display the Text Services and Input Languages dialog box shown in Figure 33.12, click Add, and click the plus sign next to the Greece (Greek) keyboard to open the selection of possible keyboards. Select one of the Greek entries (such as Greek or Greek Latin); the first item listed for a country is usually the most common, so click to select that choice if you're unsure of which option matches the keyboard you have.

Click the Preview button to display a preview of the keyboard Vista expects you to have for that selection. For example, Figure 33.13 shows a Greek keyboard that Vista assumes when you select the first Greek keyboard available in the list. If this matches the Greek keyboard you have with you, click the Close key and then click OK. Your Text Services and Input Languages dialog box will now show both the English and the Greek keyboards. Select the Default Input Language (Greek in this case) if you want Vista to assume that you're typing from the Greek keyboard when you enter data; otherwise, Vista knows the Greek keyboard is available but does not assume that you're using it.

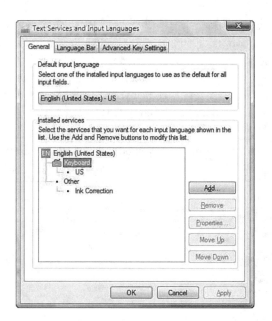

FIGURE 33.12
You can add multiple keyboards to Vista's collection and select the one you want to use, depending on what work you need to accomplish.

Don't uninstall the keyboard settings you normally use for your country when you travel and use a second keyboard. Keep your original one set up so that you can switch back to it easily when you come home.

Watch Out!

FIGURE 33.13
Make sure that the country and language whose keyboard you select matches the keyboard you have to use.

When you click OK to close the Text Services and Input Languages dialog box, Vista displays a language bar on the Windows taskbar to the left of your notification area. A button displays the first two letters of your default language and keyboard to indicate that language you're using. For example, the EN button appears when your keyboard and input language are set to English. Double-click the button and Vista pops up a selection of languages: one for each keyboard and input language you've set up so far.

Figure 33.14 shows how simple it is now to move between your English and Greek keyboards. Click the language button, select a different language, and then plug in that language's USB keyboard to your laptop to move to the second language. When you're done with the second keyboard, remove it from the Text Services and Input Languages dialog box and keep just your regular keyboard; the language bar disappears from your taskbar when you opt for a single keyboard.

Did you
Know?

You can set up more than two languages and keyboards and quickly move among them in this manner.

FIGURE 33.14
Click to switch between key-boards and lan-guages.

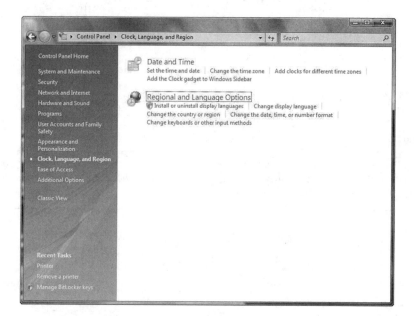

Event Sounds

Perhaps you've already heard some sounds coming out of your PC's speakers as you've worked with Windows Vista. If you like the sounds, you're going to learn here how to add new sounds and change ones that you want to change. If you don't want the sounds, you can eliminate them. Vista gives you control of your system sounds; the sounds should help point out things that are happening, such as warning messages that appear when you make a mistake, but the sounds should never be irritating.

A Windows event usually triggers a sound. An **event** is something that takes place when you use Windows, such as starting a program.

By the Way

The Windows Vista event sounds can help those who are visually impaired. The audio feedback verifies that an event took place, and can also signal that an error has occurred.

Some Windows users do not like sounds attached to events, whereas others do. You can request sounds for all the following common events:

- Dialog box opening and closing
- User errors
- Starting Windows
- Exiting Windows
- Minimizing and maximizing windows
- Starting programs
- Displaying menus
- Displaying help screens

In addition to these common events, you can assign sounds to several more events. You can attach sounds to some networking events, such as the appearance of an email message. In addition, you can customize the sounds that Windows uses.

Assign Your Own Event Sounds

If you want to assign a specific sound to every Windows Vista event, or only some Windows events, you can do so. Many kinds of sounds are available, and as you familiarize yourself with the available sounds, you can customize your Windows system so that anyone within hearing range can know it's you using Windows and nobody else. Follow these steps to assign sounds to Windows events:

1. Open your Control Panel's Hardware and Sound group. Click to select the Sound dialog box and click the Sounds page to display the window shown in Figure 33.15.

2. Scroll through the Program list to see all the events to which you can assign sounds. The event list sorts by application and the first application is Windows itself. As you scroll through the list, you'll see specific events listed for Windows Explorer, Speech Recognition, and Photo Gallery.

FIGURE 33.15
Specify event
sounds with
the Sound
dialog box.

Some of the events might seem cryptic to you, but as you use Windows more, you'll better understand each event's purpose. For example, the Windows Exclamation event occurs when an application displays a message box that shows a system error message that you should pay attention to. It signals that you can't do something you tried to do, or that Windows ran across a problem when doing something you requested (such as trying to write to a USB-based flash drive that you removed from the drive before all the data finished writing to it).

By the Way

Events that show a speaker icon to their left have associated sounds. Events without a speaker icon do not have sounds associated with them, but you can add sounds to them, as you'll do in this task.

Select the Maximize event. Unless you or someone else has changed your Vista settings, you won't see a speaker icon next to the Maximize event, meaning that the event has no assigned sound. When you click to maximize a window, Vista doesn't play a sound.

Open the Sounds drop-down list box to see a list of sounds that you can add to the event. Select Chimes (it might display as chimes.wav). A speaker icon will appear next to the Maximize event. Click the Test button to hear the chimes sound. The chimes will now sound when you maximize a window. If you want to change an event's sound, highlight the event and double-click the sound to review it or select a different sound that you want to replace the original sound with.

Add more sounds to additional Windows events if you want to. Change the sounds that are already there. When your sounds are the way you like them, you can save your custom sound settings by clicking the Save As button and entering a name for your sound scheme. (A **sound scheme** is a customized set of Windows Vista sounds saved in a file.) You can save as many sound schemes as you like. To apply a sound scheme, open the Sound dialog box and select a saved scheme from the Sound Scheme drop-down list box to apply that set of sounds.

Your sound scheme stays with your user account. So, if you share a computer with another user, you can each have your own sound scheme and the sounds you change won't interfere with the other user's sound schemes.

6. Close the Sound dialog box and test the new sounds. For example, open a program or Explorer window, minimize the window, and then maximize the window to hear the chimes play.

It's important to know that Windows Vista controls the sounds, not the individual applications listed in the Sound dialog box's Programs list. The idea of the Sounds list is for programs to list themselves in the Sound dialog box when you install them. The Sound dialog box gives you the ability, therefore, to control the sounds of all the common events found in all your programs.

The problem is that most software does not install itself as an option in your Sound dialog box. Not even the majority of Windows Vista's own programs appear there, so your ability to control the sounds your programs make is more limited than it otherwise would be.

Select the Sound Scheme named No Sounds if you want to turn off all system sounds.

Record Your Own System Sounds

If you don't like the sounds Windows Vista supplies, record your own. You can assign any wave file (with the .wav filename extension) to a listed event. Chapter 18, "Recording Simple Audio," explains how to use Vista's Sound Recorder program to make your own recordings. After you save the recordings to your disk, you can assign them to Windows events.

When you open the Sound dialog box and click the Browse button, Vista displays
the Browse for New Sound dialog box shown in Figure 33.16. The default folder for
your system sounds is the Windows/Media folder, but you can click other disk locations you have access to and locate other sound files you've saved to your disk drive.

FIGURE 33.16
You can assign
any .wav file on
your disk to sys-
tem events.

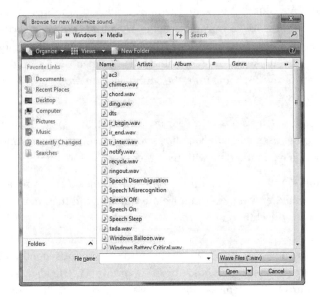

Work with Windows Themes

Throughout this book, and especially in this chapter, you've learned how to customize several Windows Vista settings so that Vista looks, sounds, and behaves the
way that you prefer. Not every user wants or requires the same customized settings.
The fact that Vista allows such a wide assortment of custom settings allows each
user to personalize his or her Vista installation.

When you customize your sounds, colors, and screen display settings, you are customizing the **theme** of your Windows Vista installation. When you get Windows
customized the way you prefer it, it's a good idea to save your custom settings as a
theme that you name. You can store several themes and use whichever one you prefer. For example, when traveling, you might opt to use a theme that doesn't include
many Windows event sounds but does include a higher-contrast display mode so
that you can read your laptop's screen in various outdoor lighting better. When you
return home from a trip, you might change your laptop's theme to one balanced
with sounds and a lower-contrast screen.

To save your current configuration settings in a named theme, open your Control Panel's Appearance and Personalization group, click to open the Personalization window, and select Theme to open the Theme Settings window shown in Figure 33.17. Click the Save As button to open a Save As dialog box, give your theme a name, and click Save. Vista adds your theme to the drop-down list of themes in the Theme Settings dialog box, and you can select that theme or a different one when you're ready to use any one of them.

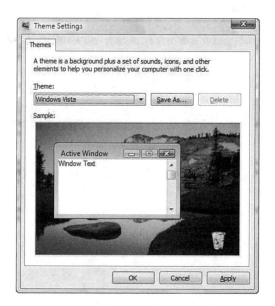

FIGURE 33.17
As you customize Windows, save your settings as a new theme that you can return or change to when you want your Vista's customized settings to differ.

Vista even allows you to forgo Vista and return to the older Windows XP themed environment! If you select Windows Classic from the Theme drop-down list and click the Apply button, your windows and colors will return to a more Windows XP–like appearance. You can always change back to your Windows Vista theme by opening the dialog box again and selecting Windows Vista or one of your saved themes.

By the Way

View All Your System Settings

It's difficult to see all your Vista settings in one place. You know to use your Control Panel to access most of them, but they are scattered all over it. You must look at your display settings to see your monitor's current settings and then move to the Printers area to see the printers installed on your computer.

Windows Vista offers a tool, named System Information, with which you can more easily view all your system's settings. Open your Start menu, select All Programs, Accessories, System Tools, and then select the System Information program. The initial System Information program, shown in Figure 33.18, is helpful in that it shows your exact operating system version. Vista comes in several flavors, or versions, such as Windows Vista Ultimate and Windows Vista Business, and each one has been released and updated, so one Windows Vista Business installation might have a later version number than another.

FIGURE 33.18
The System Information program is one place you can view nearly every customizable setting in Windows Vista.

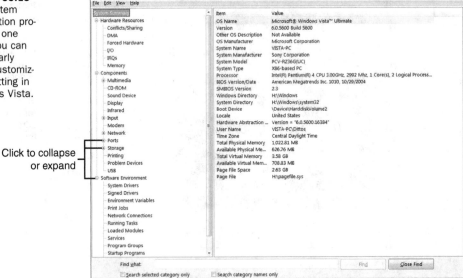

Click to collapse or expand

Clicking the plus sign next to Hardware Resources, Components, or Software Environment opens those sections so that you can quickly view your system settings. Click Display, for example, to see what resolution your screen is currently using. Click Printing to see a list of all your installed printers.

Although you cannot directly change any system setting inside the System Information program, you can view your settings from one location instead of having to hunt through several different Control Panel groups to locate a setting you want to know about.

Select File, Print and print your system information settings occasionally. If you or someone else happens to mess up your monitor or other settings, the printout serves to tell you how your system should be set up.

Chapter Wrap-Up

This chapter discussed several configuration options and settings that you might want to modify. In a way, this chapter exists to inform you of the lesser-known system settings that might come in handy some day. Even if you don't care about your system sounds, for example, it's good to know that you can customize them in the future if the need arises.

When you get your computer set the way you like it, you can store your configuration settings in a theme file that you name and can later restore, if necessary. Saving multiple themes gives you the ability to change your Windows look and behavior when you want to change how—or where—you use your computer.

In the next chapter, you'll learn about some unique settings that can actually save you money as you use Windows Vista. Vista offers several advanced power-saving features that are especially useful if you use a battery-powered laptop or tablet PC.

CHAPTER 34

Saving Power with Windows Vista

In This Chapter:

▶ Use one of Vista's Power Plans to save your laptop's battery life

▶ Customize Vista's power settings

▶ Change your computer's response when you press the Power button

▶ Learn what to do if your computer stops responding

▶ Customize your own power settings

In today's high-cost world of energy, it always helps when we can save some money. Windows Vista can help. Vista is able to monitor its power usage and shut down certain options after a preset time of inactivity. Vista's energy-saving capability is most helpful when you use a battery-powered laptop or tablet PC because Vista can lengthen the amount of time between recharges.

To get the most out of your computer and to use the least amount of energy while doing so, take advantage of some of the power-saving features you'll learn about in this chapter. Perhaps you'll save enough money in energy costs to upgrade to the next-higher version of Vista!

Power Plan Options

As you might expect, Vista's power-saving options appear in your Control Panel. Open your Control Panel and select the System and Maintenance group to locate the Power Options section. Click Power Options to open the Power Options screen shown in Figure 34.1.

FIGURE 34.1
Specify your
computer's
power settings
in the Power
Options window.

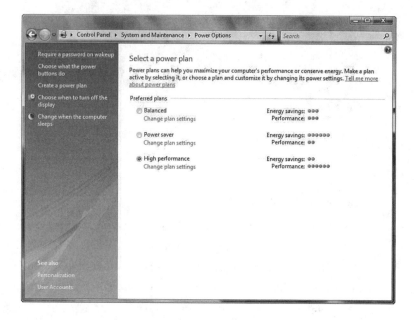

The primary way that Windows saves power is during times of inactivity; if you stop using your computer for a while, Vista swoops in and begins to shut down various items such as hard disks and your screen. Typically, you have only to press a key to take your computer out of this power-saving state and return it in the same ready state in which you left it.

Initially, the Power Options window offers a surprisingly simple interface; just select the power plan you prefer: Balanced, Power Saver, or High Performance. Vista makes some assumptions, changes some internal power-related settings, and you're off to saving that money (assuming that you didn't choose High Performance, which saves the least amount of energy but maximizes your computer's speed and performance).

These plans are a combination of hardware and software settings. For most users, one of these plans will work just fine.

Don't look for anything called Power Schemes like those in Windows XP. *Power Plans* is Vista's new name for Power Schemes.

The option you choose depends on your computing needs. If you're running Vista on an older or slower computer that begins to get really sluggish, you might have to increase your performance at the cost of decreasing your energy savings to get the speed you need to do your work. Therefore, you will probably change your power settings over time.

If energy cost is a big issue to you, select the Power Saver plan first to save as much as you can. Work with your computer a few days. If the computer's performance is adequate, there might never be a need to change the power plan again. If, on the other hand, your computer is a little slow and cranky, upgrade your power plan to Balanced to see whether you get the performance you want. If not, select High Performance and forsake the energy savings for a more robust computing experience.

Did you Know?

About Your Computer's Power Consumption

Computers don't consume a lot of power. Your printer is likely the biggest single energy consumer of your computer system, especially if you use a high-speed laser printer. If you're like most computer users, you don't need your printer turned on all the time, so your printer's power consumption doesn't have to be a primary consideration for you. In addition, printer manufacturers are getting stricter about their own products' power consumption. A heavy-duty color laser printer from Hewlett-Packard, for example, goes into an energy-saving standby mode if the printer sits idle for 20 minutes or so. The power drain when in this idle mode is minimal.

If you use an LCD flat-screen monitor, your monitor's power drain is far less than it was a few years ago with tube-based CRT monitors. Of course, many computer users now run two or more monitors on a single computer, doubling or tripling their monitor's power consumption. That could be an issue for you, and you might want to turn off your monitors when you leave. By doing so, you save a little energy, but not as much as you're used to; Vista powers down your monitors if you walk away from your computer for a while unless you instruct Vista never to do so.

Laptop manufacturers are especially cautious about balancing the power-versus-performance of the machines they sell. The length of a single battery charge is a primary consideration for many users. Travelers who use their laptops in flight, for example, want their charged laptop's power to last during an entire cross-country flight. Although it's true that more and more airplane seats are equipped with laptop power outlets (requiring a special power plug, not the kind that works in an automobile), being able to run on a battery without getting out the power cord is always nice.

Laptop makers realize that their users want the fastest laptop possible with the longest battery life available. Surprisingly little battery life extension has been seen since the first true laptops were sold almost two decades ago. Battery life typically runs between two and four hours, although some of the thinner and lighter laptops are beginning to widen that threshold in an effort to approach a solid eight-hour charge, as is possible with some smaller PDA devices and digital media players, such as iPods and Zunes.

Did you Know?

If you use a laptop, you don't have to open your Control Panel to display or change your Power Plan. Click the battery icon at the right of your taskbar. Vista displays a window showing how much battery life remains, whether you're plugged in to an AC outlet, and which Power Plan you have set. You can click any Power Plan to choose another. In addition, you can click the Windows Mobility Center to open the window shown in Figure 34.2, which displays several laptop settings related to power and your portable computer.

FIGURE 34.2
You can learn a lot about your laptop's power and other settings from the Windows Mobility Center.

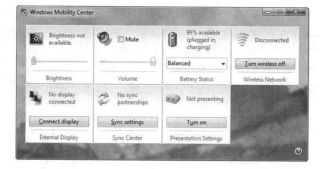

Customize Your Power Buttons

All computers have a power button with which you turn on and off your computer. Some computers have Sleep buttons on their keyboards that can put your computer into a low-power mode while you go do something; when you return, press any key (or perhaps Sleep, if required) to awaken your computer and you'll be right back where you were when you put the machine into its sleep mode.

I'm Frozen and I Can't Turn Off!

If your computer freezes and nothing you do from the keyboard seems to change anything, give your computer a couple of minutes and try once more to use your keyboard. Some downloads and some processor-intensive programs can make your computer seem as though it's frozen when it's just processing and not able to respond to you at the time. If you're sure that your computer is frozen, however, there is often little to do but resort to the last resort: turn off the power.

When you press your power button, it's possible that your computer won't power off even then. If so, here's a trick that is designed into most computers and almost always works: Hold your power button in, as though you were turning it on, but keep the button pressed all the way down for 10 or 12 seconds. Your computer should then turn off. Most systems have a built-in sensor for such a long power-down press and the hardware will take over whatever is causing the system to freeze and turn off your computer. Always let your computer settle a few seconds, preferably as much as a minute, before turning it back on because it's not good for your components to turn them on and off again without a pause.

You can control what happens when you press your computer's power or sleep button on your system unit and keyboard. To view or change what takes place when you press one of these buttons, click the Power Options window's Require a Password on Wakeup link in the left pane. (This is one of the few Vista options that isn't named well, but in Microsoft's defense, it makes the same window available when you click the next link, Choose What the Power Buttons Do.) Figure 34.3's Define Power Buttons window opens and enables you to change your button settings.

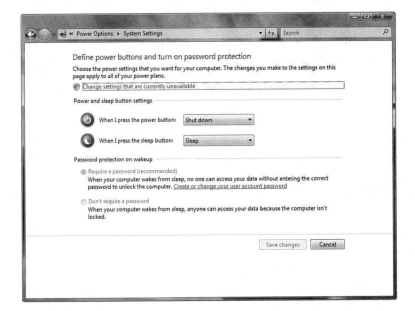

FIGURE 34.3
Determine what happens when you press your computer's power or sleep buttons.

You can change the action of your power or sleep buttons to one of the following four options by selecting from the buttons' drop-down list box:

▶ **Do Nothing**—Causes Windows to ignore any power button press. This might be useful for computers you have on display running an ad in a store or in a classroom setting, for example. Passers-by cannot turn off the computer by pressing the power button. The surprising thing about this option, however, is that it doesn't require an Administrator user account to turn on and off; if someone has access to your computer's keyboard he or she can change this to Shut Down and the power button will be active once again. In most situations in which the computer is being used as a display for information, however, the keyboard is often left unplugged or hidden.

▶ **Sleep**—On a desktop system, sleep mode saves all your current settings—including open windows and programs—to memory as well as to your disk drive. You can quickly resume working by pressing any key or moving your mouse, and all is back and you're working again within seconds. If, however, the power went out and the memory shut down, the saved state of your computer will be loaded from your disk drive the next time you power on so that, within a few more seconds than normal sleep, you can be up and running again when all is restored. For a laptop, sleep mode is usually entered by closing the laptop's lid or by pressing your laptop's power button, if you choose that option. On desktop systems, the Start menu's Power button causes your computer to enter sleep mode.

▶ **Hibernate**—Saves your data to your hard disk without using the quicker-to-restore memory-save feature that the sleep mode uses.

▶ **Shut Down**—Closes all windows and programs and shuts down your computer's power.

In almost every case, it's best to leave your desktop system unit's power button left set to the Shut Down option so that your computer shuts down—or makes an effort to shut down—when you press the power button. Vista's onscreen buttons in your Start menu's right pane allow you to select exactly what you want to happen if you want to override the power button's settings.

When you read the second half of the window, it's obvious (now) why this window was available as Require a Password on Wakeup link in Power Options. Here, if you click the Change Settings That Are Currently Unavailable link in the top half of the window, the Require a Password and Don't Require a Password options are activated. You can request that Vista not ask for your password when your computer wakes from sleep mode; obviously, doing so could allow anyone with access to your computer to get into your account's files that would still be active if someone resumes your computer from a sleep mode, so use with caution.

If you usually work by yourself all day at home, or perhaps with other family members such as a husband or wife with whom you share an account, you might want to turn off the password requirement when awakening from sleep mode. If you ever take your laptop on vacation, a coffee shop, or elsewhere, you should turn the password requirement back on.

Did you Know?

Customize the Power Plans

You're not limited to the settings in the three Power Plans you see in your Power Options window. Depending on your needs, you can customize your computer's power settings.

You can click the Change Plan Settings link that appears beneath any of the three Power Plans to change the settings for the individual Power Plans. Click the link beneath the Balanced Power Plan and Figure 34.4's window appears.

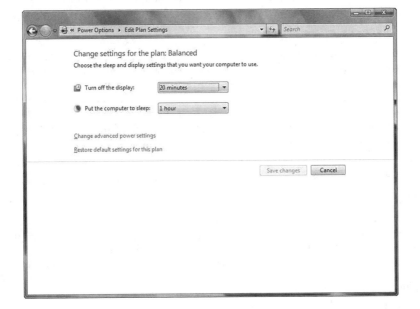

FIGURE 34.4
You can customize the settings of each Power Plan.

If you find that you often go to lunch for (at most) an hour and that sometimes you get back early and sometimes late—but you don't want your computer automatically entering the sleep state either way—you can increase the amount of idle time that must go by before your computer enters the sleep mode by clicking the drop-down list box and selecting a different time.

If you leave your desk quite a bit during the day and don't want others to see your files, you might want to require that your computer enter sleep more quickly for the Power Plan that you selected. In that case, you would reduce the amount of idle time required before entering sleep mode.

Watch Out!

> If security is an issue, you should manually put your computer into a sleep mode or log off your user account before you leave your desk. This might be the case for employees in a payroll department, for example. It's human nature, however, to forget to do this manually, or perhaps you get to talking, leave your office with someone, and just forget to put your computer into one of these safer states. By reducing the idle time required before your computer goes to sleep, and by requiring a password on awakening as the previous section explained, you help ensure that your computer is never logged on for very long without you.

You can also adjust the display settings to change the amount of time Vista waits before powering down your screen. If you're really concerned about the amount of power your screen consumes, lower the time it takes to be idle before the screen goes off. When you return to your computer and press a key to awaken the machine, Vista will power on your screen again.

Watch Out!

> Extremely old monitors don't always have the capability to be turned on and off by Vista.

Far more detailed custom settings are available for you to change if you click the Change Advanced Power Settings link on the Edit Plan Settings window. The Advanced Settings dialog box, shown in Figure 34.5, offers disk drive, wireless networking cards, and more options that you can customize to turn on and off based on idle time and your needs at the time.

Did you Know?

> If you change something too dramatically and want to return to one of the original Power Plans and start over, click the Restore Plan Defaults button.

You'll see that the Power Options window has two additional links in its left pane: Choose When to Turn Off the Display and Change When the Computer Sleeps. These both produce the Edit Plan Settings window shown in Figure 34.4.

FIGURE 34.5
Several detailed settings are available to you depending on how much control over your Power Plans you wish to have.

Your Computer Maker Can Offer Additional Power Plans

Manufacturers are free to offer their own Power Plans to augment the three that Vista provides. Depending on what your computer maker does, you might see extra options on Vista's power-related screens shown in this chapter. Some manufacturers might do this to take advantage of special hardware they developed or perhaps to use as some kind of "new and extended Power Plans to save you money" marketing material.

You can create your own Power Plan or Plans as well. In the previous section, you learned how to adjust each Power Plan's details. Instead of adjusting an existing plan, you can augment them with one or more of your own. Just as you learned in the previous chapter how to create your own Sound Schemes and save them to your disk, and your own Windows Themes and save those to your disk, you can create your own Power Plans. They can enable you to change to specific power-related settings quickly and easily without having to reset and re-establish specific options each time you want to change your power settings.

To create your own plan without changing one of the existing ones, click the Create a Power Plan link in the left pane of your Power Options window. The Create a Power Plan window shown in Figure 34.6 appears. Select the existing Power Plan that most closely matches yours and then type a name for your new plan in the Plan Name text box.

FIGURE 34.6
To create your own Power Plan, start with the plan that most closely matches the one you want to create, give your plan a name, and specify the details you require.

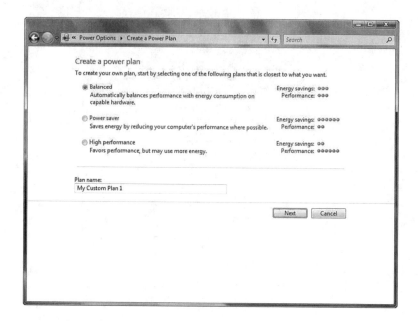

After clicking Next and specifying the computer and display time settings, your new plan will appear in the list of Power Plans that you can choose from the next time you open the Power Options window. Just as you can change the advanced details of the three supplied Power Plans, you can also change your Power Plan, click the Change Advanced Power Settings link, and modify the disk, screen, wireless networking, and other settings that affect your computer's performance and power consumption.

Chapter Wrap-Up

Finding the right balance between power and performance isn't always easy. Usually, it's an iterative process. You begin at the end of the scale you care about most, performance or power consumption, and you slowly change settings in the other direction until you find the final setting you can work with. For example, if you care more about a faster computer than power consumption, you should first set your computer to the High Performance Power Plan to see whether your computer performs to your liking. If it does, increase the Power Plan to a more balanced plan and see whether that works for you. If not, you might need to set your computer back to the highest-performing and lowest-energy savings possible to get the performance you want; otherwise, you'll still have your performance but at a better energy savings.

The correct power settings are more critical for laptops where you have a limited battery life. If your battery lasts three hours at a 20% slowdown in performance, you might prefer to take the performance hit and select your laptop's Power Saver plan even if you prefer performance over energy savings. You might do this if it means you can make it through that entire train or plane ride on a single battery charge.

In Chapter 33, "Configuring Windows Vista," you learned about themes. After you get your computer set the way you like it, you'll be able to store your configuration settings in a theme file that you name and can later restore. Saving multiple themes gives you the ability to change your Windows look and behavior when you want to change how—or where—you use your computer. In this chapter you learned how to create and save your own Power Plans. In the next chapter, you'll learn to back up more than just your theme files. You'll learn how to back up your entire computer so that you can recover from a hardware failure or other emergency that could destroy your computer's data and programs.

CHAPTER 35

Protecting Your Data and Programs

In This Chapter:

▶ Learn advanced backup strategies to guard your computer's files

▶ Master Vista's Backup program

▶ Make both full and incremental backups so that disaster recovery goes smoothly

▶ Understand the pros and cons of using external devices and off-site backups

▶ Backup with emails and USB flash drives

▶ Scheduling automated backups

Disaster recovery is an important term in the world of computing and has been for about 35 years, ever since the concept of *Information Systems* or *MIS* (for *Management Information Systems*) came into vogue in the corporate world. The idea now applies to individual computer users as well as for huge corporate networked computer systems.

It's almost cliché to mention the adage, "It's not *if* your files will get destroyed but *when.*" A corollary to that is, "It's not *if* a disk crash will occur but *when.*" Problems happen to the best of computer systems. Disk drives are mechanical and they cannot last forever. Their specifications are so exacting that the tiniest bump can put them off track (although they are designed to be rugged) and an invasion by the smallest dust particle will wreak havoc on the drive's platter.

You must plan for your own disaster recovery *now.* A single computer system often runs thousands of dollars worth of software. You can always buy a new computer; getting your data and programs back the way you like them is the challenge if something goes wrong.

Nothing should go wrong with computers, though, right? As the computer HAL made clear in the movie *2001: A Space Odyssey*, "Nothing can possibly go wrong…go wrong…go wrong…"

It's Not Always the Fault of Your Hardware

Disaster occurs to computer files in many ways. A disaster doesn't always come to you in the form of a hardware failure such as a disk crash. No matter how much design went into Vista to protect you and your system files, a glitch such as trashing an operating system file can occur. The glitch might be intended, due to spyware, or unintended, as from a bug in a program you install and run. The nastiest bugs are the ones that occur later and not immediately, long after you install the offending program, which makes tracking down the problem rather difficult.

Most of the time, software causes more problems than hardware. You go into your office and turn on your computer or start-up from a sleep state, only to find that your system won't boot and you cannot access your hard disk.

The very best thing to do immediately after you realize your computer files are gone is to restore the computer backup that you made seconds before the problem occurred. The reality is you can count the number of people in history able to do exactly that on one hand. For the rest of us, it's time to get serious about backing up your files.

You might not be able to restore a backed-up system to the full and reliable state it was in seconds before the problem, but a standard backup plan can go a long way toward protecting you and getting your computer back in action soon. Backing up isn't difficult or time-consuming. If you follow the advice in this chapter, you can set your backup plan into motion and not worry about it much after that.

By the Way

Making a backup is like getting fire insurance. Nobody wants to do it. Everybody hopes doing so is a waste of time. It's better to have a backup and not need it than to need it and not have it.

Windows Vista Backup

Ever since Windows 95, the backup program Microsoft supplied with Windows has been woefully inadequate and seemed almost like an afterthought. The all-important backup program was not intuitive, hardly updated as hardware advanced, and didn't even install automatically with some Windows installations such as Windows Me.

Windows Vista offers a new backup program. Figure 35.1 shows the opening screen that appears when you select Backup Status and Configuration from your System Tools folder on your Start menu. The backup program is an improvement from the Windows backup program that came before and might be all you ever need. Vista's backup program is not a comprehensive program and you can purchase far more complete backup programs, but Vista's isn't too bad. Along with every backup program, you also need a reliable way to restore your backed-up files if a disaster occurs. Vista's restore procedure is good, too, especially if you use one of the higher-end Vista versions that includes an advanced backup mode called *Complete PC Backup*, which saves complete mirror images of your disk drives.

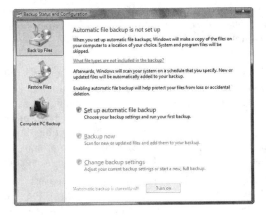

FIGURE 35.1
Windows Vista's backup and restore program is one that you can rely on.

Vista's backup program backs up selected files such as your data files or your entire computer. You'll want to back up different things at different times, and you'll learn the advantages and disadvantages of each backup style later in this chapter.

Your Backup Frequency

You can never back up too often. Monthly is almost never often enough, weekly is far better, and daily backups are vital if you want to maintain a computer system that has good redundancy and that you can put back the way it was before a failure and lose no more than a day's work.

In addition to scheduling a nightly backup, you can do some other things to back up your current work files during the day so that you potentially lose far less than one day's work. If, for example, you create and manage financial spreadsheets, you should save each spreadsheet you work on several times throughout your work session. Get in the habit of selecting File, Save every few minutes (often Ctrl+S is the shortcut key to save your files and on a toolbar there is often a Save icon you can click if you find that to be easier). I can attest that this becomes second nature after a few days, and you'll find yourself unconsciously selecting File, Save to save your most recent changes every few minutes and always before you get up from your desk.

Using an Application's Automatic Save Feature

Programs such as those in the Microsoft Office suite usually provide a feature that automatically saves your work every few minutes. You can adjust the settings so that the saving takes place at a time interval you specify. This feature works well and is dependable in most cases. I say *most cases* because it's caused some of us problems over the years.

The application expects the file to remain where it is, named what it's named, on the disk where you first saved it for the automatic save feature to operate smoothly. If you often find yourself moving files, renaming files, and swapping disk drives (as you can do, for example, with USB-based flash drives and other external disk drives), the automatic save feature *can* become confused. As a result, your files might not always save the way you expect them to or sometimes one piece of a file saves without another piece, which causes the file to become corrupted.

Having said this, many users have used the automatic save feature for years without a hitch and that's great. Perhaps some of us bitten by these one or more times over the years are in the extreme minority. If this worries you, however, or if you've had a similar experience in the past and turned off your software's automatic save feature, you don't need that feature. Computers and disk drives are fast, and manually saving your work every few minutes gets to be a habit and works like your own unconscious automatic save feature after you get used to doing it.

Of course, saving your work often—whether manually or through an automatic save feature—typically saves your work to the same disk drive. Generally, you'll use a primary disk drive for most of your work and to which you'll save your data. Typically, that drive holds your user account's Documents and other folders and files. Performing a save often to that disk makes sure that a fresh version of your work is on disk and not just in memory if something bad occurs, such as a power outage.

Run, don't walk, to your nearest computer store or electronics website and get an *uninterruptible power supply* (*UPS*). Don't skimp and get a low-end UPS; you need one rated at least 1000VA/500W. Such a system gives you a few minutes to save your work and properly power down your computer down before the backup battery drains out of the UPS and you lose power completely. Don't keep your printer plugged into the UPS or it will drain too much power if the current goes out. Keep your computer, your Internet DSL/cable/telephone modem, and at least one display plugged into the UPS so that you have full control to save your work if the power goes out.

Even with your UPS in place, don't even think about eliminating the periodic save-to-disk routine. You'll still want to save your work every few minutes if you can get into that file-saving habit (and you can). A UPS doesn't do much good if someone walks by and accidentally trips over a cord that pulls your computer power cord from your system unit. Even your own foot could do this while you sit there working. Don't risk your data; save often.

Incremental and Full Backups

Several kinds of backups are possible. Most backups fall into one of these five categories:

- ▶ **A full backup**—A backup of all your files, including your data, programs, and system files.

- ▶ **An image backup**—A bit-by-bit mirror image of your disk drive. The backup program might compress the image backup, so storing the backup does not consume as much disk space as storing as the actual, original source disk. An image backup takes the longest of all the backups to make, but provides the easiest way to get your computer back to working order if you must restore your entire disk drive.

- ▶ **An incremental backup**—A backup of all files that have changed since the most recent full backup or image backup. An incremental backup is far less time-consuming than a full or image backup. If you ever have to restore your computer, you have to restore the full backup first, and then restore each incremental backup in the order you made them to get your system back to its most recent, stable state. The more often you make a full backup, the fewer incremental backups you have to restore when you need to recover your computer.

▶ **A data backup**—A backup of your data. The easiest way to do this in Vista is to back up your user account's folders and files. Your data is far more difficult to restore from scratch than your programs. Your data includes your documents, pictures, music, and video files as well as emails, Windows Vista, and program settings. The drawback to making only data backups is that if you lose your hard disk, you have to restore Windows Vista, and install all your programs before you can work with your data again.

Reinstalling all your programs is often difficult because the sources for new programs are so varied. You buy some programs and have the CDs and DVDs they came on. Some programs you might get from friends. Some programs you might download and install from the Internet. Many programs that you originally installed from CDs or DVDs you have since updated and upgraded online. You have to install them again from their installation discs and perform all the updates and upgrades again before those programs will work reliably with the data file backup files you restore.

▶ **An individual file backup**—A backup copy of one or more files you want to protect by saving them to your disk drive, separate from their original location or on a different disk drive. As the next section explains, an individual file backup isn't a true backup, but one where you save current data as you work with that data so that you protect today's work.

A full backup of all your programs, system programs, and data actually doesn't do you a lot of good these days if it's not an image backup of your disk drive. Computer systems have several hidden files and folders and partitioned disk areas that make a complete file backup difficult to create. After you create it, restoring such a backup isn't always possible.

Image backups make far more sense than file backups in most cases because image backups include an exact image of your disk's files and settings. If your disk drive gets wiped out, you can restore the drive to the exact point in time that you backed up the disk image. If your disk drive gets damaged, you need only get an identical drive and put it in your computer, giving you a place to restore the image backup so that you'll be running smoothly once again.

The greatest thing about Vista's backup program is that its full backup routine *is* an image backup of your computer disk drive so that in a worst-case scenario you can completely restore your hard disk. The former Windows backup program could create a full backup of your data, program, and system files, but it was not an image backup and it was difficult to restore.

Vista's full disk image backup, called a *Complete PC* backup, is not available for Windows Home Basic or Vista Home Premium editions. This is a shame. If you run either of those Vista installations, you should get a backup program that does create an image backup, such as Norton Ghost. The steps necessary to run an image backup for a program such as Norton Ghost differ from Vista's Complete PC backup, but the overall process is similar and you can read the "Making a Complete Image Backup," section later in this chapter to get a feel for the steps you'll take with a third-party program such as Ghost. (The Complete PC backup procedure alone might be enough reason to upgrade your Windows to a higher version.)

Where You Back Up to Makes a Difference

After you get in the habit of saving your files often as you work with them, and when you have your UPS in place so that the power doesn't go out on you before you've had a chance to save your current work, you've only just begun to protect your files from the grave harm that is possible.

Saving your work to your disk while working during the day saves your work to one disk—a single disk—and that disk can go bad. The periodic saving technique works to protect you only if something happens to your computer's power. It does nothing to protect you if something happens to your computer's disk drive.

Using a Second Internal Drive

A relatively simple way to save your data in a second location, other than your primary work disk, is to install a second internal disk drive in your computer. You could change to that other disk drive every few times that you select File, Save. That procedure puts a recent copy of your important work in two places. If one disk drive crashes, the other will usually be okay.

There are no guarantees in life or in computing, and sometimes a problem brings down a computer system and all disks and files in that computer. Bad viruses can do this. Periodically saving your work throughout the day to a second, internal drive, however, helps to save your data and keep it fresh if the first disk drive goes bad. Internal disk drives are inexpensive these days, and after installing one in your computer's system unit, it's extremely simple and fast to save files there. Just change the drive letter and save your file. The ease of making that second copy throughout the day, combined with the extra protection of saving to a second drive, helps protect your data more than if you use only a single disk drive.

Using a USB Flash Drive

Some people are fanatical about backing up. Every hour or so, they insert a USB flash drive, save their day's work to the flash drive, remove the drive, and continue. These fanatics are *never* called fanatics when something happens to their computer, however, because their data is safe and they're back working on it within a few minutes of getting another computer to use. Although such a flash drive backup procedure might seem like a lot of work, inserting and removing a flash drive is quick and easy and might mean a lot to you someday if you ever need the files on that flash drive. Consider using this method to save your day's work at least before you leave for lunch and at the end of your work day.

Send Emails to Yourself

One of the simplest ways to back up a file quickly (as long as you have a high-speed Internet connection) is to send the file to a web-based email account. Google's Gmail and Microsoft's Hotmail accounts work well for this and when you travel it's one of the simplest ways to protect your data.

After you've worked on a file for a while, just open a Windows Explorer window, right-click the file, and select the Send To option. You can first select multiple files, as Figure 35.2 shows, before selecting the Send To option. Click Mail Recipient and Vista opens an email message window. Type your web-based email address in the To field, type a subject that describes the files you're sending there, and click Send. After they go, you have a fresh copy of your files on a highly reliable web-based email account that you can access to get your files back if something happens to your computer's disk drive before you've had a chance to make a full backup.

FIGURE 35.2
Send files to a web-based email account when you want a reliable backup.

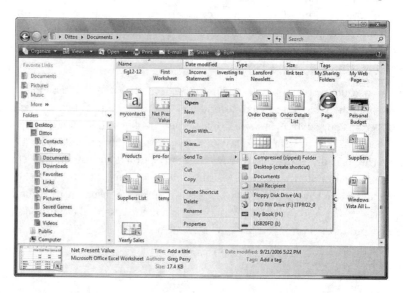

Emailing files to yourself works well as long as you don't have your computer's email system set to download email from that web-based email account. For example, if you send a file as an email attachment to your Gmail account and all that Gmail account's email downloads to your laptop or desktop the moment you open your email program, the files no longer reside on that web-based server and you're back to having all your files on one disk drive. It's simple to open a second web-based email account if you want one solely for backing up your files. You should routinely log in to your email account and delete the files that you no longer need or that are on a more complete backup DVD or external drive to keep the account cleared out.

 By the Way

Consider Online Backup Services

Some online backup service web sites exist so that you can send files to them for storage and backup. www.itronis.com and www.usdatatrust.com are two well-known sites. Although the cost to backup a large disk drive is prohibitive, backing up your important files such as financial records may be worth the cost, especially if you travel and work on the road. You can upload your files each evening to the online backup service's web storage so your files are safe in case something happens to your data.

If you use one of the Quicken products for your financial record-keeping, you can upload your Quicken data to Intuit's servers (Intuit, Incorporated produces the Quicken products) for a small monthly fee and Intuit will protect your data and make it available from a secure location that you can access only with the password and username you've first set up.

Using an External Disk Drive

External drives are plentiful, only slightly more costly than internal disk drives, and they are easy to install. In most cases, you plug a new external drive into your computer's USB or FireWire port, Vista recognizes the drive, adds the drive to your list of disk drives in all your Explorer and File Save windows, and the drive is ready for you.

Such an external disk drive works well for saving your work throughout the day because it adds yet another location in which to back up your current and fresh files. There's nothing wrong with using an external disk drive for this purpose but, in reality, external disk drives are better for a slightly different use.

External drives are far better than CDs and DVDs because they hold so much more data and you can write to them so much faster. Although you can back up onto CDs and, preferably if you must choose between them, DVDs, a typical hard disk drive might require 10 or more DVDs to hold an image backup set and such DVD-swapping makes backups far less likely to happen. You must be there to swap the DVDs as they fill up, so the process consumes your time, and you're far less likely to back up regularly. By backing up to an external disk drive you plug in to your computer, your computer can perform any backup you specify at night when you're away from your computer. You can create a weekly complete backup and a nightly incremental backup and Vista takes care of all the work. All you have to do is make sure that the drive is plugged in and large enough to hold the backups.

External disk drives provide perhaps the best location for your disk drive backups. Whether you routinely back up an incremental set of files or create a full system backup, an external disk drive makes a wise location for such backups. You can buy as many external disk drives as you like and rotate them. For example, this week you might make a full system backup and five daily incremental backups of your system, and then unplug the external drive and plug in a different one for next week. By rotating the external drives, you have a double backup set for twice the protection of a single backup.

Here is the best tip you will ever read about backing up: Use an external disk drive for your backups, rotate a second external drive as the previous paragraph explained, and then take the drive not currently in use to an off-site location where your computer is not stored. In other words, take the backup drive not currently plugged in to work with you for the week and bring it home the next week so that you can trade it for the other drive, which you then take to work for the week. This helps to ensure that if a fire breaks out and burns up your computer, the second backup drive wouldn't be sitting right there getting burned also. (Discussing backups does get serious; but remember what was said early in this chapter: Backups are like life insurance and it's better to have them and not need them than the other way around.)

Using Windows Vista Backup

Assuming that you connected an external disk drive, or perhaps have a second internal drive you want to back up to for now, you're ready to back up your computer. Keep in mind that backing up your entire system is the best place to begin. After you do that, you can create an incremental backup or perhaps just back up your data files for the next few rounds of backups until you again create a full back-up image.

To start Vista's backup program, open your Start menu, select All Programs, Accessories, System Tools, and then select Backup Status and Configuration to open Vista's backup program (refer to Figure 35.1). Backup Status and Configuration isn't necessarily the easiest name to remember so the rest of this chapter will call it simply Backup.

Making a Complete Image Backup

The first time you back up your computer, and as often as necessary after that, you should perform a complete PC backup. Vista recommends that you perform this type of backup at least monthly, but if you often modify your computer settings or install and uninstall programs and settings frequently, a weekly complete backup makes more sense.

Click the Complete PC Backup button. The window normally shows the time and date of the most recent successful complete backup and location to which it was stored. But if this is the first time for this computer, both the date and location entries show None.

Click the Create a Backup Now button and after an administrative privilege confir-mation, Vista looks for available backup drives and asks where you want to create the complete backup image as Figure 35.3 shows.

FIGURE 35.3
Tell Vista where you want the backup image to be stored.

Click to open the drive-selection drop-down list to select a hard disk or click to select the On One or More DVDs option, depending on where you want to place the back-up. If you have an external drive connected to your computer (the best choice for this kind of backup), use that drive for your backup.

Watch Out!

The external disk drive must be partitioned in the NTFS file system and not FAT or FAT32. **NTFS** stands for **New Technology File System** and offers more file storage and security than the older FAT-based disk standards did. If the backup program doesn't display your external drive, its format might not be correct. Contact your external drive's website's customer support site to learn how to convert the drive to NTFS or whether it's possible to do so. If not, you'll have to get a different, more recent external drive for your complete backups.

By the Way

You cannot place a complete PC full-image backup onto a disk drive or disc that is one gigabyte or smaller. Therefore, you cannot place the backup onto a series of CD-ROMs. You can, however, use CD-ROMs for other kinds of backups you would do incrementally, such as your data and selected file backups.

Click Next to confirm your backup settings. Vista tells you which disc drives it will back up, as Figure 35.4 shows. In Figure 35.4, Vista's system drive happens to be disc drive H: and not disc drive C: but as you can see, the Backup program doesn't care. It backs up the entire system, saving both drives. If you ever had to restore such a system, Backup would restore everything to its current state.

FIGURE 35.4
Vista needs confirmation before making the system backup.

The Confirm Your Backup Settings window shows how much disk space the backup will consume. If your selected backup drive does not have enough free space, Vista tells you so that you can cancel the process, free some space or use a different drive, and start again. When everything is ready, click Start Backup and the process begins.

> During a Complete PC Backup, you can click the Stop Backup button to stop the process. If you stop the process in the middle of a complete backup, the Backup program erases any saved data. Windows cannot work with a partial system backup, so you have to start over when you're ready to let the process finish.

Vista does allow you to work on your computer while saving the backup. If you do, however, any work you do is not included in the backup. You have to back up any changes to files, or new files you create, the next time you perform a backup.

When you see the dialog box in Figure 35.5, you can rest easy knowing that your Complete PC backup image is safe on the external drive. With that backup, you can restore your entire computer back to its present state if something happens.

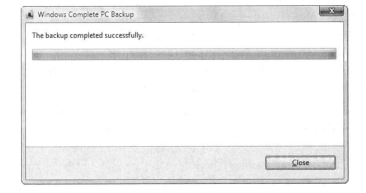

FIGURE 35.5
The Complete PC Backup finished and an image of your computer now resides on the external backup drive.

Restoring a Complete Image Backup

Suppose that you start getting system errors but you can still use Windows Vista. Perhaps settings are lost and certain programs stop working. As long as you can boot Windows Vista, restoring your entire system back to the original state it was in when you performed a Complete PC backup is rather simple.

The best news to learn is that you might not have to restore the Complete PC backup image. You might just need to restore your system files back to an earlier date using System Restore. Refer to Chapter 31, "Restoring Your Windows System to a Previous State," for details.

The sooner you spot system problems and the sooner you perform a System Restore, the more likely it is that System Restore can take care of the problem for you and you can get back to work.

If System Restore doesn't seem to be fixing things, you probably have to resort to restoring your Complete PC backup image. First, save any data files you might have changed or created since the most recent Complete PC backup, if you still have access to your disk files.

Perhaps you'll use Vista's Backup program to save those individual files as the next section explains, or perhaps there aren't too many files and you can copy them to a USB flash drive, CD, or DVD. As long as you can access the files, you should be able to save them in their newest, current state. If you have Internet access, send them to a web-based email account as explained earlier in this chapter for a reliable backup that you can retrieve after you restore the rest of your computer.

Obviously, if your system has major problems, you might not be able to back up even your most recent data. If not, be thankful you have created daily backups and know that you'll lose one day's work at most. You then must start the restore process.

The procedure you use to restore a Complete PC backup depends on how the manufacturer set up your computer and configured it to sell. If your computer came with a Windows Vista installation disc, or if you upgraded your computer to Vista using a Windows Vista installation disk, follow these steps to restore your system:

1. Remove any CD or DVD from your computer's disc drive, place your Windows installation disc there, and restart your computer. If you cannot display Vista's Start menu to restart your machine, you might have to resort to turning off your computer and turning it back on again after letting it sit in a power-off state for a minute or so.

2. If prompted to boot from the DVD drive, press any key to confirm that's what you want to do. Some systems attempt to boot automatically from any disc that is there, so you might not have to do anything to get your computer to boot to the Windows Vista installation DVD.

   The boot process will take a while longer than normal, but you will eventually see the Start button.

If you cannot get your computer to boot to the installation disc but it keeps trying to boot normally from the hard disk, you need to contact your computer's manufacturer's customer support website or check your manual to learn how to enter the computer's BIOS screen and request that the system boot from the disc drive. This usually requires pressing the keyboard's F2 key when the computer first starts until you see the BIOS screen. If this doesn't work, your only resort really is the manual or the customer support staff.

3. Click the Start button, click the arrow to the right of the Start menu right pane's Lock button, and select Restart.

4. Vista prompts you for your language settings. Select a language and click the Next button.

5. Select Repair Your Computer and click Next.

6. Finally, open the System Recovery Options menu and select the Windows Complete PC Restore option. Vista prompts you for a confirmation and perhaps asks that you select from the drive and then the restoration will begin. The Complete PC restore process takes longer than it took to create the full backup image, so have patience while Vista performs the restore. After the restore finishes, your reward is a fully working computer again.

Vista is robust and advanced enough to be able to recognize your USB-based disk drive during this recovery process even if it cannot recognize other devices, such as your printer. If you use a FireWire drive, especially one made before 2004, Vista might not be able to recognize it during the recovery process. Many external drives are both USB- and FireWire-enabled, so locate the drive's USB cable and connect it to see whether Vista recognizes the drive during this restore process. If not, you might have to get a newer USB drive, install it temporarily on another computer, temporarily install your FireWire drive on that computer, and copy the WindowsImageBackup folder to the new drive, which Vista should recognize for the restoration.

If your computer did not come with a Windows Vista installation disc but had Windows Vista preinstalled, follow these steps to restore your system:

1. Remove any CD or DVD from your computer's disc drive, and restart your computer. If you cannot display Vista's Start menu to restart your machine, you might have to turn off your computer and turn it back on again after letting it sit in a power-off state for a minute or so.

2. Turn your computer on and press F8 repeatedly, waiting about a second between F8 key presses. If asked to select an operating system, as would be the case if you have Vista and another operating system installed, use your arrow keys to highlight Vista and press F8. (If you see your Windows logo screen you didn't start pressing F8 soon enough and you need to reboot and try again.)

3. Vista will start in **safe mode**, an environment where Vista loads only enough drivers and system routines to give you control of your computer using the mouse, screen, keyboard, and your internal and external drives. You'll soon see the Advanced Boot Options menu. Select Repair Your Computer and press Enter.

4. Vista then prompts you for a keyboard layout. Select a layout and click Next.

5. If asked, select your username, enter your password, and click OK.

6. Open the System Recovery Options menu that appears and select Windows Complete PC Restore. Vista prompts you for a confirmation, perhaps asks that you select the drive, and then begins the restoration. The Complete PC restore process takes longer than it took to create the full backup image, so have patience while Windows Vista performs the restore. After the restore finishes, you should have a fully working computer again.

After restoring your computer and verifying that it works as you expect, you need to restore any incremental backups you made since you created that Complete PC backup. You should either restore an incremental backup you created (as explained in the next two sections of this chapter) or retrieve the files from a USB flash drive, CD, DVD, or web-based email. Your system should be back to where it was before the problems began.

Backing Up Selected Data Files and Folders

If you don't need a Complete PC backup image because you recently made one, you can back up selected files and folders using an incremental approach. The only kinds of files that you cannot back up, even if you use an Administrator user account, are these:

▶ Encrypting File System (EFS) files

▶ Windows system files

▶ Program files

▶ Files formatted with the older FAT or FAT32 file system

▶ Web-based email not downloaded to your computer

▶ Recycle Bin files

▶ Temporary files

▶ User Profile settings

Obviously this list poses quite a few limitations. You can't back up program files, so if you have a disk problem, you have to reinstall the programs from their original program discs or from their download site. But as long as you regularly create a Complete PC full image backup, as the previous two sections described, you won't have a need to back up your programs because they reside in your complete backup image.

Perhaps the biggest limitation—and, again, it's fixed as long as you have a complete backup—is that you cannot save your user profile settings. The backup is not intended to back up anything other than your data. Keep in mind, your data covers a lot of territory, including

▶ Program data such as Outlook contacts and emails, Word documents, and Quicken-based financial information

▶ Music stored in MP3 and other music file formats

▶ Digital videos

▶ Digital pictures

Remember that as long as you make complete backups regularly and back up your data regularly (such as daily), you can restore everything with ease.

To some Vista users' dismay, Vista is strict about backups. In fact, before Vista lets you make a backup of your files, it requires that you set up a regular backup schedule. When you first click the Back Up Files button on the Windows Backup program, Vista lets you know that you don't yet have an automatic file backup set up, as Figure 35.6 shows.

The first thing to do is the best thing: Click the Set Up Automatic File Backup option, confirm your administrative privileges, and set up your regular file backup schedule. Vista will ask where you want to store your scheduled backup. You choose from an external disk drive or a network disk drive attached to any network you're using at the time. You then must select the disk drives you want to back up. Vista always selects the system disk you're using and you can optionally keep any additional disks on your computer. Click Next after you select the drives you want to back up.

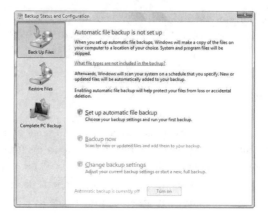

Vista now presents you with Figure 35.7's File Types window where you select which kinds of files you want to include in the scheduled backup. Typically you'll want to back up everything except some files, such as TV shows that you might have saved from the Vista Media Center software (refer to Chapter 14, "Going Multimedia with Vista"). Remember that TV shows and other video can generate extremely large files, and you might not want to back those up because your backup disk will fill quickly after only a few backups if you save that kind of data.

By the Way

Another way of looking at large digital video files like television programs, however, is that their nature (a show that you always want to see and that plays once every week) and their huge size make them difficult to capture again. You must wait for the rerun season to begin if you lose the show that you saved to watch before you're able to watch it. You should back up such a file despite its size, and the best thing to do is to make sure that you have plenty of space on your backup drive. This might require purchasing a larger, external drive than you currently have.

After making sure that you selected the files want to include, click Next to move to the scheduling window shown in Figure 35.8. There you set the time you want Vista to use to make your routine data backups. The very first time you back up your data files, Vista backs up all of them. In subsequent backups, Vista backs up only files that are new or have changed since the most recent data file backup, meaning that Vista performs an incremental backup of your data after the first complete backup.

FIGURE 35.7
Select the kind
of data you
want to back up
regularly.

The best time to run a backup is when you're not using your computer. That way, Vista can back up your data and save any changes you made before you left your computer for the day (or perhaps for lunch). The backup can begin during times you do want to use your computer, but changes you make to your data files during the backup will not be saved until the next scheduled backup. The only things you must make sure of when scheduling a backup are that your computer is powered on at that time (you don't have to be logged on) and your backup drive, such as an external USB drive, is connected to your computer.

Did you Know?

After you schedule and perform your first backup, you can create a manual backup anytime you want. Suppose that you worked a lot on your computer today before lunch, and copied other files to your computer from co-workers or family members who want you to work on their files for some reason, and you want to make a backup to protect everything even though one isn't scheduled until 3:00 a.m.

In that case, just start Vista's Backup program and select Back Up Now. Vista allows you to create a manual backup of your data files because you've already scheduled automatic backups and already performed your first backup. Simply click the Back Up Now option and make the backup.

Unlike a Complete PC backup, you can cancel a data file backup, and the files that have been written will be backed up and you can retrieve them later. Although a partial backup is never as good as a full one, if something happens in the middle of such a backup, such as the power going out in the middle of the night, you still have some files saved on the backup drive.

By the Way

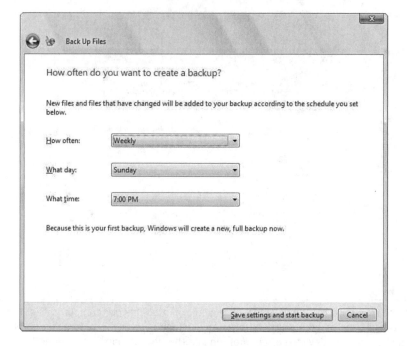

After you schedule a backup and perform your first one, you can turn off the scheduled backup if you want. Obviously, doing so puts your data at risk, but there might
be times when you want to do so. For example, perhaps you back up nightly but
want to go out of town for three days and don't want to leave your external backup
disk drive attached for that time; you would rather leave the backup disk at your
office, off-site, just in case something happened at home. You might leave your computer on while you're away for others to use, but the backup drive won't be there
and available when the scheduled backup is to take place each night.

To turn off a scheduled backup, start the Windows Backup program and click the
Turn Off button at the bottom of the window. When you return, you can click the
button now labeled Turn On and put the external drive back where the scheduled
backups expect to find it.

By the Way

When your scheduled backup is turned off, you can still manually back up your
files. Click the Back Up Now button and Vista begins the backup. Because you've
already made a full backup, Vista backs up only those files that have changed
since your last backup. Such an incremental backup goes very quickly in comparison to a full data backup.

Restoring a Data Backup

Unlike a Complete PC backup, you can select certain files and folders to restore from a data backup whether that backup was created manually or from a scheduled backup process. You can also restore the entire set of data files if you want to do so, and that might be your preference if you just had to restore your entire PC using an image backup.

To restore all your files from a backup, click the Restore Files button. Vista asks whether you want to restore files from the latest backup you made or from an earlier backup, as might be the case if you deleted a file before making your most recent backup but decided you want that file again. The Backup program asks what files and folders you want to restore, and you select either individual files and folders or select all available and restore everything.

By clicking the Advanced Restore option, shown in Figure 35.9, you can restore files that you backed up from another computer. This might be handy if you have a new laptop on which you want to place all your desktop's data files and folders.

By the Way

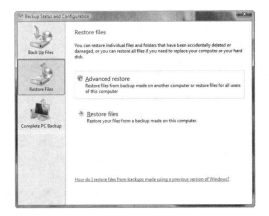

FIGURE 35.9
Select the Restore Files option when you need to grab files from a backup disk and when you need to restore a complete disk image.

Chapter Wrap-Up

This chapter described Windows Vista's Backup program, technically called the *Backup Status and Configuration program*. Take it on yourself to be responsible for your applications and data. Computers often work reliably for years, but you're still a possible victim of a disk drive failure at any unexpected moment. A copy of your files means the difference between returning to your regular routine quickly or spending hours, days, and weeks trying to restore your system to its original state.

Your disk drives are mechanical and will break down over time. Don't wait to make your first backup or you'll regret it the first time your disk has a problem.

The next chapter begins the final part of this book. The material moves away from your own computer and shows you how to connect to other computers, both on a network and the Internet. Vista's networking and Internet tools are extremely advanced, and yet Microsoft put a lot of effort into shielding the average user from the technical details. As you'll learn in the next chapter, the nicest thing about networking under Vista is that, most of the time, it just works.

PART VII

Running Windows Vista in a Connected World

CHAPTER 36

Combining Vista, Networks, and the Internet

In This Chapter:

- ▶ Learn how Vista simplifies networking
- ▶ Determine which networking hardware works best for you
- ▶ View a graphical representation of your own network
- ▶ Use Vista's Network Discovery tool to locate computers and printers available to you on your network
- ▶ Connect to XP computers on your network
- ▶ Set up file and printer sharing
- ▶ Use Public folders to make sharing information easy
- ▶ Password-protect your files and printers

In the past, a Windows book typically included a chapter about networks. Then there would be a chapter or two about the Internet. This book's outline initially included separate chapters about using a network with Vista and accessing the Internet with Vista; those chapters combined to form this single chapter.

Things change. Why should accessing files on the Internet (including web pages, which are nothing more than files stored on a collection of remote computers) be much different from accessing files on a network that happens to be located in your building?

The fact is that connecting to a network and connecting to the Internet used to require you to jump through hoops to make the connections work. Fortunately, that isn't typically the case anymore. Several things occurred to make accessing networked files and the Internet much easier: Much of the networking and Internet-based technology standardized and converged, and Vista got very smart and does most of or all the hard stuff for you.

Average users simply know that the Internet just works and the files on that networked computer appear when you need them. Well, that's the goal. Vista is able to achieve that goal for most people.

Networking Is Not as Technical as Before

By its very nature, networking is a technical subject. Anytime you must connect hardware to software and make that hardware and software talk to other computers that might not even be running the same operating system you do, the connection is going to have some challenges.

These challenges were faced and generally overcome in the past two or three decades that computer networking has become so ubiquitous. When networking first appeared on the desktop computer scene in the early 1980s, several networking technologies competed to become the world's standard networking technology. Backed by IBM, token ring networking came on the strongest, and ethernet and ARCnet were among other technologies that competed to have the biggest installed base of users.

It was obvious that one technology had to emerge to become the leader because the competing networks didn't communicate with each other very well, and users wanted a seamless method to send and receive data between their computer and others' computers. Unexpectedly, the ethernet networking technology began to grab market share from token ring and other varieties. One reason was simply that the cable used for ethernet was easier to manage than the coaxial cable required for token ring and some of the other network types. Looking like a slightly thicker telephone cable that plugged into network cards as easily as familiar phone lines plugged into phone jacks, it might have been nothing more than the familiarity of the cable and plug that turned the corner for ethernet.

In addition, the fact that a new and emerging technology called the Internet came on the scene in the 1990s and used the same kinds of networking **protocols** (communication standards) as ethernet. That certainly helped seal ethernet's place in our world today. Because the Internet uses protocols similar to ethernet networks it makes both technologies so easy for Windows Vista to access and manage.

Standards are now in place and Vista is well-configured to take advantage of them. The bottom line for you is simple: It's easy to access the Internet and other networked computers and printers using Vista. Windows XP leaped forward with making both technologies available to you, but Vista goes further and lessens the technical nature even more. In the rest of this chapter, you won't spend long, tedious sections learning about TCP/IP protocols because you don't have to. The Internet and networks just work (most of the time) under Vista. Here, you'll learn some of the things you can do with a networked Internet-based computer running Vista.

Microsoft completely rewrote the internal networking system instead of reusing and updating XP's. The code is better and runs faster. *Maximum PC* magazine published its results of testing large downloads on a Vista computer and an identical computer running XP. The testing showed a speed improvement of 15%, resulting in far faster downloads on the Vista machine (page 31, *Maximum PC* magazine, June 2006).

Did you Know?

Networking Your Environment

Many homes and offices have more than one PC. Perhaps you use a laptop on the road and a desktop at work. Perhaps you replaced an older PC with a more modern one and relegated the older PC to the kids' room. The victims of today's low-priced, high-powered PCs are yesterday's PCs. Older PCs are too expensive to throw out, they aren't powerful enough to use as a serious business or entertainment tool, and if you used them in a business you've depreciated their cost so that you cannot donate them for a tax break.

You can now begin to use that second, slower PC elsewhere in your home or office. Such PCs used to be discarded, but new advances in simple networking technology enable the home and small office user to take advantage of every computer. Although the slower machine might not be your primary computer, you can use it to access the other PC's files when you are in another room, putting the slower machine back into operation again.

The primary reason you would network PCs is to share a single printer, files, and usually an Internet connection. You can connect your home office PC to a laser printer and your bedroom PC can, through the network, print documents to the laser upstairs. Of course, the printer must be turned on for the documents to print, but if it's not, Windows Vista holds the output in its print queue until you can get there to turn on the printer. For fun, multiplayer games played over a network can be fun for several family members at once (and for co-workers who, of course, play only on their lunch breaks...).

Did you Know?

Although the printer does not have to be on, your printer's PC must be connected and turned on to accept print commands from the network. Therefore, the machine that you use for a shared printer must be powered on or the network's PCs can't print to that printer. Unlike larger, more powerful, more expensive networks, you don't have to designate a machine as a network server machine. A server isn't a computer that anyone can sit down and use. In the home-based networking system used most often, every PC on the network, including those sharing files and printers, can also be used as regular PCs on the network. The networks described here are **peer-to-peer** networks, meaning that every machine is a usable machine and one does not have to be designated as a reserved server for files and the printer.

Networking Hardware

A network used to require cabling between two or more computers. Many networks in use today still use cabling, but there are wireless options that eliminate the requirement to run cables. Right now, you can network PCs together using one or both of these two methods:

▶ **Traditional wiring**—Wired networks are generally ethernet-based, simple to install, and require a router with a switch (or hub) to which all network cables run to manage the traffic across the network. A **router** takes an Internet signal and enables it to be shared between users. Many of today's routers are wireless, sending out both wired and wireless connections to the Internet (see Figure 36.1). Routers often include switches in them so you can plug multiple devices into your router without needing to purchase a separate switch. You would only need to buy a switch with several additional network ports if you want to connect more devices to your network than your router's connections allow. The wiring between computers, such as 100Base-TX wiring (Ethernet), is similar to telephone cable, is flexible, and is easy to run through walls and under carpet.

▶ **Wi-Fi (wireless) transmission**—One or more computers includes a wireless networking card that transmits and receives network signals. Wi-Fi networks are traditionally slower than wired ethernet but provide the obvious advantage of being wireless, although new advances are improving Wi-Fi's speed and range. Wi-Fi is also known by the naming standards of its various technologies, such as 802.11b (slowest and the first widely adopted wireless standard), as well as 802.11n, 802.11a, and 802.11g (all of which are faster than 802.11b). 802.11g is currently the most popular standard but the 802.11n will likely take over during Vista's lifetime, as more users adopt it.

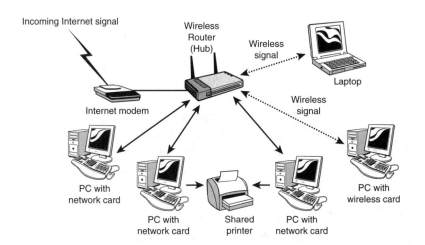

Incoming Internet signal

Wireless Router (Hub)

Wireless signal

Laptop

Internet modem

Wireless signal

PC with network card

PC with wireless card

PC with network card

Shared printer

PC with network card

FIGURE 36.1
A router sends the Internet signal wirelessly to Wi-Fi PCs and through a hub or switch that routes Internet and network information between the computers connected to the network.

When you install a network, each networked PC that will connect to the wired network requires a network interface card (NIC) that you can insert into one of the empty PC slots. Most PCs and laptops sold after 2002 already have built-in networking cards and connectors. You run the network cable from card-to-router (or external switch or hub if you use one) until all wired PCs are connected to the network.

Wireless network and Internet connections require a wireless card. Most laptops sold today have them already, but if yours does not, you can purchase one inexpensively. You can insert a wireless card in a desktop computer as well, although the increased speed of a wired network connection along with the fact that you rarely move a desktop computer from one place to another means that most people run a network cable from their desktops to the hub they use.

This discussion of networking hardware is important for you to understand, but it's almost unnecessary with modern computers. A computer running any Vista Home Premium version requires an Internet connection, and most computers that can run Vista are recent enough to include the necessary networking connections. Your job is to make sure that you get a router and possibly a hub so that you can share your Internet connection among the computers on your network.

Windows Vista Helps You Network

Fifteen years ago, managing a network of any size required a **network administrator**, a person who was responsible for maintaining the network connections, adding users to the network, and setting up security, giving access to certain files and printers. Networks were extremely cumbersome to maintain. Although larger network systems still require extensive training and procedures to operate, the home-based

PC boom turned the smaller segment of the networking market into a consumer-oriented technology segment.

One of the reasons home-based networks don't require much know-how to operate is because of the ethernet standard described in this chapter's opening section. The other reason that networking is virtually painless is due to Windows itself. Beginning with Windows 3.11 (called *Windows for Workgroups*), peer-to-peer networking became a reality instead of a difficult-to-deliver promise. More importantly, Windows 3.11 (which continued throughout all the versions until Windows XP appeared) gave the industry a standard on which to build network hardware and write network software.

Vista ups the ante as usual.

The majority of users with broadband Internet service—available over DSL or a cable modem—will find that they have to do absolutely nothing to let Vista know about the Internet connection. Long gone are the days when users had to tweak their system settings or play around with modem DIP switches to get a solid connection. Given Vista's support for more devices than any other operating system to come before it, if you use a dial-up modem (especially if it's a newer model that plugs into a USB port), Vista will probably recognize your modem when you install Vista and you'll be dialing (and faxing) with the modem, connecting to your local Internet provider, without trouble. If you have trouble connecting, it's probably because of a software problem that your Internet provider can fix after you tell the customer service representative that you're trying to connect on a Vista-based computer.

Windows Vista provides you with full control over your computer's networking connections in the Network and Sharing Center, shown in Figure 36.2. You can display your Network and Sharing Center by opening your Control Panel's Network and Internet group and selecting the Network and Sharing Center option.

The vast majority of anything you might ever need to do with your computer's network connection is available from the Network and Sharing Center. The rest of this chapter describes many of the features of your Network and Sharing Center and explores ways you can use it to your advantage.

Your Graphical Network Connection

The very top of your Network and Sharing Center window shows your computer's network and Internet modem connection. Depending on your setup, you might see a different picture from that at the top of Figure 36.2. For example, if you don't use a router, you probably have your Internet connection coming directly into your computer. You then share that connection over your network, so the globe representing the Internet might be shown connecting to your PC as well as the Network icon in your Network and Sharing Center.

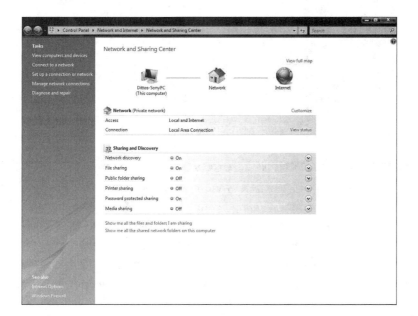

FIGURE 36.2
Just about anything you want to do with your network is available in Vista's Network and Sharing Center.

Your Network and Sharing Center will display a more detailed graphic representation of your entire network if you click the View Full Map link. Figure 36.3 shows a simple network shown in the full map view. Two computers are wired to a **switch** (which is a network hub), and the switch is connected to a **gateway** (which is typically an Internet router or modem). If your router includes a switch then your diagram won't show the switch separately.

Did you Know?

This graphical representation of your network can become huge, depending on how many connections your network has available. In addition, you might see only Vista computers on your network graphic even if you can access shared Windows XP computers connected to your network.

Press F5 to refresh the network graphic if you add or remove network devices and want to confirm that Vista recognizes them.

Did you Know?

FIGURE 36.3
View a full detailed map of your network connections.

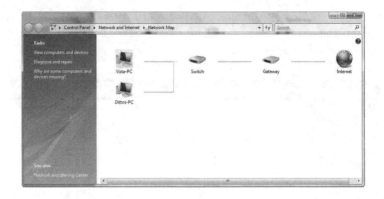

Turning On Network Discovery

If your network doesn't see one of your Vista computers, you need to turn on **network discovery**, an internal system program that makes your computer available to others on your network. In Figure 36.2, the network discovery feature is turned on, as indicated by the first entry in the Sharing and Discovery section.

If a computer on your network does not have network discovery turned on, click the arrow to expand that computer's Network Discovery group (the arrow to the right of each entry in the Network and Sharing Center) and click to select the Turn On Network Discovery option as shown in Figure 36.4.

Workgroup name   Click to collapse or expand

FIGURE 36.4
Turn on network sharing when you want others on the network to see your computer.

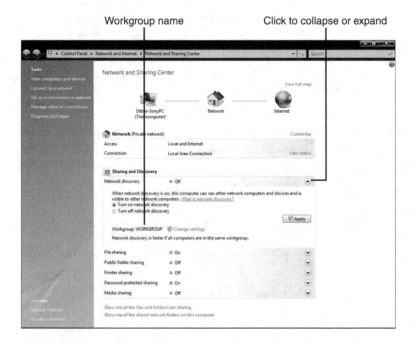

You might want to turn off network discovery on your laptop when you use it away from home. With network discovery off, your laptop can still access an Internet signal wirelessly but other computers on the network won't be able to see your computer.

After you turn on network sharing, the other computers on your network should be able to see your computer after a few seconds.

While you have your Network Discovery option open, check to see what workgroup your Vista computer is a member of. Workgroups are not the primary means of network access in Vista, but they were in versions of Windows through Windows XP. Because you might share a network connection with XP-based computers in your home or office, you might have to change the workgroup assignment of your Vista computer so that those XP computers can see your computer and share files and printers with it.

In Figure 36.4, the workgroup name is WORKGROUP, the default workgroup name. It's recommended that you change to a different workgroup name for security reasons just because changing from the common WORKGROUP name gives a hacker one more barrier of entry. To change that to the workgroup used by whatever XP-based computers you want to network to, click the Change Settings link to the right of the existing workgroup name, confirm your administrative privileges, and enter a new workgroup name. Click the Change button in the System Properties dialog box that opens, type a new workgroup name in the Workgroup text box (as shown in Figure 36.5), and close the dialog boxes. You must reboot your computer to apply the new workgroup name fully. After your computer restarts, your Vista machine will be a member of the same workgroup as your XP computers and they should be able to share files and printers.

To locate the name of a Windows XP's workgroup, right-click My Computer and select Properties to display the System Properties dialog box. Click the Computer Name tab. The workgroup name appears to the right of Workgroup in the center of the dialog box.

Vista's Network and Sharing Center won't always show an XP computer in the graphical network connection even if both it and your computer are members of the same workgroup. A workgroup enables the XP computer to see your computer, but the Network and Sharing Center is designed for Vista computers on your network. If XP computers are members of your Vista computer's workgroup, you can see them from an Explorer window (such as the one in Figure 36.6) when you click the Network folder to see all the computers and other networked devices with which you can share files and printers.

FIGURE 36.5
Set your Vista computer's workgroup name to the same name as your XP computers to share files and printers with those computers.

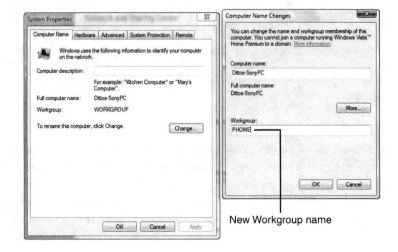

New Workgroup name

Mobile devices

FIGURE 36.6
Although the icons are the same as the Vista PCs, the computers named JAYNE-HP-PC and OFFICEDELL are not Vista-based computers. Because they're members of the same workgroup as the two Vista machines in the list, all four computers can share files and printers. The XP machines, however, don't appear in the Network and Sharing Center.

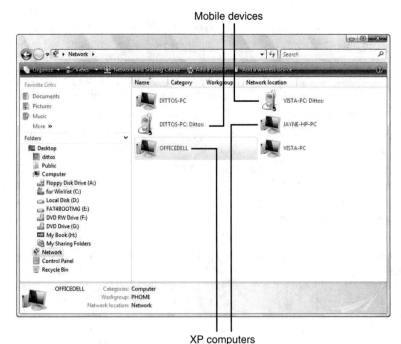

XP computers

> If a networked Vista computer doesn't show in your Network and Sharing Center map, or if an XP-based computer isn't shareable even if that XP machine shares the same workgroup name as your Vista computer, the computer that doesn't show up might have a firewall setting that blocks network access. Firewalls block and unblock local networks differently, so you have to check that computer's firewall settings and online help to learn how to unblock local area network access. In general, Vista's firewall allows local network connections through as long as you've turned on the Network Discovery option.

Did you Know?

Allow for File and Printer Sharing

You must allow file and printer sharing on any computer whose files or printers you want to share. To share your files, click to expand the File Sharing section of your Network and Sharing Center and click to select the option labeled Turn On File Sharing. Click Apply and Vista shares your computer's files as soon as you confirm your administrative privileges. Reverse this procedure if you want to turn off file sharing, as you might do if you're working in a public wireless area such as a coffee shop that offers Wi-Fi connections.

In a like manner, you can click to expand the Printer Sharing section of your Network and Sharing Center and click to select the Turn On Printer Sharing option. Click Apply and Vista shares any printer attached to your computer after you confirm your administrative privileges. Reverse this procedure if you want to stop sharing that computer's printer.

> If you have password protection turned on, as described in the "Password-Protecting Your Files and Printers" section later in this chapter, users on your network will be required to type a password anytime they request access to a file or printer on your computer.

Watch Out!

Working with Public Folders

A **Public folder** is one meant for sharing with others. You copy and move items to your Public folder when you want to make those items available to others.

> Only one Public folder exists on a Vista computer, no matter how many user accounts are set up to use that computer. Given the nature of the Public folder and its intended use as a shared folder, there is no reason to keep access from others on your computer from that folder. If you don't want to share a file, make sure that you never put that file in a Public folder. Every file in every Public folder is always available to everyone who has a user account on your computer. All network users might or might not have access to your Public folders depending on the file-sharing permissions discussed in the previous section.

Watch Out!

The Public folder contains the following subfolders:

- Public Documents
- Public Downloads
- Public Music
- Public Pictures
- Public Videos
- Recorded TV

You can create additional subfolders in the Public folder as well. The Public folder appears in your Explorer window in the left navigation pane, as Figure 36.7 shows.

FIGURE 36.7
Your computer's Public folder is always available in your Explorer window's left navigation pane.

Public folders

To control whether people on your network can access your computer's Public folders, click to the Public folder's Sharing Settings button to move to your Network and Sharing Center. Under the Public Folder Sharing option you have three choices depending on the level of Public folder access you want to grant:

- **Turn On Sharing So Anyone with Network Access Can Open Files**—Enables anyone with network access to your computer to access your Public folders and all contents within. Those users are limited to reading the files and folders (this includes copying from them), and cannot change or delete any contents of your Public folders.

▶ **Turn On Sharing So Anyone with Network Access Can Open, Change, and Create Files**—Enables anyone with network access to your computer to access your Public folders and all contents within. Those users may read the files and folders, delete files and folders, create new files and folders, and change the contents of the files and folders. In other words, they have the full access that users on your computer have to the Public folder stored there.

▶ **Turn Off Sharing**—Blocks access to your computer's Public folders to all users on your network. All users with accounts on your computer still have full access when they log in to their account.

Password-Protecting Your Files and Printers

When you password-protect your computer, anyone on your network who attempts to gain access to your shared files or shared printers won't be allowed access unless they have a user account on your computer. If they do, they must type the password when they want access or your computer will not allow file and printer sharing to take place.

To add the password requirement, click to expand the Password Protected Sharing section in your Network and Sharing Center. Click the Turn On Password Protected Sharing option and then click Apply. After Vista confirms your administrative privileges, only users who have a user account and password on your computer can access shared files and printers.

Sharing Media

The nice thing about networking Vista computers is the ease with which you can share media files among the machines. For example, if you network in a home environment, a user on another Vista computer in your home can start Media Player and access the music and videos on your machine. The access is limited to music, pictures, and videos, and the remote users only have read access. That is, the remote users cannot change them or delete the files unless they have full access to your files through the other file-sharing means described in the previous sections.

To turn on your computer's media-sharing capability, open your Network and Sharing Center, click to expand your Media Sharing section, and click the Change button to turn on the Media Sharing option. Vista displays the Media Sharing dialog box shown in Figure 36.8. Click the Share My Media option to allow others to access your media files.

FIGURE 36.8
You can allow other Vista users on your network to access your pictures, music, and videos.

By the Way

> The media files stream from your computer to your remote users' computers. **Streaming** means that when someone begins to play a video from your computer, the entire video file doesn't have to travel over the network before that user can begin watching the file; instead, once enough of the video travels to the user's computer, the video begins to play while the rest of the video arrives.

Did you Know?

> If anyone on your network uses an Xbox 360 or other digital media player, they can access your media as well. This enables you to send music and video throughout your home or office to other rooms that have an Xbox 360 or perhaps to your TV or home theater to which you've connected an Xbox 360.

After you verify that you want to turn on media sharing, Vista displays the Media Sharing dialog box (shown in Figure 36.9) that enables you to decide which Vista-based computers on your network can access your media files. In Figure 36.9, only one other computer is a Vista computer and it doesn't currently have access to the computer's media files because the option is turned off. To allow the computer named dittos-pc as well as other users with user accounts on the current computer to access the media files, you need to give those machines specific access.

By the Way

> It might seem as though you must turn on media sharing twice: once from your Network and Sharing Center (refer to Figure 36.8) and once more from the Media Sharing dialog box in Figure 36.9. Actually, when you initially turn on media sharing from the Network and Sharing Center you're giving your computer permission to share files, but you haven't specified exactly *which* computers and users on your networks will have access to the media. It's only when you select one or more computers and users from the Media Sharing dialog box (see Figure 36.9) that media sharing is actually available to those users and computers. This way, you can limit which computers have access if your network includes multiple Vista computers.

Currently not allowed to see media
Currently allowed to see media

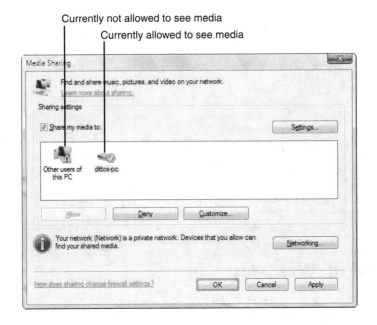

FIGURE 36.9
Select the com-
puters and
users connect-
ed to your
machine to
which you want
to offer media
files and click
Allow.

Click each computer in the Media Sharing dialog box you want to give media access to and then click the Allow button. The yellow exclamation point on those users or that computer changes to a green check mark, indicating that computer now has access to your media.

> While still inside the Media Sharing dialog box, if you click to select a networked computer and then click the Customize button, Figure 36.10's Media Sharing Customize window opens. Here you can specify more detailed options for this network computer's sharing of your media files. For example, you can limit the content that the computer can play from your machine by parental rating or media type.

Did you Know?

The networked computer now has only to open its Media Player program to access the shared content. In Windows Media Player, this means that the networked computer user clicks the arrow below the toolbar's Library button, selects Media Sharing, clicks to select the Find Media That Others Are Sharing option, and clicks OK. The user now has access on that computer to all media given from the source machine. Check the left navigation pane in the networked computer's Windows Media Player and the source computer's name appears; you can click the name to see all its allowed media files.

FIGURE 36.10
You can narrow the kinds of media another computer can access by putting limits based on media type, star ratings, or parental control ratings.

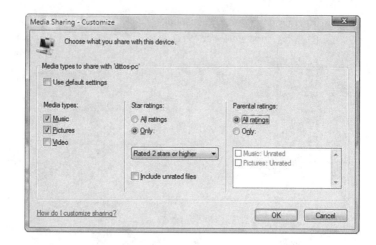

Chapter Wrap-Up

This chapter took you on a brief history of networking so that you could gain a little background to the world of networking. Network technology has come a long way in speed increases and cost decreases. The true winners in the network advances are small office and home-based PC users. Networks used to be synonymous with expensive technology that was difficult to use, hard to install, and costly to maintain.

All that has changed, and Vista really goes above and beyond the call of duty by putting your file and printer sharing setup in the Network and Sharing Center. You can easily specify who has access to what on your computer and a graphical map always lets you know how your own computer connects to the network. Other computers and users can access your digital pictures, music, and video with ease after you allow media sharing.

It's obvious that networks are now popular for two reasons: Users of multiple machines can share files and printers, and file integrity is maintained when only one disk keeps the data used by several PCs. Fortunately, Vista takes much of the mystery out of the software side of networking setup, management, and use.

In the next chapter, you'll learn how to use your computer to explore the largest network in the world: the Internet. Although you've almost surely used the Internet before, and you might be a pro at it, Windows Vista brings some new features to the Internet user's world that Windows XP didn't offer.

CHAPTER 37

Exploring the Internet with Vista and Internet Explorer

In This Chapter:

- ▶ See Vista's full support for browsing the Web
- ▶ Master Internet basics if you're new
- ▶ Use Internet Explorer's tabbed browsing window to keep track of multiple web pages
- ▶ Maximize your use of Internet Explorer's Favorites Center
- ▶ Add RSS feeds to Internet Explorer
- ▶ Manage your web-browsing history
- ▶ Change Internet Explorer settings to match the way you like to surf the Web

If you've used the Internet before, you've probably used Microsoft's Internet Explorer (IE) to surf the Web. IE has a huge market share with far more users than any other web browser.

However, IE's massive market share has dwindled somewhat in the past few years because Microsoft upgraded IE when security holes were found but for hardly any other reason. Several browser vendors, most notably Firefox (www.firefox.com), began adding features, some of which left IE in the dust. As much as 10% of Microsoft's browser market share has gone to Firefox and the trend is continuing.

Internet Explorer 7, the version that comes with Vista, might change that. For the first time in a decade, Microsoft worked to add features to IE to bring it into the new millennium. Some say that IE 7's features are just playing catch-up with Firefox and that isn't necessarily wrong on all fronts. IE 7 includes many features that have been standard in competing browsers for a long time, but IE 7 is the first browser to take advantage of Vista's Aero user interface and has a few surprises of its own, as you'll see in this chapter.

> Internet Explorer is available as a download for users of Windows XP. If you have a computer or two that you haven't yet upgraded to Vista, you can get most of the functionality of Vista's IE 7 by downloading the update from www.Microsoft.com/downloads.

The Internet and Vista

In today's world, the Internet is a much larger part of computer users' lives than ever before. In designing Windows Vista, Microsoft kept the Internet firmly in mind; the browser concept runs throughout Windows and you can access the Internet or your desktop from almost anywhere in Windows. For example, you can directly access the Internet from within the Windows Explorer window without first opening Internet Explorer.

> To jump to an Internet page directly from any Windows Explorer window, press Alt+D or click the Address bar at the top of the Explorer window and type a complete web address such as http://www.msn.com; Internet Explorer automatically opens to that web page and your Explorer window also stays open so that you can move between the windows.

> Surprisingly, the Address bar is not on your Windows Vista taskbar automatically unless you upgraded from an XP system that had the Address bar there, but you can easily add it. Doing so gives you the ability to type a web address anytime, no matter what else you're doing, without having to start Internet Explorer first. Right-click on a blank area of your taskbar, select Toolbars, Address to place the Address bar there. Type any web address and press Enter and Vista opens that web page as Figure 37.1 shows.

Although you can access the Internet throughout many areas of Vista, you'll probably access the Internet primarily from within Internet Explorer (if you're not using a competing browser). If you surf the Web a lot, you'll probably keep at least one IE window open so that you can go to it and check the Web when you need to.

> If you do enjoy a competing browser such as Firefox, you should look at Vista's Internet Explorer to see whether it now suits your needs. Some websites still work best with IE; if IE now has all the features you became used to, it might be time to switch back.

Typed web address

FIGURE 37.1
An Address bar on your Vista taskbar enables you to access a web page without starting Internet Explorer first.

The World's Shortest Internet Introduction

The vast majority of readers won't need an introduction to the Internet. If you've used the Internet for web browsing, even if you still consider yourself a novice, you can safely skim this section.

If you haven't gotten on the Internet before, but want to, this section will give you a brief background so you'll know what to expect. Don't feel bad. As unlikely as it might seem, the majority of people in the world still have *not* used the Internet to explore web pages and download content. You don't need an in-depth background to get up to speed quickly.

The Internet is a worldwide system of interconnected computers. Whereas your desktop computer is a standalone machine that might be connected to one or more other computers in your home or office in a networked system, the Internet is a worldwide online network of computers connected to computers through modems and other kinds of online connections. Hardly anyone understands the entire Internet because it is not one system but a conglomeration of systems. The Internet is so vast that nobody could access all of its information.

> No central Internet computer exists. The Internet is a system of connected computers. *Internet* is the term given to the entire system.

The Internet's fast growth almost caused its downfall. How does anyone access or find information on the Internet? Fortunately, Internet technicians began standardizing Internet information when it became apparent that the Internet was quickly growing and becoming a major information provider. A standard for the language behind web pages called *HTML* (for HyperText Markup Language) was quickly adopted and *search engines* (web sites that locate information for you) such as Yahoo.com and Google began appearing. With the Windows Vista interface now assisting Internet Explorer's search tools, locating Internet information is simpler today than ever.

> Do not confuse Internet Explorer with Windows Explorer. Internet Explorer is your Internet browser, and Windows Explorer enables you to view and manage your files. Chapter 8, "Mastering Vista's Explorer Windows," describes Windows Explorer in more detail.

The WWW: World Wide Web

The *WWW*, the *World Wide Web*, or just the *Web*, is a collection of Internet pages of information. Web pages can contain text, graphics, sound, and video. Figure 37.2 shows a sample web page. As you can see, the web page's graphics and text organize information into a magazine-like, readable, and appealing format.

Generally, a website contains more information than fits easily on a single web page. Therefore, many web pages contain links to several additional extended pages, as well as other linked web pages that might relate to the original topic. The first page you view is the website's home page. From there, you can view other pages of information.

Each web page has a unique location that includes the source computer and the page's location on that computer. The Internet has standardized web page locations with a series of addresses called **URLs**, or **uniform resource locator** addresses. You can view any web page if you know its URL. And its URL, or web address, is often a name that somewhat corresponds to the content, such as www.microsoft.com and www.ibm.com. If you do not know the URL, the Internet's search engines help you locate information.

Web address entry/display

Web page display are

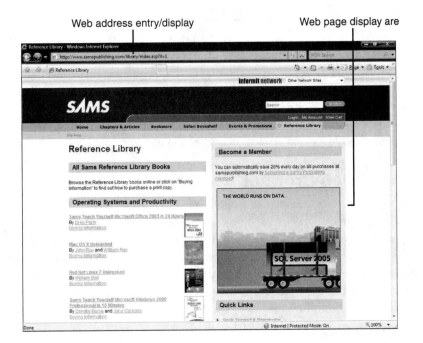

FIGURE 37.2
Web pages pro-
vide Internet
information in a
nice format.

Surely you've run across computer addresses that look like this: www.microsoft.com
and www.ebay.com. Those addresses are the URLs that access the web pages. These
two happen to be the URLs for Microsoft Corporation and an online auction house,
respectively.

You will often see http:// before a web address. When you type a web address in
Internet Explorer, your taskbar's Address bar, or in most places where a web
address is acceptable, the http:// is usually optional. Most of the time, even the
www is optional before a web address. Typing `http://www.microsoft.com` and
typing `microsoft.com` into an Address bar such as appears at the top of Internet
Explorer takes you to the same web page: Microsoft Corporation's home page.

Your Internet Provider

Before you can access the Internet's web pages, you need to get Internet access
through an **ISP**, or **Internet service provider**. The ISP provides the Internet signal
that goes in and out of your home or office. You've probably heard of such national
ISPs as America Online (AOL) and Microsoft Network (MSN). Many people can
access the Internet through a local Internet provider, such as your local cable or
phone company. Whichever provider you use, your provider will tell you how to set
up Internet Explorer to access the Internet.

You can physically access the Internet in several ways. If you use a phone line and phone modem to dial in to the Internet, your dial-up connection will work, but will not offer the benefits that a high-speed, always-on Internet service such as DSL (available through most phone companies) or a cable modem (available through most cable television companies) provides. If you have no DSL or cable modem service, you might want to check out a satellite Internet service that provides most of the advantages of a higher-speed connection and is available in rural and other areas where DSL or cable modem service isn't yet available.

Using a Web Browser

Before you can access and view web information, you need a program that can display web page information, including text, graphics, audio, and video. The program you need is a **web browser**—or just a **browser**. As stated earlier in this chapter, Internet Explorer is the web browser that comes with Vista and has been a part of Windows operating systems for many years. The web pages in Figure 37.2 use Internet Explorer. Given that IE comes with Vista, the rest of this chapter uses IE exclusively in figures that show web pages.

Internet Explorer is easy to start. You literally can access the Internet with one or two clicks by running Internet Explorer. Just click the Vista taskbar button that has an icon with a blue letter *e* on it. You can also display the Windows Start menu and select Internet Explorer.

When you first start IE, a web page appears and it might or might not be what you want to see. IE has to assume some web page because opening to a blank screen wouldn't be useful. Generally, default Vista machines open to Microsoft.com or perhaps Live.com, which is part of Microsoft's Internet service provider's home page.

By the Way

> Both websites and your web browser have a designated page known as the *home page*. A website's **home page** is the first page you view when you go to the website's base web address (such as www.microsoft.com), but *your* home page is the first page that your web browser displays when you start your web browser. Actually, today's web browsers allow for more than one home page because they support **tabbed browsing**: Multiple web pages appear, and you can view any one of them by clicking the appropriate tab. We'll talk about tabbed browsing later in this chapter.

At any time during your Internet browsing, you can return to Internet Explorer's home page by clicking the Home button on the toolbar toward the top of the IE window. You can change your browser's home page. Just browse to the web page you want to see every time you start IE, click the arrow to the right of the Home button, select Add or Change Home Page, and click to select the Use This Webpage as Your Only Home Page option if you want a single home page to appear when you start IE. If you want to add the page to your multiple home pages that appear, instead select the labeled Add This Webpage to Your Home Page Tabs option, which is available by clicking the appropriate tabs across the top of the Internet Explorer window.

Figure 37.3 shows an Internet Explorer window with four pages loaded. Only one (the eBay-related page in this case) can appear at one time in IE's window, but by clicking any of the four tabs, you can change to one of those web pages.

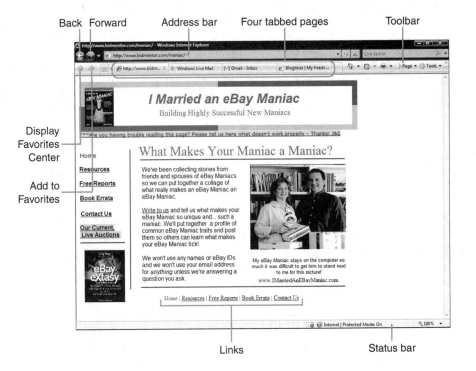

Back · Forward · Address bar · Four tabbed pages · Toolbar

Display Favorites Center

Add to Favorites

Links · Status bar

FIGURE 37.3
Four web pages are loaded in one Internet Explorer window.

Before Internet Explorer 7 arrived, tabbed browsing was available in other web browsers, but not IE. The rest of this chapter discusses tabbed browsing in more detail. The advantage of tabbed browsing is that IE loads all pages of all your tabs and makes that data available. Before IE 7, you would have to load four web pages manually, in four separate Internet Explorer windows, if you wanted to switch among four web pages.

Surfing the Internet

Remember that the Web is a collection of interconnected web pages. Almost every web page contains links to other sites. These links (also called *hot links*, *hypertext links*, and *hyperlinks*) are usually underlined. You can locate these links by moving your mouse cursor over the underlined description. If the mouse cursor changes to a hand, you can click the hand to move to that page. After a brief pause, your web browser displays the page.

Did you Know?

A link is nothing more than a URL address to another website. The link often displays a description and not a technical URL address. (As you move your mouse cursor over a link, your web browser's status bar displays the actual URL address to the link.) Therefore, you can traverse related web pages without worrying about addresses; just click link descriptions to move to those sites.

Suppose that you view the home page of your financial broker. The page might include links to other related pages, such as stock quotation pages, company financial informational pages, and order-entry pages in which you can enter your own stock purchase requests.

One of the most useful features of Internet Explorer and every other web browser is the capability to return to sites you've visited, both in the current session and in former sessions. The Back button in the upper-left corner returns you to a page you just visited, and you can keep clicking the Back button to return to pages you visited during this session. The Forward toolbar button returns you to pages from which you backed up. In addition to the Back and Forward buttons, you can click the Address drop-down list box to see a list of URL addresses you've visited.

If you know the address of a website you want to view, you can type the site's address directly in IE's Address bar. When you press Enter or click the blue arrows to the right of the web address, Internet Explorer takes you to that site and displays the web page. In addition, from the Start menu, you can enter a URL in the Run dialog box (available by pressing Windows+R) to see any page on the Web. If you want to return to your original home page, click the toolbar's Home button.

By the Way

You might not feel like a web pro after this brief introduction, but it's all you really need to begin. You can now follow the rest of this chapter and understand most or all of what it contains even if you are a newcomer to the Internet.

Mastering IE's New Features

As explained earlier in this chapter, Internet Explorer 7 is a vast improvement over the versions of IE that came before. Several features now in IE have been around in some form with other, competing web browsers. Some of the features are new to IE, however. The rest of this chapter explores IE's new features and shows you ways to take advantage of them.

Tabbed Browsing

When you open IE, you'll see that the web page has a tab at the top of it with a description of that page. By opening a series of additional web pages, each with its own tab, inside your single Internet Explorer window, IE loads each page all at once. You then can switch among the open web pages just by clicking the tab of the page you want to see. To open a page in a new tab, you can

▶ Click the small, blank tab next to the rightmost web page on your screen; IE opens a blank page for that tab and you can type a web address in the Address bar you want to use for that new tabbed web page. IE loads the web page and adds a new blank tab for the next tabbed web page you might want to add to the current group of tabbed web pages.

▶ Right-click over any web page's link and select Open in New Tab. In earlier IE versions, you might right-click and select Open in New Window to open a separate Internet Explorer window. The Open in New Window option still resides on a link's right-click menu, but you'll now select to open the page in a new tabbed page more often so that you can move between your web pages more easily just by clicking the tabs.

To close a tabbed web page, you click the tab to display that page, and then click the X (a small Close Window button) on that page's tab to close the page and eliminate its tab from view. You can also right-click the web page's tab and select Close to close its tabbed page without first displaying the menu.

To close all tabbed pages *except* the one currently showing, right-click any tab description and select Close Other Tabs.

Figure 37.4 shows an IE window with four tabbed pages. You can change to a different open web page by clicking its tab or close a tabbed page by clicking its Close button.

FIGURE 37.4
The web page tabs across the top of Internet Explorer make it simple to move from one open page to another open page.

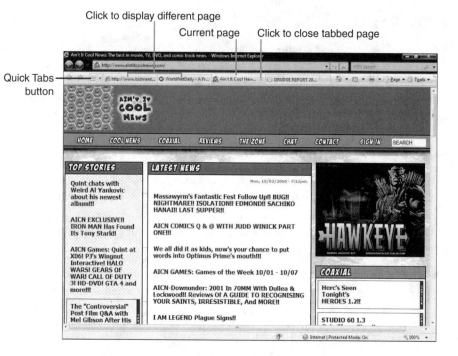

Click to display different page

Current page   Click to close tabbed page

Quick Tabs button

You can change the order of the tabbed pages that appear in your Internet Explorer. The default order in which the pages appear is the order in which you open them, but you can drag a tab to a different location to reorder them.

Internet Explorer even lets you see thumbnail images of all your open tabbed web pages. Click the Quick Tabs button and IE shows a thumbnail image of each page in a single window such as the one in Figure 37.5. You can click on any thumbnail to open that page in a full-sized, tabbed IE window.

The thumbnails take full advantage of the Aero user interface if you have the necessary hardware to run Aero. If a web page updates in real time, its thumbnail image in the Quick Tabs view also changes.

Pres Esc or click any thumbnail to leave the Quick Tabs view and return to a full-size web page view of your tabbed pages.

Tab list

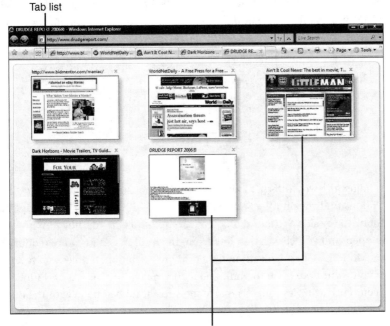

Click to view full size

FIGURE 37.5
The Quick Tabs
view gives you a
bird's-eye view
of every tabbed
web page you
currently have
open.

The Quick Tabs view is useful when you have several tabbed web pages open in your browser because the tabs aren't always wide enough to display the web pages' full description. The Quick Tabs view enables you to know what each open site contains and lets you quickly move between them. From the regular full-size web page view, you can also click the Tab List button to drop down a list of your open websites and click to select the one whose description matches the site you want to view.

Did you Know?

Tabbed, open web pages require an extra decision on your part when you click IE's Close button to close the web browser. When you click the Close button in the browser's upper-right corner, IE displays a dialog box that asks whether you want to close all the open tabs, as in Figure 37.6's window.

If you want to close all open tabbed pages now, click the Close Tabs button. If you want to close all tabbed pages every time you click IE's Close button, you can click to select the Do Not Show Me This Dialog Again option and IE won't ever ask again whether you want to close all the tabs; instead, IE will close them all without asking.

If you meant to close only the current open tabbed page, click Cancel and close the page by clicking its tab's Close button (the X next to the description in the tab).

FIGURE 37.6
Tabbed browsing offers more choices but also requires that you make more decisions.

You can adjust the way Internet Explorer handles tabbed web pages by selecting Tools, Options and clicking the Settings button in the Tabs section to display Figure 37.7's Tabbed Browsing Settings dialog box. For example, if you have Internet Explorer open and you click a web link from an email message you're reading in Windows Mail, the Open Links from Other Programs option enables you to specify whether you want IE to open the link's page in a new IE window, a new tabbed window in your current IE session, or replace the current tabbed page with the link's web page when it displays.

To display Internet Explorer's menu—the one you might be familiar with from all the previous IE versions—press Alt. The expected File, Edit, View, and other options appear above your web page viewing area. Press Alt again to hide the menu.

Working with the Favorites Center

In IE 7, the Favorites folder that appeared in previous versions is now the Favorites Center. If you find a location you really like and want to return to, save it in Internet Explorer's Favorites Center. For example, perhaps you run across a site that discusses your favorite television show and you want to return to that site again quickly. Just click the Add to Favorites button, confirm that you want to add the page to your Favorites selection, type an optional description, and click Add. When you want to see one of your favorite websites, click the Favorites button to display your Favorites Center to the left of your web page viewing area.

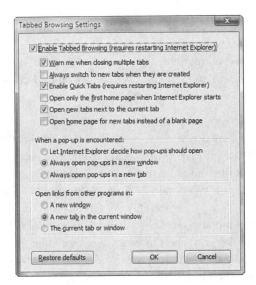

FIGURE 37.7
You can adjust the decisions and settings that IE makes when you work with tabbed web pages.

Figure 37.8 shows the Favorites Center. The Favorites Center contains a list of folders that are preinstalled as Internet Explorer favorites, followed by a few websites that the user has added to the Favorites Center.

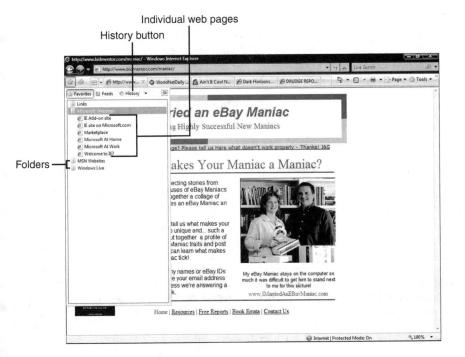

FIGURE 37.8
Store websites in your Favorites Center so that you can return to them in the future without having to hunt for them or type their web addresses.

You can add to your Favorites Center as follows:

▶ **Saved individual web pages**—You can add web pages, usually the home pages of websites you routinely visit, to your Favorites Center. To delete a site from your Favorites Center, right-click an entry and select Delete. You can also delete Favorites Center folders the same way.

▶ **Groups of web pages**—If you have several web pages open in IE with each page tabbed for easy access, you can store all the currently tabbed pages in your Favorites Center. To do this, open all the tabbed pages you want to save as a group, click the Add to Favorites button, select Add Tab group to Favorites, and type a description in the Add Group to Favorites dialog box shown in Figure 37.9. When you click Add, IE saves all the currently open tabbed pages' web addresses in their own folder and the folder has the name you gave it. The folder appears in your Favorites Center. By creating a folder this way, you store a collection of related web pages. For example, you could open all the financial websites you visit often, with each site open in its own tabbed web page, and save them as a group that you name Financial. To view the websites, you open your Favorites Center, click to expand the Financial folder, and click to display the web page or pages that you want to view from the folder.

FIGURE 37.9
Describe the group of tabbed web pages that you want to save as a new Favorites Center folder.

See More or See Less

Using a combination of your keyboard's Ctrl key and your mouse's (or trackball's) scroll wheel, you can scroll in or out of any web page. Being able to zoom out to see from afar is useful if you want to get an idea of what the full page contains, such as how much text and graphics it has, like the zoomed-out view in Figure 37.10.

If you design web pages, being able to zoom out to see how balanced your text and graphics are helps you see whether the overall design is appropriate.

FIGURE 37.10
Hold Ctrl and move your mouse's scroll wheel backward (toward you) to zoom out of a web page.

To reverse the process, hold Ctrl and move your mouse's scroll wheel toward your screen to zoom into a web page and see a close-up of your web page (as you might want to do if you want to read some small print or see a close-up of a picture). Figure 37.11 shows Figure 37.10's web page up close. You can use the scrollbars to the right and below a web page that you zoom into to see text not currently shown in the screen.

If the Ctrl+mouse wheel scroll is awkward for you, click the arrow to the right of the Page button on your IE 7 toolbar and select Zoom to increase or decrease the amount of view you are zoomed in to. You can also click your Status bar's Zoom button or the arrow to the right of the Status bar's Zoom button to change the amount of zoom you want to use.

By the Way

The F11 key changes your browser to a full-screen view where you see no window border, no toolbar, no menu, and no tabs for other open web pages. You see only the Status bar at the bottom of your screen. To return to the regular IE 7 view, press F11 once again and the border, toolbar, and other extra items reappear.

Did you Know?

FIGURE 37.11
Hold Ctrl and
move your
mouse's scroll
wheel away
from you to
zoom in on a
web page and
see its text and
graphics up
close.

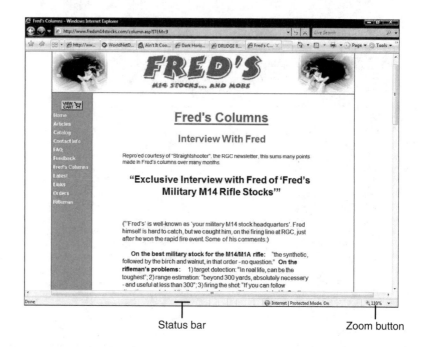

Status bar   Zoom button

Your Browsing History

To see all the pages you've visited recently, click your Favorites Center History button. The History button opens a list of time ranges such as 3 Weeks Ago, 2 Weeks
Ago, Last Week, and Today. Clicking any of these entries opens a list of all web
pages you visited during that time in alphabetical order. After a list of pages
appears in the History panel, click any page to open that page in a new tabbed IE
window.

You can also browse your history of web page visits by date, by most visited, or in
the order you visited them today by clicking the arrow to the right of your History
button, as Figure 37.12 shows.

By the
Way

Your Favorites page content won't be the same as your History. Your History
entries update over time as you visit websites, keeping at most three weeks'
worth of visited site addresses. Your Favorites Center tracks only websites you
place there.

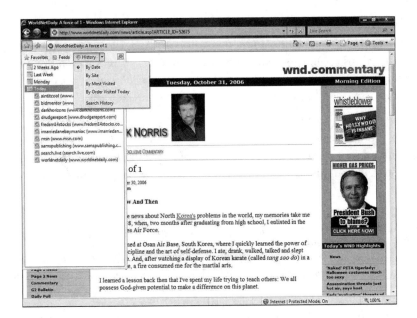

FIGURE 37.12
View any web page you've visited in the past month.

Cleaning Up Internet Explorer

To clear your history, select Delete Browsing History from your Internet Explorer's Tools menu. IE displays the Delete Browsing History dialog box shown in Figure 37.13. Obviously, you can clear far more than your browsing history from the Delete Browsing History dialog box.

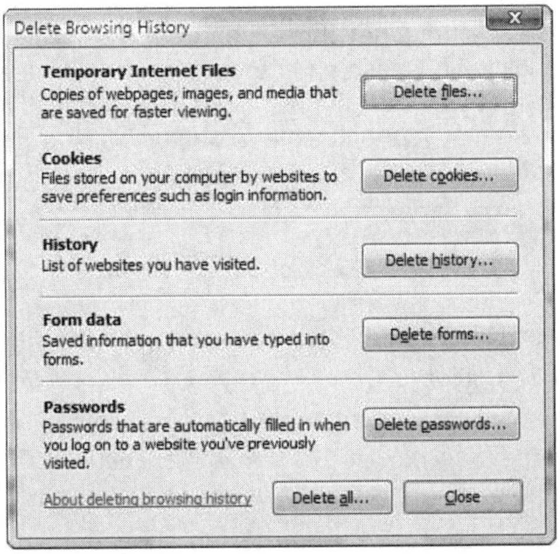

FIGURE 37.13
Internet Explorer offers to clean all your web-browsing tracks.

Deleting Temporary Internet Files

Clicking the Delete Files button in the Temporary Internet Files section deletes—after you confirm this is what you want to do—all temporary IE information stored on your computer. These temporary files are copies of web pages, pictures, audio, and video clips that IE still has saved from your recent web page visits.

To speed your Internet browsing experience, IE saves this kind of information in a **cache** (an area on your disk reserved for such information). If you revisit a web page that has not changed since your most recent visit, it's far faster for IE to load the page from your disk drive than to load the same web page from the Internet again.

Depending on your Internet Explorer settings, IE might load a page from your cache even when a fresher version appears on the Internet. If you think the page has changed from the older version you're viewing, press F5 to force IE to reload the page from the Web. Selecting Tools, Internet Options, clicking the General tab, and clicking the Settings button enables you to change how often you want Internet Explorer to load a fresh web page and its images and media content. In general, if you have a quick Internet connection, selecting the Every Time I Visit the Webpage ensures that every page you visit will be loaded fresh.

Did you Know?

Before leaving on an airplane ride, if you use your laptop to visit several web pages using your airport's wireless signal or before you leave home and then change your IE Temporary Internet Files setting to never load, you will be able to start IE and revisit those pages and thoroughly read them during your in-flight travel. IE goes to the cache and does not attempt to reload them from the Internet because you won't have an Internet connection on the airplane. (Some airlines are testing the possibility of making an Internet signal available to its passengers.) When you arrive at your destination, change the setting back to refresh web pages from the Web so that your subsequent web-browsing experience displays fresh content again.

Deleting Cookies

A **cookie** is a file that websites might store on your computer when you visit them. Many times a cookie is a great tool that helps you. For example, if you've ordered from Amazon.com in the past, when you visit Amazon.com again, the site knows who you are. This is due to a cookie that Amazon placed there in the past. Because IE looks at the cookie, you don't have to re-enter your login ID or email, only a password to confirm that you are who Amazon thinks you are and you're on your way.

Some users don't like cookies placed on their computer. Search engines can track your web-searching activities by placing cookies on your computer every time you perform a search. Often, the search engines use this data to offer products or sites that you might also be interested in. Websites can generate a profile of your likes by what you've done before.

If you don't want cookies stored on your computer, click the Delete Cookies button on the Delete Browsing History dialog box. After confirming the deletion, IE removes all cookies from your computer.

Deleting Your Website History

To delete all websites stored in your History folder, click the Delete History button. After confirming the deletion, Internet Explorer erases all your web-browsing history. When you click to open your Favorites Center, you won't see a History button until you've visited one or more web pages and started a new web-browsing history.

As you might expect, you can control whether IE stores a history of your web page visits and, if so, how much history is stored. Select Tools, Internet Options to open the Internet Options window and click the Browsing History section's Settings button to open Figure 37.14's Temporary Internet Files and History Settings window. Click the scroll button on the Days to Keep Pages in History option to increase or decrease the number of days IE is to track your browsing history.

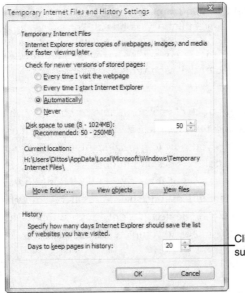

FIGURE 37.14
Specify how much, if any, web-browsing history you want Internet Explorer to track as you surf the Web.

Click to add or subtract from your history

Deleting Your Form Data

As you surf the Web, you'll fill out various forms along the way. Perhaps you'll sign up for a free emailed newsletter, or order supplies, or place an eBay auction bid. As you fill out forms, Internet Explorer keeps track of the entries you make in an effort to make filling out subsequent forms easier. For example, if you sign up for a new newsletter and enter your first name and last name on the sign-up form, IE automatically fills in your first name and last name the next time a website requests that information.

Selecting the Delete Forms button from the Delete Browsing History dialog box removes all your stored form data, requiring you to re-enter any of those values the next time you have to fill out a web form.

Internet Explorer can store the usernames and passwords you enter on forms. This is a great time-saving tool because you don't have to re-enter that data every time you revisit a site that requires it. In addition, you don't have to remember every password you save for every site you visit. Unfortunately, this poses a problem if you are using a shared computer, as might be the case at work or in an Internet cafe somewhere. At work, you should have your own user account and log in and out when you use the computer. Doing so keeps your user data protected because IE keeps form data separate for each user, but you always risk a security breach if you walk away from your computer with your account still active. When you share a computer with someone else, especially if you're using someone else's computer, as might be the case in a public Internet cafe or library, you should ensure that the AutoComplete settings have the usernames and passwords turned off. You might not always be able to access the AutoComplete Settings dialog box if the computer is set to disallow access to such system settings, as many public computers are, so you should be extra careful when entering such data on a computer that isn't yours.

Internet Explorer keeps track of your form data as part of its AutoComplete feature. **AutoComplete** is a way that IE watches what you type, such as a web address or form data, and if it sees you start to type something similar to other similar items, it displays a list of potential matches of that data. For example, in Figure 37.15, the user is starting to type SamsPublishing.com in IE's Address bar. Because the user visited SamsPublishing.com at least once before, IE offers that web address. Instead of typing the full web address, the user has only to press the Down Arrow or click the offered address with the mouse to complete the address.

FIGURE 37.15
Internet Explorer completes web addresses for sites you've visited before or saved to your Favorites Center.

If the site is a location you've visited in the past and saved in your Favorites Center, IE goes one step further and offers the site by the description you gave it instead of the sometimes-more obscure web address. Figure 37.15 shows Sams Publishing as one of the AutoComplete options because *Sams Publishing* is a description in that user's Favorites Center. If Sams Publishing didn't appear in the Favorites Center, AutoComplete would offer the full web address http://www.samspublishing.com as one of the possible websites to visit.

If a website follows the common home page pattern of http://www.*HomePage*.com, you can type only the *HomePage* portion in IE's Address bar and press Ctrl+Enter. IE fills in the rest. For example, if you type ebay and press Ctrl+Enter, IE changes the Address bar to http://www.ebay.com.

Did you Know?

You can erase the form and other AutoComplete data that IE stores by selecting Tools, Internet Options and clicking the Content tab. Click the Settings button in the AutoComplete section to display the AutoComplete Settings dialog box shown in Figure 37.16. There you specify exactly what IE is to keep track of. You can specify that you want IE to save web addresses, form data, and your username and passwords so that you don't have to re-enter those the next time you're prompted for them.

FIGURE 37.16
Tell Internet
Explorer
exactly which
AutoComplete
items you want
tracked.

You'll see on the Delete Browsing History that you can click a Delete Passwords button to erase all passwords currently stored in your account's AutoComplete history.
Storing usernames but not passwords is a safer alternative to storing both, while still
keeping your other AutoComplete information available to speed data entry on the
web pages you visit. Your usernames and web page AutoComplete entries remain,
but nobody can have access to your secure web accounts because your password
won't automatically appear when requested if you delete your passwords.

Delete your entire browsing history in one step by clicking the Delete Browsing
History's Delete All button.

Print Complete Web Pages

One welcome feature to Internet Explorer 7 is its capability to print entire web
pages. Previous versions often cut off the right side of a web page because of the
way IE printed the page. Now, when you select File, Print (or click the Print button
on the toolbar), click your Preferences button. An option that almost goes unnoticed
is the Scale to Fit option shown in Figure 37.17, clicked by default, that you select
when you click to select the Print Document On option.

Search the Web from Within Internet Explorer

In the upper-right corner of IE is a Search box much like the Search boxes you see
throughout Vista. Unfortunately, the Search box doesn't act like the other Vista
Search boxes; you cannot perform an incremental search. When you start typing
Sams Publishing, no AutoComplete entry appears and no incremental search of
the Web begins. The search of what you type starts only when you press Enter or
click the Search button (with the magnifying glass icon) that appears to the right of
the Search box.

Shrinks web page to fit paper

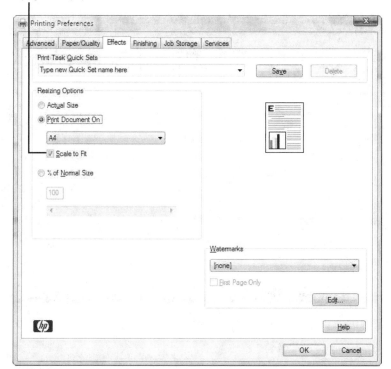

FIGURE 37.17
Internet Explorer shrinks the web page enough to fit fully on a page so that the right margin on web pages you print is no longer left off the printout.

Internet Explorer uses Live Search by default to locate your search term. This means that the search results appear on Microsoft's Live Search web page, shown in Figure 37.18. Clicking one of the links on the search results page takes you to that page.

> If you click the arrow to the right of the search button instead of clicking the Search button, three options appear. The Find on This Page option searches only the web page you're currently viewing for your search term. This is handy when you're looking at a long web page for specific information. (Ctrl+F is a shortcut key to find specific data on the current page.)

Did you Know?

To change your browser's default search engine, click the arrow to the right of the search box and select Find More Providers. IE opens a web page with several search engines on the Internet from which you can select. Figure 37.19 shows such a page of search providers.

FIGURE 37.18
Internet
Explorer uses
your default
search engine
to locate your
search term on
the Internet.

Search term

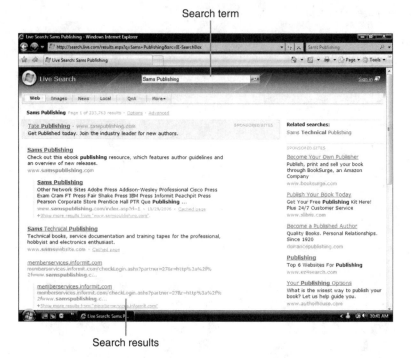

Search results

Click to add another provider

Only provider at first

FIGURE 37.19
You can add
more search
providers to
your Search box
list of search
engines.

You're not limited to only one of the providers. Click a search engine, such as Google, and after Microsoft confirms that you want to add Google as one of your browser's search providers, it appears as one of your search providers when you type a term in the Search box and click the Search box's down arrow to select the provider you want to use for your search.

To change the default search engine, click to select the Search box's Change Search Defaults option, click to select the search provider in your list that you want to make the default search provider when you search with IE, and click the Set Default button. Then click OK to set the new search engine as your primary, default search provider in Internet Explorer.

Guarding Against Pop-Ups

Since version 6, Internet Explorer has offered the capability to hide pop-up windows. A **pop-up window** is an extra, usually smaller window that appears when you visit a website. A pop-up window typically displays an ad and can appear *under* (in spite of its name) your open web page, so you don't see it until you close the original page that triggered its appearance.

By default, Internet Explorer blocks such pop-up windows. If a website triggers such a window, your IE Information bar (a yellow bar that appears below your web page tabs) lets you know what happened and gives you a choice of whether you want the blocked pop-up window to appear. When the Information bar appears, you'll hear a beep as an audible signal in case you didn't notice the bar itself.

To let you know more about the Information bar, when you first begin to use Internet Explorer 7 and surf to a web page with a pop-up window, IE displays a message box such as the one shown in Figure 37.20 that tells you that the Information bar appeared. You can click the Don't Show This Message Again option to hide the message window in the future so that only the Information bar appears.

By clicking the Information bar, a series of options drop down from which you can select how you want to handle the pop-up window. You can select Temporarily Allow Pop-Ups to see the pop-ups produced by the underlying website until you close that site. (The next time you visit that or any other site, the process begins anew if a pop-up is available.) If you select Always Allow Pop-Ups from This Site, IE stops blocking all pop-up windows from the current site from this point forward when you visit the site.

FIGURE 37.20
Internet
Explorer blocks
pop-up windows
unless you
specifically want
to see them.

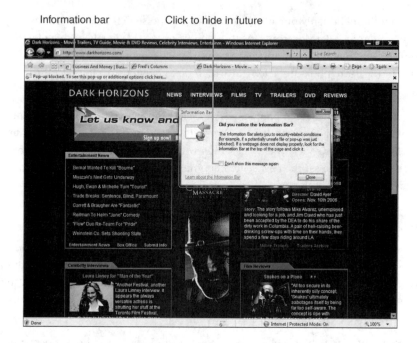

The Settings option displays options that enable you to determine the future settings
of IE's pop-up blocker. If you select Turn Off Pop-Up Blocker, IE stops blocking all
pop-up windows from all sites until you turn the pop-up blocker back on again. By
selecting Show Information Bar for Pop-Up (the default setting), the Information bar
appears at the top of your IE window every time a pop-up window attempts to open
as described here. The More Settings option opens Figure 37.21's Pop-Up Blocker
Settings dialog box. There you can add sites you trust and whose pop-up windows
you want to allow, and remove those sites you allowed in the past but no longer
want to allow. The options at the bottom of the dialog box further control what
occurs when a pop-up is available on a site you visit.

No pop-up blocking for these sites

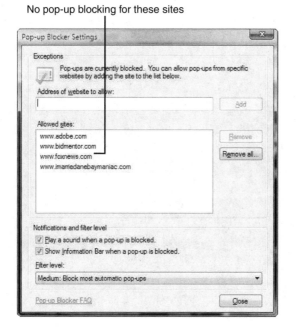

FIGURE 37.21
Add new websites to your allowed pop-up settings so that IE won't stop pop-ups from appearing when triggered by the websites in your Allowed Sites list.

Chapter Wrap-Up

This chapter explored Internet Explorer and showed you how to take advantage of IE and the new features that arrived with version 7 and Vista. It took Microsoft far too long to update IE's feature set, but with version 7, some users who switched to a different web browser will come back and use Internet Explorer. Its tabbed browsing windows, simplified interface, and easier-to-set options, such as deleting your browsing history, make for a pleasant web-browsing experience.

Microsoft added more than just whiz-bang features to Internet Explorer, however. As you learned in Chapter 27, "Managing Your Windows Security," Internet Explorer comes with anti-phishing technology and supports Vista parental controls that determine which websites certain family members can visit.

Internet Explorer also became up-to-date with its integrated support for RSS technology, as the next chapter will explain. With RSS, you can make website data come to you instead of having to check your favorite websites to see what new information is there.

CHAPTER 38

Staying in Touch with RSS and Instant Messaging

In This Chapter:

▶ Learn what RSS is really all about

▶ Subscribe to RSS feeds from within Internet Explorer

▶ View your feed details

▶ Use Instant Messaging to stay in touch

One of the features that web users have now used and relied on for several years is RSS, which stands for *Really Simple Syndication*, as you learned in Chapter 9, "Working with the Sidebar and Gadgets." Websites that support RSS make their content available to you and everyone else who has an RSS reader of some kind. The bottom-line advantage of RSS is that your favorite website's content, if that site supports RSS, will come to you instead of you having to go to the website to see whether anything is new. Although you can use a Sidebar gadget to access RSS feeds, Internet Explorer's RSS technology is simpler to use and puts your feeds where you're most likely to want them: in your web browser.

After you set up RSS, you can stay in touch with websites. To stay in touch with people, you can use instant messaging (IM). Instant messaging gives you instant, online communication to others that use IM and to whom you want to chat when the two of you are online. IM isn't specific to Windows Vista; any Windows version and any non-Windows operating system can use instant messaging. Instant messaging complements your online experience, and this chapter introduces you to IM technology in case you've been a holdout and didn't want to take the IM plunge before now.

All About Really Simple Syndication

As Chapter 9 explained, when you use RSS, you request that one or more websites send information to you. Internet Explorer offers a uniform RSS feed reader, and most people seem to like reading RSS feeds in IE as opposed to using the Sidebar and the RSS gadget.

In general, the RSS information sent to your computer comprise the newest entries on the site. For example, if you want to keep track of your favorite news site, and that website offers RSS support, you can subscribe to its RSS service.

By the
Way

> You don't have to worry about personal information being sent when you sub-scribe to a site's RSS feed. You don't have to give any user information or create a password to grab RSS feeds; you let Internet Explorer know you want to sub-scribe to a site's RSS feed and then IE takes over. It grabs those feeds and dis-plays the RSS data when the site makes the data available.

When IE begins to grab RSS feeds from the RSS-based websites you've subscribed to, those feeds might come to your computer in small snippets and not full articles, or the full articles may appear depending on the RSS service available at that site. For example, if a news site supports RSS feeds and you subscribe to that news site, the RSS data that comes to you is often nothing more than the headline of each new article that appears on the site. The headline is a link to the page with the full arti-cle. In a way, an RSS feed is a synopsis of something more detailed that you can go to if you want to see more details.

Learning Whether a Site Supports RSS Feeds

If you want to know whether a site offers RSS subscriptions, visit that site and look at Internet Explorer's toolbar. Your IE toolbar includes an orange RSS feed icon that is active if the site offers an RSS subscription and is grayed out if the site does not. Internet Explorer can retrieve different kinds of RSS feeds, including Atom feeds. Figure 38.1 shows the Address bar and toolbar areas of two Internet Explorer win-dows. The top IE window supports RSS feeds; its RSS icon is visible. The bottom IE window does not support RSS feeds because its RSS icon is grayed out. (In this book, you don't see figure colors so the distinction won't be as great here as it will be in your own browser.)

Active RSS icon

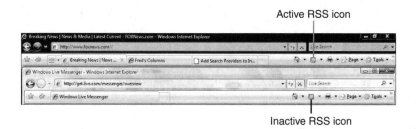

Inactive RSS icon

FIGURE 38.1
Internet Explorer's own toolbar lets you know whether a site supports RSS subscriptions.

Subscribing to an RSS Feed

Before subscribing to a site's RSS feed, you can usually click the active RSS button to see a web page that displays all current RSS feeds for the site. Figure 38.2 shows the FoxNews.com website's RSS feed page that appears when you click IE's RSS button while viewing www.FoxNews.com.

On the RSS page, you'll see the headlines that appear in IE's RSS reader area when you subscribe to that site. The feeds will be little more than linked headlines that take you to the more complete web content.

Click to subscribe   Change display order of feeds

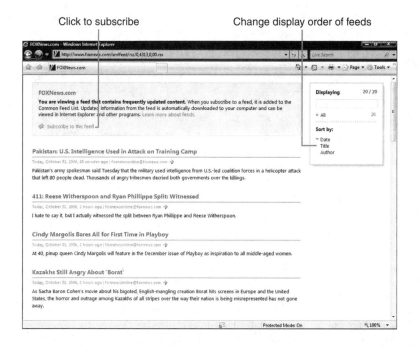

FIGURE 38.2
View the site's recent RSS feeds.

You don't have to view the web feeds for the site before subscribing; doing so, however, gives you an idea of the kinds of feeds that site provides.

If the feeds are the kind you want to subscribe to, click the plus sign next to the Subscribe to this Feed link and Internet Explorer begins grabbing data fed from that site. The Subscribe to This Feed box appears as shown in Figure 38.3. There you can type your own description for the feeds or keep the website's address for the description. You can store the feeds in IE's default Feeds folder or create a new folder by clicking the New Folder button and typing a new name.

FIGURE 38.3
Subscribe to the feed after deciding on a name and folder for the feed.

If you subscribe to several feeds, you'll want to organize them into folders by feed type. For example, you might want to store your news-related feeds in a folder named News and your entertainment-related website feeds in a folder named Entertainment. To narrow down to the feeds you're interested in viewing at the time, you can expand or collapse the feed folders when you view all your feeds.

Click Subscribe to finish subscribing to a feed. At that moment, Internet Explorer begins to grab feeds from that site and stores them in your Feeds folder. If you opted to store the feed in a new folder, that folder appears as a subfolder under your regular Feeds folder.

Some websites use an RSS feed that contains XML code called *Document Type Definitions* (*DTDs*) that Internet Explorer 7 doesn't support at the time of this writing. The fact that IE doesn't support that kind of feed might limit you from eventually grabbing feeds from certain websites. This means that either Microsoft will update IE to support DTD-based feeds or those websites that use DTD feeds will change to IE's more universal, non-DTD feed type. Only time will tell. Microsoft is making an attempt to become more XML-centric, especially with Office 2007's support for XML data, so it's a surprise that Microsoft didn't find a way to access DTD-based feeds.

When you use Internet Explorer to subscribe to an RSS feed, your Sidebar RSS Reader gadget also knows about that same feed. One alerts the other when you subscribe using one of those RSS feed readers and both track the same RSS feeds you subscribe under either program.

Viewing Your Feeds

To see your feeds, click to open your Favorites Center. There a Feeds button appears. When you click Feeds, your subscribed feeds appear in a list of individual site feeds and folders as shown in Figure 38.4.

Click to see folder's feeds

Click to see feeds

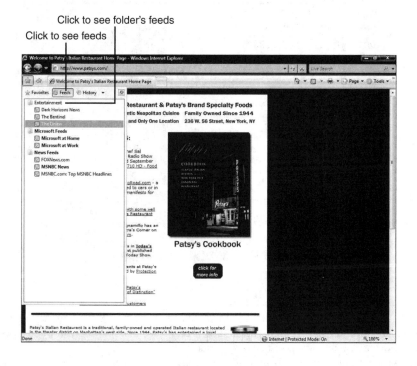

FIGURE 38.4
IE gathers all your web feeds into one location where you can click for details you want to know more about.

Hopefully you're beginning to get the idea that RSS feeds can save you a tremendous amount of web-surfing time. In the past, you had to go check all the sites you're interested in. You had to scour the site to see whether there was anything new and, if so, you would then read the new information. It was easy to miss something. It was time-consuming. You might have to check 15 to 25 sites each morning just to catch the new information in them.

Now, you can simply look at your RSS feed folders in Internet Explorer. Nothing that isn't new will be listed for a given site. Quickly scan the new feeds, and click to read the ones you want to know more about.

Did you Know?

RSSfeeds.com (see Figure 38.5) and several other sites provide a list of hundreds of RSS-based websites, organized by subject. Use Google or another search engine to locate other RSS feed lists; they're all over the Web.

FIGURE 38.5
RSSFeeds.com provides listings of many RSS-based sites you can subscribe to, organized by subject.

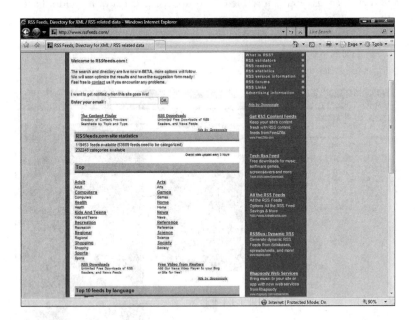

Did you Know?

Outlook 2007 was the first version of Outlook to support RSS feed subscriptions. You can view subscribed feeds in Outlook (see Figure 38.6) giving you three ways to view feeds using Microsoft-based products that are in common use: Vista's gadgets, Internet Explorer 7, and Outlook 2007. If you want to view RSS feeds differently from the way that the Microsoft products display them, you can choose from several feed reading programs from websites such as www.BlogLines.com.

Watch Out!

You must be logged on to the Internet to receive RSS feeds. Dial-up users receive the feeds only when they connect to the Internet.

Individual feed window pane   A feed's article appears here

Feeds

FIGURE 38.6
You can also
view feeds in
Outlook if you
use version
2007 or later.

Managing Your RSS Feeds

Use Internet Explorer's Favorites Center to manage your RSS feeds. You can move
them around, rename them, and change which folders they appear in. In addition,
you can completely delete an RSS feed from your subscribed list of feeds.

Click your Favorites button to open your Favorites Center. Click the Feeds button if
your feeds are not showing. To move a feed from one location to another, even to a
different folder, click and drag that feed to another location.

Use the right-click menu to rename or delete a feed. Figure 38.7 shows the right-click
feed menu. Select Delete to remove a feed from your subscribed list. After IE confirms
that you truly want to remove the feed, the feed goes away, you are unsubscribed,
and all of that feed's content that was available from your feed folders is deleted
from your computer.

FIGURE 38.7
Right-click over any subscribed feed and select Delete to remove that feed from your list.

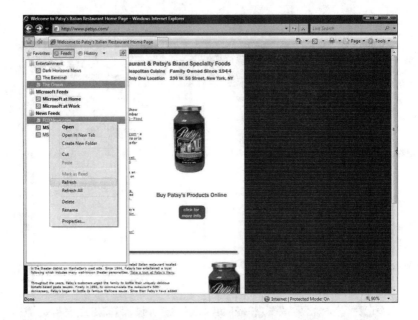

Instant Messaging Lets You Stay in Touch with Others Online

The first instant messaging programs used to provide users who were online at the same time a way to chat with each other. You typed back and forth and the online connection sent your messages back and forth.

Today's versions of instant messaging programs do far more than send typed chat messages back and forth. Most support some kind of video and audio messaging service. Many support VoIP technology that allows you to use your Internet connection to make phone calls. Some even go so far as to allow you to take over someone else's computer—when given permission to do so!—so that you can troubleshoot a problem a friend of yours might be having; you'll see their screen in your instant messaging window and use your keyboard to control their machine until you solve the problem.

By the Way

Instant messaging is useful today even if none of your friends or associates are online at the same time you are. IM programs often serve up news, weather, and other information while you're online, alerting you to different events you've requested such as new emails arriving and can even tell you when you win an eBay auction.

For the first time in years, Microsoft chose not to include an instant messaging program in Windows Vista. This is most strange considering instant messaging is more popular than ever before.

Recent versions of Windows included Microsoft's own Messenger. Microsoft Messenger has had several names through the years including Windows Messenger, MSN Messenger, and the current iteration, Windows Live Messenger. If you have a Microsoft Passport, Microsoft Live ID, or use Hotmail, MSN, or live.com for email, you can download and use Microsoft's Messenger program.

Yahoo! and AOL have their own competing instant messaging programs. Until recently, they didn't talk well to one another, so if you wanted to communicate with an AOL user but you used Yahoo! Messenger, you had to install AOL's messenger as well or send an email. As time goes by, companies that provide IM programs are relaxing their protocols to allow other services to communicate with them. The current Windows Live Messenger can chat back and forth with Yahoo! Messenger and perhaps more instant messaging services will be available to use with Windows Live Messenger by the time you read this.

Installing Your Instant Messaging Program

Because Vista doesn't come with an IM program, you must find your own.

The following steps explain how to locate and install Microsoft's Live Messenger. If you use a different IM service, that's fine. If you don't yet use an IM but want to try, Microsoft's works well and has a good feature set. In addition, Microsoft's is sure to work with your Windows Vista operating system. Probably the other IM programs (sometimes called *IM clients*) will also work under Vista, but Microsoft certainly has the most to gain by making Microsoft Live Messenger fully compatible and respectful of Vista so that's the one described here.

To install Windows Live Messenger, go to the http://get.live.com/messenger/overview web page shown in Figure 38.8. Click the Get It Free button to begin downloading the Windows Live Messenger program.

IE offers to run or save the downloaded file. In case you need to reinstall Windows Live Messenger in the future, click Save and create a folder for Windows Live Messenger in your Downloads folder. This makes installing Windows Live Messenger on other computers in your home or business faster because after you save it on your disk, you can copy the downloaded installation file to a CD or USB flash drive and install on all your other computers without waiting for the download again. When the file downloads to your folder, click Open to run the installation program and follow the prompts.

FIGURE 38.8
Vista doesn't come with an IM program, so you must locate and download one yourself.

During installation, you must agree to the typical, wordy, cloudy legal agreement. In addition, Windows Live Messenger offers, in a dialog box like the one shown in Figure 38.9, to make all sorts of changes to your system. Unless you live and breathe instant messaging, the settings and programs Windows Live Messenger offers to set up for you can be intrusive. For example, do you want your home page changed to MSN.com?

FIGURE 38.9
Windows Live Messenger offers to change several items on your computer; unselecting these options before continuing might save you from having to reverse their effects later.

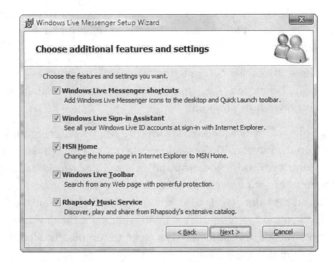

Did you
Know?

Keeping the option labeled Windows Live Sign-In Assistant might be the only one most users should consider leaving checked. If you get additional Windows Live Messenger accounts (they are free), checking this option enables Windows Live Messenger to sign you on to all your accounts to check email and messages in each one from the same Windows Live Messenger window.

After clicking to uncheck any or all Windows Live Messenger's suggested options, click Next to continue with the installation. Windows Live Messenger has to verify your administrative privileges during the installation and Windows Live Messenger will finish installing. When the installation finishes, Windows Live Messenger opens in its own window, as shown in Figure 38.10.

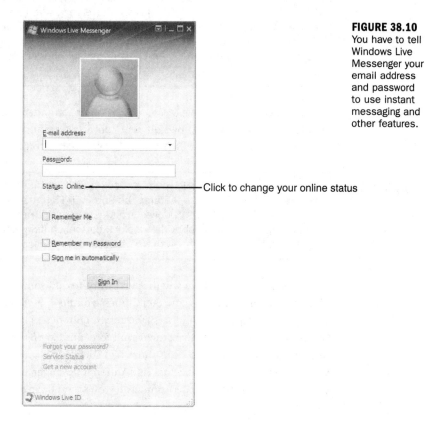

FIGURE 38.10
You have to tell Windows Live Messenger your email address and password to use instant messaging and other features.

Click to change your online status

Type your Windows Live Messenger email address and password in the boxes provided. Remember, these are from your Hotmail or MSN email account, or perhaps your MSN Passport or Windows Live ID. Click Remember Me if you want Windows Live Messenger to remember your email name, and click Remember My Password if you want Windows Live Messenger to remember your password so that you don't later have to enter your username or password. Click the option labeled Sign Me In Automatically if you want Windows Live Messenger to sign you on every time you log in to your user account. Click Sign In to log in to Windows Live Messenger.

When you sign in to Windows Live Messenger, others who have added you as a contact to their Windows Live Messenger system can see that you just signed on because they can set their IM to notify them when friends and family sign in. This means that you might get lots of instant messages the moment you sign in to Windows Live Messenger. It's great to have friends, but sometimes you need to get some work done. Click the arrow to the right of the Online status and change your status to Busy or Away, Be Right Back, Out to Lunch, In a Call, or Appear Offline if you don't want it made known to everyone who has you as a contact in their IM programs that you just signed in. You can easily change your online status to Online whenever you're ready to chat by right-clicking the Windows Live Messenger Notification Area icon on your taskbar and requesting the status change.

If you've used Windows Live Messenger on other computers, your newly installed Windows Live Messenger knows all your contacts, so you don't have to start from scratch every time you install Windows Live Messenger on a new computer.

By the Way

If you use Windows Firewall, you might see a warning that it blocks some of Windows Live Messenger's features, as shown in Figure 38.11. As long as you don't mind allowing all of Windows Live Messenger's features to work without dampening any of them, click the Unblock button, confirm your administrative privileges, and Vista gives Windows Live Messenger full access.

If you get a question asking whether you want to add sharing folders on your computer, it's usually okay to allow them unless you have high security concerns and you share a computer with others who might gain access to your Windows Live Messenger account if you walk away and forget to log off your user account. By allowing shared folders, you can share files such as pictures and videos with others who use Windows Live Messenger and Yahoo! Messenger, and who you've added to your Windows Live Messenger contacts list and who have given you access to theirs.

Adding Contacts

Even though today's IM programs provide far more than keyboard-based chat sessions, such online chats are still the most popular use for IM programs. People from all over the world can chat by typing messages back and forth with each other as long as both log on to the Internet and their IM programs at the same time.

FIGURE 38.11
Let Windows Vista's firewall know that Windows Live Messenger is a program you want to give full access to; otherwise, some features such as being able to share files over your own network might be blocked.

In my home, we use Windows Live Messenger constantly. We have one computer upstairs and another downstairs, and it's too far to talk to each other and we'd get hoarse yelling. Therefore, when two of us are on, we can easily send an instant message to each other, telling that dinner is ready or perhaps asking whether the mail has arrived. When we travel separately, we can be in different states but if we're both logged in to Windows Live Messenger, we chat by typing messages and the response time seems to be identical to the response time (virtually instant) when we're in the same house. About once a week, an Italian friend of my wife's who lives in Messina, Italy sees Jayne sign in and sends a *Ciao!* (Hi!) message and chats for a few moments. We would miss IM if we lost the ability to use it, and if you give it a chance, you will like it too. You'll find new ways to use it all the time.

Unlike most text messaging sent over cell phones, IM messages don't cost money to send. You can, by the way, send a cell phone a text message from most IM and email programs; the cell phone provider can supply the email address to use.

By the Way

To chat with someone, you need to add that person to your IM's contacts list. To do this in Windows Live Messenger, click the Add a Contact button to display the Add a Contact dialog box shown in Figure 38.12, and fill in as many details as you can. The email address is required. Click Type A Personal Invitation if you don't want to use the standard IM invite that Windows Live Messenger sends requesting that your contact add *you* to *their* contacts list if you're not there already. (Both of you must accept the other as a contact before you can chat.)

FIGURE 38.12
Let Windows
Live Messenger
know the con-
tact's email
address you
want to invite to
be a chat
buddy.

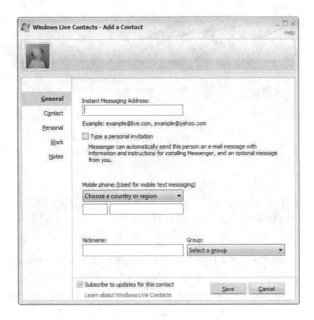

As you can see in Figure 38.12, you enter your contact's text messaging number in this Add a Contact window when you want to be able to send instant messages to their cell phones. Be warned though, this might cost your contacts a dime or so for each message you send, depending on the cell phone plan they have.

The Nickname and Group entries allow you to give your contact a nickname and assign that person to one of three groups: Coworkers, Family, Friends. By grouping your contacts properly, you can more easily locate people you want to chat with as your contacts list grows.

Talking to Others

To chat with one of your contacts, that contact must have approved your invitation to be one of your contacts. After the person does that, you can chat. When that contact signs in to Windows Live Messenger, you'll see a pop-up box like the one shown in Figure 38.13 telling you that person is online. You can click the name in the pop-up box or right-click the contact in your Windows Live Messenger window and select Send an Instant Message to open a message window and chat.

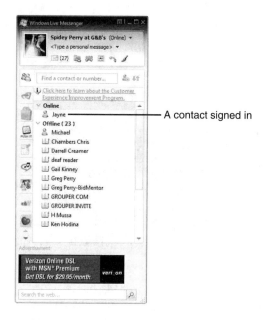

FIGURE 38.13
When one of
your contacts
comes online,
Windows Live
Messenger tells
you; click their
name to chat.

A contact signed in

> You'll soon notice that Windows Live Messenger opens *two* windows when you sign on: a Windows Live Messenger window with your contacts and a Today window that displays some news headlines, entertainment information, and a bunch of ads. You can keep the Today window from opening every time you sign in to Windows Live Messenger by clicking your name at the top of the smaller Windows Live Messenger window and selecting Personal Settings. Click the General tab and click to uncheck the Show Windows Live Today After signing in to Messenger option. The Today window won't automatically appear the next time you sign in to Windows Live Messenger.

By the Way

After you request a chat with one of your contacts, the chat window opens. The top of the window shows your complete chat session as each of you types messages back and forth to one another. The lower text box is where you type messages to your chat contact.

Figure 38.14 shows a chat session taking place. To send a message, type in the lower text box and press Enter or click Send. Your contact sees your message and can reply the same way. In Figure 38.14, the chat goes back and forth in real time as each person types messages to the other. You'll also see two **emoticons**, icons that portray emotion, one being a happy face licking his lips after the food reference. In the past, you indicated an emoticon with a symbol such as :) to represent a happy face; those symbol-based emoticons are read sideways, but if you type such a symbol, Windows Live Messenger turns it into an actual colorful icon.

Emoticons

FIGURE 38.14
Send messages
back and forth
and include
emoticons for
an extra-special
effect.

Full conversation
appears here

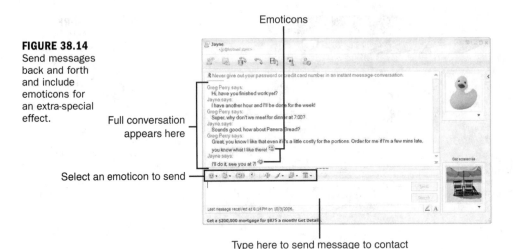

Select an emoticon to send

Type here to send message to contact

Instead of knowing which symbols produce which emoticons, you can click the Select an Emoticon drop-down icon and choose from several that Windows Live Messenger makes available.

Play around with the symbols and options on the message window. You can send a wink or a nudge to your Windows Live Messenger contact. A wink makes a large icon move and appear on your contact's screen (they're funny), and a nudge completely shakes your contact's IM window and makes a buzzing sound in case you suspect your contact didn't notice that you just sent an instant message. Other tools are available to format your text, change the picture that appears when you chat, and place a background image on your IM chat session to make the experience more pleasant.

Additional IM Options

If you're in the middle of a chat and want to invite a third contact into the chat, click the Invite Someone to This Conversation button in the upper-left corner of your chat session's toolbar. As long as that person is online and is a contact of one or both of you in the current conversation, you can add that person and more to join in.

It's simple to send files back and forth and often gets around email spam filters and file size limits that still plague email. Click the Share Files button on the instant message's toolbar, select Open Your Sharing Folder to select files from your shared folder or select Send a Single File if you want to send a file that's not in a shared folder or if you don't yet have shared folders set up. After you select a file, Windows Live Messenger sends it to your contact's computer.

Did you Know?

If one of you does not have shared folders set up, you can set up shared folders from the Personal Settings window. The shared folders are simpler to access from Windows Live Messenger, but make sure that you make available only files you want to share with any or all of your contacts. When you open a shared folder and are online with a contact, that contact can see all files you store there and can download any or all of them.

If you want to hold a video conversation with your contact, click the chat toolbar's Start or Stop a Video Call. The first time you select this option, Windows Live Messenger presents you with the Audio and Video Setup window shown in Figure 38.15. Generally this ensures that both of you have a webcam connected to your computer so that the other can watch you and you can watch them as you talk. As you might expect, the quality and speed of the video isn't bad but certainly isn't broadcast quality; nevertheless, being able to hold video-based conversations with any contact in the world, without incurring a charge, is an amazing testament to instant messaging.

FIGURE 38.15
You have to set up your audio and video equipment before having a video-based conversation with a contact.

You can even play games with your contacts. Click your toolbar's Games button and select a game to play. Windows Live Messenger connects to the Internet and downloads the game to both your computers, and you are playing in no time. If you're playing chess, for example, you'll both make moves and see your opponent's moves in real time.

When you send a file or offer to play a game with a contact, Windows Live
Messenger sends a request to your contact that your contact can accept or reject.

The first time you end a conversation with someone, Windows Live Messenger displays the Windows Live Messenger dialog box shown in Figure 38.16. Your response
to this dialog box determines whether you want Vista to keep a transcript of your
online chats. By selecting Yes, you inform Vista that you might want to read the
transcript of a keyboard chat session you have had in the past. As long as you're
okay with that, save the transcript. If you see no reason to save or if you want the
privacy (as you might if you're, say, a politician), don't save copies of your chat
sessions.

FIGURE 38.16
Tell Windows
Live Messenger
whether to save
transcripts of
your instant
messages.

When you finish a chat, the Windows Live Messenger window remains on your
screen although you can close this window and remain online with Windows Live
Messenger. Closing the window gets rid of it from your screen, but your taskbar's
notification area still displays the instant message icon that you can right-click to
start a chat or view email (for the web-based email system connected to the chat
such as Hotmail). Double-click the Windows Live Messenger icon to open your
Windows Live Messenger window again in case you need to set some Windows Live
Messenger options or talk with someone using that interface.

Along the left edge of the Windows Live Messenger window appears a list of icons
that you can scroll through. You'll find an eBay icon that displays a subset of
eBay.com that you can search through for something to buy. Click the Rhapsody
icon to see the Rhapsody music website from which you can purchase and download music to your computer. Other icons represent financial and news websites as
well as offer activities that might interest you as a Windows Live Messenger user.

Viruses and spyware can infect instant messaging programs, and some people send out blanket contact requests using randomly generated IM addresses hoping you respond to a request. As with email, use care. These kinds of problems aren't as common as they are with email, and a good antivirus and spyware protection program that you update regularly should keep you from any problems.

Chapter Wrap-Up

This chapter explored ways you can keep touch with websites (RSS feeds) and ways you can keep in touch with friends and family (instant messaging) while online.

By using RSS feeds, you take control of when you want to view content without running the risk of missing content. The summaries go to your Favorites Center's Feeds folders regularly and await your attention there. You don't have to browse through all the websites you normally peruse to see new updates to those sites.

Communicate instantly with friends by downloading and installing an instant-messaging program. You can send keyboarded instant messages back and forth or even communicate by video and voice, free of charge, to others in your contacts list. IM is a way for anyone online to chat with anyone else in real time and demonstrates the true power of today's wired world.

This and the previous chapter explored ways that you and your computer keep in touch with others over the Internet. Sometimes you want your computer to keep in touch with other devices, such as your cell phone and PDA (personal data assistant). Synchronizing such devices with some of your pertinent computer files keeps your needed data with you when you're on the go.

CHAPTER 39

Synchronizing Your Computer with Other Devices

In This Chapter:

- ▶ Synchronize the files among your computers and mobile devices
- ▶ Let Windows Vista update the files on your mobile device before you leave on a trip
- ▶ Learn the established communication rules to get the most out of your synchronized connections
- ▶ Use the Mobile Device Center to set up sync partnerships
- ▶ Manage your Mobile Favorites folder
- ▶ Use sync to manage multiple synchronizations

It's an electronic world. Computers are everywhere, even in the cars driven and the televisions and stereos played. Not only are computers obvious, with laptops and desktops in homes and businesses and coffee shops and everywhere else all around the world, but small hidden computers also appear in cell phones, pocket PCs, MP3 players, watches, and calculators.

The need to have information available to use night and day prompted a growth of small, handheld computing devices, often called **PDAs** for **Personal Digital Assistants** several years ago. PDAs kept track of our appointments, phone numbers and other contacts, and held some data also. Some are little computers—with names such as Pocket PC, Treo, and Blackberry—that can access Internet web pages and show us our emails when an Internet signal is available. And they can do so even when an Internet signal *isn't* readily available because many of these devices also act as cell phones that can call the nearest cell tower to access an Internet data feed when requested to do so.

In fact, it's often difficult to distinguish between a cell phone, a PDA, and an MP3 player because they all seem to share the same subset of features in one way or another.

The key to making those small devices truly useful is that you want your information with you when you travel. This means you must transfer your desktop's data files, such as email, contacts, and important financial and other data that you want with you, to the device before you leave your desk. Windows Vista helps keep your larger computers and your small mobile devices in sync with each other. In this chapter, you'll see how Vista does that. It's a short chapter, but these are small devices and synchronizing your computer and mobile devices is easy thanks to Vista.

Establishing a Mobile Device Connection

Before your computer can synchronize data with your mobile device, you must set up a sync partnership between your larger computer (which might be a desktop or your laptop) and your mobile device. That partnership defines a profile that describes how information is to pass between these devices. For example, on one of your mobile devices you might want your contacts and emails downloaded from the larger computer, but on a different mobile device you might just want a set of MP3 files. (What? You do have more than one mobile device, don't you?)

The real problem with synchronizing information is that information can get scattered among your devices. After you send data to your mobile device and you leave for a trip, it's not only possible but probable that you'll update or change the data in some way while you're gone, perhaps adding new contacts for the people you meet. Accepting Vista's help in synchronizing data between all your computing devices will seem a welcome feature indeed. Vista helps you put changed data where it needs to go and keeps fresh data placed wherever it needs to be, even if that means that Vista uses your newer mobile device files to update your desktop computer when you get home.

By the Way   Vista uses the accepted, abbreviated term *sync* for the communication and reconciliation of files among computers and mobile devices.

Obviously you need a way to connect your devices together before a sync can take place. Often this means connecting a base unit for your mobile device into your computer's USB port, or perhaps using a wireless connection such as Bluetooth so that the two devices can communicate with each other.

The two devices cannot magically sync with each other unless you connect them together using a wired or wireless method. If you're using your mobile device on vacation, your desktop computer back home won't be synced to the changes you make while away from home until you return and sync the devices. As you might now expect, the sync rules must be set up so that the mobile device's changes can update the desktop.

To establish a sync partnership, you must connect your mobile device to your computer. The connecting hardware that comes with your mobile device determines how you plug your mobile device into your computer. If your mobile device plugs into your computer with a USB cable, connect your cable now if you haven't already done so. If your mobile device uses a wireless signal instead of USB, check your user manual to see the best way to set up the device so that your computer gets the signal at the appropriate time.

If you connect your mobile device to your computer using a USB cable, the USB connection often acts as both a charger and as a data path for the sync partnerships you establish. If your device has no remaining charge, however, you might need to give it an initial charge and turn it on before inserting the device into the USB-based port before Vista can sense the unit. For a wireless connection, your mobile device must have some battery charge or be plugged into an AC outlet to send its signal to your desktop.

If you've used Windows XP's ActiveSync to synchronize your mobile devices in the past, you cannot use ActiveSync with Vista. Vista includes the Windows Mobile Device Center which replaces the ActiveSync program used in previous Windows versions.

After connecting your mobile device, turn it on. When you do, Vista senses the device's presence and opens the Windows Mobile Device Center shown in Figure 39.1. If the Mobile Device Center doesn't open automatically, open your Control Panel and open the Network and Internet group. Select Windows Mobile Device Center to open the program's window. (Although the Sync Center appears earlier in the list, you'll need to visit the Mobile Device Center the first few times you set up your device.)

FIGURE 39.1
Vista's Mobile Device Center is where you manage sync partnerships between your computer and your mobile device.

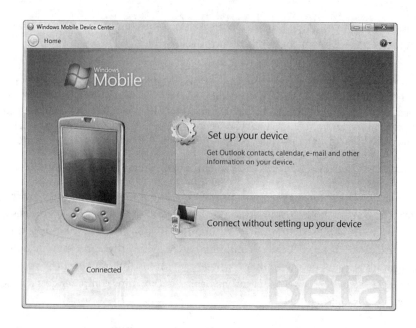

The Mobile Device Center is where you manage partnerships that you establish between your computer and one or more mobile devices.

Let Vista Handle Your Post Trip Information Overload

You can establish multiple sync partnerships with multiple devices. For example, you might establish a partnership for times before you go on a trip that sends certain data to your mobile device. The partnership then allows for a two-way sync when you return and want to update your desktop computer with any data changes you made on your mobile device while traveling.

One change might be a new contact you met, added to your mobile device's list of contacts, and that you want stored on your desktop. By letting sync take care of the details, you don't have to save that business card and type the same data twice: once in your mobile device while on the road and again when you get back from your trip.

When you first plug your mobile device into your Vista-based computer, your mobile device often displays a message and shows an icon to indicate that the connection is being established or has been made. In addition, you might see an AutoPlay window open such as the one shown in Figure 39.2. This is the result of an internal Windows file called the *mobile device base driver*. With this base driver's window, you get simple Explorer-like access to your device and you can copy files to and from the device.

For example, you can select what you want to do if one of the AutoPlay options provides the primary reason you normally connect the mobile device to your computer.

FIGURE 39.2
Some mobile devices are simple and require very little interaction and no sync partnership connection.

If the device is a portable digital music player (with optional video), you might always want to sync its files with your Windows Media Player's files, so you'd select the Sync Digital Media Files to This Device option and never use the Mobile Device Center. If the mobile device has a digital camera and you use the device to take or store pictures you get elsewhere, select the Import Pictures option. You might just select the Open Device to View Files option to open a Windows Explorer window and copy files manually to or from the device.

Leave the Always Do This for This Device option checked if you want Vista to remember your selection and never ask again. Click to uncheck this option if you want to select one of the AutoPlay options this time, but you don't necessarily want Vista to assume that's what you will want to do in the future.

As explained in Chapter 24, "Controlling Windows Vista," you can change any AutoPlay option you set from your Control Panel's Hardware and Sound group.

Setting Up Your Device

If you want to do more with your device than the simple AutoPlay interface allows, you can work from the Mobile Device Center to set up more complicated partnerships. The first time you connect your mobile device to your computer and view the Mobile Device Center program window, you have to set up your device so that your computer knows what kind of partnership you want to establish.

> By the way, the Mobile Device Center's picture won't necessarily match your
> mobile device. The picture might not look like the cell phone you just plugged in.
> In fact, you might not have even plugged in a cell phone but, instead, connected a
> Pocket PC or other kind of nonphone PDA device to your computer, but the picture
> might show a cell phone anyway. None of that matters because the purpose of the
> initial Mobile Device Center picture is just to make it clear you're working with a
> mobile device connected to your desktop or laptop computer.

The Mobile Device Center sees that you've plugged your mobile device into your
computer and that you have not yet set up that device. The Set Up Your Device and
the Connect Without Setting Up Your Device options make themselves available
automatically in the Mobile Device Center as shown in Figure 39.1.

When you first connect a mobile device to your computer, the Set Up Your Device
option appears. But after you perform the setup, that option goes away and a list of
routine sync options appear that you can use to manage your mobile device's synchronization settings.

Using the Set Up Your Device Option to Establish an Initial Partnership

When you first connect a mobile device to your computer, select the Set Up Your
Device option on the Mobile Device Center and answer the prompt shown in Figure
39.3 that asks how many computers you'll want to connect the mobile device to.
Most users will be setting up a single sync partnership with their mobile device and
if you're one of them you'll select the first, default option. If the mobile device
already has a partnership set up with another computer, you will need to select the
second option, No I Want to Synchronize with Two Computers, so Vista doesn't
monopolize your mobile device and remove other partnerships.

Given the vast differences among computer software configurations and mobile
devices, your combination of hardware and software determines what you can sync
and how that takes place.

Several synchronization rules limit how much you can take advantage of Vista's
sync capabilities that Mobile Device Center offers. Among these are the following:

▶ To be able to access all the Mobile Device Center features, you should use a
mobile device that runs Windows Mobile Operating System 5 or later. Users of
devices that run operating systems such as the Pocket PC 2003 Edition can
access many of the sync features, but some sync services might be more limited than available for devices running Windows Mobile 5 and later.

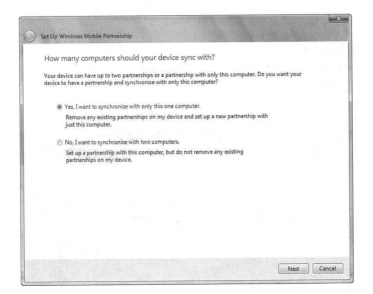

FIGURE 39.3
Tell Vista how this device shares partnerships with others.

- One computer can have partnerships with many different mobile devices: cell phones, PDAs, and MP3 players.

- A mobile device can have a partnership with only two computers at most. For example, you can keep your contacts up-to-date among your PDA and desktop and laptop, but not a third computer.

- You can synchronize email between only one mobile device and one computer. This holds true even if you're syncing to a computer on a Microsoft Exchange email network; only one Exchange computer can sync email with each mobile device connected to any computer on the network.

- For full syncing of Outlook data, you have to upgrade to Outlook with Business Contact Manager.

- If your mobile device connects using a wireless signal instead of a USB connection, a Change Schedule Settings option will appear on the Mobile Device Center sync data screen that you can select to determine when the sync should take place. When wired with a USB cable, the sync takes place when you connect the device.

The Mobile Device Center makes you aware of any limitations you might have based on the hardware and software it sees. After clicking Next from the Set Up Windows Mobile Partnership window, for example, you're asked what kinds of data you wish to synchronize your mobile device to and the options include Outlook email. You may run into problems, however, if everything isn't as expected. For example, in Figure 39.4, an attempt was made to establish a sync between a Pocket PC and Outlook without Business Contacts Manager installed. It would be more helpful if the message beneath Contacts, Calendar, E-mail, Tasks, and Notes actually said the lack of the Business Contacts Manager was the reason the sync was not configured for those Outlook items, however.

FIGURE 39.4
You might find that you cannot synchronize all your data, depending on your software and hardware combination.

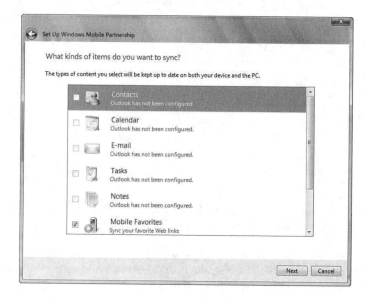

No matter what kind of software and hardware combination you have to synchronize, you can almost always sync your Mobile Favorites folder (use Windows Explorer to open your user account's Favorites folder to see the Mobile Favorites subfolder there) and files that you select by clicking the Files link in the setup window.

Did you Know?

To keep the latest music on your mobile settings, routinely copy MP3 files that you want to listen to on your mobile device to your computer's Mobile Favorites folder. The next time you plug your mobile device into the USB-based connector or achieve a wireless connection, Mobile Device Center will synchronize all the music in your Mobile Favorites to your mobile device. By using the Mobile Favorites folder as your only shared folder when you establish syncs with your mobile device, you achieve easier control over the files that you take with you because any synced file is in your Mobile Favorites folder.

After you check the items you want to sync for the new partnership, Mobile Device Center asks for a name to save the defined partnership under so that later you can more easily locate and remove specific partnerships you no longer need on your computer.

When you create and save a partnership, Mobile Device Center immediately synchronizes your files. That means selected data on your mobile device that doesn't appear on your computer makes its way there, and selected items found only on your computer makes its way to your mobile device. During a sync, the message Syncing appears in your Mobile Device Center's lower-left window corner as shown in Figure 39.5.

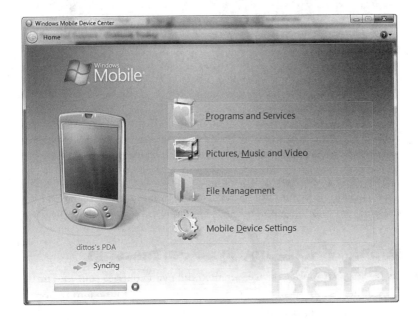

FIGURE 39.5
Mobile Device Center tells you when syncing is taking place.

After the sync finishes, a green check mark appears in place of the Syncing message and Mobile Device Center tells you the time of the most recent sync. Figure 39.6 shows this area of the Mobile Device Center window. If you want to force a manual sync because you changed some selected data and sync doesn't recognize you did so, click the green Sync button and Mobile Device Center will review both your mobile device and desktop settings to see whether a sync needs to occur once again.

Until you change some of the files associated with a partnership, Mobile Device Center never syncs again on its own. However, the next time you connect your mobile device to your computer, a sync occurs just to make sure that everything is up-to-date in both places.

FIGURE 39.6
The Syncing message goes away when a sync finishes and the synchronized data is properly established on both your mobile device and computer.

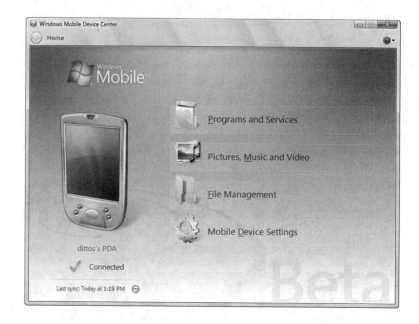

To end a partnership between your computer and a mobile device, open your Mobile Device Settings menu option and click the More link. Select the End a Partnership option and select one or more named partnerships you want to delete.

Managing an Existing Sync Partnership

After you set up your mobile device, the next time you connect your mobile device to your computer the Mobile Device Center window opens to the four options shown in Figure 39.6, described in the next few sections.

Connecting to Mobile Programs and Services

The Programs and Services option takes you to the Internet and opens a page in your web browser where you can download programs and updates from Microsoft's Windows Mobile website shown in Figure 39.7. The website is a full-featured mobile device site from which you can download updates to your mobile device's software, download programs you can use with your mobile device (such as games and business applications), and get support if you have trouble using your mobile device with Windows Vista.

Watch Out!

The Windows Mobile site is a retail site that charges for most programs you download to use with your device. You have to select the kind of device you'll be using the programs on, such as a cell phone or Pocket PC, and not every program is available for every type of device.

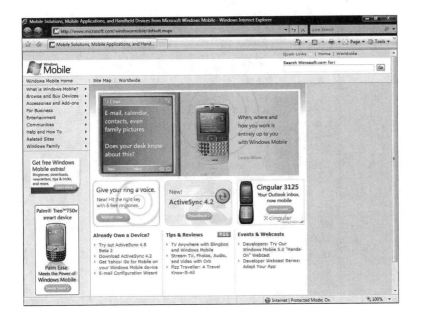

FIGURE 39.7
Mobile Device Center's Programs and Services option opens the Windows Mobile web page where you can get support and programs related to mobile computing.

After you download one or more programs from the Windows Mobile website, you can manage your mobile-based programs by again selecting Programs and Services and clicking the More button. A window appears inside Mobile Device Center; from there, you can add and remove mobile device-related programs, as you might need to do to put the downloaded programs on and remove downloaded programs from your mobile device.

Did you Know?

Connecting to Pictures, Music, and Video

By selecting Mobile Device Center's second menu option, Pictures, Music, and Video, you can easily send or retrieve media-related content to your mobile device from your computer. The following three options appear when you select and open the Pictures, Music, and Video Mobile Device Center menu option:

▶ **Import Pictures/Video From Your Device**—If your mobile device has pictures, digital music, or digital sound, you can import that content to your computer. If Mobile Device Center doesn't locate any media content on your mobile device, a message box tells you there is no media content found on the device that doesn't already appear on your computer.

▶ **Pictures/Video Import Settings**—Clicking this option opens the Import Settings dialog box shown in Figure 39.8. There you determine which folders to store shared content that you grab from connected mobile devices.

FIGURE 39.8
Determine files,
folders, and
other settings
to match when
you move media
content
between your
mobile device
and computer.

▶ **Add Media to Your Device From Windows Media Player**—Opens Media Player where you can select music and videos, and use its Sync drop-down list to synchronize your computer and your mobile device.

After Media Player opens on your computer you can play music and video stored on your mobile device from Windows Vista on your computer, using your computer's speakers to hear the sound.

Managing Mobile Device Files

When you open the File Management menu option and click the Browse the Contents of Your Device option, a Windows Explorer window opens to reveal the contents of your mobile device. Be warned that you might see more devices than you expect. For example, Figure 39.9 shows an Explorer window open for a Pocket PC. Even though the Pocket PC is the only device attached to the computer, Mobile Device Center shows three items in the Explorer window: Memory, a Flash ROM disk, and a CF card.

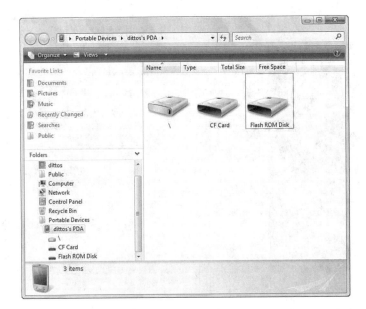

FIGURE 39.9
All memory areas of your mobile device show in the Explorer window when you wish to view your mobile device's contents.

The Pocket PC attached to this computer contains both a memory to process data, internal ROM (for *read-only memory*) that holds the Pocket PC's system startup and program-loader (collectively called a *BIOS* for *basic input/output system* and referred to only as \ in Explorer), and a removable memory card that's the CF Card (for *Compact Flash card*) format. The bulk of any media content is most often stored on the removable CF Card for such a device, so double-clicking the Explorer window's CF Card icon displays a list of any files stored on the Pocket PC's CF Card currently installed there.

> Selecting the next Quick Connect menu, Mobile Device Settings, opens the same window as the initial Mobile Device Center's Set Up Your Device option that you see the very first time you connect your device to your computer and no sync settings have been made.

By the Way

Visiting the Sync Center

In spite of its name, Vista's Sync Center is not where you specify and adjust your mobile device's synchronization partnerships. Instead, the Sync Center, shown in Figure 39.10, is a central location where you can view results of your mobile device synchronization.

FIGURE 39.10
The Sync Center is just a shell to manage mobile device syncs.

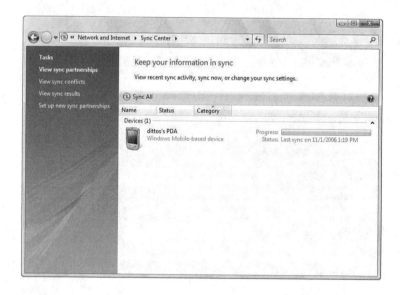

As with most users, you probably have at most one mobile device to connect to your computer. Figure 39.10 shows the same device partnership shown earlier in the chapter throughout the Mobile Device Center's discussion.

The Sync Center has no sync software available. Sync Center only manages other synchronizing software. If you only have one mobile device and you use the Mobile Device Center to set up your partnerships, you don't use Sync Center to change the partnership but only to trigger syncs when you need to sync and view results. For example, a problem may occur if your mobile device is set to sync to a specific file folder on your computer and you delete that folder. If this occurs, the Sync Center's View Sync Conflicts option displays the problem that occurred.

If you happen to connect multiple mobile devices to your computer, you may find more use for Sync Center than if you just connect one. By connecting all your devices to your computer and viewing the sync results from within Sync Center, you get a bird's eye view reporting of all that took place. The Sync Center keeps track of a synchronization history of when your syncs began and ended for each device you connect. You can view that history (from the View Sync Results option) to troubleshoot potential problems if a sync doesn't go as expected.

Chapter Wrap-Up

Mobile devices are not only handy; they are usually fun, too. You can synchronize certain folders to include music that you want to take on a trip, and sync the tunes to your mobile device as well as with more important information such as your business contacts and email and appointments from your Outlook Calendar.

Synchronizing files and folders and Outlook data items manually takes a lot of effort. So much manual effort is required that you will rarely leave with your mobile device and have everything you need on it. By setting your mobile device's partnership settings and periodically reviewing those settings, you can help ensure that you have whatever data you need when you leave home or the office.

The next chapter introduces you to Windows Mail, a program that manages both email and newsgroups on your Vista computer. Windows Mail is an improved version of the Outlook Express program that came with earlier versions of Windows.

CHAPTER 40

Mailing with Windows Mail

In This Chapter:

- ▶ See how Windows Mail relates to Outlook Express
- ▶ Set up a Windows Mail email account
- ▶ Import data from Outlook or Outlook Express
- ▶ Create new email messages to send
- ▶ Send entire web pages to someone
- ▶ Receive and reply to email in Windows Mail
- ▶ Manage your message folders
- ▶ Create an email signature that gets read
- ▶ Manage spam and other junk email

Vista includes Windows Mail, a program that replaces Outlook Express found in previous Windows versions. As with Outlook Express, Windows Mail offers support for email and **newsgroups**—electronic bulletin boards where you can exchange ideas and files.

With Windows Calendar (refer to Chapter 20, "Dating with Windows Calendar") and Windows Mail, you really don't *need* a separate program such as Microsoft Outlook for your email and scheduling. The truth is, however, that Windows Mail is not an extremely sophisticated email program and Windows Calendar isn't an extremely sophisticated scheduling program. It wasn't Microsoft's intent to make these programs everyone's answer to scheduling and email; as with Outlook Express, the adequate (and free with previous versions of Windows) Windows Mail can handle day-to-day email tasks and will do the job without all the bells and whistles that a program such as Microsoft Outlook provides. (In addition, Windows Mail provides a newsreader and Outlook does not.)

In this chapter, you'll learn how Windows Mail works to handle your email. You'll set up your email account and send emails in no time. The next chapter shows you how to use Windows Mail to access newsgroups for information about various topics that interest you.

Introducing Windows Mail

To start Windows Mail, open your Start menu and select the Windows Mail option. Figure 40.1 shows the screen that awaits you after Windows Mail loads. Even if you have set up no email accounts, Microsoft stuck an email message in your Inbox to tell you a little about Windows Mail. (Depending on your version and release date of your specific Windows Vista system, you might see a slightly different email message from Microsoft.)

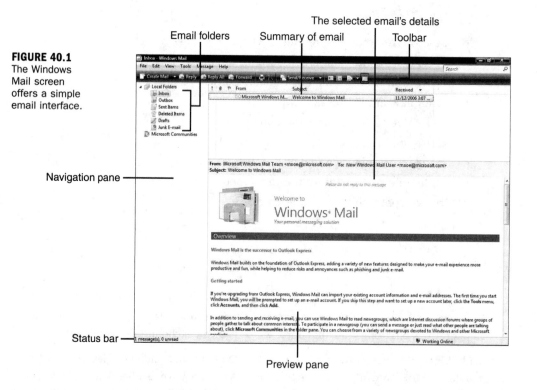

FIGURE 40.1
The Windows Mail screen offers a simple email interface.

As with most email programs Windows Mail provides you with the following folders in the navigation pane:

▶ **Inbox**—Holds your incoming email.

▶ **Outbox**—Holds your outgoing mail; if you're online, items don't remain in your Outbox folder very long. As soon as you send an email message, it goes to your Outbox and Windows Mail begins sending the message. As soon as it sends the message, Windows Mail moves the email message from your Outbox folder to your Sent Items folder. If you're not online, as might be the case when working on a laptop while traveling on a plane, you can send emails and Windows Mail stores them in your Outbox until you get to a live Internet connection. At that point, after you start Windows Mail, it sends those messages to their intended recipients.

▶ **Sent Items**—Holds email you've successfully sent previously.

▶ **Deleted Items**—Holds email you've deleted; until you empty your Deleted Items folder, you can undelete email messages. The Deleted Items folder works like your Recycle Bin and holds messages you want to delete.

▶ **Drafts**—Holds email you have started to write but not yet finished.

▶ **Junk E-mail**—Holds email you've received that you or a junk email filter has determined is possible **spam** (an unsolicited ad arriving in an email), or an email infected with spyware, or a virus that Windows Defender or an antivirus program you've installed detected as being a threat.

To view all the items in a navigation pane folder, double-click the folder and the items will appear in the email summary area. You can move items from folder to folder and create your own folders to sort and store your messages.

Setting Up an Email Account

The first thing you have to do to use Windows Mail is set up an email account in the program. Most often, an email account falls into one of two categories:

▶ **HTML-based email**—A web-based email account such as Microsoft's Hotmail or Google's Gmail.

▶ **POP3 email**—A service-based email usually provided by your Internet service provider such as Microsoft's MSN or AOL. In the past, a program such as Windows Mail or Outlook was required to access POP3-based email.

Both kinds of email accounts are set up in slightly different ways, depending on the service, but for Windows Mail, you can only set up an email account that offers a POP3 connection. Therefore, you'll have a problem with Hotmail and some other web email services because many email programs, such as Windows Mail, require a POP3 email account to access the email there.

Many web-based email services such as Gmail provide you with a free POP3 connection to your web-based email account so that you can use Windows Mail to send and retrieve a Google account's email. Surprisingly, however, Microsoft's own Windows Mail won't read Microsoft's own Hotmail email because the free version of Hotmail doesn't allow a POP3 connection.

> Microsoft assumes that if you get free Hotmail, you should use the Hotmail web-based interface to read ads that appear along the edges of your Hotmail screen at various times. If you pay to upgrade to Hotmail Plus, Microsoft adds a POP3 connection to your Hotmail account so that you can use Windows Mail to access your email.

A third kind of email account, IMAP, is available as well as a web-based and POP3 email account, but IMAP is generally limited to large corporate network computers like those you'd find at a large company's headquarters or a university. The *IT* staff (IT stands for *Information Technology*, a name often used for a company's computer support staff) for that organization can supply the details you need to configure Windows Mail for your mail account if you use an IMAP account.

> Windows Mail makes it easy to work with more than one email account. You can add one or more email accounts and you can send and receive from all your accounts from within Windows Mail. In addition, you can create separate folders to hold email messages sent to each account so that you can keep your accounts separate.

Before you set up a new email account in Windows Mail, you need the following information, most of which you know, but some of which you will probably have to obtain from your email account's customer support website:

▶ **Name you want others to see**—Your first name and last name or a nickname you want others to see in the From field of the email messages you send. This field is commonly referred to as your *display name,* and if you choose to leave your display name blank, your email address will appear in the From field instead of your name.

▶ **Email address**—Your email address which generally follows the pattern, *MyEmail@isp.com.*

▶ **Email server**—Your email provider's POP3 server value (see the note that follows this list), which generally follows the pattern of pop3.*isp*.com, where *isp* is your Internet service provider, or smtp.*isp*.com. The POP3 value is your email's incoming server and the SMTP value is your email's *outgoing server.* To be able to send and receive emails from your email account, you must have both these values. They usually have to be supplied by your ISP because many email providers don't follow any naming standards for their email servers.

▶ **Username**—The username that you chose or were assigned when you received your email account from your email provider. This is the name that appears before *@email*.com, so MarilynWheeler@mantlemin.com's username would be *MarilynWheeler*.

▶ **Password**—The password that you chose or were assigned when you received your email account from your email provider.

ISPs' POP3 and SMTP information is readily available, and if you don't know your email account's POP3 and SMTP values that is information your email account provider will almost always make readily available on its customer support website and phone centers. The information is so often requested that it's usually faster to go online and locate it on your ISP's website than to call its help staff. Companies that provide email account service understand the importance of making it easy for you to find these values so that you can set up email programs such as Windows Mail.

Setting Up an Email Account in Windows Mail

As long as you use a POP3-based email account, or a web-based email account that offers POP3 access, such as Gmail, it's simple to set up Windows Mail to send and receive your email. Windows Mail is a more structured way to manage your email than the Gmail website because Windows Mail runs on your own computer, and you're not limited to an Internet connection speed when all you want to do is read and manage and sort and delete the email messages that you went online to send and receive.

To add a new email account to Windows Mail, follow these steps:

1. Select Tools, Accounts to open the Internet Accounts window.

2. Click Add.

3. Select E-mail Account and click Next.

You will see Directory Service as one of the kinds of accounts you can create in addition to an email and newsgroup account. A **directory service** is an address book for contacts and is often made available in a large organization.

4. Type your display name, such as Marilyn Wheeler, and click Next.

5. Type your email address, such as Zucchi77@Hotmail.com, and click Next to display the E-mail Server Names window.

6. Assuming that you are setting up a POP3-based email account, leave the Incoming Server setting as POP3 and type your email account's POP3 server information in the top text box. Type your email account's SMTP server information in the bottom text box. Click the My Server Requires Authentication option if your email account requires it, and your E-mail Server Names window should look like the one in Figure 40.2. Click Next to move to the Internet Mail Logon window.

FIGURE 40.2
Your email account's provider will inform you of the POP3, SMTP, and authentication settings you must use.

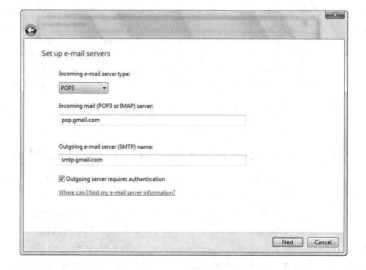

7. At the Internet Mail Logon window, enter your email username and password. Remember that your username will be the leftmost part of your email name, so Samantha-9-Pick@aol.com's username would be Samantha-9-Pick. Type the password for your account in the Password field. Without these values, Windows Mail has no access to your email account. Keep the Remember Password option checked unless you share a computer and user account with someone else; in that case you should type your email account's password every time you check email instead of leaving the option checked and letting Windows Mail enter the password for you. Click Next to move to the final email setup window.

8. Click to check the option Do Not Download My E-Mail at This Time if you don't want to download all email stored in your account at the time you set

up Windows Mail to read your email. With the option checked, Windows Mail reads only new email that comes to your account and stores that email in your Windows Mail Inbox. Generally, most people want to download any current email in the account to Windows Mail and that is why the option defaults to being clear. Click Finish and, assuming that you entered all your email account correctly, Windows Mail goes to the Internet and retrieves any email waiting for you there.

Some Words About Importing Data

One of the things you'll probably want to do is move contacts and possibly old email that you've received in the past into Windows Mail. There are so many options, depending on what you've used in the past for email, that to cover them all would be impossible. So, a brief overview of what you'll go through will be helpful.

One of the nicest things about Windows Mail is that when you upgrade a computer from Windows XP to Windows Vista, Windows Mail imports all your Outlook Express contacts and email addresses (as well as newsgroups) so that you don't have to do anything special after you install Vista. Windows Mail will already have all your contacts and email information and you're ready to continue where you left off with Outlook Express.

If you have not used an email system on your current computer because it's new, one of the things you'll certainly want to do first is to get your past emails and contacts into Windows Mail. The contacts will include your names, email addresses, and other contact information you might have kept track of elsewhere or on another computer, such as a desktop where you use Outlook or Outlook Express.

It might be nice to keep Outlook on your desktop and use Windows Mail for your laptop's email. By doing that, you save the cost of a second copy of Microsoft Outlook but you can still use Outlook's contacts and even import its email messages into Windows Mail. You will need to select Outlook's File, Import and Export command and export your Outlook Contacts to a CSV (comma-separated value) file and your email data to a PST personal folder file. These files might be large if you have lots of contacts and emails, so you might have to save the files onto a CD-ROM or perhaps burn a DVD. You need a way to get the files to your laptop. If you run a network between your laptop and the desktop on which you installed Outlook, you can store Outlook's exported files in a Public folder and copy that folder to your laptop.

If you already have Outlook on the Windows Mail machine, you might not have the need or desire to use Windows Mail. Even though its interface is simpler than

Outlook's, you will lose functionality. Getting your contacts and email from another computer that uses Outlook, however, is a need that you might have.

If you use Outlook Express on your desktop and have a new laptop that you didn't upgrade, you'll want to get your Outlook Express email and contacts to Windows Mail. From Outlook Express, you must select File, Export and export your OE messages to one file and your OE contacts to another file.

After you copy your exported contacts and messages to your laptop, select Windows Mail's File, Import, Messages option. Then select the program that holds the email you want to import from using the Select Program dialog box shown in Figure 40.3.

FIGURE 40.3
You can import your Outlook or Outlook Express settings from a desktop to a new Vista laptop if you want to get your contacts and emails on your laptop.

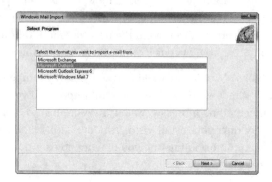

Given that Windows Mail is Microsoft's product, Microsoft doesn't offer options to import from non-Microsoft email programs. Select a program such as Microsoft Outlook or Microsoft Outlook Express 6 and click Next. Windows Mail leads you through a window or two where you locate the imported file (the one you exported from the other program and copied to your laptop). Select the items you want to import (such as the mail folders you want to import) and the import process begins. To import the contacts that you exported from Outlook as a CSV file, select File, Import, Windows Contacts, CSV; click Import and locate the file to import.

This example has assumed an existing desktop and a new Vista laptop, but the same procedure holds if you're transferring mail data from one desktop to another, too.

After you import Outlook or Outlook Express email and contacts into Windows Mail, a new folder hierarchy appears in the Windows Mail navigation pane, like the one in Figure 40.4. Windows Mail stores all imported folders in a new folder named Imported Folder. You can keep whatever imported folders you want to keep and remove those you don't want to use with Windows Mail by right-clicking the folder and selecting Delete.

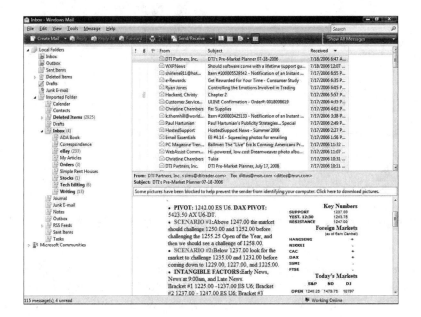

FIGURE 40.4
After Windows Mail imports your folders, you'll see your familiar folders and their contents in a new folder named Imported Folder.

If you've used the Vista program called Windows Contacts and manually added contacts there or perhaps imported them from Outlook Express, you can import those contacts into Windows Mail as well. Even better, when you import contacts from Outlook or Outlook Express into Windows Mail, Vista also uses those same contacts for Windows Contacts, a program that does nothing but manage your contacts, as Figure 40.5 shows. Windows Contacts serves up your contacts to various Vista programs that can access those contacts.

Did you
Know?

FIGURE 40.5
The Windows
Contacts pro-
gram, which
automatically
updates when
you update your
Windows Mail
contacts,
makes your con-
tacts available
to other Vista
programs, and
acts as a stand-
alone contact-
management
tool for you to
manage names
and addresses
of associates,
family, and
friends.

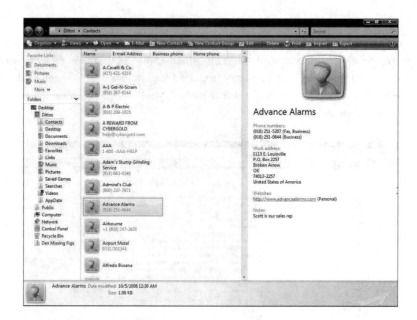

Sending Mail with Windows Mail

Obviously you'll use Windows Mail to send emails to others. The following steps
show you how to send various forms of email to recipients. Windows Mail probably
works exactly the way you expect it to if you've used other email programs in the
past. Windows Mail has several options, but you can send email messages and files
to others very easily without worrying too much about what else is under Windows
Mail's hood.

1. Click Windows Mail's Create Mail button to open the New Message window.

2. Type your recipient's email address in the To field or click the To button to
   select the recipient if the name appears in your Windows Mail contacts list.

3. Use the Cc (Carbon copy) field to send copies of your message to another
   recipient. The recipient will know that the message was copied to him. If you
   enter an email address in the Bcc (Blind carbon copy) field, the To and Cc
   recipients will not know that the Bcc recipients got copies of the message.

If you do not see the Bcc box, select View, All Headers, and the Bcc field will
appear beneath your carbon copy field.

4. Enter a subject line. Get in the habit of entering a subject so that your recipients can file your messages by subject.

5. Press the Tab key or Shift+Tab to move from field to field. When you type the message in the message area, a scrollbar enables you to scroll through messages that don't completely fit inside the window. Use the formatting toolbar above the message area to apply formatting, color, and even numbered and bulleted lists to your message. You must be careful, however, to make sure that your recipients have an email program capable of reading all the formatting that Windows Mail can produce. Unless you send plain text messages, your recipient might not be able to read your message clearly without Windows Mail or a fully compatible email program.

6. If you want to attach one or more files to your message, select Insert, File and select a file from the Open dialog box that appears. (The Attach toolbar button, the one with the paper clip icon, also attaches a file to your email.)

7. Windows Mail supports email formatting. You can change your font and other formatting details, create bulleted and numbered lists, and insert pictures and hyperlinks using the formatting toolbar above the message body area.

Windows Mail supports spell-checking! Click the top toolbar's spell-check button (the one with the letters *ABC* on it) to make sure that your message's spelling is correct before sending your email.

Did you Know?

---

8. Your message might look something like the one in Figure 40.6. As you can see from the name in the To field, when you select one of your contacts, as opposed to typing an email address, Windows Mail fills in your recipient's name as well. To send the message, click the Send button and the message goes on its way toward the recipients.

Sending email messages and attached files to the right recipients, as you can see, requires only that you know the person's email address or locate that person's email address from your list of email addresses in Windows Mail.

You can send an email to multiple recipients (or multiple Cc- or multiple Bcc-filled recipients) by separating multiple email addresses with a semicolon.

Did you Know?

Spell-check button┐ ┌File attachment button

FIGURE 40.6
Your new email
message is
ready to send.

Attachment included ──

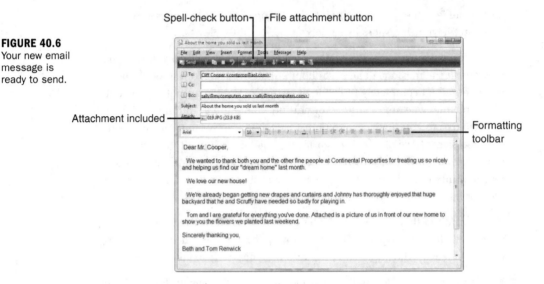

Formatting
toolbar

Send Web Pages in Emails

You can send entire web pages to any recipient using Windows Mail. The reason you
might do this is that you want someone to see something firsthand on a web page
you just visited. By sending the page in an email, you act a little like your own RSS
service, sending web content to specific people whose email address you know.

Before sending a web page with Windows Mail, make sure that Windows Mail is
your default email program by opening the Control Panel's Programs group and
selecting Default Programs. Select the Set Your Default Programs option, choose
Windows Mail, click the Set as Default option, and close the window.

> The default email program you set will be the one displayed at the top of your
> Start menu in the slot labeled E-mail. Outlook places your default web browser
> (usually Internet Explorer) and email program in the top two Start menu slots
> because of the frequency that most users run those two programs.

Follow these steps to use Windows Mail to send an entire web page to someone:

1. Start Internet Explorer.

2. Display the web page that you want to send to somebody. (You can send the
   page to your own email account for a test if you want to see how such an
   email arrives.)

3. Click the arrow to the right of the toolbar's Page button to display a drop-down list of options.

4. Select Send Page by E-mail. When Vista confirms that you want to send the web page as an email, click Allow. (If you select Send Link by E-mail, Internet Explorer opens a new email message and inserts a hyperlink to the web page in the email.)

5. The email window opens so that you can select a recipient and add copies to others if you like. You can see the web page in your message body, like the one shown in Figure 40.7. Now *that's* quite a fancy email message!

Embedded web page

FIGURE 40.7
Your recipient will see the web page you sent when viewing this email.

6. Click the Send button to send the web page.

Remember that your recipient must also use an email program, such as Windows Mail or Outlook Express, that can display formatted email as web-based HTML code; otherwise, the recipient will get garbage in the message. Your recipient will be able to read the mail's text, but the email will be messed up because the recipient will see all the HTML formatting codes that are normally hidden.

Receiving Email in Windows Mail

You can receive and organize the email that people send to you by taking advantage of Windows Mail's folder structure. Windows Mail automatically checks for new email messages every 30 minutes, but you can change this frequency. To set the email check frequency so that Windows Mail checks every 5 minutes, select Tools, Options and click the General tab to display the page shown in Figure 40.8.

Change frequency here

FIGURE 40.8
You can request
that Windows
Mail check for
new email mes-
sages more
often.

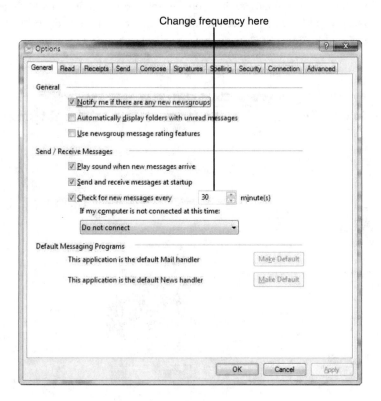

Even if Windows Mail hasn't checked for emails, you can. Click the toolbar's Send/Receive button to refresh your email account, send any emails that might be in your Outbox folder, and receive any emails that have been sent to you since your most recent send and receive action.

As you click the headers in the Inbox, a preview appears for that message in the lower pane. (Drag the center bar up or down to make more or less room for the headers.) If you double-click an Inbox item, a window opens so that you can view the message from a larger window without the other screen elements getting in the way.

Managing Email and Folders

Delete mail you do not want by selecting one or more message headers and dragging them to the Deleted Items icon. The Deleted Items area acts like the Windows Recycle Bin. Mail does not really go away until you delete items from the Deleted Items area by clicking the Deleted Items icon and removing unwanted mail. You can also delete mail by clicking the mail item and pressing the Delete key.

You can easily reply to an email message's author, or to the entire group if you are one of several who was sent mail, by clicking the Reply or Reply All toolbar button. In addition, when reading email, you can compose a new message by clicking the toolbar's Create Mail button.

You can create new folders to store email that you want to keep for future reference. Select File, New, Folder to display the Create Folder window in Figure 40.9. Type a folder name in the Folder Name field and click the folder where you want to insert the new one. The new folder will be a subfolder of the one you click.

If you're unsure where the new folder should go, put it in your Inbox folder.

By the Way

FIGURE 40.9
Create new folders so that you can organize your messages by subject.

You can drag any folder from one location to another.

Did you Know?

If an email arrives with an attachment, you'll see a paper clip icon to the left of the email's From recipient in your Inbox. Figure 40.10 shows a series of emails, four of which have attachments. All have been read before except the top one from DTI Partners. The envelope icon to the left of a message's sender's name or email indicates whether you've read—indicated by an open envelope—or haven't yet read that email.

FIGURE 40.10
A paper clip icon indicates that an email has a file attached to it.

Click to open attachment

Attachments   Unread message

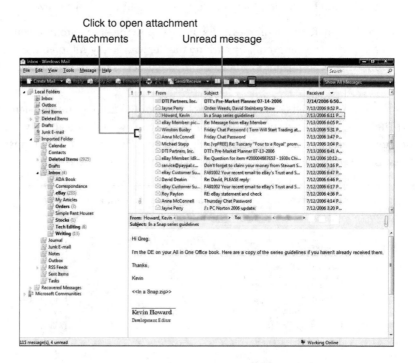

To open the attachment, click the email's paper clip icon and click the filename. To save the attached file to your disk, click the email's attachment paperclip, select Save Attachments, and enter a filename. Windows Mail stores the attachment to the folder you select.

Watch Out!

Don't open attachments from unknown sources. Nasty viruses often arrive as email attachments. Even if someone you know sends you an email with an attachment, it doesn't mean that the email is safe. Some Trojan programs hijack a user's contacts list and, in the background, sends email to everyone in the contacts list from the computer owner's email address without the owner knowing it's happening. Keep your antivirus and spyware programs up-to-date because they should catch most of or all the problems you might have.

Your Blocked Senders and Junk Email Options

Windows Mail maintains a list of blocked senders. If you receive junk email or other email you no longer want to receive, right-click the message, select Junk E-mail, and select Add Sender to Blocked Senders List to add the email's sender to your blocked emails. In the future, any emails you receive from that sender automatically go to your Junk E-mail folder. You should periodically click your Junk E-mail folder to view the mail there. Windows Mail's Junk E-mail filter, although good, isn't perfect and it sometimes happens that a valid email gets sent to your Junk E-mail folder by mistake.

You can ask Windows Mail's help in cleaning up your Inbox by setting Windows Mail's Junk E-mail filter to a higher-than-default setting. To do this, select Tools, Junk E-mail Options to open your Junk E-mail Options dialog box shown in Figure 40.11.

FIGURE 40.11
Select the level of junk email filtering that Windows Mail is to perform.

If you select the No Automatic Filtering option, Windows Mail sends only email you've requested to be blocked to your Junk E-mail folder. By raising the level of junk email filtering from Low to High, you greatly increase the number of emails that Windows Mail sends to your Junk E-mail folder, but it also sends some valid emails there by mistake. That is why it's incumbent on you to check your Junk E-mail folder every day or two to make sure that you don't miss a valid email.

If you select Safe List Only, Windows Mail sends *all* email you receive to your Junk E-mail folder except those emails sent by people in your Safe Senders list. You maintain the Safe Senders list by clicking the Junk E-Mail Options dialog box's Safe Senders tab and adding new email addresses.

Did you Know?

All email addresses in your Windows Contacts folder are assumed safe and Windows Mail will not block any of their emails unless you click to uncheck the option labeled Also Trust E-mail from My Windows Contacts. If you click the option labeled Automatically Add People I E-mail to the Safe Senders List, Windows Mail monitors to whom you send emails. Windows Mails adds everyone you send an email to your Safe Senders list so that they won't be blocked in the future.

If you receive an email that contains graphics and the sender is not part of your Safe Senders list, Windows Mail blocks the graphics and puts a red *X* inside a box to indicate that it is blocking the graphic image from view. Windows Mail does this because viruses and spyware software can arrive in an email disguised as a graphic image; by blocking the image, Windows Mail blocks that kind of danger from infecting your computer. Figure 40.12 shows such an email. The email is from Amazon.com, a trusted source that sends email with lots of graphics that are safe from such problems.

FIGURE 40.12
Windows Mail blocks pictures from unknown email recipients.

When you receive such an email, you can click the yellow information bar above the previewed email with the blocked pictures to request that Windows Mail load the pictures and display the email as the sender intended it to display. If you then add the sender to your Safe Senders list, Windows Mail never again blocks the graphic images that come inside emails from that sender.

Create an Email Signature

You can add a message to the bottom of every email you send by creating an email signature. If, for example, you routinely sell on eBay, you might want to direct all readers of your email to a list of your current auctions—an email signature could do just that. A business might require that all emails sent from the company's domain include a privacy clause or perhaps an equal-opportunity employment clause, and an email signature is great for that purpose By creating a signature to appear automatically, the sender never has to worry about forgetting to type the message.

After you create a signature, every time you create a new email message, Windows Mail automatically adds your signature to the bottom of the email. You don't need to do anything except send the email. To really catch the reader's eye, you can highlight your email signature in color or format the signature to look the way you want it to look.

> For that rare email you might not want to send a signature with, you can delete the signature's text before sending the email.

By the Way

To add a signature, select Tools, Options and click to select the Signatures tab. Click the New button to type a new signature in the Edit Signature box. Click Rename to rename the signature something other than Windows Mail's default name so that you can select the signature from a list of additional signatures you might add in the future. Click the Add Signatures to All Outgoing Messages to make sure that your new email signature appears at the bottom of every email you send. You can also make sure that your email signature appears at the bottom of every email you reply to or forward, assuming that you want your signature on such emails, by unchecking the Don't Add Signatures to Replies and Forwards option. Figure 40.13 shows the creation of a signature. After you finish the signature, click OK to save it.

FIGURE 40.13
Create an email signature that you want to appear at the bottom of every email you send.

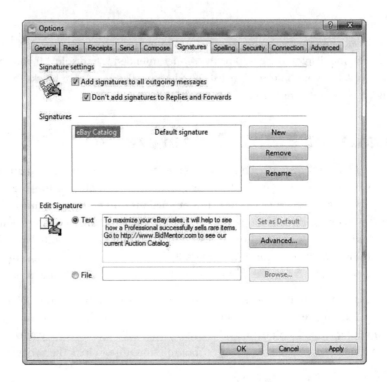

> **By the Way**
>
> The Advanced button displays a list of all email accounts currently set up in Windows Mail so that you can select which account's email you want the signature test to appear on.

> **Did you Know?**
>
> If your goal for your signature is to get the email's recipient to click a link, that's great because if you include a hyperlink in a signature, Windows Mail turns that link's text into an active and clickable link. Some senders find that formatting the entire signature text as a hyperlink is more likely to grab that click than an embedded hyperlink. You'll have to test this to see which works best in your situation.

The next time you create a new email message, Windows Mail places your default signature at the bottom of the message. Figure 40.14 shows such a message.

Adding a few blank spaces above a signature or using a smaller signature font size helps to distinguish the signature from your email message.

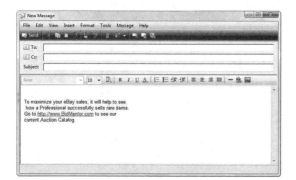

FIGURE 40.14
Windows Mail does all the signature's work by placing the signature at the bottom of every email you create.

If you want a really fancy signature, such as one with a yellow background and perhaps a small picture, use your word processor or other web page creation program, such as Microsoft Publisher, to create a nicely formatted signature. Save the signature as an HTML file. You can use that file as your email signature in Windows Mail by clicking the File option on the Signatures dialog box and browsing to that HTML file. Select the HTML file and Windows Mail loads the HTML code and formats your signature accordingly.

Did you Know?

Chapter Wrap-Up

This chapter explained how to use Windows Mail, Windows Vista's free email program and newsgroup manager. Email is a major part of every Internet user's life, and you'll appreciate Windows Mail's advanced support and email management simplicity. You can import all your existing email and contacts so that you'll be ready to send emails to family and friends in no time.

If you want detailed information on a subject, you can search the Web for all kinds of data, but you'll want to keep newsgroups in mind as another source. Windows Mail doesn't do only mail well—it is also known as a *newsreader client* that enables you to access thousands of messages and files on subjects that interest you. In the next chapter, you'll learn how to set up and use Windows Mail as a newsgroup reader.

CHAPTER 41

Accessing a World of Information in Newsgroups

In This Chapter:

- ▶ See how newsgroups bring millions of messages to you, all organized by topics that might interest you
- ▶ Locate a newsgroup provider
- ▶ Subscribe to newsgroups
- ▶ Read messages, tips, and advice about your hobbies, TV shows, and interests
- ▶ Download newsgroup attachments that you want to work with
- ▶ Place your own messages and files on a newsgroup to help others

What is your favorite hobby? Start Windows Mail, click on one of the newsgroup servers, and type your hobby name in the newsgroup list to see whether any matching newsgroups appear. Probably more than one newsgroup that's all about your hobby will appear, sometimes dozens. Welcome to the world of newsgroups, where hundreds and possibly thousands of people are sending messages and files to each other related to items that interest them.

Newsgroups are fun to monitor and you will often find a wealth of information that interests you there. Newsgroups comprise the big secret jewel of Internet information. A loosely based, somewhat organized by topic, massively large database resides in newsgroups and all you need is Windows Mail—and a subscription to a newsreader service—to access that data.

Introducing the World of Newsgroups

Using the Internet, you primarily share information with others in one of three ways:

▶ Web pages

▶ Email

▶ Newsgroups

Data put on a web page gets read only when someone browses to that page or clicks a link to get there. Email messages generally arrive at their destination within a few seconds or minutes, and if the recipients are online they can read a message as soon as they see that one arrived and they take steps to read it. Newsgroups offer a different kind of messaging center for messages you want to communicate publicly about a topic. You can post newsgroup topics, surveys, articles, questions, answers, music, videos, and read similar information from others who are interested in the same subjects you are.

By the Way

Newsgroups typically have little or nothing to do with the daily news, unless of course a newsgroup is named and set aside to discuss current events. In a way, a newsgroup acts like a combination of a slow email program and a community bulletin board. Newsgroups are thousands of lists, arranged by subject, that hold messages and files that you and others can post and read.

Suppose that you are interested in rollerblading and want to trade information you have with others who are interested in the sport. You could find one of the several newsgroups related to skating and read the hundreds of messages and files posted to that newsgroup. Depending on the Internet service you use and the newsgroup-filing rules, you might find messages months old or only from the past few days. Often, the larger newsgroups can keep only a limited number of days' worth of messages and files available, especially if pictures and videos are common in that group.

This is how newsgroups act like slow email services: If someone posts a question to which you know the answer, you can post a reply. Everyone in the newsgroup who wants to read your reply sees it. There's no guarantee that the person who submitted the question will ever go back to the newsgroup to read the answer, but the postings are for anybody and everybody who is interested.

If you've used Outlook Express in previous versions of Windows to read news-groups, Windows Mail works the same way. Windows Mail, however, uses a differ-ent file structure that will not freeze if your message storage for a newsgroup grows to more than 2GB as Outlook Express did.

By the Way

Locating a Newsgroup Provider

Different newsgroup providers (also called *news servers* and *newsgroup servers*) are available to sell access to the thousands and thousands of newsgroups in existence. To see newsgroups available in a newsgroup service, you can scan the newsgroup provider's website to see which groups it offers. Perform an Internet search on *news-group servers* to locate newsgroup providers. Costs range from free for some more limited web-based newsgroup providers (such as http://groups.google.com/) to more than $20 per month for the more comprehensive newsgroup providers. Several of the well-established newsgroup providers are

- ▶ Newsfeeds.com
- ▶ Newsdemon.com
- ▶ Newsrover.com

In the early days of the Internet, Internet service providers gave away free news-group access to their members. For example, MSN.com, ATT.com, and AOL.com each offered free newsgroup access to anyone who subscribed to their ISP and got Internet service from them. These days, ISPs rarely if ever give away full news-group access. Some might offer a limited set of newsgroups, but those groups are usually limited to groups about that provider such as Microsoft's own msnews.microsoft.com newsgroup that is free and manned by Microsoft's own support staff some of the time to provide support on various Microsoft products. You will find a few ISPs around the country that still provide this valuable service, such as Comcast and Insight.

By the Way

Before you can access any newsgroup, you must contact a newsgroup provider and sign up for service. You then must set up Windows Mail so that Windows Mail can access the newsgroups offered by the newsgroup provider.

The procedure for setting up a new newsgroup inside Windows Mail differs depend-ing on which newsgroup provider you sign up with, but the basic method is similar to setting up a new email account (which you learned to do in the previous chap-ter). Newsgroups follow a slightly less universal standard, however, and you must rely on your newsgroup provider to send you instructions for connecting Windows

Mail to your provider's newsgroups. After Windows Mail makes your newsgroup provider's newsgroups available, you're ready to access the groups.

Subscribing to Newsgroups

Keep in mind that tens of thousands of newsgroups exist, ranging from subjects as universal as music and books to obscure subjects such as medical practitioners who use Corel's WordPerfect software. After you set up Windows Mail to read your provider's newsgroups, you can display a list of the thousands of newsgroups available any time you want. To read from one or more of them, however, you must subscribe to a newsgroup. The subscription doesn't cost money (other than your monthly newsgroup provider's fee), you can subscribe to as many newsgroups as interest you, and you don't give any personal information when you subscribe. To **subscribe**, in this instance, simply means you want to see all the individual messages and files located within that newsgroup.

After you set up Windows Mail to read your newsgroup provider's newsgroups, that newsgroup provider's news server name appears in the Windows Mail Navigation window pane below your email folders. For example, if you sign up to get your newsgroup access from Newsfeeds.com, a news.newsfeeds.com entry appears at the bottom of your Windows Mail navigation pane as shown in Figure 41.1.

Indicates no newsgroups are subscribed to

FIGURE 41.1
You have to subscribe to a newsgroup to read the individual messages inside that group.

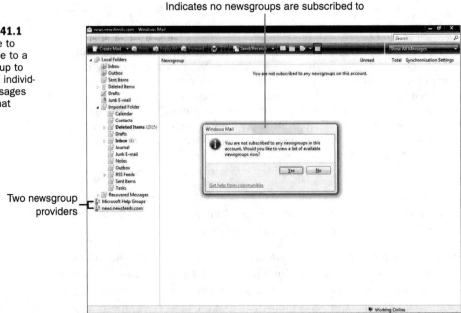

Two newsgroup providers

Actually, you don't *have* to subscribe to a specific newsgroup to read its messages; you can visit there without subscribing. In doing that, however, you will have to select the newsgroup again the next time you want to read its messages. By subscribing, Windows Mail remembers your subscription and you can more quickly access that newsgroup the next time you want to read the group's messages.

By the Way

As Figure 41.1 shows, if you click to select your newsgroup provider's name, Windows Mail pops up a message box telling you that you haven't yet subscribed to any specific newsgroup.

Click Yes to view a full list of your provider's available newsgroups. After a brief pause, an alphabetical list of all newsgroups available from your newsgroup provider appears. Figure 41.2 shows such a list. Scroll through the list and you will see tens of thousands of groups. Keep in mind, these are not the actual messages, but the available *subjects*; within each subject can reside thousands of messages and files that you can access to the moment you subscribe to that group.

Click to see newsgroups currently subscribed to

Selected newsgroup server

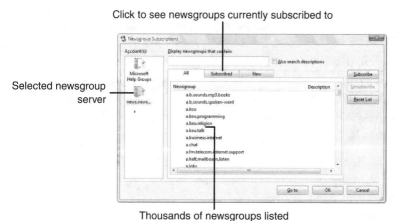

Thousands of newsgroups listed

FIGURE 41.2
Scroll through the list of numerous subjects you'll find.

With the good comes the bad. Tens of thousands of newsgroups await you, and maybe half of them have junk and spam or nothing at all in them. Most of the ones that are left have something in them that resembles the newsgroup name to some extent. The facts that you have tens of thousands to choose from, and that more than half might not be worth much and probably shouldn't even exist shouldn't sway you from the fact that many thousands *do* have information of interest to whomever wants to discuss or know more about that newsgroup's topic.

Watch Out!

By the Way

> In general, nobody monitors newsgroups. In certain newsgroups, called *moderated newsgroups*, some people do delete messages that don't pertain to the subject, remove any spam that might appear, and generally keep the group on topic. The people who do this are often the very people who created the newsgroup to begin with. The reason there are so many newsgroups is because anyone can create one. You can, too, by clicking the New button at the top of the list of available newsgroups.

Although your newsreader provider gives you access to the tens of thousands of newsgroups you see in your Newsgroup Subscription window's list, subscribe only to those groups that interest you.

Newsgroups have strange names, such as rec.pets.dogs and alt.algebra.help. Table 41.1 describes what the more common newsgroup prefixes stand for. Elsewhere in the newsgroup name you can often glean more information about the newsgroup's primary topic; for example, a newsgroup named rec.sport.skating.roller would probably contain skating news, and alt.autos.italian would contain files and messages pertaining to Italian cars (*i macchine italiani!*).

TABLE 41.1   Common Newsgroup Prefixes Describe the Nature of the Newsgroup

Prefix	Description
alt	Groups that allow informal content and are not necessarily as widely distributed as the other newsgroups
biz	Business-related newsgroups
comp	Computer-related newsgroups
misc	Random newsgroups
rec	Recreational and sporting newsgroups
sci	Scientific newsgroups
soc	Social issue-related newsgroups
talk	Debate newsgroups

Scroll through the newsgroup list to find the newsgroups you want to see. When you find one or more newsgroups that might contain items you want to view, subscribe to those newsgroups by double-clicking the newsgroup name, or highlight the name and click Subscribe.

Did you Know?

Windows Mail is good about searching through the newsgroups when you type a few letters about a subject. For example, type **adobe** (the case doesn't matter so **ADOBE** returns the same results as **Adobe** and **adobe**) to see every newsgroup with the word *adobe* in its name. Some will be obvious; adobe.photoshop.windows is a newsgroup related to using the Windows version of Adobe Photoshop.

By the Way

Even though a Description column appears next to each newsgroup name, almost no newsgroup has the description filled in, so you must rely on the newsgroup name to figure out what you want to view.

If you click the Subscribe tab, you'll see the list of newsgroups to which you subscribe. After subscribing to some newsgroups, click the OK button to close the Newsgroups window and prepare to read the news.

Enter a search topic in the text box at the top of the Newsgroups window to display newsgroups that contain that topic. As you type more of the topic for which to search, the list below the text box shrinks to include only those newsgroups that include the text you enter.

Reading Messages in Newsgroups

After you subscribe to one or more newsgroups, you want to view them. Follow these general steps to read messages in your subscribed newsgroups:

1. After subscribing to several newsgroups, a list of your subscribed newsgroups appears, as shown in Figure 41.3. Unless you've already visited one or more of the newsgroups, you will see 0 in the Unread and Total count columns. When you've visited newsgroups that you've subscribed to and read messages, the count columns will reflect that activity.

By the Way

Keep in mind that a message might be a short note or an entire file. As with email, if a news posting contains a file, the file will come as an attachment to the message.

2. To read messages in a newsgroup, double-click that newsgroup name. Figure 41.4 appears showing the newsgroups in the upper window and the text for the selected newsgroup in the lower window. Some long messages take a while to arrive, and you won't see any of the messages until the entire message downloads to your PC.

FIGURE 41.3
Your newly sub-
scribed news-
groups appear
in the middle of
your screen.

Subscribed newsgroups

Only one subscribed newsgroup
has been viewed on this PC

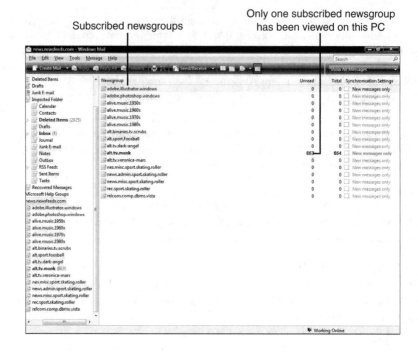

FIGURE 41.3
Your newly sub-
scribed news-
groups appear
in the middle of
your screen.

Click to read message's thread   Selected newsgroup name

Individual message headers

FIGURE 41.4
Scroll through
the news mes-
sage headers
and see detail
in the lower
pane.

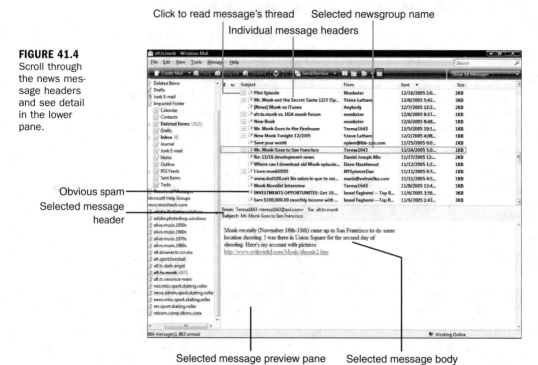

Obvious spam
Selected message
header

Selected message preview pane   Selected message body

Windows Mail downloads the first 300 messages in a newsgroup when you visit that group. After you go through the messages, you can select Tools, Get Next 300 Headers to load another 300 messages. Actually, Windows Mail downloads only the message *header* and not each of the 300 message bodies or attachments if any attachments are associated with a message. (A newsgroup message's header corresponds to an email's Subject field in that the header should describe the contents of the message.)

Select Tools, Options and click the Read tab to increase the number of messages Windows Mail downloads. Change the Get value to a number as high as 999. Windows Mail will download 999 headers every time you select Tools, Get instead of only 300 when you change the value to 999 in the Options Read tabbed page. If a newsgroup happens not to have 999 message headers left to display, Windows Mail will download as many headers as there are and you can scroll through them.

If a message has a plus sign next to it, click the plus sign to open all related messages. The messages form a *thread*, meaning that they relate to each other. If someone posts a question, for example, and several people reply to that posting, those related messages group themselves under the first question's message, and you can see the replies only after you click the plus sign. The plus sign becomes a minus sign when you expand the newsgroup item so that you can collapse the item again.

As mentioned earlier, some newsgroups are moderated better than others. Keep this in mind because you'll often find unrelated messages throughout all newsgroups. Just expect that you'll find such unrelated items and you'll be pleased when you run across the wealth of messages that *do* relate to the newsgroup's subject. Newsgroups have lots of spam messages in them, but your antivirus program won't remove the spam or send the message to a junk folder because the message is on a newsgroup server somewhere and not on your computer unless you download an attachment and run it. Be careful, obviously, about running anything you download from a newsgroup although an MP3, picture, or message body is usually safe.

3. Check the Size column to determine whether you can read the message in the lower window or whether you should open a new window to view the message. If a message is more than 2 or 3KB, you should probably double-click the message header to view the message inside a scrollable window. The window contains a menu that enables you to save the message in a file on your disk for later retrieval. If a message has an attachment, you must open the message in a separate window to save the attachment as a file on your disk.

After you read a message inside the preview pane, you can click another message header to view another message. If you view a message in a separate window, you can close the window to view a different message.

4. If you want to reply to a message, you have two options: reply to the group, in which case everybody who subscribes to the newsgroup can read your reply; or reply to the author privately via email. The Reply Group and Reply toolbar buttons accomplish these purposes. Each copies the original message at the bottom of your reply.

You can reply to a message or start a new message topic. You can also start a new message thread (related postings) by clicking the Write Message button (the far-left toolbar button) and typing a new message. The message window looks a lot like an email message that you create in Windows Mail, as Figure 41.5 shows.

When you click Send, after a while, your message appears in the newsgroup as a new post and not part of a chain of previous postings.

Newsgroup to post in   Click to attach file to message

FIGURE 41.5
Talk to the world (or at least those in the world who visit newsgroups) by sending messages to a newsgroup to ask questions, answer questions, or visit and share information about your interests.

Message header

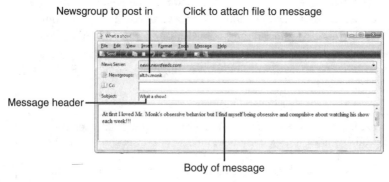

Body of message

Probably the biggest problem with newsgroups is the time you waste in them! You might hop over to a newsgroup to see whether the group contains an answer you need, and two hours later you're still reading the postings. Newsgroups can provide a wealth of information on thousands and thousands of topics. Although the Web is great for organizing information into collections of pages, newsgroups are most useful for the messages and files that people want to share with each other.

Cleaning Up the Newsgroup Clutter

As you download message headers and message bodies and attachments, your disk drive can quickly become cluttered with files and messages you don't necessarily need. Although today's disk drives are huge, having a lot of old, extra newsgroup message-related content will slow down your backups and make Windows Mail clunkier when you access newsgroups that you have weeks of data stored for.

To clean all or part of Windows Mail's newsgroup storage area, select Tools, Options, click Advanced, and then click the Maintenance button to open the Maintenance dialog box. Click the Clean Up Now button to display Figure 41.6's Local File Clean Up dialog box.

FIGURE 41.6
Regularly clean up Windows Mail's file area to keep your disk drive running at its best, your newsgroups loading at their quickest, and your backups taking less time and space when you perform a complete backup of your computer.

Click the Select button and select the news server you want to clean up. If you subscribe to only one newsgroup server, the choice isn't difficult to make. (You can also clean up your email using this maintenance screen when you select Windows Mail to clean up instead of a newsgroup server.)

Click the Remove Messages button to remove all downloaded message bodies and attachments but leave the headers downloaded so that you don't have to load several days or weeks worth of messages when you want to search the newsgroup for something. Click the Delete button to delete both message headers and bodies, but still leave message headers that you've downloaded in the past marked as read so that you know which messages you read in the past. Click the Reset button to completely erase all message headers, bodies, and attachments (assuming that you didn't save the message attachments to one of your user account's folders such as Documents) and to reset all the headers as unread so that the next time you visit the newsgroup, all messages download as though you've never been there before.

How Can I Locate an Old Newsgroup Message?

Sometimes you read a newsgroup message but later you are unable to locate that message in that newsgroup again. It's frustrating when you want to reread a message that you didn't save and you've cleaned up your Windows Mail newsgroups so that the headers and message bodies no longer appear in your newsgroup reading pane.

Depending on how long ago you saw the message, you might or might not be able to locate and download the message again. Each news server holds a limited number of messages. As you know, Windows Mail downloads, at most, 999 messages at any one time. Sometimes the newsgroup server will have more than 999 messages available and sometimes not.

As a news server's reaches its newsgroup limits, that news server begins to erase the oldest messages (including headers, bodies, and attachments) to make room for newer messages. If the message you want to reread isn't too old, it might be there, but you might have to select Tools, Get Next 999 Headers several times before you can find it. (The Edit, Find, message menu command is helpful to locate messages from the headers you've loaded with the Get command. In addition, the Search box works to quickly locate message headers that match your search term.) If the message is one of the older ones that your news server had to erase to make room for new messages, you'll never retrieve the message. Therefore, if you read a message that you might want to have around later, select File, Save and save the message to your Documents folder. All messages use the .nws filename extension, and usually any word processor or text reader such as Vista's Notepad can read the messages you save.

Chapter Wrap-Up

This chapter explained how to use Windows Mail's newsgroup feature, the half of Windows Mail not connected to email. When you want detailed information on a subject, you can search the Web for all kinds of data, but remember to look for newsgroups on the topic as well. Whereas some websites are often consumer-related collections of merchandise and hype, newsgroups often contain thousands of messages from people like you who have questions and answers for others with the same interest.

The next chapter begins Part VIII, "Making Vista Work Better for You." You're about finished with the beginning of your Vista education and you've mastered far more in this book than most users who use Vista for several years will know. Congratulations! The next few chapters round out your Vista education with a few tips that will make Vista work better for you and some traps that you should avoid.

PART VIII

Making Vista Work Better for You

CHAPTER 42

Vista's Ten Best Tips That Save You Time and Grief

The format of this chapter is a little different from the chapters that came before. Instead of the more traditional sections, you'll find exactly ten sections here and in each is a tip. The tip might be short or long but no matter its length, each tip aims to give you an insightful way to use Vista and your computer together for a better and more pleasant experience.

You worked hard to master Windows Vista. You've now mastered the basics and more, so now you're ready to move up to the level of official *Windows Vista Guru*. This chapter teaches several practical tips that you are ready for now that you understand the ins and outs of Vista.

By the Way

There are so many things you can do with Vista that it's impossible to rank tips in order of coolness! There's no order of importance in these tips. Just read them, use them, and save enough time and frustration with them that you have more time to watch videos with Windows Media Player.

Eliminate User Account Control Message Boxes

Okay, security is just wonderful until you *don't* need it—then it gets in your way. After you install your antivirus program, your spyware protection, and turn on a firewall, you have gone above and beyond what many people do and protected yourself against the nasties that want to rob your computer's data and files.

When you've done all that, it seems that Vista still asks you to confirm your Administrator user account privileges every time you try to do anything reasonable like create a restore point. The User Account Control (UAC) message pops up and gets in your way. It's almost as though Vista forgot that the very first thing you did when you sat down at the keyboard was log in as an Administrator.

Vista didn't forget. As explained in Chapter 27, "Managing Your Windows Security," the UAC is there on both Administrator user and Standard user accounts to remind you that what you're about to do has some potential to harm the system or other users. As long as you confirm your administrative privileges, you're on your way. You can even perform administrative-level tasks when logged in as a standard user as long as you know the password of one or more administrative user accounts on your computer. But still, the messages get frustrating.

You can turn the annoying messages off. You probably shouldn't, but let's face it: Many other users who know how to do it probably will.

One thing you can do is create a new Administrator user account, perhaps called *Freedom*, and turn off the UAC in that one account. Then you use your other account for computing when you want to be more careful and when you're less likely to need one of the administrative-level programs.

To turn off the UAC, follow these steps:

1. Log in to an Administrator user account.

2. Open your Control Panel's User Accounts and Family Safety group.

3. Click User Accounts to modify the account.

4. Click the Turn On or Off User Account Control (UAC) On or Off link. After one final UAC message box confirmation (good riddance!), you can click to uncheck the Use User Account Control option on the window that appears (shown in Figure 42.1), click OK and reboot, and you won't be hassled by those pesky messages again.

5. To turn UAC back on if you miss the messages, repeat the process.

FIGURE 42.1
Say goodbye to
UAC messages.

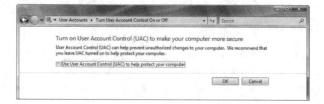

Rearrange Your Start Menu

If you don't like the location of a menu item on one of your Start menus, drag that item to another location. When you've opened one of the Start submenus, such as the All Programs, Accessories submenu, you can click and drag any item to another menu. To drag a menu item such as the Command Prompt from the Accessories menu to the System menu, display the menu and locate Command Prompt. Drag it to the System Tools menu folder; after a brief pause (while you continue holding the drag) System Tools opens, and you can release the Command Prompt selection inside the System menu where it will remain.

When you make such a move, Vista warns you with Figure 42.2's message window that this move affects all users of the system, but that's fine. Just remember that other users might be confused if they expect to find the menu item on the Start menu's top level, for example, and it's not there because you moved the item further down into the menu structure.

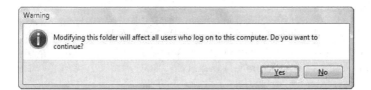

FIGURE 42.2
Some menu restructuring moves menu items from locations other users have become familiar with, so confirm that you want to do this.

Make Yourself More Comfortable

What's the most important component in your PC system? It's not your system unit, your CPU, the speed with which Vista performs, your hard disk, or your printer. Your most important component is the very chair you sit in. Smart computer users spend almost as much money on their chair as they do on their operating systems.

If you spend an hour or more a day at your PC, run, don't walk, to your local office furniture store and check out their desk chair selection. If you've never paid much attention, you'll be shocked at how many kinds of chairs that you find. Your back, arms, shoulders, and wrists (not to mention the body part on which you sit), deserve far better than the average chair most people place in front of their computers. You'll be more productive, work more accurately, and you'll feel better.

The better desk chairs provide separate controls for the arm rests, back and lumbar support, and height. Make sure that you can adjust these components easily *while sitting in the chair*. Look for a chair on wheels that rolls easily so that you can move between your PC and other work areas.

Did you Know?

Stop a Copy or Move

This one is so easy to do, yet it's often forgotten. It's been around since early versions of Windows, but if you've never heard of it you'll be grateful to learn about it.

Sometimes you begin a copy or move operation with your mouse by dragging something from one location to another, and you realize that you want to cancel the copy or move. What do you do when you've got the items dragged over a folder where you first thought you wanted them? If you release the files, they are put in the folder whether or not you want them there. If you move your mouse pointer back to the original location where you dragged from, Vista creates a copy of the files in that same folder.

All you do to end a drag or copy operation that you've begun is press Esc. Vista cancels the current copy or move in progress and all your files and folders are in the same state they were in before you began.

Instantly Speed Up Any Computer with ReadyBoost

Truly one of the most amazing tips to help just about any Vista user whose computer is sluggish uses a simple ubiquitous USB flash drive.

One of the ways you can improve the speed of an older computer is to add memory to the machine. That means locating and purchasing the correct memory chips, opening the system unit, and installing the new memory. The process isn't always as straightforward as it should be and you risk damaging something when you insert the memory because such electronics are extremely fragile.

Instead of buying memory, just buy a USB flash drive. Better yet, wait for a post-Christmas sale and you can often find them free after rebate. With such a drive, and the more memory it has the better (at least 512MB is a great place to begin), plug the flash drive into a spare USB port. Use one on the back of your computer because this isn't something you'll be removing once you see what happens.

When you plug a USB flash drive into a Vista machine, Vista displays the expected AutoPlay dialog box shown in Figure 42.3. (Your AutoPlay options might differ slightly.)

FIGURE 42.3
A simple and cheap USB flash drive instantly speeds up almost any Vista computer.

Select the option labeled Speed Up My System to activate Vista's ReadyBoost feature. Vista begins using your flash drive as extra memory, eliminating the need for you to buy, add, and go to the trouble of installing memory chips.

> If your computer has already more than a gigabyte or more of memory, it probably has enough memory and a flash drive won't make as big a speed improvement as it will on Vista machines running 512MB.

By the Way

Type an Application's Name to Run It

Many of us appreciate Vista's one-column menu over the cascading Start menu that XP gave us. The one-column menu stays in place, allows everybody to see the rest of the screen, and seems to be more manageable in general. Nevertheless, the improvements to the Start menu don't help when you need to locate a program buried deep in the menu structure.

Programs you commonly run, such as Word, probably appear on your Start menu's Recent Items list (see Figure 42.4). Those programs are simple to find because they're right there when you click Start or press your Windows key on your keyboard.

FIGURE 42.4
Your recently
run items are
only a click
away.

Programs you've
recently run

To run programs that aren't on your recent items list without having to click menu folder after menu folder to locate them, just type a keyword from the program's name. For example, to run the Chess Titans program, you *could* find it on Vista's Start menu structure or you can display your Start menu, type chess, and press Enter. When you type, your letters appear in your Start menu's Search box and when you press Enter, Vista looks for the closest match. Unless you have more than one chess program on your computer, the Chess Titans game will start.

Save Paper

When printing a draft of anything, you can save paper, ink, energy, and time. Most printers support this feature so get in the habit of printing multiple pages of output on a single page.

Select File, Print from any Vista application and when the Print dialog box appears, click the Properties button. On one of the tabbed pages (usually called Finishing or Layout) you should see an option labeled Pages per Sheet. Click to display a drop-down list of options. Figure 42.5 shows such a list.

Preview

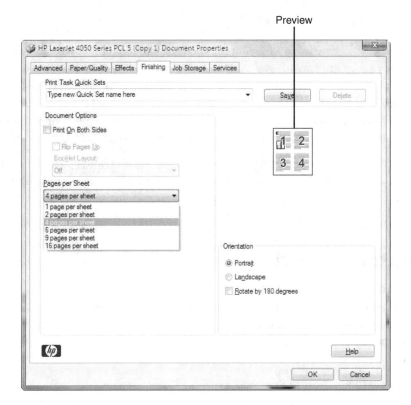

FIGURE 42.5
Print more than
one page of
output on a sin-
gle sheet of
paper to save
paper, energy,
ink, and time.

When you click OK and print the document, you will see four (if you selected 4
Pages Per Sheet) pages of output printed on one page of output. The pages are exact
reproductions of their full-page equivalents. Sometimes the text can be small and
you might have to print only two pages per page to keep everything readable, but
some people are able to print up to eight pages per sheet and still comfortably read
the output.

The document you print has as much to do with how readable the multiple printed
pages will be as your eyesight does. Some eBooks, for example, have very little
text and lots of whitespace on each page relative to a regular book, and printing
eight pages per sheet of such an eBook is more readable than you might expect.

By the
Way

Print to a Hotel Fax

When you write something with your laptop while you're on the road, you probably don't have your printer with you. Although you can back up your files to a flash drive or send yourself an email to a web-based email account with the files attached, you might feel better if you print the document. You'll then have the printed **hardcopy** (a term used for a printed document) in case something happens to your laptop and you can later edit the printed hardcopy at your convenience.

If you don't want to lug a printer on your trip, open Vista's Windows Fax and Scan program (open your Start menu, and type fax, and press Enter to use a tip from earlier in this chapter), and fax your document to the hotel fax machine. You will, in a few seconds, have a printout of your document.

Laptop Security

If you use a laptop, you can help get your laptop back if you lose it. Right now, before you forget, tape your business card to the bottom of your laptop. If you leave the laptop in an airport or hotel, the finder of your PC will be able to contact you to return the laptop. Sure, if a thief steals your laptop, he will know whom to thank, but many people are honest and it's worth the cost of a business card to try.

Don't wait; tape your card there *right now*.

> As a bonus tip, you can also use the Vista Paint program to create a background image for your Vista-based laptop. Use whatever image you want, but click the Text tool and type If found, call (111) 222-3333 or send an email to me at *MyName@ISP*.com. Anyone who finds your laptop will then easily be able to contact you.

Chapter 10, "Exploring the Windows Vista Accessories," explains how to start and use Vista's Paint program.

Spend Some Time in Windows Explorer

In Chapter 8, "Mastering Vista's Explorer Windows," you learned how Vista improved on the more stodgy Windows Explorer features that came before. Many windows in Vista now take on Explorer-like features, including the Control Panel, Computer Explorer window, Network Explorer, and more. New features such as live thumbnail previews (assuming that you have Aero) and zoom controls are common throughout most of the Explorer windows and the Search box is always present.

Pay attention to the icons when viewing an Explorer window and you'll glean a lot of information about the contents of your files and folders before you open them. For example, Figure 42.6 shows several folders inside a user's account and although you can look at the names of the folders, the icons used for each one gives a quicker representation of what the folder contains (videos, music, pictures, documents, and you can even see which folders are currently empty).

Empty   Multiple folders reside in this folder

FIGURE 42.6
Quickly scan your Explorer window's icons to learn what's there.

If you find yourself changing a folder's view by clicking its View button, the next time you change the folder's view you can make Vista retain that view in the future. Click to open the Organize drop-down list and select Folder and Search Options to open the Folder Options dialog box. Click the View tab and scroll to the option labeled Remember Each Folder's View Settings. Click to select the option (see Figure 42.7) and every time you subsequently close an Explorer window, Vista remembers the view you set and puts you back into that same view.

If the live icons don't provide enough detail for you when you search through your files and folders, you can request a preview pane and Vista displays an instant preview of your document that you can scroll through. This means you don't have to open the application that produced that document to read its contents.

FIGURE 42.7
Vista retains
your folder's
view for the
next time you
visit that folder.

Click to set ──

Vista isn't always able to preview a file's contents depending on how universal the application is. For example, you can preview PowerPoint, Excel, and Word documents, but you cannot get a preview of data files from a program such as InfoSelect that is less known and not one whose data files are available as a preview to Vista's Explorer windows.

By the
Way

Figure 42.8 shows a preview of a document. The Explorer window tells a lot about the file just by glancing at it: The document is a Word document, which you know from the small flying-*W* icon in the thumbnail. The thumbnail gives a preview of the document's contents, and by clicking the Organize drop-down list and selecting Layout, Preview Pane, a readable preview of the document appears to the right of the file list.

Did you
Know?

As a bonus Windows Explorer tip, remember that a slideshow is only a click away whenever you view pictures. When viewing a list of digital graphic images in a Windows Explorer window, click the toolbar's Slide Show button. Vista instantly changes to a full-screen, changing montage moving from image to image. Right-click the slideshow to change its speed and slide order. Press Esc to end the slideshow and return to your Explorer window.

Click to display preview   Preview pane

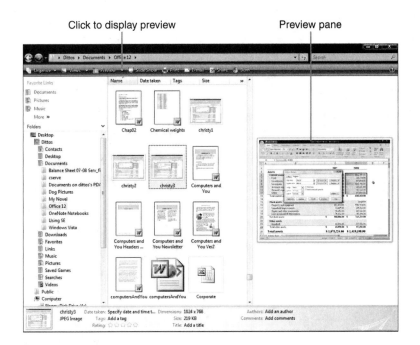

FIGURE 42.8
Not only can you use live thumbnail images to see what's in a file, but Explorer's preview pane shows actual, readable content that you can scroll through.

Chapter Wrap-Up

So, are you maximizing your Vista-powered computer?

This chapter showed you ways to do just that. These were just a sampling of tips that even the pros often forget about. Make Vista work smarter so that you can, too.

In the next chapter, you'll learn additional tips as well as some traps to avoid related to working online.

CHAPTER 43

Ten Terrific Online Tips to Help and Traps to Avoid

Many people use computers online more than they use them offline. They surf the Web, manage email, browse newsgroups, and chat with instant messaging. The time consumed by those activities often adds up to be more than the time they spend in traditional computing activities such as word processing, electronic spreadsheets, and financial record-keeping.

This chapter shows you ten ways to take your online experience to the next level without sacrificing safety and speed.

Stay Up-to-Date

Although this chapter's tips and traps aren't ranked in any specific order of importance, keeping your computer up-to-date is the primary means of helping most people to ensure their security and to keep their web-browsing experience safe. In addition, you're less likely to experience problems because your system programs remain up-to-date and running using the latest available versions.

When you select Windows Update from your Vista Start menu, you *should* see something like Figure 43.1. In the figure, it's obvious that the computer's Windows Vista is up-to-date and that no updates are available.

Vista offers to maintain an up-to-date computer for you. When you click the Change Settings link in the Windows Update's left window pane, you can click to select the option Install Updates Automatically and then select a frequency and time that's best for you. To really keep things updated, select Every Day and choose a time that won't conflict with anything you're doing, such as 3:00 a.m.

Choose a time when your computer will be turned on and connected to the Internet or the updates cannot occur until you next connect to the Internet.

Watch Out!

FIGURE 43.1
Keeping your computer up-to-date is the best way to guard against threats.

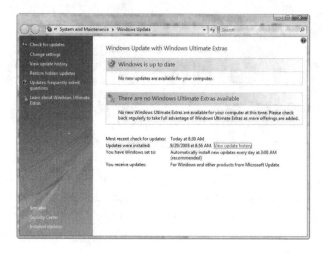

If you choose any of the other options, you open yourself up for problems unless you routinely and consistently check the updates manually and install them when they're available.

The great thing about Windows Update is that it checks your computer to see which Microsoft products you've installed, such as Microsoft Office and Windows Defender, and updates those when updates become available.

In the past, some updates have had bugs that caused more problems than the updates fixed. Just because this happened infrequently doesn't mean you should stop updating your computer with the latest security and program updates. You can always return to a system restore point saved the day before the update occurred if that happens. If you're really concerned about the possibility of an update causing a problem, select Download Updates But Let Me Choose Whether to Install Them from the Windows Update window and manually install any update made available to you after you've checked the latest technology news (such as www.cnet.com) to see whether an update has caused reported problems.

Review Internet Explorer's Options

Select Tools, Internet Options from Internet Explorer's menu. Remember, IE displays a menu across the top of your web page when you press Alt. Click the Advanced tab to display the customization list shown in Figure 43.2. Each item in the list describes a different aspect of Internet Explorer that you can control, from browsing tasks to toolbar information.

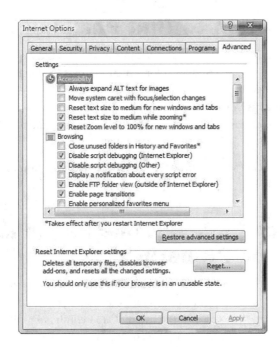

FIGURE 43.2
You can completely customize Internet Explorer.

You'll find options that change the way IE responds as you browse the Internet, and the list of options is huge. Some are technical in nature, such as Disable Script Debugging, and if you don't know what an option is for, it's best to leave it alone. For the others, you can change them to suit your preferences.

Many Internet Explorer pros forget about some of the options that would benefit them. For example, the option for printing background colors and images is usually unchecked, so when you print web pages and wonder where the color went, the option to print the background color is turned off. Clicking to uncheck the Do Not Search from the Address Bar option means that you don't have to go to the Search box to search the Internet; just type your search term in the Address bar where you'd normally type a web address, and IE performs the search.

As a bonus tip, remember that Alt+D sends your text cursor to the Address bar. Your hands don't have to leave the keyboard to enter a web address or a search term.

Did you Know?

Pay Attention to That Phishing Detector

As explained in Chapter 37, "Exploring the Internet with Vista and Internet Explorer," your Address bar changes colors when Internet Explorer senses that you're viewing a phony website that's masquerading as another. If you click an email link that's supposed to take you to eBay.com, but IE displays a red background in the Address bar, you're almost surely *not* on an eBay.com page and you should not enter your username or password.

This one tip alone *could* save your bank and PayPal accounts from being robbed of every cent in them.

Save Your Tabbed Home Pages and Order Them Properly

If you find yourself returning to the same site almost every time you start Internet Explorer, you might want to make that page your home page so that IE automatically displays it every time you surf the Internet. You can have multiple home pages open in tabs across IE every time you start the program.

Adding one or more home pages to IE is simple and many people do it. Just click the down arrow to the right of the Home button at the top of IE's toolbar and select Add or Change Home Page when you surf to a web page you want to add to your tabbed set of home pages.

As a bonus tip, remember that if you don't like the order of your tabbed pages you can drag a tab left or right to change its position. If your home page tabs don't appear in the order you want them in when you start IE, drag to change their order and open the toolbar's Home button's drop-down list of options. Click to select Use the Current Tab as Your Home Page and then click OK. The next time you start IE, the tabs will be in your preferred order.

Links Take You There Fast

Used less frequently than tabbed home pages but often just as helpful are page links that you can add to the top of your Internet Explorer window. Normally, the links aren't displayed, but by right-clicking on a blank area of your IE toolbar (such as to the left of the Home page icon), and clicking to check the Links option, the Links bar appears above your tabs.

Your Links bar can hold one or more web page links. Click a link and IE takes you right there. Figure 43.3 shows a Links bar with five link buttons. When you click a button, the corresponding page opens in your current browser page.

Five link buttons   Links bar

FIGURE 43.3
A Links bar keeps your frequently visited web pages just a click away.

Click your Add to Favorites button to add web pages to your Links bar. (Ctrl+D is the shortcut key for opening the Add to Favorites box.) Instead of adding to a traditional Favorites folder, however, add the link to the Links folder as shown in Figure 43.4.

The web page title, not the URL, appears as the link for that page and some titles can get long. For example, when you add eBay.com to your Links bar, eBay's home page web title *eBay – New & used Electronics, Cars, Apparel, Collectibles, Sporting Goods & More at Low Prices* appears instead of just *eBay*. Right-click the link's title, select Rename, and change it to a more manageable size so that more links can appear on your Links bar at one time. At the time you add a link, you can shorten the title if you want to, but the link often has to appear on your Links bar before you can determine whether it's taking too much space.

To remove a link, right-click the link and select Delete. One of the first links you now should remove is the one that appears when you first use Internet Explorer: Customize Links, a link to a page that tells how to add links to your Links bar.

FIGURE 43.4
Add a web page
to your Links
bar from within
your Add to
Favorites
dialog box.

Add Your Links to Your Taskbar Too

When you create IE links, Vista keeps track of those links and makes them available on your Windows taskbar, too.

Right-click a blank area on your taskbar, point to Toolbars, and select Links to place a check mark next to the option. A Links area appears on your taskbar and it holds all your web link buttons. Whether or not IE is open, you need only to display your Windows taskbar and click any link to cause Vista to open IE to that link's site.

If your taskbar begins to get full, the Links buttons won't all have room to appear. Just click the arrow to the right of the links to display a pop-up list of the rest of your links that there wasn't room for on your taskbar, as Figure 43.5 shows. Click a link to open that web page.

FIGURE 43.5
Click any link on
your taskbar's
Links bar to open
that website.

Keep Windows Mail's Deleted Folder Clean

Like files you delete that go to Windows Vista's Recycle Bin, email messages that you delete from your Inbox and other Windows Mail folders don't really go away; they move to your Deleted Items folder. If you want to free space of unwanted, old email messages completely, routinely open your Deleted Items folder and delete the messages there. You have to confirm the delete because Windows Mail wants you to remember that the files are truly gone when you delete them from the Deleted Items folder.

Keeping Windows Mail's Deleted Items folder clear keeps hundreds and even thousands of messages from potentially appearing there and slowing down Windows Mail. If you send something to your Deleted Items folder by accident, or later decide you want to keep something there before you empty the Deleted Items folder, you can drag messages from your Deleted Items folder to any other folder at the left of the Windows Mail screen. A clean Deleted Items folder, a folder that routinely gets very large if you don't monitor it, also decreases the time it takes to back up your computer.

> Remember that you can always create a new folder to move the item to if the item doesn't belong in your Inbox folder any longer.

By the Way

If you select Windows Mail's Tools, Options menu option and click Advanced, the Settings dialog box opens. Click the Maintenance button in the dialog box's lower-right corner to open Figure 43.6's Maintenance dialog box.

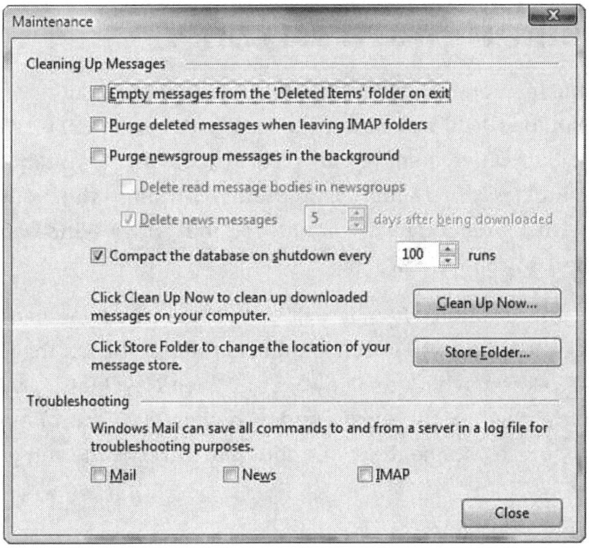

FIGURE 43.6
Keep Windows Mail running smoothly by cleaning up old, deleted items periodically.

At the top of the Maintenance dialog box is the Empty Messages from the Deleted Items Folder on Exit option. If you click to check this option, every time you exit Windows Mail, Windows Mail erases all your Delete Items folder's contents. This is a convenient way to keep major clutter from piling up in Windows Mail; of course, it also means that if you delete something by accident and realize you've done so later, you won't be able to get the message back. Most users prefer to leave this option unchecked and manually handle the Deleted Items folder.

Your Inbox Should Also Be Cleared

In addition to keeping your Deleted Items folder clear, if you keep your Inbox folder cleared of most of its messages you will be better off. An organized email system is a productive email system. Making it a priority to read each incoming message as soon as you can and moving that message to another folder when you finish with it—or deleting the message—keeps your Inbox clear so that you know that whatever is in your Inbox needs your attention.

If you'd like, create a new folder named Follow-Up and move emails that you need to respond to later, but don't currently have time for, from your Inbox to there. This maintains your cleared Inbox goal and gives you a one-stop place to go when you have time to correspond and follow-up to emails you've received that need your attention. (Some email systems, such as Google's Gmail, do not use multiple folders to store messages. Because there is only a single Inbox folder, mail organization is done using various sorting and searching tools.)

Check Email More Often

If you receive much email throughout the day, select Tools, Options and decrease the time that Windows Mail waits before checking for new email on the General tabbed page. If you read your email only once or twice a day, you might want to check for new email less often than the 30-minute default so that your system runs more efficiently when you don't want email. You must have Windows Mail running before it can check for new email.

Windows Mail emits a sound when new email arrives. When you hear that sound, it's time to check the Windows Mail Inbox for new messages. On the Options General page, check or uncheck the Play Sound When New Messages Arrive option to request or cancel the new message sound. (Chapter 24, "Controlling Windows Vista," explains how to change the sound that plays every time you get a new message.)

Take an Internet Refresher

With today's programs filled to the brim with features and options, it seems as though no matter how long you use something, there are commands and features that you miss that could help you do something faster or simpler. In the olden days of computers when software came with helpful manuals, you could skim through the manual every few months, and another new tip or procedure that you forgot about or never knew before would jump out.

Windows Word 1.0 came with a thick, hardback manual written in a friendly style with lots of text and step-by-step guides. Those were the days of manuals!

Because software no longer comes with comprehensive manuals, you can turn to the Web for the same information. You can get an Internet Explorer refresher from within Internet Explorer itself by selecting Help, Internet Explorer Tour. IE opens the IE tour website window, shown in Figure 43.7, and guides you through a tour of IE features to show you new ways to use the product you might not have thought of before.

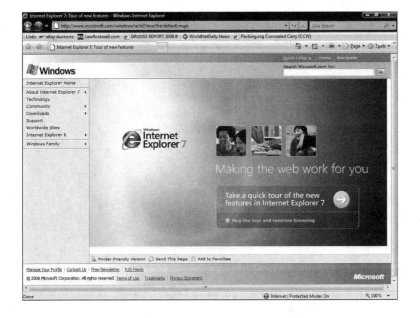

FIGURE 43.7
Use Internet Explorer to learn about features you might have forgotten about or never known.

Microsoft updates the tour site regularly, so your tour window might not look like the one in Figure 43.7. In addition, as Microsoft releases new versions of IE, it updates the tour for the new versions.

Chapter Wrap-Up

You've now protected yourself while online and you have learned some insider's secrets to achieving a better online experience.

Your initial Windows Vista education is over, so now it's time to really get started mastering the operating environment. The only way to really learn Vista is to use Vista. You have all the tools necessary to do just that. After a brief concluding chapter that discusses the future of you and Vista, you'll be done with this book's journey.

CHAPTER 44

Your Windows Vista Future

Now that you've mastered the basics (and more) of Windows Vista, what's next to conquer? If you're asking yourself that question, you'll either be relieved or frustrated to learn that there is a *lot more* to learn! You've only scratched the Windows Vista surface. Although you now know more about Windows Vista than most people, don't let Vista's simple-to-use environment fool you—there is much more waiting for you to master "under Vista's hood."

The chapter winds down your current track of Vista training. Instead of covering specific details, this chapter reviews Vista's goals and explains how you might approach Vista in the future to improve the way you work.

Vista and Software

More and more companies are writing application software for Windows Vista. Although Windows XP software usually works well with Vista, there is no way that software written for the older versions of Windows can take advantage of the many Vista features. In this book, you've seen examples of Vista software and how Vista improves the way you work. Software can be written to honor the parental control settings, respect Vista's other security measures such as specifying the type of user account that can use the program, and allow their data files to save thumbnail images for the Aero interface's Live Preview mode.

> Software developers have to do a lot to write programs that take advantage of Vista's features. Microsoft makes available a list of requirements before a program can be officially called a Vista-compatible program. For example, a program must come with an install routine and an uninstall routine, and is supposed to create a restore point before installing itself to protect you, the user, from harm.

By the Way

As Windows Vista sells on more and more new computers, and as more Windows XP users upgrade to Vista, software makers have even more incentive to write specifically for Vista and take advantage of Vista's feature set. That's good news for you because software written for Vista is often more robust and offers more features than software written for a more universal Windows platform.

Fortunately, Vista is friendly when it comes to running software written for XP and even systems earlier than Windows XP. Windows Vista can actually run some DOS-based software from the 1980s and earlier, although this is never guaranteed to work glitch-free.

> You're welcome to install all your older, pre-Vista games and programs. You don't have to limit the programs you install on a Vista machine to Vista-compatible only. Just be warned, however, that you should never install a utility program such as an antivirus, spyware, disk drive optimization, or other system utility on a computer running Vista. In the best of worlds, Vista *might* refuse to run the program but far worse things can happen if something goes wrong. So, limit your use of Vista-only system utility programs, but feel free to run your traditional applications on Vista even if they were written for Windows XP or earlier versions.

Vista's Understanding of Data Flow

More than a decade before this book was written, I wrote the following in an older Windows book:

"There are many in the computer industry who believe that all of the following items will be integrated into one unit some day:

▶ Your computer

▶ A television

▶ A telephone

▶ Stereo equipment

▶ Pager equipment

▶ Cellular communications

▶ Fax communications"

With the exception of the pager, which has far less importance today with instant messaging and text messaging available on most computers and cell phones, the prediction wasn't too far off. Today, one box offering access to all those features is almost commonplace with Media Center–ready PCs offering television tuners and sound cards providing Dolby sound enhancement and PC speaker systems that include subwoofers.

It wasn't my brilliance that made the prediction so accurate. It was obvious that data used to be thought of as numbers and letters, but it was realized early in the 1990s that data can take on far more properties than letters and numbers. Data is any collection of symbols that can represent anything, including sound and video. A digital image, a digital phone call, a digital fax transmission, and a digital video image are all composed of nothing more than streams of data that a computer can process. Combining all that into one central repository only makes sense.

Windows Vista is the first true operating environment that can access all that data and make it usable to nontechnical computer users.

Your Vista Version Is Always Upgradeable

Microsoft changed its software model when it released Vista. When you buy a DVD with Vista on it, you actually get *every Vista version* available from Windows Vista Home Basic to Windows Vista Ultimate. It's the way you activate Vista when you install it and the activation code given to you on the package that determines which version installs.

The chances are good that you'll upgrade to a higher version of Vista someday, and Microsoft knows this. That's why your Start menu's Extras and Updates submenu enables you to upgrade to another version by paying a fee difference and unlocking the version you want. You could start with Windows Vista Home Premium and start a small business in your home only to realize that Windows Vista Business has a few features you could really use.

When you upgraded to a different Windows version in the past—even a version within the same family such as moving from Windows XP Home to Windows XP Professional—you had to purchase a separate installation disc and upgrade your system. The time and effort were far greater than the effort required to take Windows Vista up an upgrade notch or two. By giving you every version on a single DVD, Microsoft eliminated the need for you to download or go purchase an upgrade in person.

When you do upgrade, Windows Update might require you to download several updates for the version you upgrade to in order to become as current as possible with all the patches and updates released since your installation DVD was published.

By the Way

Check the www.microsoft.com/windows website often to see what new goodies Microsoft makes available to you as a Vista user. Check the Downloads link in the Resources section of the page's left window pane because Microsoft offers a surprising number of games and tools and add-ons to other programs you probably already use, such as Office. Many of these downloads are not available automatically through Windows Update because they don't actually update Windows, but they provide extras for those who use Windows applications. In addition to many freebies, Microsoft offers trial downloads so that you can try programs to see whether they do the job for you before you pay for them.

Chapter Wrap-Up

This is more than a chapter wrap-up—it's a book wrap-up as well. You are now well-educated in Windows Vista and you have all the fundamentals that you need to move forward. You will experience Vista far more effectively than many others who use Vista because you now have a better understanding of Vista's internals and what Vista is capable of doing.

Now close the book and open some windows.

PART IX

Appendix

APPENDIX A

Common Vista Keyboard Shortcuts

As you master Windows Vista, you'll find yourself performing the same actions repeatedly. Vista includes numerous shortcut keys that enable you to get things done faster than you otherwise would by using the traditional way of selecting from menus.

Here you'll find several tables that list the shortcut keys Windows Vista supports. You might never need to learn most of them, but you *should* peruse this list regularly and add new shortcut keystrokes to your keyboarding repertoire. Even Windows veterans find that if they review Windows' list of shortcut keys every once in a while, they pick up a shortcut key they had forgotten existed or that they overlooked the first time.

TABLE A.1   Ease of Access Shortcut Keys

Press This Key...	To Perform This Action
Right Shift for eight seconds	Turn Filter Keys on or off
Left Alt+Left Shift+Print Screen	Turn High Contrast on or off (or PrtScrn)
Left Alt+Left Shift+Num Lock	Turn Mouse Keys on or off
Shift five times	Turn Sticky Keys on or off
Num Lock for five seconds	Turn Toggle Keys on or off
Windows logo key+U	Open the Ease of Access Center window

> For additional Ease of Access coverage, refer to Chapter 22, "Making Windows More Accessible."

By the Way

TABLE A.2   General Windows Vista Shortcut Keys

Press This Key...	To Perform This Action
Ctrl+C	Copy the selected item
Ctrl+X	Cut the selected item
Ctrl+V	Paste the selected item
Ctrl+Z	Undo your most recent action
Delete	Delete the selected item and move it to the Recycle Bin
Shift+Delete	Delete the selected item but do not move it to the Recycle Bin
F2	Rename the selected item
Ctrl+Right Arrow	Move the text insertion point to the beginning of the next word
Ctrl+Left Arrow	Move the text insertion point to the beginning of the previous word
Ctrl+Down Arrow	Move the insertion point to the beginning of the next paragraph
Ctrl+Up Arrow	Move the insertion point to the beginning of the previous paragraph
Ctrl+Shift+any arrow key	Select a block of text
Shift+any arrow key	Select more than one item in a window or on the desktop, or select text within a document
Ctrl+A	Select all items in a document or window
F3	Search for a file or folder
Alt+Enter	Display properties for the selected item
Alt+F4	Close the active item or exit the active program
Alt+Spacebar	Open the shortcut menu for the active window
Ctrl+F4	Close the active document (in programs that allow you to have multiple documents open simultaneously)
Alt+Tab	Switch between open items
Alt+Esc	Cycle through items in the order they were opened
F6	Cycle through screen elements in a window or on the desktop
F4	Display the Address Bar list in Windows Explorer
Shift+F10	Display the shortcut menu for the selected item
Ctrl+Esc	Open the Start menu
Alt+underlined letter	Open the corresponding menu

TABLE A.2   Continued

Press This Key...	To Perform This Action
Alt+underlined letter	Perform the menu command when a menu is displayed
F10	Activate the menu bar in the active program
Right Arrow	Open the next menu to the right or open a submenu
Left Arrow	Open the next menu to the left or close a submenu
F5	Refresh the active window
Backspace	View the folder one level up when using Windows Explorer
Esc	Cancel the current task
Ctrl+Shift+Esc	Open the Task Manager
Windows logo key+Break	Display the System Properties dialog box
Windows logo key+D	Display the desktop
Windows logo key+M	Minimize all windows
Windows logo key+Shift+M	Restore minimized windows to the desktop
Windows logo key+E	Open Computer
Windows logo key+F	Search for a file or folder
Ctrl+Windows logo key+F	Search for computers (if you're on a network)
Windows logo key+L	Lock your computer (if you are connected to a network domain) or switch users (if you are not connected to a network domain)
Windows logo key+R	Open the Run dialog box
Windows logo key+T	Cycle through programs on the taskbar
Windows logo key+U	Open Ease of Access Center
Windows logo key+X	Open Windows Mobility Center
Shift when you insert a CD	Prevent the CD from automatically playing

TABLE A.3   Useful Shortcut Keys When Working in Dialog Boxes

In Dialog Boxes, Press This Key...	To Perform This Action
Ctrl+Tab	Move forward through tabbed pages
Ctrl+Shift+Tab	Move back through tabbed pages
Tab	Move forward through controls
Shift+Tab	Move back through controls
Alt+underlined letter	Perform the command (or select the option) associated with that letter

TABLE A.3   Continued

In Dialog Boxes, Press This Key...	To Perform This Action
Enter	Replace clicking the mouse for many selected commands
Spacebar	Select or clear the check box if the active option is a check box
Arrow keys	Select a button if the active option is a group of option buttons
F1	Display Help
F4	Display the items in the active list
Backspace	Open a folder one level up if a folder is selected in the Save As or Open dialog box

TABLE A.4   Windows Explorer Shortcut Keys

In Explorer Windows, Press This Key	To Perform This Action
End	Display the bottom items in the active window
Home	Display the top items in the active window
Num Lock+Asterisk (*) on numeric keypad	Display all subfolders under the selected folder
Num Lock+Plus Sign (+) on numeric keypad	Display the contents of the selected folder
Num Lock+Minus Sign (-) on numeric keypad	Collapse the selected folder
Left Arrow	Collapse the current selection (if it is expanded) or select the parent folder
Right Arrow	Display the current selection (if it is collapsed) or select the first subfolder

Index

Security option, 428-430

System and Maintenance
option, 425-428

User Accounts and Family
Safety option, 433-435

opening, 418

option locations, 421-422

searching, 420-421

Security Center, 475-478

warnings about, 423-424

control panel (Photo Gallery),
302-303

cookies, deleting, 644-645

copying

Calculator values, 173

files/folders, 138-141

copying files, stopping, 730

copyright issues, 493

crashes. See freezes

Create a Power Plan window, 583

credits, adding to movies,
341-342

Crop Picture tool (Photo
Gallery), 306

cropping photos, 306, 526

Curve tool in Paint, 184

Customer Experience
Improvement Program in Media
Center, 254-255

Customize Start Menu dialog box,
53-56

customized settings, saving as
themes, 571

customizing

desktop, 107

adding desktop icons,
106-107

background image,
111-112

color schemes, 110-111

deleting desktop icons,
105-106

display settings, 107-108

hiding desktop icons, 104

mouse properties,
117-121

moving desktop icons,
102-103

screensavers, 112-115

sounds, 115-117

themes, 109-110

view settings for desktop
icons, 103-105

power button settings,
579-581

power plans, 581-583

Start menu, 52

Classic Start menu, 53

from context menus,
58-60

Internet browser/email
program links, 57-58

recent programs list, 53

right pane, 53-55

with Customize Start
Menu dialog box, 55-56

taskbar, 89-91

user interface, 35-36

Windows Explorer, 141-146

D

data, System Restore and, 533

data backups, 592. See also
incremental backups

data CDs, 279

data integration in Windows
Vista, 750-751

date

browsing by, in Media Player,
266-267

searches by, 230-231

date/time settings

changing, 559-560

synchronizing with Internet
time, 561-562

daylight savings time,
setting, 559

default printer

overriding, 510-511

setting, 510

default Start menu, restoring, 56

defaults

AutoPlay, changing, 440-442

program-related defaults,
442-443

file type associations,
445-449

running programs,
449-451

defragmentation with Disk
Defragmenter, 542-545

protecting from power failure,
545-546

Delete Browsing History dialog
box, 643

Deleted Items (Windows
Mail), 693

Deleted Items folder (Windows
Mail), cleaning, 744-745

deleting. See also uninstalling

appointments, 362

calendars, 357

cookies, 644-645

N

P

Paint, 169, 179-185
Paragraph dialog box, 178
parallel cables, 506
parallel printers, installing, 508-510
parental controls, 14, 485-487
  on DVDs, 284
  on games, 203-204
password protection, file and printer sharing, 623
passwords
  assigning, 456-458
  deleting, 458
  for sleep mode, 580
  in Windows Mail, 695
  saving in Internet Explorer, 646-648
pasting video clips into movies, 336-337
paths, breadcrumbs, 134-136
PDAs (Personal Digital Assistants), 675
peer-to-peer networks, 614
Pencil tool in Paint, 181
Percentages in Calculator, 173
performance improvements, Welcome Center information, 29-31
performance utilities
  Disk Cleanup, 546-550
  Disk Defragmenter, 542-545
    protecting from power failure, 545-546
Personal Digital Assistants (PDAs), 675. See also mobile devices

Personalize Windows option (Welcome Center), 35-36
personalizing. See customizing
phishing, 19
phishing filter in Internet Explorer, 742
phishing websites, 472-473
phone lines for faxes, 521
Photo Gallery, 241-244
  adding folders to, 298-299
  control panel, 302-303
  displaying photos in, 299-302
  editing tools, 304-307
  emailing photos, 316-317
  exporting photos to Movie Maker, 316
  fixing photos with, 304-307
  importing photos from digital cameras, 291
    importing directly into Photo Gallery, 293-296
    with memory card and card reader, 291-292
    with USB cable connection, 292-293
  importing photos over network, 288-290
  Media Player versus, 248, 284
  new features, 20-21
  overview, 287
  printing photos from, 308-309
  saving photos to DVD, 312
    backup data DVDs, 312
    video DVDs, 313-315
  scanning photos into, 293-296

sending photos to professional photo services, 310-312
  starting, 297
photos. See digital photos
pictures. See digital photos
Pictures window, 123, 146-147
Pictures, Music, and Video option (Mobile Device Center), 685-686
pinning, 57-59
pixels, 107
playlists
  creating in Media Player, 272-275
  defined, 269
Polygon tool in Paint, 183
pop-up menus. See context menus
pop-ups, blocking, 651-653
POP3 email, 693
  Hotmail and, 694
portable computers. See laptop computers
ports, 470
Power button, 52
  customizing settings, 579-581
  icons for, 66
  sleep mode, 64-66
  troubleshooting freezes, 578-579
power consumption of hardware, 577-578
power failure
  protecting Disk Defragmenter from, 545-546
  UPS (uninterruptible power supply), 591

movie properties,
349-350

narration, 350-351

pasting video clips into
movies, 336-337

publishing movies,
344-348

rearranging video
clips, 338

saving projects, 344

special effects, 340-341

storyboard, 336

Tasks pane, 333

Timeline, 343-344

titles, 341-342

transitioning between
video clips, 338-340

trimming video clips,
337-338

versions, 330

workspace, 333-334

Photo Gallery

adding folders to,
298-299

control panel, 302-303

displaying photos in,
299-302

displaying photos in, 300

editing tools, 304-307

emailing photos, 316-317

exporting photos to Movie
Maker, 316

fixing photos with,
304-307

importing photos directly
into Photo Gallery,
293-296

importing photos from
digital cameras,
291-293

importing photos over
network, 288-290

overview, 287

printing photos from,
308-309

saving photos to DVD,
312-315

scanning photos into,
293-296

sending photos to
professional photo
services, 310-312

starting, 297

security tools, list of,
469-471

Sound Recorder, 319

hardware requirements,
322

microphones, 322-323

recording sound, 324-326

recording tips and
techniques, 327

visual displays, 323-324

.wav file properties,
321-322

.wma file properties, 321

when to use, 319-321

**Tools menu commands (Movie
Maker), Narrate Timeline, 350**

tour of Internet Explorer, 746-747

**TPM (trusted platform
module), 488**

training

computer for speech
recognition, 411-412

voice for speech recognition,
412-416

transcripts of chat sessions,
saving, **672**

**Transfer File and Settings option
(Welcome Center), 32-33**

translucent windows, 76-77

transmitters for faxes, 521

tricks in Hearts, 197

trimming video clips, 337-338

troubleshooting

date/time settings, 560

freezes, 578-579

mobile device
connections, 677

print jobs, 516

printer installation, 509-510

shutting down Windows Vista,
70-71

startup, 555-557

**trusted platform module
(TPM), 488**

two-way firewalls, 14

U

**UAC (User Account Control), 13,
462-464**

disabling messages from,
727-728

underlined text in WordPad, 176

Undo command in Paint, 182

**Undo command (Movie Maker
Edit menu), 341**

undoing

restore points, 539

System Restore, 534

**uniform resource locators (URLs),
630-631**

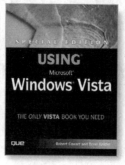